JOHN WILLIS'

THEATRE
WORLD

1974-1975 SEASON

Volume 31

CROWN PUBLISHERS, INC.
419 PARK AVENUE SOUTH
NEW YORK, N.Y. 10016

PN
2277
.N5
A17
1974/75

792
T34
96050
Feb. 1976

with Phyllis Konstam in
"Murder on the Second Floor"
(1929)

with Katharine Cornell in
"No Time for Comedy" (1939)

with James Dale in "The Gr
Bay Tree" (1933)

with Vivien Leigh in
"Romeo and Juliet" (1940)

as Oedipus
(1946)

as Caesar in "Caesar and
Cleopatra" (1951)

with Vivien Leigh in "Antony
and Cleopatra" (1951)

as "Becket"
(1960)

in "The Entertainer"
(1958)

1931   1946   1958   1972

T O
LAURENCE OLIVIER

who is one of the most brilliant, versatile, and truly great English-speaking actors of this century; an object of profound admiration and respect by other performers, and the idol of millions of fans throughout the world.

**Anthony Hopkins, Peter Firth, Everett McGill
in "Equus"
*Winner of 1975 "Tony" and New York
Drama Critics Circle Awards for Best Play***

CONTENTS

EDITOR: JOHN WILLIS

Assistant Editor: Stanley Reeves

Staff: Alberto Cabrera, Don Nute, Evan Romero

Staff Photographers: Bert Andrews, Friedman-Abeles, Al Husted, Van Williams

THE SEASON IN REVIEW
June 1, 1974–May 31, 1975

What a wonderfully surprising season! It began with the first booking jam in several years, and made it necessary for some new productions to wait for others to close. In the deepest national economic recession in 30 years, the theatre experienced an increase in financial and artistic success that was a surprise for almost everyone. Even though tickets were relatively expensive (a $15 top for several productions), more were being bought than in several previous seasons. *Variety* reported a 24% gross increase on Broadway over the dreary 1973–74 season. It was a richly varied year that offered many English imports, and few new American plays. For the records, there were 42 Broadway productions: 17 were new plays, 14 were revivals, and 9 were musicals.

Many angry protests accompanied the announcement of the Antoinette Perry (Tony) Awards nominations, but the majority seemed to be in agreement as to the best play of the season. The British import "Equus," with brilliant performances by Anthony Hopkins and Peter Firth, received not only the Tony, but also the New York Drama Critics Circle Award for best play. The New York Drama Critics voted "The Taking of Miss Janie" the best American play, and Off Broadway's "A Chorus Line" the best musical. It was a unique, beautifully conceived, produced, and performed musical. The entire cast and company of creative artists deserved awards. It will be moved to Broadway early next season. The Tony Award musical was "The Wiz," and cast members Dee Dee Bridgewater and Ted Ross received Tonys for best supporting actress and actor in a musical. Winners of Tonys for best musical actor and actress were John Cullum of "Shenandoah," and Angela Lansbury of the revival of "Gypsy." Ellen Burstyn received a Tony for best actress for her performance in the wonderfully ingenious two-character hit play "Same Time, Next Year." The Tony for best actor was shared by John Kani and Winston Ntshona in Off-Broadway's Afro-British imports "Sizwe Banze Is Dead" and "The Island" in repertory. Supporting performers receiving Tonys were Rita Moreno for "The Ritz" and Frank Langella for "Seascape"—the Pulitzer Prize play for 1975. Alexander H. Cohen again beautifully produced the Tony Award telecast at the Winter Garden Theatre, using its history as the theme. During the evening special Theatre Awards were presented to playwright Neil Simon and caricaturist Al Hirschfield.

Usually treacherous, revivals and British imports met generally with popular and critical success this season. Imports and British revivals included "Scapino," "London Assurance," "Sherlock Holmes," "The Misanthrope," "Love's Labour's Lost" with an all-male cast, "Absurd Person Singular," "The Constant Wife," "Brief Lives," "In Praise of Love," and "The National Health." Revivals of American playwrights included "Cat on a Hot Tin Roof" with a beautiful performance by Elizabeth Ashley, and "Of Mice and Men" with James Earl Jones in another of his widely acclaimed characterizations. The greatly anticipated "Miss Moffatt" (a musical based on "The Corn Is Green") starring Bette Davis folded during its tryout tour. In addition to outstanding performers already cited, the following also deserve accolades for the season: Charles Grodin, Diana Rigg, Alec McCowen, Joel Grey, Maureen Anderman, Cleavon Little, Julie Harris, Bernadette Peters, Robert Preston, Ron O'Neal, Rex Harrison, Donald Sinden, Geraldine Page, Richard Kiley, Roy Dotrice, John Wood, Deborah Kerr, Henry Fonda, and Maggie Smith.

Joseph Papp's New York Shakespeare Festival season, both at the downtown Public Theater and at Lincoln Center, was disappointing again. Except for the unanimously praised "A Chorus Line," his only other success was the completely sold out limited engagement of Liv Ullmann in "A Doll's House." He has promised this formula for future productions at Lincoln Center: stars in revivals of classics. Off Broadway has declined not only in influence, but also in quantity of productions. Off Off Broadway is now the center of experimental theatre, and is steadily increasing its number of productions and showcases. The most noteworthy Off Broadway presentations this season were "What Every Woman Knows" at the Roundabout's beautiful new theatre, "Battle of Angels" at Circle Repertory Theatre, "Enter a Free Man" at St. Clement's Theatre, all three presented for limited runs only, "Kid Champion," the double bill of "Rubbers" with "Yankees 3, Detroit 0," "The Wager," "Naomi Court," and the revues "Gay Company" and "Pretzels." The Brooklyn Academy of Music again hosted the Royal Shakespeare Company in impressive productions of "Summerfolk," "Love's Labour's Lost," "Lear," and "He That Plays the King."

During the year, other events worth noting were the retirement of Richard Watts, Jr., as daily drama critic for the *New York Post;* however, he will continue to write a column for the weekend edition. Martin Gottfried took the daily assignment. The First American Congress of Theatre assembled at Princeton University and brought into the spotlight the common interests and problems of Broadway, Off Broadway, and regional theatres. The venerable and historic Belasco Theatre was defaced and converted into a cheap cabaret theatre for the brief run of "The Rocky Horror Show." Because of the recession, a decline in construction of office buildings happily saved some theatres that had been marked for demolition. Ticketron, a computerized boxoffice system, established over 90 outlets for ticket buyers in New York, Connecticut, and New Jersey. The Theatre Development Fund, and the Times Square Ticket Booth for impulsive or last-minute theatregoers were wooing new and younger audiences interested in live theatrical entertainment. There was an appreciable increase in black participation not only from behind the footlights, but also from the audience. Happily, the theatre was out of the doldrums and in its healthiest condition in several years, with encouraging prospects for an even brighter year ahead.

Elizabeth Ashley

Joel Grey

NO. _____ $ 6.00

_____ 19 ___

TO _____

	DOLLARS	CENTS
BAL. FOR'D		
DEPOSITS		
"		
TOTAL		
THIS CHECK		
BAL. FOR'D		

ADWAY CALENDAR

74 through May 31, 1975

John Cullum

lmann

Maggie Smith

Michael Moriarty

WINTER GARDEN
Opened Monday, September 23, 1974.*
Barry M. Brown, Edgar Lansbury, Fritz Holt, Joseph Beruh
present:

GYPSY

Book, Arthur Laurents; Suggested by memoirs of Gypsy Rose
Lee; Music, Jule Styne; Lyrics, Stephen Sondheim; Director, Arthur
Laurents; Original Jerome Robbins choreography reproduced by
Robert Tucker; Scenery and Lighting, Robert Randolph; Costumes,
Raoul Pene du Bois; Musical Director, Milton Rosenstock; Orches-
trations, Sid Ramin, Robert Ginzler, Dance Music arranged by John
Kander; Miss Lansbury's costumes, Robert Mackintosh; Sound De-
signer, Jack Mann; Hairstylist, Vincent Prestia; Assistant Music
Director, Phil Fradkin

CAST

Uncle Jocko/Kringelein/Cigar	John C. Becher
George/Mr. Goldstone	Don Potter
Clarence	Craig Brown
Balloon Girl	Donna Elio
Baby Louise	Lisa Peluso
Baby June	Bonnie Langford
Rose	Angela Lansbury
Chowsie	Peewee
Pop/Phil	Ed Riley
Newsboys	Craig Brown, Anthony Marciona, Sean Rule
Weber	Charles Rule
Herbie	Rex Robbins
Louise	Zan Charisse
June	Maureen Moore
Tulsa	John Sheridan
Yonkers	Steven Gelfer
L. A.	David Lawson
Little Rock	Jay Smith
San Diego	Dennis Karr
Boston/Bourgeron-Couchon	Serhij Bohdan
Gigolo	Edith Ann
Waitress	Patricia Richardson
Miss Cratchitt/Mazeppa	Gloria Rossi
Hollywood Blondes	Pat Cody, Jinny Kordek, Jan Neuberger, Marilyn Olson, Patricia Richardson
Agnes	Denny Dillon
Pastey	Richard J. Sabellico
Tessie Tura	Mary Louise Wilson
Electra	Sally Cooke
Maid	Bonnie Walker

STANDBYS AND UNDERSTUDIES: Rose, Mary Louise Wilson;
Louise, Patricia Richardson; Herbie, Ed Riley; Tessie, Mazeppa,
Electra, Bonnie Walker; June, Jan Neuberger; Baby June, Baby
Louise, Donna Elio; Tulsa, Steven Gelfer; Cratchitt, Sally Cooke;
Uncle, Pop, Weber, Don Potter; Kringelein, Goldstone, Charles
Rule; George, Richard J. Sabellico

MUSICAL NUMBERS: "Let Me Entertain You," "Some People,"
"Small World," "Baby June and Her Newsboys," "Mr. Goldstone,"
"Little Lamb," "You'll Never Get Away from Me," "Dainty June
and Her Farmboys," "If Momma Was Married," "All I Need Is the
Girl," "Everything's Coming Up Roses," "Toreadorables," "To-
gether," "You Gotta Get a Gimmick," "The Strip," "Rose's Turn"

A Musical in two acts. The action takes place in various cities in
the U. S. A. from the early 1920's to the early 1930's.

General Management: Marvin A. Krauss
Company Manager: Charles Willard
Press: Merlin Group, Sandra Manley
Stage Managers: Kathleen A. Sullivan, Moose Peting, Serhij
Bohdan

* Closed January 4, 1975 after 120 performances and 4 previews.
Miss Lansbury received a 1975 "Tony" Award for Best Actress
in a Musical. Original production opened May 21, 1959 and ran
for 702 performances with Ethel Merman, Jack Klugman, Sandra
Church. See THEATRE WORLD V15.

Martha Swope Photos

**Top Right: Lisa Peluso, Angela Lansbury,
Bonnie Langsford Below: Mary Louise Wilson,
Zan Charisse, Angela Lansbury**

Zan Charisse

Angela Lansbury

ANTA THEATRE
Opened Tuesday, September 24, 1974.*
The American National Theatre and Academy presents the American Shakespeare Theatre (Michael Kahn, Artistic Director) production of:

CAT ON A HOT TIN ROOF

By Tennessee Williams; Director, Michael Kahn; Setting, John Conklin; Costumes, Jane Greenwood; Lighting, Marc B. Weiss

CAST

Margaret	Elizabeth Ashley †1
Brick	Keir Dullea †2
Mae	Joan Pape
Gooper	Charles Siebert
Big Mama	Kate Reid
Sookey	Sarallen
Dixie	Deborah Grove
Big Daddy	Fred Gwynne
Reverend Tooker	Wyman Pendleton
Doctor Baugh	William Larsen
Children	Jeb Brown, Susannah Brown, Amy Borress

STANDBYS AND UNDERSTUDIES: Margaret, Mae, Caroline McWilliams; Brick, Michael Zaslow; Big Mama, Patricia Grove; Big Daddy, William Larsen; Dr. Baugh, Rev. Tooker, Charles Kindl; Dixie, Amy Borress

A Drama in three acts. The action takes place in 1954 on a delta plantation.

General Manager: Oscar Olesen
Press: Seymour Krawitz, Patricia McLean Krawitz, Fred Hoot
Stage Managers: Edward Dimond, Charles Kindl

* Closed Feb. 8, 1975 after 160 performances and 2 previews. Original production opened March 24, 1955 and played 694 performances with Barbara Bel Geddes, Ben Gazzara, Burl Ives, Mildred Dunnock. See THEATRE WORLD V11.

† Succeeded by: 1. Caroline McWilliams, 2. Michael Zaslow

Martha Swope Photos

Elizabeth Ashley, Keir Dullea
Top Right: Keir Dullea, Fred Gwynne

Kate Reid, Keir Dullea

MAJESTIC THEATRE
Opened Sunday, October 6, 1974.*
David Merrick presents:

MACK AND MABEL

Book, Michael Stewart; Music and Lyrics, Jerry Herman; Directed and Choreographed by Gower Champion; Scenery, Robin Wagner; Costumes, Patricia Zipprodt; Lighting, Tharon Musser; Musical Director and Vocal Arrangements, Donald Pippin; Orchestrations, Philip J. Lang; Incidental and Dance Music, John Morris; Associate Choreographer, Buddy Schwab; Production Supervisor, Lucia Victor; Associate Producer, Jack Schlissel; Based on an Idea by Leonard Spigelgass; In association with Edwin H. Morris; Hairstylists, Ted Azar, Hector Garcia, Charles LaFrance; Film Coordinator, Andy Stein; Wardrobe Supervisors, Gene Wilson, Kathleen Foster; Assistant to the Director, Pat Cummings; Dance Captain, Sandra Brewer; Associate Conductor, Skip Redwine; Original Cast Album by ABC Records

CAST

Eddie, the watchman	Stanley Simmonds
Mack Sennett	Robert Preston
Lottie Ames	Lisa Kirk
Ella	Nancy Evers
Freddie	Roger Bigelow
Charlie Muldoon	Christopher Murney
Wally	Robert Fitch
Frank Wyman	Jerry Dodge†
Mabel Normand	Bernadette Peters
Mr. Kleiman	Tom Batten
Mr. Fox	Bert Michaels
Iris, the wardrobe mistress	Marie Santell
William Desmond Taylor	James Mitchell
Phyllis Foster	Cheryl Armstrong
Serge	Frank Root

THE GRIPS: John Almberg, Roger Bigelow, George Blackwell, Frank Bouley, Gerald Brentte, Lonnie Burr, Chet D'Elia, Igors Gavon, Jonathan Miele, Don Percassi, Frank Root

MACK SENNETT BATHING BEAUTIES: Cheryl Armstrong, Claudia Asbury, Sandahl Bergman, Chrystal Chambers, Nancy Dafgek, Prudence Darby, Elaine Handel, Paula Lynn, Patricia Michaels, Carol Perea, L. J. Rose, Rita Rudner, Marianne Selbert, Jo Speros, Pat Trott, Geordie Withee

UNDERSTUDIES: Mack Sennett, Igors Gavon; Mabel, Marie Santell; Lottie, Patricia Michaels; Taylor, Roger Bigelow; Wyman, Frank Root; Muldoon, Lonnie Burr; Kleiman, Frank Bouley; Fox, Jonathan Miele; Ella, L. J. Rose; Wally, Don Percassi; Watchman, George Blackwell; Swing Dancers, Helen Butleroff, Richard Maxon

MUSICAL NUMBERS: "Movies Were Movies," "Look What Happened to Mabel," "Big Time," "I Won't Send Roses," "I Wanna Make the World Laugh," "Wherever He Ain't," "Hundreds of Girls," "When Mabel Comes in the Room," "My Heart Leaps Up," "Time Heals Everything," "Tap Your Troubles Away," "I Promise You a Happy Ending"

A Musical in fourteen scenes, performed without intermission. The action takes place between 1911 and 1938 in New York and Hollywood.

Press: Solters/Roskin, Bud Westman, Joshua Ellis
Stage Managers: Marnel Sumner, Tony Manzi, Pat Trott

* Closed Nov. 30, 1974 after 66 performances and 5 previews.
† Succeeded by Frank Root, Jess Richards

Top Left: Robert Preston, Christopher Murney, Bernadette Peters, Lisa Kirk Below: James Mitchell, Bernadette Peters

Robert Preston, also above with Igors Gavon, Christopher Murney, Bernadette Peters, Jerry Dodge

BILTMORE THEATRE
Opened Monday, October 7, 1974.*
Herman and Diana Shumlin and Merrold Suhl in association
with Larry Parnes present:

FLOWERS

Devised, Designed and Directed by Lindsay Kemp; Lighting, Mr.
Kemp, John Spradbery; Sound Composed by Andrew Wilson; Scenery Supervised by Leo B. Meyer; Lighting Supervision, John Gleason; Special Assistant to the Producers, Julie Chanova; Wardrobe
Supervisor, Frank Green; Musical Supervisor, Earl Shendell

CAST

The Boy	David Meyer
The Groom	Neil Caplan
The Mother	Arlene Phillips
Woman in Silver	Lindsay Kemp
Woman in Red	Jack Birkett
A Waiter	Tony Maplés
Tap Dancer	Robert Anthony
The Angel	David Haughton

A theatre piece presented without intermission. The action takes place in a prison, a cemetery, a cafe in Montmartre, a garret, and a theatre.

General Manager: William Orton
Press: Gifford/Wallace, Tom Trenkle
Stage Managers: John Spradbery, Timothy Wales

* Closed Oct. 26, 1974 after 24 performances.

Avery Willard Photos

Top and Right: Lindsay Kemp (C)

Lindsay Kemp

David Haughton, Lindsay Kemp

11

THE MUSIC BOX
Opened Tuesday, October 8, 1974.*
The Theatre Guild and the John F. Kennedy Center for the
Performing Arts in association with Michael Codron present:

ABSURD PERSON SINGULAR

By Alan Ayckbourn; Director, Eric Thompson; Scenery, Edward
Burbridge; Costumes, Levino Verna for Laurence Gross; Lighting,
Thomas Skelton; Produced by Philip Langner, Armina Marshall;
Production Associate, Mary Jane Vineburgh; Wardrobe Supervisor,
Lillias Norel; Production Assistants, Robert Cohn, Eve Langner,
Lola Langner; Coiffures, Michael of New York

CAST

Jane	Carole Shelley
Sidney	Larry Blyden †1
Ronald	Richard Kiley †2
Marion	Geraldine Page †3
Eva	Sandy Dennis †4
Geoffrey	Tony Roberts†5

STANDBYS: Jane, Marion, Eva, Marilyn Clark; Sidney, Ronald,
Geoffrey, Wayne Carson

A Comedy in three acts. The action takes place on a Christmas
Past, a Christmas Present, and a Christmas to Come, in a town in
England.

General Manager: Victor Samrock
Press: Joseph Wolhandler Associates
Stage Managers: Frederic de Wilde, Wayne Carson

* Still playing May 31, 1975.

† Succeeded by: 1. Paul Shyre, 2. Fritz Weaver, Scott McKay, 3.
Sheila MacRae during vacation, 4. Carol Lynley, 5. Curt Dawson

Friedman-Abeles Photos

**Right: Tony Roberts, Fritz Weaver, Sandy
Dennis Above: Richard Kiley, Larry Blyden,
Geraldine Page Top: Richard Kiley, Larry
Blyden, Carole Shelley, Geraldine Page, Sandy
Dennis, Tony Roberts**

Larry Blyden, Fritz Weaver, Carole Shelley

Paul Shyre, Curt Dawson, Geraldine Page, Fritz
Weaver, Carol Lynley, Carole Shelley

CIRCLE IN THE SQUARE/JOSEPH E. LEVINE THEATRE
Opened Thursday, October 10, 1974.*
Circle in the Square, Inc. (Theodore Mann, Artistic Director;
Paul Libin, Managing Director) presents the Long Wharf The-
atre production of:

THE NATIONAL HEALTH

By Peter Nichols; Director, Arvin Brown; Setting, Virginia Dancy
Webb; Costumes, Whitney Blausen; Lighting, Ronald Wallace;
Original Music, Terrence Sherman; Production Associate, E. J.
Oshins; Wardrobe Supervisor, Latonia Baer; Hairstylist, Roberto
Fernandez; Production Assistants, Nancy Cook, Johnny Clontz,
Gordon Bendall; Dialect Coach, Elizabeth Smith

CAST

Staff Nurse Norton, Puerto Rican	Rita Morena †
Ash, Bristolian patient	Richard Venture
Rees, Welsh patient	William Swetland
Foster, London patient	George Taylor
Flagg, Hertfordshire patient	Louis Beachner
Mackie, a patient	Emery Battis
Tyler, London patient	Stephen Mendillo
Ken, London patient	Paul Rudd
Nurse Sweet, Londoner	Suzanne Lederer
Loach, London patient	John Braden
Nurse Lake, Jamaican	Olivia Cole
Woman	Mary Fogarty
Barnet, Londoner, orderly	Leonard Frey
Dr. Boyd, Scottish	Richard McKenzie
Neil, Boyd's son, a doctor	Sean G. Griffin
Sister McPhee, Scottish nurse	Veronica Castang
West Indian Student	Tazewell Thompson
Dr. Bird	Shirley Bryan
Matron	Joyce Ebert
Chaplain	David H. Leary
Nurses and Orderlies	Carlos Carrasco, David Derosa, Alice Nagel, Christinea Whitmore

A Play in two acts. The action takes place at the present time in
the men's ward of a British hospital.

Company Manager: William Conn
Press: Merle Debuskey, Leo Stern
Stage Managers: Anne Keefe, Randall Brooks

* Closed Nov. 24, 1974 after 53 performances and 23 previews.

† Succeeded by Patricia Mauceri

Martha Swope Photos

**Right: Rita Moreno Top: Leonard Frey, Suzanne
Lederer, Olivia Cole, Louis Beachner, George Taylor,
Rita Moreno**

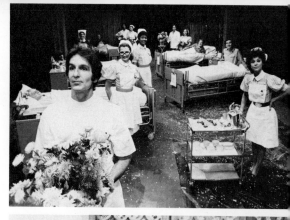

**lliam Swetland, Stephen Mendillo, Richard Venture,
ery Battis, Paul Rudd, George Taylor, John Braden**

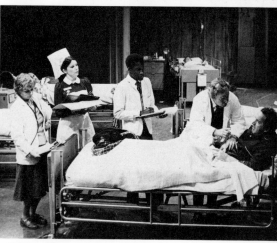

**Shirley Bryan, Veronica Castang, Tazewell Thompson,
Richard McKenzie, Richard Venture**

MINSKOFF THEATRE
Opened Tuesday, October 15, 1974.*
Lee Guber, Shelly Gross and Joseph Harris present:

CHARLES AZNAVOUR ON BROADWAY

Musical Director, Aldo Frank; Production Manager, Levon Sayan; A Music Fair-Enterprises Inc. Production; Music Coordinator, Mel Rodnon; Technical Director, Michael Cadieux; Lighting, Marc B. Weiss; Production Assistant, Marilyn Cuttler

PROGRAM

PART I: "Le Temps," "Happy Anniversary," "I Live for You," "Un Par Un," "Our Love, My Love," "The Ham," "La Mamma," "To Die of Love," "No I Could Never Forget," "I Have Lived," "La Boheme," "What Makes a Man," "Emmenez-Moi"

PART II: "La Baraka," "Reste," "We Can Never Know," "You've Let Yourself Go," "Trousse Chemise," "The 'I Love You' Song," "She," "Que C'est Triste Venise," "And I in My Chair," "Yesterday When I Was Young," "Isabelle," "The Old Fashioned Way," "Les Comediens," "You've Got to Learn"

Company Manager: James O'Neill
Press: Solters/Roskin, Milly Schoenbaum

* Closed Oct. 27, 1974 after limited engagement of 16 performances.

Charles Aznavour

URIS THEATRE
Opened Wednesday, October 16, 1974.*
Nederlander presents:

ANDY WILLIAMS
with
MICHEL LEGRAND

Musical Director, Jack Feierman; Associate Conductor, Armand Migiani; Soloist, Eileen Duffy; Set, Neil Peter Jampolis; Lighting, Jane Riesman; Stage Director, Jerry Grolinek; Sound Consultant, Pat Baroo

Management: Leonard A. Mulhern
Press: Michael Alpert, Warren Knowlton, Anne Weinberg, Solters & Roskin, Florence Semon

* Closed Oct. 27, 1974 after limited engagement of 15 performances.

Left: Andy Williams, Michel Legrand

BOOTH THEATRE
Opened Wednesday, October 16, 1974.*
Triumph Theatre Productions, Ellen Brandt, David Lonn present:

BRIEF LIVES

Adapted from the writings of John Aubrey by Patrick Garland, and Directed by Mr. Garland; Designed by Julia Trevelyan Oman; American Supervisor, Neil Peter Jampolis

CAST
ROY DOTRICE
as John Aubrey

A theatre piece in two acts. The action takes place in Mistress Byerley's lodgings in Dirty Lane, Bloomsbury, in 1697, the last year of John Aubrey's life.

General Manager: C. Edwin Knill
Company Manager: Virginia Snow
Press: Jean Dalrymple
Stage Manager: Wally Peterson

* Closed Dec. 1, 1974 after 54 performances and one preview.

Roy Dotrice

ETHEL BARRYMORE THEATRE
Opened Thursday, October 17, 1974.*
David Merrick presents:

DREYFUS IN REHEARSAL

By Jean-Claude Grumberg; Adapted and Directed by Garson Kanin; Scenery, Boris Aronson; Costumes, Florence Klotz; Lighting, Jennifer Tipton; Translator Consultant, Daphne Swabey; Associate Producer, Jack Schlissel; Musical Number Staged by Sandra Devlin; Music Consultant, Ruth Rubin; Musical Arrangements, Dorothea Freitag; Production Assistant, Richard Corneilius Skinner III; Wardrobe Master, Clarence Sims; Assistant to Director, Melissa Sutherland

CAST

Morris	Allan Arbus
Michael	Peter Kastner
Mendl	Avery Schreiber
Arnold	Sam Levene
Zina	Ruth Gordon
Zalman	Harry Davis
Myriam	Tovah Feldshuh
Dr. Wasselbaum	Anthony Holland
Yanek	Michael Pendrey
Bronislaw	Rex Williams

UNDERSTUDIES: Zina, May Muth; Michael, Morris, Yanek, Wasselbaum, Jerry Sroka; Myriam, Ellen Sherman; Arnold, Zalman, Bronislaw, Mendl, Loney Lewis

A Play in two acts and seven scenes. The action takes place in 1931 in Vilna, Poland during March, April and May.

Press: Solters/Sabinson/Roskin, Bud Westman, Nini Finkelstein, Edith Kean
Stage Manager: May Muth

* Closed Oct. 26, 1974 after 12 performances.

Top Right: Peter Kastner, Tovah Feldshuh, Allan Arbus

Tovah Feldshuh, Peter Kastner, Allan Arbus, Ruth Gordon, Anthony Holland, Harry Davis, Sam Levene, Avery Schreiber

Avery Schreiber, Sam Levene, Ruth Gordon

PLYMOUTH THEATRE
Opened Thursday, October 24, 1974.*
Kermit Bloomgarden and Doris Cole Abrahams in association with Frank Milton present:

EQUUS

By Peter Shaffer; Director, John Dexter; Scenery and Costumes, John Napier; Lighting, Andy Phillips; Sound, Marc Wilkinson; Mime, Claude Chagrin; American Supervision of Scenery and Lighting, Howard Bay; Costumes, Patricia Adshead; Production Assistant, Scott Rudin; Wardrobe Supervisor, Eric Harrison; Assistant to the Director, Gabriel Oshen.

CAST

Martin Dysart	Anthony Hopkins †1
Alan Strang	Peter Firth †2
Nurse	Mary Doyle
Hesther Salomon	Marian Seldes
Frank Strang	Michael Higgins
Dora Strang	Frances Sternhagen
Horseman/Nugget	Everett McGill
Harry Dalton	Walter Mathews †3
Jill Mason	Roberta Maxwell †4
Horses	Gus Kaikkoen, Philip Kraus,
	Gabriel Oshen, David Ramsey, John Tyrrell

STANDBYS AND UNDERSTANDINGS: Dysart, Alan Mixon; Alan, Thomas Hulce; Frank, Don Plumley; Dora, Hesther, Mary Doyle; Jill, Nurse, Dale Hodges; Harry, Horseman, Philip Kraus; Horses, Michael Wieben

A Drama in two acts. The action takes place in Rokeby Psychiatric Hospital in Southern England at the present time.

General Manager: Max Allentuck
Press: John Springer Associates, Louis Sica
Stage Managers: Robert L. Borod, Nicholas Russiyan, Michael Wieben

* Still playing May 31, 1975. Winner of 1975 Best Play awards from New York Drama Critics Circle, "Tony," Drama Desk, New York Outer Critics, also "Tony" and Drama Desk Awards for Best Director.

† Succeeded by: 1. Anthony Perkins, 2. Thomas Hulce, 3. Don Plumley, Page Johnson, 4. Jeanne Ruskin

Van Williams Photos

Left: Roberta Maxwell, Peter Firth
Top: Anthony Hopkins, Peter Firth

Peter Firth on Everett McGill

Anthony Hopkins, Thomas Hulce, Everett McGill

MINSKOFF THEATRE
Opened Wednesday, October 30, 1974.*
Lee Guber, Shelly Gross and Joseph Harris present:

TONY BENNETT & LENA HORNE
SING

Music Directors, Torrie Zito, Robert Freedman; Technical Director, Serge Descheneaux; Production Coordinator, Sherman Sneed; Wardrobe for Miss Horne, Georgio Sant'Angelo; Music Coordinator, Mel Rodnon; Production Assistant, Marilyn Cuttler; Personal Management for Mr. Bennett, Jack Rollins; For Miss Horne, Ralph Harris

Company Manager: James O'Neill
Press: Solters/Roskin, Milly Schoenbaum

* Closed Nov. 24, 1974 after limited engagement of 37 performances.

Tony Bennett   **Lena Horne**

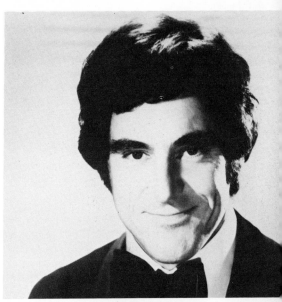

URIS THEATRE
Opened Thursday, october 31, 1974.*
Nederlander presents:

ANTHONY NEWLEY/HENRY
MANCINI

Lighting and Sound, Jerry Grollnek, Pat Barso; Conductor for Mr. Newley, Ian Fraser; Set Designed by Neil Peter Jampolis; Theatre Lighting, Jane Reisman

Management: Leonard A. Mulhern
Press: Michael Alpert, Marilynn LeVine, Ellen Levene, Warren Knowlton, Anne Weinberg

* Closed Nov. 10, 1974 after limited engagement of 15 performances.

Anthony Newley

PALACE THEATRE
Opened Monday, November 25, 1974.*
Nederlander presents:

EDDIE ARNOLD

* Closed Nov. 30 after limited engagement of 8 performances. No other details available.

Henry Mancini

17

LYCEUM THEATRE
Opened Sunday, November 10, 1974.*
Samuel H. Schwartz presents the Lenox Arts Center/Music-Theater Performing Group production of:

MOURNING PICTURES

By Honor Moore; Director, Kay Carney; Music, Susan Ain; Setting, John Jacobsen; Lighting, Spencer Mosse; Costumes, Whitney Blausen; Producers, Lyn Austin, Mary Silverman; Wardrobe Supervisor, Florence Aubert; Assistant to the Director, Ellyn Marshall; Music Supervisor, Larry Abel

CAST

Margaret	Kathryn Walker
Maggie	Leora Dana
Philip	Donald Symington
Abigail	Leslie Ackerman
David	Daniel Landon
Singer	Dorothea Joyce
Doctors Rumbach, Cassidy, Berryman, Potter	Philip Carlson

UNDERSTUDIES AND STANDBYS: Maggie, Carol Teitel; Singer, Ann Duquesnay; David, Duane Mazey; Margaret, Abigail, Allison Brennan; Philip and Doctors, Joseph Daly

A Drama in two acts. The action takes place between March and September in Connecticut, New York and Washington, D.C.

Company Manager: Robert P. Cohen
Press: Merlin Group, Harriett Trachtenberg, Elizabeth Rodman
Stage Managers: Frank Marino, Duane Mazey

* Closed Nov. 10, 1974 after one performance and four previews.

Martha Swope Photos

Kathryn Walker, Leora Dana, Donald Symington
Top Right: Leslie Ackerman, Donald Symington, Leora Dana, Kathryn
Walker, Daniel Landon, Dorothea Joyce, Philip Carlson

18

HELEN HAYES THEATRE
Opened Monday, November 11, 1974.*
Phoenix Theatre presents the New Phoenix Repertory Company (T. Edward Hambleton, Michael Montel, Managing Directors; Stephen Porter, Harold Prince, Artistic Directors) in:

LOVE FOR LOVE

By William Congreve; Director, Harold Prince; Scenery, Douglas Higgins; Costumes, Franne Lee; Lighting, Ken Billington; Incidental Music, Paul Gemignani; Songs, Hugh Wheeler, Paul Gemignani; Assistant Director, Ruth Mitchell; Wardrobe Supervisor, Helen McMahon; Hairstylist, Lynn Quiyou; Assistant Managing Director, Daniel Freudenberger; Assistant General Manager, Gregory W. Taylor

CAST

Streetsweeper	Clarence Felder
Jeremy	Munson Hicks
Valentine	Joel Fabiani
Scandal	David Dukes
Trapland	Nicholas Hormann
Snap	Ernest Thomas
Buckram	Fred Morsell
Tattle	Charles Kimbrough
Mrs. Frail	Charlotte Moore
Foresight	John McMartin
Nurse	Jeanette Landis
Angelica	Glenn Close †1
Sir Sampson	George Ede
Mrs. Foresight	Ellen Tovatt
Miss Prue	Marybeth Hurt
Ben	Peter Friedman
Jenny	Patricia Conwell †2
Servant	Marge Eliot
The Elizabethan Enterprise	Lucy Cross, David Hart, Mary Springfels

UNDERSTUDIES: Sampson, Buckram, Clarence Felder; Valentine, Ben, Nicholas Hormann; Scandal, Trapland, Fred Morsell; Tattle, Foresight, Munson Hicks; Jeremy, Ernest Thomas; Mrs. Foresight, Mrs. Frail, Jeanette Landis; Nurse, Marge Eliot.

A Comedy in three acts. The action takes place in Valentine Legend's lodgings in London and the Foresight country home in Kensington.

General Manager: Marilyn S. Miller
Press: Mary Bryant, Bill Evans
Stage Managers: Robert Beard, Jonathan Penzner, Elisabeth W. Seley

* Closed Nov. 30, 1974 after limited engagement of 24 performances and 4 previews.

† Performed in previews by: 1. Mary Ure, 2. Glenn Close

Van Williams Photos

**Right: David Dukes, Ellen Tovatt
Top: Glenn Close**

John McMartin, George Ede

Peter Friedman, Charlotte Moore

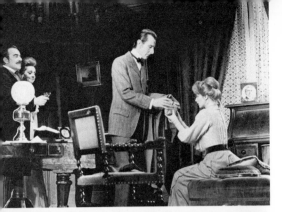

BROADHURST THEATRE

Opened Tuesday, November 12, 1974.*

James Nederlander, Inc., The Shubert Organization, Kennedy Center Productions, Inc., Adela Holzer, Eddie Kulukindis, Victor Lurie by arrangement with the Governors of the Royal Shakespeare Theatre, Stratford-upon-Avon, England, present the Royal Shakespeare Company (Trevor Nunn, Artistic Director) in:

SHERLOCK HOLMES

By Arthur Conan Doyle and William Gillette; Director, Frank Dunlop; Scenery and Costumes, Carl Toms; Music Arranged by Michael Lankester; Lighting, Neil Peter Jampolis; Production Associates, Susan Gustafson, Lee Howard; Wardrobe Supervisor, Rosalie Lahm; Hairstylist, Tiv Davenport; Scenery and Costumes Supervised by Mason Arvold

CAST

Madge Larrabee	Barbara Leigh-Hunt †1
John Forman	Harry Towb †2
James Larrabee	Nicholas Selby †3
Terese	Pamela Miles †4
Sidney Prince	Trevor Peacock †5
Alice Faulkner	Mel Martin †6
Sherlock Holmes	John Wood †7
Professor Moriarty	Philip Locke †8
John	Michael Mellinger †9
Alfred Bassick	Martin Milman †10
Billy	Sean Clarke †11
Doctor Watson	Tim Pigott-Smith †12
Jim Craigin	Morgan Sheppard †13
Thomas Leary	Keith Taylor †14
"Lightfoot" McTague	Joe Marcell †15
Parsons	Arthur Blake †16
Sir Edward Leighton	John Keston †17
Count von Stalburg	John Bott †18
Newsboy	Robert Cook †19
Violinist	Christopher Tarle
Londoners and others	Wendy Bailey †20, Joseph Charles, Alan Coates, Robert Cook, Joe Marcell, Michael Walker
Trumpet	Dick Perry

A Mystery in two acts and five scenes. The action takes place in London in 1891 in the Larrabees' drawing-room, Prof. Moriarty's underground office, Sherlock Holmes' apartment in Baker Street, Stepney gas chamber, Dr. Watson's consulting room in Kensington.

General Manager: Nelle Nugent
Company Manager: James Turner
Press: Michael Alpert, Marilynn LeVine, Ellen Levene, Anne Weinberg, Warren Knowlton
Stage Managers: George Rondo, Frank Bayer, Robert Walter, Barbara-Mae Phillips, John Handy, Rock Townsend, Joe Muzikar

* Still playing May 31, 1975. Winner of 1975 "Tony" Awards for Best Scenic Designer, and Best Lighting Designer.

† Succeeded by: 1. Christina Pickles, 2. Richard Lupino, 3. Ron Randell, 4. Diana Kirkwood, 5. Tony Tanner, 6. Lynn Lipton, 7. Patrick Horgan, John Neville, 8. Clive Revill, 9. Matthew Tobin, 10. Robert Phalen, 11. Tobias Haller, 12. Dennis Cooney, 13. Richard Woods, 14. Arthur Burghardt, 15. Richard Council, Kim Herbert, 16. Matthew Tobin, 17. Patrick Horgan, Richard Woods, Patrick Horgan, 18. Fred Stuthman, 19. Rock Townsend, 20. all Londoners succeeded by Michael Hawkins, Joe Muzikar, Susan Merril-Taylor, Robert Perault, Rock Townsend

Martha Swope Photos

Top Left: Nicholas Selby, Barbara Leigh-Hunt, John Wood, Mel Martin Below: Philip Locke, John Wood

John Neville, Clive Revill Above: Morgan Sheppard, Keith Taylor, Nicholas Selby, John Wood, Mel Martin

URIS THEATRE
Opened Wednesday, November 13, 1974.*
Ron Delsener and Nederlander present:

JOHNNY MATHIS
and
The Miracles

Musical Conductor, Jim Barnett; Associate Producer for Ron Delsener, Jonathan Scharer; Lighting, Jane Reisman; Setting, Neil Peter Jampolis

Management: Leonard A. Mulhern
Press: Michael Alpert Associates

* Closed Nov. 24, 1974 after limited engagement of 15 performances.

Top Right: Johnny Mathis
Below: The Miracles

JOHN GOLDEN THEATRE
Opened Monday, November 18, 1974.*
James J. C. Andrews and Tony Zanetta for Mainman present:

FAME

Written and Directed by Anthony J. Ingrassia; Set, Douglas W. Schmidt; Costumes, Jeffrey B. Moss; Lighting, Martin Aronstein; Sound, Chuck London; Hairstylist and Makeup Concept, Hari Van Wyngerge; Associate Producer, Shirley Rappoport; Wig Styles, Hector Garcia; Wardrobe Supervisor, Mallory Abramson

CAST

Studio Official	Rudy Hornish
Diane Cook	Ellen Barber
Makeup Man	Robert Miano
Eunice (Diane's mother)	Bibi Besch
Madge (Diane's foster mother)	Nancy Reardon
Bill (Diane's first husband)	Lawrie Driscoll
Louella O. Parsons (a helper)	Nancy Reardon
Young Gable (an adopted father)	Robert Miano
Helen Harvey (modeling agent, helper)	Nancy Reardon
Ed Aimes (casting director, helper)	Jeremy Stevens
Louis B. Mayer (an enemy)	Rudy Hornish
Ned (a lover)	Lawrie Driscoll
Eva (a teacher, confidante)	Bibi Besch
Private Dick	Jeremy Stevens
Danny Grant (a lover, career planner)	Jeremy Stevens
Tadlock (a matchmaker)	Rudy Hornish
Milton (Diane's third husband)	Lawrie Driscoll
Meg (a secretary, a confidante)	Christine Lavren
Sonny (Diane's second husband)	Lawrie Driscoll
TV News Reporter	Rudy Hornish
Walter (another TV news reporter)	Jeremy Stevens
An Established Actress (an enemy)	Christine Lavren
Richard Ronson (a business associate)	Robert Miano
Young Priest (an enemy)	Robert Miano
Sam (a teacher, confidante)	Jeremy Stevens
Luba (a coach, confidante)	Bibi Besch
Telephone Operator	Christine Lavren
Newspaper Reporter	Jeremy Stevens
Woman with fur at party	Christine Lavren
Mrs. Hodges	Christine Lavren

STANDBYS AND UNDERSTUDIES: Bibi Besch, Christine Lavren, Nancy Reardon - Audre Johnston; Ellen Barber, Christine Lavren; Lawrie Driscoll, Robert Miano - Douglas Travis

A Comedy in two acts. Place: America. Time: See the U.S.A. in your Chevrolet

General Manager: Norman Kean
Company Manager: Laurel Ann Wilson
Press: Les Schecter Associates
Stage Managers: R. Derek Swire, Peter von Mayrhauser

* Closed Nov. 18, 1974 after one performance and eleven previews.

Ellen Barber

MARTIN BECK THEATRE
Opened Thursday, November 21, 1974.*
Barry M. Brown, Fritz Holt, S. Spencer Davids present:

SATURDAY SUNDAY MONDAY

By Eduardo de Filippo; English Adaptation, Keith Waterhouse, Willis Hall; Presented by arrangement with the National Theatre of Great Britain; Directed and Designed by Franco Zeffirelli; Lighting, Roger Morgan; Costumes, Raimonda Gaetani; Hairstylist, Ted Azar; Associates to the Producers, Amos Abrams, Jan Walchko

CAST

Antonio	Walter Abel
Rosa	Sada Thompson
Peppino	Eli Wallach
Aunt Meme	Jan Miner
Raffaele	Michael Vale
Attilio	Amos Abrams
Maria	Susan Merson
Roberto	William McCauley
Rocco	Jeff Giannone
Giulianella	Francesca Bartoccini
Virginia, the maid	Minnie Gordon Gaster
Frederico, Giulianella's fiance	Gary Sandy
Luigi Ianniello, the accountant	Ron Holgate
Elena, his wife	Nina Dova
Catiello, the tailor	Michael Enserro
Michele	Terry Hinz
Dr. Cefercola	Sam Gray

STANDBYS: Rosa, Aunt Meme, Nina Dova; Antonio, Catiello, Peppino, Sam Gray; Elena, Virginia, Maria, Saax Bradbury; Giulianella, Susan Merson; Attilio, Rocco, Robert, Federico, Richard DeFabees; Dr. Cefercola, Michele, Luigi, Raffaele, John Grigas.

A Comedy in three acts. The action takes place at the present time on Saturday, Sunday, and Monday in the Priore Family's apartment in Naples.

General Management: Marvin A. Krauss Associates
Company Manager: David Wyler
Press: Merlin Group, Cheryl Sue Dolby
Stage Managers: William Dodds, John Grigas

* Closed Nov. 30, 1974 after 12 performances and 4 previews.

Ken Howard Photos

Right: Sam Gray, Jeff Giannone, Walter Abel Top: Sada Thompson, Sam Gray

William McCauley, Susan Merson, Eli Wallach

Eli Wallach, Ron Holgate, Terry Hinz

22

Opened Wednesday, November 27, 1974.*
Marc Gordon Productions in association with Nederlander presents:

THE 5th DIMENSION
with
Jo Jo's Dance Factory

Musical Director, John Myles; Choreography, Jo Jo Smith; Lighting, Jane Reisman; Setting, Robin Wagner; Choreography for The 5th Dimension, Bert Woods; Costumes, Michael Travis; Production Coordinator, Brian Avanet; Coordinator, Sylvia Brown; Musical Director for Jo Jo's Dance Factory, William Daniel

Management: Leonard A. Mulhern
Press: Michael Alpert Associates

* Closed Dec. 8, 1974 after a limited engagement of 15 performances.

The Fifth Dimension

URIS THEATRE
Opened Thursday, December 19, 1974.*
Nederlander presents:

RAPHAEL IN CONCERT
with
The Voices of New York

Lighting Design, Jane Reisman; Set Designed by Neil Peter Jampolis; Personal Manager, Fred Harris; Spanish Manager, Francisco Bermudez

Management: Leonard A. Mulhern
Press: Michael Alpert Associates, Marilyn LeVine, Warren Knowlton

* Closed Dec. 22, 1974 after limited engagement of 6 performances.

Raphael

MARK HELLINGER THEATRE

Opened Tuesday, December 3, 1974.*

Hurok in association with Herman and Diana Shumlin by arrangement with The National Theatre of Great Britain presents:

AS YOU LIKE IT

By William Shakespeare; Director, Clifford Williams; Designed by Ralph Koltai; Lighting, Robert Ornbo; Music Composed by Marc Wilkinson; Fight Director, William Hobbs; Associate Producer, Sheldon Gold

CAST

Duke Senior, Jacques living in exile	Michael Beint
Frederick, his brother	Gilbert Wynne
Lords attending on the exiled duke:	
Amiens	Ian Hanson
Jacques	John Nettleton
Le Beau, a courtier	Dennis Edwards
Charles, a wrestler	John Flint
Son of Sir Rowland de Boys:	
Oliver	David Howey
Jacques	Adam Kurakin
Orlando	Paul Hastings
Oliver's servants:	
Adam	Blake Butler
Dennis	Rod Willmott
Touchstone, a clown	Nigel Hawthorne
Sir Oliver Martext, a vicar	Christopher Robb
Corin, a shepherd	John Gay
Silvius, a shepherd	Geoffrey Burridge
William, a country boy	John Dallimore
First forest lord	David Mace
Hymen	Ian Hanson
Rosalind, daughter of the exiled duke	Gregory Floy
Celia, daughter of Frederick	David Schofield
Phebe, a shepherdess	Christopher Neame
Audrey, a country girl	Gordon Kaye
Lord and Pages .... John Dallimore, Raymund Dring, Andrew Johns, Adam Kurakin, David Mace, Jeff Murray, Christopher Robb, Rob Willmott	

A Comedy presented in two acts.

General Manager: William Orton
Press: Sheila Porter, Gifford/Wallace, Tom Trenkle
Stage Managers: Robert Findlay, Michael Joyce

* Closed Dec. 7, 1974 after seven performances.

Top: David Schofield, Gregory Floy, John Nettleton,
24   **Paul Hastings**

David Schofield, Gregory Floy, Nigel Hawthorne
Above: Geoffrey Burridge, Christopher Neame

PALACE THEATRE

Opened Thursday, December 5, 1974.*
James M. Nederlander, Roger L. Stevens, Eddie Kulukindis by arrangement with Eddie Kulukindis present The Royal Shakespeare Company's:

LONDON ASSURANCE

By Dion Boucicault; Adapted and Directed by Ronald Eyre; Assistant Director, Howard Panter; Designed by Alan Tagg; Lighting, Robert Ornbo; Costumes, David Walker, Michael Stennett; Music Arranged by Guy Woolfenden; Costume Supervisor, Frances Roe; Wig Supervisor, Janet Archibald; Wardrobe Supervisor, Billie White; Hairstylist, Roy Helland; Set and Costume Supervisor, Mason Arvold

CAST

Cool, a valet	Anthony Pedley
Martin	Tom Owen
Charles Courtly	Roger Rees
Dazzle	Bernard Lloyd
Sir Harcourt Courtly	Donald Sinden
Maximilian Harkaway	Glyn Owen
Solomon Isaacs	Leon Sinden
Pert	Sue Nicholls
James, a butler	Andy Mulligan
Grace Harkaway	Polly Adams
Mark Meddle	John Cater
Lady Gay Spanker	Elizabeth Spriggs
Adolphus Spanker	Sydney Bromley
Jenks	Douglas Anderson

STANDBYS AND UNDERSTUDIES: Grace, Marion Lines; Cool, Stephen Gordon; Meddle, Douglas Anderson, Cool, Solomon, Jenks, Martin, James, Stephen Gordon; Dazzle, Andy Mulligan; Lady Gay, Sue Nicholls; Charles, Tom Owens; Sir Harcourt, Anthony Pedley; Maximilian, Adolphus, Leon Sinden

A Comedy in two acts and six scenes. The action takes place in Sir Harcourt Courtly's house in Belgrave Square, London, and in and around Oak Hall, Gloucestershire.

General Manager: Nelle Nugent
Production Manager: John Wallbank
Company Managers: Howard Panter, Joseph Grossman
Press: Michael Alpert Associates, Anne Weinberg, Warren Knowlton Ellen Levene, Marilynn LeVine
Stage Managers: Michael Cass Jones, Keith Oldfield

Closed Jan. 12, 1975 after limited engagement of 45 performances and 2 previews.

Zoe Dominic Photos

Donald Sinden, Anthony Pedley

Top: Bernard Lloyd, Roger Rees Right: Elizabeth Spriggs Below: Polly Adams, Donald Sinden

25

LUNT-FONTANNE THEATRE
Opened Monday, December 9, 1974.*
Alexander H. Cohen and Bernard Delfont present:

WHO'S WHO IN HELL

By Peter Ustinov; Director, Ellis Rabb; Scenery, Douglas W. Schmidt; Costumes, Nancy Potts; Lighting, John Gleason; Production Associate, Hildy Parks; Associate Producer, Roy Somlyo; Production Supervisor, Jerry Adler; Staff Assistants, Meg Simon, Penny Franks; Wardrobe Supervisor, Elonzo Dann

CAST

Elbert C. Harland	George S. Irving
Arlo Forrest Buffy	Beau Bridges
Ilse	Olympia Dukakis
Samuel E. McWhirter	Bob Lawrence
Sir Augustus Ludbourne	Joseph Maher
Boris Vassilievitch Krivelov	Peter Ustinov
Arnold J. Pilger	Josef Sommer
The Frenchman	Jim Oyster
Galina Chubkina	Christina Pickles
General Mike O'Henry	G. Wood
Bundy Harris	Erin Connor

STANDBYS: Krivelov, Pilger, O'Henry, Jim Oyster; Harland, Lubourne, Miller Lide; McWhirter, Dino Shorte; Galina, Ilse, Jane Groves; Bundy, Barbara Cohen

A Drama performed without intermission.

General Manager: Roy Somlyo
Associate Manager: Seymour Herscher
Press: Richard Hummler
Stage Manager: Barbara Cohen

* Closed Dec. 14, 1974 after 8 performances and 8 previews.

Martha Swope Photos

Erin Connor, Beau Bridges, Peter Ustinov, Joseph Maher, George S. Irving
Top Right: Peter Ustinov, Beau Bridges, George S. Irving

MOROSCO THEATRE
Opened Tuesday, December 10, 1974.*
Arthur Cantor presents:

IN PRAISE OF LOVE

By Terence Rattigan; Director, Fred Coe; Scenery and Lighting, Jo Mielziner; Costumes, Theoni V. Aldredge; Assistant to the Producer, Arline Mann; Assistant to the Director, Tom Greene; Wardrobe Mistress, Agnes Farrell; Production Assistants, Jason Buzas, Craig Smith; Hairstylist, Ray Iagnocco; Wigs, Paul Huntley

CAST

Lydia Cruttwell	Julie Harris
Sebastian Cruttwell	Rex Harrison
Mark Walters	Martin Gabel
Joey Cruttwell	Peter Burnell

STANDBYS AND UNDERSTUDIES: Sebastian, Mark, Paul Sparer; Lydia, Joan Bassie; Joey, Bill Biskup

A Play in two acts. The action takes place during the past year in the Cruttwell flat in the Islington section of London on a spring evening.

Company Manager: Maurice Schaded
Press: Arthur Cantor Associates, C. George Willard, Carl Samrock
Stage Managers: Mortimer Halpern, Bill Biskup

* Closed May 31, 1975 after 200 performances and 7 previews.

Martha Swope Photos

**Right: Julie Harris, Peter Burnell
Top: Rex Harrison, Julie Harris**

Martin Gabel, Julie Harris, Rex Harrison

EUGENE O'NEILL THEATRE
Opened Wednesday, December 11, 1974.*
Emanuel Azenberg and Eugene V. Wolsk present:

GOD'S FAVORITE

By Neil Simon; Director, Michael Bennett; Settings, William Ritman; Costumes, Joseph G. Aulisi; Lighting, Tharon Musser; Assistant Director, Bob Avian; Production Supervisor, Tom Porter; Wardrobe Supervisor, Josephine Zampredi; Hairstylist, Howard Rodney; Production Assistant, Helen Kira

CAST

Joe Benjamin	Vincent Gardenia
Ben Benjamin	Lawrence John Moss
Sara Benjamin	Laura Esterman
Rose Benjamin	Maria Karnilova
David Benjamin	Terry Kiser
Mady	Rosetta LeNoire
Morris	Nick LaTour
Sidney Lipton	Charles Nelson Reilly

STANDBYS AND UNDERSTUDIES: Sidney, Ben, Ken Olfson; Rose, Jo Flores Chase; Joe, Richard Kuss; David, Philip Cusack; Mady, Mary Rio Lewis; Sara, Ellen Ruskin; Morris, Phil Lindsay

A Comedy in two acts and three scenes. The action takes place in the Benjamin mansion on the North Shore of Long Island.

Manager: Jose Vega
Company Manager: Martin Cohen
Press: Solters/Roskin, Milly Schoenbaum, Bud Westman, Nini Finkelstein
Stage Managers: Tom Porter, Philip Cusack

* Closed Mar. 23, 1975 after 116 performances and 7 previews.

Sheldon Secunda Photos

Nick LaTour, Rosetta LeNoire, Maria Karnilova, Laura Esterman, Lawrence John Moss, Vincent Gardenia, Terry Kiser Top Left: Maria Karnilova, Vincent Gardenia, Charles Nelson Reilly

HELEN HAYES THEATRE

Opened Thursday, December 12, 1974.*

Phoenix Theatre presents the New Phoenix Repertory Company (T. Edward Hambleton, Michael Montel, Managing Directors; Stephen Porter, Harold Prince, Artistic Directors) in:

THE RULES OF THE GAME

By Luigi Pirandello; Translated by William Murray; Director, Stephen Porter; Scenery, Douglas Higgins; Costumes, Nancy Potts; Lighting, Ken Billington; Wardrobe Supervisor, Helen McMahon; Hairstylist, Lynn Quiyou; Assistant General Manager, Gregory W. Taylor

CAST

Silia Gala	Joan Van Ark
Guido Venanzi	David Dukes
Clara	Jeanette Landis
Leone Gala	John McMartin
Marquis Miglioriti	Peter Friedman
Coco	Nicholas Hormann
Meme	Munson Hicks
Filippo	George Ede
Dr. Spiga	Charles Kimbrough
Barelli	Joel Fabiani
Neighbors	Clarence Felder, Glenn Close, Fred Morsell, Ellen Tovatt

UNDERSTUDIES: Leone, Munson Hicks; Silia, Glenn Close; Guido, Peter Friedman; Spiga, Filippo, Clarence Felder; Barelli, Nicholas Hormann; Clara, Marybeth Hurt

A Black Comedy in two acts and three scenes. The action takes place in 1918 in Silia's apartment, and in Leone's house.

General Manager: Marilyn S. Miller
Assistant Managing Director: Daniel Freudenberger
Press: Mary Bryant, Bill Evans
Stage Managers: Robert Beard, Jonathan Penzner, Elizabeth W. Seley

Closed Dec. 21, 1974 after limited engagement of 12 performances and 8 previews.

Van Williams Photos

: John McMartin, David Dukes Below: (C) Joan Van Ark, Ellen Tovatt

Joel Fabiani, John McMartin, Charles Kimbrough
Top: Joan Van Ark

29

BROOKS ATKINSON THEATRE

Opened Wednesday, December 18, 1974.*

Elliot Martin in association with Mortimer Levitt presents:

OF MICE AND MEN

By John Steinbeck; Director, Edwin Sherin; Scenery, Costumes, and Lighting, William and Jean Eckart; Assistant to the Director, Charles Richter; Wardrobe Supervisor, Joseph Busheme; Production Assistant, Allen Heaton; Sound and Musical Effects, Mark Hardwick

CAST

George	Kevin Conway
Lennie	James Earl Jones
Candy	Stefan Gierasch
The Boss	David Clarke
Curley	Mark Gordon
Curley's Wife	Pamela Blair
Slim	David Gale
Carlson	Pat Corley
Whit	James Staley
Crooks	Joe Seneca

STANDBYS AND UNDERSTUDIES: Curley's Wife, Linda Martin; Lennie, Crooks, Frankie Faison; George, Pat Corley; Candy, David Clarke; Curley, James Staley; Carlson, Whit, Slim, Boss, Lanny Flaherty

A Drama in two acts and six scenes. The action takes place in southern California in the 1930's, on the bank of the Salinas River in the bunkhouse, in Crook's room, in the hayloft.

General Manager: Leonard A. Mulhern
Associate General Manager: David Relyea
Company Manager: James Mennen
Press: Seymour Krawitz, Patricia McLean Krawitz, Fred Hoot
Stage Managers: Harry Young, Frankie Faison

* Closed Feb. 9, 1975 after 62 performances and 12 previews and began touring.

Martha Swope Photos

James Earl Jones, Kevin Conway

Top: James Earl Jones, Kevin Conway, Pamela Bla[i]
Left Center: David Gale, Conway, Jones, Mark Gor[don]

CIRCLE IN THE SQUARE THEATRE
Opened Thursday, December 19, 1974.*
Circle in the Square, Inc. (Theodore Mann, Artistic Director;
Paul Libin, Managing Director) presents:

WHERE'S CHARLEY?

Book, George Abbott; Based on Brandon Thomas' play "Charley's Aunt"; Music and Lyrics, Frank Loesser; Director, Theodore Mann; Scenery, Marjorie Kellogg; Lighting, Thomas Skelton; Costumes, Arthur Boccia; Choreography, Margo Sappington; Musical Direction and New Arrangements, Tom Pierson; Dialect Coach, Marjorie Phillips; Hairstylist, Roberto Fernandez; Wardrobe Supervisor, Latonia Baer; Assistant to the Director, Ted Snowdon; Production Associate, E. J. Oshins; Production Assistants, Nancy Cook, Johnny Clontz, Gordon Bendall

CAST

Brassett .... Louis Beachner
Jack Chesney .... Jerry Lanning
Charley Wykeham .... Raul Julia
Kitty Verdun .... Carol Jo Lugenbeal
Amy Spettigue .... Marcia McClain
Sir Francis Chesney .... Peter Walker
Mr. Spettigue .... Tom Aldredge
Donna Lucia D'Alvadorez .... Taina Elg
Reggie .... Dennis Cooley

STUDENTS AND YOUNG LADIES: Pamela Burrell, Jacqueline Clark, Dennis Cooley, Karen Jablons, Jack Neubeck, Craig Sandquist, Leland Schwantes, Miriam Welch

UNDERSTUDIES: Charles, Dennis Cooley; Amy, Miriam Welch; Jack, Jack Neubeck; Kitty, Karen Jablons; Donna Lucia, Pamela Burrell; Spettigue, Leland Schwantes; Sir Francis, Craig Sandquist; Brassett, Male Chorus, David-James Carroll; Female Chorus, Martha Deering

MUSICAL NUMBERS: "Where's Charley?," "Better Get out of Here," "The New Ashmolean Marching Society and Students Conservatory Band," "My Darling, My Darling," "Make a Miracle," "Serenade with Asides," "Lovelier than Ever," "The Woman in His Room," "Pernambuco," "Once in Love with Amy," "The Gossips," "At the Red Rose Cotillion," Finale

A Musical in two acts and five scenes. The action takes place during the summer of 1892 at Oxford.

Company Manager: Willian Conn
Press: Merle Debuskey, Susan L. Schulman
Stage Managers: Randall Brooks, James Bernardi

* Closed Feb. 23, 1975 after 78 performances and 20 previews. Original production opened Oct. 11, 1948 at the St. James and ran for 792 performances with Ray Bolger, Allyn Ann McLerie, Byron Palmer, and Doretta Morrow. See THEATRE WORLD, Vol. 5

Martha Swope Photos

Top Right: Raul Julia

Raul Julia (C), Jerry Lanning (R)

Marcia McClain, Raul Julia

ST. JAMES THEATRE
Opened Monday, December 23, 1974.*
Harry Rigby and Terry Allen Kramer present:

GOOD NEWS

Book, Laurence Schwab, B. G. DeSylva, Frank Mandel; Words and Music, DeSylva, Brown and Henderson; Adapted by Garry Marshall; Director, Michael Kidd; Associate Choreographer, Gary Menteer; Settings, Donald Oenslager; Costumes, Donald Brooks; Lighting, Tharon Musser; Orchestrations, Phillip J. Lang; Musical Direction, Liza Redfield; Sound, Tony Alloy; Musical Supervision and Vocal Arrangements, Hugh Martin, Timothy Gray; Dance Music and Incidental Music Composed and Arranged by Luther Henderson; Hairstylist and Makeup, Masarone; Associate Producers, Robert Anglund, Stan Hurwitz, Frank Montalvo; Wardrobe Supervisor, Anthony Karniewich; Production Coordinator, Linda Mann Reed; Production Associate, Kathy Lowe; Assistant Conductor, Mel Pahl; Production Assistant, Penny Pritchard

CAST

Bill Johnson	Gene Nelson †
Tom Marlowe	Scott Stevensen
Beef Saunders	Joseph Burke
Bobby Randall	Wayne Bryan
Pooch Kearney	Stubby Kaye
Flo	Rebecca Urich
Millie	Paula Cinko
Pat	Jana Robbins
Babe O'Day	Barbara Lail
Windy	Terry Eno
Slats	Jimmy Brennan
Sylvester	Tommy Breslin
Professor Kenyon	Alice Faye
Connie Lane	Marti Rolph
Muffin	Margaret
Colton Player	Ernie Pysher
Happy Days Quartet	Tim Cassidy, Randall Robbins, Scott Stevensen, David Thome
Acrobats	Lisa Guignard, Mary Ann Lipson, Ernie Pysher, Jeff Spielman
Baton Twirlers	Tim Cassidy, Lynda Goodfriend, Lisa Guignard
Tap Dancers	Terry Eno, Jimmy Brennan

COEDS: Paula Cinko, Robin Gerson, Lynda Goodfriend, Lisa Guignard, Anne Kaye, Mary Ann Lipson, Sally O'Donnell, Rebecca Urich, Marcia Lynn Watkins

BOYS: Michael Austin, Jimmy Brennan, Tim Cassidy, Ernie Pysher, Randall Robbins, Jeff Spielman, David Thome

UNDERSTUDIES: Prof. Kenyon, Jana Robbins; Bill, Randall Robbins; Pooch, Jimmy Brennan; Connie, Anne Kaye; Tom, Terry Eno; Pat, Paula Cinko; Babe, Rebecca Urich; Bobby, Tommy Breslin; Beef, Ernie Pysher; Millie, Marcia Lynn Watkins; Sylvester, Jimmy Brennan; Flo, Sally O'Donnell; Windy, David Thome; Slats, Tim Cassidy; Margaret, Mini; Alternates, Kathie Carson, David Fredericks

MUSICAL NUMBERS: Overture, "He's a Ladies' Man," "The Best Things in Life Are Free," "Just Imagine," "Happy Days," "Button up Your Overcoat," "Lucky in Love," "You're the Cream in My Coffee," "Varsity Drag," "Together," "Tait Song," "Today's the Day," "Girl of the Pi Beta Phi," "Good News," "Keep Your Sunny Side Up," "Life Is Just a Bowl of Cherries," "The Professor and the Students," Finale

A Musical Comedy in two acts. The action takes place in the mid-1930's on and around the campus of Tait College.

General Managers: Joseph Harris, Ira Bernstein
Company Managers: Archie Thomson, George Boras
Press: Henry Luhrman Associates, Terry Lilly
Stage Managers: Phil Friedman, Craig Jacobs, Judy Olsen

* Closed Jan. 4, 1975 after 16 performances and 51 previews. Original production opened Sept. 6, 1927 at the 46th Street Theatre and ran for 551 performances

† Played by John Payne during previews and pre-Broadway tour

Martha Swope Photos

Top Left: Alice Faye, Marti Rolph
Below: Stubby Kaye (L), Gene Nelson (R)

Tommy Breslin Above: Scott Stevensen, Jana Robbins

BOOTH THEATRE
Opened Sunday, December 29, 1974.*
Adela Holzer presents:

ALL OVER TOWN

By Murray Schisgal; Director, Dustin Hoffman; Scenery, Oliver Smith; Costumes, Albert Wolsky; Lighting, John Gleason; Production Supervisor, Mitche Miller; Wardrobe Supervisor, Kenneth E. Gelow; Assistant to the Director, Theresa Curtin; Hairstylist, Paul Huntley; Production Assistants, Kim Cruse, Bruce MacCallum

CAST

Millie	Pamela Payton-Wright [1]
Sybil Morris	Jill Eikenberry [2]
Dr. Lionel Morris	Barnard Hughes [3]
Beebee Morris	Carol Teitel
Charles Kogan	Jim Jansen [4]
Colonel Martin Hopkins	William LeMassena
Lewis	Cleavon Little [5]
Louie	Zane Lasky [6]
Michael Boyssan	Joseph Leon
Jackie Boyssan	Patti Perkins
Laurent	Gerrit de Beer
Philomena Hopkins	Polly Holliday [7]
Demetrius	Richard Karron
Mr. Harold P. Hainsworth	Every Hayes
Francine	Hershey Miller
Maharishi Bahdah	Michael Gorrin
Detective Peterson	Barney Martin [8]
Detective Kirby	Richard Karron

UNDERSTUDIES: Morris, Hopkins, Maharishi, Peterson, Joseph Leon; Philomena, Beebee, Ruth Baker; Lewis, Hainsworth, Joseph Keyes; Sybil, Millie, Jackie, Francine, Carol Nadell; Michael, Demetrius, Joel Wolfe; Charles, Louie, Kirby, Laurent, Chip Zien; Lewis, Every Hayes

A Comedy in two acts and five scenes. The action takes place at the present time in the Morris Family's duplex apartment on Manhattan's Upper East Side.

General Management: Theatre NOW
Company Manager: Leo K. Cohen, Robb Liady
Press: Michael Alpert Associates, Ellen Levene, Marilynn LeVine, Warren Knowlton
Stage Managers: Frank Marino, Barbara-Mae Phillips, Ron Abbott, Richard Karron

* Closed July 20, 1975 after 233 performances and 12 previews.

† Succeeded by: 1. Beth Hattub, 2. Mary Nealie, 3. George S. Irving, Thomas Toner, 4. Philip Polito, 5. Ron O'Neal, 6. Chip Zien, 7. Sarah Saltus, 8. Joel Wolfe

Martha Swope Photos

Left: Zane Lasky, Cleavon Little
Top: Cleavon Little, Barnard Hughes

**Pamela Payton-Wright, Barnard Hughes,
Cleavon Little**

**Polly Holliday, Barnard Hughes,
Richard Karron**

33

HELEN HAYES THEATRE
Opened Thursday, January 2, 1975.*
Phoenix Theatre presents the New Phoenix Repertory Company (T. Edward Hambleton, Michael Montel, Managing Directors; Stephen Porter, Harold Prince, Artistic Directors) in:

THE MEMBER OF THE WEDDING

By Carson McCullers; Director, Michael Montel; Scenery, Douglas Higgins; Costumes, Donald Brooks; Lighting, Ken Billington; Incidental Music, Charles Strouse, Assistant Managing Director, Daniel Freudenberger; Assistant to the Director, Donna Sontheimer; Wardrobe Supervisor, Helen McMahon; Hairstylist, Lynn Quiyou

CAST

Berenice Sadie Brown	Marge Eliot
Frankie Addams	Marybeth Hurt
John Henry West	Eamon MacKenzie
Jarvis	Nicholas Hormann
Janice	Glenn Close
Mr. Addams	George Ede
Mrs. West	Charlotte Moore
Doris	Jeanette Landis
Sis Laura	Marcella Lowery
T. T. Williams	Fred Morsell
Honey Camden Brown	Ernest Thomas
Barney MacKean	Tim Wilson

UNDERSTUDIES: Berenice, Marcella Lowery; Frankie, Glenn Close; John Henry, John E. Dunn; Mr. Addams, Clarence Felder; T. T., Honey, Charles Turner; Mrs. West, Jeanette Landis

A Drama in three acts and five scenes. The action takes place during August of 1945 in a small Southern town.

General Manager: Marilyn S. Miller
Assistant General Manager: Gregory W. Taylor
Press: Mary Bryant, Bill Evans
Stage Managers: Robert Beard, Jonathan Penzner, Elizabeth W. Seley

* Closed Jan. 11, 1975 after a limited engagement of twelve performances and four previews.

Van Williams Photos

Eamon MacKenzie, George Ede, Marybeth Hurt, Glenn Close, Nicholas Hormann Top Right: Marybeth Hurt, Marge Eliot, Eamon MacKenzie Below: George Ede, Nicholas Hormann, Charlotte Moore, Glenn Close, Marybeth Hurt

Opened Sunday, January 5, 1975.*
Ken Harper presents:

THE WIZ

Book, William F. Brown; Based on L. Frank Baum's "The Wonderful Wizard of Oz"; Music and Lyrics, Charlie Smalls; Direction and Costumes, Geoffrey Holder; Setting, Tom H. John; Lighting, Tharon Musser; Orchestrations, Harold Wheeler; Musical Direction and Vocal Arrangements, Charles H. Coleman; Dance Arrangements, Timothy Graphenreed; Choreography and Musical Numbers staged by George Faison; Wardrobe Supervisor, Yvonne Stoney; Assistant to Choreographer and Dance Captain, John Parks; Music Coordinator, Earl Shendell; Wigs, Stanley James

CAST

Aunt Em	Tasha Thomas
Toto	Nancy
Dorothy	Stephanie Mills
Uncle Henry	Ralph Wilcox †
Tornado	Evelyn Thomas
Munchkins	Phylicia Ayers-Allen, Pi Douglass, Joni Palmer, Andy Torres, Carl Weaver
Addaperle	Clarice Taylor
Yellow Brick Road	Ronald Dunham, Eugene Little, John Parks, Kenneth Scott
Scarecrow	Hinton Battle
Crows	Wendy Edmead, Frances Morgan, Ralph Wilcox †
Tinman	Tiger Haynes
Lion	Ted Ross
Kalidahs	Phillip Bond, Pi Douglass, Rodney Green, Evelyn Thomas, Andy Torres
Poppies	Lettie Battle, Leslie Butler, Eleanor McCoy, Frances Morgan, Joni Palmer
Field Mice	Phylicia Ayers-Allen, Pi Douglass, Carl Weaver, Ralph Wilcox †
Gatekeeper	Danny Beard
The Wiz	Andre De Shields
Evillene	Mabel King
Lord High Underling	Ralph Wilcox †
Soldier Messenger	Carl Weaver
Winged Monkey	Andy Torres
Glinda	Dee Dee Bridgewater

EMERALD CITY CITIZENS: Lettie Battle, Leslie Butler, Wendy Edmead, Eleanor McCoy, Frances Morgan, Joni Palmer, Evelyn Thomas, Phillip Bond, Ronald Dunham, Rodney Green, Eugene Little, John Parks, Kenneth Scott, Andy Torres

PIT SINGERS: Frank Floyd, Sam Harkness, Jozella Reed, Tasha Thomas

STANDBYS AND UNDERSTUDIES: Dorothy, Arnetia Walker; Addaperle, Jozella Reed, Butterfly McQueen; Tinman, Ralph Wilcox; Scarecrow, Pi Douglass; Evillene, Tasha Thomas; Aunt Em, Dee Dee Bridgewater; Glinda, Phylicia Ayers-Allen; Swing Dancer-Singers, Cynthia Ashby, Otis Sallid

MUSICAL NUMBERS: "The Feeling We Once Had," "Tornado Ballet," "He's the Wizard," "Soon as I Get Home," "I Was Born on the Day before Yesterday," "Ease on down the Road," "Slide Some Oil to Me," "Mean Ole Lion," "Kalidah Battle," "Be a Lion," "Lion's Dream," "Emerald City Ballet (Pssst)," "So You Wanted to Meet the Wizard," "To Be Able to Feel," "No Bad News," "Funky Monkeys," "Everybody Rejoice," "Who Do You Think You are?," "Believe in Yourself," "Y'All Got It!," "A Rested Body Is a Rested Mind," "Home"

A Musical in 2 acts and 16 scenes, with a prologue.

General Managers: Emanuel Azenberg, Eugene V. Wolsk
Manager: Jose Vega
Company Manager: Susan Bell
Press: The Merlin Group, Sandra Manley, Elizabeth Rodman

Still playing May 31, 1975. Winner of 1975 "Tony" Awards for Best Musical, Best Musical Score, Best Supporting Actor and Actress in a Musical (Ted Ross, Dee Dee Bridgewater), Best Director of a Musical, Best Costumes, Best Choreographer

Succeeded by Albert Fann

Martha Swope Photos

Top Right: Stephanie Mills, Hinton Battle, also below with Tiger Haynes (top), Ted Ross Right: Andre De Shields, Tiger Haynes

Mabel King Above: Clarice Taylor, Dee Dee Bridgewater

ALVIN THEATRE
Opened Tuesday, January 7, 1975.*
Philip Rose, Gloria and Louis K. Sher present:

SHENANDOAH

Book, James Lee Barrett, Peter Udell, Philip Rose; Based on Screenplay of the same title by James Lee Barrett; Music, Gary Geld; Lyrics, Peter Udell; Director, Philip Rose; Choreography, Robert Tucker; Scenery, C. Murawski; Lighting, Thomas Skelton; Costumes, Pearl Somner, Winn Morton; Orchestrations, Don Walker; Musical Direction, Lynn Crigler; Dance Arrangements, Russell Warner; Hairstylist, Werner Sherer; Technical Advisor, Mitch Miller; Wardrobe Supervisor, Lee Decker; Production Assistant, Rosemary Troyano

CAST

Charlie Anderson	John Cullum
Jacob	Ted Agress
James	Joel Higgins
Nathan	Jordan Suffin
John	David Russell
Jenny	Penelope Milford †
Henry	Robert Rosen
Robert (The Boy)	Joseph Shapiro
Anne	Donna Theodore
Gabriel	Chip Ford
Reverend Byrd	Charles Welch
Sam	Gordon Halliday
Sergeant Johnson	Edward Penn
Lieutenant	Marshall Thomas
Tinkham	Charles Welch
Carol	Casper Roos
Corporal	Gary Harger
Marauder	Gene Masoner
Engineer	Ed Preble
Confederate Sniper	Craig Lucas

ENSEMBLE: Tedd Carrere, Stephen Dubov, Gary Harger, Brian James, Robert Johanson, Sherry Lambert, Craig Lucas, Gene Masoner, Paul Myrvold, Dan Ormond, Casper Roos, J. Kevin Scannell, Jack Starkey, E. Allan Stevens, Marshall Thomas, Matt Gavin

UNDERSTUDIES: Charlie, Edward Penn; Jacob, Gene Masoner; James, Marshall Thomas, Paul Myrvold; Nathan, Craig Lucas, Matt Gavin; John, Matt Gavin, Robert Johanson; Jenny, Betsy Beard; Henry, Robert Johanson, Craig Lucas; Robert, Jeffrey Rea; Anne, Kay Coleman; Gabriel, Brent Carter; Rev. Byrd, Ed Preble; Sam, Robert Rosen; Sgt. Johnson, Casper Roos; Lt., Tedd Carrere; Tinkham, Ed Preble; Carol, J. Kevin Scannell; Corporal, Robert Johanson; Marauder, Engineer, E. Allan Stevens

MUSICAL NUMBERS: "Raise the Flag of Dixie," "I've Heard It All Before," "Pass the Cross to Me," "Why Am I Me," "Next to Lovin' I Like Fightin'," "Over the Hill," "The Pickers Are Comin'," "Meditation," "We Make a Beautiful Pair," "Violets and Silverbells," "It's a Boy," "Freedom," "Papa's Gonna Make It Alright," "The Only Home I Know," "Pass the Cross to Me"

A Musical in two acts with a prologue. The action takes place during the Civil War in the Shenandoah Valley of Virginia.

General Manager: Helen Richards
Assistant General Manager: Steven Suskin
Press: Merle Debuskey, Leo Stern
Stage Managers: Steve Zweigbaum, Arturo E. Porazzi, Sherry Lambert

* Still playing May 31, 1975. Received 1975 "Tony" Awards for Best Musical Book, and Best Actor in a Musical (John Cullum).
† Succeeded by Maureen Silliman

Friedman-Abeles Photos

John Cullum, Donna Theodore
Above: John Cullum, Penelope Milford

Top: John Cullum, David Russell, Joseph Shapiro, Donna Theodore, Joel Higgins, Ted Agress, Penelope Milford, Gordon Halliday

36

LONGACRE THEATRE
Opened Monday, January 20, 1975.*
Adela Holzer presents:

THE RITZ

By Terrence McNally; Director, Robert Drivas; Scenery and Costumes, Lawrence King, Michael H. Yeargan; Lighting, Martin Aronstein; Hairstylist, Vidal Sassoon; Production Supervisor, Mitch Miller; Wardrobe Supervisor, Mariane Torres; Assistant to the Director, Tony de Santis; Production Assistant and Assistant to the Director, Gary Keeper

CAST

Abe	George Dzundza
Claude Perkins	Paul B. Price
Gaetano Proclo	Jack Weston †1
Chris	F. Murray Abraham †2
Googie Gomez	Rita Moreno †3
Maurine	Hortensia Colorado
Michael Brick	Stephen Collins
Tiger	John Everson †4
Duff	Christopher J. Brown
Carmine Vespucci	Jerry Stiller †5
Vivian Proclo	Ruth Jaroslow †6
Pianist	Ron Abel
Policeman	Bruce Bauer †7
Crisco	Richard Boccelli
Sheldon Farenthold	Tony de Santis
Patron in Chaps	John Remme †8
Patron from Sheridan Square	Steve Scott

STANDBYS AND UNDERSTUDIES: Vivian, Vera Lockwood; Gaetano, Carmine, George Dzundza; Googie, Hortensia Colorado; Brick, Bruce Bauer; Tiger, Duff, Steve Scott; Chris, Claude, John Remme; Abe, Richard Boccelli

A Comedy in two acts. The action takes place at the present time in The Ritz Baths.

General Managers: Edward H. Davis, William Court Cohen
Company Manager: Leo K. Cohen
Press: Michael Alpert Associates, Marilynn LeVine, Ellen Levene, Anne Weinberg, Warren Knowlton
Stage Managers: Larry Forde, Steve Beckler

* Still playing May 31, 1975. Rita Moreno received a 1975 "Tony" Award for Best Supporting Actress in a play.
† Succeeded by: 1. George Dzundza for 2 weeks, 2. Robert Drivas for 2 weeks, 3. Chi Chi Navarro during illness, Hortensia Colorado, 4. Larry Gilman, 5. Mike Kellin, 6. Antonia Rey, 7. Thomas Leopold, 8. John Mintun.

Friedman-Abeles Photos

Right: Jerry Stiller, Jack Weston Top: Tony DeSantis, Ruth Jaroslow, Jerry Stiller, Stephen Collins, F. Murray Abraham, Steve Scott

Rita Moreno, Jerry Stiller, Jack Weston

Paul B. Price, Jack Weston

SAM S. SHUBERT THEATRE
Opened Sunday, January 26, 1975.*
Richard Barr, Charles Woodward, Clinton Wilder present:

SEASCAPE

By Edward Albee; Directed by the author; Scenery and Lighting
James Tilton; Costumes, Fred Voelpel; Assistant to General Manager, Michael O'Rand; Assistant to the Producers, Jerry Sirchia
Assistant to the Director, William Martin; Wardrobe Supervisor
Sophie Fields; Production Assistant, Christopher Cara; Special
Sound Effects, Garry Harris; Movement Technique Consultant, William Rhys; Hairstylist, Paul Huntley; Miss Anderman's and Mr
Langella's Makeup, Carl Fullerton

CAST

Nancy	Deborah Kerr
Charlie	Barry Nelson
Leslie	Frank Langella
Sarah	Maureen Anderman

STANDBYS: Nancy, Sarah, Augusta Dabney; Charlie, William
Prince; Leslie, Allen Williams

A Comedy in two acts. The action takes place at the present time
on a beach.

General Manager: Michael Kasdan
Press: Betty Lee Hunt Associates, Maria C. Pucci, Stanley F.
Kaminsky

* Closed March 22, 1975 after 63 performances and 7 previews
Winner of 1975 Pulitzer Prize. Mr. Langella received a 197
"Tony" Award for Best Supporting Actor in a Play. Opened Apri
1, 1975 at the Shubert Theatre in Los Angeles for a five week run

Friedman-Abeles Photos

Deborah Kerr, Barry Nelson
Top Left: Maureen Anderman, Frank Langella

Opened Thursday, February 6, 1975.*
Arthur Cantor by arrangement with H. M. Tennent, Ltd. presents:

PRIVATE LIVES

By Noel Coward; Director, John Gielgud; Sets, Anthony Powell; Costumes, Germinal Rangel, Beatrice Dawson; Lighting, H. R. Poindexter; Wardrobe Supervisor, John Whitmore; Assistant to the Producer, Arline Mann; Production Assistant, Craig Smith; Hairstylist, Richard Sabre; Wigs, Ken Lintott; Production Manager, Mitchell Erickson

CAST

Sybil Chase	Niki Flacks
Elyot Chase	John Standing
Victor Prynne	Remak Ramsay
Amanda Prynne	Maggie Smith
Louise	Marie Tommon

STANDBYS AND UNDERSTUDIES: Amanda, Laura Stuart; Elyot, Victor, Colin Hamilton; Sybil, Marie Tommon; Louise, Nancy Aiello

A Comedy in three acts. The action takes place in the late 1920's, on the terrace of a hotel in France, and in Amanda's flat in Paris.

Company Manager: Ronald Bruguiere
Press: Carl Samrock, C. George Willard
Stage Managers: Robert Crawley, Colin Hamilton, Nancy Aiello

Closed April 26, 1975 after 92 performances and 2 previews. Original production opened Jan. 27, 1931 at the Times Square Theatre with Noel Coward, Gertrude Lawrence, Laurence Olivier and played 256 performances. Tallulah Bankhead revived it at the Plymouth Theatre Oct. 4, 1948 for 248 performances. (See THEATRE WORLD, Vol. 5) Last revival (Dec. 4, 1969) with Tammy Grimes and Brian Bedford ran for 199 performances at the Billy Rose Theatre. (See THEATRE WORLD, Vol. 26)

Zoe Dominic Photos

John Standing, Maggie Smith

Top: Maggie Smith, Remak Ramsay
Right: John Standing, Niki Flacks

39

JOHN GOLDEN THEATRE
Opened Tuesday, February 11, 1975.*
Jay Julien in association with Sidney Eden presents:

<h1 style="text-align:center">HUGHIE
and
DUET</h1>

"Hughie" by Eugene O'Neill; "Duet" by David Scott Milton; Director, Martin Fried; Scenery, Kert Lundell; Costumes, Ruth Morley; Lighting, Marc B. Weiss; Associate Producer, Norman A. Levy; Wardrobe Supervisor, Arlene Konowetz; Production Assistant, Mary Shortkroff

CAST

"Hughie"

A Night Clerk .... Peter Maloney
"Erie" Smith .... Ben Gazzara

The action takes place in the lobby of a small hotel off Times Square in New York City. It is between 4 and 5 A.M. of a day in the summer of 1928.

"Duet"

Leonard Pelican .... Ben Gazzara

The action takes place at the present time in the lobby of the Forty-third Street Hotel off Times Square in New York City.

General Manager: Max Allentuck
Company Manager: James Awe
Press: Merle Debuskey, Leo Stern
Stage Managers: Franklin Keysar, Rudolph Bond

* Closed March 8, 1975 after 31 performances and 6 previews.

Ben Gazzara in "Duet"

Ray Fisher Photos

Top: Peter Maloney, Ben Gazzara in "Hughie"

ETHEL BARRYMORE THEATRE
Opened Wednesday, February 26, 1975.*
Edgar Lansbury and Joseph Beruh in association with The
Shubert Organization present:

THE NIGHT THAT MADE AMERICA FAMOUS

Music and Lyrics, Harry Chapin; Director, Gene Frankel; Choreographer, Doug Rogers; Scenery, Kert Lundell; Costumes, Randy Barcelo; Lighting, Imero Fiorentino; Lighting Supervision, Fred Allison; Multi-Media Development Consultants, Imero Fiorentino Associates; Multi-Media Executed by Jim Sant'Andrea; Multi-Media under the Direction of Joshua White; Musical Direction, Stephen Chapin; Dance Arrangements, John Morris; Audio Design, Michael Solomon; Associate Producer, Nan Pearlman; Dance Captain, Bonnie Walker; Technical Director, George B. Honchar; Wardrobe Master, Joe Busheme; Assistant to Producers, Darrell Jonas; Assistant to the Director, Linda Swenson; Assistant Choreographer, Mercedes Ellington; Production Assistants, Linda Canavan, Jo Marie Wakefield, Lee Minter; Musical Coordinator, Joseph Stecko

CAST

Harry Chapin	Delores Hall
Kelly Garrett	Sid Marshall
Gilbert Price	Ernie Pysher
Bill Starr	Lynne Thigpen
Alexandra Borrie	Tom Chapin
Mercedes Ellington	Stephen Chapin

MUSICAL NUMBERS: Prologue, "Six String Orchestra," "Give Me a Road," "Sunday Morning Sunshine," "It's My Day," "Give Me a Cause," "Welfare Ray," "Better Place to Be," "Give Me a Wall," "Peace Teachers," "Pigeon Run," "Changing of the Guard," "When I Look Up," "Sniper," "Great Divide," "Taxi," "Cockeyed John," "Mr. Tanner," "Maxie," "Fugue: Love Can't, When Maudey Wants a Man, I'm a Wonderfully Wicked Woman," "Battleground Bummer," "Stoopid," "Cat's in the Cradle," "Cockeyed John, Give Me a Dream," "Too Much World," "As I Grow Older," "Beginning of the End," "The Night That Made America Famous."

A Musical in two acts. The action takes place during the last fifteen years.

General Management: Marvin A. Krauss Associates
Company Managers: Al Isaac, Bob Skerry
Press: Gifford/Wallace, Tom Trenkle
Stage Managers: Herb Vogler, Bonnie Walker

* Closed April 6, 1975 after 75 performances.

Kenn Duncan Photos

Delores Hall, Harry Chapin, Kelly Garrett

Harry Chapin (also above)

Ann Reinking, Joel Grey, Jay Garner

PALACE THEATRE
Opened Monday, March 3, 1975.*
Max Brown and Byron Goldman in association with Robert
Victor and Stone Widney present:

GOODTIME CHARLEY

Book, Sidney Michaels; Music, Larry Grossman; Lyrics, Hal
Hackady; Director, Peter H. Hunt; Dances and Musical Numbers
Staged by Onna White; Associate to Miss White, Martin Allen;
Scenery, Rouben Ter-Arutunian; Costumes, Willa Kim; Lighting,
Feder; Orchestrations, Jonathan Tunick; Incidental Music, Arthur
B. Rubinstein; Dance Music, Daniel Troob; Production Manager,
Peter Stern; Hairstylist, Ted Azar; Original Cast Album by RCA
Records; Assistant to the Director, Stuart H. Ross; Production As-
sistant, Virginia Lim; Wardrobe Supervisor, Adelaide Laurino; Mu-
sical Conductors, Arthur B. Rubinstein, Lawrence J. Blank

CAST

Henry V	Brad Tyrrell
Charles VI	Hal Norman
Isabella of Bavaria	Grace Keagy
Queen Kate	Rhoda Butler †1
Phillip of Burgundy	Charles Rule †2
Yolande	Peggy Cooper
Marie	Nancy Killmer
Pope	Ed Becker
Charley	Joel Grey
Archbishop Regnault de Cartres	Jay Garner
General George de La Tremouille	Louis Zorich
Servants	George Ramos, Ross Miles, Pat Swayze, Cam Lorendo
Agnes Sorel	Susan Browning
Jesters	Andy Hostettler, Gordon Weiss
Joan of Arc	Ann Reinking
Minguet	Richard B. Shull
First English Captain	Charles Rule
Second English Captain	Hal Norman
Third English Captain	Kenneth Bridges
Herald	Hal Norman
Trio	Kenneth Bridges, Brad Tyrrell, Ed Becker
Louis	Dan Joel
Chef	Charles Rule
First Soldier	Kenneth Bridges
Second Soldier	Brad Tyrrell
Third Soldier	Hal Norman
Guard	Charles Rule
Estelle	Kathe Dezina

SINGERS: Rhoda Butler, Peggy Cooper, Kathe Dezina, Nancy
Killmer, Jane Ann Sargia, Ed Becker, Kenneth Bridges, Hal Norman, Charles Rule, Brad Tyrrell

DANCERS: Andy Hostettler, Cam Lorendo, Dan Joel, Glen
McClaskey, Ross Miles, Tod Miller, Sal Pernice, George Ramos, Pat
Swayze, Gordon Weiss, Jerry Yoder

STANDBYS AND UNDERSTUDIES: Charley, Austin Pendleton;
Joan, Susan Browning; Agnes, Rhoda Butler; Minguet, Kenneth
Bridges; Archbishop, Hal Norman; General, Charles Rule; Isabella,
Peggy Cooper; Yolande, Nancy Killmer; Kate, Marie, Estelle, Jane
Ann Sargia; Henry Charles, Philip, Pope, Kenneth Bridges

MUSICAL NUMBERS: "History," "Goodtime Charley," "Visions
and Voices," "Bits and Pieces," "To Make the Boy a Man," "Why
Can't We All Be Nice," "Born Lover," "I Am Going to Love the
Man You're Going to Be," "Castles of the Loire," "Coronation,"
"You Still Have a Long Way to Go," "Merci, Bon Dieu," "Confes-
sional," "One Little Year," "I Leave the World"

A Musical in 2 acts and 17 scenes. The action begins in France
March 6, 1429 and ends February 28, 1461.

General Manager: Ralph Roseman
Company Manager: Ken Myers
Press: Max Eisen, Barbara Glenn, Judy Jacksina
Stage Managers: Bruce W. Stark, Lee Murray

* Closed May 31, 1975 after 104 performances and 12 previews.
† Succeeded by: 1. Maureen Maloney, 2. Kenneth Bridges

Kenn Duncan Photos

Top Left: Joel Grey, Susan Browning (seated)

MINSKOFF THEATRE
Opened Monday, March 3, 1975.*
Mike Merrick and Don Gregory present:

HENRY FONDA AS CLARENCE DARROW

By David W. Rintels; Based on "Clarence Darrow for the Defense" by Irving Stone; Directed by John Houseman; Scenery and Lighting, H. R. Poindexter; Production Coordinator, Ed Goldstein; Assistant to the Producers, Rita Colecchio, Cheryl Lawrence; Mr. Fonda's Wardrobe, Carmen Lamola; A Dome Production

A one-man show presented in two parts.

Company Manager: David Hedges
Press: Seymour Krawitz, Patricia McLean Krawitz, Fred Hoot
Stage Managers: George Eckert, Berny Baker

* Closed March 22, 1975 after 18 performances. This production opened originally March 26, 1974 at the Helen Hayes Theatre, but was forced to close after 29 performances because of Mr. Fonda's illness, and toured after his recovery.

Top Right: Henry Fonda as Clarence Darrow

Right: Nancy King Zeckendorf, Diosa Costello, Walter Willison Below: Ethel Merman, Dorothy Stickney, Dorian Harewood

IMPERIAL THEATRE
Sunday, March 9, 1975.*
Friends of the Theatre and Music Collection of the Museum of the City of New York present:

A GALA TRIBUTE TO JOSHUA LOGAN

Conceived and Produced by Anna Sosenko; Staged by Donald Saddler; Musical Direction, Colon Romoff; Lighting Design, Jane Reisman; Sound Designed by Abe Jacob; Assistants to Mr. Saddler, Arthur Faria, Francois Marie Benard, S. Robert Goodman; Production Assistants, Merle Hubbard, Mark Reynolds, Dale Carter; Scenic Consultant, Neil Peter Jampolis

CAST

Larry Blyden, Sheila Bond, Nell Carter, Diosa Costello, Douglas Fairbanks, Jr., Jose Ferrer, Henry Fonda, Stanley Glover, Lee Goodman, Dolores Gray, Albert Hague, Dorian Harewood, Maria Karnilova, Jane Pickens Langley, Avon Long, Patricia Marand, Ethel Merman, James Michener, Phyllis Newman, Betsy Palmer, Tom Perkins, Harold Rome, Walter Slezak, James Stewart, Dorothy Stickney, Tom Tryon, Ray Walston, Walter Willison, Nancy King Zeckendorf, Zorina

DANCERS AND SINGERS: Gian Carlo Esposito, Debby Feezel, Vicki Geyer, Yolande Graves, Richard Hamilton, Richard T. Herd, Helen Jennings, Christy Laurence, Geoffrey Leon, Johanna Lockwood Lester, Rudolf Lowe, Betty Lynd, Randy Martin, Justin McDonough, John Otis, Pamela Palluzzi, Lacy Darrell Phillips, Sandra Phillips, Janet Power, Orrin Reilly, Kenneth H. Roberts, Gil Robins, Arlen Dean Snyder, Peter Turgeon, Jaison Walker

Manager: Victor Samrock
Press: Robert Ullman, Louise Weiner Ment
Stage Managers: Edward Preston, Robert Schear, Bob Buzzell

One performance only.

Henry Fonda, James Stewart, Joshua Logan

LYCEUM THEATRE
Opened Sunday, March 9, 1975.*
Joseph S. Kutrzeba and Spofford J. Beadle present:

THE LIEUTENANT

By Gene Curty, Nitra Scharfman, Chuck Strand; Director, William Martin; Choreography, Dennis Dennehy; Scenery and Costumes, Frank J. Boros; Lighting, Ian Calderon; Musical Direction, Chuck Strand; Music Arranged by Chuck Strand and Gus Montero; Sound, Bill Merrill; Music Coordinator, Earl Shendell; Wardrobe Mistress, Latonia Baer; Hairstylist, Edward Cohen; Production Assistant, Paul Andrecovich

CAST

Lieutenant	Eddie Mekka
Judge	Gene Curty
Recruiting Sergeant	Joel Powers
First General	Chet D'Elia
Second General	Eugene Moose
Third General	Danny Taylor
OCS Sergeant	Gene Curty
Chaplain	Don McGrath
Captain	Walt Hunter
Sergeant "C" Company	Jim Litten
"C" Company	Steven Boockvor, Clark James, Jim-Patrick McMahon, Joseph Pugliese, Burt Rodriguez, Tom Tofel
G. I.	Tom Tofel
Senator	Joel Powers
First Congressman	Don McGrath
Clergyman	Jim Litten
Second Congressman	Burt Rodriguez
First Reporter	Jim Litten
Second Reporter	Tom Tofel
Third Reporter	Jo Speros
Prosecutor	Burt Rodriguez
Defense Attorney	Gordon Grody
New Recruit	Alan K. Siegel
Dance Captain	Jim-Patrick McMahon

STANDBYS AND UNDERSTUDIES: D. A., Dan Kruger; Swing Dancer, Marius Hanford; OCS Seargeant, Steven Boockvor; Prosecutor, Gene Curty; Judge, D.A., Walt Hunter; Third General, Clark James; Third Reporter, Beth Kennedy; G. I., 2nd Congressman, Dan Kruger; Clergyman, Reporter, Jim-Patrick McMahon; Chaplain, Eugene Moose; Lieutenant, Joseph Pugliese; Captain, Burt Rodriguez; Recruiting Sgt., Senator, Congressman, Danny Taylor; New Recruit, Tom Tofel

MUSICAL NUMBERS: "The Indictment," "Join the Army," "Look for the Men with Potential," "Kill," "I Don't Want to Go over to Vietnam," "Eulogy," "At 0700 Tomorrow," "Massacre," "Something's Gone Wrong," "Twenty-Eight," "Let's Believe in the Captain," "Final Report," "I Will Make Things Happen," "He Wants to Put the Army in Jail," "There's No Other Solution," "I'm Going Home," "We've Chosen You, Lieutenant," "The Star of This War," "On Trial for My Life," "The Conscience of a Nation," "Damned No Matter How He Turned," "The Verdict," Finale

A Rock Opera in Two acts. The action alternates between Vietnam and the United States over a three-year period.

Company Manager: James O'Neill
Press: Alan Eichler, Marilyn Percy
Stage Managers: Phillip Moser, Marius Hanford

* Closed March 16, 1975 after 9 performances and 7 previews.

Bert Andrews Photos

Top Right: Burt Rodriguez, Eddie Mekka
Below: Eddie Mekka

Jim Litten, Tom Tofel, Eddie Mekka, Jo Speros

Meat Loaf
Right: Abigale Haness, Bill Miller

BELASCO THEATRE
Opened Monday, March 10, 1975.*
Lou Adler presents the Michael White Production of:

THE ROCKY HORROR SHOW

Book, Music, and Lyrics, Richard O'Brien; Director, Jim Sharman; Designed by Brian Thomson; Costumes, Sue Blane; Lighting, Chipmonck; Set Supervisor, Peter Harvey; Costume Supervisor, Pearl Somner; Sound Design, Abe Jacob; Musical Director, D'Vaughn Pershing; Assistant Director, Nina Faso; Associate Producer, John Beug; Arrangements, Richard Hartley; Special Effects, Robert E. McCarthy; Hairstylist, Ramon Gow

CAST

Narrator	Graham Jarvis
Belasco Popcorn Girl (Trixie)	Jamie Donnelly
Janet	Abigale Haness
Brad	Bill Miller
Riff-Raff	Ritz O'Brien
Columbia	Boni Enten
Magenta	Jamie Donnelly
Frank	Tim Curry
Rocky	Kim Milford
Eddie/Dr. Scott	Meat Loaf

UNDERSTUDIES: Eddie/Dr. Scott, David P. Kelly; Janet, Magenta, Pamela Palluzzi; Brad, Rocky, Robert Rhys.

MUSICAL NUMBERS: "Science Fiction," "Wedding Song," "Over at the Frankenstein Place," "Sweet Transvestite," "Time Warp," "The Sword of Damocles," "Charles Atlas Song," "What Ever Happened to Saturday Night," "Eddie's Teddy," "Once in Awhile," "Planet Shmanet Janet," "It Was Great When It All Began," "Super Heroes," Finale

A Rock Musical in 2 acts and 17 scenes.

General Management: Avnet & Krauss
Company Manager: Brian Avnet
Press: Michael Alpert Associates, Ellen Levene, Marilyn LeVine, Anne Weinberg, Warren Knowlton
Stage Managers: David H. Banks, August Amarino, Judy Burns

* Closed April 6, 1975 after 45 performances and 4 previews. The Belasco was converted into a cabaret theatre.

Martha Swope Photos

**Tim Curry, Kim Milford (on hands),
Boni Enten**

45

URIS THEATRE
Opened Tuesday, March 11, 1975.*
Marcia Day and Marc Lemkin present:

SEALS AND CROFTS
with
Walter Heath

Executive Producer, Marc Lemkin; Sound and Lighting, Nine House Productions; Production Direction, Bud Becker, Rich Cohen; Stage Direction, Tim McCarthy, Randall Woods; Personal Manager, Marcia Day; Road Manager, Gloria Sanchez; Lighting Consultants, Jay Baker, Ron Cohen; Sound Consultants, Gary Stouffer, Randy Ezritti

A concert with Jimmy Seals and Dash Crofts, and special guest star Walter Heath.

Press: Susan Joseph, Florence Towers

* Closed March 16, 1975 after limited engagement of 6 performances.

ST. JAMES THEATRE
Opened Wednesday, March 12, 1975.*
David Merrick and The John F. Kennedy Center present The National Theatre of Great Britain in:

THE MISANTHROPE

By Moliere; Adapted by Tony Harrison; Director, John Dexter; Designed by Tanya Moiseiwitsch; Lighting, Andy Phillips; Music Arranged by Marc Wilkinson; Production Supervisor, Lucia Victor; Lighting Supervisor, Jennifer Tipton; Wardrobe Supervisor, Gene Wilson; Wardrobe Mistress, Kathleen Foster; Production Assistant, Sandra Mandel; Staff Associates, Penny Franks, Mary T. Smith; Hairdressers, Phyllis Della, Tony Marrero

CAST

Alceste	Alec McCowen
Philinte	Robert Eddison
Oronte	Gawn Grainger
Celimene	Diana Rigg
Eliante, Celimene's cousin	Louie Ramsay
Arsinoe	Gillian Barge
Acaste	Nicholas Clay
Clitandre	Albert Roffrano
Basque, Celimene's servant	Daniel Thorndike
Official of Academie Francaise	Stephen Williams
Dubois, Alceste's valet	Peter Needham

UNDERSTUDIES: Alceste, Alfred Karl; Celimene, Carole Monferdini; Philinte, Basque, John Straub; Oronte, Official, Dubois, Tom McLaughlin; Acaste, Josef Warik; Clitandre, Patrick Watkins; Arsinoe, Elaine, Claudia Wilkens

A comedy in two acts. The action takes place in 1966 in Celimene's house in Paris.

General Manager: Helen L. Nickerson
Company Manager: Gino Giglio
Press: Solters/Roskin, Bud Westman
Stage Managers: Alan Hall, Claudia Wilkens

* Closed May 31, 1975 after 94 performances.

Carl Samrock Photos

Top Left: Diana Rigg, Alec McCowen

Diana Rigg, Gawn Grainger, Alec McCowen, Louie Ramsay

BROOKS ATKINSON THEATRE
Opened Thursday, March 13, 1975.*
Morton Gottlieb, Dasha Epstein, Edward L. Schuman, Palladium Productions present:

SAME TIME, NEXT YEAR

By Bernard Slade; Director, Gene Saks; Scenery, William Ritman; Costumes, Jane Greenwood; Lighting, Tharon Musser; Hairstylist, Steve Atha; Associate Producers, Ben Rosenberg, Warren Crane; Production Assistant, Alyssa Levy

CAST

Doris .... Ellen Burstyn †1
George .... Charles Grodin †2

Standbys: Rochelle Oliver, Joe Ponazecki

A Comedy in two acts and six scenes. The entire action of the play takes place in a guest cottage of a country inn in Northern California, from 1951 to 1975.

Company Manager: Martin Cohen
Press: Solters/Roskin, Milly Schoenbaum
Stage Manager: Kate Pollock

* Still playing May 31, 1975. Miss Burstyn received a 1975 "Tony" Award for Best Actress in a Play.
† Succeeded by: 1. Joyce Van Patten, Loretta Swit, 2. Conrad Janis, Ted Bissell

Martha Swope Photos

Right: Charles Grodin, Ellen Burstyn
(also below)

Ellen Burstyn

Charles Grodin, Ellen Burstyn

HELEN HAYES THEATRE

Opened Tuesday, March 18, 1975.*
Charles Bowden, Slade Brown, Jim Milford present:

DON'T CALL BACK

By Russell O'Neil; Director, Len Cariou; Setting, Oliver Smith;
Costumes, Whitney Blausen; Lighting, John Gleason; Electronic
Sound, Ken Guilmartin; Miss Francis' gown by Egon von Fursten-
berg; Associate Producer, Morgan Holman; Wardrobe Supervisor,
Cindy Chock; Production Associate, David Hadden

CAST

Jason Croydon	Richard Niles
Miriam Croydon	Arlene Francis
Gregory Schaeffer	Stanley Grover
Clarence	Dorian Harewood
Crowbar	Mark Kologi
Trucker	Robert Hegez
Claire	Catherine Byers

STANDBYS AND UNDERSTUDIES: Miriam, Claire, Lynne
Stuart; Gregory, Chet Gould; Jason Crowbar, Frank Di Elsi; Clarence, Trucker, James Weaver

A Thriller in 2 acts and 5 scenes. The action takes place at the
present time in a Park Avenue duplex apartment in New York City.

General Manager: James Walsh
Press: Seymour Krawitz, Patricia McLean Krawitz, Barbara
Carroll, Fred Hoot
Stage Managers: Donald Christy, Frank Di Elsi, James Weaver

* Closed March 18, 1975 after one performance and 13 previews.

Friedman-Abeles Photos

Right: Dorian Harewood, Arlene Francis
Below: Richard Niles, Robert Hegez, Arlene
Francis, Dorian Harewood

Arlene Francis

Arlene Francis, Catherine Byers

WINTER GARDEN
Opened Wednesday, March 19, 1975.*
Cyma Rubin presents:

DOCTOR JAZZ

Book, Music and Lyrics (mostly by) Buster Davis; Direction and Choreography, Donald McKayle; Scenery and Costumes, Raoul Pene duBois; Lighting, Feder; Sound, Abe Jacob; Principal Orchestrator, Luther Henderson; Associate Orchestrators, Dick Hyman, Sy Oliver; Dance Music Arranger and Incidental Music Composer, Luther Henderson; Musical Director and Vocal Arrangements, Buster Davis; Associate Musical Director, Joyce Brown; Scenic Coordinator, Mason Arvold; Costume Coordinator, David Toser; Hairstylist, Randy Coronato; Entire Production Supervised by John Berry; Assistants to the Director, Gail Benedict, Michele Simmons; Dance Captain, Gail Benedict; Wardrobe Supervisor, Jack Kopera; Assistant Conductor, Sande Campbell; Assistant to the Producer, Lenore Edis; A Pyxidium Ltd. Production

CAST

Steve Anderson	Bobby Van
Spasm Band	Quitman D. Fludd III, Bruce Heath, Hector Jaime Mercado, Jeff Veazey
Jonathan Jackson, Jr.	Jack Landron
Henry	Paul Eichel
Harriet Lee	Peggy Pope †
Georgia Sheridan	Lillian Hayman
Edna Mae Sheridan	Lola Falana
Georgia's Girls	Bonita Jackson, Michele Simmons, Annie Joe Edwards
Harriet's Girls	Gail Benedict, Sarah Coleman, Maggy Gorrill, Kitty Jones, Diana Mirras, Sally Neal, Yolanda R. Raven, Catherine Rice
Lead Dancer	Hector Jaime Mercado
The Group	Bruce Heath, Bonita Jackson, Sally Neal, Yolanda R. Raven, Michele Simmons
Rudy	Paul Eichel
Pete	Eron Tabor
Harry	Paul Eichel
Showgirls	Sarah Coleman, Kitty Jones

SINGERS: James Braet, Annie Joe Edwards, Paul Eichel, Marian Haraldson, Evelyn McCauley, Eron Tabor

DANCERS: Gail Benedict, Quitman D. Fludd III, Maggy Gorrill, Bob Heath, Bruce Heath, David Hodo, Bonita Jackson, Michael Lichtefeld, Hector Jaime Mercado, Diana Mirras, Sally Neal, Yolanda R. Raven, Catherine Rice, Michele Simmons, Dan Strayhorn, Jeff Veazey

ONSTAGE MUSICIANS: George Davis, Jr., Dennis Drury, John Gill, Vince Giordano, Haywood Henry, Danny Moore, San Pilafian, Candy Ross, Bob Stewart, Allan Vache, Warren Vache, Jr., Earl Williams, Francis Williams

UNDERSTUDIES: Steve, Eron Tabor; Edna Mae, Sally Neal; Georgia, Annie Joe Edwards; Harriet, Evelyn McCauley; Jonathan, Quitman D. Fludd III; Swing Dancers, Marshall Blake, JoAnn Ogawa

MUSICAL NUMBERS: "Dr. Jazz," "We've Got Connections," "Georgia Shows 'Em How," "Cleopatra Had a Jazz Band," "Juba Dance," "Charleston Rag," "I've Got Elgin Watch Movements in My Hips," "Blues My Naughty Sweetie Gave to Me," "Good-Time Flat Blues," "Evolution Papa," "Rehearsal Tap," "I Love It," "Anywhere the Wind Blows," "Those Shiek-of-Araby Blues," "Look Out for Lil," "Swanee Strut," "All I Want Is My Black Baby Back," "Everybody Leaves You," "Free and Easy"

A Musical in 2 acts and 20 scenes.

General Manager: C. Edwin Knill
Company Manager: James Mennen
Press: David Powers
Stage Managers: Michael Turque, Marnel Sumner, Harrison Avery

* Closed March 22, 1975 after 5 performances and 42 previews.
† Played by Joan Copeland in previews.

Martha Swope Photos

Top Right: Bobby Van, Lillian Hayman
Below: Lola Falana, Hector Jaime Mercado

Bobby Van, Joan Copeland
Above: Lola Falana, Bobby Van

CIRCLE IN THE SQUARE THEATRE

Opened Thursday, March 20, 1975.*
Circle in the Square (Theodore Mann, Artistic Director; Paul Libin, Managing Director) presents:

ALL GOD'S CHILLUN GOT WINGS

By Eugene O'Neill; Director, George C. Scott; Sets, Ming Cho Lee; Costumes, Patricia Zipprodt; Lighting, Thomas Skelton; Associate Designer, Marjorie Kellogg; Hairstylist, Roberto Fernandez; Wardrobe Supervisor, Sydney Brooks; Production Associate, E. J. Oshins; Assistant to the Managing Director, Alan Wasser; Production Assistants, Nancy Cook, Johnny Clontz, Gordon Bendall, Bernard Ferstenberg, Atsumi Kolba, Anne Oberbroeckling

CAST

Mickey, as a child	Jimmy Baio
Joe, as a child	Robert Lee Grant
Jim, as a child	Carl Thomas
Shorty, as a child	Tommy Gilchrist
Ella, as a child	Susan Jayne
Shorty	Ken Jennings
Joe	Tim Pelt
Mickey	Tom Sminkey
Jim Harris	Robert Christian
Ella Downey	Trish Van Devere
Wino	Chuck Patterson
Mrs. Harris	Minnie Gentry
Hattie Harris	Vickie Thomas
Harmonica Player	Craig Wasson
Singers	Chuck Patterson, Craig Wasson

CHILDREN: Ginny Binder, Beatrice Dunmore, Helen Jennings, Kathy Rich, Derrel Edwards

STREET PEOPLE: Alice Nagel, Ted Snowdon, Arthur French, Verona Barnes, Robert Earl Jones, Gracie Carroll

UNDERSTUDIES AND STANDBYS: Ella, Judith Barcroft; Jim, Joe, Chuck Patterson; Shorty, Mickey, Craig Wasson; Jim, Joe as children, Derrel Edwards; Ella as a child, Ginny Binder; Hattie, Mrs. Harris, Verona Barnes

A Drama in two acts and seven scenes. The action takes place in lower New York City, years ago.

Company Manager: William Conn
Press: Merle Debuskey, Susan L. Schulman
Stage Managers: Randall Brooks, James Bernardi

* Closed May 4, 1975 after 53 performances and 23 previews. First presented at the provincetown Playhouse in New York City on May 15, 1924.

Mary Ellen Mark Photos

Robert Christian, also top
with Trish Van Devere

Trish Van Devere, Robert Christian

50

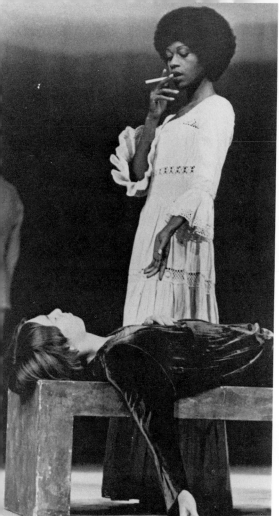

ANTA THEATRE

Opened Saturday, March 22, 1975.*
The Byrd Hoffman Foundation, Inc. presents:

A LETTER FOR QUEEN VICTORIA

Written and Directed by Robert Wilson; Music, Alan Lloyd in collaboration with Michael Galasso; Choreography, Andrew DeGroat; Scenery and Costume Supervision, Peter Harvey; Lighting Supervision, Beverly Emmons, Carol Mullins; Musical Direction, Michael Galasso; Sound Supervisor, R. O. Willis

CAST

SINGERS: Sheryl Sutton, Cynthia Lubar, George Ashley, Stefan Brecht, Kathryn Cation, Alma Hamilton, Christopher Knowles, James Neu, Robert Wilson

DANCERS: Andrew DeGroat, Julia Busto

MUSICIANS: Michael Galasso, Susan Krongold, Kevin Byrnes, Laura Epstein, Kathryn Cation

An Opera in four acts performed with one intermission. Entractes by Robert Wilson and Christopher Knowles.

Company Manager: C. Edwin Knill
Press: The Merlin Group, Sandra Manley
Stage Managers: Terrence Chambers, Carol Mullins

* Closed April 5, 1975 after 18 performances and 3 previews.

Beatrice Heyligers Photos
**Top: Kathryn Cation, Sheryl Sutton
Right: Robert Wilson Below: Christopher
Knowles, Sheryl Sutton**

Sheryl Sutton, Cindy Lubar, Scotty Snyder

AMBASSADOR THEATRE
Opened Tuesday, April 2, 1975.*
Alexander H. Cohen presents:

WE INTERRUPT THIS PROGRAM

By Norman Krasna; Director, Jerry Adler; Scenery, Robert Randolph; Costumes, Pearl Somner; Lighting, Marc B. Weiss; Sound, Jack Shearing; Production Associate, Hildy Parks; Associate Producer, Roy A. Somlyo; Presented in association with ABC Entertainment; Audio production by Dan Aron for No Soap Radio; Associate Manager, Seymour Herscher; Assistants to Producer, Julie Hughes, Kim Sellon; Production Assistant, Meg Simon; Staff Assistant, Michael Lonergan; Wardrobe Supervisor, Elonzo Dann

CAST

Amanda Williams	Holland Taylor
Sam Williams	Brandon Maggart
Benny	Tony Major
Dave	Dino Shorte
Kenny	Charles Turner
Howie	Howard Rollins, Jr.
Jim	J. W. Smith
Luke	Taurean Blacque
Al Seaver	Dick Anthony Williams
Stage Manager	Stanley Brock
Man in brown suit	Taylor Reed
Gunga Din	Miller Lide
Jason Taylor	Marshall Borden
Father Murray	George Hall
Lt. Burke	Frederick Coffin
Sonny Seaver	Albert Hall
Louise Fletcher	Theta Tucker
Patrolman Walker	Don Creech
Mr. Johnson	John D. Seymour
Mrs. Johnson	Abby Lewis
Laura Woodley	Susan Kendall Newman
Albert Woodley	James Ray Weeks
Detective Louis Harris	Lloyd Hollar

UNDERSTUDIES: Al, Howard Rollins, Jr.; Sonny, Dino Shorte; Burke, Stanley Brock; Luke, Tony Major; Harris, Charles Turner; Benny, Dave, Jimmy Smith; Stage Manager, Jason, Father, Johnson, Jim Cavanaugh; Amanda, Mrs. Johnson, Esther Benson; Louise, Stephannie Hampton Howard; Walker, Woodley, Miller Lide; Laura, Barbara Cohen

A Mystery Thriller performed without intermission. The action takes place on the stage of the Ambassador Theatre in New York City tonight.

Company Manager: Joel Wyman
Press: David Powers, Martha Mason, Richard Hummler
Stage Managers: Murray Gitlin, Robert O'Rourke

* Closed April 5, 1975 after 7 performances and 21 previews.

Martha Swope Photos

Marshall Borden, Albert Hall, Fred Coffin, Taurean Blacque, Dino Shorte, Miller Lide, Stanley Brock, Lloyd Hollar, Tony Major, Dick Anthony Williams Top Right: Blacque, Coffin, Hall, Williams Below: Abby Lewis, John D. Seymour

52

JOHN GOLDEN THEATRE
Opened Monday, April 7, 1975.*
Richard Barr, Charles Woodward, Terry Spiegel present:

P.S. YOUR CAT IS DEAD!

By James Kirkwood; Director, Vivian Matalon; Setting and Lighting, William Ritman; Costumes, Frank J. Boros; Associate Producer, Neal Du Brock; Produced in cooperation with the Buffalo Studio Arena Theatre; Assistant to the Producers, Jerry Sirchia; Technical Consultant, John Maher; Wardrobe Supervisor, Sophie Fields; Production Assistant, Christopher Cara

CAST

Vito	Tony Musante
Kate	Jennifer Warren
Jimmy	Keir Dullea
Fred	Peter White
Carmine	Antony Ponzini
Janie	Mary Hamill
Wendell	Bill Moor

STANDBYS AND UNDERSTUDIES: Jimmy, Peter White; Vito, Antony Ponzini; Kate, Janie, Sharon De Bord; Fred, Wendell, Carmine, Duncan Hoxworth

A Comedy in two acts and three scenes. The action takes place at the present time in Jimmy Zoole's loft apartment in New York City on New Year's Eve.

General Manager: Michael Kasdan
Assistant to General Manager: Michael O'Rand
Press: Betty Lee Hunt, Maria Pucci, Stanley Kaminsky
Stage Managers: Mark Wright, Duncan Hoxworth

* Closed April 20, 1975 after 16 performances and 5 previews.

Friedman-Abeles Photos

Right: Jennifer Warren, Keir Dullea
Top: Jennifer Warren, Peter White, Tony Musante, Keir Dulea

Keir Dullea, Tony Musante

Bill Moor, Antony Ponzini, Mary Hamill

SAM S. SHUBERT THEATRE
Opened Monday, April 14, 1975.*
Arthur Cantor by arrangement with H. M. Tennent, Ltd.,
presents:

THE CONSTANT WIFE

By W. Somerset Maugham; Director, John Gielgud; Designed by
Alan Tagg; Costumes, Beatrice Dawson; Lighting, H. R. Poindexter;
Production Manager, Mitchell Erickson; Assistant to the Producer,
Arline Mann; Wardrobe Supervisor, Kathe Long; Hairstylist, Joseph Osofsky; Production Assistant, Craig Smith; American Scenic
Production Supervised by H. R. Poindexter; Costumes Supervised
by Jane Greenwood

CAST

Mrs. Culver .... Brenda Forbes
Bentley .... Richard Marr
Martha Culver .... Delphi Lawrence
Barbara Fawcett .... Marti Stevens
Constance Middleton .... Ingrid Bergman
Marie-Louise Durham .... Carolyn Lagerfelt
John Middleton FRCS .... Jack Gwillim
Bernard Kersal .... Paul Harding
Mortimer Durham .... Donald Silber

STANDBYS AND UNDERSTUDIES: Constance, Jillian Lindig;
Mrs. Culver, Martha, Constance Dix; Middleton, Joe Hill; Barbara,
Jillian Lindig; Marie-Louise, Sigourney Weaver; Kersal, Mortimer,
Richard Marr

A Comedy in three acts. The action takes place in John Middleton's house in Harley Street, London, in the late 1920's.

Company Manager: Marshall Young
Press: Gertrude Bromberg, C. George Willard
Stage Managers: David Taylor, Joe Hill, Sigourney Weaver

* Closed May 10, 1975 after limited engagement of 32 performances
to continue touring.

**Left: Ingrid Bergman, Carolyn Lagerfelt,
Donald Silber Top: Ingrid Bergman,
Brenda Forbes**

Ingrid Bergman

Jack Gwillim, Ingrid Bergman, Paul Harding

54

MINSKOFF THEATRE

Opened Monday, April 14, 1975.*
Aaron Russo in association with Ron Delsener presents:

BETTE MIDLER'S
CLAMS ON THE HALF SHELL

Directed and Choreographed by Joe Layton; Settings and Costumes, Tony Walton; Lighting, Beverly Emmons; Sound, Stan Miller; Musical Director, Don York; Associate Choreographer, Andre De Shields; Orchestrations, Jimmie Haskell; Production Coordinator, Fritz Holt; Assistant to the Producers, Jerry Wynn; Special Material, Bruce Vilanch, Bill Hennessy, Jerry Blatt; Additional Lyrics, Jerry Blatt, Bette Midler; Wardrobe Supervisor, Sydney Smith; Hairstylist, Terry Foster; Producer, Aaron Russo; Associate Producer, Ron Delsener

CAST

BETTE MIDLER
with
Lionel Hampton

THE HARLETTES: Charlotte Crossley, Robin Grean, Sharon Redd

THE MICHAEL POWELL ENSEMBLE: Michael Powell, Charlene Ricks, Doretha Doctor, Jeannie Paige, Clifford Jamerson, Peggy Williams, Ricardo Portlette, Joey Coleman, Vinson Cunningham, Shirley Underwood, Lee Roy Cooks, Norman P. Hawkins

General Management: Brian Avnet/Marvin A. Krauss Associates
Press: Howard Atlee Associates
Stage Manager: George Boyd

* Closed June 22, 1975 after limited engagement of 80 performances. No production photos available.

Top Right: (front) Barbara Andres, Tovah Feldshuh, Virginia Sandifur, Rebecca York, Mary Sue Finnerty, Jamie Donnelly, (back) Jimmy Brennan, Stephen Lehew, Jim Litten, Wayne Bryan, Laurence Guittard
Right: "The Cakewalk"

HELEN HAYES THEATRE

Opened Tuesday, May 13, 1975.*
Lester Osterman Productions (Lester Osterman-Richard Horner) in association with Worldvision Enterprises Inc. presents:

RODGERS & HART

Music, Richard Rodgers; Lyrics, Lorenz Hart; Concept by Richard Lewine and John Fearnley; Director, Burt Shevelove; Choreography, Donald Saddler; Music Direction and Vocal Arrangements, Buster Davis; Principal Orchestrator and Dance Music Arranger, Luther Henderson; Additional Orchestrations, Jim Tyler, Bill Brohn, Robert Russel Bennett; Setting, David Jenkins; Costumes, Stanley Simmons; Lighting, Ken Billington; Assistant Choreographer, Arthur Faria; Hairstylist, Ted Azar; Production Manager, Mortimer Halpern; Wardrobe Supervisor, Joseph Busheme; Assistant to the Director, Drew Hill; Production Assistant, Jeffrey Schissler; Dance Captain, Pamela Peadon; Assistant Conductor, Jay Brower

CAST

Barbara Andes	Mary Sue Finnerty
Jimmy Brennon	Laurence Guittard
Wayne Bryan	Stephen Lehew
David-James Carroll	Jim Litten
Jamie Donnelly	Virginia Sandifur
Tovah Feldshuh	Rebecca York

STANDBYS: Kevin Daly, Pamela Peadon, David Thome, Judi Rolin

A program of songs by Rodgers and Hart presented in two acts.

General Manager: Leonard Soloway
Press: Seymour Krawitz, Patricia McLean Krawitz, Barbara Carroll
Stage Managers: Mortimer Halpern, Bryan Young, Kevin Daly

* Closed Aug. 16, 1975 after 108 performances and 22 previews.

Friedman-Abeles Photos

Jimmy Brennan, Jamie Donnelly, Jim Litten

BROADWAY PRODUCTIONS FROM PAST SEASONS
THAT RAN THROUGH THIS SEASON

BROADHURST THEATRE
Opened Wednesday, June 7, 1972.*
(Moved November 21, 1972 to Royale Theatre)
Kenneth Waissman and Maxine Fox in association with Anthony D'Amato present:

GREASE

Book, Music and Lyrics, Jim Jacobs and Warren Casey; Director, Tom Moore; Musical Numbers and Dances Staged by Patricia Birch; Musical Supervision and Orchestrations by Michael Leonard; Musical Direction, Vocal and Dance Arrangements, Louis St. Louis; Scenery, Douglas W. Schmidt; Costumes, Carrie F. Robbins; Lighting, Karl Eigsti; Sound, Jack Shearing; Hairstyles, Jim Sullivan; Production Assistant, Carolyn Ciplet; Original Cast Album by MGM Records; General Management, Theatre Now, Inc.

CAST

Miss Lynch	Dorothy Leon†1
Patty Simcox	Ilene Kristen‡2
Eugene Florczyk	Tom Harris†3
Jan	Garn Stephens†4
Marty	Meg Bennett†5
Betty Rizzo	Adrienne Barbeau†6
Doody	James Canning†7
Roger	Walter Bobbie†8
Kenickie	Timothy Meyers†9
Sonny LaTierri	Jim Borrelli†10
Frenchy	Marya Small†11
Sandy Dumbrowski	Carole Demas†12
Danny Zuko	Barry Bostwick†13
Vince Fontaine	Gardner Hayes†14
Johnny Casino	Alan Paul†15
Cha-Cha Gregorio	Kathi Moss
Teen Angel	Alan Paul†15

UNDERSTUDIES: Female Roles, Joy Rinaldi, Alaina Warren; Male Roles, John Fennessy, Albert Insinnia, Tony Shultz

MUSICAL NUMBERS: "Alma Mater," "Summer Nights," "Those Magic Changes," "Fredd, My Love," "Greased Lightnin'," "Mooning," "Look at Me," "I'm Sandra Dee," "We Go Together," "Shakin' at the High School Hop," "It's Rainin' on Prom Night," "Born to Hand-Jive," "Beauty School Dropout," "Alone at a Drive-In Movie," "Rock 'n' Roll Party Queen," "There Are Worse Things I Could Do," "All Choked Up," Finale.

A Musical in two acts and twelve scenes. The action takes place at the reunion of the Class of 1959 of Rydell High School.

General Manager: Edward H. Davis
Company Managers: Edward H. Davis, Robb Lady
Press: Betty Le Hunt, Henry Luhrman, Harriett Trachtenberg, Maria C. Pucci, Stanley F. Kaminsky, Kevin Ottem
Stage Managers: T. Schuyler Smith, John Fennessy, Tom Harris, Larry Forde, Paul Bengston, John Everson, M. William Lettich, Lynne Guerra

* Still playing May 31, 1975. For original production, see THEATRE WORLD, Vol. 28,

† Succeeded by: 1. Sudie Bond, Ruth Russell, 2. Joy Rinaldi, Carol Culver, 3. Barry Smith, Stephen Van Benschoten, Lloyd Alann, 4. Jamie Donnelly, Rebecca Gilchrist, 5. Denise Nettleton, Marilu Henner, 6. Elaine Petricoff, Randee Heller, 7. Barry J. Tarallo, 8. Richard Quarry, John S. Driver, Ray DeMattis, Michael Tucci, 9. John Fennessy, Jerry Zaks, 10. Matt Landers, 11. Ellen March, Joy Rinaldi, 12. Ilene Graff, Candice Earley, 13. Jeff Conaway, John Lansing, 14. Jim Weston, John Holly, Walter Charles, 15. Bob Garrett, Philip Casnoff, Joe Rifici

Friedman-Abeles Photos

Top Right: Ilene Graff, John Lansing
Below: Ellen March and beauty school choir

John Lansing, Walter Charles

IMPERIAL THEATRE

Opened Monday, October 23, 1972.*
Stuart Ostrow presents:

PIPPIN

Book, Roger O. Hirson; Music and Lyrics, Stephen Schwartz;
Director-Choreographer, Bob Fosse; Scenery, Tony Walton; Costumes, Patricia Zipprodt; Lighting, Jules Fisher; Musical Direction, Stanley Lebowsky, Rene Wiegert; Orchestrations, Ralph Burns; Dance Arrangements, John Berkman; Sound, Abe Jacob; Hairstyles, Ernest Adler; Original Cast Album by Motown Records.

CAST

Leading Player	Ben Vereen†1
Pippin	John Rubinstein†2
Charles	Eric Berry
Lewis	Christopher Chadman†3
Fastrada	Leland Palmer†4
Musician/Swordbearer	John Mineo†5
The Head	Roger Hamilton
Berthe	Irene Ryan†6
Beggar	Richard Korthaze†7
Peasant	Paul Solen†8
Noble	Gene Foote†9
Field Marshal	Roger Hamilton
Catherine	Jill Clayburgh†10
Theo	Shane Nickerson

STANDBYS AND UNDERSTUDIES: Pippin, Dean Pitchford; Leading Player, Northern J. Calloway; Berthe, Fay Sappington; Catherine, Joy Franz; Theo, George Parry; Charles, Roger Hamilton; Fastrada, Mitzi Hamilton; Dance Alternates, Jill Owens, Andy Keyser

MUSICAL NUMBERS: "Magic to Do," "Corner of the Sky," "Welcome Home," "War Is a Science," "Glory," "Simple Joys," "No Time at All," "With You," "Spread a Little Sunshine," "Morning Glow," "On the Right Track," "Kind of Woman," "Extraordinary," "Love Song," Finale.

A Musical in eight scenes, performed without intermission. The action takes place in 780 A.D. and thereabouts, in the Holy Roman Empire and thereabouts.

General Managers: Joseph Harris, Ira Bernstein
Press: Solters/Roskin, Milly Schoenbaum, Joshua Ellis
Stage Managers: Phil Friedman, Lola Shumlin, Paul Phillips, Roger A. Bigelow, Herman Magidson, Edward Preston

* Still playing May 31, 1975.
† Succeeded by: 1. Northern Calloway, Samuel E. Wright, 2. Dean Pitchford, Michael Rupert, 3. Justin Ross, 4. Priscilla Lopez, Patti Karr, 5. Ken Urmston 6. Lucie Lancaster, Dorothy Stickney, 7. Larry Merritt, 8. Chet Walker, 9. Larry Giroux, 10. Betty Buckley

Top Right: Michael Rupert, Patti Karr, Eric Berry (R) Below: Samuel E. Wright

Lucie Lancaster

Michael Rupert, Shane Nickerson, Betty Buckley

Ralph Carter, Virginia Capers, Ernestine Jackson

FORTY-SIXTH STREET THEATRE
Opened Thursday, October 18, 1973.*
(Moved to Lunt-Fontanne Theatre January 14, 1975)
Robert Nemiroff presents:

RAISIN

Book, Robert Nemiroff, Charlotte Zaltzberg; Based on Lorraine Hansberry's play "A Raisin in the Sun"; Music, Judd Woldin; Lyrics, Robert Brittan; Director-Choreographer, Donald McKayle; Scenery, Robert U. Taylor; Costumes, Bernard Johnson; Lighting, William Mintzer; Musical Director-Conductor, Howard A. Roberts, Margaret Harris; Orchestrations, Al Cohn, Robert Freedman; Vocal Arrangements, Joyce Brown, Howard Roberts; Dance Arrangements, Judd Woldin; Incidental Arrangements, Dorothea Freitag; Associate Producers, Sydney Lewis, Jack Friel; Production Associates, Irving Welzer, Will Mott, Charles Briggs; Consultant to Producer, Joseph Burstin; Technical Adviser, Mitch Miller; Assistant Manager, Duke Kant; Sound, James Travers; Wardrobe Supervisors, Lee Decker, Mary Eno; Hairstylists, Stanley James, Bruce Clark; Associate Conductor, Robert Freedman; Assistant Conductor, Joseph Cali; Dance Captain, Zelda Pulliam; Production Assistant, Cassandra Harris; Assistant to Director, Dorene Richardson; Original Cast Album, Columbia Records

CAST

Pusher	Al Perryman†1
Victim	Loretta Abbott
Ruth Younger	Ernestine Jackson
Travis Younger	Ralph Carter†2
Mrs. Johnson	Helen Martin
Walter Lee Younger	Joe Morton
Beneatha Younger	Deborah Allen
Mama Lena Younger	Virginia Capers
Bar Girl	Elaine Beener
Bobo Jones	Ted Ross†3
Willie Harris	Walter P. Brown
Joseph Asagai	Robert Jackson†4
African Drummer	Chief Bey
Pastor	Herb Downer†5
Pastor's Wife	Marenda Perry†6
Karl Lindner	Richard Sanders

PEOPLE OF THE SOUTHSIDE: Chuck Thorpes, Eugene Little, Karen Burke, Zelda Pulliam, Elaine Beener, Renee Rose, Paul Carrington, Marenda Perry, Gloria Turner, Don Jay, Glenn Brooks, Marilyn Hamilton, Edward Love, Keith Simmons, Eric Townsley, Alyce Elizabeth Webb, Vanessa Shaw, Clinton Keen

STANDBYS AND UNDERSTUDIES: Mama, Barbara Montgomery; Walter, Herb Downer; Ruth, Vanessa Shaw; Walter, Joseph, Autirs Paige; Beneatha, Renee Rose; Mama, Mrs. Johnson, Alyce Elizabeth Webb; Karl, Will Mott; Willie, Bobo, Pastor, Don Jay; Travis, Eric Townsley; Bar Girl, Zelda Pulliam

MUSICAL NUMBERS: "Prologue," "Man Say," "Whose Little Angry Man," "Runnin' to Meet the Man," "A Whole Lotta Sunlight," "Booze," "Alaiyo," "African Dance," "Sweet Time," "You Done Right," "He Come Down This Mornin'," "It's A Deal," "Sidewalk Tree," "Not Anymore," "Measure of the Valleys"

A Musical in two acts. The action takes place in Chicago in the 1950's.

General Managers: John Corkill, Helen Richards
Press: Max Eisen, Maurice Turet, Barbara Glenn, Judy Jacksina
Stage Managers: Helaine Head, Nate Barnett, Anthony Neely, Autris Paige

* Still playing May 31, 1975. Winner of 1974 "Tonys" for Best Musical, and Best Musical Actress (Virginia Capers)
† Succeeded by: 1. Chuck Thorpes, 2. Paul Carrington, Darren Green, 3. Irving Barnes, 4. Herb Downer, 5. Milt Grayson, 6. Alyce Elizabeth Webb

Top Left: Virginia Capers, Joe Morton, Ernestine Jackson Below: Joe Morton, Deborah Allen

The Chelsea Theater Center of Brooklyn (Robert Kalfin, Artistic Director; Michael David, Executive Director; Burl Hash, Productions Director) presents:

CANDIDE

Book adapted from Voltaire by Hugh Wheeler; Music, Leonard Bernstein; Lyrics, Richard Wilbur; Additional Lyrics, Stephen Sondheim, John LaTouche; Director, Harold Prince; Choreography, Patricia Birch; Setting, Eugene Lee; Costumes, Franne Lee; Lighting, Tharon Musser; Musical Direction, John Mauceri, Paul Gemignani; Orchestrations, Hershy Kay; Produced in association with Harold Prince and Ruth Mitchell; Assistant Conductor, Joseph D. Lewis; Hairstylist, Sondra Muir; Wardrobe Supervisor, Kathy Dee Zasloff; Assistant to Director, Annette Brafman Meyers; Assistant to Choreographer, Lynne Gannaway; Production Supervisor, Ruth Mitchell

CAST

Dr. Voltaire/Dr. Pangloss/Governor Host/Sage	Lewis J. Stadlen†1
Coolie/Soldier/Priest/Spanish Don/ Sailor/Lion/Guest	Jim Corti
Candide	Mark Baker
Huntsman/Recruiting Officer/Agent/Spanish Don/Cartagenian/Sailor/Eunuch	David Horwitz
Paquette	Deborah St. Darr
Baroness/Harpsichordist/Penitente/ Steel Drummer/Houri	Mary-Pat Green
Baron/Grand Inquisitor/Slave Driver/ Captain/Guest	Joe Palmieri
Cunegonde	Maureen Brennan
Maximilian	Sam Freed
Servant/Agent of Inquisition/Spanish Don/ Cartagenian Sailor	Robert Hendersen
Recruiting Officer/Aristocrat/ Cartagenian	Peter Vogt
Penitente/Whore/Houri	Gail Boggs†2
Aristocrat/Cartagenian/Second Sheep	Carolann Page
Bulgarian Soldier/Aristocrat/Vendor/ Sailor/Pygmy/Cow	Carlos Gorbea
Bulgarian Soldier/Penitente/Cartagenian/ Sailor/Cow	Kelly Walters
Westphalian Soldier/Agent/Governor's Aide/Pirate/Guest	Chip Garnett
Rich Jew/Judge/Man in black/Cartagenian/ Pirate/German/Botanist/Guest	Jeff Keller
Aristocrat/Cartagenian/Houri	Becky McSpadden
Aristocrat/Whore/Houri/Cunegonde alternate for matinees	Kathryn Ritter
Lady with knitting/Cartagenian/First Sheep	Renee Semes
Old Lady	June Gable†3
Swing Girl	Rhoda Butler†4

UNDERSTUDIES: Charles Kimbrough, Sam Freed; Mark Baker, Kelly Walters; Maureen Breenan, Kathryn Ritter; Sam Freed, Robert Hendersen; June Gable, Renee Semes; Deborah St. Darr, Lynne Gannaway; Joe Palmieri, Jeff Keller, David Horwitz

MUSICAL NUMBERS: "Life Is Happiness Indeed," "The Best of All Possible Worlds," "Oh Happy We," "It Must Be So," "O Miserere," "Glitter and Be Gay," "Auto da Fe (What a Day)," "This World," "You Were Dead, You Know," "I Am Easily Assimilated," "My Love," "Alleluia," "Sheep's Song," "Bon Voyage," "Make Our Garden Grow."

A Musical performed without intermission.

General Manager: Howard Haines
Assistant Manager: Terry Grossman
Press: Betty Lee Hunt, Maria C. Pucci, Stanley F. Kaminsky
Stage Managers: George Martin, Errol Selsby, Carlos Gorbea

Still playing May 31, 1975. Opened Tuesday, Dec. 11, 1973 at the Chelsea Theater Center, Brooklyn Academy of Music, and played a limited engagement of 48 performances before moving to Broadway. Received 1974 "Tony" Awards for Best Book of a Musical, Best Director of a Musical, Best Scenic Design, Best Costume Designer; also voted Best Musical by NY Drama Critics Circle. Succeeded by: 1. Charles Kimbrough, 2. Lisa Wilkinson, 3. Niki Flacks, 4. Lisa Wilkinson, Rhoda Butler Blank

Top Right: Joe Palmieri, Mark Baker, Maureen Brennan Below: Charles Kimbrough (C)

Carlos Gorbea, June Gable

CORT THEATRE
Opened Tuesday, May 28, 1974.*
Edgar Lansbury, Joseph Beruh, Ivan Reitman present:

THE MAGIC SHOW

Book, Bob Randall; Songs, Stephen Schwartz; Magic Doug Henning; Direction and Dances, Grover Dale; Setting, David Chapman; Costumes, Randy Barcelo; Lighting, Richard Nelson; Musical Director, Stephen Reinhardt; Dance Arrangements, David Spangler; Assistant to Director, Jay Fox; Associate Producer, Nan Pearlman; Audio Design, Phil Ramone; Assistant to Producers, Jo Marie Wakefield; Wardrobe Supervisor, Virginia Sylvain; Production Assistants, Sam Christensen, Darrell Jonas, Walter Wood

CAST

Manny	Robert Lupone†1
Feldman	David Ogden Stiers†2
Donna	Annie McGreevey
Dina	Cheryl Barnes
Cal	Dale Soules
Doug	Doug Henning†3
Mike	Ronald Stafford
Steve	Loyd Sannes†4
Charmin	Anita Morris
Goldfarb	Sam Schacht

UNDERSTUDIES: Cal, Donna, Baillie Gerstein; Charmin, Dina, Sharron Miller; Feldman, Goldfarb, Garnett Smith; Mike, Steve, Christopher Lucas; Manny, Jay Fox

MUSICAL NUMBERS: "Up to His Old Tricks," "Solid Silver Platform Shoes," "Lion Tamer," "Style," "Charmin's Lament," "Two's Company," "Goldfarb Variations," "Doug's Act," "A Bit of Villainy," "West End Avenue," "Sweet, Sweet, Sweet," "Before Your Very Eyes"

A magic show with music performed without intermission.

General Management: Marvin A. Krauss
Company Manager: Gary Gunas
Press: Gifford/Wallace, Tom Trenkle
Stage Managers: William Dodds, Herb Vogler, Jay Fox, John Actman

* Still playing May 31, 1975. For original production, see THEATRE WORLD, Vol. 30.
† Succeeded by: 1. Clifford Lipson, 2. Kenneth Kimmins, 3. Jeffrey Mylett during vacation, 4. T. Michael Reed

Kenn Duncan Photos

Right: Kenneth Kimmins (C)
Top: Anita Morris, Doug Henning

BROADWAY PRODUCTIONS FROM OTHER SEASONS THAT CLOSED THIS SEASON

Title	Opened	Closed	Performances
A Little Night Music	2/25/73	8/3/74	601
Irene	3/13/73	9/7/74	594
Good Evening	11/14/73	11/30/74	438
Over Here	3/6/74	1/4/75	341
Lorelei	1/27/74	11/3/74	320
Thieves	4/7/74	1/5/75	313
A Moon for the Misbegotten	12/29/73	11/17/74	313
Scapino	5/18/74	3/2/75	298
My Fat Friend	3/31/74	12/8/74	288
Bad Habits	5/5/74	10/5/74	176
Noel Coward in Two Keys	2/28/74	6/29/74	140
Words & Music	4/16/74	8/3/74	127

OFF BROADWAY PRODUCTIONS

KAUFMANN CONCERT HALL
Tuesday and Wednesday, June 3–4, 1974
S. Hurok presents:

CLAUDE KIPNIS MIME THEATRE

Director, Claude Kipnis; Designers, Dina Kipnis, Amiran Shamir; Sound Production, Eddie Korvin; Stage Manager, Michael Filisky

CAST
Claude Kipnis

Rudy Benda
Doug Day
Robert Griffard

Rita Nachtmann
Jay Natelle
Christina Swing

PROGRAM
PART I: "Men and Dreams" (Music, Noam Sheriff): Hello!, Eve and the Serpent, The Village, Fantasy in Wax, Main Street, The Bottle, Goodbye!
PART II: Premiere of "Pictures at an Exhibition" (Music, Moussorgsky): The Visitor, The Guard, The Gnome, The Castle, The Tuileries Park, The Ox-cart, Chick in its Shell, Samuel and Schmuyle, The Market, The Catacombs, Baba Yaga, The Great Gate

Right and Top: Claude Kipnis Mime Theatre

CITY CENTER 55th STREET THEATER
Opened Tuesday, June 4, 1974.*
VICMAN Productions present:

THE MERRY WIDOW

Book, Victor Leon, Leon Stein; Spanish Translation, Miguel Padilla; Music, Franz Lehar; Director, Miguel De Grandy; Scenery, Cormani di Milano; Costumes, Stivanello; Lighting, Lawrence Metzler; Musical Director and Conductor, Alfredo Munar; Chorus Master, Juan Viccini; Choreographer, Armando Suez; Special Consultant, Raymond R. Norat; Assistant to Producers, Maria Tadei; Producers, Victor del Corral, Manolo Alonso, Henry Boyer; Wardrobe Supervisor, Ray Durso; Hairstylist, Pedro of Coiffure 1089; Makeup, Paul Brito; Prompter, J. Carliny Osorio

CAST

Viscount Zancada	Hernando Chaviano
Baron Mirko Zeta	Miguel de Grandy
Kromow	Rosendo Gali Menendez
Raul de Saint Brioche	Carlos de Leon
Olga Kromow	Nydia del Rivero
Bogdanovitch	Ruddi Fanetti
Pritzky	Jesus Zubizarreta
Valencienne	Puli Toro
Camilo De Rosillon	Rafael Le Bron
Pascovia	Lolina Gutierrez
Negus	Manolo Alvan
Ana De Glavari	Georgina Granados
Count Danilo	Tomas Alvarez
Sylviana Bogdanovitch	Lisette Palacio
Waiters	Pablo Alamo, Eddie Gonzales, Mario Santisteban, Pedro Trujillo

CHORUS: German Acosta, Frank Acosta, Jose Calazan, Nina Cruz, Frank Cruz, Isis Figueroa, Lourdes Galaya, Luis Gotay, Ilka Gutierrez, Ernesto Gutierrez, Hector Lomba, Maria Mainery, Rafael Morales, Amparo Navarro, Josefa Navarro, Soledad Navarro, Luis Pena, Juan Sabache, Flora Santana, Antonio Terazona, Amparo Viccini, Elda Zubizarreta, Mercedes Zubizarreta

DANCERS: Kate Antrobus, Joan Baker, Marissa Benetsky, Sandy Galiano, Barbara Klein, Henry Boyer, Marcos Dinnerstein, Daryl Gay, Gerald Moreno, Stephen Rockford

An Operetta in three acts. The action takes place in Paris in the '00s

General Manager: Jesus Alonso
Press: Howard Atlee, Cecilia Soler, Clarence Allsopp, Meg Gordean, Owen Levy, Efrain Hidalgo
Stage Managers: Janet Beroza, Sonia Rodriguez

*Closed June 9, 1974 after limited engagement of 7 performances.

**Puli Toro, Rafael Le Bron
in "The Merry Widow"**

VANDAM THEATRE
Opened Thursday, June 6, 1974.*
Bari and Bennett Productions present:

M. GORKY: A PORTRAIT
with
Michael A. Del Medico

Written and Directed by Michael A. Del Medico; Production and Costume Design, L. Bari; Lighting Design, Joy Lilly; Sound Technician, P. Brandstein; General Manager, Jeanne Bennett

PROGRAM

Part I: The World, Part II: Revolution, Part III: The Past, Part IV: Home

* Closed June 30, 1974 after a limited engagement of 24 performances.

MANHATTAN THEATRE CLUB
Opened Friday, June 7, 1974.*
Ruth Kalkstein and Sidney Annis present:

SOME PEOPLE, SOME OTHER PEOPLE, AND WHAT THEY FINALLY DO

By Jordan Crittenden; Director, Charles Aidman; Incidental Music, Stephen Lawrence; Setting, John Lee Beatty; Lighting, Joel Grunheim; Costumes, Reet Pell; Associate Producer, John Allen; Stage Manager, Duane Mazey

CAST

Jordan Crittenden
Lois Battle
Rod Browning
Carol Morley

A Revue in fifteen scenes "with hardly any music."

* No other details available.

PROVINCETOWN PLAYHOUSE
Opened Friday, June 7, 1974.*
The Italian Ministry of Culture and Tourism with a grant from Monmouth College and Quaigh Theatre presents:

LE POSEUR

By David Lifson; Director, Joseph Siracuse; Stage Design and Lighting, Curtis LaBon; Special Lighting Consultant, Charles Embry; Special Assistant, Kevin Reed; Costumes, Adrienne Boyd; Songs sung by Novella Nelson

CAST

Steve Lewis	Russell Costen
Edward Bolt	Daniel Ziskie
Sandy Johnson	Joan Rue
Dr. Daniel Adams	James Newell
Maxine Adams	Edith Greenfield
Hester	Shirley Brown

A Play in three acts and eleven scenes performed with one intermission. The action takes place in the living room of Steve's small house on the campus of a college in Eastern Pennsylvania in mid-January at the present time.

Stage Manager: Kyle Duncan

THE SEDUCERS

Book, Mario Fratti; Music and Lyrics, Ed Scott; Director, Will Lieberson

CAST

Nick Angotti	Thom Koutsoukos
Chris Gampel	Danton LaPenna
Annette Hunt	Garret Nichols
Deborah Johansen	Ira Rappaport
	Harris Shore

* Closed June 23, 1974 after limited engagement of 9 performances.

Michael A. Del Medico as M. Gorky
(Irene Fertik Photo)

PLAYERS THEATER
Opened Tuesday, June 11, 1974.*
Norman Twain in association with Michael Liebert by special arrangement with Marvin Worth presents:

THE WORLD OF LENNY BRUCE

Adapted from the material of Lenny Bruce by Frank Speiser; Production Designed by Richard Masur; Assistant to the Producer, Sue Factor; Vocalist, Ellen Kearney; Voice of the Judge, Sherwin Weiss

FRANK SPEISER†
as
Lenny Bruce

PART I: A nightclub in New York in the late 1950's
PART II: Criminal Court of the city of New York in 1965

General Manager: Sherman Gross
Press: The Merlin Group, Jay Bernstein, Jeff Richards

* Closed Oct. 6, 1974 after 137 performances.
† Succeeded by Ted Schwartz

Ken Howard Photo

Above: Frank Speiser as Lenny Bruce

JONES BEACH THEATRE
Opened Thursday, June 27, 1974.*
Guy Lombardo presents:

FIDDLER ON THE ROOF

Book, Joseph Stein; Based on Sholem Aleichem stories by special permission of Arnold Perl; Music, Jerry Bock; Lyrics, Sheldon Harnick; Director, John Fearnley; Original Choreography of Jerome Robbins reproduced by Robert Patent; Scenery, John W. Keck; Costumes, Winn Morton; Lighting, Thomas Skelton; Orchestrations, Don Walker; Musical Director, Jay Blackton; Entire Production under the supervision of Arnold Spector; Assistant Conductor, Paul Cianci; Choral Director, Robert Monteil; Wardrobe, Agnes Farrel, Lee Decker; Makeup Supervision, William H. Zauder; Religious Consultant, Zvee Scooler

CAST

The Fiddler	Geoffrey Webb
Tevye	Norman Atkins
Golde, his wife	Geraldine Brooks
Yente, a matchmaker	Honey Sanders
Avram, a bookseller	Lee Cass
Nahum, a beggar	Tony Slez
Lazar Wolf, a butcher	Ted Thurston
Rabbi	Zvee Scooler
Mendel, his son	David Ellin
Constable	Stan Page

Tevye's Daughters:

Tzeitel	Sherry Lambert
Hodel	Christine Andreas
Shprintze	Christine Miller
Bielke	Celeste Miller
Chava	Robin Hoff
Motel Kamzoil, a tailor	Bruce Adler
Mordcha, an innkeeper	Ralph Vucci
Fyedka	Bjarne Buchtrup
Perchik, a student	Richard Ianni
Grandma Tzeitel, Golde's grandmother	Sherry Lambert
Fruma-Sarah, Lazar Wolf's first wife	Barbara Cowley
Shandel, Motel's mother	Jeanne Grant
Sasha	Barry Ball
Yosel	Robert Monteil

VILLAGERS: Dru Alexandrine, Lisa Berg, Jean Busada, Barbara Cowley, Mona Elgh, Doris Galiber, Jeanne Grant, Mickey Gunnersen, Gail Malmuth, Irma Rogers, Renee Spector, Dixie Stewart, Sara Swanson, Marsha Tamaroff, Russell Anderson, Barry Ball, James Braet, Jeff Cahn, Peter Clark, Paul Flores, Nickolas Frank, Mark Goldman, Frank Mastrocola, Robert Monteil, George Pesaturo, Sal Provenza, Brian Ross, Tony Slez, Mark Tollefson, Arthur Whitfield, Ed Zimmerman

STANDBYS AND UNDERSTUDIES: Tevye, Ted Thurston; Golde, Jeanne Grant; Lazar, Tony Slez; Yente, Irma Rogers; Perchik, Sal Provenza; Motel, Mark Goldman; Rabbi, Brian Ross; Fyedka, Barry Ball; Hodel, Gail Malmuth; Tzeitel, Barbara Cowley; Chava, Dru Alexandrine; Constable, Lee Cass; Avram, Ed Zimmerman; Mordcha, Robert Monteil; Fiddler, George Pesaturo; Mendel, Peter Clark; Shprintze, Mona Eigh; Bielke, Christine Miller

MUSICAL NUMBERS: Grand Opening, "Tradition," "Matchmaker, Matchmaker," "If I Were a Rich Man," "Sabbath Prayer," "To Life," "Tevye's Monologue," "Miracle of Miracles," "The Dream," "Sunrise, Sunset," "Wedding Dance," "Now I Have Everything," "Tevye's Rebuttal," "Do You Love Me?," "The Rumor," "Far from the Home I Love," "Chavaleh," "Anatevka," Epilogue

A Musical in two acts. The action takes place in Anatevka, a village in Russia, in 1905, on the eve of the revolutionary period.

Company Manager: Sam Pagliaro
Press: Saul Richman
Stage Managers: Mortimer Halpern, Bertram Wood, Stan Page, Tony Slez

* Closed Sept. 1, 1974 after 67 performances.

(Ken Howard Photo)

Top Right: Geraldine Brooks, Norman Atkins in "Fiddler on the Roof" Below: Helen Hanft, teven Davis, Mary Carter in "Why Hanna's Skirt Won't Stay Down"

TOP OF THE VILLAGE GATE
Opened Monday, July 1, 1974.*
Michael Harvey presents The Theatre of the Eye Repertory Company in:

WHY HANNA'S SKIRT WON'T STAY DOWN

By Tom Eyen; Directors, Neil Flanagan, Tom Eyen; Lighting, Gary Weathersbee; Sets, T. E. Mason; Costumes, Patricia Adshead

CAST

Barker	William Duff-Griffin†1
Hanna	Helen Hanft
Arizona	Steven Davis
Sophie	Mary Carter†2

Standbys: Julia Curry, Ron Carrier

A carnival sideshow beginning in the believable 40's and freezing in the fantasy of the mid-60's.

General Management: Albert Poland
Press: Alan Eichler, Marilyn Percy
Stage Managers: Duane F. Mazey, Lee Cotterell

* Closed Oct. 27, 1974 after 136 performances.
† Succeeded by: 1. Joseph C. Davies, 2. Madeleine le Roux

63

Wushu Troupe

(Richard Braaten Photo)

NEW YORK PUBLIC LIBRARY
Opened on Tuesday, July 9, 1974.*
The Triad Playwrights Company presents:

THE GIRL WHO LOVED THE BEATLES

By D. B. Gilles; Director, Alan Mixon; Costumes, James Berton Harris; Producer, Milan Stitt; Assistant Producer, Richard Greene

CAST

Young Man . . . . Paul Carpinelli†
Young Woman . . . . Jane Campbell

A play performed without intermission.

Stage Manager: Richard Tirotta

* Closed December 19, 1974 after 17 performances in various branches of the New York Public Library.
† Succeeded by Eugene Blythe

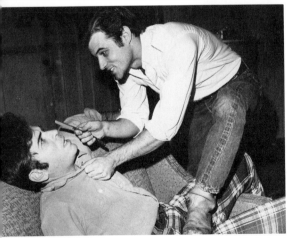

(Avery Willard Photo)

64   **Jordan Charney, Brad Davis**
         Above: Sally Gracie, Michael Ryan

MADISON SQUARE GARDEN FELT FORUM
Opened Thursday, July 4, 1974.*
The City Center of Music and Drama, Inc. (Norman Singer Executive Director) and the National Committee on United States-China Relations, Inc. present:

WUSHU TROUPE
of The People's Republic of China

Producers for City Center, Robert P. Brannigan, Chuck Eisler For National Committee, Jan Carol Berris, Douglas P. Murray Technical Director, Lowell Sherman; Secretary, Kate Stone

Wushu is the most popular sport of long historical tradition in China. The performance was presented in two parts.

Company Manager: Morry Efron
Press: Dan Langan
Stage Manager: Jeff Chambers

* Closed July 7, 1974 after limited engagement of four performances.

**Eugene Blythe, Jane Campbell
in "The Girl Who Loved the Beatles"**

STAGE 73
Opened Wednesday, August 21, 1974.*
Leonard Schlosberg in association with Jean Dalrymp presents:

NAOMI COURT

By Michael Sawyer; Director, Ira Cirker; Set and Light Desig Andrew Greenhut; Production Assistant, Greta Rauch; Technic Director, Brett Lewis; Props, Sheila Keminsky

CAST

Lenny . . . . Terry Alexand
David . . . . Jordan Charn
Miss Dugan . . . . Sally Grac
Mr. Berry . . . . Michael M. Ry
Harper . . . . Brad Dav

A Drama in 2 acts and 4 scenes with a prologue and epilogue. T action takes place at the present time outside Naomi Court, in M Dugan's apartment, and in David's apartment.

General Manager: Homer Poupart
Press: Saul Richman, Fred Nathan
Stage Manager: K. C. Schulberg
* Closed Nov. 10, 1974 after 84 performances.

WEST SIDE THEATER
Opened Wednesday, September 11, 1974.*
The Commedia Company of Chicago presents:

ISABELLA'S FORTUNE
and
PEDROLINO'S REVENGE

Composed by William Russo; Produced and Directed by William Russo; Set, Jann Courey, Terry Jenkins; Costumes, Marianne Blossom; Assistant Director, Albert Williams; Lighting, John Formanek; Sound, Debbie Gilbert; Action and Dance Sequences, Joseph Martinez; Technical Director, B. J. Sharp

CAST

"Isabella's Fortune"
Text by Albert Williams; Based on scenario of same title by Flaminio Scala

Argentina, the innkeeper's wife................ Linda Wesley
Pantalone, wealthy old merchant .... Mareo Mulet
Flavio, son to Pantalone..................... Stephen Sturk
Isabella, Genoese gentlewoman .... Sandy Grant
Burrattino, servant to Isabella......... Thomas Caufield Goltz
Punchinello, the innkeeper.............. Sherman Washington
Flaminia, a young lady....................... Barbara Cody
Capitano, a Spanish soldier .... Douglas Hoekstra
Arlecchino, servant to Capitano .... Kat Buddeke

The action takes place in the courtyard of Punchinello's inn in Rome circa 1600.

"Pedrolino's Revenge"
Text by Jonathan Abarbanel; Based on scenario "The Dentist" by Flaminio Scala

Lavinia, a young widow..................... Kat Buddeke
Pedrolino, servant to Zanobio .... Douglas Hoekstra
Leandro, son of Zanobio .... Thomas Caufield Goltz
Magnifico, a wealthy old lawyer .... Bill Leubrie
Francesca, servant to Lavinia .... Debbie Gilbert
Silvio, a young gentleman .... Stephen Sturk
Cortellino, servant to Silvio .... Mareo Mulet
Sangre y Fuego, a Spanish captain .... Arv Rocans
Silvia, daughter to Zanobio .... Stefani Hirsch
Gratiano, an old doctor .... Marty Plocke

The action takes place in Rome circa 1600 in a town square, with the house of Zanobio to one side and the house of Silvio on the other.

Production Manager: Deborah Howard
Press: Arts Counterparts, Jan Hash
Stage Manager: Taylor Greuel

Closed Sept. 22, 1974 after limited engagement of 15 performances.

Kat Buddeke in "Isabella's Fortune"

THE PERFORMING GARAGE
Opened Wednesday, September 18, 1974.*
The Performing Garage presents The Body Politic Dream Theater of Chicago in:

PURE DESIRE

Director, Jim Shiflett; Music and Sound Composed and Arranged by Melissa Shiflett; Lighting Design and Technical Direction, David Moore, Eric Gustafson; Sets, Mary McBain; Associate Director, David Moore

ENSEMBLE

Beth Leonard	Barbara Robin
David Moore	Jim Shiflett
Rod Nesbitt	Harold Yee
Yasha Novak	

Five dream stories in two acts: The Cracker Dream, We Dream of Tours, The Peep Show, The Bear Dream, A Country Doctor, Epilogue.

Press: Harold Yee, Beth Leonard
Stage Managers: Steve Meyer, Bob Eisen

* Closed Sept. 29, 1974 after limited engagement of 16 performances.

**Rod Nesbitt, Barbara Robin, David Moore,
Yasha Novak, Beth Leonard, Harold Yee
in "Pure Desire"**

TOP OF THE VILLAGE GATE

Opened Thursday, September 17, 1974.*
Michael Harvey presents The Theatre of the Eye Repertory Company in:

WHAT IS MAKING GILDA SO GRAY?
(or, It Just Depends on Who You Get)

By Tom Eyen; Director, Michael Posnick

CAST

France .... Carleton Carpenter†1
Gilda .... Alix Elias†2
Sound Effects People .... Amanda Davies, Ron Carrier

A play performed without intermission. "A bitter Valentine to all those who grew up in the '50's, fell in love in the '60's, and are still married in the '70's."

Press: Alan Eichler, Marilyn Percy
Stage Managers: Lee Cotterell, Duane Mazey

* Closed Oct. 17, 1974 after limited engagement of 15 performances.
† Succeeded by: 1. Peter Bartlett, 2. Helen Hanft

Alix Elias, Carleton Carpenter
(Zarko Kalmic Photo)

AMERICAN MUSEUM OF NATURAL HISTORY

Saturday, September 28, and Wednesday, October 23, 1974.
Kazuko Hillyer presents:

NATIONAL SHADOW THEATRE OF MALAYSIA

PROGRAM: First and Second Episodes from the "Ramayana"

National Shadow Theatre of Malaysia

THE LITTLE THEATRE

Opened Wednesday, October 2, 1974.*
Catherine Ellis presents:

MEDEA AND JASON

Freely Adapted from the "Medea" of Euripides by Robinson Jeffers; Director, Eugenie Leontovich; Choreography, Nora Peterson; Set, Alan Beck; Lighting, Lee Goldman; Costumes-Sound-Music, Thom Edlun; Production Coordinator, Tatiana Survillo; General Management, Theatre NOW, Inc.; Assistant to the Director, Mark MacCauley

CAST

Nurse .... Lilia Skala
Herikles .... Philip McKeon
Helios .... James Spies
Tutor .... Al Hill
First Woman .... Glen Lincoln
Second Woman .... Millette Alexander
Third Woman .... Roz Vallero
Fourth Woman .... Diane Burak
Fifth Woman.............................. Ellen Farran
Medea...................................... Maria Aho
Creon .... Chet Doherty
Jason.............................. Richmond F. Johnson
Messenger .... David MacEnulty
Soldiers............... David MacEnulty, E. Lynn Nickerson,
Faustino Rothman, Henry Tunney

UNDERSTUDIES: Medea, Catherine Ellis; Tutor, Mark MacCauley; Jason, Messenger, E. Lynn Nickerson; Creon, Henry Tunney; Nurse, Roz Vallero

A Drama in two acts with a prologue and epilogue. The action takes place in a Greek Bistro at the present time, and in Corinth in 431 B.C.

General Manager: Edward H. Davis
Company Manager: Robb Lady
Press: Solters/Sabinson/Roskin, Milly Shoenbaum, Joshua Ellis
Stage Managers: Susan Chase, E. Lynn Nickerson

* Closed Oct. 2, 1974 after one performance.

**Maria Aho, Chet Doherty
in "Medea and Jason"**

PROVINCETOWN PLAYHOUSE

Opened Thursday, October 3, 1974.*
Nicholas John Stathis presents the American Premiere of The Classic Theatre production of:

THE ADVERTISEMENT

By Natalia Ginzburg; Translated by Henry Reed; Director, David Black; Designed by Donald L. Brooks; Consultant, Maurice Edwards; Associate Designer, Mary V. Moran; Assistant to the Director, Ali Jones

CAST

Teresa.. Julia Curry
Elena .... Maria Ruberto
Lorenzo .... Harvey Solin
Giovanna .... Ali Jones

A play in three acts. The action takes place at the present time in Teresa's apartment in Rome.

Press: Alan Eichler, Marilyn Percy
Stage Managers: Karen Sundbergh, Rana Arons

* Closed Oct. 20, 1974 after limited engagement of 12 performances and 4 previews.

Julia Curry in "The Advertisement"

GRAMERCY ARTS THEATRE

Opened Friday, October 4, 1974*
The Spanish Theatre Repertory Company (Gilberto Zaldivar, Producer) presents:

O CASI EL ALMA

By Luis Rafael Sanchez; English Translation, Charles Pilditch; Director, Rene Buch; Scenery, Robert Federico; Costumes, Maria Ferreira; Lighting, Russell Krum; Production Manager, Jorge Amud

CAST

The Woman .... Isabel Segovia
The Man .... Raul Davila
The Lady .... Ofelia Gonzalez†
The Envoy .... Fernando Miyares

A Drama in two acts.

Press: Marian Graham
Stage Manager: Vivian Deangelo

Closed February 2, 1975 after 15 performances in repertory with the English version that opened Friday, October 20, and closed November 7, 1974 after 3 performances. Other productions presented in repertory were "Los Soles Truncos" by Rene Marques, with Mirtha Cartaya, Vivian Deangelo, and Maria Norman; "O. K." by Isaac Chocron, with Xonia Benguria, Fini Moreno, and Jose Juan Baldini.
†Succeeded by Silvia Brito. Charlotte Jones played the role in the English version, titled "A Miracle for Maggie."

Bert Andrews Photo

Isabel Segovia, Raul Davila

NATIONAL ARTS CLUB

Thursday, October 10, 1974.*
The National Arts Club (Mrs. G. Walter Zahn, President; Jason de Montmorency, Chairman of Drama Committee) presents:

CHEKHOV ON THE LAWN

An Entertainment from the works of Anton Chekhov; Devised, adapted and directed by Elihu Winer; Sound, William Mason

CAST

WILLIAM SHUST

Presented in two parts. The action takes place on the lawn of Chekhov's home in Yalta on the afternoon of April 17, 1900.
Presented for one performance only.

William Shust as Anton Chekhov

NEW YORK THEATRE ENSEMBLE

Opened Thursday, October 17, 1974.*
The Theatre of the Eye Repertory Company presents:

WOMEN BEHIND BARS

By Tom Eyen; Directed and Designed by Ron Link; Lighting, David Andrews; Make-up, Paul Hamlin; Production Manager, Liza Persky

CAST

Blanche Kaminsky	Hope Stansbury
Cheri Netherland	Sharon Barr
Shirel Spligingate	Ann Collier
Gloria Jean Kojax	Mary Woronov
Sarah Lee Crocker	Mary Boylan
Ada Morris	Madeleine le Roux
Guadalupe Maria Therese Santanos	Hortense Colorado
Matron	Pat Ast
Mary-Eleanor O'Connelly	Mary-Jenifer Mitchell
Louise Stanley	Sweet William Edgar
Paul Glickman	Walker Stuart

* Closed November 17, 1974 after 20 performances.

BIJOU THEATRE

Opened Monday, October 15, 1974.*
Norman Kean in association with John C. Goodwin presents:

HOSANNA

By Michael Tremblay; Translated by John Van Burek and Bill Glassco; Director, Bill Glassco; Designed by John Ferguson; Lighting, Vladimir Svetlovsky; Lighting, Ken Billington; Scenery, Stuart Wurtzel; Costumes, Molly Harris Campbell; Presented in association with Tarragon Theatre, Toronto, Can.; Production Associate, Paul Rackley; Technical Director, Richard Borman

CAST

Hosanna	Richard Monette
Cuirette	Richard Donat

A play in two acts. The action takes place at the present time in a Montreal apartment.

Company Manager: Maria Di Dia
Press: Les Schechter Associates, Henry Luhrman
Stage Manager: Penelope Ritco

* Closed Nov. 3, 1974 after 24 performances and 4 previews.

Left: Richard Monette, Richard Donat

EDEN THEATRE

Opened Sunday, October 20, 1974.*
Harry Rothpearl and Jewish Nostalgic Production Inc. present:

THE BIG WINNER

By Sholom Aleichem; Adapted and Directed by David Opatoshu; Music, Sol Kaplan; Choreography, Sophie Maslow; Lyrics, Wolf Younin; Musical Director, Jack Easton; Sets and Costumes, Jeffrey B. Moss; Lighting, Tom Meleck; Sound, Elliot Rothpearl; Assistant to the Director, Bryna Wasserman; Assistant to Choreographer, Lynne Kothera; Wardrobe Supervisor, Sylvia Friedlander; Technical Director, Sol Dexter

CAST

Old Man	Bruce Adler
Kopel	Stan Porter
Motel	Diane Cypkin
Bailke	Miriam Kressyn
Ety-Meny	David Opatoshu
Shimele Soroker	David Carey
Solomon Fine	Herschel Rosen
Osher Fine	Shifra Lerer
Perel	Jack Rechtzeit†1
Solovaitchik	William Gary
Goldentaller	Elia Patron
Mendel	Shmulik Goldstein
Rubinchik	Jaime Lewin†2
Vigdorchik	Reizl Bozyk
Madame Fine	Shifra Lerer
Madame Flaum	Jaime Lewin†2
Sexton	

TOWNSPEOPLE, GUESTS: Richard Ammon, Winifred Berg, Susan Fox, Joseph Goode, Cheryl Hartley, Marcus Williamson

UNDERSTUDIES: Susan Beitchman, Alan Skolnick

MUSICAL NUMBERS: "How Can I Tell Him She Loves Me?", "We're the People," "Lottery Celebration," "Money, Wealth, Gold," "It's Delicious," "Movie Montage," "I Am a Tailor's Daughter," "Tango Rehearsal," "The Tango," "In-Laws," "Love Song," "Winners, Losers," "Wedding Dance."

A Musical in 2 acts and 4 scenes performed in Yiddish with narration in English. The action takes place in 1910 in a Jewish town in Russia.

General Manager: Seymour Rexite
Press: Max Eisen
Stage Manager: Bryna Wasserman

* Closed Feb. 2, 1975 after 119 performances.
† Succeeded by: 1. Jaime Lewin, 2. Jack Rechtzeit

Diane Cypkin, Bruce Adler, David Opatoshu, Stan Porter, Miriam Kressyn

Socorro Cruz in "La Carpa de los Rasquachis"

EASTSIDE PLAYHOUSE
Opened Monday, October 21, 1974.*
Richard Lee Marks, Henry Jaffe, William Craver present:

THE WAGER

By Mark Medoff; Director, Anthony Perkins; Scenery, David Mitchell; Lighting, Neil Peter Jampolis; Costume Coordinator, Mary Beth Regan; Production Assistant, Alan Zimmerman; Wardrobe, Carol Hurlburt

CAST

Leeds .... Kristoffer Tabori
Ward .... Kenneth Gilman
Honor .... Linda Cook
Ron .... John Heard
Understudy: Christopher Curry

A Comedy in 3 acts and 5 scenes. The action takes place at the present time in the apartment of two graduate students at a university in northern California.

Company Manager: Patricia Bartolotta
Press: Marilyn LeVine, Warren Knowlton
Stage Managers: Tom Sawyer, Christopher Curry

*Closed Jan. 19, 1975 after 104 performances and 13 previews.

Left: Kristoffer Tabori
(Ken Howard Photo)

KAVOOKJIAN AUDITORIUM
Opened Tuesday, October 22, 1974.*
The Armenian Diocese presents:

ARMENIANS

By William Saroyan; Director, Ed Setrakian; Sets and Lighting, John Brennan, Eric Cowley, Torkom Demirjian, Bob Doran; Costumes, Ruth Thomason; Production Coordinator, Alice Eminian; Props, Anne Setrakian

CAST

Casparian .... Ed Setrakian
Knadjian .... Warren Finnerty
Papazian .... Luis Avalos
Almast .... Terese Hayden
Sexton .... Nicholas Daddazio
Dr. Jivelekian .... Joseph Ragno
Farmer .... Murray Moston
Man from Bitlis .... Vahagn Hovannes
Man from Moush .... Raymond Cole
Man from Van .... Harold Cherry
Man from Harpoot .... David Patch
Vasken .... Bob Doran
Man from Erzeroum .... Rudy Bond
Man from Dikranagert .... Sal Carollo
Man from Giligia .... Robert Coluntino

A play in two acts. The action takes place in 1920 in the office of the Red Brick Church on Ventura at M Street in Fresno, California; and in the Patriotic Club.

Stage Manager: Susan Gregg

* Closed Nov. 14, 1974 after limited engagement of 8 performances.

Left Center: Ed Setrakian, Luis Avalos, Warren Finnerty
(Garbis Boghossian Photo)

WESTSIDE THEATER
Opened Thursday, October 24, 1974.*
The Chelsea Theater Center of Brooklyn presents El Teatro Campesino's production of:

LA CARPA DE LOS RASQUACHIS

(The Tent of the Underdogs)

A play written, produced, directed, and performed by El Teatro Campesino de Aztlan (Luis Valdez, Founder-Director)

* Closed Nov. 18, 1974 after limited engagement of 32 performances.

Robert Tananis, Candice Earley, Rick Garner

(Ken Howard Photo)

THEATRE FOUR
Opened Tuesday, October 29, 1974.*
Gil Adler and Jack Temchin present The Low Moan Spectacular's production of:

BULLSHOT CRUMMOND

By Ron House, John Neville-Andrews, Alan Shearman, Diz White, Derek Cunningham; From an idea by Ron House and Diz White; Scenery and Costumes, Mary Moore; Production Manager, Jonathan Gardner; Associate Producers, Allen Stanton, Howard Bellin; Managerial Associate, Patricia Bartolotta; Wardrobe Supervisor, Mary Beth Regan; Sound, Gary and Timmy Harris

CAST

Capt. Hugh Bullshot Crummond	Alan Shearman
Algy Longwort	John Neville-Andrews
Otto von Bruno	Ron House
Lenya von Bruno	Louisa Hart
Rosemary Fenton	Diz White
Policeman/Prof. Rupert Fenton/Inspector Scabbard/Wolfgang Schmidt/Marovitch/Waiter	John Neville-Andrews

"A Satiric Reminder" in 2 acts and 8 scenes. The action takes place somewhere over England, Chambers in Mayfair, Netherington Abbey, the Carlton Tea Rooms, somewhere in Kent, "The Larches," Turnbridge Wells, and dungeons of Netherington Abbey.

General Manager: William Craver
Press: David Powers, William Schelble

* Closed Nov. 3, 1974 after 8 performances and 14 previews.

Right Center: Ron House, Diz White, John Neville-Andrews, Alan Shearman, Louisa Hart

Calvin Culver, Jake Everett, Walter Holiday
in "Tubstrip"

THE LITTLE HIPPODROME
Opened Tuesday, October 29, 1974.*
The Little Hippodrome presents:

GAY COMPANY

Music and Lyrics, Fred Silver; Director, Sue Lawless; Music Director, John Franceschina; Designed by Michael J. Hotopp an Paul de Pass; Associate Lighting Designer, Cheryl Thacker; Co tume Coordinator, Laura Thompson; Assistant Musical Directo Dennis Buck; Additional Dialogue, Les Barkdull; Artistic Produ tion Assistants, Rita Mandl, Jerry Kuehner

CAST

Candice Earley
Rick Gardner
Cola Pinto
Gordon Ramsey
Robert Tananis

MUSICAL NUMBERS AND SKETCHES: "Welcome," "Begi ners Guide to Cruising (Pilgrim's Primer)," "A Special Boy "Handsome Stranger," "True Confession," "Where There Smoke," "I Met My Love," "Lament," "Phantom of the Opera "Your Home away from Home," "Two Strangers," "Remen brances," "Days of the Dancing Are Gone," "I've Just Been to Wedding," "If He'd Only Be Gentle," "Freddy Liked to Fugue Finale

"A Try-Sexual Musical Revue" in two acts.

Press: Gene Webber Associates, Gifford/Wallace
Stage Manager: Less Barkdull

* Closed Feb. 23, 1975 after 24 4 performances.

MAYFAIR THEATRE
Opened Thursday, October 31, 1974.*
K. G. Productions Ltd. in association with Mark Seg presents:

TUBSTRIP

By A. J. Kronengold; Director, Jerry Douglas; Setting, Leo Meyer; Costumes, Jim Faber; Lighting, Edward I. Byers; Associa Producer, Fred Walker; Technical Assistant, Paul Harkins; Produ tion Assistant, Marshall Ballou

CAST

Brian	Calvin Culv
Darryl	Jade McC
Andy	Walter Holid
Wally	Jake Evere
Tony	Gerald Gra
Kevin	Michael Kear
Richie	Edward Rambe
Dusty	John Bruce Deav
Bob	Dick Josl

A Comedy performed without intermission. The action tak place at the present time in Boys Town Bath House.

General Manager: Jim Gordon
Company Manager: Ken Gaston
Press: Max Eisen, Tom Wilner
Stage Manager: Robert Lo Bianco

* Closed Nov. 17, 1974 after 21 performances and 3 previews.

THE IMPROVISATION
Opened Thursday, October 31, 1974.*
Stoner Arts Inc. in association with The Improvisation presents:

I'LL DIE IF I CAN'T LIVE FOREVER

Music, Lyrics, and Musical Staging by Joyce Stoner; Original Book Concept, Karen Johnson; Additional Music, Musical Arrangements, and Musical Director, William Boswell; Designed by Irving · Milton Duke; Additional Book Material, William Brooke; Technical Director, Dale Lally; Assistant Musical Director, Mark T. Long; Hairstylist, Jonathan Bavaro; Technical Assistant, Alan Selevan; Adviser, Budd Friedman

CAST

Gabrielle Schwartz .... Gail Johnston
Heather O'Malley .... Maureen Maloney
Jenette Morrison .... Nancy Reddon
Dan Craig .... Don Bradford
Jonathan Winslow .... Tom Hastings
Ted Thornton .... Michael David Laibson
Pianist .... Mark T. Long

MUSICAL NUMBERS: "The Opening Number," "The Improvisation," "Joys of Manhattan Life," "Where Would We Be without Perverts?," "My Life's a Musical Comedy," "We're Strangers Who Sleep Side by Side," "The Roommate Beguine," "A Is For," "Take Me!," "There's Always Someone Who'll Tell You No," "24 Hours from This Moment," "Ode to Electricity," "I'm in Love," "I'm So Bored," "My Place or Yours?," "Who Do We Thank!," "Let's Have a Rodgers and Hammerstein Affair," "Less Is More and More," "I Hate Football," "They Left Me," "It's Great to Be Gay," "I'll Die if I Can't Live Forever," "The Finale," "The Great White Way"

"A Stage Struck Revue" in two acts.

Press: Al Davis
Stage Manager: Dale Lally

* Closed Feb. 2, 1975 after 81 performances.

BROOKLYN NAVY YARD
Opened Thursday, November 7, 1974.*
The Chelsea Theater Center of Brooklyn presents:

THE MADHOUSE COMPANY OF LONDON

Hamlet MacWallbanger
Marcel Steiner
Oscar Oswald
Tommy Shand
Nina Petrova

Press: Betty Lee Hunt Associates
Closed Mar. 15, 1975 after 129 performances.

Don Bradford, Michael Laibson, Tom Hastings, Gail Johnston
(Holly Knup Photo)

Marcel Steiner, Hamlet MacWallbanger, Oscar Oswald, Tommy Shand, Nina Petrova

TRUCK AND WAREHOUSE THEATRE
Opened Wednesday, November 6, 1974.*
Ron Link and Alan Eichler present a Theatre of the Damned Production of:

TURQUOISE PANTOMIME

Production Devised, Designed, Directed, and Performed by Lindsay Kemp; Stage Director and Lighting, John Spradbury; Ballet Mistress, Arlene Phillips; Assistant to the Director, David Haughton; Wardrobe and Costumes, Robert Anthony; Musical Director and Accompaniment, Henry Krieger; Assistant to the Producers, Lisa Persky; Technical Assistant, Lawrence Eichler; Production Coordinator, Jonathan Gardner; Sound, E. Michael Meade

with
LINDSAY KEMP

PROGRAM: Overture, "The Incredible Orlando," "Circus," "Aimez-Vous Bach?," "The Flower," "Orlando at the Palais," "Adam and Eve," "The Albatross," "Burlesque"

General Manager: Marilyn Percy
Press: Alan Eichler
Stage Managers: Neil Caplan, Tony Maples, Robin Martin

* Closed Dec. 15, 1974 after limited engagement of 30 performances.

Incredible Orlando, Lindsay Kemp in "Turquoise Pantomime"

Daniel Asher Photo

HUNTER COLLEGE PLAYHOUSE
Opened Thursday, November 7, 1974.*
Hunter College Concert Bureau presents:

THE AMERICAN MIME THEATRE

Paul J. Curtis, Director

COMPANY: Jean Barbour, Charles Barney, Paul Curtis, Deda Kavanagh, Marion Knox, Marc Maislen, Mike O'Brien, Toni Stanley, Arthur Yorinks, and Mr. Bones

PROGRAM: "The Lovers," "The Scarecrow," "Dreams," "Hurlyburly," "Evolution," "Sludge," "Six"

* Closed November 9, 1974 after limited engagement of 3 performances.

The American Mime Theatre in "Dreams"
(Jim Moore Photo)

EDISON THEATRE
Opened Wednesday, November 13, 1974.*
By arrangement with the English Stage Company Ltd, Hillard Elkins, Lester Osterman Productions, Bernard Delfont, Michael White present the Royal Court Theatre Production of:

SIZWE BANZI IS DEAD

Devised by Athol Fugard, John Kani and Winston Ntshona; Director, Athol Fugard; Scenic Design, Stuart Wurtzel; Lighting, Ronald Wallaxe; Costumes, Bill Walker; Design Consultant, Douglas Heap; Wardrobe Mistress, Peggy Paparone; Production Assistants, Jamie Gallagher, Astrid Ronning

CAST

Styles . . . . John Kani
Buntu . . . . John Kani
Sizwe Banzi . . . . Winston Ntshona

Performed without intermission. The action takes place in South Africa.

Opened Sunday, November 24, 1974.*

THE ISLAND

Devised by Athol Fugard, John Kani, Winston Ntshona; Director, Athol Fugard

CAST

John . . . . John Kani
Winston . . . . Winston Ntshona

Performed without intermission. The action takes place on Robben Island, seven miles from Cape Town, South Africa, and the maximum security prison for African political offenders.

General Manager: Leonard Soloway
Press: Solters/Roskin, Bud Westman, Ted Goldsmith
Stage Managers: Nina Seely, Bryan Young

* Closed May 18, 1975 after 209 performances and 6 previews. John Kani and Winston Ntshona received 1975 "Tony" awards for Best Actor in a Play.

John Kani, Winston Ntshona in "The Island"
above in "Sizwe Banzi Is Dead"

72

NEIGHBORHOOD HOUSE
Opened Friday, November 15, 1974.*
Riverdale Community Theatre presents:

THE PIRATE

Book, Lawrence Kasha, Hayden Griffin; Based on play by S. N. Behrman, and Screenplay by Albert Hackett and Frances Goodrich; Music and Lyrics, Cole Porter; Directed and Choreographed by Jeffery K. Neill; Production and Costumes Designed by Charles W. Roeder; Musical Direction and Special Arrangements, Wendell Kindberg; Producers, Celia and Robert Kornfeld; Assistant to the Producers, Jean Bonniol

CAST

Serafin	Norb Joerder
Manuela	Cynthia Meryl
Don Pedro Vargas	Jeffrey Wallach
Aunt Inez Alva	Patricia Brooks
Uncle Capucho Alva	Sumner E. DeMar
Gumbo	Rhea Plotka
Trillo	Robert Sinclair
Estraban	Edwin A. Folts
Casilda	Ruth Lewin
Lizarda	Lila Koven
Isabella	Kris Koczur
Mercedes	Jean Bonniol
Advocate	Thomas F. Lee
Viceroy	Jim Ryan
Captain	Thomas F. Lee

A Musical in 2 acts and 7 scenes with a prologue. The action takes place in the Town Square of the village of Calvados, in Panama City, in Manuela's sitting room.

Press: Jean Bonniol, Colby Woeltz, Frances Bander
Stage Managers: Marilyn Grossman, Mary Mansfield, Harriet Miller

* Closed Nov. 23, 1974 after limited engagement of 5 performances.

Aixa Clemente (front), Angel Martin, Anita Tamaino
(Susan Cook Photo)

UPSTAGE AT JIMMY'S
Opened Saturday, November 16, 1974.*
WPG presents:

JUST LIBBY

Written by Libby Morris and Leslie Lawton; Special Musical Numbers, Bill Solly; Musical Arrangements, Chuck Mallett; Musical Direction, Geoffrey Brawn; New York Production, Jordan Hott; Production Associate, Billie Biederman; Production Manager, Lee Cotterel; Hairstylist, Roger Thompson

with
LIBBY MORRIS

A one-woman musical revue presented in two acts.

Press: Saul Richman

* Closed Dec. 7, 1974 after 32 performances.

Norb Joerder, Cynthia Meryl in "The Pirate"
(Robert Kornfeld Photo)

PROVINCETOWN PLAYHOUSE
Opened Saturday, November 16, 1974.*
The Peoples Performing Company presents:

STREET JESUS

Book and Lyrics, Peter Copani; Music, Chris Staudt, Peter Copani; Musical Direction, Ed Vogel; Choreography, John Werkheiser; Sets, Lights and Costumes, Gary Langley; Entire Production Conceived and Directed by Peter Copani; Production Manager, Richard Kayne; Production Assistant, John Paul Copani

CAST

Larry Campbell	Michael D. Knowles
Robin Cantor	Angel Martin
Regina Cashone	Vernon Spencer
Aixa Clemente	Anita Tomaino
Joe Garrambone	Meri Weiner

MUSICAL NUMBERS: "Bad But Good," "The Good News," "Manufacture and Sell," "Today Will Be," "Strawberries, Pickles and Ice Cream," "Hail, Hail," "If Jesus Walked the Earth Today," "L'America Ha Fato per Te," "Who Can Say," "Down on Me," "Wait and See," "God's in the People," "Street Jesus," "Flame of Life," "Corruption," "For the Good Times," "Special Man," "Dance," "A Better Day," "Friends," "In the Name of Love," "Make Them Hate," "Riot," "One of Us," "Love Is Beautiful"

"An American Street Musical" in two acts.

Press: Robert Ganshaw
Stage Managers: Ralph Thomas, Paul Huck

* Closed Jan. 4, 1975 after 52 performances.

Libby Morris

Ted Neeley, Alaina Reed
(Michael Childers Photo)

ASTOR PLACE THEATRE
Opened Sunday, November 17, 1974.*
3W Productions Inc. present:

HOW TO GET RID OF IT

Book, Lyrics, Direction, Eric Blau; Based on Eugene Ionesco's "Amedee"; Music, Mort Shuman; Scenery and Costumes, Don Jensen; Arranged and Conducted by Wolfgang Knittel; Lighting, Ian Calderon; Executive Producer, Stan Swerdlow; Production Assistants, Stephen Boyle, Giorgio Costa, Anita Kelman; Sound, George Jacobs

CAST

Amedee Buccinioni	Matt Conley
Lady Super	Carol L. Hendrick
Shirley, a prostitute	Lorrie Davis
Mr. Helliker, Apt. 3A	David Vogel
Mr. Provan, Apt. 5D	Joseph Neal
Lucinda, a prostitute	Janet McCall
Ms. Cohen, Apt. 2C	Vilma Vaccaro
Harry, the bartender	James Doerr
Police Sergeant O'Hanley	Mike Dantuono
Police Sergeant Ramirez	Edward Rodriguez
Vietnam Veteran	Joe Masiell
Madeleine Buccinioni	Muriel Costa-Greenspon
Postman	Joseph Neal
Mushrooms	Mike Dantuono, Lorrie Davis, Carol L. Hendrick, Janet McCall, Joseph Neal, Edward Rodriguez, Vilma Vaccaro, David Vogel

Alternates: Janet McCall for Muriel Costa-Greenspon, Joseph Neal for Joe Masiell
Understudies: Harriet Scalici, Jan Ewing

MUSICAL NUMBERS: "Mind Your Business," "The Old Man Says to the Old Woman," "The Mushrooms Are Coming in Here," "Good Morning, I'll Put You Through," "At the End of a Period of Time," "Are You the Man Whose Name Is on the Paper," "Almost Everybody Suffers More than Us," "You've Got to Get Rid of It," "Suite for a Growing Corpse," "I Am Here at the Place Where Time Began," "I Am a Vietnam Veteran," "Well, Yes, He's a Friend," "What an Evening," "Five to One," "Amedee, Amedee, It Isn't Too Late," "The Late, Late Show"

A Musical in two acts. The action takes place at the present time in the apartment of Mr. and Mrs. Buccinioni on Barrow Street, and somewhere in Greenwich Village, in New York City.

General Manager: Lily Turner
Press: Saul Richman, Fred Nathan
Stage Manager: G. Allison Elmer

* Closed Nov. 24, 1974 after ten performances.

BEACON THEATRE
Opened Sunday, November 17, 1974.*
Robert Stigwood in association with Brian Avnet and Scarab Productions presents:

SGT. PEPPER'S LONELY HEARTS CLUB BAND ON THE ROAD

Music and Lyrics, John Lennon, Paul McCartney; Production Conceived and Adapted by Robin Wagner, Tom O'Horgan; Directed and Staged by Tom O'Horgan; Associate Producers, Gatchell and Neufeld; Scenic Design, Robin Wagner; Lighting, Jules Fisher; Costumes, Randy Barcelo; Sound, Abe Jacob; Arranged and Conducted by Gordon Lowry Harrell; production Supervisor, Richard Scanga; Executive Producer, Peter Brown; Presented by Steven Singer, Steve Metz, Howard Dando

CAST

Maxwell's Silver Hammermen:	
Jack	Allan Nicholls
Sledge	William Parry
Claw	B. G. Gibson
Billy Shears	Ted Neeley
Lucy	Alaina Reed
Flattop	Walter Rivera
Sun Queen/Lovely Rita/Polythene Pam/Sgt. Pepper	David Patrick Kelly
Strawberry Fields	Kay Cole
Hammeroids	Blake Anderson, Edward Q. Bhartonn, Arlana Blue, Ron Capozzoli, Michael Meadows, Stoney Reece, Jason Roberts

UNDERSTUDIES: Billy, David Patrick Kelly; Strawberry, Lucy, Stoney Reece; Sgt. Pepper, Polythene Pam, Michael Meadows

MUSICAL NUMBERS: "Sgt. Pepper's Lonely Hearts Club Band," "With a Little Help from My Friends," "Nowhere Man," "Lucy in the Sky with Diamonds," "I Want You," "Come Together," "Sun Queen," "Lovely Rita," "Polythene Pam," "She Came in through the Bathroom Window," "You Never Give Me Your Money," "Her Majesty," "A Day in the Life," "She's Leaving Home," "Strawberry Fields Forever," "Getting Better," "Because," "When I'm 64," "Good Morning, Good Morning," "Being for the Benefit of Mr. Kite," "Oh Darling," "Fixing a Hole," "Mean Mr. Mustard," "Maxwell's Silver Hammer," "Carry That Weight," "Golden Slumbers," "The Long and Winding Road," "Get Back"

"A Rock Spectacle" in two acts.

General Management: Gatchell & Neufeld
Press: Rogers & Cowan
Stage Managers: Marc Cohen, Bruce Mason, Galen McKinley, Laura Rambaldi

* Closed Jan. 5, 1975 after 66 performances.

Muriel Costa-Greenspon, Matt Conley, Joe Masiell
(Olliverre-Kharem Photo)

WESTSIDE THEATRE
Opened Wednesday, November 20, 1974.*
The Chelsea Theater Center of Brooklyn presents the San Francisco Mime Troupe in:

THE MOTHER

By Bertolt Brecht; Translated by Lee Baxandall; Adapted from the novel by Maxim Gorky; Directed, Designed, Performed, and Produced by the San Francisco Mime Troupe; Music, Hanns Eisler, and the Mime Troupe

CAST

Company of twelve
(Names not submitted)

Performed in fourteen scenes.

Opened Wednesday, November 27, 1974*

Top Right: "The Mother"

Right: Frances Salisbury, Louise Stubbs in "The Prodigal Sister"

(Bert Andrews Photo)

THEATRE DE LYS
Opened Monday, Nov. 25, 1974.*
Woodie King, Jr. presents:

THE PRODIGAL SISTER

Book and Lyrics, J. E. Franklin; Music and Lyrics, Micki Grant; Director, Shauneille Perry; Musical Director, Neal Tate; Choreographer, Rod Rodgers; Designer, C. Richard Mills; Costumes, Judy Dearing; Associate Producer, Ed Pitt; Wardrobe Mistress, Katherine Roberson; Technical Director, Jack Magnifico; Originally presented July 11, 1974 at Henry Street Settlement's New Federal Theatre; Presented by special arrangement with Lucille Lortel Productions

CAST

Jackie .... Paula Desmond
Mother .... Frances Salisbury
Mrs. Johnson .... Esther Brown
Sissie/Prostitute/Third Employment Girl .... Ethel Beatty
Jack .... Leonard Jackson
Essie/Baltimore Bessie .... Louise Stubbs
Lucille/Dowah .... Saundra McClain
Slick/Pallbearer .... Kirk Kirksey
Rev. Wynn/Employment Man .... Frank Carey
Hot Pants Harriet/Dowah/First
    Employment Girl .... Joyce Griffen
Dr. Patton/Caesar/Jackie's
    Boyfriend .... Victor Willis
Jackie's Spirit/1st City Girl/2nd
    Employment Girl/1st Country Girl .... Judy Dearing
Second Prostitute/Second City Girl .... Yolande Graves
Dowah/Policeman/City Man/Country Boy .... Larry Lowe
2nd Policeman/2nd City Man/2nd
    Country Boy .... Rael Lamb

MUSICAL NUMBERS: "Slip Away," "Talk, Talk, Talk," "Ain't Marryin' Nobody," "If You Know What's Good for You," "First Born," "Woman Child," "Big City Dance," "Employment Office Dance," "Sister Love," "Hot Pants Dance," "Remember Caesar," "Superwoman," "Flirtation Dance," "Look at Me," "I Been up in Hell," "Thank You, Lord," "Remember," "Celebration," "The Prodigal Has Returned"

A Musical performed without intermission in 8 scenes.

General Manager: Paul B. Berkowsky
Company Manager: Charles Artesona
Press: Samuel Lurie
Stage Managers: Dan Early, Regge Life

Closed Dec. 29, 1974 after 42 performances and 8 previews.

Bert Andrews Photos

Frances Salisbury, Frank Carey, Esther Brown

GREEK ART THEATRE

Opened Tuesday, November 26, 1974.*
The Greek Art Theatre (George Arkas, Executive Director) presents:

ELECTRA

Written and Directed by George Arkas; Based on play by Sophocles; Managing Director, Yannis Simonides; Music, Dimitris Dragatakis; Lighting, Larry Jacobs; Set, Nick Ikaris; Costumes, Maria Stefanatos; Executive Producer, Max Gottfried; Administrative Director, Richard Wienecke; Associate Directors, Christopher Tanner, Yannis Simonides

CAST

Gypsy	Tanny McDonald
Clytaemnestra	Robin Howard
Aegisthus	Eric Sinclair
Electra	Yula Gavala
Beggar	R. Patrick Sullivan
Orestes	Reno Roop
Pylades	Peter Alzado
Tutor	William Robertson
Singer	Irma Sandrey
Chrysothemis	Olga Sorok

UNDERSTUDIES: Electra, Olga Sorok; Clytaemnestra, Tanny McDonald; Orestes, Peter Alzado; Gypsy, Irma Sandrey; Pylades, Reno Roop; Beggar, William Robertson; Tutor, R. Patrick Sullivan; Chrysothemis, Gypsy, Singer, Nomi Mitty

A Tragedy performed without intermission.

General Manager: Christopher Tanner
Press: Bernard Bennett
Stage Manager: Jon Polito

* Closed Dec. 8, 1974 after 16 performances.

Yula Gavala

ALICE TULLY HALL

Opened Friday, November 29, 1974.*
Arthur Shafman International Limited and Lincoln Center for the Performing Arts present:

MUMMENSCHANZ

Entire Production Conceived and Directed by the Company.

CAST

Andres Bossard
Florianna Frassetto
Bernie Schurch

Program presented in two parts: Part I Evolution, Part II Relationships.

* Closed Nov. 31, 1974 after limited engagement of 5 performances to resume tour.

Mummenschanz

THEATRE AT THE LAMBS

Opened Saturday, December 7, 1974.*
Theatre at the Lambs (Gene Frankel, Creative Director) in association with Ben Shaktman presents:

THE OLD ONES

By Arnold Wesker; Director, Ben Shaktman; Scenery, Ed Wittstein; Costumes, David Toser; Lighting, Tony Quintavalla; Associate Producer, Edith O. Rea; Technical Director, Larry Rappaport; Sound, Martin John Kralik; Wardrobe, Rita Calabro; Technical Assistants, Barbara Rosoff, Susan Vick-Davis, Keith Wylie; Properties, Sal Miraldi; Production Assistant, Michael Diamond; Production Coordinator, Flori Werbin; Asssociate Producer, Pamela Mitchell

CAST

Emanuel	Lou Gilbert
Gerda, his wife	Eda Reiss Merin
Boomy, his younger brother	Norman Rose
Sarah, his sister	Tresa Hughes
Teressa, Sarah's friend	Carol Teitel
Millie, Sarah's friend	Sylvia Gassell
Jack, Sarah's neighbor	John A. Coe
Rosa, Sarah's daughter	Carol Mayo Jenkins
Rudi, Sarah's nephew	Jean-Pierre Stewart
Martin, Boomy's son	David Garfield
Two Youths	Alex Funtow, Harry Santiago

A play in two acts. The action takes place in early autumn at the present time in the backyards, kitchens, rooms, classrooms, and streets of New York's lower East Side.

Press: Joyce O'Brian
Stage Managers: Marjorie Horne, Tim O'Donnell

* Closed Dec. 15, 1974 after limited engagement of 8 performances.

Lou Gilbert, Norman Rose, Eda Reiss Merin

Bert Andrews Photo

THEATRE FOUR

Opened Monday, December 16, 1974.*
Burry Fredrik and Walter Boxer present the Phoenix Theatre Production of:

PRETZELS

Music and Lyrics, John Forster; Written by Jane Curtin, Fred Grandy, Judy Kahan; Director, Patricia Carmichael; Scenery, Stuart Wurtzel; Costumes, Clifford Capone; Lighting, Ken Billington; Dance Sequence, Francis Patrelle; Projections, Eugene Lowery; Assistant Managing Director, Daniel Freudenberger; Assistant General Manager, Gregory W. Taylor; Production Assistant, Michel Choban; Assistant to Producers, Alan Sobek

CAST

Jane Curtin
John Forster
Timothy Jerome
Judy Kahan
Jane Ranallo

MUSICAL NUMBERS AND SKITS: "Pretzels," "Unemployment," "Take Me Back," "Cosmetology," "Sing and Dance," "Wild Strawberries," "Jane's Song," "The Waitress," "The Cockroach Song," "Richie and Theresa," "Classical Music," "Monologue," "Tim Vander Beek," "Loehmann's," "The Reunion"

A Revue presented in two parts.

General Managers: Marilyn S. Miller, David Lawlor
Company Managers: David Lawlor, Fred Walker
Press: Mary Bryant, Carl Samrock, Bill Evans, Shirley Herz
Stage Managers: Susie Cordon, Mary Burns

* Closed Mar. 23, 1975 after 120 performances.

Top Right: John Forster, Timothy Jerome, Judy Kahan, Jane Curtin in "Pretzels"

(Ken Howard Photo)

INTERNATIONAL CABARET

Opened Tuesday, December 17, 1974.*
International Cabaret Theatre presents:

BROADWAY DANDIES

Producer-Director, Robert Johnnene; Choreographer, Henry Le-Tang; Music Director, Don Whisted; Set, Wilfredo Surita; Lighting, Barry Arnold; Assistant to the Director, Ellie LeTang; Assistant Choreographer, Gingy Kroner; Vocal Coach, James E. Gassett; Pianist, Don Manor; Women's Gowns, Julian Starr of London; Lighting and Sound, Tom field

CAST

Tour Guide	Robert Fitch
Cabaret Host	Hal James Pederson
Cabaret Performer	Diane Nicole
Dance Hall Hostess	Suzi Swanson
Recording Artist	Michael Radigan
Opera Star	Hal James Pederson
Club #1	Teddy Williams
Club #2	Marilyn Anderson
Club #3	Janet Saunders
Club #4	Hal James Pederson
Dance Team	Don Swanson, Suzi Swanson
Send in the Clowns	Sharon Bruce

MUSICAL NUMBERS: "On Broadway," "Lullaby of Broadway," "Give Our Regards to Broadway," "Wilkomen," "Cabaret," "Carousel," "Standing on the Corner," "Big Spender," "Ten Cents a Dance," "I'm All Smiles," "Questa Quela," "Let's Dance," "Ain't Misbehavin'," "Honeysuckle Rose," "Adelaide's Lament," "Summertime," "I Never Have Seen Snow," "Night and Day," "Too Darn Hot," "Sisters," "Aquarius," "Send in the Cowns," "That's Entertainment," "Another Opening"

"A Musical Romp through New York" in two acts.

Press: Saul Richman, Dick Falk

* Closed Dec. 22, 1974 after 8 performances.

Right Center: Marilyn Anderson, Sharon Bruce, Hal James Pederson, Suzi Swanson, Diane Nicole, Janet Saunders

(Tucker Photo)

TOP OF THE GATE

Opened Wednesday, December 25, 1974.*
Phil Oesterman and Jim Sink present:

THE CHARLES PIERCE SHOW

Material by Charles Pierce; Director, Phil Oesterman; Lighting, Gary Weathersby

A one-man show presented in two parts.

Press: Saul Richman, Fred Nathan

* Closed May 18, 1975 after 169 performances.

Above: Charles Pierce

EXCHANGE THEATRE
Opened Monday, December 30, 1974.*
Lyn Austin, Mary Silverman and Charles Hollerith present th
Music-Theatre Performing Group production of:

HOTEL FOR CRIMINALS

Conceived, Written and Directed by Richard Foreman; Com
posed by Stanley Silverman; Musical Direction, Roland Gagnon
Costumes, Whitney Blausen; Orchestrations, Stanley Silverman
Scenery and Lighting, Richard Foreman; Production Associate
Kenneth James; Technical Director, Duane Mazey

CAST

Judex, the detective .... Ken Bel
Fantomas, the evil .... Paul Uken
Helene, his innocent daughter .... Lyn Ger
Irma Vep, the vampiress .... Lisa Kirchne
Max, the young journalist .... Gene Wes
M. Gaston .... Luther Enstac
Alain Duchamp .... Robert Schle
Julot L'Enjoleur .... Ray Murce
Dr. Lacloche .... Paul Ukena, Jr
Parisians .... Victor Abravaya, Katherine Alport
          Glenn Barrett, Roxy Dawn, Steven Guimon

A Musical performed without intermission.

General Manager: Kenneth Jansen

* Closed Jan. 12, 1975 after limited engagement of 16 performances

---

Lyn Gerb, Gene West
(Clemens Kalischer Photo)

BIJOU THEATRE
Opened Friday, January 3, 1975.*
Jon Voight and Susan Bloom present:

THE HASHISH CLUB

By Lance Larsen; Director, Jerome Guardino; Entire Production
and Special Effects Designed by Russell Pyle; Supervising Designers:
Scenery, Stuart Wurtzel; Lighting, Ken Billington; Costumes, Sara
Brook; Associate Producers, Terence Shank and Robert Waters; An
Elmer and Jalmia Production; Originally produced by the Company
Theatre; Production Assistant, Laurence Cohen

CAST

Tom Eren .... Lance Larsen
Jack (The Cutter) Cutter .... Jack Rowe
Dean (The Potter) Potter .... Gar Campbell
Doc Trane .... Dennis Redfield
Maston (The Canner) Kantaylis .... Michael Stefani
with the participation of T. W. Blackburn

STANDBYS: Tom, Maston, Michael Hawkins; Jack, Dean, Doc,
Dan Plucinski

A play performed without intermission.

General Management: Gatchell & Neufeld
Press: Betty Lee Hunt Associates, Stanley F. Kaminsky
Stage Managers: Robert Vandergriff, Michael Hawkins

* Closed Jan. 11, 1975 after 11 performances and 3 previews.

(John Rose Photo)

**Right Center: Jack Rowe, Gar Campbell, Lance
Larsen, Dennis Redfield, Michael Stefani in
"The Hashish Club"**

TRUCK AND WAREHOUSE THEATRE
Opened Saturday, January 4, 1975.*
The New York Theater Ensemble (Lucille Talayco, Artistic
Director) presents:

SALOME

Based on play by Oscar Wilde; Directed, Designed, and Illumi
nated by Lindsay Kemp; Music Composed and Performed by Wil
liam Hellermann; Technical Director, David Andrews; Producers
Ron Link, Alan Eichler

CAST

Acrobat/Salome's Page .... Robert Anthony
Bride/Young Syrian .... Tony Maples
Fool/Narraboth .... Neil Caplan
Man with whip/Naaman .... Robin Martin
Salome .... Lindsay Kemp
Blind Angel/Jokaanan .... David Haughton
Mad King/Herod .... David Meyer
Horse/Herodias .... The Incredible Orlando

Press: Alan Eichler, Marilyn Percy
Stage Manager: Jeremy Switzer

* Closed Dec. 15, 1974 after 30 performances in repertory with
"Turquoise Pantomime."

Tom Bair, Richard Spore, Bill Roberts,
Patricia Hodges, Patricia Conwell,
Fred Martell (foreground) in "The Devils"
(Joel Gordon Photo)

DIRECT THEATRE
Opened Friday, January 10, 1975.*
Direct Theatre presents:

THE DEVILS

By John Whiting; Director, Allen R. Belknap; Music, Jason McAuliffe; Setting and Costumes, Frank Julian Boros; Lighting, Richard Winkler

CAST

Mannoury	Bob Del Pazzo
Adam	Michael Haney
Ninon	Patricia Hodges
The Governor	Paul Collins
Chief Magistrate	Jim R. Sprague
Father Grandier	Fred Martell
Sewerman	Ralph Pape
The Cardinal	Richard Spore
Father Barre	Tom Bair
Phillipe	Patricia Carney Conwell
Sister Jeanne	Glynis Bell
The Commissioner	Bill Roberts
Sister Claire	Jo Lynn Palmer
Sister Louise	Patricia Mertens
Father Mignon	David Kousser
The Prince	George Maguire
The Jailer	Chris Hughes
Acolyte	Takashi Kazunari

Press: Les Schecter, Barbara Schwei
Stage Managers: Barbara Herzog, Chris Hughes, Takashi Kazunari

* Closed Jan. 26, 1975 after limited engagement of 15 performances.

WESTSIDE THEATRE
Opened Tuesday, January 14, 1975.*
The Chelsea Theater Center of Brooklyn presents:

DIAMOND STUDS

(The Life of Jesse James)

Book, Jim Wann; Original Music and Lyrics, Bland Simpson, Jim Wann; Musical Numbers Staged by Patricia Birch; Director, John L. Haber; Music Consultant, Mel Marvin; Design Adviser, Larry King; Sound, Laddy Savetin; Production Assistant, Ceci Conway

CAST

The Southern States Fidelity Choir:

Jesse James/Guitar	Jim Wann
Gov. Thomas Crittendon/Piano	Bland Simpson
Bob Ford/12-string guitar	John Foley
Allen Pinkerton/Percussion	Mike Sheehan
Major Edwards/Bass	Jan Davidson

The Red Clay Ramblers:

Zerelda Samuels/Cole Younger/Banjo	Tommy Thompson
Jim Younger/Mandolin	Jim Watson
Bob Younger/Fiddle	Bill Hicks
Dr. Reuben "Pappy" Samuels/Piano	Mike Craver

And Friends:

William Clark Quantrill	Scott Bradley
Zee James	Joyce Cohen
Frank James	Rick Simpson
Belle Starr	Madelyn Smoak
Tourist	Frances Tamburro

MUSICAL NUMBERS: "Jesse James Robbed This Train," "These Southern States That I Love," "The Year of Jubilo," "The Unreconstructed Rebel," "Mama Fantastic," "Saloon Piano," "I Don't Need a Man to Know I'm Good," "Northfield, Minnesota," "King Cole," "New Prisoner's Song," "K. C. Line," "Cakewalk into Kansas City," "When I Was a Cowboy," "Pancho Villa," "Put It Where the Moon Don't Shine," "Sleepy Time Down South," "Bright Morning Star," "When I Get the Call"

"A Saloon Musical" in two acts.

Company Manager: Catherine Boyer
Press: Betty Lee Hunt Associates, Stanley F. Kaminsky
Stage Manager: Brenda Mezz

Closed Aug. 3, 1975 after 232 performances.

Tom Victor Photos

Right Center: Joyce Cohen, Jim Wann

**Jim Wann, Rick Simpson, Tommy Thompson,
Jim Watson, Bill Hicks**

CHERRY LANE THEATRE
Opened Thursday, January 16, 1975.*
Edgar Lansbury, Joseph Beruh and Torquay Company present:

BLASTS AND BRAVOS

An Evening with H. L. Mencken

Adapted by Paul Shyre; Production Designed by Eldon Elder; Incidental Music, Robert Rines; Production Coordinator, Gail Bell; Production Assistant, Wayne Maxwell

with
Paul Shyre as H. L. Mencken

Performed with one intermission. The action takes place in the study of H. L. Mencken's home in Baltimore, Md., in 1930.

General Manager: Al J. Isaac
Company Manager: Ron Bunker
Press: Gifford/Wallace, Tom Trenkle
Stage Manager: Clint Jakeman

* Closed Feb. 23, 1975 after 46 performances.

ALL SOULS UNITARIAN CHURCH
Opened Monday, January 20, 1975*
The All Souls Players present:

IT'S NOT WHERE YOU START ...

(A Musical Tribute to Dorothy Fields)

Conceived and Directed by Tran William Rhodes; Choreography, Don Madison; Lighting, Bill Pietrucha, Martin Smith; Photography/Slide projectionist, Mary Lumsden, Costumes, Fran Loccisano

CAST

Barbara Coggin
Meredith Kelly
Don Madison
Tran William Rhodes
Tim Sheahan
Norb Joerder
Kris Koczur
Paul Merrill
Jinny Sager
Roger Whitmarsh

Pianos, David Lahm and Tran William Rhodes; Percussion, James Erwin

A selection of 41 songs and 2 scenes written by the late lyricist/librettist, Dorothy Fields.

Stage Manager: Lou Pavone

* Closed January 23, 1975 after a limited run of 3 performances.

MAYFAIR THEATRE
Opened Thursday, January 23, 1975.*
Ted Ravinett and Steve Rubenstein present:

DANCE WITH ME

Written and Composed by Greg Antonacci; Directed and Choreographed by Joel Zwick; Scenery and Lighting, Scott Johnson; Costumes, Susan Hum Buck; Sound, Theatre Technology; Musical Consultant, Peter Frumkin; Assistant Director, Philip Shafer; Associate Producer, Barry Cornet; Technical Director, Mike Moran; Production Assistants, Tammie Temptation, Eileen Markoe, Diane Blumberg

CAST

Tommie Sincere	Annie Abbott
Honey Boy	Greg Antonacci†
Jimmy Dick II	John Bottoms
Thumbs Bumpin	Peter Frumkin
Judy Jeanine	Patricia Gaul
Wendell Crunchall	Scott Robert Redman
Goldie Pot	Deborah Rush
Smitner Tuskey	Stuart Silver
Don Tomm	Skip Zipf
Bulldog Allen	Joel Zwick

Understudy: Wendy Ellen

"A Comedy with Music" in two acts. The action takes place in a subway station in New York City at the present time.

Press: Max Eisen, M. J. Boyer, Judy Jacksina
Stage Manager: Robert H. Keil, Jr.

* Still playing May 31, 1975.
† Succeeded by Peter Riegert

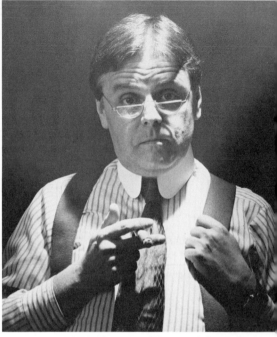

Paul Shyre in "Blasts and Bravos"
(Kenn Duncan Photo)

Barbara Coggin, Don Madison, Norb Joerder, Meredith Kelly

John Bottoms, Stuart Silver, Joel Zwick, Greg Antonacci, Deborah Rush, Patricia Gaul, Annie Abbo (back) Peter Frumkin, Scott Redman, Skip Zipf

PLAYERS THEATRE
Opened Monday, January 27, 1975.*
Phillip Graham-Geraci and Michael Brown present:

LOVERS

Book, Lyrics, Direction by Peter del Valle; Music, Steve Sterner;
Lighting, Paul Sullivan; Costumes, Reve Richards; Set, Eugene Hide

CAST

Freddie	Martin Rivera
Eddie	Michael Cascone
Harry	John Ingle
Dave	Richard Ryder†
Spencer	Reathel Bean
George	Gary Sneed

MUSICAL NUMBERS: "Lovers," "Look at Him," "Make It," "I
Don't Want to Watch TV," "Twenty Years," "Somebody, Some-
body Hold Me," "Belt and Leather," "There Is Always You,"
"Hymn," "Somehow I'm Taller," "Role-Playing," "Argument,"
"Where Do I Go from Here?," "The Trucks," "Don't Betray His
Love," "You Came to Me as a Young Man"

"A Really Gay Musical Revue" in 2 acts and 17 scenes.

Press: Henry Luhrman Associates, Les Schecter
Stage Manager: Rick Claflin

* Closed May 11, 1975 after 118 performances.
† Succeeded by Robert Sevra

Martha Swope Photos

**Top Right: Gary Sneed, Reathel Bean, Martin Rivera,
Michael Cascone, John Ingle, Robert Sevra**

THE LITTLE THEATRE
Opened Wednesday, January 29, 1975.*
Andy Warhol in association with Richard Turley presents:

MAN ON THE MOON

Book, Music and Lyrics by John Phillips; Director, Paul Mor-
rissey; Sets, John J. Moore; Costumes, Marsia Trinder; Lighting,
Jules Fisher; Musical Director, Karen Gustafson; Musical Arrangements, Michael Gibson, Tim Tyler; Sound, Gary Harris; Costume
Design Supervised by Michael Yeargan; Hairstyles and Makeup,
Roberto Vega, Pablo Fortunato; Wardrobe, Kathleen Shearer, Loraine Lang; Production Assistant, Jeanette Chastonay

CAST

Dr. Bomb	Harlan S. Foss
Ernie Hardy	Eric Lang
Leroy (Little Red Box)	Mark Lawhead
President and King Can	Dennis Doherty
Angel	Genevieve Waite
Venus	Monique Van Vooren
Celestial Choir:	
Mercury/Miss America	Brenda Bergman
Mars	John Patrick Sundine
Neptune	Jennifer Elder
Pluto	E. Lynn Nickerson
Saturn	Jeanette Chastonay

STANDBYS: President, King Can, Scientist, John Patrick Sundine;
Venus, Miss America, Brenda Bergman; Angel, Jennifer Elder; Mer-
cury, Neptune, Jeanette Chastonay

MUSICAL NUMBERS: Prologue, "Boys from the South," "Mid-
night Deadline Blastoff," "Mission Control," "Speed of Light,"
"Though I'm a Little Angel," "Girls," "Canis Minor Bolero Waltz,"
"Starbust," "Penthouse of Your Mind," "Champagne and Kisses,"
"Star Stepping Stranger," "Convent," "My Name Is Can," "Ameri-
can Man on the Moon," "Welcome to the Moon," "Sunny Moon,"
"Love Is Coming Back," "Truth Cannot Be Treason," "Place in
Space," "Family of Man," "Yesterday I Left the Earth," "Stepping
the Stars"

A Musical performed without intermission.

General Manager: Ashton Springer
Company Manager: Chester Fox
Press: Michael Sean O'Shea, Robert M. Zarem
Stage Managers: Michael Maurer, Thomas Vivian

*Closed Feb. 1, 1975 after 5 performances and 21 previews.

Bert Andrews Photo

**Monique Van Vooren, Eric Lang
in "Man on the Moon"**

81

Lillian Lux, Pesach Burstein
in "A Wedding in Shtetel"

THEATRE DE LYS

Opened Monday, February 17, 1975.*

Michael Harvey presents:

FOUR FRIENDS

By Larry Kramer; Director, Alfred Gingold: Scenery and Lighting Designed by Duane F. Mazey; Costumes, Tom Fallon; Production Manager, Duane F. Mazey; Assistant to the Director, David Kneuss

CAST

Charlie	Robert Stattel
Dick	Ronald Hale
Ben	John Colenback
Edward	Jeremiah Sullivan
Annie	Jill Andre
Mike	Brad Davis
Laura	Hallaren
Elizabeth	Sharon Laughlin

A play in two acts. The action takes place at the present time in the apartments of Charlie, Dick, Ben, and Edward, a street, and a restaurant.

General Manager: Jay Kingwill
Press: Alan Eichler, Marilyn Percy
Stage Manager: Brad Davis

* Closed Feb. 17, 1975 after one performance.

Cast of "Four Friends"
(Friedman-Abeles Photo)

EDEN THEATRE
Opened Sunday, February 9, 1975.*

A WEDDING IN SHTETEL

Libretto, William Siegel; Music, H. Wohl; Director, P. Burstein; Adapted by Lillian Lux; Musical Director, Renee Solomon

CAST

Narrator	David Carey
Malka, the Rabbi's maid	Janece Martel
Eli Melach, the Rabbi's Shames	Pesach Burstein
Mike, Rabbi's American nephew	David Carey
Feigele, the bride	Gerri-Ann Frank
Shimon, Rabbi's son	Karol Latowicz
Ruben, Rabbi's son	Robert Wayne
Levi, Rabbi's son	Shmulik Goldstein
Rabbi Issor'l of Brinitz	Elia Patron
Yossele, his youngest son	Mike Burstein
The Rebbitzin, Yossele's mother	Rochelle Relis
Guzik, a theatre director	Jaime Lewin
Ruzha, his wife	Reizl Bozyk
Regina, their primadonna	Lillian Lux
Dr. Boris Lazarow	William Gary

Standby for Yossele, David Carey

MUSICAL NUMBERS: "A Chasens in Shtetel," "Az Men Zicht, gefint men," "Feigalach Tzvei," "Oy Vay Tate," "Yossele and Feigele," "Wedding Ensemble," "An Actor's Life," "Without Him," "Yossele Entrance," "Sing a Happy Song," "Feigele, My Love," "Shabes nuchn Kiegel," "Yossele's Dream," "Efsher Vet Geshen a ness"

A Musical Comedy in two acts, and three scenes. The action takes place in the village of Brinitze, Russia, before World War I, and in Kretshma, in the town of Zhmerkinka.

Press: Max Eisen

* Closed March 2, 1975 after limited run of 12 performances.

NEW PALLADIUM
Opened Friday, February 21, 1975.*
Ivan Reitman presents:

THE NATIONAL LAMPOON SHOW

Music Composed and Performed by Paul Jacobs; Words and Lyrics By The Cast (overlooked by Sean Kelly); Director, Martin Charnin; Production Supervised by Dale Anglund; Lighting, Lowell Sherman; Costume Coordinator, Patricia Britton; Sound, Abe Jacob

CAST

John Belushi
Brian Doyle-Murray
Bill Murray
Gilda Radner
Harold Ramis

A Satirical Revue performed without intermission.

General Management: David Wyler, Marvin A. Krauss
Press: Gifford/Wallace, Tom Trenkle
Company Manager: Robyn Watson

*Closed June 29, 1975 after 180 performances.

**Above: Bill Murray, John Belushi, Brian
Doyle-Murray, Harold Ramis**

Sadayo Kita in "Hagoromo"
(Thomas Haar Photo)

RT WHEELER THEATRE
Opened Tuesday, March 12, 1975.*
Allan Brown, Renee Semes Herz and Bill Vitale present:

APE OVER BROADWAY

ook, Mary McCartney, Bart Andrews; Music, Stephen Ross; cs, Bill Vitale; Director-Choreographer, Jeffery K. Neill; Set gn and Lighting, Dan Leigh, Gail Van Voorhis; Costumes, t J. Porter; Musical Direction, Dance Music and Arrangements, lerick S. Roffman; From an original idea and story by Andrew z; Produced in association with Octagon: The American Musical atre Company; Assistant Musical Director/Piano, David Rada; inical Director, Timothy Farmer; Assistant to the Producers, Ci og; Assistant to the Director, Norb Joerder

CAST

e	Jacqueline Reilly
ord Gotham	Robert Calvert
ona/Smitty/Jungle Jill/Evans/Flamingo Fusser/	
tty/Mrs. O'Hara	Phylis Ward
e/Miss Frump/Jungle Jill/Shirley/Flamingo	
usser/Pinky Chiffon	Freyda-Ann Thomas
very Boy/Pilot/Native Guide/Higgins/Flamingo	
usser/Johnson/Cop	Jim Cyrus
st Boles	Robert Lydiard
Stud/Martini/Stevens/King/Delivery	
an/TV Announcer	Norb Joerder
Peskowitz	Barbara Coggin
....	Curt Ralston

SICAL NUMBERS: "Nude-Lewd," "The Star Number," adway," "I've Had Everything but a Man," "The Man Eating Waltz," "Saga of Men and Marriage," "An Ape Can Save the ld," "Mixed-Up Media," "I'm in Like with You," "Flamingo s," "Triangle Song," "Just Whistle," "My Friend," "Ape over adway," Finale

A New Gorilla Musical" in 2 acts and 8 scenes. The action takes e in New York City, and in Deepest Darkest Africa.

General Managers: Gatchell and Neufeld
Press: Max Eisen
Stage Managers: Jeanne Fornadel, Tony Slez

losed March 23, 1975 after limited engagement of 11 performances.

Cast of "Wings"
(Martha Swope Photo)

JAPAN HOUSE
Wednesday, February 19, 1975.*
Japan Society presents:

THE KITA NOH TROUPE

Sadayo Kita
Yasunobu Uchida
Shigeyoshi Mori
with musicians and chanters

PROGRAM: "Hagoromo," "Kumasaka"

* Presented for one performance only.

Norb Joerder, Freyda-Ann Thomas, Jacqueline Reilly, Robert Lydiard, Curt Ralston, Robert Calvert, Barbar Coggin, Phylis Ward, Jim Cyrus
(Paddy Briglio Photo)

EASTSIDE PLAYHOUSE
Opened Sunday, March 16, 1975.*
Stephen Wells presents:

WINGS

Book, Music and Lyrics, Robert McLaughlin, Peter Ryan; Based on Aristophanes' "The Birds"; Director, Robert McLaughlin; Scenery and Lighting, Karl Eigsti; Costumes, Shadow; Associate Producers, R. E. Lee, Jr., Charles Walton; Musical Direction, Larry Hochman; Orchestrations and Vocal Arrangements, Bill Brohn; Musical Numbers Staged by Nora Christiansen; Managerial Associate, Patricia Bartolotta; Production Assistant, Steve Harris

CAST

Pisthetairos	Jerry Sroka
Euelprides	David Kolatch
Butler Bird/Insurance Salesman/	
Hercules	David Pursley
Epops	Jay E. Raphael
Procne	Mary Sue Finnerty
Cardinal/Barbarian God	Peter Jurasik
Male Tanager	James Howard Laurence
Female Tanager/Birdwatcher	Maureen Sadusk
Large-Breasted Bushtit/Poet	Barbara Rubenstein
Dickcissel	Nicholas Stannard
Eagle/Construction Boss/Prometheus	Dan Held
Macaw	Brenda Gardner
Parrot/Iris	Robin Wesley
Flamingo/Soothsayer	Sally Mitchell
Penguin/Land Developer/Zeus	Stuart Pankin

MUSICAL NUMBERS: "Wings," "Call of the Birds," "O Sacrilege," "The Human Species," "Time to Find Something to Do," "First I Propose," "Comfort for the Taking," "You'll Regret It!," "How Great It Is to Be a Bird," "Rah Tah Tah Tio Beep Doo Doo," "The Wall Song," "Take to the Air," "Iris the Fleet," "The Great Immortals," "We're Gonna Make It," Finale

A Musical Comedy in two acts. The action takes place on a mountain top.

General Manager: William Craver
Press: Mary Bryant, Bill Evans
Stage Managers: Peter Lawrence, Dan Held

* Closed March 23, 1975 after 9 performances.

LA MAMA ANNEX

Opened Tuesday, March 18, 1975.*
Mel Howard, Ninon Tallon Karlweis and The Festival of the Third World Corporation presents from Nigeria, Duro Ladipo's Yoruba Folk Opera:

OBA KOSO

Produced, Written and Directed by Duro Ladipo; Lighting, Olatunde Oguntola; Settings, Oshogbo Artists of Mbari Mbayo; Tour Director, Atlee Stephan III

CAST

Duro Ladipo
with
Duro Ladipo's National Theatre
and
Musicians

A Yoruba Musical in 8 acts and 11 scenes.

Stage Manager: Lanrewaju Ladipo

* Closed March 22, 1975 after limited engagement of 5 performances. Returned Thursday, April 17–19, 1975 for 4 additional performances at Madison Square Garden.

(Satomeor Photo)

Top Right: Duro Ladipo in "Oba Koso"

BELMONT THEATRE

Opened Sunday, March 23, 1975.*
J. Arthur Elliot presents:

BE KIND TO PEOPLE WEEK

Book, Music and Lyrics, Jack Bussins, Ellsworth Olin; Produce Director, Quinton Raines; Musical Direction, Jeremy Stone; Ch reography, Bobby Lee; Vocal Arrangements, John Franceschin Musical Arrangements, Jack Gale; Scenery, Bruce Monroe; Ligh ing, Anguss Moss; Wardrobe, Kathy Dyas; Production Assistar Barry Blaustein; Fashions by Gimbels

CAST

Hope Healy	Naura Hayd
Norman	Kenneth Co
Alan	Alan Ka
Dan	Daniel Brov
Nell	Nell N. Cart
Judy	Judy Congre
Grenoldo	Grenoldo Frazi
Bobby	Bobby L
Dana	Dana Lor
Randy	Randy Mart
Maureen	Maureen Moc

MUSICAL NUMBERS: "What Ever Happened to the Good O Days," "I Will Give Him Love," "Mad about You, Manhattan," Have a Friend at the Chase Manhattan Bank," "All I Got Is You "I'm in Like with You," "When We See a Pretty Girl We Whist Ecology," "I Need You," "To Love Is to Live," "Freud Is a Fraud "Black Is Beautiful," "A Smile Is Up," "You're Divine," "Be Kir to People Week"

"A Smiling Musical" in 2 acts and 22 scenes. The action tak place at the present time in New York City.

General Manager: Bob MacDonald
Press: Saul Richman, Herb Striesfield
Stage Manager: John Brigleb

* Closed June 14, 1975 after 100 performances.

CITY CENTER 55th STREET THEATER

Opened Tuesday, March 24, 1975.*
Ronald Wilford presents:

MARCEL MARCEAU

with
Pierre Verry

Administrative Director, Alain Mangel; Assistant to Mr. Ma ceau, Yancy Bukovec; Lighting Director, Geoffrey Taylor; To Direction, Columbia Artists Management Inc.

A program of pantomime presented in two parts.

Company Manager: John Scott
Stage Manager: Antoine Casanova

* Closed April 13, 1975 after limited engagement of 24 perfo mances.

Marcel Marceau

UPSTAIRS AT NEW JIMMY'S
Opened Friday, March 28, 1975.*
MCB Productions presents:

IN GAY COMPANY

Lyrics and Music by Fred Silver; Director, Sue Lawless; Designed by Michael J. Hotopp and Paul De Pass; Musical Director, John DeMaio; Assistant Musical Director, Dennis Buck; Production Assistant, Bonnie Sue Schloss

CAST

Rick Gardner
Bob Gorman
Ann Hodapp
Gordon Ramsey
Robert Tananis

MUSICAL NUMBERS: "Welcome, Welcome," "A Pilgrim's Primer," "A Special Boy," "Handsome Stranger," "Ode to a Hard Hat," "Fahrenheit 451," "Loew's Sheridan Square," "Lament for a Man in Blue," "Opera Buffa," "A House Is Not a Home," "Two Strangers," "Remembrance of Things Past," "The Days of Dancing," "I Remember Mama," "If He'd Only Be Gentle," "Freddy Liked to Fugue," "Thank You, Thank You"

A Musical Revue in two acts.

Press: Shirley Herz
Stage Manager: Les Barkdull

Closed April 5, 1975 after 8 performances. Presented at the Little Hippodrome Oct. 29, 1974 as "Gay Company" with other cast members and musical numbers.

BERT WHEELER THEATRE
Opened Sunday, April 13, 1975.*
Hyperion Productions presents:

THE RAINBOW RAPE TRICK

Book, Greg Reardon; Music, Ann K. Lipson; Lyrics, Greg Reardon, Ann K. Lipson; Director, Robert Davison; Costumes, Mary Ann Tolka; Choreography, Robin Raseen; Lighting, Chaim Gitter; Scenic Designer; Francis Pezza; Technical Director, Marlene Schwartz; Props, Rose Auringer; Wardrobe Mistress, Marilyn Block; Musical Director, Elliot Ames

CAST

Billy Redfeather .... Bob Bosco
Randy McGee .... Vincent Millard
Tim McGee .... Patrick O'Sullivan
Peggy McGee .... Lois Hathaway
Ruth Robbins .... Deidre Lynn
Abie, the Robot .... John Blanda
Clovis Taylor .... Anthony Dileva
Marcus Schmidt .... Jerry Rodgers
Hugo Caporello .... Joseph Tripolino
Michael Taylor .... Jeremy Stockwell
Minerva Taylor .... Jean Greer
Ken. Merryweather/Rainbow
Village Assassin .... John Blanda

MUSICAL NUMBERS: "Zip Community," "Free," "Itch to Be a Bitch," "Most Confused Prince," "Stay with Me," "Northchester," "Democracy Is Lunacy," "Little Blue Star," "Crush on You," "'Tis Thee," "Love Me, Baby!," "Three Fierce Men," "Divorce of Course," "Act Like a Villager," "Empty World of Power," Finale

A Musical in 2 acts and 7 scenes. The action takes place in the future in Rainbow Village.

Press: Lisa Lipsky, David Lipsky
Stage Manager: Marjorie Dundas

Closed April 15, 1975 after 4 performances.

Joseph
Tripolino

Jean
Greer

Jeremy
Stockwell
in "The Rainbow Rape Trick"

Gordon Ramsey   Ann Hodapp   Robert Tanar
in "In Gay Company"

UNITARIAN CHURCH OF ALL SOULS
Opened Friday, April 11, 1975.*
The All Souls Players presents:

CAN-CAN

Book, Abe Burrows; Music and Lyrics, Cole Porter; Directed and Choreographed by Jeffery K. Neill; Designed by Robert Edmonds; Costumes, Charles Roeder; Lighting, Tony Santoro; Musical Direction and Special Arrangements, Wendell Kindberg; Producers, Dorothy Harris, Howard Van Der Meulen; Assistant to the Director, and Dance Captain, Jean Turney; Technical Director, Disbrow Hadley; Wardrobe Mistress, Jean Bonniol

CAST

Bailiff/Prosecutor	Jim-Bob Williams
Registrar/Customer/Photographer/Doctor	Michael Palmer
Judge Barriere/Monarchist	Jim Ryan
Court President	Tim Kennedy
Judge Aristede Forestiere	Bob Sikso
Claudine	Kathleen W. Gray
Gabrielle	Kris Koczur
Marie	Linda Lipson
Celestine	Lila Koven
Laundress/Mimi	Marilyn Anderson
Laundress/Model	Lavinia Plonka
Policeman/Waiter	Bill Fowle
Policeman/Waiter/Jussac's Second	Michael Williamson
Policeman/Waiter	Philip Gerson
Policeman/Waiter/Customer/Turnkey	Norb Joerder
Court Attendant/Customer/Judge Chambrun	Don Madison
Hilaire Jussac	James LeVaggi
Boris Adzinidzinadze	Robert D. Kane
Hercule	Joe Aronica
Theophile	Ed Folts
Etienne	Tran Rhodes
La Mome Pistache	Mary Lynne Metternich
Nun	Jean Turney
Cafe Musician	Julio Rivas
Laundresses	Kathryn Burke, Bobbie Gevas, Suzanne Kaszynski

MUSICAL NUMBERS: "Maidens Typical of France," "The Law," "I Do," "What a Fair Thing Is a Woman," "Never Give Anything Away," "C'est Magnifique," "Quadrille," "Her Heart Was in Her Work," "Come Along with Me," "Live and Let Live," "I Am in Love," "If You Loved Me Truly," "Garden of Eden Ballet," "Montmartre," "Allez-vous-en," "Never, Never Be an Artist," "It's All Right with Me," "Every Man Is a Stupid Man," "Apache Specialty," "A Man Must His Honor Defend," "I Love Paris," "To Think This Could Happen to Me," "Can-Can," Finale

A Musical in two acts. The entire action takes place in Paris in 1893.

Press: James E. V. Butler, Mary McCartney
Stage Managers: Eve Sorel, Harry Blum, Steve Matos

* Closed April 19, 1975 after a limited engagement of 5 performances.

Ed Folts, Linda Lipson, Robert D. Kane, Kathleen W. Gray, Tran Rhodes, Kris Koczur, Joe Aronica, Lila Koven in "Can-Can"

William Schilling in "Singly None"
(Danny Lowenthal Photo)

CARNEGIE HALL
Wednesday, Thursday, April 16–17, 1975
The Carnegie Hall Corporation and Kazuko Hillyer International present:

KYOGEN

National Comic Theatre of Japan

PROGRAM: "Boshibari (Tied to a Pole)," "Urinusubito (The Melon Thief)," and "Kusabira (Mushrooms)"

**Nanci Addison, Ray Rantapaa, Jane Cook
in "Agnes and Joan"**
(Frank Derbas Photo)

WESTSIDE THEATER
Opened Monday, April 14, 1975.*
The Labor Theater Inc. (C. R. Portz, Artistic Director; Bette Craig, Executive Director) presents:

... SINGLY NONE'

Written and Directed by C. R. Portz; Set Design, James Singelis; Costumes, Arlene Gold; Assistant Designer, Linda Skipper; Lighting, Gabe Gabrielsky; Assistant Producer, William Grange

CAST

John L. Lewis .... William Schilling
Kathryn Lewis .... Reva Cooper
Mother Jones/Woman .... Dorothy Lancaster
Singers .... Gloria Goldman, Mark Ross

Stage Manager: William Grange

* Closed April 28, 1975 after a limited engagement of 3 performances. The production had been previously presented for 12 performances at various union halls, and Henry Street Settlement.

Kyogen Theatre of Japan

ALL ANGELS CHURCH
Opened Thursday, April 17, 1975.*
The Lab Theatre Company (Matt Conley, Artistic Director; Don Joslyn, Executive Director) presents:

AGNES AND JOAN

By Gyorgy Sebestyen; Translated and Directed by Peter Sander; Costumes, Georgia Baker; Sets, Boots Davis, Richard Talcott; Lighting, Jeff Davis; Music, Daniel Jahn; Choreography, Dee Bagley; Production Manager, John Brigleb; Wardrobe, Ike Feather, Bill Taylor; Props, Charles Caron; Lighting, Terry Brockbank; Pianist, Frank Echols

CAST

Charles, the Dauphin .... Ray Rantapaa
Philippine .... Susan Johnson
Jacobine .... Kathy Dyas
Isabeau of Bavaria .... Norma Justin
Agnes Sorel .... Nanci Addison
Isabella of Lorraine .... Dee Bagley
Maria of Anjou .... Amy Wright
Joan of Domremy .... Jane Cook
The Musician .... Greg Godeke
Charles of Valois .... John Miranda

A play in three acts. The action takes place at Chinon Castle.

Press: Howard Atlee Associates, Clarence Allsop
Stage Manager: John Brigleb

* Closed May 3, 1975 after limited run of 12 performances.

**Jeffrey DeMunn, Faith Catlin, Kenneth Harvey
in "Augusta"**

(Friedman-Abeles Photo)

IERRY LANE THEATRE
Opened Friday, April 25, 1975.*

HUSTLERS

Written and Directed by A. J. Kronengold; Lighting, Tina Char-
y; Costumes Faber Inc.; Production Coordinator, Marshall Ballou

CAST

▸ger De Jonge	Warren Pincus
▸nine	Susan Valentino
▸rrie	Eve Adams
▸uitfly	Kathryn Hultsberg
▸e Johns	David Cargill
▸ry	Jim Faber
▸sh	Sonny Landham
▸ C. Starr	Dennis Walsh
▸rry Bloomingdale	Gary Faga

"A New Erotic Comedy" in two acts. The action takes place at
▸ present time during a 72 hour period of time on Eighth Avenue
▸ New York city, in a restaurant, and in Roger DeJonge's walkup
▸ement apartment.

General Manager: Michael Woods
Company Manager: Ken Gaston
Press: Max Eisen, Barbara Glenn
Stage Manager: Paul Harkins

Closed April 27, 1975 after 5 performances and 16 previews.

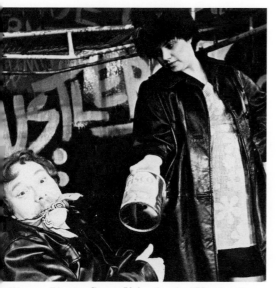

Warren Pincus, Susan Valentino in "Hustlers"
(Ron Schubert Photo)

THEATRE DE LYS
Opened Sunday, April 20, 1975.*
Gerald Seiff and Geoffrey Winters present:

AUGUSTA

By Larry Ketron; Director, David Black; Scenic Design, Barry F.
Williams; Lighting, Daniel Flannery; Costumes, Jennifer von Mayr-
hauser; Production Supervisor, Peter von Mayrhauser; Production
Coordinator, Assistant to the Director, Allie Jones

CAST

Laureen	Jill Andre
Jud	Anthony Call
Champion	Kenneth Harvey
Betty	Faith Catlin
Boyd	Jeffrey DeMunn
Marilyn	Elizabeth Franz

A play in 2 acts and 7 scenes. The action takes place at the present
time in the woods of Georgia just outside Augusta

General Manager: Gatchell & Neufeld
Press: Betty Lee Hunt Associates, Maria C. Pucci, Stanley F.
Kaminsky, Bill Evans
Stage Managers: Peter von Mayrhauser, Patti King

* Closed April 27, 1975 after 9 performances.

PLAYHOUSE
Opened Sunday, April 27, 1975.*
Jeff Britton presents:

A MATTER OF TIME

Book, Hap Schlein, Russell Leib; Music and Lyrics, Philip F.
Margo; Directed and Choreographed by Tod Jackson; Designed by
David Guthrie; Lighting, Martin Aronstein; Sound, Jack Shearing;
Orchestrations, Elliot Gilman; Musical Direction, Vocal and Dance
Arrangements, Arnold Gross; Assistant Choreographer, Leland
Schwantes; Assistant to the Producer, James Struthers; Assistant to
the Director, Rick Podell; Music Coordinator, Earl Shendell; Ward-
robe Supervisor, Michael Dennison

CAST

Next	David-James Carroll
Lily	Jane Robertson
Blaze	Glory Van Scott
"D"	Joe Masiell
Pansy/Candy	Carol Estey
Tulip/Fatima	Miriam Welch
Rose/Cynthia	Joyce Nolen
Leroy/Harry	Leland Schwantes
Mervyn	Dennis Michaelson
Harvey	Ronnie De Marco
Jordon	Douglas Bentz
Kate	Charlise Harris
Paul	Donald M. Griffith
The Flasher	Elliott Lawrence
Young Girl	Suellen Arlen
Fifi	Rosamond Lynn
Louise	Linda Willows
The Flames	Carol Estey, Rosamond Lynn, Miriam Welch
The Furies	Douglas Bentz, Ronnie De Marco, Leland Schwantes
The Voice of "G"	Elliott Lawrence

UNDERSTUDIES: Next, Ronnie De Marco; Blaze, Miriam Welch;
"D", Douglas Bentz; Kate, Carol Estey; Paul, Elliott Lawrence;
Cynthia, Rosamond Lynn; Louise, Suellen Arlen

MUSICAL NUMBERS: "Me God, Please God," "It's Not Easy
Being Next," "The Ritual," "Welcome to Hell," "Purgatory U,"
"Snake," "If This Were My World," "A Matter of Time," "This
Moment," "Don't Let Me Bother You," "Oh, What a Wonderful
Plan," "Sex Is a Spectator Sport," "Winner," "It Will Be My Day,"
"Time Is a Travellin' Show," "I Can Give You Music," "This Is
Your Year 1976," "The Devil in Your Eyes," "Oh, World," "I Am
the Next"

A Musical in 2 acts and 13 scenes with a prologue and epilogue.
The action takes place on December 31, 1975.

Company Manager: Gloria Alter
Press: Max Eisen, M. J. Boyer, Judy Jacksina
Stage Managers: Janet Beroza, Pat DeRousie

* Closed April 27, 1975 after one performance. (no photos available)

WASHINGTON SQUARE CHURCH

Opened Monday, April 28, 1975.*
Lois D. Sasson and Olive F. Watson present:

PARTO

Based on "The Three Marias: New Portugese Letters" by Maria Isabel Barreno and Gilda Grillo; Director, Gilda Grillo; Costumes and Settings, Hortense Guillemard; Lighting, Marilyn Rennagel; Music, Emilia Biancardi Ferreira; Organist, Marie Truran; Percussionist, Edwina Tyler.

CAST

Mother Abbess	Natalie Gray
Maria	Carole Leverett
Coleta	Coleta
Ana	Ruth Truran
Dona Brites	Muriel Miguel
Eunuchs	Loremil Machado, Jelom Vieira
Mariana	Sherry Mathis
Joana	Donna Faye Isaacson
Monica	Carol Cole

A play in twelve scenes without intermission.

General Manager: Berenice Weiler
Press: Shirley Herz
Stage Managers: Elizabeth Holloway, P. Delurier

* Closed May 18, 1975 after 24 performances and 8 previews. Reopened at La Mama for 4 performances June 5–8, 1975.

Natalie Gray, Ruth Truran, Donna Faye Isaacs Carol Cole, Carole Leverett, Coletta in "Parto
(Martha Swope Photo)

(Top) Madeleine le Roux, Helen Hanft, Sharon Ann Barr, (Center) Leslie Edgar, Hope Stansbury, Mary-Jenifer Mitchell, Ann Collier, (Front) Mary Boylan, Maria De-Landa, Pat Ast

ASTOR PLACE THEATRE

Opened Thursday, May 1, 1975.*
Craig Baumgarten, Alan Eichler and Ron Link present:

WOMEN BEHIND BARS

By Tom Eyen; Director, Ron Link; Set, Herbert Nagle; Lightin Lawrence Eichler; Associate Managers, Phyllis Restaino, Thelm Cooper; Technical Director, G. Allison Elmer; Production Assi tant, Lisa Persky; Title Song by Tom Eyen; Sung by Larry Pauler.

CAST

Matron	Pat A
Louise	Leslie Edg
Blanche	Hope Stansbu
Jo-Jo	Ann Colli
Cheri	Sharon Ann Ba
Granny	Mary Boyl
Gloria	Helen Han
Ada	Madeleine le Ro
Guadalupe	Maria DeLan
Mary-Eleanor	Mary-Jenifer Mitch
The Men	Walker Stua

A play performed without intermission. The action takes place the Women's House of Detention between 1952 and 1960.

General Management: Dorothy Olim Associates
Company Manager: Donald Tirabassi
Press: Alan Eichler, Marilyn Percy
Stage Managers: Jack Kalman, Walker Stuart

* Closed June 15, 1975 after 54 performances.

Arthur Weinstein Photo

88

Opened Sunday, May 11, 1975.*
Jane Manning and Carol McGroder in association with Wendell Minnick present:

THE GLORIOUS AGE

Book, Cy Young in collaboration with Mark Gordon; Music and Lyrics, Cy Young; Director, John-Michael Tebelak; Scenery, Stuart Wurtzel; Lighting, Barry Arnold; Costumes, Jennifer von Mayrhauser; Arranged and Orchestrated by Stephen Reinhardt; Musical Director, Robert W. Preston; Special Movement, Dick Stephens; Assistant to the Director, Janet Sonenberg; Management Associates, Phyllis Restaino, Donald Tirabassi, Thelma Cooper; Assistant to the Producers, Barbara Bryan; Production Assistant, Stuart H. Ross; Wardrob, Bonnie Baker

CAST

Blacksmith/Student/Hunchback Man/	
Crusader/Bear	Stuart Pankin
Doctor/Town Crier/Student/Crusader	George Riddle
Scientist/Student/Relic Seller/Crusader	Clyde Laurents
Madame Duncan/Crusader	Susan Willis
Theologian/Merchant/Professor/	
Commissioner/Crusader	Barry Pearl
Theologian/Merchant/Professor/	
Commissioner/Crusader	Paul Kreppel
Theologian/Merchant/Professor/	
Commissioner/Crusader	Laurie Faso
Henrietta/Student/Crusader	Robin Wesley
Jana/Student/Crusader	D'Jamin Bartlett
Drum Girl/Student/Commissioner's Wife/	
Crusader	Carol Swarbrick
Peter the Crusader/Student	W. M. Hunt
Matthew/Crusader	Don Scardino

MUSICAL NUMBERS: "Glorious Age," "Teach the Children," "Stay on the Path," "Mother Love," "All about the Plum," "Relic Seller Theme," "Theologian Theme," "The Turn My Life Is Taking," "Rah, Rah," "Whoop De Doo," "Must Be a Witch in Town," "Everyone Should Play a Musical Instrument," "The Future Looks Promising," "Maybe There's a Place," "La La La," "Child of the Age"

A Musical in two acts that takes "a light look at the Dark Ages." The action takes place in and around a town square during the Glorious Age.

General Management: Dorothy Olim Associates
Press: Gifford/Wallace, Tom Trenkle
Stage Managers: Suzanne Egan, Laurie Faso

Closed May 18, 1975 after 14 performances.

D'Jamin Bartlett, George Riddle, Barry Pearl, Paul Kreppel, Clyde Laurents, Carol Swarbrick, Laurie Faso, Stuart Pankin
(Bert Andrews Photo)

GREEK ART THEATRE
Opened Wednesday, May 14, 1975.*
The Aristophanes Meets Zorba Production Company of Athens, Greece (Fondas Lalaounis, Executive Producer) and The Lemos Greek Repertory Theater present:

THE WOMEN'S TRIBUNAL

An Adaptation by Alexis Solomos of "The Thesmophoriazusae" of Aristophanes; Director, Dinos Eliopoulos; Choreography, Yannis Nikitakis; Musical Coordination, Asteris Matakos; English Narrative, George Lendrihas; Lighting, George Avgerakis; Costumes, Diana; Sound, Kimon Danos; Advisory Producer, George Lendrihas; Production Assistant, Stella Manesiotis

CAST

Dancer/First Guard	Yannis Nikitakis
Narrator/Kerikena	Lytha Miranda
Euripides	Adamandios Lemos
Mnesilochus	Dinos Eliopoulos'
Servant of Agathon/Skythis	Kostas Aiolos
Agathon/Cleisthenes/2nd Guard	Nikos Kapsokefalos
First Muse/Mika	Eleni Saniou
Critylla	Mari Karavia
Kerikena	Lytha Miranda
Mika	Eleni Saniou
Cleisthenes	Nikos Kapsokefalos
Elafion	Linda Dobson

CHORUS OF WOMEN: Charlotte Christen, Linda Dobson, Nedra Marlin-Harris, Nadia Haritou, Wanda Lowe, Doris Pasteleur

Performed without intermission. The action takes place 450 B.C. to forever. . . . and thereabouts A.D. in an Athenian marketplace near the Pnyx, a hill opposite the Acropolis.

Press: Alan Eichler, Zanis Zakinthinos, Mitzi Dallas, Georgia Generalis, Kostas Theodorakos
Stage Manager: Stella Manesiotis

* Closed May 25, 1975 after limited engagement of 20 performances.

Adamandios Lemos, Dinos Eliopoulos in "The Women's Tribunal"
(Wagner International Photo)

THE ACTORS STUDIO

Lee Strasberg, Artistic Director
Arthur Penn, Executive Producer

ACTORS STUDIO
Opened Wednesday, October 16, 1974.*
Theatre at the Actors Studio presents:

OLD TIMES

By Harold Pinter; Lighting, Sara Schrager; Technical Directors, John Branon, Eric R. Cowley; Producers, Marilyn Fried, Alan Mandell, Elizabeth Stearns; Production Assistants, Chaz McCormack, Dione Messina, Jeffrey Miller, Pam Seamon, Alice Strong, Harry Cohen, Gaynelle Clements, Bob Doran, James Langford, Robert Laterza, Marion Levine

CAST

Kate . . . . Sandra Seacat
Deeley . . . . Will Hare
Anna . . . . Hildy Brooks

A play in two acts. The action takes place in a converted farmhouse on an autumn night.

Press: Alan Eichler, Ellen Chenoweth
Stage Managers: Jay Nelson, Margery Nelson, Deborah Roe

* Closed Oct. 26, 1974 after limited engagement of 10 performances.

Susan Peretz, Lily Lodge, Arlene Golonka, Doris Roberts, Elaine Aiken in "Ladies at the Alamo" Above: "The Masque of St. George. . . ."

90

ACTORS STUDIO
Opened Thursday, December 19, 1974.*
Theatre at the Actors Studio presents:

THE MASQUE OF SAINT GEORGE AND THE DRAGON

Anna Strasberg, Director

CAST

Clown . . . . Dolores Aguanno
Father Christmas . . . . John Massimiano
King Alfred . . . . Nick Mariano
Bride . . . . Jackie Jacobus
King Cole . . . . Jeff Boucher
King William . . . . Billy Summerfield
Giant Blunderbore . . . . Dwayne Tucker
Little Man Jack . . . . Jamie Cutler
Saint George . . . . Mel Bernstein
Fair Sabra . . . . Julie Newmar or Hildy Maze
King of Egypt . . . . Marshall Hutchinson
Turkish Knight . . . . Paul Thomas
Doctor Ball . . . . Susan Peretz
The Dragon . . . . Eric Kohner

MINSTRELS. Jamie Cutler, Saralyn Myers, Patsy Moss, Irene Wagner

MERRY MEN: Billy Vignari, Gary Springer, Aixa Fiedler, Susan Jobson, Ann Johns, Debbie Roe, Jose Enriquez, Shelley Mitchell, Gail Lomax

* Closed Dec. 29, 1974 after limited engagement of 17 performances.

ACTORS STUDIO
Opened Thursday, May 29, 1975.*
The Actors Studio (Lee Strasberg, Artistic Director) presents:

LADIES AT THE ALAMO

Written and Directed by Paul Zindel; Scenic Designer, Bil Mikulewicz; Lighting, Arden Fingerhut; Executive Producer, Arthur Penn; Producers, Marilyn Fried, Elizabeth Stearns, J. J. Quinn; Associate Director, J. J. Quinn; Technical Director, Ron Pies; Sound, Linda Harrison; Properties, Neva Thornton; Production Assistants, Kim Novick, Diana Davisson, Harry Cohn; Assistant to the Director, Mary Flynn

CAST

Dede . . . . Doris Roberts
Bella . . . . Elaine Aiken
Suits . . . . Susan Peretz
Joann . . . . Lily Lodge
Kim . . . . Arlene Golonka

A play in three acts. The action takes place at the present time in the Alamo Theatre in Texas.

Press: Barbara Ligeti, Honey Becker
Stage Managers: Linda Harris, Lee Pucklis

* Closed June 8, 1975 after limited engagement of 9 performances.

"God's Trombones" at Amas Repertory Theatre
(Ambur Hiken Photo)

AMAS REPERTORY THEATRE

Rosetta LeNoire, Artistic Director
Anita L. Thomas, Administrative Director
Third Season

CHURCH OF ST. PAUL & ST. ANDREW
Opened Friday, October 18, 1974.*
The Amas Repertory Theatre Inc. presents:

TWO DAUGHTERS
and
All OVER NUTHIN'

Sets designed by Douglas Carver; Costumes, Katharine Cook, Cynthia Powell; Lighting Designers, Shirley Prendergast, Douglas Murray; Props, Reyno Crayton; Production Intern, Derrick Robinson; Production Coordinator, Anne Einhorn.

CAST

"Two Daughters" by Roy W. Bush
Director, Charles Briggs

Bill Hamilton .... Dan Barbaro
Mary Jefferson .... Gertrude Jeannette
Barbara Hamilton .... Eve Packer
Steven Anderson .... Bill Tatum
Jessie Jefferson .... Venida Evans

"All Over Nuthin' " by Frederick L. Lights
Director, Charles Kakatsakis

Emerson .... Roy Inniss
Mattie Bea .... Amanda Robinson
Stella .... Yvette Freeman
Gertie .... Irene Datcher
Joe .... Ken Foree
Bill .... Manny Thompson

Stage Managers: Regge Life, Fred Berry

Closed Nov. 3, 1974 after limited engagement of 12 performances.

CHURCH OF ST. PAUL & ST. ANDREW
Opened Friday, January 10, 1975.*
AMAS Repertory Theatre presents:

BAYOU LEGEND

By Owen Dodson; Director, Shauneille Perry; Music and Lyrics, Jack Landron; Musical Director, Neal Tate; Choreographer, Debbrah Allen; Set, C. Richard Mills; Lighting, Paul Sullivan; Costumes, Sherri Brewer; Assistant Choreographer, Clinton Turner Davis; Props, Taft Richards

CAST

Naomi, Bijou's mother .... Carolyn Byrd
Maud .... Zaida Coles
Teaka/Betsue/Tulip .... Lori Chinn
Willie Silver/2nd Councellor .... Billy Davis
Yancey/3rd Councellor .... Clinton T. Davis
Bijou's Father/Ballon/Molder .... Erni Adano
Grave/Zempoaltepec .... Ted Goodridge
Sophie-Louise .... Karen Grannum
Bijou/Oleander .... Yvette Johnson
Reve .... Jack Landron
Troy/1st Councellor .... Edward Love
Apocalypse/Old Priest .... Emett "Babe" Wallace
King Loup/Man .... Tom White
Charlotte/Clove .... Dorian Williams
Mrs. Candymayme .... Sundra Williams
Methabella/Woman .... Binky Wood

MUSICAL NUMBERS: "Alligator Dance," "Rice Hulling Song," "I Wasn't Born to Die No Common Way," "You Only Fool Me Cause I Want You To," "Le Carabine," "Sophie-Louise," "I'm Bad," "King of the Rock," "I Belong Right Here," "My Only Son," "I Cut Their Throats," "Teaka's Dance," "Hello Out There," "Reamon Died Last Night," "Something in the Wind," "Graveyard Chant," "Another Day"

A Musical in 2 acts and 8 scenes. The action takes place in the 1800's.

Stage Manager: Femi Sarah Heggie

Closed Jan. 26, 1975 after limited engagement of 12 performances.

CHURCH OF ST. PAUL & ST. ANDREW
Opened Friday, February 14, 1975.*
AMAS Repertory Theatre Inc. presents:

BUBBLING BROWN SUGAR
"A Musical Journey through Harlem"

By Loften Mitchell, Rosetta LeNoire; Director, Robert M. Cooper; Musical Director, Danny Holgate; Choreographer, Fred Benjamin; Assistant Choreographer, Karen Burke; Set, Gene Fabricatore; Lighting, Ian Johnson; Costumes Coordinated by Carol Luiken; Production Manager, Ian Johnson

CAST

Sophie/Mrs. Roberts .... Spence Adams
Checkers/Rusty .... Joseph Attles
Ella/Club Singer .... Ethel Beatty
Bud/M.C. .... Thommie Bush
Neighbor/Club Singer .... Sandi Hewitt
Neighbor/Stroller/Club Singer .... Yvette Johnson
Neighbor/Stroller/Club Singer .... Alton Lathrop
John Sage/Bert Williams/Dusty .... Avon Long
Irene Paige .... Mary Louise
Judy/Club Singer .... Julienne Marshall
Joe/Count .... Dale McIntosh
Jim/Lunky/Singer .... Howard Porter
Joyce/Georgia Brown/Club Singer ..... Vivian Reed
Mr. Roberts/Dutch/Waiter .... Anthony Whitehouse
Standby for Mary Louise: Emme Kemp

MUSICAL NUMBERS: "Bubbling Brown Sugar," "Harlem Sweet Harlem," "I Ain't Never Done Nothing To Nobody," "Some of These Days," "Through the Years," "Strolling," "Honeysuckle Rose," "I'm Going to Tell God All My Troubles," "His Eye Is on the Sparrow," "Swing Low Sweet Chariot," "Sweet Georgia Brown," "Stormy Monday Blues," "Rosetta," "S'posin'," "Solitude," "Stompin' at the Savoy," "A Train," "Love Will Find a Way," "Crying My Heart Out," "Dutch's Song," "Pray for the Lights to Go Out," "Brown Boy," "Memories of You," "Moonlight Cocktail," "I Got It Bad," "Harlem Tour," "Jim Jam Jumping Jive," "It's All Your Fault," "God Bless the Child," "It Don't Mean a Thing"

A Musical in two acts. The action takes place in Harlem between 1910 and 1940.

General Manager: Ashton Springer
Stage Manager: Alan Crawford

* Closed March 2, 1975 after limited engagement of 12 performances.

CHURCH OF ST. PAUL & ST. ANDREW
Opened Friday, April 11, 1975.*
AMAS Repertory Theatre Inc. presents:

GOD'S TROMBONES

By James Weldon Johnson; Director, John Barracuda; Musical Director, J. Hamilton Grandison; Choreographer, Juliet Seignious; Lighting, Phillip Almquist; Set and Costumes, Linda Day; Production Coordinator, Anne Einhorn

CAST

Dorothea Anderson	Dee Dee Levant
John Barracuda	John McCurry
Pamela Carpenter	Fran Salisbury
Joe Crawford	Juliet Seignious
Mary Cunningham	Barbara Sloane
Michael Ebbin	Joseph Smith
Mel Edmondson	Tad Truesdale
Juanita Greene	Pauline Weekes
Katherine Kelly	Carlton Williams
John LeGros	

MUSICAL NUMBERS: "He Brought Me Out," "Prayer," "Ol' Time Religion," "Sweet Hour of Prayer," "My God Looked Down," "There Comes a Time," "Young Man, Young Man," "Death Come to My House," "Soon-ah Will Be Done," "Steal Away," "Weep Not," "Noah," "The Ol' Ark's A-Moverin'," "Fire, Fire," "Take My Mother Home," "Were You There," "Let My People Go," "See the Sign of the Judgment," "In Dat Great Gittin' Up Mornin'," "Work On, Pray On"

Performed without intermission.

Stage Manager: James L. Mulligan

* Closed April 27, 1975 after limited engagement of 12 performances.

AMERICAN PLACE THEATRE

Wynn Handman, Director
Julia Miles, Associate Director
Eleventh Season

AMERICAN PLACE THEATRE
Opened Friday, October 25, 1974.*
The American Place Theatre presents:

THE BEAUTY PART

By S. J. Perelman; Director, James Hammerstein; Scenery, Fred Voelpel; Lighting, Roger Morgan; Costumes, Pearl Somner; Technical Director, Henry Millman; Wardrobe, Maria Schweppe; Production Assistants, Francie Thompson, Pamela White, Dianne Babb

CAST

Armand Assante
Joseph Bova
Ron Faber
Cynthia Harris
Mitchell Jason
Peter Kingsley
Bobo Lewis
Susan Sullivan
Jerrold Ziman
Understudy: Michael Tucker

A Comedy in 2 acts and 11 scenes. The action takes place at the present time in the library of Mr. and Mrs. Milo Weatherwax; April Monkhood's apartment; office of Hyacinth Beddoes Laffoon; Goddard Quagmeyer's studio; The Rising Sun Employment Agency, Santa Barbara; kitchen of the Fingerhead residence; the conservatory of the Pasadena estate of Nelson Smedley; Whirlaway Scenic Studio, Los Angeles,; a television studio, Los Angeles,; a wedding chapel in New York City.

Press: David Roggensack
Stage Managers: Gigi Cascio, Mary E. Baird

* Closed Nov. 23, 1974 after limited engagement of 36 performances.

Joseph Bova, Cynthia Harris Above: Susan Sullivan, Peter Kingsley in "Beauty Part"
(Martha Holmes Photos)

AMERICAN PLACE THEATRE
Opened Friday, February 21, 1975.*
The American Place Theatre (Wynn Handman, Director; Ju Miles, Associate Director) presents:

STRAWS IN THE WIND

With Pieces and Songs by Donald Barthelme, Marshall Brickm Cy Coleman, Betty Comden and Adolph Green, Ira Gasman, G MacDermot, Lanny Meyers, Billy Nichols, Stephen Schwartz, Pe Stone; Director, Phyllis Newman; Scenery, Peter Harvey; Lighti Roger Morgan; Costumes, Ruth Morley; Musical Direction, Lan Meyers; Assistant to Director for Musical Staging, Otis A. Sall Piano and Associate Musical Director, Jeremy Stone; Techni Director, Henry Millman; Wardrobe Mistress, Maria Schwep Production Assistants, Peri Frost, Lynn Hardin, Patricia Diaz, I Pucklis, David Evans

CAST

Tovah Feldshuh
Carol Jean Lewis
Brandon Maggart
Josh Mostel
George Pentecost

MUSICAL NUMBERS AND SKITS: "Opening," "My Doct the Box," "Noah," "In Which to Marry Me," "The Photograph "Lost Word," "Dick's Last Tape," "Goin' Home," "Discovery Earth ... October 12, 1992," "Suffrage," "Simplified Language "It's Not Such a Brave New World, Mr. Huxley," "The Schoc "You'll Have Your Moment," "Finale"

"A Theatrical Look Ahead" in two acts.

Press: David Roggensack
Stage Managers: Gigi Cascio, Mary E. Baird

* Closed Mar. 22, 1975 after 33 performances.

Brandon Maggart, Tovah Feldshuh, Carol Jean Lewis, George Pentecost, Josh Mostel

92

Martha Holmes Photo

AMERICAN PLACE THEATRE
Opened Friday, April 4, 1975.*
The American Place Theatre (Wynn Handman, Director; Julia
Miles, Associate Director) presents:

KILLER'S HEAD and ACTION

By Sam Shepard; Director, Nancy Meckler; Scenery, Henry Mill-
[ma]n; Lighting, Edward M. Greenberg; Costumes, Susan Denison;
[Wa]rdrobe Mistress, Marla Schweppe; Production Assistants, Kim
[Al]en, Patricia Diaz

CAST

"[K]iller's Head"
[Ma]zon .... Richard Gere

"[A]ction"
[Sho]oter .... R. A. Dow
[Lu]pe .... Marcia Jean Kurtz
[Liz]a .... Dorothy Lyman
[Je]p .... Richard Lynch

Press: David Roggensack
Stage Managers: Gigi Cascio, Mary E. Baird

Closed May 3, 1975 after limited engagement of 34 performances.

Marcia Jean Kurtz, R. A. Dow, Dorothy Lyman,
Richard Lynch in "Action" Left: Richard Gere
in "Killer's Head"
(Martha Holmes Photos)

AMERICAN PLACE THEATRE
Opened Friday, May 16, 1975.*
The American Place Theatre (Wynn Handman, Director; Julia
Miles, Associate Director) presents:

RUBBERS
and
YANKS 3 DETROIT 0 TOP OF THE SEVENTH

By Jonathan Reynolds; Director, Alan Arkin; Scenery, Henry
Millman; Lighting, Roger Morgan; Costumes, Susan Denison;
Wardrobe, Marla Schweppe; Swedish Adviser, Ted Chapin; Produc-
tion Assistants, Gretchen Wengenroth, Patricia Diaz

CAST

"Rubbers"
Republicans:
Mr. Clegg, Majority Leader .... Charles Siebert†1
Mr. Mutrix, Acting Speaker .... Lou Criscuolo†2
Mr. Damiano .... Robert Lesser†3
Mr. Tomato .... Michael Prince
Mr. P. Vlitsiak .... Mitchell Jason
Mr. Bapp .... William Bogert
Mr. Fermrlnr .... Michael Prince
Democrats:
Mrs. Brimmins .... Laura Esterman
Mr. Pard .... MacIntyre Dixon
Mr. Townsend .... Albert Hall†4
Mr. Austin .... John Horn†5
Miss Sinkk, Clerk of the Assembly .... Lane Binkley
Pages .... Warren Sweeney†6, Jaime Tirelli

Place: The Assembly Chamber of the State Legislature.

"Yanks 3 Detroit 0 Top of the Seventh"
Emil "Duke" Bronkowski .... Tony LoBianco
Lawrence "Beanie" Maligma .... Lou Criscuolo†2
Old Salt .... Mitchell Jason
Lucky Johnson .... John Horn†5
Donna Luna Donna .... Lane Binkley
Lincoln Lewis III .... Albert Hall†4
Guido Morosini .... Robert Lesser†3
Brick Brock .... William Bogert
Baseball Players .... Warren Sweeney†6, Jaime Tirelli

Press: David Roggensack
Stage Managers: Franklin Keysar, Mary E. Baird

* Still playing May 31, 1975.
† Succeeded by: 1. Ed Herlihy, 2. Merwin Goldsmith, 3. Armand
Assante, 4. Fred Morsell, 5. George Bamford, 6. Peter Mainguy

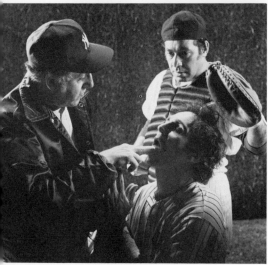

Mitchell Jason, Tony LoBianco, Lou Crisuolo
in "Yanks 3 ..." Above: Laura Esterman, Charles
Siebert in "Rubbers"

Martha Holmes Photos

Opened Friday, December 6, 1974
The American Puppet Arts Council (Arthur Cantor, Executive Producer) presents:

BIL BAIRD'S MARIONETTES
Ninth Season

Artistic Associate, Frank Sullivan; Associate Producer, Susanna Lloyd; Scenery, Howard Mandel

COMPANY

Peter Baird, Rebecca Bondor, Mary Case, Tim Dobbins, Olga Felgemacher, Steve Hansen, Bill Tost, Steven Widerman

PRODUCTIONS

PETER AND THE WOLF: Book, A. J. Russell;Music, Serge Prokofiev; Incidental Music, Paul Weston; Lyrics, Ogden Nash; As Adapted and Arranged by Paul Weston; Assistant to Mr. Weston, Sheldon Harnick; Lighting, Carl Harms; Musical Director and Special Arrangements, Alvy West; Director, Paul Leaf; Singing Voice of the Wolf, George S. Irving; Conceived, Designed and Produced by Bil Baird; Followed by HOLIDAY ON STRINGS: Created and Designed by Bil Baird; Written by Alan Stern; Opened Friday, Dec. 6, 1974 and closed Feb. 9, 1975 after 77 performances.
ALICE IN WONDERLAND: Book, A. J. Russell; Music, Joe Raposo; Lyrics, Sheldon Harnick; Lighting, Peggy Clark; Director, Paul Leaf; Designed and Produced by Bil Baird; Based on the classic by Lewis J. Carroll; Production Manager, Carl Harms; Singing Voices, George S. Irving, Sheldon Harnick, Rose Marie Jun, Ivy Austin, Margery Gray, William Tost, Margery Gray, Bil Baird. Followed by BIL BAIRD'S VARIETY. Opened Wednesday, February 19, 1975 and closed April 13, 1975 after 64 performances.

**Bil Baird's Marionettes
in "Peter and the Wolf"**

THE BILLY MUNK THEATRE

Barry Moss, Executive Director
Barbara Loden, Mary Tierney, Artistic Directors

THE BILLY MUNK THEATRE
Opened Monday, March 17, 1975.*
The Billy Munk Theatre presents:

HOME IS THE HERO

By Walter Macken; Director, Barbara Loden; Producers, Pat and Moss Cooney; Set, Robertson Carricart; Lighting, Brett Landow Lewis; Costumes, Susan Harris

CAST

Paddy O'Reilly	Pat McNamara
Daylia	Janet Ward
Willie	John Burke
Josie	Mary Tierney
Trapper O'Flynn	Walt Gorney
Dovetail	Diarmuid McNamara
Bid	Audrey Bel
Mrs. Green	Maggie Burke
Lily Green	Allison Corbett-Smith
Manchester Monaghan	James Handy

The action takes place circa 1950 in the downstairs living-room in a house in the town of Galway, Ireland.

Stage Managers: Ellen Casey, Estelle Fennell

* Closed Apr. 14, 1975 after limited engagement of 16 performances.

THE BILLY MUNK THEATRE
Opened Friday, May 23, 1975.*
The Billy Munk Theatre Presents:

LOVE TWO

Director, Arthur Sherman; Producers, Moss and Pat Cooney; Set, Kert Lundell; Lighting, Brett Landow Lewis; Costumes, Robert Joel Schwartz; Portraits, Lawrence Eisler

CAST

"The Lover" by Harold Pinter

Richard	Ron Leibman
Sarah	Linda Lavin
John	Jack Kehler

"Score" by Lyndon Brook; Presented through the courtesy of Alexander H. Cohen; American Premiere

Harry	Ron Leibman
Sheila	Linda Lavin

Press: Langan Communications
Stage Managers: Leslie Kimble, Jack Kehler

* Closed June 16, 1975 after limited engagement of 16 performances.

Above: Ron Leibman, Linda Lavin in "Score"
(Robertson Carricart Photo)

THE BILLY MUNK THEATRE
Opened Friday, April 25, 1975.*
The Billy Munk Theatre presents:

AN O'CASEY COMEDY FESTIVAL

Three one-act plays by Sean O'Casey; Director, Mary Tierney Setting, Robertson Carricart; Lighting and Sound, Estelle Fennell Technical Director, Brett Landow Lewis

CAST

"End of the Beginning"

Husband	Brian Denneh
Wife	Audrey Bel
Friend	Chris Carrick

"Bedtime Story"

John Jo Mulligan	James Handy
Angela	Judith McGilliga
Dan Halibut	Robertson Carricar
Miss Mossie	Audrey Bel

"A Pound on Demand"

Postmistress	Gayle Green
Jerry	Pat McNamara
Sammy	Moss Cooney
Policeman	Stephen Lan
Young Woman	Ellen Case

Stage Managers: Jean Davidson, Frank Levan

* Closed May 12, 1975 after limited engagement of 12 performances.

BROOKLYN ACADEMY OF MUSIC

Harvey Lichtenstein, Executive Director

BROOKLYN ACADEMY OF MUSIC
Opened Wednesday, February 5, 1975.*

The Brooklyn Academy of Music presents the Royal Shakespeare Company (Trevor Nunn, Artistic Director) in:

SUMMERFOLK

By Maxim Gorky; English Version, Jeremy Brooks, Kitty Hunter Blaire; Director, David Jones; Designed by Timothy O'Brien and Tazeena Firth; Music Composed and Arranged by Carl Davis; Lighting, Stewart Leviton; Assistant Director, Howard Davies

CAST

The Bassov Household:

Bassov, Sergei Vassilich, a lawyer	Norman Rodway
Varvara Mikhailovna, his wife	Estelle Kohler
Vlass Mikhailich, her brother	Mike Gwilym
Zamislov, Nikolai Petrovich, Bassov's assistant	David Suchet
Kaleria Vassilievna, Bassov's sister	Susan Fleetwood
Sasha, the Bassov's maid	Annette Badland

Their Neighbors:

Suslov, Pyotr Ivanich, an engineer	Tony Church
Yulia Filipovna, his wife	Lynette Davies
Dudakov, Kirill Akimovich, a doctor	Patrick Godfrey
Olga Alekseyevna, his wife	Janet Whiteside
Ryumin, Pavel Sergeyich	Robert Ashby
Maria Lvovna, a doctor	Margaret Tyzack
Sonya, her daughter	Louise Jameson
Zimin, Maxin, a student	Michael Ensign
Dvustobaika, watchman of the villas	Norman Tyrrell
Kropilkin, a watchman	Gavin Campbell
Woman with a bandaged cheek	Maroussia Frank

New Arrivals:

Shalimov, Yakov Petrovich, a writer	Ian Richardson
Dvoetochie, Semyon Semyonich, Suslov's uncle	Sebastian Shaw
First Beggar	Doyne Byrd
Second Beggar	John Labanowski
Lady in a yellow dress	Janet Chappell
Man in a check suit	Wilfred Grove
Gentleman in a top hat	Roger Bizley
Semyonov	Albert Welling
The Cadet	Mark Cooper
Young Lady in pink	Emma Williams

A Drama in 3 acts and 4 scenes. The action takes place at the Bassov's summer villa.

Tour Manager: Hal Rogers
Press: Carol Jennings, Charles Ziff
Stage Managers: Maggie Whitlum, Giles Barnabe, Diana Bruce, Peter Sofroniou, Tony Vanden Ende

Closed Feb. 9, and returned in repertory Feb. 25–Mar. 2, 1975. (15 performances)

Estelle Kohler, Ian Richardson
in "Love's Labour's Lost"

Estelle Kohler, Ian Richardson, Mike Gwilym,
Janet Whiteside, Susan Fleetwood in "Summerfolk"

BROOKLYN ACADEMY OF MUSIC
Opened Tuesday, February 11, 1975.*

The Brooklyn Academy of Music by arrangement with the Governors of the Royal Shakespeare Theatre, Stratford-upon-Avon, England, presents the Royal Shakespeare Company (Trevor Nunn, Artistic Director) in:

LOVE'S LABOUR'S LOST

By William Shakespeare; Director, David Jones; Designed by Timothy O'Brien and Tazeena Firth; Music, William Southgate; Lighting, Stewart Leviton; Sound, Julian Beach

CAST

Court of Navarre

Ferdinand King of Navarre	David Suchet
Longaville	Robert Ashby
Dumaine	Michael Ensign
Berowne	Ian Richardson
Don Adriano de Armado	Tony Church
Moth, his page	Martin Lev

French Embassage

Princess of France	Susan Fleetwood
Boyet	Patrick Godfrey
Maria	Lynette Davies
Katharine	Janet Chappell
Rosaline	Estelle Kohler
French Lord	Wilfred Grove
Marcade	John Labanowski

Local Inhabitants

Dull, a constable	Denis Holmes
Costard, a clown	Mike Gwilym
Jaquenetta, a country wench	Louise Jameson
A Forester	Gavin Campbell
Holofernes, a schoolmaster	Norman Rodway
Sir Nathaniel, a curate	Jeffrey Dench
Lords, Villagers	Annette Badland, Doyne Byrd, Gavin Campbell, John Labanowski

Performed in two acts.

Stage Managers: Maggie Whitlum, Giles Barnabe, Diana Bruce, Peter Sofroniou, Tony Vanden Ende

* Closed Feb. 23, 1975 after 15 performances.

95

BROOKLYN ACADEMY OF MUSIC
Opened Tuesday February 25, 1975.*
The Brooklyn Academy of Music presents the Royal Shakespeare Company in:

LEAR

By William Shakespeare; Director, Buzz Goodbody; Designed by Anna Steiner; Music, Michael Tubbs; Lighting, Brian Harris; Music Performed by Robin Weatherall

CAST

Lear, King of Britain	Tony Church
Earl of Kent	Roger Bizley
Earl of Gloucester	Jeffrey Dench
Edgar, Gloucester's son	Mike Gwilym
Edmund, Gloucester's bastard son	Charles Keating
The Fool	David Suchet
Goneril	Sheila Allen
Regan	Lynette Davies
Cordelia	Louise Jameson
Servant	Anthony Vanden Ende

A shortened version of Shakespeare's tragedy presented in two acts.

* Closed Mar. 30, 1975 after limited engagement of 17 performances.

Top Right: David Suchet, Tony Church, Lynette Davies Below: Sheila Allen, Lynette Davies in "Lear"

BROOKLYN ACADEMY OF MUSIC
Opened Saturday, March 29, 1975.*
The Brooklyn Academy of Music by arrangement with the Governors of the Royal Shakespeare Theatre presents the Royal Shakespeare Company in:

HE THAT PLAYS THE KING

Compiled by Ian Richardson from the works of William Shakespeare; Music Composed by Guy Woolfenden; Performed by Robin Weatherall

CAST

Ian Richardson
Susan Fleetwood
Mike Gwilym
Tony Church

A recital of scenes from Shakespeare's tragic and historic kings. Presented in two parts.

Company and Stage Manager: Hal Rogers
Press: Carol Jennings, Charles Ziff

* Closed April 6, 1975 after limited engagement of 8 performances.

(from top) Tony Church, Susan Fleetwood, Ian Richardson, Robin Weatherall, Mike Gwilym in "He That Plays the King"

OOKLYN ACADEMY OF MUSIC
Opened Monday, April 7, 1975.*
The Brooklyn Academy of Music presents The O'Neill Center's
National Theatre of the Deaf (Producing Director, David
Hays) in a double bill:

THE DYBBUK

y S. Ansky; Director, John Broome; Based on the Translation
oseph Landis; Sign Master, Bernard Bragg; Setting, David Hays;
stumes, Fred Voelpel; Lighting, Guy Bergquist; Tour Director,
ck Scism; Wardrobe Mistress, Liz Quinn; Company Interpreter,
ki Kilpatrick; Music Composed by the Company with Robert
menfeld

CAST

bi Azrielke	Patrick Graybill
nnakh	Ed Waterstreet, Jr.
yer	Joseph A. Castronovo
Man	Andrew Vasnick
ssenger	Joe Sarpy
erly Woman	Gunilla Wagstrom
onnon	Timothy Scanlon
e	Freda Norman
rse to Leye	Julianna Field
tel	Linda Bove
Sender	Bernard Bragg
ung Woman/Voice	Elaine Bromka
ce for Leye	Timothy Near
ce for Rabbi	Rico Peterson
ce for Khonnon	Robert Blumenfeld

with

PRISCILLA, PRINCESS OF POWER

ased on a script by James Stevenson; Adapted by The Company;
der the Supervision and Direction of Ed Waterstreet, Jr.

CAST

scilla	Linda Bove
Schlock	Bernard Bragg
y Bean Boss	Patrick Graybill
ıck	Timothy Scanlon
ntal Assistant	Timothy Near
s. Colson	Julianna Field
rrator	Elaine Bromka

LLOONS AND GANGSTERS: Robert Blumenfeld, Joseph A.
tronovo, Freda Norman, Rico Peterson, Joe Sarpy, Andrew Vas-
k, Gunilla Wagstrom, Ed Waterstreet, Jr.
General Manager; George Thorn
Company Manager: Nancy Van Rijn
ress: Arts Counterparts, Jan Henry James, William Schelble
Stage Managers: Guy Bergquist, Jerry Kelch

Closed April 13, 1975 after limited engagement of 8 performances
o resume national tour.

"The $ Value of Man"

**Linda Bove, Patrick Graybill, Elaine Bromka
in "Priscilla" Above: "The Dybbuk"**

BROOKLYN ACADEMY OF MUSIC
Opened Thursday, May 8, 1975.*
The Brooklyn Academy of Music presents:

THE $ VALUE OF MAN

Written and Directed by Christopher Knowles and Robert Wil-
son; Music, Michael Galasso; Choreography, Andrew De Groat;
Assistant Director, Ralph Hilton; Production Coordinator, James
Finguerra; Vaudeville Script Coordinator, Carol Mullins; Casino
Script Coordinator, James Neu; Tape Constructions, Jacob Burc-
khardt; Additional Movement, Steven Crawford; Lighting, Carol
Mullins; Props, Mayra Levy; Scenery Supervision, Gregory Payne,
Terence Chambers, Charles Dennis; Costumes, Richard Roth;
Sound, Jan Kroeze; Technical Assistants, Bill Hammond, Bruce
Hoover

CAST

Catherine Allport, Eric Appel, George Ashley, Ellen Benson, Robyn
Brentano, Ritty Burchfield, Jacob Burckhardt, Julia Busto, Kevin
Byrnes, Kathryn Cation, Steven Crawford, Roger Curtis, Frank
DeGregorie, Andrew De Groat, Dale De Groff, Sandra Delaney,
Charles Dennis, Laura Epstein, Nasar and Fahimeh Farhangfar,
James Finguerra, Meredith Gang, Karin Greenblatt, Andy Gurian,
Ester Grite, Edward Hadas, Julia Hanlon, Ralph Hilton, Melissa
Homan, Arnold Horton, Julia Hymen, Maria Karrell, Christopher
Knowles, Jan Kroeze, Robert Levithan, Mayra Levy, Robert Liebo-
witz, Cynthia Lubar, Elaine Luthy, Paul Mann, Richard Morrison,
Carol Mullins, James Neu, Gregory Payne, Liz Pasquale, Ewa Piet-
kiewcz, Alfredo Godot Pinhiero, Kathryn Ray, Marin Riley, Mi-
chael Rivlin, Richard Roth, Valda Setterfield, Shirley Soffer, Chris
Stevens, Rosetta Stone, Ruth Tepper, Paul Thek, Ann Wooster,
Sally Wormer, Shelley Valfer, Scotty Snyder

* Closed May 18, 1975 after limited engagement of 8 performances.
No photos available.

CHELSEA THEATER CENTER OF BROOKLYN

Robert Kalfin, Artistic Director
Michael David, Executive Director
Burl Hash, Productions Director
Tenth Season

BROOKLYN ACADEMY OF MUSIC
Opened Wednesday, October 23, 1974.*
The Chelsea Theater Center of Brooklyn presents:

HOTHOUSE

By Megan Terry; Director, Rae Allen; Scenery, Lawrence King; Costumes, Vernon Yates; Lighting, William Mintzer; Production Coordinator, Deborah Leschin; Technical Director, Jim Burke; Costumer, Carol Spier; Assistant Director, Kathy Talbert; Sound, Gary Harris

CAST

Jody Duncan	Kathleen Tolan
David Gordon	Michael Cornelison
Ma Sweetlove	Dorothy Chace
Banty	Dermot McNamara
Roz Duncan	Helen Gallagher
Andy Anderson	R. A. Dow
Doll Jensen	Carol Morley
Lorna	Barbara Tarbuck
Scoogie	Kelly Fitzpatrick
Jack Duncan	Brad Sullivan

UNDERSTUDIES: Ma, Kathryn Eames; Andy, Jack, Kelly Fitzpatrick; Jody, Kathleen Heaney; David, Richard Manheim; Roz, Doll, Barbara Tarbuck

A play in three acts. The action takes place in the fishing village of Edmonds, near the city of Seattle, Washington, in late spring of 1953.

Press: Leslie Gifford
Stage Managers: Clint Jakeman, Richard Manheim

* Closed Nov. 10, 1974 after limited engagement of 21 performances.

**Helen Gallagher, Brad Sullivan
in "Hothouse"**
(Thomas Victor Photo)

BROOKLYN ACADEMY OF MUSIC
Opened Friday, December 20, 1974.*
The Chelsea Theater Center of Brooklyn presents:

YENTL THE YESHIVA BOY

By Isaac Bashevis Singer; Adapted for the stage by Leah Napo? Isaac Bashevis Singer; Director, Robert Kalfin; Music, Mel Marv Scenery, Karl Eigsti; Costumes, Carrie F. Robbins; Lighting, W liam Mintzer; Production Consultant, Leonard Kaplan; Assist. Director, Ron Logomarsino; Production Coordinator, Deborah L chin; Technical Director, James Burke; Sound, Gary Harris; Ha tylist, Joe Stephen, John de Laat

CAST

Yentl	Tovah Feldsh
Red Todrus/Fulcha/Musician	Bernie Passelti
Cantor/Shepsel/Necheleh/	
Chambermaid	Mary Ellen Ash
Lemmel/Yussel/Jester/Mohel	Leland M
Reb Nata/Musician/Groinem Zelig	Reuben Sch
Nehemiah/Rabbi	Albert M. Oppenhein
Mordecai/Feitl	Hy An
Zisheh/Shmuel/Dr. Chanina	Stephen de Pi
Nachum/Chaim/Musician	Charles McKe
Gershon/Luzer/Laibish/Musician	Elliot Burt
Moshe/Coachman/Lazar/Feivl	
Musician/Dr. Solomon	Ron Lagomarsi
Treitl/Reb Alter	Herman O. Arb
Avigdor	John V. Sh
Pelte/Raizeleh	Susan An
Berel/Finkl	Kathleen Hear
Avriam/David	Brian Kanna
Shimmel/Zelda-Leah	Madeline Sh
Hadass	Neva Sm
Frumka	Natalie Pri
Pesheh	Blanche D
Yachna	Rita Ka
Zlateh	Elaine Grollm

UNDERSTUDIES: Hadass, Susan Andre; Yentl, Kathleen Hean Avigdor, Charles McKeane

A play in two acts. The action takes place in the villages of Yan Zamosc and Bechev, Poland in the year 1873.

Press: Leslie Gifford, Penny Peters
Stage Managers: Ginny Freedman, Richard Manheim

* Closed Jan. 26, 1975 after 35 performances.

**John Shea, Tovah Feldshuh in "Yentl the
Yeshiva Boy"**

(Thomas Victor Photo)

Opened Tuesday, February 18, 1975.*
The Chelsea Theater Center of Brooklyn (Robert Kalfin, Artis-
tic Director; Michael David, Executive Director; Burl Hash,
Productions Director) presents:

SANTA ANITA '42

y Allan Knee; Director, Steven Robman; Scenery, Jeremy
er; Costumes, Carol Oditz; Lighting, David Sackeroff; Produced
pecial arrangement with Claire Nichtern; Sound, Gary Harris;
luction Coordinators, Deborah Leschin, Ginny Freedman;
nical Director, James Burke

CAST

d Imigration Official/FBI Agent/	
ublic Address Announcer	Frank Anderson
cher	Henry Kaimu Bal
nd Immigration Official/Dressmaker/Citizen's	
rvice Committeewoman	Beth Dixon
t Immigration Official/Barker/Racetrack	
nnouncer/FBI Agent/Public Address	
nnouncer	William Knight
er/Serenader	Tom Matsusaka
ako	Lani Gerrie Miyazaki
her/Serenader/Mrs. Yamato	Mary Mon Toy
	Stephen D. Newman
hael	Sab Shimono
ru	Michael
Chi	Peter Yoshida

DERSTUDIES: Roger Brown for W. Knight, F. Anderson, S.
Newman; Judith Burke for B. Dixon; Tisa Chang for L. G.
asaki, M. Mon Toy; Tom Matsusaka for H. K. Bal, S. Shimono,
oshida, C. Yama; Peter Yoshida for T. Matsusaka

, play in two acts.

Press: Leslie Gifford, Penny Peters
Stage Managers: Abbe Raven, Judith Burke

losed Mar. 16, 1975 after limited engagement of 32 perfor-
ances.

**Lani Gerrie Miyazaki, Stephen D. Newman
in "Santa Anita '42"**
(Thomas Victor Photo)

BROOKLYN ACADEMY OF MUSIC
Opened Thursday, May 8, 1975.*
The Chelsea Theater Center of Brooklyn (Robert Kalfin, Artis-
tic Director: Michael David, Executive Director; Burl Hash,
Productions Director) presents:

POLLY

Being a Sequel to "The Beggar's Opera" by John Gay; With Music
newly realized by Mel Marvin; Adapted and Directed by Robert
Kalfin; Scenery, Robert U. Taylor; Costumes, Carrie F. Robbins;
Lighting, William Mintzer; Musical Staging, Elizabeth Keen; Musi-
cal Director, Clay Fullum; Orchestrations by Mel Marvin, Ken
Guilmartin; Fight Director, R. D. Colter; Dialect Coach, Gordon A.
Jacoby; Technical Director, James Burke; Costumer, Carol Spier;
Assistant to the Director, Mitchell Engelmeyer; Production Assis-
tant, Joan Friedman; Hairstylist, Ken Davis; Production Coordina-
tor, Ginny Freedman

CAST

Poet/Morano (alias Macheath)	Stephen D. Newman
1st Player/Old Woman Cook/LaGuerre	Roy Brocksmith
2nd Player/Culverin	Alexander Orfaly
3rd Player/Flimzy/Old Woman Maid/	
Indian Wife	Prudence Wright Holmes
Signora Crochetta/Jenny Diver	Patricia Elliott
4th Player/Capstern/Indian	John Long
Diana Trapes	Lucille Patton
Ducat	Edward Zang
Polly Peachum	Betsy Beard
Damaris/Indian Wife	Mary Ellen Ashley
Mrs. Ducat	Fran Stevens
Reginald	Ruff Ruff
1st Footman/Vanderbluff	Igors Gavon
2nd Footman/Dagger/Indian	Brent Mintz
Messenger Indian	Robert Manzari
Hacker	George F. Maguire
Cutlace/Indian	Brian James
Cawwawkee, the Indian Prince	Richard Ryder
Pohetohee, the Indian King	William J. Coppola

UNDERSTUDIES: Mary Ellen Ashley, Roger Brown, Brian James,
Lynn Anne Leveridge, John Long, Robert Manzari, Brent Mintz

A Musical in 3 acts and 9 scenes. The action takes place in the
West Indies in the past.

Press: Leslie Gifford, Penny Peters
Stage Managers: Lewis Rosen, Michael W. Schaefer

* Closed May 25, 1975 after limited engagement of 32 performances.

**Roy Brocksmith, Alexander Orfaly, Betsy Beard,
George F. Maguire, John Long in "Polly"**
(Thomas Victor Photo)

CIRCLE REPERTORY COMPANY

Marshall W. Mason, Artistic Director
Jerry Arrow, Executive Director
Marshall Oglesby, Coordinating Director
Sixth Season

CIRCLE REPERTORY THEATRE
Opened Sunday, November 3, 1974.*
The Circle Repertory Company presents:

BATTLE OF ANGELS

By Tennessee Williams; Director, Marshall W. Mason; Set, John Lee Beatty; Lighting, Dennis Parichy; Costumes, Jennifer von Mayrhauser; Music, Norman L. Berman; Technical Director, Earl R. Hughes; Assistant to the Director, Peter Schneider; Assistant Technical Director, Bob Yanez

CAST

Conjure Man	Lance Taylor, Jr.
Dolly Bland	Sharon Madden
Pee Wee Bland	Baxter Harris
Beulah Cartwright	Rheatha Forster
Sheriff Talbott	Jack Davidson
Cassandra Whiteside	Trish Hawkins
Vee Talbot	Conchata Ferrell
Val Xavier	Max
Blanch Temple	Maryellen Flynn
Eva Temple	Berrilla Kerr
Myra Torrance	Tanya Berezin
Loon	Elliott C. Moffitt
Jabe Torrance	Ron Seka
Edna Mae	Suzanne Golden
Jane	Diana Malchin
Sherri-lee	Julie Wakefield
David Anderson	Alan Jordan
Bennie	Matthew McDonald
Mrs. Regan	Debra Mooney
Townspeople	Alan Jordan, Allan Goldstein, Alan Fox

A Drama in three acts. The action takes place at the present time in February and April at the Torrance Mercantile Store in Two River County, Mississippi.

Company Manager: Barbara Darwall
Press: Herb Striesfield, Sharon Madden
Stage Managers: Alan Fox, Allan Goldstein

* Closed Dec. 1, 1974 after limited engagement of 32 performances.

Trish Hawkins, Sharon Madden Above: Tanya Berezin, Max in "Battle of Angels"
(Ken Howard Photos)

CIRCLE REPERTORY COMPANY THEATRE
Opened Sunday, February 2, 1975.*
Circle Repertory Company (Marshall W. Mason, Artistic Director; Jerry Arrow, Executive Director) presents:

THE MOUND BUILDERS

By Lanford Wilson; Director, Marshall W. Mason; Setting, John Lee Beatty; Lighting, Dennis Parichy; Costumes, Jennifer von Mayrhauser; Sound and Visual Effects, Chuck London, George Hansen; Technical Director, Earl R. Hughes; Production Coordinator, Marshall Oglesby; Assistant to the Director, Peter Schneider

CAST

Dr. August Howe, archeologist	Rob Thirkield
D. K. Eriksen, his sister	Tanya Berezin
Cynthia, his wife	Stephanie Gordon
Kirsten, his daughter	Lauren Jacobi
Dr. Dan Loggins, his associate	Jonathan Hogan
Dr. Jean Loggins, Dan's wife	Trish Hawkins
Chad Jasker, son of the landowner	John Strasberg

A Drama in two acts. The action takes place at the university, and the past summer at the site of the dig in Southern Illinois.

Company Manager: Barbara Darwall
Press: Sharon Madden, Herb Striesfield
Stage Managers: Peter Schneider, Jerry W. Roberts, Marilyn Baum

* Closed Mar. 2, 1975 after limited engagement of 29 performances and 6 previews.

Jonathan Hogan, Tanya Berezin in "The Mound Builders"
(Ken Howard Photo)

CIRCLE REPERTORY COMPANY THEATRE

Opened Sunday, March 23, 1975.*

Circle Repertory Company (Marshall W. Mason, Artistic Director; Jerry Arrow, Executive Director) presents:

DOWN BY THE RIVER WHERE WATERLILIES ARE DISFIGURED EVERY DAY

By Julie Bovasso; Director, Marshall Oglesby; Setting, John Lee Beatty; Lighting, Richard Winkler; Costumes, Jennifer von Mayrhauser; Music, Norman L. Berman; Choreography, Ginger Darnell; Duel Staged by R. Mack Miller; Sound, Chuck London, George Hansen; Technical Directors, Earl R. Hughes, Bob Yanez; Wardrobe, Patti King; Properties, Robin Tagliente; Production Assistants, Cathy Rennich, Gail Molerio

CAST

Phoebe	Bobo Lewis
Clement	Neil Flanagan
Count Josef	Ryland Merkey
Constantine	Linda Hunt
Herschel	Ruth Hermine
Count Junior	Charles T. Harper
Sissy	Verna Hobson
Missy	Saraellen
Prince Percy	Harry Browne
Count Junior/Smithers	Charles T. Harper
Queen Nell/Countess Elizabeth	Cathryn Damon
Barry Zap/General Buckley	Baxter Harris
King Arnie/Admiral Duncan	Brian Calloway

A play in two acts. The action takes place at the present time—anywhere.

Company Manager: Barbara Darwall
Press: Sharon Madden, Herb Striesfield
Stage Managers: Robert W. Pitman, Jason Buzas, Charlie Coco

* Closed April 13, 1975 after 30 performances and 6 previews.

"Down by the River Where Waterlilies are Disfigured Every Day"
(Ken Howard Photo)

Kevin McCarthy, Lois Smith in "Harry Outside"
(Ken Howard Photo)

HARRY OUTSIDE

By Corinne Jacker; Director, Marshall W. Mason; Setting, John Lee Beatty; Costumes, Jennifer von Mayrhauser; Lighting, Dennis Parichy; Sound, Chuck London, George Hansen; Original Music, Jonathan Hogan; Production Coordinator, Marshall Oglesby; Technical Director, Earl R. Hughes; Assistant to the Director, Peter Schneider

CAST

Susan	Denise Lute
Irene	Tanya Berezin
"Harry" Harrison	Kevin McCarthy
Fred Crosley	Alfred Hinckley
George	Jonathan Hogan
Lois	Shelly Batt
Gabby	Lois Smith

A play in 3 acts and 5 scenes. The action takes place at the present time in mid-August in a civilized clearing in the woods.

Company Manager: Barbara Darwall
Press: Sharon Madden, Herb Striesfield
Stage Managers: Marlyn Baum, Dennis L. Schneider

* Closed June 8, 1975 after limited engagement of 30 performances and 6 previews.

COUNTERPOINT THEATRE COMPANY

Howard Green, Executive Artistic Director
Gonzalo Madurga, Artistic Director
Paulene Reynolds, Managing Director

COUNTERPOINT THEATRE
Opened Friday, September 27, 1974.*
Counterpoint Theatre Company presents:

SPOON RIVER ANTHOLOGY

By Edgar Lee Masters; Director, Gonzalo Madurga; Costumes, Ernesto Leston; Lighting, Robert Brigham; Lighting Assistant, Dean Languell

CAST

Howard Green	Al Secunda
Jean Greer	G. Todd Ortone
Sharon Shayne	Nina Dova
Paulene Reynolds	Murray Moston

Stage Managers: Stuart Schwartz, Reyno Crayton

* Closed Oct. 14, 1974 after limited run of 12 performances. (No photos available)

COUNTERPOINT THEATRE
Opened Friday, November 29, 1974.*
The Counterpoint Theatre Company presents:

FINGERNAILS BLUE AS FLOWERS
and
THE BURIAL OF ESPOSITO

By Ronald Ribman; Directors, Howard Green, Gonzalo Madurga; Costumes, Ernesto Leston; Scenery, Minda Chipurnoi; Lighting, Robert Brigham

CAST

"Fingernails Blue as Flowers"
Eugene Naville .... Howard Green
Waiter .... Rawle Brome
Estelle Singer .... Ellen Bry
Jesse .... Dan Grimaldi
Rosemary .... Hayley Altman or Timothi-Jane Graham

"The Burial of Esposito"
Nick Esposito .... Gonzalo Madurga
His Wife .... Tina Mandas
His Brother-in-law .... Dan Grimaldi
His Son .... Joseph Guardino

Stage Managers: Mimi Jordan, Fred Berry, Dean Languell

* Closed Dec. 15, 1974 after limited run of 12 performances.

Tracey Phelps, Sharon Shayne, Gonzalo Madurga in "No Exit" Above: Howard Green in "Fingernails .

COUNTERPOINT THEATRE
Opened Friday, April 18, 1975.*
Counterpoint Theatre Company presents:

NO EXIT

By Jean-Paul Sartre; Director, Howard Green; Scenery, Minda Chipurnoi; Costumes, Ernesto Leston; Lighting, Dean Languell; Production Supervisor, Paulene Reynolds

CAST

Cradeau .... Gonzalo Madurga
Bellboy .... James Dybas
Inez .... Tracey Phelps
Estelle .... Sharon Shayne

Stage Managers: Fred Berry, Charles Trent

* Closed May 4, 1975 after limited run of 12 performances.

COUNTERPOINT THEATRE
Opened Thursday, February 13, 1975.*
Counterpoint Theatre Company presents:

UNCLE VANYA

By Anton Chekhov; Director, Gonzalo Madurga; Costumes, Ernesto Leston; Lighting, Dean Languell

CAST

Astrov .... Howard Gree
Marina, the nurse .... Gisella Ansk
Vanya .... Gonzalo Madurg
Alexandre .... Anton Spaet
Telyegin .... Valentin Smirno
Sonya .... Paulene Reynold
Yelena .... Linda Geise
Marya .... Luba Marshalo
Petya .... Charles Tre

Stage Managers: Fred Berry, Charles Tyndall, Charles Trent

* Closed March 9, 1975 after limited run of 16 performances.

**Paulene Reynolds, Linda Geiser
in "Uncle Vanya"**

THE CUBICULO

Philip Meister, Artistic Director
Elaine Sulka, Managing Director

E CUBICULO
June 5–22, 1974
(12 performances)
E KISS-OFF by John Herzfeld; Director, Sara Harte; General
nager, Albert Schoemann; Press, Pamela Hare; Setting, Bob
winger; Costumes, Christina Katz; Lighting, Orin Charm; Stage
nager, Danny Fishkin; Production Assistants, Michael Meany,
orah Falcone, Christine Doherty; Coordinator, Haig Shepherd.
ST: Connie Forslund (Daisy), William Andrews (Ted)
UEBERRY MOUNTAIN by John Herzfeld. CAST: Ryan List-
 (Jesse), David Pendleton (Leroy), Lynn Lowry (Honey Baby)
June 13–29, 1974
(12 performances)
ITH, HERE! by Edward Greenberg; Director, Donald Auspitz;
, Dan Leigh; Lighting, Scott Johnson; Props, Jean Brett; Stage
nagers, Charles Carney Conwell, Susan Baum; Program Direc-
Maurice Edwards; Resident Designer, Brian Jayne. CAST: Stan-
Brock
SENSWEIG F. C. by Edward Greenberg. CAST: Susan Baum
rs. Halperin), Robert Dale Martin (Rosie Rosensweig), Norman
nple (Abe), Lee Terri (Wilma)
July 15–16, 1974
(2 performances)
 PEDENT by Flaminio Scala; Director, Barry Magnani; Set,
Truitt, Tricia Barkley; Technical Director, Oriole O'Neill; The
ni Street Theater Production. CAST: Tom Russo (Oratio), Ted
on (Pantelone), Robert Wilson (Cataldo), William Forbes (Pe-
no), Heather Lupton (Isabella), W. David Watson (Capitano),
y Magnani (Arlechino), Sherry Meccariello (Flaminia), Joel
nan (Dr. Gratiano)
E CUBICULO
September 17–21, 1974
(5 performances)
 RISE AND FALL OF BURLESQUE HUMOR FROM
ISTOPHANES TO LAUGH-IN by Dick Poston; General Man-
, Albert Schoemann; Administrative Director, Mark Page; Ad-
istrative Assistant, Pamela Hare; Technical Director, Bob
brill. CAST: Josep Elic (The Comic), Dick Poston (Straight
), Marilyn Wassell (Talking Lady)
September 27–28, 1974
(2 performances)
ME OF THE ANCIENT MARINER AND OTHER SEA STO-
S performed by Richard Clairmont and Peter Lobdell; Lighting,
 Charney, Bob Gambrell; Tone Poems, Charles Horwitz; Mask,
Stein; Set, Shop II
Tuesday, October 22, 1974
(1 performance)
ING INTO THE 16th ROUND: Poetry by Peggy Garrison and
cy Scott
E CUBICULO
October 25–26, 1974
(2 performances)
ON directed by Charles Howard; with Scott Thornton and Betsy
hony in "In the Whisper Ride the Lash" and "Love Run";
sented by the Icon Theatre Group
October 31–November 2, 1974
(3 performances)
GRAN JUAN WAYNE by Bob Santana; Directed by the au-
; Sound-Stage Manager, Tom Aberger; Lighting, Sanford Mor-
Production Assistant, Jackie Russ; Set, John Q. Anonymous.
ST: Michael Fraguada (Ralphie), Domingo Ambriz (Polo-
ng), Richard Reber (Juan), Andrew Schneider (Governor),
en Edelman (Jessica), Patricia Triana (Lupe), Gary Adler
ry), Gerardo Finiello (Al), Gloria (Secretary), Ray Baden (TV
nerman)

**Dick Poston, Marilyn Wassell, Josep Elic
in "The Rise and Fall of Burlesque Humor . . ."**
(Conrad Ward Photo)

THE CUBICULO
November 1–2, 1974
(2 performances)
TRANSFORMING: Mime with Peter Lobdell; Lighting, Mark
Ammerman; Music and Tone Poem, Charlemoon; Poetry read by
Maurice Edwards
November 4–6, 1974
(3 performances)
THE FIRST GILBERT & SULLIVAN QUARTETTE: Sandra
Darling, James Wilson, Nell Evans, John Carle, Shirley Sequin (pia-
nist)
November 7–24, 1974
(12 performances)
FALLING APART by Monte Merrick; Director, John Henry Da-
vis; Music Composed and Performed by Brad Fiedel; Set, Jane
Thurn; Lighting, Todd Lichtenstein; Projections, Deborah Roth;
Stage Manager, Moneer Zarou; Electrician, Judy Rude. CAST:
James Alexander, Jo Anne Belanger, Mark Blankfield, Brandis
Kemp, Tina Sattin, Adam Wade, Voice of Gordon A. Jacoby
November 12–16, 1974
(7 performances)
CIRCUS: Book and Lyrics, Martin Calabrese; Music, Jason McAu-
liffe; Director, Jason McAuliffe; Choreography, Robert Anderson;
Sets and Lights, Mark Kaufman; Musical Director, Jeffrey Roy;
Costumes, Mary Ann Tolka, Fran Bradfield; Stage Manager, Sherry
Caldwell; Presented by The Circus Company in association with
Richard Eber; Props, Ruth Slattery; Musical Arrangements, Jeffrey
Roy; Assistant Director, Steve Jobes; Assistant Choreographer, Bar-
bara McKay. CAST: Frank Anderson (Ringmaster), Jean Busada
(Charlotte), Leonard John Crofoot (Chris), Patti Farmer (Sandy),
Spence Ford (Mincemeat), Nick Jolley (Bob), George Maguire
(Tom), Frank Mastrocola (Phoofie), Jayme Mylroie (Joan), Donna
Rossini (Oziemandarin), Marcia Savella (Linda), Mary Lee Stahl
(Faye)
November 29–December 15, 1975
(11 performances)
THE DARK MOON AND THE FULL by Joe Hart; Director,
Albert Takazauckas; Set, Michael Massee; Lighting, Mark Ammer-
man; General Manager, Albert Shoemann; Administrative Director,
Mark Page; Administrative Assistant, Pamela Hare. CAST: Audree
Rae (Helen), Shirley O'Key (Grandma), Mary M. Manzi (Patsy),
Anthony Manionis (Michael), Carol Rosenfeld (Loretta)
SUNDAY MORNING BRIGHT AND EARLY by Joseph Hart;
Director, Albert Takazauckas. CAST: Anthony Manionis (Son),
Dermot McNamara (Father)
December 5–21, 1974
(11 performances)
THE SEA GULL by Anton Chekov; Director, Philip Meister; Set,
Edgardo Franceschi; Costumes, Holly Hollinger; Stage Manager,
Richard L. Abel; Lighting, Mark Ammerman. CAST: Bill Errigo
(Yakov), Ann Sweeny (Masha), Carl Trone (Semyon), Paul Andor
(Pyotr), Leo Schaff (Konstantin), Eren Ozker (Nina), Mark Shapiro
(Yevgeny), Marcia Mohr (Polina), Elaine Sulka (Irina), James Gal-
lery (Ilya), Robert Elston (Boris)

**Scott Thornton, Betsy Anthony
in "Icon"**

103

THE CUBICULO

December 18–21, 1974
(6 performances)
THE FIRST THE LAST THE MIDDLE by Israel Horowitz; Performed by the Dartmouth Players; Director, Eric Forsythe; Stage Managers, Merle Gordon, Deborah Cafolla; Technical Production, Allin Tallmadge; Sound, Jennifer Warren; Choreographer, David Briggs. CAST: John Battle (Fleming), Peter Parnell (Stephen), Christine Crawfis (Molly), Normand Beauregard (Dolan), Peter Hackett (Arnall), Mark Arnott (The Man), Ray Paolino (Kiley), Mark Gamell (Goldstein), Laura Cuetara (Evelyn), Kathleen Laskey (Gracie)

THE CUBICULO

January 2–19, 1975
(12 performances)
WILD MAN OF BOREO by Allen Sternfield; Director, Bret Lyon; Sets, Cliff Simon; Lights, Ira Landau; Costumes, Linda Jackson; Sound, Marvin Adler; Assistant Set Designer, Tavia Trusch; Props, Elaine Barlas; Bust, Edmond Felix. CAST: Larry Swansen (Victor), Mari Rovang (Diane), Bob Zay (Ralph), Robert Tennenhouse (Harry), Eileen Davis (Cora), John H. O'Keefe (Hodgkins), Dennis Kelly (Wild Man), Peter Yoshida (Inspector Chin), Dennis Sakamoto (#2 Son), John Aquin (Inspector Muldoon)
HOLMES AND MORIARTY by Allen Sternfield. CAST: Ken Starret (Holmes), John Aquino (Watson), Carl Trone (Moriarty), Mari Rovang (Mrs. Hudson), Bob Zay (Inspector Lestrade), Robert Tennenhouse (Colonel Moran)
January 9–26, 1975
(12 performances)
HEARTBREAK HOUSE by G. B. Shaw; Director, Robert Elston; Set and Costumes, John McGroeder; Lighting, David Bosboom; Stage Managers, David Bosboom, Sue Fabrykant; General Manager, Albert Schoemann; Administrative Director, Pamela Hare. CAST: Josie O'Donnell (Nurse), Joanna Rotte (Ellie), Robert Gaus (Captain), Elizabeth Perry (Lady Utterwood), Catherine Byers (Hessione), Robert McIlwaine (Mazzini), David Tress (Hector), Frank Bara (Boss), Kent Broadhurst (Randall), Pierre Epstein (Burglar)
February 2–16, 1975
(10 performances)
RAFFERTY ONE BY ONE by Rolf Fjelde; Director, John Henry Davis; Set, John Walker; Lighting, Barbara Kopit; Costumes, Kim Beckwith; Stage Manager, Annie Rech; Props, Eliza Beckwith, Michel Tulier. CAST: Sheldon Feldner (Lorn), Sturgis Warner (Minotaur), Bill Nunnery (Shoengut), Paul McMaster (Budge), Stephen Everett (Francis), Eve Packer (Winifred), Gary Allan Poe (Bo), Lin Shaye (Donna), Norman Jacob (Pentacost), Mark Margolis (Mex), Bill Britten (Judge), John David Clarke (Prosecutor), Dave Konig (Boy), Eve Packer (Operator/Nurse)
February 3–4, 1975
(2 performances)
ATTEMPTED RESCUE ON AVENUE B by Megan Terry; Director, Lynn Rogoff; Design, Tom Meleck. CAST: Trazana Beverly (Maxine), Gloria Chetwynd (Mira), Michael Dattorre (Landy), Alex Duncan (Mendel), Glenn Kezer (Taverniti), Muriel Mason (Mrs. Line), Lenore Sherman (Mrs. Taverniti), Diane Shuman (Helen)
February 25–March 8, 1975
(10 performances)
JUDAS by Robert Patrick; The Orion Repertory directed by Eric Concklin; Set and Lighting, David Adams; Stage Manager, Mysti Michelles; Production Coordinator, Les Benda; Crown of Thorns, Lohr Wilson; Costumes, Fashions Fabulous Compendium. CAST: Neil Flanagan (Pilate), Perrin Ferris (Philus), William Duff-Griffin (Herod), Jeffrey Herman (Judas), Madeleine le Roux (Mary), George Wolf Reily (Joseph), Lee Kissman (Jesus), John Albano (Peter)

John Aquino, Ken Starrett, Bob Zay, Robert Tennenhouse in "Holmes and Moriarty"

(Conrad Ward Photo)

THE CUBICULO

Marth 6–22, 1975
(12 performances)
BLOOD WEDDING by Federico Garcia Lorca; Director, Phil Meister; Movement, Rudy Perez; Original Music, Charles Gros Setting, Jane Thurn; Costumes, Mary McDonough; Lighting, Mar Ammerman; Stage Manager, Deborah Teller; Production Assistan Duncan Brine; Lighting Technician, Lynda Corso; Translated b James Graham-Lujan and Richard L. O'Connell. CAST: Elair Sulka (Mother), Joanna Rotte (Bride), Peter Jacob (Leonardo), Ke Kliban (Bridegroom), Carlo Grasso (Bride's Father), Carol Emsho (Servant), Nina Dova (Neighbor), Ruth Klinger (Mother-in-law Myra Malkin (Leonardo's Wife), Nina Dova (Death), Sturg Warner (Moon), Michael S. Williamson (Young Man), Young Girl Jennifer Carroll, Claire Rosenberg, Jayne Shaw
March 11–22, 1975
(12 performances)
STICK OF INCENSE by Michael McGrinder; Director, Hugh Gi tens; Sets and Lighting, David Adams; Technical Director, Le Banda; Technical Coordinator, Richard Zangrillo; Technical Assi tant, Neva Weschenfelder; CAST: Alice Hedberg (Kathleen), Nicl Kaplan (Sister McSweeney), Robert Burke (Padraig)
MADAM ZODIAC by Michael McGrinder; Director, M McGrinder; Costumes Supervisor, and Set Decor, Judy Pendleto CAST: Julia Curry (Evangeline), George Wolf Reily (Clark), Wi liam Perley (Prosecutor), Gary Swartz (George/Cheiro), Arlen Young (Suzie/Louise), Sherrie Berk (Sheila), Donald Carte (Judge), Bill Maloney (Professor/Doctor/Announcer)
April 8–19, 1975
(10 performances)
AIN'T THAT A SHAME—the Saga of Richard Nixon by Josep Renard; Director, Neil Flanagan; Set and Lights, David Adam Music, Henry Krieger; Choreography, Lisa Jacobson; Stage Mana ers, Les Banda, Joel Russ. CAST: Marilyn Amaral, Sherrie Ber Robert Burke, Ron Carrier, Constance Clarke, Julia Curry, Willia Duff-Griffin, Perrin Ferris, Lisa Ingalls, Bert Kruse, Marcia Moh William Perley, David Plummer, Gary Swartz, Lou Trapan George Wolf Reily, Diane Cina (Alternate Pianist)
April 17–May 3, 1975
(12 performances)
THINGS ARE GETTING BETTER by Van Joyce; Direction an Musical Staging, Donnis Honeycutt; Musical Direction, Stanle Wietrzychowski; Sets and Costumes, Danny Morgan; Lightin Randy Becker; Special Choreography, Sandifer Sanders; Stage Ma ager, Randy Becker; Props, Suelen Fabrykant; Production Assistan Duncan Brine; Design Assistants, Peggy Haugh, Tommy Hanse Amalia Pietri, Billy Puzo. CAST: Tim Cahill, Dana Coen, Sharc Hess, Gail Johnston, Charles Leipart, Jean Palmerton, Susan Riche son, Tony Travis, Louise Turner

Ken Kliban, Joanna Rotte in "Blood Wedding"

(Conrad Ward Photo)

DUME SPANISH THEATRE

Herberto Dume, Producer-Artistic Director
Fifth Season

DUME SPANISH THEATRE
Opened Saturday, November 9, 1974.*
Dume Spanish Theatre presents:

LA DAMA DE LAS CAMELIAS

By Alexandre Dumas; Adapted and Directed by Herberto Dume;
Sets, Guido Betancourt; Costumes, Serge Pinckney; Lighting, Wilfredo Zagal; Sound, Dume; Make-up, Hair Styles, Rolando
Zaragoza; Wigs, Bob Kelly, Hollywood Joe; Assistant Director,
Manuel Bachs

CAST

Arturo de Varville . . . . Julio Ambros
Nanine . . . . Emma Vilvas
Prudencia Duvernoy . . . . Camelis Marin
Margarita Gautier . . . . Virginia Arrea
Olimpia . . . . Otilia Galis Menendez
Saint Gaudens . . . . Emilio Garcia De Soto
Gaston Rieux . . . . Rene Troche
Armando Duval . . . . Andres Nobregas
Valentin . . . . Manuel Bachs
Jorge Duval . . . . Guillermo Rosales

A Melodrama in 2 acts and 5 scenes.

Press: Enrique Gomez

* Closed Dec. 23, 1974 after limited run of 23 performances.

DUME SPANISH THEATRE
Opened Saturday, March 15, 1975.*
Dume Spanish Theatre presents:

MEDEA

By Euripides; Producer-Director, Herberto Dume; Sets, Guido
Betancourt; Costumes, Serge Pinckney; Lighting, Wilfredo Zagal;
Make-up, Rolando Zaragoza; Assistant Director, Wilfredo Zagal

CAST

Medea . . . . Virginia Arrea
Jason . . . . Enrique Gomez
Nodriza . . . . Sol
Mensajero . . . . Rene Troche
Maestro . . . . Emilio Rodriquez
Ninos . . . . Emma Vilvas, Manuel Bachs, Cristina Castanon
Corifeo . . . . Rafael Delgado
Egeo . . . . Rene Troche
Coro . . . . Christina Castanon,
Manuel Bachs, Emma Vilvas
Creonte . . . . Juan Troya

A Tragedy performed without intermission.

Press: Enrique Gomez

Closed Apr. 27, 1975 after limited run of 13 performances.

**Virginia Arrea, Andres Nobregas in "La Dama
de las Camelias"**
(Rafael Llerena Photo)

DUME SPANISH THEATRE
Opened Friday, February 28, 1975.*
Dume Spanish Theatre presents:

EL ROBO DEL COCHINO

By Abelardo Estorino; Producer-Director, Herberto Dume; Sets,
Guido Betancourt; Costumes, Serge Pinckney; Lighting, Wilfredo
Zagal; Make-up, Rolando Zaragoza; Hairstylist, Julio Ambros; Assistant to the Director, Wilfredo Zagal

CAST

Cristobal . . . . Juan Troya
Rosa . . . . Isabel Segovia
Juanelo . . . . Rene Troche
Lola . . . . Mercedes Enriquez
Rodriguez . . . . Emilio Rodriguez
La Maestra . . . . Idalia Diaz

A Drama in three acts.

Press: Enrique Gomez

* Closed Apr. 13, 1975 after limited run of 13 performances.

**Left Center: Isabel Segovia, Juan Troya
in "El Robo del Cochino"**
(Rafael Llerena Photo)

**Enrique Gomez, Virginia Arrea
in "Medea"**
(Rafael Llerena Photo)

THE ENSEMBLE STUDIO THEATRE

Curt Dempster, Director
Robert Saidenberg, Anne Wadsworth, Associate Directors

ENSEMBLE STUDIO THEATRE
Opened Thursday, December 5, 1974.*
The Ensemble Studio Theatre presents:

PARADES SHALL FOLLOW

By Donald Marcus; Created by Gary Nebiol and Donald Marcus;
Set, Kert Lundell; Lighting, Michael Watson; Technical Director,
Steve Crowley; Sound, Leah Mark, John Grenon; Props, Bill Luhrs;
Costumes, Karen Miller; Producer, Jerry Zaks

CAST

Chi-Chi .... Gary Nebiol
Montesquieu .... Donald Marcus

A play in 5 scenes performed without intermission. The action
takes place two weeks before the Investiture Ball in Chi-Chi's wind-
mill on the far side of the swamp in the farthest corner of the
kingdom.

Press: Gerald Siegal

* Closed Dec. 15, 1974 after limited run of 11 performances.

ENSEMBLE STUDIO THEATRE
Opened Thursday, February 6, 1975.*
The Ensemble Studio Theatre presents:

THE DOG RAN AWAY

By Brother Jonathan; Director, Curt Dempster; Setting, Kert
Lundell; Music and Sound, Jesse Miller; Lighting, Geoffrey Dunbar;
Producer, Robert Saidenberg; Associate Designer, Paul Eads; Cos-
tumes, Gertrude Sloan; Sound, Leah Mark; Props, Megan Robinson;
Assistant Producer, Anne Wadsworth

CAST

David .... Joseph Ponazecki
William .... Josef Sommer
Joseph .... John Wardwell

A play in 2 acts and 11 scenes. The action takes place in December
of 1973 in the gatekeeper's house for a large estate on Long Island
now owned by a Franciscan order.

Press: Gerald Siegel

* Closed Feb. 16, 1975 after limited run of 8 performances.

ENSEMBLE STUDIO THEATRE
Opened Thursday, April 3, 1975.*
The Ensemble Studio Theatre presents:

THE TRANSFIGURATION OF BENNO BLIMPIE

By Albert Innurato; Setting and Lighting, Charles Cosler; Costumes, Sheila Roman; Producer, Curt Dempster; Production Associate, Kimberly Kearsley

CAST

Benno .... Martin Shakar
Young Girl .... Lynn Ritchie
Grandfather .... Michael Tucker
Mother .... Melodie Somers
Father .... Paul Austin

A play performed without intermission. The action takes place in
the 1950's in South Philadelphia.

Press: Gerald Siegal
Stage Manager: Charlene Harrington

* Closed Apr. 13, 1975 after limited run of 8 performances.

Jacqueline Brookes, Will Hare
in "Dream of a Blacklisted Actor"
(Michael Landrum Photo)

ENSEMBLE STUDIO THEATRE
Opened Friday, March 7, 1975.*
The Ensemble Studio Theatre (Curt Dempster, Director)
presents.

AMNESIA

By Michael Shaffer; Director, Charles Parks

CAST

Bill Cwikowski   Bill Snickowsk
Lyle Kessler   Richard Sherma
Bevya Rosten   Melodie Somer

* Closed March 9, 1975 after limited run of 3 performances.

ENSEMBLE STUDIO THEATRE
Open Thursday, May 1, 1975.*
The Ensemble Studio Theatre (Curt Dempster, Director)
presents:

DREAM OF A BLACKLISTED ACTOR

By Conrad Bromberg; Director, Harold Stone; Setting, John Jackson: Costumes, Libby Palmer; Lighting, Geoffrey Dunbar; Assistant
Set Designer, Mary Ann Neilson

CAST

Edward Morris .... Will Hare
Cookie Morris .... Jacqueline Brookes
Teresa Morris .... Paula Marchese
Joe Morris .... Jerry Zaks
Richard Kiehl .... Joseph Ponazecki
Grace .... Sarah Harris
Mr. Bennett .... Louis Pietig
Paul Warren .... Adam Keefe
Al Goodman .... Rudy Bond
Charlie Allman .... James Tolkan

A play in three acts. The action takes place in New York City in
1951.

Press: Gerald Siegal
Stage Manager: Barry Kearsley

* Closed May 11, 1975 after limited run of 8 performances.

EQUITY LIBRARY THEATRE

George Wojtasik, Managing Director
Lynn Montgomery, Production Director
Ann B. Grassilli, Producer ELT Informals
Thirty-second Season

EQUITY LIBRARY THEATRE
Opened Thursday, October 17, 1974.*
Equity Library Theatre presents:

ARMS AND THE MAN

By George Bernard Shaw; Director, Russell Treyz; Scenery Design, Billy Puzo; Lighting Design, Victor En Yu Tan; Costumes, Mary McDonough; Production Director, Lynn Montgomery; Technical Director, Isaac Waksul; Assistant Musical Director, Jim Coleman

CAST

Raina Petkoff .... Ellen Fiske
Catherine Petkoff .... Margaret Gwenver
Louka .... Naomi Robin
Captain Bluntschli .... Chet Carlin
Russian Officer .... Robert Lehman
Nicola .... Irwin Atkins
Major Paul Petkoff .... George Hall
Major Sergius Saranoff .... Richard Council

A Comedy in three acts. The action takes place in a lady's bedchamber in Bulgaria in a small town near the Dragoman Pass, late November of 1885; the garden of Maj. Petkoff's house on March 1886; and the library after lunch.

Press: Lewis Harmon, Sol Jacobson
Stage Manager: Bob Jaffe

Closed on Oct. 27, 1974 after limited engagement of 16 performances.

LIBRARY & MUSEUM OF PERFORMING ARTS
Monday, Tuesday, Wednesday, October 21–23, 1974
Equity Library Theatre presents:

HEATHEN PIPER

By Michael McGrinder; Directed by Cyprienne Gabel; Lighting, Cecile Fallat; Stage Manager, David Rosenberg; Uilleann Pipes, Bill Ochs

CAST

Author .... J. C. Hoyt
Kevin .... Robert Burke
Laurie .... Christy Virtue
Dermott .... Michael Dennis Moore
Sam .... Bruce French
Barney .... Robert Einenkel
Nora .... Nancy Nutter
Mick .... Michael Bright

Chet Carlin, Ellen Fiske
in "Arms and the Man"
(Gene Coleman Photo)

EQUITY LIBRARY THEATRE
Opened Thursday, November 7, 1974.*
Equity Library Theatre presents:

THE BOY FRIEND

By Sandy Wilson; Director, Nancy Z. Rubin; Dances and Musical Numbers Staged by Joe Davis; Musical Direction, Jim Coleman; Scenery, Ernie Smith; Lighting, Gregg Marriner; Costumes, David Charles; Hairstylist, Edward Cohen; Wardrobe, B. J. Porter; At the piano, Jim Coleman; Percussionist, Edward G. Zacko

CAST

Hortense .... Janet MacKenzie
Maisie .... Marilyn Seven
Dulcie .... Linda Poser
Fay .... Liz Marks
Nancy .... Deborah Combs
Phoebe .... Jo Ann Yeoman
Polly Browne .... Neva Rae Powers
Marcel .... Roger Neale
Pierre .... Jerry Senter
Alphonse .... Robert Raye
Georges .... Christopher Coles
Mme. Dubonnet .... Carolyn Chrisman
Bobby .... Cameron Mason
Percival Browne .... Joseph Jamrog
Tony .... Richard Cooper Bayne
Lord Brockhurst .... Herb Aronson
Lady Brockhurst .... Rose Roffman

A Musical in three acts. The action takes place in the spring of 1926 in the drawing room of the Villa Caprice near Nice, the plage, the terraces of the Cafe Pataplon.

Press: Sol Jacobson, Lewis Harmon
Stage Managers: Jerry Roberts, Jennifer Parichy, Ellen Zalk

* Closed Nov. 24, 1974 after a limited engagement of 22 performances.

Liz Marks, Roger Neale, Neva Rae Powers, Robert
Raye, Linda Poser, Jo Ann Yeoman, Christopher
Coles, Deborah Combs, Jerry Senter in "Boy Friend"

Gene Coleman Photo

EQUITY LIBRARY THEATRE

Opened Thursday, December 5, 1974.*
Equity Library Theatre presents:

THE DESPERATE HOURS

By Joseph Hayes; Director, Robert Brink; Scenery, Jane E. Thurn; Lighting, Sander R. Gossard; Costumes, Patrice Elaine Alexander; Technical Director, Isaac Waksul

CAST

Tom Winston	Bob Gunton
Jesse Bard	Woody Eney
Harry Carson	Douglas Hayle
Eleanor Hilliard	Patricia Mertens
Ralphie Hilliard	Barney Miller
Dan Hilliard	Michael B. Miller
Cindy Hilliard	Kathy Connell
Glenn Griffin	Steve Simpson
Hank Griffin	Bill Cwikowski
Robish	Joe LoGrippo
Chuck Wright	Chris Romilly
Mr. Patterson	Michael Robert Zaccaro
Lt. Carl Fredericks	Robert Tennenhouse
Miss Swift	Pamela Wild Marsen

A Drama in three acts. The action takes place at the present time in the city of Indianapolis, Indiana.

Press: Lewis Harmon, Sol Jacobson
Stage Managers: David Semonin, Mary Murphy, Susan Scida

* Closed Dec. 15, 1974 after limited engagement of 14 performances.

LIBRARY & MUSEUM OF PERFORMING ARTS

Monday, Tuesday, Wednesday, December 9–11, 1974
Equity Library Theatre presents:

TWO BY LINNEY

Written by Romulus Linney; Director, Lou Rodgers; Scenery and Lighting Design, and Stage Manager, Terrence B. Rodney; Production Assistant and Understudy, C. A. Hutton; Assistant Stage Manager, and Understudy, Ellen Mait; Original Music, Lou Rodgers; Sound, Alan Yorinks

CAST

"The Seasons"

He	Stuart Michaels
She	Lenore Loveman
Girl	Rebecca Dobson
Boy	Tom Cuff

"Man's Estate"

Old Woman	Carolyn Chrisman
Cardell	Tom Cuff
Mary	Rebecca Dobson
Herschel	Arne Gunderson
Griswold	Oliver Malcolmson

Steve Simpson, Michael B. Miller, Patricia Mertins, Barney Miller in "The Desperate Hours"

108

(Gene Coleman Photo)

Scot Stewart, John Dorrin, Livia Genise in "New Girl in Town"
(Gary Wheeler Photo)

EQUITY LIBRARY THEATRE

Opened Thursday, January 9, 1975.*
Equity Library Theatre (George Wojtasik, Managing Director; Lynn Montgomery, Production Director) presents:

NEW GIRL IN TOWN

Book, George Abbott; Music and Lyrics, Bob Merrill; Director, Richard Michaels; Based on play "Anna Christie" by Eugene O'Neill; Settings, Kenneth Foy; Costumes, Brent J. Porter; Lighting, Isaac Waksul; Choreography, Lynne Gannaway; Assistant Choreographer, Richard Maxon; Musical Direction, Michael Dansicker; Percussion, Edward G. Zacko

CAST

Chris Christopherson	John Dorrin
Anna Christopherson	Livia Genise
Johnson	Gerald Haston
Larry, the bartender	Roger Kozol
Pearl	Rosamond Lynn
Marthy Owen	Peggy Pope
Lil	Maureen Sadusk
Matt Burke	Scot Stewart

MUSICAL NUMBERS: "Sunshine Girl," "Anna Lilla," "Flings," "On the Farm," "Good to Be Alive," "Look at Her," "Roll Yer Sox Up," "You're My Friend," "There Ain't No Flies on Me," "You Might Get to Like Me," "Did You Close Your Eyes," "Red Check Apron Ball," "When We Waltz," "If That Was Love," Finale.

A Musical in 2 acts and 9 scenes. The action takes place during 1900 in Johnny-the-Priest's Saloon on the waterfront of New York City, and in the cabin aboard Chris's coal barge.

Press: Sol Jacobson, Lewis Harmon
Stage Managers: Barry Steinman, Lee Geisel, Mark Varian

* Closed Jan. 26, 1975 after limited engagement of 22 performances.

Opened Thursday, February 6, 1975.*
Equity Library Theatre (George Wojtasik, Managing Director;
Lynn Montgomery, Production Director) presents:

BUS STOP

By William Inge; Director, Richard Mogavero; Scenery, Richard
B. Williams; Lighting, Guy J. Smith; Costumes, Marianne Powell-
Parker; Sound, Nancy Bain.

CAST

Elma Duckworth, a waitress	Alice Elliott
Grace Hoylard, owner of restaurant	Dolores Kenan
Will Masters, a sheriff	Dick Bonelle
Cherie, a chanteuse	Darlene Parks
Dr. Gerald Lyman, a former college professor	Jim Hillgartner
Carl, a bus driver	Duane Tucker
Virgil Blessing, a ranch hand	Michael Zeke Zaccaro
Bo Decker, young rancher and cowboy	Treat Williams

A play in three acts. The action takes place in a street-corner
restaurant in a small town about thirty miles west of Kansas City.

Press: Lewis Harmon, Sol Jacobson
Stage Managers: Judy Goldstein, Robert Kahn, Karen Shapiro

* Closed Feb. 16, 1975 after a limited engagement of 14 performances.

LIBRARY & MUSEUM OF PERFORMING ARTS
Monday, Tuesday, Wednesday, February 24–26, 1975
Equity Library Theatre presents:

MANDRAGOLA

By Niccolo Machiavelli; Director, Thomas Molyneaux

CAST

Callimaco	Bill Cwikowski
Siro	James Allan Bartz
Nicia	Herman K. Tuider
Ligurio	Edmund Lyndeck
Sostrata	Fran Anthony
Friar Timoteo	Malcolm Gray
Woman	Lynn Webster
Lucrezia	Kim Ameen

Darlene Parks, Treat Williams, Michael Zeke
Zaccaro in "Bus Stop"
(Gary Wheeler Photo)

EQUITY LIBRARY THEATRE
Opened Thursday, March 6, 1975.*
Equity Library Theatre (George Wojtasik, Managing Director;
Lynn Montgomery, Production Director) presents:

DO I HEAR A WALTZ?

Book, Arthur Laurents; Based on his play "The Time of the
Cuckoo"; Music, Richard Rodgers; Lyrics, Stephen Sondheim; Di-
rector, Dolores Ferraro; Musical Direction, Jim Coleman; Choreog-
raphy, Peter J. Humphrey; Settings, James L. Joy; Lighting, Joseph
P. Dziedzic; Costumes; Louise Krozek; Wardrobe, Jim Woolley;
Technical Director, Isaac Waksul; Technical Assistants, Robert
Strohmeier, Steve Goldstein; Properties, Nancy Bain

CAST

Mauro	David Craig Moskin
Leona Samish	Rosalind Harris
Jennifer Yeager	Melanie Chartoff
Eddie Yeager	Joel Colodner
Guide	Robie Braun
Blonde Tourist	Lynn Marlowe
Red Haired Tourist	Betty Jo Doolan
Edith McIlhenny	Judith Tillman
Lloyd McIlhenny	John Hallow
Fioria	Barbara Lea
Giovanna	Gail Oscar
Alfredo	Russ Beasley
Vito	Steven Gelfer
Renato DiRossi	Donald Craig
Man on the bridge	Robie Braun
Mrs. Victoria Haslam	Betty Jo Doolan
and Friend	Robie Braun

MUSICAL NUMBERS: "Someone Woke Up," "This Week Ameri-
cans," "What Do We Do? We Fly!," "Someone Like You," "Bar-
gaining," "Here We Are Again," "Thinking," "No Understand,"
"Take the Moment," "Moon in My Window," "We're Gonna Be All
Right," "Do I Hear a Waltz?," "Stay," "Perfectly Lovely Couple,"
"Last Week Americans," "Thank You So Much"

A Musical in 2 acts and 11 scenes. The action takes place at the
present time in Venice, Italy.

Press: Sol Jacobson, Lewis Harmon
Stage Managers: Michael R. Martorella, Emily E. Garlick,
Nancy Bain

* Closed Mar. 23, 1975 after limited engagement of 22 performances.

Melanie Chartoff, Joel Colodner, Rosalind Harris,
dith Tillman, John Hallow in "Do I Hear a Waltz?"
(Gary Wheeler Photo)

MASKS

Three one-act plays by Ted Pezzulo; Director, Bill Herndon; Set and Lighting, Bob Phillips; Assistant Director, Erik Boles; Sound, Gary Granatoor; Stage Managers, Ted Chapin, Gideon Davis

CAST

"Family Circle"
Irate Woman .... Alice McLane
Stanley .... Hal Holden
Jack .... Bob Shields
Inquisitive Man .... Gideon Davis
Cashier .... Jim Carruthers

"The Demand"
Nick .... Richard Zavaglia
Andy .... Jim Dybas

"The Good Citizen"
Rose Jenkins .... Alice McLane
Walter Frazier .... Jim Carruthers
Mr. Maeda .... M. B. Miller
Peter Curran .... Matthew Arkin

EQUITY LIBRARY THEATRE
Opened Thursday, April 10, 1975.*
Equity Library Theatre presents:

THE ZYKOVS

By Maxim Gorky; Director, Isaac Schambelan; Scenery, Christopher A. Thomas; Lighting, Gary Porto; Costumes, Cheryl Lovett; Russian Consultant, Mary Mlynar

CAST

Anna Markovna .... Saax Bradbury
Sophia Ivanovna, Antipa's sister .... Delphi Harrington
Palageya, Anna's servant .... Beege Barkett
Mikhail, Antipa's son .... James Seymour
Shokhin, a forest warden .... Gaetano Bongiovanni
Antipa Ivanovich Zykov, a timber merchant .... Louis Turenne
Pavla (Pasha) .... Susan Sharkey
Vassily Pavlovitch Muratov, a forester .... Richard Greene
Matvey Ilich Tarakanov, bookkeeper .... William Robertson
Styopka, Sophia's servant .... Kathy K. Gerber
Gustav Yegorovich Hevern, Antipa's partner ..... Robert Hitt

A drama in four acts. The action takes place in 1913 in the Russian countryside, Anna Markovna's house, the Zykov garden, Sophia's office.

Press: Lewis Harmon, Sol Jacobson
Stage Managers: Terry Malone, Donald Pitkin

* Closed April 20, 1975 after limited engagement of 14 performances.

Delphi Harrington, Susan Sharkey, James Seymour, Saax Bradbury, Louis Turenne in "The Zukovs"

(Gary Wheeler Photo)

MISS PETE

By Andrew Glaze; Director, Arlen Dean; Sound, Alan Yorin Stage Manager, Dallas Coke; Co-Produced with The Players Cl

CAST

Miss Pete .... Ronnie Claire Edwar
Bo .... Richard Hamilt
George Stringer .... Mason Adar

GALLOWS HUMOR

By Jack Richardson; Director, Rena Down; Stage Manager, E Sorel

CAST

Warden .... Robert Mottingdorf
Lucy .... Lorraine Serabia
Walter .... Kenneth Tig

EQUITY LIBRARY THEATRE
Opened Thursday, May 8, 1975.*
Equity Library Theatre presents:

THE THREE MUSKETEERS

Adapted by William Anthony McGuire; Music, Rudolf Frin Lyrics, P. G. Wodehouse, Clifford Grey; Directed and Chore graphed by Charles Abbott; Musical Direction and Vocal Arrang ments, Jim Coleman; Settings, Sandi Marks; Costumes, Mir Maxmen; Lighting, Francis J. Webb; Duels Choreographed by E ward Easton; Production Supervisor, Robert Bennett; Assistant D rector, Alan Rust; Production Assistants, Melissa Taylor, Jan Crean

CAST

Zoe .... Doreen Dun
Zoe's Beau .... Michael Genna
Innkeeper .... Charles Maggio
Jussac .... Richard Christoph
First Guard .... Alan Ru
Rochefort .... Jose Rodrigue
Milady .... Jane Altma
Two Musketeers .... Ed Oster, Cameron Smi
Athos .... Michael A. Mauric
Porthos .... David Pursle
Aramis .... Ray Co
Constance .... Tricia Ell
Planchet .... Roger Fawce
D'Artagnan .... Jason McAulif
DeTreville .... Charles Maggio
Queen Anne .... Karen Zenke
Nuns .... Gwen Arment, Ruth Ellen Sherma
Buckingham .... Robert Frisc
Cardinal Richelieu .... Russell Coste
Louis XIII .... Roger McIntyr
Brother Joseph .... Richard Ebe
King's Attendant .... MichaelJohn McGan
Mother M .... Greta Newkir
Bohemian Dancer .... Yuye Fernande
Bosun .... William Van Hunte
Patrick .... Robert Lintne

MUSICAL NUMBERS: "Summertime," "All for One and One fo All," "The He for Me," "Gascony," "My Sword and I," "Vespe Bells," "Dreams," "March of the Musketeers," "The Colonel an the Major," "Love Is the Sun," "Your Eyes," "Welcome to th Queen," "Red Wine," "Ma Belle," "One Kiss from You," "Quee of My Heart," "Each Little While," "The Court Dance," Finale

An Operetta in 2 acts and 10 scenes.

Press: Sol Jacobson, Lewis Harmon
Stage Managers: Roger Pippin, Harold Hyman

* Closed May 25, 1975 after limited engagement of 22 perfor mances.

HAMM & CLOV STAGE COMPANY

David Villaire, Artistic Director

Associate Directors, Holly Villaire, Alvah Stanley, Tom Tarpey, John Beary; Musical Director, Ed Summerlin; Coordinator, Inez M. Kirby; Stage Managers, Lynn Gutter, Steve Zuckerman; Set Designs, Roger LaVoie, Guy J. Smith, David A. Koch; Costumes, Mimi Maxmen, Richard Graziano, Pegi P. Goodman; Composers, Ed Summerlin, Matthew Yasner, David Ferguson; Technical Director, Lynn Gutter; Administrative Director, Maribeth Gilbert; Business Manager, Jim Hosbein; Box Office Manager, Leslie Hosbein; Press, C. J. Boyer

MDA THEATRE
June 13–30, 1974
(12 performances)
THE WIDOW'S HOUSE by David Ferguson; Director, David Villaire; Sets, Roger LaVoie; Costumes, Mimi Maxmen; Lighting, Lynn Gutter. CAST: Ferrie Lani Miyazaki (Meihua), Arabella Hong Young (Young Mrs. Yen), Alvin Lum (Lee), Ernest Abuba (Captain), Tisa Chang (Old Mrs. Yen), Marion Jim (Lehua), Tom Matsusaka (Regular), Calvin Jung (Kung), Peter Yoshida (Chou), Tom Matsusaka (Messenger)

ST. CLEMENTS
June 14–23, 1974
(12 performances)
THE FALL AND REDEMPTION OF MAN by John Bowen (see Theatre at St. Clement's Series)

MDA THEATRE
November 1–17, 1974
(12 performances)
STRINDBERG by Colin Wilson; Director, David Villaire; Sets, David A. Koch; Costumes, Mimi Maxmen; Lighting Lynn Gutter; Music, Ed Summerlin. CAST: Alvah Stanley (Strindberg), Larry Carpenter, Maria Cellario, Vivien Ferrara, Julia MacKenzie, Stephen Randolph, Tom Tarpey

MDA THEATRE
December 6–22, 1974
(12 performances)
TREES IN THE WIND by John McGrath; Director, John Beary; Sets, Guy J. Smith; Lighting, Lynn Gutter. CAST: Polly Adams, Kelly Fitzpatrick, Susan Stevens, Jennifer Warren

MDA THEATRE
December 13–29, 1974
(12 performances)
THE TRUE HISTORY OF SQUIRE JONATHAN AND HIS UNFORTUNATE TREASURE by John Arden; Director, David Villaire; Set, David A. Koch; Costumes, Pegi P. Goodman; Lighting, Lynn Gutter; Music, Ed Summerlin. CAST: Ian Trigger (Squire Jonathan), Jill Tanner (Blond Woman)

Jennifer Warren, Kelly Fitzpatrick, Polly Adams
Susan Stevens in "Trees in the Wind"

David Pursley, Tricia Ellis, Ray Cox, Gwen Arment in "Three Musketeers" (ELT)
(Gary Wheeler Photo)

Jill Tanner, Ian Trigger in "The True History of Squire Jonathan. ..."

111

INTAR:
INTERNATIONAL ARTS RELATIONS

Max Ferra, Artistic Director

Executive Directors, Elsa Ortiz Robles, Frank Robles; Public Relations, Joel Kudler, Walter Price; Coordinators, Lourdes Casal, Doris Castelanos, Eloisa Castellanos, Andres R. Hernandez; Administrator, Ilka Tanya Payan; Production Manager, Don Pelletier

INTAR HISPANIC THEATRE
October 12–November 3, 1974
February 22–March 23, 1975
(16 performances)
LITTLE RED RIDING HOOD: Director, Manuel Martinez; Assistant Director, John Monge; Original Music, Ed Wogel; Choreography, Phyllis Richmond; Costumes, Set, Eloisa Castellanos; Lighting, Max Ferra; Sound, Manuel Martinez; Make-up, Rolando Zaragoza. CAST: Fanny Rybin (Mother), Jose Herminio Gonzalez (Tinoco), Susan Rybin (Little Red Riding Hood), Emilio Rodriguez (Hunter), Juan Granda (Wolf), Teresa Yenke (Grandmother), Trees: Elizabeth Pena, Jorge Alvarado, Robert Lope, Edwin Avila

INTAR HISPANIC THEATRE
November 23, 1974–February 2, 1975
(24 performances)
THE ZOO STORY by Edward Albee; Director, Max Ferra; Translation by Lourdes Casal; Assistant Director, Gloria Zelaya; Set, Sound, Lighting, Steven Jan-Hoff; Production Manager, Hiran Oritz; Press, Walter Price, Joel Kudler. CAST: Luis Avalos (Jerry), Norberto Kerner (Peter)

INTAR HISPANIC THEATRE
January 18–February 2, 1975
(8 performances)
ABOUT GOYA: Book and Direction, Tony Benitez, Eloisa Castellanos; Translation and Adaptation, Eloisa Castellanos; Lighting, Edy Sanchez; Recording, Alberto Zaldivar; Costumes, Amada Benitez; Set Construction, Don Pelletier; Press, Joel Kudler. CAST: Haydee Zambrana (Person O), Teresa Yenke (Person #1), Victor Romero (Person #2), J. Herminio Gonzalez (Person of Light), Eloisa Castellanos, Manuel Martinez (Voices)

INTAR HISPANIC THEATRE
February 15–March 16, 1975
(22 performances)
FORTUNE AND MEN'S EYES by John Herbert; Director, Eduardo Corbe; Assistant Director, John Monge; Set, Eloisa Castellanos, Don Pelletier; Costumes, Angel Martinez; Lighting, Edy Sanchez; Sound, Eduardo Corbe; Choreography, Antonio Pantojas; Production Manager, Don Pelletier; Press, Joel Kudler. CAST: Raul Carbonell (Rocky), Manuel Martinez (Queenie), Jaime Montilla (Juan), Ernest Ross (Guard), Andres Nobregas (Smitty), John Monge (Catsolino), Paul Caban (Cholo)

MATINEE SERIES

Lucille Lortel, Artistic Director
Nineteenth Season

THEATRE DE LYS
Monday Evening, November 11, 1974
Tuesday Matinee, November 12, 1974
FIRE AND ICE By Robert Frost: A Cycle of Rhymes and Masque of Reason; Arranged and Directed by John Genke; Song Composed and Sung by Wendy Erdman; Music, Teiji Ito, Dan Erkkila; Choreographed by Jean Erdman; Poems Spoken by John Fitzgibbon, John Genke, Lee McClelland.
PROGRAM: "The Road Not Taken," "To the Thawing Wind," "Blue Butterfly Day," "Fragmentary Blue," "The Telephone," "Nothing Good Can Stay," "Tree at My Window," "The Death of the Hired Man," "Lines Written in Dejection on the Eve of Great Success," "A Time to Talk," "Not All There," "Lodged," "A Reflex," "Any Size We Please," "The Pasture," "The Silken Tent," "To Earthward," "The Subverted Flower," "Wind and Window Flower," "Home Burial," "Fire and Ice," "I Could Give All to Time," "Come In," "After Apple-Picking," "Stopping by Woods on a Snowy Evening."
A MASQUE OF REASON: Job, John Genke; Thyatria, his wife, Lee McClelland; God, John FitzGibbon; Satan, Dan Erkkila; Director, Albert Takazauckas

THEATRE DE LYS
Monday Evening, December 2, 1974
Tuesday Matinee, December 3, 1974
DRUMS AT YALE: by Walter A. Fairservis, Jr.; Director, Isaiah Sheffer; Production Associate, Marjorie Martin; Production Assistants, Kim Beckwith, Denah Gordon, Michel Tullier. CAST: Prof. Stephen Hull (George Washington), Walter A. Fairservis; Alice, Linda Martin; John Conway, Lon Clark; Prof. Paul Longworth (Gen. William Howe), Matthew Tobin; Peter (Nathan Hale), Gary Cookson; Charles Martin (Montressor), Joseph Jamrog. The action takes place during the present and in September of 1776 in New Haven Connecticut, and Manhattan.

THEATRE DE LYS
Monday Evening, January 6, 1975
Tuesday Matinee, January 7, 1975
THE LONG VALLEY by John Steinbeck; Adapted and Directed by Robert Glenn; Choreographic Aid, Rachael Lampert; Production Assistant, John Krug; Language Consultant, Ruth Wong Lyon; Production Design Consultant, Edward Haynes; Original Music Composed and Directed by Wendy Erdman; Ballads, Woody Guthrie; Stage Manager, Linda Harris. CAST: Aurelia DeFelice, Will Hare, J. Frank Lucas, Brandon Maggart," Robert Glenn, Andrea Masters, Dina Paisner. THE STORIES: "The Chrysanthemums," "The Vigilante," "The Sisters Lopez," "Breakfast," "The Raid," "Johnny Bear" (no photos available)

Norberto Kerner, Luis Avalos in "The Zoo Story"

Jaime Montilla, Manuel Martinez, Raul Carbonell, Andres Nobregas in "Fortune and Men's Eyes"

(Ilka Payan Photo)

112

LOOM:
LIGHT OPERA OF MANHATTAN

William Mount-Burke, Producer-Director

Associate Director, Raymond Allen; General Manager, Steve Simon; Stage Manager, Choreographer, Jerry Gotham; House Manager, Don Barker; Sets, William Schroder, Tad Motyka, Milton Duke; Costumes, William Schroder, George Stinson; Lighting, Tom O'Shea; Wardrobe, Barbara Callahan, Susan Ehinger; Accompanist, Brian Molloy; Props, Laura Bernard; Press, Steve Simon, Charley Kyle, Steve Kluger

COMPANY

Raymond Allen, Lynne Greene, Lloyd Harris, Nancy Hoffman, Florence Levitt, Georgia McEver, Nancy Papale, Vashek Pazdera, Gary Pitts, Larry Raiken, Julio Rosario, James Weber, Eleanor Wold, Steve Anderson, Don Barker, Susan Beitchman, Del Bach, Laura Bernard, Chris Biehn, Thomas Brooks, Steve Brown, Betsy Cohen, Mary Lou Crivello, Eleanor Davis, Dennis English, Linda Ferraro, Marilyn Florez, Amy Guvirty, Barbara Guerard, Margaret Hurley-Chace, Joanne Jamieson, Peter Kellogg, Deborah Kelly, Steve Kluger, Marilyn Komisar, Joan Lader, Debbie Laurie, Barbara Lorenc, Brian Malone, Migdalia Mercado, Valerie Mondini, Mary Murphy, Regina McIlvain, Peter McLaughlin, Neal Newman, John Palmore, Bill Park, Clarisse Persanyi, Gomer Pound, Frank Prieto, Kathy Quinn, Gary Ridley, Fina Rogers, Cheryl Savitt, Rhanda Spotton, Diane Stobaeus, Dorothy Tanerdi, Sandra Teller, William Wesbrooks, Ray Willingham
GUEST ARTIST: Joan Sena-Grande for "Naughty Marietta"

PRODUCTIONS
October 2, 1974–May 25, 1975

"H.M.S. Pinafore," "Ruddigore," "The Pirates of Penzance," "Princess Ida," "Iolanthe," "The Gondoliers," "The Mikado," "The Yeoman of the Guard," "Patience," "Trial by Jury," "Naughty Marietta"
PREMIERES: "Princess Ida" (Nov. 6–10, 1974), "The Mikado" (Jan. 15–19, 1975), "Naughty Marietta" (Apr. 30–May 4, 1975)

David Chase, Arlene Avril Photos

Right: "Iolanthe" Above: Gary Pitts, Larry Raiken, Gary Ridley in "Princess Ida" Top: Gary Pitts, Raymond Allen in "Yeoman of the Guard"

Raymond Allen, Patricia Irmen
in "The Gondoliers"

Nancy Hoffman, Julio Rosario
in "Iolanthe"

THE MANHATTAN THEATRE CLUB

Lynne Meadow, Artistic-Executive Director

Managing Director, Kathleen Norris; Associate Director, Thomas Bullard; Casting and Literary Director, Stephen Pascal; Adjunct Director, Carole Rothman; Public Relations Director, Joel Wald; Assistant to the Managing Director, Trudy Brown; Series Director Chamber Theatre, Barry Moss; Technical Director, William D. Anderson; Administrative Assistant, Laura Resnikoff; Technical Assistant, Jonathan Lawson

MANHATTAN THEATRE CLUB

June 6–23, 1974
(12 performances)
TWO BY TENNESSEE: "This Property Is Condemned" and "Portrait of a Madonna" by Tennessee Williams; Director, Dolores Ferraro. CAST: Jason Buzas, Cynthia Darlow, Olive Deering, Haskell Gordon, Alex Mann, Richard Marr, Jonathan Millner
June 14–29, 1974
(15 performances)
THE MORNING AFTER OPTIMISM by Thomas Murphy, Director, Robert Mandel; Set, Marjorie Kellogg; Costumes, Carol Oditz; Technical Director, Peter Dowling; Stage Manager, Beth Weissman; Lighting, Arden Fingerhut; Sound, Robert Dennis; Fencing Choreography, Stu Pankin. CAST: Sharon Spelman (Rosie), Kevin O'Connor (James), Jill Eikenberry (Anastasia), Allan Carlsen (Edmund)
June 27–July 14, 1974
(12 performances)
NIGHT MUST FALL by Emlyn Williams; Director, Stephen Levi; Stage Manager, Andrea Simon; Associate Series Director, Kevin Barkhausen. CAST: Alice Scudder Emerick (Mrs. Bramson), Joanne Dorian (Olivia), James Gallery (Hubert), Barbara Rubenstein (Nurse), Jo Anne Belanger (Mrs. Terence), Candace Coulston (Dora), Robert Foley (Inspector), Jay Bell (Dan)
July 18–August 4, 1974
(12 performances)
THE CARETAKER by Harold Pinter; Director, Joel Wald; Assistant Director, Nancy Alexander; Technical Director, Brett Lewis; Stage Manager, Ellen Murray; Production Assistant, Sheila Kaminsky. CAST: Peter Burnell (Mick), Edward Herrmann (Aston), Will Hare (Davies)
August 8–18, 1974
(8 performances)
ONE SUNDAY AFTERNOON by James Hagan; Director, Barbara Loden; Stage Manager, Steven Friedman; Technical Director, Eric Cowley; Assistant Technical Director, Sharon O'Donnell. CAST: Steve Railsback, Clinton Allmon, J. J. Quinn, Eileen Manley, Wende Sherman, Lenny Grodin, Michael Railsback, Linda DiCerb, Nancy Zala
August 22–September 1, 1974
(8 performances)
BLUES FOR MR. CHARLIE by James Baldwin; Director, Nick LaTour; Stage Manager, David E. Freeman; Technical Director, Nancy Hart; Lighting, Brett Lewis. CAST: Carl Moebus (Lyle), Ken Foree (Richard), Shelton Franklin (Meridan), Jinaki Milele (Mother Henry), Marcia McBroom (Juanita), Obaka Adedunyo (Lorenzo), Make Bray (Peter), Jessie Eccles (Student), Robert Abbott (Parnell), Michael Dorn (Papa D), Lucia Lewis (Jo), Raymond W. Cline (Judge), Ray Suideau (Rev. Phelps), Carrie Jiler (Susan), Larry Guardino (Ralph), Mary Ellen Davis (Hazel), Susan Heidi Arbiter (Lillian), Ike Williams (State Counsel)

MANHATTAN THEATRE CLUB

September 5–22, 1974
(12 performances)
THE SUBJECT WAS ROSES by Frank D. Gilroy; Director, Barry Moss; Lighting, Brett Landow-Lewis; Stage Manager, David Freeman. CAST: Kevin Barkhausen (Timmy), Paul Larson (John), Georgia Southcotte (Nettie)
October 3–13, 1974
(8 performances)
THE PRIME OF MISS JEAN BRODIE by Jay Presson Allen; Adapted from the novel by Muriel Spark; Director, Tony Slez; Associate Producer, Walter Barnett. CAST: Shelly Batt, Judy Curcio, Eugene Draper, Dorothy Fielding, Margot Hastings, Carole Hochman, Megan Hunt,, Leslie Jarmon, Judy Jensen, Eleanore Knapp, Ron Millkie, Gerianne Raphael, Bruce Robinson
OCTOBER 7–November 3, 1974
(12 performances)
LOOK BACK IN ANGER by John Osborne; Director, Paul Schneider; Modular Scenic Elements, Peter Larkin; Lighting, Brett Landow-Lewis; Original Music, Bob Dennis; Stage Manager, Louis Mascolo. CAST: Will Mackenzie (Jimmy), Peter Rogan (Cliff), Carolyn Lagerfelt (Alison), Diana de Vegh (Helena), Edward Holmes (Colonel)
October 8–27, 1974
(15 performances)
AN EVENING WITH COLE PORTER: Conceived and Directed by Norman L. Berman; Words and Music, Cole Porter; Sets and Costumes, John Lee Beatty; Choreography, Bick Goss; Lighting, William D. Anderson; Vocal and Instrumental Arrangements, Norman L. Berman. CAST: David Brummel, Jeanne Lehman, Elaine Petricoff, Bob (B. J.) Slater, Margaret Warncke, Cindy Meche (Pianist)
November 5–17, 1974
(12 performances)
BITS AND PIECES by Corinne Jacker; Director, Lynne Meadow; Modular Scenic Elements, Peter Larkin; Lighting, Arden Fingerhut; Costume Supervision, Carol Oditz; Assistant to the Director, Clay Kee; Production Assistant, Gina Pressman; Stage Managers, Richard Hoge, Larry Aronson; Narration, Joe Silver. CAST: David Sne (Philip), James DeMarse (Doctor), Sloane Shelton (Technician/Mrs. Eberly), Rochelle Oliver (Iris), Chevi Colton (Helen), James DeMarse (Farley/Antonio/Monk)
November 12–30, 1974
(15 performances)
BLESSING by Joseph Landon; Director, Tom Bullard; Set, Salvatore Tagliarino; Lighting, Wayne J. Chouinard; Costumes, Lee Austin III; Sound, Jeffrey Alden; Stage Manager, Gray McKee. CAST: F. Murray Abraham (Sal), K. Callan (Agnes), Robert Hitt (Johnny), Louis Plante (Lyle), Charles Bartlett (Fred), Lois Battle (Rosalie)
November 21–December 8, 1974
(12 performances)
END OF SUMMER by S. N. Behrman; Director, Ronald Roston; Set and Costumes, Greg Etchison; Lighting, Brett Landow-Lewis; Stage Managers, Pat DeRousie, Ruth Cohen. CAST: Bruce French (Will), Judith Elder (Mrs. Wyler), Laurie Kennedy (Paula), Joan Copeland (Leonie), Forrest Compton (Sam), Humbert Allen Astredo (Dr. Rice), Roy London (Dennis), Bernie Passeltiner (Dexter), Chet Doherty (Count)

Jeanne Lehman, David Brummel, Elaine Petricoff, B. J. Slater, Margaret Warncke in "An Evening with Cole Porter" *(Ken Howard Photo)*

Top: Robert Hitt, F. Murray Abraham, K. Callan in "Blessing" *(Ken Howard Photo)*

114

December 6–19, 1974
(10 performances)
SIGNOR DELUSO by Thomas Pasatieri and SAVITRI by Gustav
Holst; Director, David Shookhoff; Musical Director and Conductor,
Peter Leonard; Sets and Costumes, Steven Rubin; Lighting, William
D. Anderson; Assistant Director, Caroline Suen; Stage Managers,
Gray McKee, Clark Kee. CAST: "Signor Deluso": Sheri Greena-
wald (Celie), David Anchel (Gorgibus), Annie Lynn Bornstein (Ro-
sine), Harlan Foss (Deluso), Stephanie Cotsirilos (Clara), Modesto
Crisci (Leon); (Savitri) Joy Blackett (Savitri), Patricia Deckert
(Savitri"): Modesto Crisci (Satyavan), Harlan Foss (Death), Chorus:
Natalie Campbell, Caroline Geer, Lauren Gerken, Molly Grose,
Linda J. Hayden, Susan Jefferies, Ann Pike, Cindy Ralph, Elizabeth
Usher, Lynn Weaver

December 10–29, 1974
(17 performances)
THE RUNNER STUMBLES by Milan Stitt; Director, Austin Pen-
dleton; Lighting, Cheryl Thacker; Coordinators, Gina Pressman,
Ann Granger, Robert Bishop; Company Manager, Trudy Brown;
Stage Managers, Kimothy Cruse, Richard Tirotta. CAST: Alan
Mixon (Rivard), Katrina Commings (Erna), Ken Costigan (Law-
yer), Nancy Donohue (Sister Rita), Sloane Shelton (Mrs. Shandig),
Lobb Webb (Prosecutor), Joseph Mathewson (Secretary), Marilyn
Pfeiffer (Louise)

January 21–February 16, 1975
(24 performances)
THE SEAGULL by Anton Chekhov; New English Version by Jean-
Claude van Itallie; Director, Joseph Chaikin; Sets, Philip Gilliam;
Costumes, Gwen Fabricant; Lights, Arden Fingerhut; Production
Manager, Jon Teta; Production Assistant, Ellie Renfield; Produced
in association with The Other Theatre; Technical Director, William
D. Anderson; Stage Managers, Michael Bongar, Peter Littlefield;
Design Assistant, Jeremy Lebensohn. CAST: Murray Moss (Med-
vedenko), Margo Lee Sherman (Masha), Daniel Seltzer (Pyotr),
Bernard Duffy (Konstantine), Michael Bongar (Yakov), Tina She-
pard (Nina), Elia Braca (Pauline), Thomas Barbour (Dr. Dorn),
Boris Basenko (Ilyia), Leueen MacGrath (Irina), Ron Seka (Boris)

January 23–February 9, 1975
(12 performances)
BUS STOP by William Inge; Director, Jeff Bricmont; Lighting,
Jonathan Lawson; Costumes, Jody Beth Barrett; Modular Scenic
Elements, Peter Larkin; Stage Manager, Jonathan Sand, Susan A.
Brown; Technical Director, Jonathan Lawson; Company Manager,
Trudy Brown; Sound, Jeffrey Alden. CAST: Toni Kalem (Elma),
Janice Fuller (Grace), Alice White (Grace), Douglas R. Nielson
(Will), Lynn Lowry (Cherie), Hansford Rowe (Dr. Lyman), Vic
Polizos (Carl), James Hilbrandt (Virgil), Peter Brouwer (Bo)

MANHATTAN THEATRE CLUB

February 11–23, 1975
(6 performances)
THE BEST IS YET TO BE by Margie Appleman; Director, Dolores
Ferraro; Scenic Elements, Peter Larkin; Scenic Consultant, James
Joy; Lighting, Joseph P. Dziedzic; Sound, Jeffery Alden; Stage Man-
ager, Belle Baxter, Gretchen Metzloff; Assistant to the Director,
Nancy Alexander; Technical Director, Ron Woods; Company Man-
ager, Trudy Brown CAST: Carl Low (Marvin), Berrilla Kerr (Irma),
Marcia Taranto (Red), George Ayer (Junior)

February 12–March 2, 1975
(15 performances)
THE PORNOGRAPHER'S DAUGHTER by Jonathan Levy; Di-
rector, John Pleshette; Sets, Christina Weppner; Costumes, Anne
Wolff; Lights, Cheryl Thacker; Stage Managers, Gray McKee, Joel
Besner; Sound, Jeffrey Alden. CAST: Jack Aaron (Jack), Michael
Vale (Leon), Frantz Turner (Tony), Anna Shaler (Elaine), Elaine
Kerr (Valerie), Kathleen Tolan (Annaliese), Neil Flanagan (Randy),
Kathleen Shearer (Lady), Frantz Turner (Hazleton)

February 18–February 23, 1975
(6 performances)
THE AUTUMN LADIES AND THEIR LOVERS' LOVERS by
Susan Nanus; Director, Jan Eliasberg; Sound, Jeffrey Alden; Com-
pany Manager, Trudy Brown; Technical Director, Ron Woods;
Stage Manager, Belle Baxter. CAST: Judith Elder (Rose), Margot
Stevenson (Rachel), William DaPrato (Torellini)

February 20–March 2, 1975
(8 performances)
BLOODSHOT WINE by Jim Steinman; Lyrics, Jim Steinman,
Barry Keating, Michael Weller, Ray Fox; Director, Barry Keating;
Associate Musical Director, Jez Davidson; Costumes, Bosha John-
son. CAST: Joanna Albrecht, Dorian Harewood, Sarah Harris,
Barry Keating, Andre De Shields, Dale Soules

February 27–March 16, 1975
(12 performances)
OFFENBACH COUNTRY: Two musical farces by Jacques Offenbach; Translated and Directed by Michael Feingold; Music Arranged and Conducted by Gregory Sandow; Setting, John Lee
Beatty; Lighting, Ron Woods; Costumes, Tony Negron; Stage Managers, Sari Weisman, Lee Jines; Company Manager, Trudy Brown;
Technical Director, Ron Woods. CAST: "Two Fishermen": Edmond Dante (Bigmaus), Michael Hume (Baskin), "Marriage by
Lanternlight": Stephen Rydell (Willie), Roberta Vatske (Jennie),
Lin Speer (Mary-Sue), Vilma Vaccaro (Emmaline), Lee Jones (Policeman)

March 12–30, 1975
(15 performances)
THE SEA by Edward Bond; Director, Robert Mandel; Sets, Marjorie Kellogg, Phil Eickhoff; Lighting, Arden Fingerhut; Costumes,
Carol Oditz; Stage Managers, Mark Paquette, Richard Hoge, Lind-
sey Foland; Wardrobe, Mary Anne DeStefano; Sound, Jeffrey Al-
den; Production Assistants, Ian McColl, John Streppone, Dinah
Carlson; Dialect Coach, Gordon A. Jacoby; Hairstylist, Edith Tilles.
CAST: Arnold Soboloff (Evens), John Heffernan (Hatch), Paul Col-
lins (Willy), Grayson Hall (Louise), Virginia Payne (Jessica), David
Cromwell (Holarcut), Munson Hicks (Thompson), Bill Nunnery
(Carter), Julie Garfield (Mafanwy), Linda Kampley (Jilly), Melinda
Tanner (Rachel), Paul Milikin (Vicar), Susan Sharkey (Rose), Lind-
sey Foland (Davis)

Jack Aaron, Michael Vale in "The Pornographer's
Daughter"

(Ken Howard Photo)

Top: Boris Bosenko, Tina Shepard, Leueen
MacGrath in "The Seagull"   115

(Ken Howard Photo)

MANHATTAN THEATRE CLUB

March 18–30, 1975
(12 performances)
DEATH STORY by David Edgar; Director, Carole Rothman; Set, Mary Chase; Lighting, Lewis Mead; Costumes, Luanne Aronen; Stage Managers, Larry Bussard, Mary Ellen MacDonald; Company Manager, Trudy Brown; Technical Director, Ron Woods; Combats staged by Rick Casorla. CAST: Tom Berenger (Soldier/Tybalt/A Montague), Elizabeth Owens (A Capulet/Juliet's Mother/A Woman), Jennifer Reed (A Montague/Rosaline), Robert Grillo (Colonel/A Man), Ronald C. Frazier (Captain/Priest), Jerry Zaks (Mercutio), Vic Polizos (Benvolio), John Heard (Romeo), Kathleen Tolan (Juliet)

April 3–20, 1975
(12 performances)
STAIRCASE by Charles Dyer; Director, Tom Bullard; Sets, John Vallone; Costumes, Anne Wolff; Stage Manager, Matthew Connors. CAST: Michael Allinson (Charles), John Clarkson (Harry)

April 22–May 4, 1975
(12 performances)
BATTERING RAM by David E. Freeman; Director, Stephen Pascal; Set, Sani Marks; Lights, Ron Woods; Assistant Director, Kitty Chen; Stage Managers, Lindsey Foland, Donna Cook. CAST: Scotty Bloch (Irene), Eda Zahl (Nora), John V. Shea (Virgil)

April 27–May 11, 1975
(13 performances)
THE PAST IS THE PAST by Richard Wesley, and THE BREAK-OUT by Oyamo; Director, Harold Scott; Sets, William D. Anderson; Lighting, Arden Fingerhut; Costumes, Bernard Johnson; Company Manager, Gray McKee; Stage Manager, 'Femi; Assistant to the Director, David Juaire; Sound, Chuck London; Technical Assistants, John Jeffries, John Streppone. CAST: "The Past Is the Past": Bill Cobbs (Earl), Brent Jennings (Eddie), "The Break Out": Brent Jennings (Slam), Terry Alexander (Feet), Bill Cobbs (Voice), Joe LoGrippo (Sgt. Hack), Chase Williams (Pvt. Hack), Bill Cobbs (Cat), Palmer Deane (Reporter), Jim Mallette (Reporter), Deloris Gaskins (Reporter), Marilyn Berry (Reporter), Obba Babatunde (Dollarbill), Maurice Woods (Malcolm X)

May 8–24, 1975
(12 performances)
EAST LYNNE by David Chambers; Director, Mr. Chambers; Lighting, Ron Woods; Costumes, Millie Cox; Stage Managers, Belle Baxter, Maria J. Grieco. CAST: David Cromwell (Joyce), Julie Garfield (Cornelia), Donovan Sylvest (Archibald), Christopher Guest (Sir Francis), Mary Wright (Isabel), Monica Merryman (Emma), Jerrold Ziman (Raymond), Caroline Kava (Barbara), Richard Niles (Richard), Cynthia Crumlish (Little Willie)

MANHATTAN THEATRE CLUB

May 27–June 8, 1975
(12 performances)
VALENTINE'S DAY with Book and Lyrics by Ron Cowen; Music, Saul Naishtat; Director, Seth Glassman; Musical Director, Thomas Babbitt; Costumes and Props, Richard Westby-Gibson; Lighting, Sari Weisman; Stage Managers, Bonnie Sue Schloss, Barbara Chack; Technical Director, Pat Hummel; Sound, Jeffrey Alden; Company Manager, Trudy Brown. CAST: Jeanne Arnold (Libby), Jerry Jarrett (Sam), Alice Playten (Young Libby), Chip Zien (Young Sam)

May 29–June 15, 1975
(12 performances)
OPERETTA! Director, Christopher Alden; Musical Director, Ethan Mordden; Designed by Paul Steinberg; Lighting, William D. Anderson; Stage Manager, Michael McMahon. CAST: Sheri Greenawald, Stephen Dickson, Ed Dixon, Wayne Turnage

John Clarkson, Michael Allinson in "Staircase
(Laura W. Pettibone Photo)

John V. Shea, Scotty Bloch in "Battering Ram
(Laura W. Pettibone Photo)

**Terry Alexander, Brent Jennings
in "The Breakout"** *(Ken Howard Photo)*

Gretchen Cryer, Nancy Ford performing their songs
(Laura W. Pettibone Photo)

NEGRO ENSEMBLE COMPANY

Douglas Turner Ward, Artistic Director
Robert Hooks, Executive Director
Frederick Garrett, Administrative Director
Eighth Season

T. MARKS PLAYHOUSE
Opened Tuesday, June 4, 1974.*
The Negro Ensemble Company presents:

IN THE DEEPEST PART OF SLEEP

By Charles Fuller; Director, Israel Hicks; Sets and Costumes,
Mary Mease Warren; Lights, Susan Chapman; Technical Director
and Sound, Dik Krider; Wardrobe, Beverly Bracey; Production Assistant, Sandra Ross; Administrative Assistants, Coral Hawthorne,
Alice Whitman

CAST

Maybelle .... Mary Alice
Reuben .... Todd Davis
Tyla .... Michele Shay
Moshe .... Charles Weldon

A Drama in two acts. The action takes place in Philadelphia, Pa.,
on a Wednesday in April of 1956.

Company Manager: Frederick Garrett
Press: Howard Atlee, Clarence Allsopp, Meg Gordean, Owen
Levy
Stage Manager: Harrison Avery

Closed June 30, 1974 after 32 performances.

**Right: Todd Davis, Mary Alice, Michelle
Shay (on steps) in "In the Deepest Part
of Sleep"**

(Bert Andrews Photo)

T. MARKS PLAYHOUSE
Opened Sunday, March 2, 1975.*
The Negro Emsemble Company in association with Woodie
King, Jr. presents:

THE FIRST BREEZE OF SUMMER

By Leslie Lee; Director, Douglas Turner Ward; Scenery, Edward
Burbridge; Costumes, Mary Mease Warren; Lighting, Sandra L.
Ross; Production Assistant, Cleveland Bennett; Assistant to the
Director, Anderson Johnson; Technical Director, Dik Krider

CAST

Gremmar .... Frances Foster
Nate Edwards .... Charles Brown
Lou Edwards .... Reyno
Aunt Edna .... Barbara Montgomery
Milton Edwards .... Moses Gunn
Hattie .... Ethel Ayler
Lucretia .... Janet League
Sam Greene .... Carl Crudup
Briton Woodward .... Anthony McKay
Reverend Mosely .... Lou Myers
Hope .... Petronia
Joe Drake .... Peter DeMaio
Gloria Townes .... Bebe Drake Hooks
Harper Edwards .... Douglas Turner Ward
Understudies: Roland Sanchez, Martha Short-Goldsen

A Drama in two acts. The action takes place at the present time
in a small city in the Northeast.

Company Manager: Frederick Garrett
Press: Howard Atlee, Clarence Allsopp, Meg Gordean, Owen
Levy
Stage Manager: Horacena J. Taylor

Closed Apr. 27, 1975 after 70 performances to move to Broadway.

**Frances Foster, Ethel Ayler, Moses Gunn
in "The First Breeze of Summer"**

(Bert Andrews Photo)

117

Opened Monday, April 28, 1975.*
The Negro Ensemble Company presents:

A SEASON-WITHIN-A-SEASON

Coordinator, Steve Carter; Lighting, Sandra Ross; Technical Director, Dik Krider; Production Assistant, Fai Walker Davis

LIBERTY CALL

By Buriel Clay II; Director, Anderson Johnson; Sound, Wayne Elbert; Wardrobe, Shirley Garrett Smith.

CAST

Boatswain Mate 1C John Wilheart	Samm Williams
H. O. B. Rothschild III (Double Wiggy)	Michael Jameson
Mama Sun	Thelma Carter
Lt. Priest	Ramon Rafur
Opium Man	George Campbell
First Girl	Naola Adair
Second Girl	Elaine Jackson
First Marine	Sam Finch
Second Marine	Suavae Mitchell
Bartender	George Campbell

A play in two acts. The action takes place in Southeast Asia during the 1960's

Press: Howard Atlee Associates, Clarence Allsopp, Meg Gordean, Owen Levy
Stage Manager: Michael Fleming

* Closed May 4, 1975 after limited run of 8 performances.

ST. MARKS PLAYHOUSE
Opened Tuesday, May 6, 1975.*
The Negro Ensemble Company presents:

TWO PLAYS BY DON EVANS

Director, Helaine Head

CAST

"Orrin"

Wilma	Lea Scott
Orrin	Taurean Blacque
Kenny	Eric Coleman
Alex	Carl Gordon

and

"Sugar-Mouth Sam Don't Dance No More"

Verda-Mae Hollis	Lea Scott
Sammy	Carl Gordon

* Closed May 11, 1975 after limited run of 8 performances.

ST. MARKS PLAYHOUSE
Opened Tuesday, May 13, 1975.*
The Negro Ensemble Company presents:

TWO BY RUDY WALLACE

Director, Osborne Scott; Sound, Wayne Elbert; Wardrobe, Shirley Garrett Smith; Props, Denise Gray

CAST

"The Moonlight Arms"

Rena	Charliese Drakeford
Roy	Charles Brown

"The Dark Tower"

Joe	Arthur French
Philip	Charles Brown

* Closed May 18, 1975 after limited run of 8 performances.

ST. MARKS PLAYHOUSE
Opened Sunday, May 18, 1975.*
The Negro Ensemble Company presents:

WAITING FOR MONGO

By Silas Jones; Director, Douglas Turner Ward; Scenery Costumes, Mary Mease Warren; Lighting Sandra L. Ross; Production Assistant, Cleveland Bennett; Technical Director, Dik Kri Wardrobe, Ramona King

CAST

Virgil	Re
Preach/Mongo	Bill Co
Viana	Bebe Drake Ho
Sadie Mae	Barbara Montgom
Bill	Roland Sanc
Teach	Ethel A
Doodybug	Adolph Cae
Doc	Graham Bro
Argus	Samm-Art Willia
Klansman #1	Samm-Art Willia
Klansman #2	George Camp
Klansman #3	Sam Fi
Offstage Voices	George Campbell, Sam Fi

"A Nightmare Comedy" performed without intermission. action takes place on the outskirts of Deliverance, Mississippi, so time in the recent past during the twilight of the Civil Rights inside the cellar and main body of Deliverance A. M. E. Chu

Company Manager: Frederick Garrett
Press: Howard Atlee Associates, Clarence Allsopp, Meg Gord
Stage Manager: Horacena J. Taylor

* Closed May 25, 1975 after limited run of 8 performances.

ST. MARKS PLAYHOUSE
Opened Tuesday, May 20, 1975.*
The Negro Ensemble Company presents:

WELCOME TO BLACK RIVER

By Samm Williams; Director, Dean Irby

CAST

Mama Liza	Juanita Be
Lou Mae	Marcella Low
Anna Lee	Lea S
D. J.	Taurean Blac
David Jack	Clayton Cor
Billy	Frankie Fai
Mordicah	Peter De M
Amos	Carl Gor

A Drama in two acts. The action takes place in 1958 in Bl River, North Carolina.

Press: Howard Atlee Associates, Clarence Allsopp, Meg Gordean, Owen Levy
Stage Manager: Michael Fleming

* Closed May 25, 1975 after limited run of 8 performances.

Top: Bill Cobbs, Adolph Caesar, Graham Brow Samm Williams in "Waiting for Mongo"
(Bert Andrews Photo)

THE NEW DRAMATISTS INC.

Friday, June 21, 1974
(1 performance)
IGHTLIGHT by Barry Berg; Stage Director, Eugene Kallman.
AST: Judy Jordan (Joan), Fred Morsell (Simon), Haig Shepherd
arry), Holland Taylor (Barbie)

Tuesday, June 25, 1975
(1 performance)
HE BEACH CHILDREN by John von Hartz; Director, Ron Ros-
n. CAST: Humbert Allen Astredo (Morales), Ron Faber (Max),
ancy Franklin (Margaret), Ric Mancini (Domingo), Mark Metcalf
mmy), Robin Rose (Sherry), Catherine Wolf (Alma)

Tuesday, July 16, 1974
(1 performance)
HE RAG DOLL by Allen Davis III; Stage Directions, Eugene
allman. CAST: David Aaron (Timmy), Ruth Baker (Gretchen),
lice Beardsley (Sabine), Jonathan Bolt (Wolfe), Anne Countryman
Mrs. Vickery), Margaret Impert (Teacher), Judy Jordan (Jere),
atthew Lewis (Minister), Jane Minion (Carol/Waitress), Haig
epherd (Tommy), Peggy Winslow (Clerk)

September 18–22, 1974
(5 performances)
HE SHAFT OF LOVE by Charles Dizenzo; Music, Terence
awes; Lighting, Bob Phillips; Stage Managers, Betty Martin,
onna Van Winkle. CAST: Serena Seacat (Jean), Vivian Schindler
Mary), Dino Narizzano (Dr. Burns), Arlene DeCoveny (Nurse
ack), Sarah Hofman (Nurse Norse), Allyn Monroe (Maxine), Tom
annum (Brad), Clifford Lipson (Doug), Anne Ribar (Missie), Ke-
n O'Meara (Hank), Soames Bantry (Dr. Joyce), Donna Van Win-
e (Tess)

October 1–5, 1974
(6 performances)
OVE ONE ANOTHER by Rose Leiman Golemberg; Director, C.
. Alexander; Original Music, C. K. Alexander, Choreography,
arole Schweid; Sets and Lighting, Guy J. Smith; Costumes, Patrice
lexander; Stage Manager, Eugene Kallman; Sound, Ruth Tand-
rg. CAST: Richard Fancy, Ingrid Sonnichsen

October 15–19, 1974
(6 performances)
HE RAG DOLL by Allen Davis III; Director, Bolen High; Light-
g, Joel Grynheim; Costumes and Dolls, Barbara Naomi Cohen;
age Manager, Joel Grynheim. CAST: Sharon Laughlin (Jere),
ott Sorrels (Timmy), Gene Lindsey (Wolfe), Ivy Bottini
retchen), Dorothy Levine (Sabine), Barbara Coggin (Sales Clerk),
arion Lindell (Waitress), Saundra MacDonald (Mrs. Vickery),
udrie Zerul (Teacher), Robert Tennenhouse (Minister), Joann
own (Carol), Don Paul (Tommy)

Gene Lindsey   **Sharon Laughlin**

Holland Taylor   **David Aaron**

NEW DRAMATISTS INC.

October 29,–November 2, 1974
(5 performances)
A SAFE PLACE by C. K. Mack; Director, B. J. Whiting; Set, Clay
Coyle; Lighting Stephen Harty; Music, Barbara Beckler Reis; Lyr-
ics, Carol Mack; Stage Manager, David Kraut; Sound, Peter Mack;
Technical Director, Victor Gelb. CAST: Toni Kalem (Nadia), Thom
Molyneaux (Arthur), Elsa Raven (Miss Lieder), Edmund Lyndeck
(Henry), Nancy Franklin (Elizabeth), Anne O'Sullivan (Jennifer),
Betsy Beard (Boo), Linda Lodge (Charlie), Mary Gallagher (Anna),
Jayne Wenger (Gloria), Deborah Moldow (Cissy), Alice Micci
(Florence), Penelope Safranek (Convert), Carolan R. Workman
(Convert)

November 20–23, 1974
(5 performances)
GIVE MY REGARDS TO BROADWAY by Dennis Turner; Di-
rector, Dolores Ferraro; Set and Lighting, Clarke Dunham; Stage
Manager, Eugene Kallman; Electrician, Mary DeMartino. CAST:
Brian Brownlee (Artie), David Christmas (Louis), Will Gregory
(Lawrence), Annie Kravat (Beverly), Richard Buck (Bryce)

December 17–21, 1974
(5 performances)
BREADWINNER by Marian Winters; Lighting, Stage Manager,
Sara Schrager; Assistant Stage Manager, Robert Kanner. CAST: Jo
Henderson (Sara), Rod Browning (Mark), Lillah McCarthy (Laura),
Valerie Beaman (Judy), Darius Narizzano (Robert), Monica Moran
(Harriet), Robert Kanner (Mailman/Chester), Darren Kelly (Paul)

December 19, 1974
(1 performance)
THE PINK PALACE by Aldo Giunta; Stage Directions, Robert
Kramer. CAST: Joseph Daly (Harold), Elizabeth Reavey
(Lizabeth), Anne Murray (Ellen), Frank Rohrbach (Teller), Devin
Scott (Phillip)

January 9–12, 1974
(6 performances)
LEAVE OF ABSENCE by Stephen Foreman; Director, Robert
Lowery; Scenic Consultant, Kenneth N. Kurtz; Lighting, Rick
Belzer; Costumes, Roberta Baker; Assistant Director, Jo-Dee Mer-
curio; Stage Manager, Diane Davis; Technical Assistant, Kevin Wil-
liam Meyer; Music, Buzz Brusletten; Lyrics, Thomas Hardy. CAST:
John Hartnett (Daniel), Lenora May (Bianca), Bill Braden (Barrett),
Freddie Dawson (David), Jo-Dee Mercurio or Pat Weaver (Kip),
Ray Liotta (Joel), Sally Harrison (Krista)

January 19, 1975
(1 performance)
CAKES WITH THE WINE by Edward M. Cohen. CAST: Francine Beers (Rose), Helen Hanft (Blossom), Pierre Epstein (Itchy),
Gretchen Oehler (Ida), Adam Redfield (Milton), Willy Switkes
(Maxie), Joe Silver (Moe), Frank Nastasi (Sholom), Andres Jarkow-
ski (Benny)

**Will Gregory, David Christmas in "Give My
Regards to Broadway"**
(Ben Asen Photo)

NEW DRAMATISTS INC.

January 20, 1975
(1 performance)
CARNIVAL DREAMS by Conn Fleming; Director, Robert Brewer. CAST: Polly Holliday (Wolverine/June/Valerie), John Mintun (Charles), Ed Kuczeski (Alfred), Earle Hyman (Grady)

January 28–February 1, 1975
(5 performances)
NIGHTLIGHT by Barry Berg; Director, Craig Anderson; Lighting, Richard W. Jeter; Costumes, Betty Martin; Stage Managers, Will Maitland Weiss, Jill Wisoff, Jonathan Bloch. CAST: John Medici (Larry), Jeff Peters (Ernie), David Darlow (Simon), Lucinda Constable (Barbie), Ann Sweeny (Joan)

February 6–9, 1975
(5 performances)
BETWEEN NOW AND THEN by Leslie Lee; Director, Dana Roberts; Lighting, Joel Grynheim; Set, Clay Coyle; Choreography, Francine Storey, Jerry MacLaughlin; Stage Managers, David Kraut, Richard Zigun; Production Assistant, Jill Wisoff. CAST: Charles Regan (Denny), Charmian Sorbello (Jo), Chris Tenney (Jonathan), David Kerman (Dan), Nick Roberts (Denny), Marion Levine (Darby), Greg Godeke (Gilbert), Jorge Johnson (Linwood), Bruce Bouchard (Billy), Henry Ferrentino (Ike)

February 18–22, 1975
(5 performances)
THE INN AT LYDDA by John Wolfson; Director, Philip Taylor; Lighting, Rick Belzer; Choreography, Carole Schweid; Costumer, Jill Wisoff; Stage Managers, Richard Zigun, Cindy Cannell; Incidental Music, Stuart Oderman, Peter Tchaikovski; Musical Consultant, Bob Margulies. CAST: Bernard Pollock (Balthasaar), Dennis Helfend (Casper), Bill Roulet (Melchior), Brie Salzman (Musician), Albert Verdesca, Dan Huntoon, Augustine Dunn (Guards), Bill Nunnery (Quintius), Paul Lipson (Tiberius Caesar), John Mintun (Thrysullus), Nina Stern (Musician), Helen Hale-Brandt, Marianne Chick, Arlene Miller (The 3 Marys), Jeffrey Pomerantz (Jesus of Nazareth), Jon Stevens (John), Alan Court (Mnester), Devin Scott (Caligula), JoAnn Lehmann (Helen of Tyre), William Rohrig (Lucas), Kyle Cittadin (Marcus), Robert Kanner (Innkeeper), Arlene Miller (Xenia), Helen Hale-Brandt (Antonia), Marianne Chick (Livia)

February 27, 1975
(1 performance)
BREADWINNER by Marian Winters; Stage Directions, Bernard Pollack. CAST: Alice Hirson (Sara), Rod Browning (Mark), Lillah McCarthy (Laura), Valerie Beaman (Judy), Darius Narizzano (Robert), Monica Moran (Harriet), Bernard Pollack (Mailman/Chester), Sam McMurray (Paul)

March 5, 1975
(1 performance)
ESTHER by C. K. Mack; Stage Directions, Victor A. Gelb. CAST: Fred Morsell (Ahasuerus), Stephen Mark Weyte (Haman), Steve Vinovich (Daniel), Gordon Hammett (Chaim), William E. Dauphin (Mordecai), Sharon Laughlin (Esther), Bonnie Kaiden (Hadassah), John Mintun (Heghe), Victor A. Gelb (Scribe)

NEW DRAMATISTS INC.

March 26, 1975
(1 performance)
AMOUREUSE adapted by Stuart and Anne Vaughan; Stage Directions, Kathy Dyas. CAST: Louis Edmonds (Etienne), Patricia Falkenhain (Mme. de Chazal), Janet Kapral (Germaine), Edmond Lyndeck (Pascal), Monica May (Catherine), Anne Murray (Mme Henriet), Kathy Dyas (Madelaine)

April 1–5, 1975
(5 performances)
THE SALTY DOG SAGA by David Epstein; Director, Alan Fox; Lighting, Scott Johnson; Costumes, LuAnne K. Aronen; Stage Managers, Robert Bennett, Kenneth Christian. CAST: David Dukes (Billy), Daniel F. Keyes (Orrie), Robyn Goodman (Thoosa)

April 9, 1975
(1 performance)
OAKVILLE U.S.A. by Frieda Lipp; Stage Directions, Robert Coluntino. CAST: Kelly Fitzpatrick (Wayne), Victoria Boothby (Cynthia), Stephen Butler (Steven), Eren Ozker (Louise), Sybil Gorden (Amy), Frank Biancamano (Joseph), Daniel Pollack (Prosecutor), Pawnee Sills (Marianne), Charles Pegeus (Lester), Robert Coluntino (Judge/Guard/Deputy)

April 16–17, 23–24, 1975
(4 performances)
HOCUS-POCUS by Joseph Scott Kierland; Director, Gene Montanino. CAST: Andrea Frierson (Sara), Pawnee Sills (Mama), Thommie Blackwell (Willy), Vernon Washington (Screwy), Kenneth Parker (Harvey), Jane Hoffman (Gladys), Kitty Parks (Debbie)

April 24, 1975
(1 performance)
HAPPY HALLOWEEN by Kit Jones. CAST: Aaron Schwartz (Charles), John Mintun (Peter), Francine Middleton (Marble), Charles Regan (Stanley)

May 7–10, 1975
(4 performances)
THE PINK PALACE by Aldo Giunta; Director, Richard Place; Lighting, Patrika Brown; Costumes, Nancy Johnson; Sound, Paul Gadebusch; Stage Manager, Don Pitkin. CAST: Addison Powell (Harold), Anne Murray (Ellen), Elizabeth Reavey (Lizabeth), Devin Scott (Phillip), Quinn Halford (Teller), Basil Gray (Hopper), Laura Ilene (Rana), Alex Wagner (David), Peter Gelblum (Ingram), Jim Boerlin, Alex Wagner, Roy Thomas (Beggars), Roy Thomas (Gladiator), Jim Boerlin (Cowboy), Alberta Hutchinson (Mass-Beast)

May 20–24, 1975
(5 performances)
ESTHER by C. K. Mack; Director, Philip Taylor; Lighting, Joel Grynheim; Music, Jason Shulman; Stage Managers, Victor A. Gelb, Robin Maxwell. CAST: Wil Albert (Chaim), John Henry Davis (Daniel), Nancy Foy (Hadassah), Christine Jones (Esther), Jeremy Lawrence (Heghe), Matthew Lewis (Ahasuerus), John Mintun (Haman), Kerry Welch (Mordecai)

Matthew Lewis, Christine Jones in "Esther"
(Jeanie Black Photo)

Top: Anne Murray in "The Pink Palace"
(Gary Bisig Photo)

NEW YORK SHAKESPEARE FESTIVAL AT LINCOLN CENTER

Joseph Papp, Producer

MITZI E. NEWHOUSE THEATER
Opened Sunday, October 20, 1974.*
The New York Shakespeare Festival at Lincoln Center presents:

RICHARD III

By William Shakespeare; Director, Mel Shapiro; Designed by John Conklin; Lighting, Roger Morgan; Setting, Santo Loquasto; Associate Producer, Bernard Gersten; Production Manager, Ron Abbott; Hairstylist, Dorman Allison; Fights arranged by Ron Manavite; Special Makeup, Connie Couch; Production Assistants, Richard Hirsch, Bryna Wasserman.

CAST

Richard, Duke of Gloucester, afterwards Richard III	Michael Moriarty
George, Duke of Clarence	George Hearn
Sir Robert Brakenbury	John Wardwell
Lord Hastings	Tom Toner
Lady Anne	Marsha Mason†1
King Edward IV	Patrick Hines
Anthony Woodeville, Earl Rivers	Howard Chamberlin
Elizabeth, Queen to Edward IV	Barbara Colby
Marques of Dorset, her son	Robert Lesser
Lord Grey, her son	Martin Shakar
Duke of Buckingham	Paul Winfield†2
Lord Stanley, also Earl of Derby	Maury Cooper
Margaret, widow of Henry VI	Bette Henritze
Mistress Shore	Robyn Goodman
Murderer 1	Barry Snider
Murderer 2	David Tabor
Sir William Catesby	Stephen D. Newman
Richard, Duke of York	Stephen Austin
Edward, Prince of Wales, afterwards Edward V	David Jay
Lord Mayor of London	Patrick Hines
Cardinal Bourchier	David Tabor
Sir Richard Ratcliffe	Barry Snider
Messenger	Gregg Almquist
Priest	Joseph Corral
John Morton, Bishop of Ely	John Wardwell
Duke of Norfolk	David Downing
Page	Gregg Almquist
Sir James Tyrrel	George Hearn
Henry, Earl of Richmond, afterwards Henry VII	Marco St. John
Earl of Oxford	Kurt Garfield
Sir James Blunt	K. C. Wilson
Sir Walter Herbert	Powers Boothe
Earl of Surrey	Joseph Corral
Sir William Brandon	Steve Karp

UNDERSTUDIES: Dorset, Murderer, Gregg Almquist; Stanley, Norfolk, Powers Boothe; Edward IV, Mayor, Maury Cooper; Grey, Joseph Corral; Prince Edward, Duke of York, Rodman Flender; Ratcliffe, Hastings, Kurt Garfield; Lady Anne, Robyn Goodman; Buckingham, George Hearn; Catesby, Richmond, Steve Karp; Clarence, Tyrrel, Robert Lesser; Margaret, Elizabeth, Shore, Parker McCormick; Richard III, Stephen D. Newman; Rivers, Brakenbury, C. Wilson

Presented in two acts.

General Manager: Robert Kamlot
Manager: Alison Harper
Press: Merle Debuskey, Faith Geer
Stage Managers: Jason Steven Cohen, Mark Paquette

Closed Dec. 22, 1974 after 90 performances.
Succeeded by: Jane Marla Robbins, Robyn Goodman, 2. Stephen D. Newman

Friedman-Abeles Photos

Michael Moriarty, Bette Henritze

Top Right: Michael Moriarty
Below: Powers Boothe, Robert Lesser, Michael Moriarty, Kurt Garfield, K. C. Wilson

VIVIAN BEAUMONT THEATER
Opened Thursday, October 31, 1974.*
New York Shakespeare Festival Lincoln Center (Joseph Papp,
Producer) presents:

MERT AND PHIL

By Anne Burr; Director, Joseph Papp; Setting, Santo Loquasto;
Costumes, Theoni V. Aldredge; Lighting, Martin Gersten; Sound
Tapes, Roger Jay; Special Makeup, Carl Fullerton; Production Man-
ager, Ron Abbott; Wardrobe Supervisor, James McGaha

CAST

Mert	Estelle Parsons
Phil	Michael Lombard
Mother	Marilyn Roberts
Lucille	Rhoda Gemignani
George	Norman Ornellas
Lavoris	Beverlee McKinsey
Beauty Lady	Marie Wallace

STANDBYS AND UNDERSTUDIES: Mert, Lucille, Marcia Hau-
frecht; Phil, George, George Dzundza; Mother, Lucy Lee Flippen;
Lavoris, Beauty Lady, Elaine Kerr.

A Comedy in Two acts. The action takes place Here and Now.

General Manager: Robert Kamlot
Company Manager: Patricia Carney
Press: Merle Debuskey, Faith Geer
Stage Managers: D. W. Koehler, Michael Chambers

* Closed Dec. 8, 1974 after 41 performances and 14 previews.

Friedman-Abeles Photos

Top: **Marilyn Roberts, Estelle Parsons,
Rhoda Gemignani**

**Marilyn Roberts, Estelle Parsons, Norman Ornell
Beverlee McKinsey, Michael Lombard**

VIVIAN BEAUMONT THEATER
Opened Monday, January 6, 1975.*
New York Shakespeare Festival at Lincoln Center (Joseph
Papp, Producer) presents:

BLACK PICTURE SHOW

Written and Directed by Bill Gunn; Music Composed and Conducted by Sam Waymon; Scenery, Peter Harvey; Costumes, Judy Dearing; Lighting, Roger Morgan; Associate Producer, Bernard Gersten; Production Assistant, Kathy Roberson

CAST

Vocalist	Sam Waymon
J. D., Alexander's son	Albert Hall
Alexander, a Black artist	Dick Anthony Williams
Norman, Alexander's companion	Graham Brown
Hospital Attendants	William Leet, Marvin Beck
Rita, Alexander's second wife	Carol Cole
Philippe, a movie producer,	Paul-David Richards
Jan, Philippe's wife	Linda Miller

UNDERSTUDIES: Philippe, Attendants, Doug Rowe; Rita, Ethel Ayler; Jane, Hilary Beane; J. D., Tucker Smallwood; Alexander, Norman, Bill Cobbs

A play performed without intermission. The action takes place at the present time in a hospital psychiatric unit in The Bronx, N. Y.

General Manager: Robert Kamlot
Company Manager: Patricia Carney
Press: Merle Debuskey, Faith Geer, Sally Campbell
Stage Managers: Dyanne Hochman, Osborne E. Scott, Jr.

Closed Feb. 9, 1975 after 40 performances and 21 previews.

Friedman-Abeles Photos

Marvin Beck, Dick Anthony Williams, Linda Miller,
Albert Hall, Carol Cole, Paul-David Richards

Linda Miller, Dick Anthony Williams

123

MITZI E. NEWHOUSE THEATER
Opened Sunday, January 19, 1975.*
New York Shakespeare Festival at Lincoln Center (Joseph Papp, Producer) presents:

A MIDSUMMER NIGHT'S DREAM

By William Shakespeare; Director, Edward Berkeley; Musical Staging, Donald Saddler; Music Composed by William Penn; Lighting, Jennifer Tipton; Designed by Santo Loquasto; Associate Producer, Bernard Gersten; Assistant to the Director, Craig Impink; Assistant Choreographer, Arthur Faria; Wardrobe Supervisor, Alfred Calamoneri

CAST

Hippolyta, Queen of the Amazons	Marlene Warfield
Theseus, Duke of Athens	Dan Hamilton
Philostrate, Master of the Revels	William Robertson
Egeus, father to Hermia	Jack Davidson
Lysander, beloved of Hermia	Michael Sacks
Demetrius, in love with Hermia	Richard Gere†
Helena, in love with Demetrius	Lucy Lee Flippin
Snug, a joiner	Jack R. Marks
Robin Starveling, a tailor	David Harshcheid
Tom Snout, a Tinker	Roberts Blossom
Francis Flute, a bellows mender	Edward Herrmann
Nick Bottom, a weaver	Richard Ramos
Peter Quince, a carpenter	Tom Toner
Cobweb	Stephen Austin
Puck, or Robin Goodfellow	Larry Marshall
Titania, Queen of the Fairies	Kathleen Widdoes
Oberon, King of the Fairies	George Hearn
Peaseblossom	Timmy Michaels
Moth	Arthur De Lorenzo
Mustardseed	Gwendolyn Smith
Attendants on Theseus and Hippolyta	Frank Ammirati, Michael Cornelison, Tom Everett, Carolyn McCurry, Ellen Novack

UNDERSTUDIES: Snug, Snout, Quince, Starveling, Frank Ammirati; Demetrius, Lysander, Michael Cornelison; Puck, Flute, Tom Everett; Oberon, Theseus, Philostrate, Steve Karp; Bottom, Jack R. Marks; Helena, Hippolyta, Carolyn McCurry; Titania, Hermia, Ellen Novack; Egeus, William Robertson

Performed in two acts.

General Manager: Robert Kamlot
Manager: Alison Harper
Press: Merle Debuskey, Faith Geer, Sally Campbell
Stage Managers: Jason Steven Cohen, Penny Gebhard

* Closed March 16, 1975 after 62 performances and 25 previews.
† Succeeded by David Haskell

Friedman-Abeles Photos

George Hearn, Kathleen Widdoes Top Right: Michael Sacks, Toni Wein, Richard Gere, Lucy Lee Flippin

Edward Herrmann, Roberts Blossom, Richard Ra
Above: Tim Michaels, Arthur DeLorenzo, Steph
Austin, Gwendolyn Smith, Kathleen Widdoes

VIVIAN BEAUMONT THEATER
Opened Wednesday, March 5, 1975.*
New York Shakespeare Festival at Lincoln Center (Joseph Papp, Producer) presents:

A DOLL'S HOUSE

By Henrik Ibsen; New Version by Christopher Hampton; Director, Tormod Skagestad; Scenery, Santo Loquasto; Costumes, Theoni V. Aldredge; Lighting, Martin Aronstein; Associate Producer, Bernard Gersten; Choreography, Donald Saddler

CAST

Torvald Helmer	Sam Waterston
Nora, his wife	Liv Ullmann
Mrs. Kristine Linde	Barbara Colby
Dr. Rank	Michael Granger
Nils Krogstad	Barton Heyman
Anne-Marie, the nursemaid	Helen Stenborg
Helene, the maid	Judith Light
Errand Boy	Michael Chambers

The Helmers' Children:

Bob	Gibby Gibson
Emmy	Paula Gibson
Ivar	Wayne Harding

STANDBYS AND UNDERSTUDIES: Nora, Virginia Vestoff; Torvald, Drew Snyder; Rank, Krogstad, James Gallery; Kristine, Zina Jasper; Anne-Marie, Helene, Sloane Shelton

A play in three acts. The action takes place in the Helmers' flat on Christmas Eve, Christmas Day, and the day after Christmas.

General Manager: Robert Kamlot
Company Manager: Patricia Carney
Press: Merle Debuskey, Faith Geer, Sally Campbell
Stage Managers: Barnett Epstein, D. W. Koehler, Michael Chambers

* Closed Apr. 20, 1975 after 54 performances and 14 previews.

Friedman-Abeles Photos

ight: Judith Light, Michael Chambers, Liv Ullmann

Ullmann, Sam Waterston, Barbara Colby Above: Paul
ibson, Gibby Gibson, Wayne Harding, Liv Ullmann

Liv Ullmann, Barton Heyman

MITZI E. NEWHOUSE THEATER
Opened Sunday, May 4, 1975.*
New York Shakespeare Festival Lincoln Center (Joseph Papp, Producer) and Henry Street Settlement's New Federal Theatre (Woodie King, Jr., Producer) present:

THE TAKING OF MISS JANIE

By Ed Bullins; Director, Gilbert Moses; Set Design, Kert Lundell; Costumes, Judy Dearing; Lighting, Richard Nelson; Associate Producer, Bernard Gersten; For Henry Street Settlement: Executive Director, Bertram Beck; Director Arts for Living, Mark Tilley

CAST

Monty	Adeyemi Lythcott
Janie	Hilary Jean Beane
Rick	Kirk Kirksey
Len	Darryl Croxton
Peggy	Robbie McCauley
Sharon	Lin Shaye
Lonnie	Sam McMurray
Flossy	Dianne Oyama Dixon
Mort Silberstein	Robert B. Silver

UNDERSTUDIES: Peggy, Flossy, Shezwae Powell; Monty, Len, Rick, Howard Rollins; Janie, Sharon, Paula Wagner; Lonnie, Mort, David Haskell

A play performed without intermission. The action takes place in the 1960's in California and elsewhere.

General Manager: Robert Kamlot
Manager: Alison Harper
Press: Merle Debuskey, Faith Geer, Sally Campbell
Stage Managers: Osborne Scott, Howard Rollins

* Closed June 15, 1975 after 42 performances and 11 previews. Received 1975 New York Drama Critics Circle Award as Best American Play.

Friedman-Abeles Photos

Robbie McCauley, Dianne Oyama Dixon, Adeyemi Lythcott
Top Left: Dianne Oyama Dixon, Hilary Jean Beane, Adeyemi Lythcott

IVIAN BEAUMONT THEATER
Opened Wednesday, May 7, 1975.*
The New York Shakespeare Festival Lincoln Center (Joseph
Papp, Producer) presents:

LITTLE BLACK SHEEP

By Anthony Scully; Director, Edward Payson Call; Scenery, Da-
d Mitchell; Costumes, Theoni V. Aldredge; Lighting, Martin
ronstein; Associate Producer, Bernard Gersten; Assistant to the
irector, Mary Flynn

CAST

riests of the Society of Jesus:

ather Finley .... Joseph Warren
ck Hassler .... Ken Howard
hnnie Rock .... Edward Grover
nnie Caputo .... Gastone Rossilli
ichael George, A Jesuit Scholastic ... John Christopher Jones
illie Schmidt, the housekeeper .... Stefan Schnabel
ster Mary Charles, a Dominican Nun .... Diane Kagan
enry Morlino, a civil servant .... Pierre Epstein

NDERSTUDIES: Michael, Vinnie, Douglas Jones; Jack, Johnnie,
ill Lyman; Finley, Schmidt, Morlino, Tom Toner

A play in two acts. The action takes place in the Jesuit House of
udy in New Haven, Connecticut in June of 1968.

General Manager: Robert Kamlot
Company Manager: Patricia Carney
Press: Merle Debuskey, Faith Geer, Sally Campbell
Stage Managers: Jason Steven Cohen, John Beven

Closed June 1, 1975 after 33 performances and 14 previews.

Friedman-Abeles Photos

Stefan Schnabel, Joseph Warren, John Christopher
s, Gastone Rossilli, Diane Kagan, Edward Grover,
Howard Right Center: Ken Howard, Diane Kagan

Edward Grover, Pierre Epstein

127

NEW YORK SHAKESPEARE FESTIVAL PUBLIC THEATER

Joseph Papp, Producer
Bernard Gerstein, Associate Producer

PUBLIC THEATER
Opened Friday, June 14, 1974.*
The New York Shakespeare Festival and The Chicago Project present:

NAKED LUNCH

Based on book by William Burroughs; Artistic Director, Don Sanders
* Closed July 14, 1974 after a limited engagement of 15 performances. No other details available.

PUBLIC/LITTLE THEATER
Opened Tuesday, October 15, 1974.*
New York Shakespeare Festival Public Theater (Joseph Papp, Producer) presents The Shaliko Company's production of:

THE MEASURES TAKEN

By Bertolt Brecht; Translated by Eric Bentley; Director, Leonardo Shapiro; Music, Hans Eisler; Pianist, Warren Swenson

CAST

The Control Commission:
Tom Crawley
Susan Topping
Mary Zakrzewski

The Agitators:
Jim Carrington
Chris McCann
Jane Mandel
Jerry Mayer
Press: Merle Debuskey, Bob Ullmann, Norman L. Berman

* Closed Jan. 19, 1975 after 88 performances.

Tom Crawley, Jerry Mayer, Jim Carrington, Chris McCann, Susan Topping in "Measures Taken"

Jane Sanford, Gabriel Dell, Kenneth McMillan, J Dengel in "Where Do We Go from Here?"
(Friedman-Abeles Photo)

PUBLIC/NEWMAN THEATER
Opened Sunday, October 27, 1974.*
The New York Shakespeare Festival Public Theater (Josep Papp, Producer) presents:

WHERE DO WE GO FROM HERE?

By John Ford Noonan; Director, David Margulies; Setting an Costumes, Robert Yodice; Lighting, Roger Morgan; Music, Kin Nurock; Associate Producer, Bernard Gersten; Wardrobe Mistres Alyce Gilbert; Assistant to the Producer, Gail Merrifield; Production Supervisor, Tom Gardner; Technical Director, Mervyn Haine Jr.; Production Associate, Meir Zvi Ribalow; Music Coordinato Herbert Harris

CAST

Remo Weinberger	Gabriel De
Johann Sebastian Fabiani	Jake Deng
Whimsey	Danny DeVi
Corialanus T. O'Shea	Kenneth McMilla
Robert M. Cleery	Charles Parl
Winnifred Winowski	Jane Sanfor
Heather Weinberger	Anna Shal

UNDERSTUDIES: Fabiani, Whimsey, Larry Block; Weinberge O'Shea, Cleery, James Gallery; Winnifred, Heather, Diane Simk

A Farce in two acts. The action takes place at the present tim during mid-December in the living room of a four room apartmei two stories above the streets of a downtown section of Boston, Mas

General Manager: David Black
Press: Merle Debuskey, Norman L. Berman
Stage Managers: Richard S. Viola, John J. D. Sheehan

* Closed Nov. 3, 1974 after 8 performances and 27 previews.

PUBLIC/THE OTHER STAGE
Opened Sunday, November 3, 1974.*
New York Shakespeare Festival Public Theater (Joseph Pap Producer) presents:

SWEET TALK

By Michael Abbensetts; Director, Novella Nelson; Setting, Marj rie Kellogg; Costumes, Mary Warren; Lighting, Victor En Yu Ta Associate Producer, Bernard Gersten

CAST

Al Freeman, Jr.	Garrett Mor
Arthur French	Ellen Park
Anna Horsford	Arlene Quiy

* Closed Nov. 10, 1974 after limited run of 10 performances. I photos available.

PUBLIC THEATER/OTHER STAGE
Opened Tuesday, November 5, 1974.*
The New York Shakespeare Festival Public Theater (Joseph Papp, Producer) presents:

THE LAST DAYS OF BRITISH HONDURAS

By Ronald Tavel; Director, David Schweizer; Setting, Paul Zalon; Costumes, Timothy Miller; Lighting, Ian Calderon; Associate Producer, Bernard Gersten; Wardrobe, Ken Yount; Production Manager, Andrew Mihok; Production Supervisor, Tom Gardner; Technical Director, Mervyn Haines, Jr.; Production Associate, Meir Zvi Ribalow

CAST

Captain Henry	Hannibal Penney
Danyon Paron, Jr.	Stephen Collins
Ah Balam	Marc Vahanian
The Prisoner	Don Blakely
The Amerind	Ray Barry
Lornette Wilson	Lisa Richards
Angel Ruz Covarrubias	Daniel Hedaya
Walter	Frankie Faison
Joseph Austin	Norman Matlock
Dennis Simons	F. M. Kimball
Suzanne	Sheila Gibbs
Charlie	Leroy Lessane

A play in two acts. The action takes place on September 9 and 10, 1970 in British Honduras, C.A.: Stann Creek Town; The Humingbird Forest; Lubaantun, Steps of the Pyramid.

General Manager: David Black
Press: Merle Debuskey, Bob Ullman, Norman L. Berman
Stage Manager: Jack Caputo

* Closed Dec. 15, 1974 after 32 performances.

Friedman-Abeles Photo

Lisa Richards, Stephen Collins in "The Last Days of British Honduras"

PUBLIC/ANSPACHER THEATER
Opened Wednesday, December 4, 1974.*
The New York Shakespeare Festival Public Theater (Joseph Papp, Producer) presents:

IN THE BOOM BOOM ROOM

By David Rabe; Director, Robert Hedley; Setting, David Mitchell; Costumes, Milo Morrow; Lighting, Martin Aronstein; Choreography, Baayork Lee; Associate Producer, Bernard Gersten; Wardrobe, Alyce Gilbert; Sound, David Congdon, Michael Lawrence

CAST

Chrissy	Ellen Greene
Harold	Tom Quinn
Susan	Gwendolyn Brown
Guy	Philip Polito
Eric	Fred Grandy
Sally	Lynn Oliver
Melissa	Patricia Gaul
Vikki	Missie Zollo
Ralphie	David Cromwell
Al	Christopher Lloyd
Helen	Helen Hanft
Rene	Aleta
The Man	Peter Victor
Bar Patrons	Madison Arnold, Ken Kliban, Gloria Lord

UNDERSTUDIES: Sally, Melissa, Vikki, Aleta; Harold, Al, Man, Madison Arnold; Chrissy, Patricia Gaul; Eric, Guy, Ken Kliban; Helen, Gloria Lord; Susan, Lynn Oliver; Ralphie, Peter Victor

A play in two acts. The action takes place in Philadelphia in the mid 1960's.

General Manager: David Black
Press: Merle Debuskey, Bob Ullman, Norman L. Berman
Stage Managers: Ken Glickfeld, Kate Pollock

Closed Dec. 15, 1974 after 32 performances.

Friedman-Abeles Photo

Ellen Greene, Helen Hanft, Tom Quinn in "In the Boom Boom Room"

PUBLIC/MARTINSON HALL
Opened Wednesday, January 8, 1975.*

The New York Shakespeare Festival (Joseph Papp, Producer) presents The Manhattan Project's Production of:

SEA GULL

By Anton Chekhov; Consultant on Translation, Laurence Senelick; Director, Andre Gregory; Producer, Lyn Austin; Set, Ming Cho Lee; Costumes, Nanzi Adzima; Lighting, Victor En Yu Tan

CAST

Irina Nikolayevna Arkadina,
  an actress .... Saskia Noordhoek Hegt
Constantine Gavrilovitch Trepleff, her son .... Larry Pine
Peter Nikolayevitch Sorin, her brother ...... John Ferraro
Nina Zaretchnaya, daughter of a neighbor .. Angela Pietropinto
Shamraev, retired lieutenant, manager
  of Sorin's estate .... John Holms
Paulina, his wife .... Avra Petrides
Masha, his daughter .... Karen Ludwig
Boris Alexeyevitch Trigorin, a writer .... Gerry Bamman
Eugene Sergeyevitch Dorn, a doctor .... Tom Costello
Semyonovitch Medvedenko, a teacher .... David Laden

A Drama in four acts, with two intermissions. The action takes place at Sorin's country estate.

Production Manager: Jeff Hamlin

Opened Thursday, January 9, 1975.*

OUR LATE NIGHT

By Wallace Shawn; Director, Andre Gregory; Producer, Lyn Austin; Set, Douglas W. Schmidt; Costumes, Ara Gallant; Lighting, Victor En Yu Tan

CAST

Gerry Bamman
Tom Costello
John Ferraro
Saskia Noordhoek Hegt
Karen Ludwig
Angela Pietropinto
Larry Pine

Performed without intermission. The action takes place in an apartment high above the city at the present time.

Production Manager: Jeff Hamlin

* Closed Apr. 20, 1975 after 119 performances in repertory. No photos available.

**Christopher Walken, Anna Levine, Matthew Coles
in "Kid Champion"**

(Friedman-Abeles Photo)

PUBLIC/ANSPACHER THEATER
Opened Tuesday, January 28, 1975.*
New York Shakespeare Festival Public Theater (Joseph Papp, Producer) presents:

KID CHAMPION

By Thomas Babe; Director, John Pasquin; Setting, Douglas W. Schmidt; Costumes, Theoni V. Aldredge; Lighting, William Mintzer; Music, Jim Steinman; Lyrics, Thomas Babe, Jim Steinman; Musical Direction and Arrangements, Steven Margoshes; Sound, David Congdon, Bill Dreisbach; Wardrobe, Alyce Gilbert, Kenneth Yount; Associate Producer, Bernard Gersten

CAST

Tom .... Christopher Allport
Lord Jim .... Matthew Cowles
Manager Harvey .... David Margulies
Kid Champion .... Christopher Walken
Zinko .... Don Scardino
Cop .... Anthony Mannino
Stage Manager .... Gene Fanning
Fan .... Tom Happer
Marylou .... Mary Elaine Monti
Devoted Hack Paulie .... Jerry Zaks
Porter .... Flloyd Ennis
Alice .... Anna Levine
Simon L. Renfrew .... Kenneth McMillan
Celebrity .... Patricia Stewart
Photographer .... T. Richard Mason
Groupie .... Shelly Batt
Cop .... T. Richard Mason
Narcs .... Flloyd Ennis, Gene Fanning, Tom Happer
Jill McDill .... Kathryn Walker
Mailboy .... Tom Happer
Woman .... Patricia Stewart
Mom .... Sasha von Scherler

ROADIES, GROUPIES, ETC.: Kevin Geer, Bertina Johnson, Anthony Mannino, Anne O'Sullivan, William Russ, Ilsebet Tebesli

UNDERSTUDIES: Alice, Marylou, Shelly Batt; Renfrew, Harvey, Gene Fanning; Tom, Paul, Tom Happer; Zinko, Lord Jim, T. Richard Mason; Jill, Mom, Patricia Stewart

A play in 2 acts and 12 scenes. The action takes place between late 1969 and Spring of 1970.

General Manager: David Black
Press: Merle Debuskey, Bob Ullman, Norman L. Berman
Stage Managers: Richard S. Viola, Peter von Mayrhauser

* Closed March 9, 1975 after 48 performances.

**David Margulies, Christopher Walken
in "Kid Champion"**

(Friedman-Abeles Photo)

PUBLIC/NEWMAN THEATER

Opened Wednesday, February 12, 1975.*
New York Shakespeare Festival Public Theater (Joseph Papp, Producer) presents:

FISHING

By Michael Weller; Director, Peter Gill; Setting and Costumes, Pat Woodbridge; Lighting, Ian Calderon; Associate Producer, Bernard Gersten; Wardrobe Mistress, Mary Beth Regan

CAST

Robbie	Guy Boyd
Bill	Tom Lee Jones
Shelly	Lindsay Crouse
Rory	Raymond J. Barry
Mary-Ellen	Kathryn Grody
Dane	John Heard
Reilly	Edward Seamon

UNDERSTUDIES: Rory, Bill, Bryan Gordon; Robbie, Dane, Anthony McKay; Mary-Ellen, Shelly, Ellen Sandler; Reilly, Tom Spartley

A play in 2 acts and 4 scenes. The action takes place in 1974 in the Pacific Northwest, in and around Bill and Shelly's cabin.

General Manager: David Black
Press: Merle Debuskey, Bob Ullman, Norman L. Berman
Stage Managers: John Beven, Robert Lowe

* Closed Mar. 2, 1975 after 38 performances.

PUBLIC/THE OTHER STAGE

Opened Sunday, March 16, 1975.*
New York Shakespeare Festival Public Theater (Joseph Papp, Producer) presents:

TIME TRIAL

By Jack Gilhooley; Director, Peter Maloney; Setting, John Pitts; Costumes, Pat McGourty; Lighting, Spencer Mosse; Associate Producer, Bernard Gersten

CAST

Graham Beckel
Robert Burgos
Jayne Haynes
Jeffrey Pomerantz
Ellen Sandler
Diane Stilwell
Tracey Walter

Closed March 23, 1975 after limited run of 10 performances. No photos available.

John Heard, Guy Boyd, Tom Lee Jones, Kathryn Grody, Lindsay Crouse in "Fishing"
(Friedman-Abeles Photo)

John Heard, Tom Lee Jones in "Fishing"
(Friedman-Abeles Photo)

PUBLIC/LITTLE THEATER

Opened Wednesday, April 2, 1975.*
The New York Shakespeare Festival (Joseph Papp, Producer) presents The Shaliko Company's production of:

GHOSTS

By Henrik Ibsen; English Translation by Rolfe Fjelde; Directed by Leonardo Shapiro; Production Design, Jerry Rojo; Costumes, Theodora Skiptares; Production Coordinator, Jim Carrington; Technical Director, Darrell Ziegler; Production Assistants, Michael Mason, Paul Fitzmaurice

CAST

Regina Engstrand	Jane Mandel
Jacob Engstrand	Jerry Mayer
Pastor Manders	Tom Crawley
Mrs. Helen Alving	Mary Zakrzewski
Osvald Alving	Chris McCann

A drama in three acts.

* Closed May 16, 1975 after 37 performances.

Michel Stuart, Donna McKechnie, Carole Bishop,
Thomas J. Walsh, Nancy Lane

PUBLIC/NEWMAN THEATER

Opened Wednesday, May 21, 1975.*
New York Shakespeare Festival Public Theater (Joseph Papp,
Producer) presents:

A CHORUS LINE

Conceived, Choreographed and Directed by Michael Bennett;
Book, James Kirkwood, Nicholas Dante; Music, Marvin Hamlisch;
Lyrics, Edward Kleban; Co-choreographer, Bob Avian; Setting,
Robin Wagner; Costumes, Theoni V. Aldredge; Lighting, Tharon
Musser; Orchestrations, Bill Byers, Hershy Kay, Jonathan Tunick;
Music Coordinator, Robert Thomas; Musical Direction and Vocal
Arrangements, Don Pippin; Associate Producer, Bernard Gersten;
Wardrobe, Alyce Gilbert; Sound, Roger Jay; Production Assistant,
Katherine Talbert

CAST

Roy	Scott Allen
Kristine	Renee Baughman
Sheila	Carole Bishop
Val	Pamela Blair
Mike	Wayne Cilento
Butch	Chuck Cissel
Larry	Clive Clerk
Maggie	Kay Cole
Richie	Ronald Dennis
Tricia	Donna Drake
Tom	Brandt Edwards
Judy	Patricia Garland
Lois	Carolyn Kirsch
Don	Ron Kuhlman
Bebe	Nancy Lane
Connie	Baayork Lee
Diana	Priscilla Lopez
Zach	Robert LuPone
Mark	Cameron Mason
Cassie	Donna McKechnie
Al	Don Percassi
Frank	Michael Serrecchia
Greg	Michel Stuart
Bobby	Thomas J. Walsh
Paul	Sammy Williams
Vicki	Crissy Wilzak

UNDERSTUDIES: Alan, Scott Allen; Paul, Richie, Chuck Cissel;
Kristine, Connie, Maggie, Donna Drake; Don, Mark, Brandt Edwards; Cassie, Sheila, Carolyn Kirsch; Mike, Don Percassi; Diana,
Judy Bebe, Carole Schweid; Larry, Greg, Bobby, Michael Serrecchia; Val, Judy, Crissy Wilzak

MUSICAL NUMBERS: "I Hope I Get It," "Joanne," "And . . .,"
"At the Ballet," "Sing!," "Hello 12, Hello 13, Hello Love," "Nothing," "Dance: Ten, Looks: Three," "The Music and the Mirror,"
"One," "The Tap Combination," "What I Did for Love"

A Musical performed without intermission. The action takes place
at the present time at an audition for a musical.

General Manager: David Black
Press: Merle Debuskey, Bob Ullman, Norman L. Berman
Stage Managers: Jeff Hamlin, Frank Hartenstein

* Closed July 13, 1975 after 101 performances to move to Broadway
Friday, July 25, 1975. Cited by NY Drama Critics Circle as Best
Musical of the season.

Martha Swope Photos

**Top Left: Donna McKechnie, Robert LuPone Below
Michel Stuart, Donna McKechnie, Carole Bishop
Thomas J. Walsh, Nancy Lane, Patricia Garland
Ronald Dennis, Don Percassi, Renee Baughman
Pamela Blair, Cameron Mason, Sammy Williams
Priscilla Lopez**

Kay Cole, Sammy Williams, Pamela Blair, Michel Stuart, Nancy Lane, Cameron Mason, Renee Baughman, Ron Kuhlman, Donna McKechnie, Thomas J. Walsh, Patricia Garland, Don Percassi, Ronald Dennis, Priscilla Lopez, Above: Pamela Blair, Donna McKechnie, Robert LuPone, Top: Priscilla Lopez, Sammy Williams

OCTAGON: THE AMERICAN MUSICAL THEATRE COMPANY

Joseph Lillis, Producer
Donald Oliver, Artistic Director

BERT WHEELER THEATRE
June 21–30, 1974
(12 performances)
A FUNNY THING HAPPENED ON THE WAY TO THE FORUM with Music and Lyrics by Stephen Sondheim; Book, Burt Shevelove, Larry Gelbart; Staged by Joseph Lillis; Musical Direction, Toni Hoffman; Costumes, Jill Peterson, Louis DeSimone; Scenic Design, Marc Surver. CAST: James Gallagher (Pseudolus), Michael Brown (Hysterium), David Korkov (Hero), Michelle Rosenberg (Philia), Peter Turcin (Senex), Rochelle Sporn (Domina), Tony Reilly (Miles), Karen Magid, Stuart Zagnit, Natalia Chuma, Helene Leonard, Joanne Baron, Mindy Levy, Liesl Tribble, Cliff Watters, Frank Juliano, Philip Jostrom
July 5–14, 1974
(11 performances)
THE APPLE TREE with Book by Jerry Bock, Sheldon Harnick, Jerome Coopersmith; Music, Jerry Bock; Lyrics, Sheldon Harnick; Directed and Choreographed by Michael Brown; Musical Direction, Toni Hoffman; Costumes, Jill Peterson; Scenery, Michael Brown. CAST: Frank Juliano (Adam), Arlene Miller (Eve), Mary Boyer (Snake), Rochelle Sporn (Barbara), Tony Reilly (Sanjar), Stephen Dunne (King Arik), Dudley Layne (Balladeer), Philip Jostrom, Laurie Dunlap, Joanne Baron (Passionella), Daniel Gerrity (Flip)
July 17–21, 1974
(5 workshop performances)
ANYONE CAN WHISTLE with Book by Arthur Laurents; Music and Lyrics, Stephen Sondheim; Director-Choreographer, Joseph Lillis; Musical Direction, John J. Gaughan, Jr.; Scenery, Marc Surver; Costumes, Jill Peterson. CAST: Karen Magid (Cora), James Gallagher (Schub), Philip Jostrom (Cooley), Robert Polenz (Magruder), Barbara Hartman (Fay Apple), Leslie Minski (Hapgood), Cliff Watters, Bill Hedge, Ann Jarrell, Jolly King, Fred Edwards, Toni Hoffman, Pat Lacurrubba, Natalia Chuma, Ann Williams, Deborah Magid, Diane Duncan, Linda Megale, Stanley Carr, Cynthia Wilson
July 24–26, 1974
(3 performances)
POT LUCK: a musical revue conceived by Joseph Lillis. CAST: identical to "Anyone Can Whistle"
August 14–September 15, 1974
(25 performances)
110 IN THE SHADE with Book by N. Richard Nash; Music, Harvey Schmidt; Lyrics, Tom Jones; Director, Leslie Magerman; Choreographer, Diane Duncan; Design, Ken Sansone, Beverly Gross; Stage Manager, Christopher Baker. CAST: Jon Winder, Marty Algaze, Leslie Minski (File), James Gallagher (H. C.) Bill Hedge (Noah), Cliff Watters/Scott Farrell (Jimmy), Barbara Hartman (Lizzie), Daniel Gerrity (Starbuck), Ann Jarrell (Snookie), Natalia Chuma, Diane Duncan, Robin Jacober, Lester Johnson, Ross Ronson, Ann Williams
September 27–October 6, 1974
(4 performances)
THE APPLE TREE (New Production) Book, Jerry Bock, Sheldon Harnick, Jerome Coopersmith; Music, Jerry Bock; Lyrics, Sheldon Harnick; Entire Production Supervised by Joseph Lillis; "Diary of Adam and Eve" directed by Ira Schlosser; Costumes, Aileen Kinney; Scenery, Marc Surver; Lighting, Bill Parry. CAST: John Aller (Adam), Robin Jacober (Eve), Daniel Gerrity/Lenore Vincent (Snake), John Medford (God), Ann Williams/Lenore Vincent (Barbara), Daniel Gerrity/Bill Baron (Sanjar), David Rambo (King Arik), Scott Farrell (Balladeer), Richard Beck-Meyer, Joanne Baron (Passionella), John Aller (Flip), Stanley Carr, David Goldberg
October 14–November 13, 1974
(24 performances)
DRAT! THE CAT! Book and Lyrics, Ira Levin; Music, Milton Schafer; Director-Choreographer, Joseph Lillis; Musical Director, Donald Oliver; Assistant to the Director, Christopher Baker; Scenery, Marc Surver; Costumes, Richard Gaines. CAST: Lenore Vincent (Alice), John Aller (Bob), Alan Abrams ("Bulldog"/Lucius), Marilyn Robbins/Barbara Hartman (Matilda), Stanley Carr, Philip Jostrom, Ed Prostak, Joanne Kaplan, Robin Jacober, Audrey Lavine, Gary Krasny, Richard Beck-Meyer, Bill Baron, David Rambo, Anne Shaheen, Kathleen Smith, John Medford, Robert Haggerty, Davi Loren, Deirdre Tinker, Deborah Salem

John Aller, Lenore Vincent in "Drat! The Cat
(Nancy Gray Photo)

BERT WHEELER THEATRE
November 8–16, 1974
(4 performances)
PARK with Book and Lyrics by Paul Cherry; Music, Lance M cahy; Director, Anthony Baksa; Associate Producer, Christop Baker; Choreography, Diane Jerger; Musical Director, Leon Ode Scenery, Stephen Laurier Weagle; Lighting, Mimi Jordan; Pr Michael Shepley. CAST: Michael Bahr, Reed Birney, Larry Sta Irene Frances Kling, Gloria Lambert, Diane Jerger
November 20–December 8, 1974
(12 performances)
ZORBA with Book by Joseph Stein; Music, John Kander; Ly Fred Ebb; Director-Choreographer, Robert Nigro; Musical Di tion, Roger Anderson; Lighting, Linda Schulz; Press, Rich Kornberg. CAST: Jim Pappas (Zorba), Mary Rocco (Horten Lauren White (Leader), Lenore Vincent (Widow), Richard Lohr (Nikos), Alan Abrams, Eddie Barnes, Dan Enright, Kathy Ha Ken Kantor, Steven Laurier, Mara Mellin, Anne Shaheen, Rich Grady, Charles Ryan, Davia Sacks
December 13–14, 1974
(2 performances)
KABARETT An American Experience in the European tradi Written and Composed by Herbert Nelson; Production Assista Linda Schulz, Richard Beck-Meyer. CAST: Eva Nelson, Hert Nelson
December 19–29, 1974
(8 performances)
THE SURVIVAL OF ST. JOAN with Book and Lyrics by Jar Lineberger; Music, Hank and Gary Ruffin; Director-Choreograph Ray Miller; Musical Direction, Richard DaMone; Scenery, G Langley; Costumes, Tom McKinley; Lighting, Jesse Ira Berger; G tar, Gary Hermes; Press, Richard Kornberg. CAST: Naomi Ro (Joan), Vicki Bennett, Clancy Cherry, Greg Macosko, Michael V liamson, Michael More, Michael Penna, David Rambo
January 10–19, 1975
(4 performances)
THE RAY MILLER MIME SHOW—Devised and Directed Ray Miller; Stage Manager, Clancy Cherry. CAST: Ray Mil David Rambo
January 19–26, 1975
(8 performances and 4 previews)
KNICKERBOCKER HOLIDAY with Book and Lyrics by M well Anderson; Music, Kurt Weill; Director, Dallas Alinder; M cal Director, Uel Wade; Choreographer, Edie Cowan; Associ Producer, Donald Oliver; Scenery, Patricia Van Brandenstein; C tumes, Robert Joel Schwartz; Lighting, Eugene Lowery; Stage M agers, Doug Laidlaw, David Seminon; Press, Richard Kornbe Casting, Edmund Gaynes, Pamela Hall. CAST: Alexander Orf (Pieter Stuyvesant), Christine Andreas (Tina), John Almberg (Br Broeck), Richard Niles (Washington Irving), Douglas Fisher (Ti hoven), Lou Bullock, Tony Scaddia, John O'Creagh, Tom Smink Betty Wragge, Valerie Genise, Martha Jean Sterner, Cynthia We Jean Andalman, Barbara Niles, David Vogel, John Welsh, J. Ri ard Beneville, Otto Walberg, David Tillman, Michael Walker, J Kramer, Larry Rosler, Ted Theoharous

BERT WHEELER THEATRE

February 6–15, 1975
(11 performances)

HOLLYWOOD HATTIE AND HER CELLULOID DREAM—Conceived, Directed and Choreographed by Jack Dyville; Musical Direction, John J. Gaughan, Jr. CAST: Wanda Drew (Hattie), Michael Petro (Harry), Joseph Tripolino (Harold), Noreen Bartolomeo (Hollie), Gregg Weiler (Harvey)

February 18–March 9, 1975
(12 performances)

110 IN THE SHADE (New Production) Book, N. Richard Nash; Music, Harvey Schmidt; Lyrics, Tom Jones; Director, Albert Harris; Choreographer, Richard Casper; Musical Director, Donald Mannon; Scenic Consultant, Margaret Tobin; Costumes, Michael Massee; Lighting, Harmon Leste; Press, Richard Kornberg. CAST: Robert Dennison (File), David Vogel (H. C.), Alan Gruet (Noah), Michael Bruck (Jimmy), Livia Genise (Snookie), Barbara Hartman (Lizzie), Scott Stevenson (Starbuck), Terry Jablonski, Valerie Genise, Richard Casper, Ed Koury, Don Eike, Carolann Mary, Elizabeth Usher

February 19–March 9, 1975
(12 performances)

TURKEY SALAD—Conceived and Directed by John Weeks; Choreographer, Rick Atwell; Costumes, Gussie Watson; Musical Supervision, Lawrence J. Blank; Stage Manager, Richard Beck-Meyer. CAST: Rick Atwell, Joan Bell, Ronn Hansen, Ross Petty, Thea Ramsey, Marsha Warner

March 25–April 12, 1975
(12 performances)

THE KANDER AND EBB COLORING BOOK—Conceived and Directed by Joseph Lillis; Musical Director, Rick Cummins; On-Stage Artwork, Richard Beck-Meyer; Press, Richard Kornberg. CAST: Christopher Carroll, Carolann Mary, Timothy Staton, Sandra Wheeler, Barbara Hartman

March 25–April 9, 1975
(12 performances)

TURKEY SALAD RETOSSED—Conceived and Directed by John Weeks; Musical Direction, Ian Herman; Choreographer, Rick Atwell. CAST: Rick Atwell, Joan Bell, Richard Casper, Ronn Hansen, Thea Ramsey, Marsha Warner

March 28–April 19, 1975
(12 performances)

THE HAPPY TIME with Book by N. Richard Nash; Music, John Kander; Lyrics, Fred Ebb; Director, J. Perry MacDonald; Musical Director, Rita McNally/Donald Oliver; Choreographer, Terpsie Toon. CAST: Ross Petty (Jacques), David Rambo (Bibi), Richard Broadhurst (Philippe), Betty Bennett (Felice), Lois Saunders (Suzanne), J. R. Horne/Alex Molina (Louis), Susan Koch, Thomas Guisinger (Grandpere), Shelley Wyant, Nita Michaels, Kelly O'Brien, Nancy Frangione (Laurie), Eddie Dudek, Richard Beck-Meyer, Don Johanson, Kenny Branch, Roger Spear

May 30–31, 1975
(2 performances)

THE TERI RALSTON SHOW—Musical Director, Shelley Markham; Scenic Design, Marc Surver; Stage Manager, Michael McMahon; Press, Richard Kornberg. CAST: Teri Ralston, Shelley Markham, John Miller

PHOENIX SIDESHOWS

T. Edward Hambleton, Managing Director

PLAYHOUSE II

January 23–26, 1975
(6 performances)

KNUCKLE by David Hare; Director, Daniel Freudenberger; Scenery and Lighting, James Tilton: Costumes, Clifford Capone; Musical Arrangements, Joe Castellon; Stage Manager, Margaret Ransom. CAST: Kitty Winn (Jenny), Frederick Major (Barman), Perry King (Curly), Jacqueline Brookes (Grace), Humbert Allen Astredo (Patrick), Joseph Lambie (Max)

February 6–9, 1975
(6 performances)

DANDELION WINE by Ray Bradbury; Adapted by Peter John Bailey; Director, William Woodman; Lighting, Ken Billington; Costumes, Lee Austin; Stage Managers, Linda Laundra, Munson Hicks. CAST: Matthew Anton (Douglas), Doug McKeon (Tom), Andrew Tolan (John), Michael Miller (Father), Charles White (Grandfather), Jo Henderson (Lena), Deirdre Owens (Helen), Bill McCutcheon (Colonel), Eleanor Wilson (Helen)

April 24–27, 1975
(6 performances)

MEETING PLACE by Robert Lord; Director, Michael Montel; Lighting, David F. Segal; Costumes, Donna Jo Sontheimer; Stage Manager, Margaret Ransom. CAST: Linda Carlson, Munson Hicks, Sarah Saltus, Charles Tenney

May 8–11, 1975
(6 performances)

MACRUNE'S GUEVARA by John Spurling; Director, Daniel Freudenberger; Scenery and Lighting, James Tilton; Music, Joe Castellon; Choreography, Francis Patrelle; Stage Manager, Margaret Ransom. CAST: Christopher Allport, Christine Baranski, Donny Burks, James Greene, Jennifer Harmon, Joseph Lamie, Mark Metcalf, Franklyn Seales, Tucker Smallwood

May 22–27, 1975
(6 performances)

FLUX by Susan Miller; Director, Michael Montel; Lighting, Ken Billington; Costumes, Donna Jo Sontheimer; Stage Manager, Elisabeth W. Seley. CAST: Naola Adair, Peter Alzado, Nedra Deen, Mary Elaine Monti, Thomas A. Stewart, Kathleen Tolan, Michael Wager

Alexander Orfaly in "Knickerbocker Holiday"
Right Center: Perry King, Kitty Winn in "Knuckle"

Joseph Lambie, Franklyn Seales, Christopher Allport in "MacRune's Guevara"

135

PLAYWRIGHTS HORIZONS

Robert Moss, Executive Director

Production Coordinator, Kathleen Chalfant; Press, Joan Lowell; Technical Director, Charles Tyndall; Technical Consultant, Jon Knudsen; Music Consultant, Jeremiah Murray; Fund Raising, Alvin T. Kraizer; Librarian, Louisa Anderson

PLAYWRIGHTS HORIZONS

June 19–29, 1974
(11 performances)
COWBOY PICTURES by Larry Ketron; Director, Robert Moss; Sets, Marty Henderson; Lighting, Jeff Miller; Stage Manager, David Rosenberg. CAST: Kathleen Chalfant, Lowell Gottstein, David Himes, Charles McCaughan, Keith McDermott, Susan Sullivan, Douglas Travis

January 30–February 4, 1975
(6 performances)
CARCASS CHROME by Dennis E. Hackin; Directed by Mr. Hackin; Sets, Chris Gregson; Lighting, Jeff Miller; Costumes, Liz Wood; Stage Managers, Chris Gregson, Steve Ivester. CAST: Peter Alzado, Max Braverman, Ed Clein, Mitchell Cohen, J. Victor Lopez, Willard Morgan, Andrew Potter, Susan Rosenthal, Jonathan Segal, Jill Skaist, Barbara Slone, Rebecca Westberg

February 15–22, 1975
(10 performances)
THE FIRST WEEK IN BOGOTA by Robert Cessna; Director, Charles Maryan; Set, Steve Duffy; Lighting, Jon Knudsen; Costumes, Brent J. Porter; Stage Managers, Michael Heaton, Carl Cohen. CAST: Peter Alzado, Virginia Downing, Cyprienne Gabel, Peter Simpson, JoAnne Sedwick, Casey Walters

March 1–8, 1975
(8 performances)
MISSION by Len Jenkin; Director, Leland Moss; Music, Michael Levenson; Lighting, Marilyn Rennagel; Costumes, Susan Denison; Set, Dan Leigh; Stage Manager, Robert Tomlin. CAST: Mary Carter, Jayne Haynes, Leland Moss, Marilyn Redfield, John Ross, Sheila Russell, Ron Van Lieu, Jamil Zakkai

March 7–9, 1975
(4 performances)
AUGUSTA by Larry Ketron; Director, David Black; Assistant Director, Ali Jones; Costumes, Felipe Gorostiza; Set, Robert Franklyn; Lighting, Jeff Miller; Stage Managers, Merrie Handfinger, Kristin Jolliff. CAST: Kenneth Harvey, Faith Catlin, Jeffrey DeMunn, Elizabeth Franz, Mark Curran, Renee Orin

March 15–22, 1975
(10 performances)
AN EVENING WITH MA BELL by Tony Giordano; Director, Joseph R. Cali; Set, Sandi Marks; Lighting, David Kissel; Costumes, Lorri Schneider; Stage Manager, Joseph Kavanagh, Jim Swaine. CAST: Scotty Bloch, John Clarkson, Margaret Gwenver, Christine Lavren, David McCarver, Donald Silva

Kathleen Chalfant, David Himes, Keith McDermott, Su Sullivan, Douglas Travis, (rear) Lowell Gottstein, Chuc McCaughan, Harlan Cary Poe in "Cowboy Pictures"

Cyprienne Gabel, Peter Alzado, Peter Simpson, Cas Walters, Virginia Downing in "First Week in Bogot

PLAYWRIGHTS HORIZONS

March 21–23, 1975
(4 performances)
THE EDSEL WAS A MISTAKE by Paul Hodes; Director, Rober Lowe; Set, Lon Kaufman; Lighting, David Kissel; Stage Manage Georgia Fleenor. CAST: Bill Conway, Kristin Jolliff, Peter Johl, Te Kubiak, Oliver Malcolmson, Parker McCormick, Sharon Talbot

March 29–April 5, 1975
(8 performances)
RHINEGOLD by Barry Keating, Jim Steinman; Music, Jim Stein man; Lyrics, Barry Keating; Direction and Choreography, Barr Keating; Musical Direction, Jez Davidson; Costumes, Bosha Joh son; Set, Calvin Churchman; Lighting, Jim Chaleff; Stage Manage Joel Brehm. CAST: Johanna Albrecht, George Ayer, Alan Brau stein, Sarah Harris, Mary Hendrickson, Pat Lavelle, Lester Maliz Howard Meadow, Edwin Owens, Ellen Parks, Chuck Richie, Ti Sheahan, Frank Thompson, Ron Van Lieu

April 4–6, 1975
(4 performances)
DEMONS: A POSSESSION by Robert Karmon; Director, Dav Darlow; Stage Manager, Ellen Raphael. CAST: Jim Campbell, B Cortes, Linda Carlson, Elizabeth Jones, Fred Major, Douglas Sta

April 12–19, 1975
(12 performances)
THE CORONER'S PLOT by David Shumaker; Director, Alfr Gingold; Set, Richard B. Williams; Costumes, David Murin; Ligh ing, Jeff Miller; Stage Manager, Judy Goldstein. CAST: Marga Ann Bauer, Kathleen Chalfant, Bruce Detrick, Carole Doshc Ronald Hale, Jayne Haynes, Alice Elliott, Jen Jones, Keith McD mott, Alex Reed, Patricia Richardson, H. Frederick Wessler, R ald Willoughby

April 18–20, 1975
(4 performances)
CASSEROLE by Jack Heifner; Director, Garland Wright; C tumes, David James; Set, Jemimah; Lighting, Jeff Miller; Stage M ager, Andy Lopata. CAST: John Arnone, Kathy Bates, Patri Callahan, Richard Casper, Celia Howard, Martha Miller, Gene N Tom Rodman

Edwin Owens, Pat Lavelle, Ellen Parks, Frank Thompson, Timothy Sheahan in "Rhinegold"

Nathaniel Tileston Photos

136

PLAYWRIGHTS HORIZONS

April 26–May 3, 1975
(10 performances)
NEW YORK! NEW YORK! by Dennis Andersen, David Epstein, Allan Knee, Philip Magdalany, Kenneth Pressman, Steven Shea, Marsha Sheiness, Martin Sherman; Directors, Michael Posnick, Russell Treyz, Robert Moss, Caymichael Patten, Joseph R. Cali; Producers, Dennis Andersen, Alice Elliott; Lighting, Jon Knudsen; Costumes, Jody Berke; Stage Managers, Georgia Fleenor, Jim Swaine, Joseph Kavanagh. CAST: Sudie Bond, Maria Cellario, Dana Gladstone, Barbara Lee Govan, Kristin Jolliff, Jeffrey Kramer, Roy London, Mitchell McGuire, Linda Robbins, Timothy Sheahan

May 2–4, 1975
(4 performances)
THE CATCH by Philip Valcour; Director, Jonathan Alper; Stage Manager, Roy DeNunzio. CAST: Douglas Travis, Richard Greene, George Ayer, Frances McCaffrey, Kay Michaels, John Gould Rubin, Bob Lawrence, Jong Stein, Cam Kornman

May 10–17, 1975
(8 performances)
BRAIN DAMAGE by Steven Shea; Director, Paul Cooper; Set, Ilse Kritzler; Lighting, Jeremy Lewis; Stage Managers, Robert Tomlin, Christie Heiss. CAST: Alan Rosenberg, Leland Moss, Charles Harper, Marilyn Redfield, Rosemary Quinn

May 15–18, 1975
(6 performances)
I REMEMBER THE HOUSE WHERE I WAS BORN by Dennis Andersen; Director, Susan Einhorn; Set and Costumes, Christina Weppner; Lighting, Jeremy Lewis; Stage Managers, Lillah McCarthy, Bill Phillips. CAST: George Hall, Margaret Gwenver, Peter Bartlett, Rose Lischner, Mary Frances Walsh, Daniel Pollack, Alan Jordan, Carolyn Cope

May 24–31, 1975
(8 performances)
BEETHOVEN/KARL by David Rush; Director, Edward M. Cohen; Set, Calvin Churchman; Costumes, Susan Sudert; Lighting, Joel Cartiglia; Stage Manager, Andy Lopata. CAST: Charles Carshon, Rosemary DeAngelis, Peter Johl, Tom Leo, Keith McDermott, F. William Parker, Grace Roberts, Martha Schlamme, Fred Wolinsky

May 30–June 1, 1975
(4 performances)
LEANDER STILLWELL based on a play by David Rush; Director, Joseph Kavanagh; Choreography, John Scoullar; Music, Marc Dorfmann; Sung by Johanna Gallo; Stage Manager, Cathy Rennich. CAST: George Ayer, Bill Barrett, Marianne Chick, Joseph Kavanagh, Anita Khanzadian, Joseph Ostopak, Preston Pryor, Stanleigh Williams

Nathaniel Tileston Photos

Right: Mitchell McGuire, Linda Robbins, Barbara Lee GoVan, Dana Gladstone, Sudie Bond, Jeffrey Kramer, Roy London, Maria Cellario, Timothy Sheahan, Kristin Jolliff in "New York! New York!"
Above: Martha Schlamme, Charles Carshon, Keith McDermott in "Beethoven/Karl"

Carolyn Cope, Peter Bartlett, Mary Frances Walsh, D
Pollack, George Hall, Rose Lischner, Margaret Gwen
Alan Jordan in "I Remember the House Where I Was

ene Nye, Martha Miller, Thomas Rodman, Richard Caspar,
ohn Arnone, Kathy Bates, Patricia Callahan, Celia Howard
in "Casserole"

Leland Moss, Charles Harper, Marilyn Redfie
Alan Rosenberg in "Brain Damage" 1

PORTFOLIO STUDIO

Tom Jones and Harvey Schmidt, Producing Directors

PORTFOLIO STUDIO
Opened Friday, December 6, 1974.*
Tom Jones and Harvey Schmidt present:

PORTFOLIO REVUE

Words, Tom Jones; Music, Harvey Schmidt; Costumes, Charles Blackburn; Musical Staging, Janet Kerr; Producers, Drew Katzman, John Schak

CAST
David Cryer
Tom Jones
Jeanne Lucas
Harvey Schmidt
Kathrin King Segal

A Musical Revue in two acts.

Press: David Powers

Closed Dec. 29, 1974 after limited engagement of 12 performances.

Robert Alan Gold Photo

Tom Jones, Kathrin King Segal, David Cryer, Jeanne Lucas, Harvey Schmidt in "Portfolio Revue"

PORTFOLIO STUDIO
Opened Friday, January 3, 1975.*
Portfolio Productions presents:

PHILEMON

Words by Tom Jones; Music by Harvey Schmidt; Staging, Lester Collins (Harvey Schmidt); Musical Direction, Ken Collins (Tom Jones); Costumes, Charles Blackburn; Keyboard, guitar, Ken Collins; Percussion, French horn, Bill Grossman; Keyboard, Recorder, Penna Rose; Musical Staging, Janet Kerr

CAST
Andos .... Michael Glenn-Smith
Marsyas .... Virginia Gregory
Servillus .... Charles Blackburn†
Cockian .... Dick Latessa
The Wife .... Leila Martin
The Commander .... Howard Ross
Kiki .... Kathrin King Segal

A Musical in two acts. The action takes place in Antioch in 287 A.D.

Company Manager: Bob MacDonald
Press: David Powers
Stage Manager: Janet Watson

* Closed Jan. 26, 1975 after limited engagement of 12 performances. Re-opened Tuesday, Apr. 8, 1975 and closed May 18, 1975 after 48 additional performances.
† Succeeded by Drew Katzman

Dick Latessa, Leila Martin Above: Latessa, Charles Blackburn, Howard Ross in "Philemon"

Robert Alan Gold Photo

PORTFOLIO STUDIO

Opened Friday, January 31, 1975.*

Portfolio Productions presents:

CELEBRATION

Words, Tom Jones; Music, Harvey Schmidt; Direction and Choreography, Vernon Lusby; Musical Direction, Ken Collins; Production Design, Ed Wittstein; Additional Costumes, Charles Blackburn; Assistant Director, Janet Kerr; Producers, Drew Katzman, John Schak

CAST

Potemkin	Gene Foote
The Boy	Michael Glenn-Smith
Angel	Virginia Gregory
Rich	Ted Thurston
Revelers	Bruce Cryer, James Dahlman, Doreen Dunn, Deborah Gordon, Melanie Kinnaman, Nick Munson, Jacqueline Reilly, Charles Whiteside

A Musical in two acts.

Press: David Powers

* Closed Feb. 23, 1975 after limited engagement of 12 performances.

Robert Alan Gold Photos

Top Right: Doreen Dunn, Virginia Gregory, Jacqueline Reilly   Below: Ted Thurston, Michael Glenn-Smith in "Celebration"

ohn Cunningham, Susan Watson Above: Cunningham, Ray Stewart, Watson in "The Bone Room"

PORTFOLIO STUDIO

Opened Friday, February 28, 1975.*

Portfolio Productions present:

THE BONE ROOM

A work in progress; Words, Tom Jones; Music, Harvey Schmidt; Director, John Schak; Choreography, Janet Kerr; Musical Direction, Ken Collins; Costumes, Charles Blackburn; Producers, Drew Katzman, John Schak

CAST

Male Lecturer	John Cunningham
Smith	Ray Stewart
Female Lecturer	Susan Watson

A play performed without intermission.

Press: David Powers

* Closed Mar. 23, 1975 after limited engagement of 12 performances.

PUERTO RICAN TRAVELING THEATRE

Miriam Colon, Founder/Executive Director

XPERIMENTAL LABORATORY
Opened Thursday, June 6, 1974.*
The Puerto Rican Traveling Theatre presents:

SCRIBBLES/THE INNOCENT/THE GUEST

By Pedro Juan Soto; Director, Reinaldo Arana; Set Designer, nibal Otero; Costumes, Benito G. Soto; Lighting, Larry Johnson; ssistant Directors, Lui Marquez, Guillermo Rosales; Producer, iriam Colon

CAST

icribbles" translated by Victoria Ortiz; Adapted by Miriam Colon
raciela .... Olga Mercedes Molina
osendo .... Ricardo Matamoros
ino I .... Andrew Rodriguez
ino II .... Mario Laboy
luchacho .... Julio Abinader

The Innocent" translated by Carlos Hortas, Suzanne Jill Levine; Adapted by Miriam Colon

ipe .... Ricardo Matamoros
ladre .... Iraida Polanco
lortensia .... Elizabeth Soto

The Guest" translated by Jeannie Hutchins

ictoria .... Iraida Polanco
ucia .... Olga Mercedes Molina
rma .... Elizabeth Soto
)ona Antonia .... Fini Moreno
adre .... Edelmiro Borras or Guillermo Rosales
lombre (comprador) .... Eduardo Corbe

The action of the plays takes place at the present time in New 'ork City.

Company Manager: Steve Miller Associates
Press: Alan Eichler, Marilyn Percy

Presented in Spanish and English. Closed July 1, 1974 after 28 performances.

**Ricardo Matamoros, Olga Mercedes Molina
in "Scribbles"**
(Robert Percy Photo)

PUERTO RICAN TRAVELING THEATRE
Opened Tuesday, August 6, 1974.*
The Puerto Rican Traveling Theatre (Miriam Colon, Executive Director) presents:

PAYMENT AS PLEDGED

By Alfredo Dias Gomes; Translated by Oscar Fernandez; Director, Angel F. Rivera; Choreography, Mercedes Batista; Set, Peter Harvey; Lighting, Beverly Emmons; Costumes, Maria Ferreira; Administrator, Allen Davis III; Producer, Miriam Colon; Technical Director, Michael Cummings; Production Consultant, Charles Creasap; Production Assistant, Herb Sevush; Assistant to the Producer, Jorge Gonzalez; Props and Costumes, Lauren Barnes; Sound, Gary Harris

CAST

Joe Burro .... Luis Avalos
Rosa .... Ilka Tanya Payan
Marli .... Doris De Mendez
Pretty Boy .... Tony Diaz
Priest .... J. Zakkai
Policeman .... Art Vasil
Galician .... Larry Ramos
Reporter .... Shelly Desai
Photographer .... Lui Marquez
Ray-the-Rimer .... Milo Timmons
Secret Police Agent .... Luis Montalvo
Police Commissioner/Monsignor .... Kurt Garfield

TOWNSPEOPLE, ETC.: William Barnes, Tuika Lagos, Pamela Roach, Terry Marshall-Stephen, Felix Ayer, Louis Cantres, Tony Negroni, Abigail De Lamadrid, Hugo Lan, Naomi Francis, Manuel Ramos

The action takes place at the present time in the square of a town in Northern Brazil.

Press: Alan Eichler, Marilyn Percy
Stage Managers: Paul Wyatt Davis, Allen Davis III

* Closed Aug. 25, 1974 after limited run of 18 performances at city parks and playgrounds.

**Ilka Tanya Payan, Luis Avalos
in "Payment as Pledged"**

PUERTO RICAN TRAVELING THEATRE
Opened Wednesday, February 12, 1975.*
The Puerto Rican Traveling Theatre (Miriam Colon, Executive
Director) presents:

TWO BY FERNANDO ARRABAL

Translations from French to English, Phil James; from French to
Spanish, Nelly Vivas, Miriam Colon, Jaime Sanchez; Set Design,
John Branon; Lighting, Larry Shields; Costumes, Maria Ferreira

CAST

"The Two Executioners"
Director, Norberto Kerner

Frances	Ilka Tanya Payan
Ben	Jose Vega
Maurice	Jose Rodriguez
John, the father	Guillermo Rosales
Executioners	Nelson Landrieu, Caonabo Matias Brito

"Ceremony for an Assassinated Black Man"
Director, Miriam Colon

Geronimo	Norberto Kerner
Vicente	James Victor
Francisco	Phil Saunders
Lucy	Ada Rodriguez
Corpse	Jose Pacheco
Neighbors	Tony Farro, Caonabo Matias Brito, Jose Pacheco

Company Manager: Steve Miller
Press: Alan Eichler, Marilyn Percy
Stage Manager: Michael Schaefer

* Closed March 16, 1975 after limited run of 20 performances, in
English and Spanish.

Ken Howard Photos

**Right: James Victor, Norberto Kerner in "Ceremony for
an Assassinated Black Man" Above: Ilka Tanya Payan,
Jose Vega, Jose Rodriguez in "Two Executioners"**

PUERTO RICAN TRAVELLING THEATRE LAB
Opened Thursday, April 17, 1975.*
The Puerto Rican Traveling Theatre (Miriam Colon, Executi
Director) presents:

PIRI, PABLO AND PEDRO

Director, Pablo Cabrera; Producer, Miriam Colon

CAST

Piri Thomas
Jesus Papoleto Melendez
Pedro Pietri
Mila Conway
Sandra Gallardo
Carla Pinza
Jose Rodriguez
Jose Vega

The poetry of Piri Thomas, Jesus Papoleto Melendez, and Pedr
Pietri interpreted by the poets.

Press: Alan Eichler, Marilyn Percy

* Closed May 4, 1975 after limited engagement of 12 performances

**eated: Jesus Papoleto Melendez, Piri Thomas, Pedro Pietri
standing: Jose Vega, Mila Conway, Carla Pinza, Jose
Rodriguez, Pablo Cabrera**

QUEENS PLAYHOUSE

Joseph S. Kutrzeba, Producer

QUEENS PLAYHOUSE
Opened Saturday, May 25, 1974.*
Queens Playhouse presents:

THE AMOROUS FLEA

Book, Jerry Devine; Based on Moliere's play "School for Wives"; Music and Lyrics, Bruce Montgomery; Staged by Clinton Atkinson; Musical Direction, Leslie Harnley; Designed by John Lee Beatty; Lighting and Costumes, Lee Watson; Assistant to the Producer, Barbara Darwall; Technical Directors, John Sheehan, Tom Negelow; Technicians, Kenneth Hahn, Charles Tyndall; Wardrobe Mistress, Maria K. Schweppe; Production Assistants, Bob Eberle, Dean Garfinkel, Larry Kolodny, Jesse Levy, Scarlett Sabo, Karen Varcchio

CAST

Arnolphe .... John High
Chrysalde .... Ed Preble
Alain .... Arthur Anderson
Georgette .... Patti Allison
Agnes .... Ann Hodapp
Horace .... Gary Brubach
Oronte .... Alan Brasington
Enrique .... Warren Pincus
Musicians .... Lesley Harnley, David Lang,
Barry McVinney

UNDERSTUDIES: Arnolphe, Ed Preble; Alain, Warren Pincus; Horace, Chrysalde, Alan Brasington

MUSICAL NUMBERS: "All about Me," "All about He," "All about Him," "Learning Love," "There Goes a Mad Old Man," "Dialogue on Dalliance," "March of the Vigilant Vassels," "Lessons in Life," "Man Is a Man's Best Friend," "The Other Side of the Wall," "Closeness Begets Closeness," "Too Soon the Day," "When Time Takes Your Hand," "The Amorous Flea," Finale

A Musical in three acts. The action takes place in Paris in Arnolphe's house, and on the street in front of it.

General Manager: Jerry Arrow
Press: Alan Eichler, Marilyn Percy
Stage Managers: Lewis Rosen, Shan Covey

* Closed July 21, 1974 after a limited engagement of 32 performances.

John High, Gary Brubach, Ann Hodapp in "The Amorous Flea"
(Bert Andrews Photo)

QUEENS PLAYHOUSE
Opened Tuesday, July 23, 1974.*
The Queens Playhouse (Joseph S. Kutrzeba, Producer) presents:

ROOM SERVICE

By John Murray and Allen Boretz; Director, Ron Richards; Scenic Design, John Lee Beatty; Costumes, R. J. Graziano; Lighting, Lee Watson; Assistant Manager, David Ehrlich; Assistant to the Producer, Barbara Darwall; Technical Director, John Sheehan

CAST

Sasha Smirnoff .... Ronn Carroll
Gordon Miller .... Shelley Berman
Joseph Gribble .... Matthew Tobin
Harry Binion .... Jerry Matz
Faker Englund .... Rik Colitti
Christine Marlowe .... Susan Gailey
Leo Davis .... Saylor Creswell
Hilda Manney .... Jennifer W. Blood
Gregory Wagner .... Robert Gaus
Simon Jenkins .... Jon Richards
Timothy Hogarth .... Robert Nesbitt
Dr. Glass .... Ben Yaffee
Bank Messenger .... Ron Piretti
Senator Blake .... Ronn Carroll

STANDBYS AND UNDERSTUDIES: Gordon, Richard Kline; Leo, Faker, Ron Piretti; General Understudy, Don Creetch

A Comedy in three acts. The action takes place in the spring of 1939 in Gordon Miller's room in the White Way Hotel.

General Manager: Jerry Arrow
Press: Alan Eichler, Marilyn Percy
Stage Managers: Lewis Rosen, Joel Foster

* Closed Aug. 18, 1974 after limited engagement of 32 performances.

Shelley Berman, Saylor Cresswell, Susan Gailey in "Room Service"

(Bert Andrews Photo)

QUEENS PLAYHOUSE
Opened Tuesday, August 20, 1974.*
Queen's Playhouse (Joseph S. Kutrzeba, Producer) presents:

COME BACK, LITTLE SHEBA

By William Inge; Director, Marshall W. Mason; Scenic Design, John Lee Beatty; Costumes, R. J. Graziano; Lighting, Dennis Parichy; Production Coordinator, David Ehrlich; Assistant to the Producer, Barbara Darwall; Technical Director, John Sheehan; Technicians, Kenneth Hahn, Charles Tyndall; Wardrobe, Maria K. Schweppe; Music Composed by Norman L. Berman; Production Assistant, Mary Baird; Sound, Leon Pucklis

CAST

Doc	Gil Rogers
Marie	Trish Hawkins
Lola	Jan Sterling
Turk	Roger Hill
Postman	Jon Richards
Mrs. Coffman	Shirl Bernheim
Milkman	Max
Bruce	David Sederholm
Ed Anderson	Mark Weston
Elmer Huston	Ron Seka

A Drama in two acts and six scenes. The action takes place at the present time in an old house in a mid-Western city in late spring.

General Manager: Jerry Arrow
Press: Alan Eichler, Marilyn Percy
Stage Manager: Peter Schneider

* Closed Sept. 15, 1974 after limited engagement of 32 performances.

Bert Andrews Photos

Roger Hill, Gil Rogers, Trish Hawkins, Jan Sterling
Top Right: Gil Rogers, Jan Sterling

THE RIDICULOUS THEATRICAL COMPANY

Charles Ludlam, Artistic Director—Playwright
Seventh Season

EVERGREEN THEATRE
Opened Sunday, December 8, 1974.*
The Ridiculous Theatrical Company presents:

STAGE BLOOD

Written and Directed by Charles Ludlam; Set, Bobjack Collejo;
Lighting, Richard Currie; Costumes, Arthur Brady

CAST

Carleton Stone .... Jack Mallory
Carleton Stone, Jr. .... Charles Ludlam
Helga Vain .... Lola Pashalinski
Jenkins .... John D. Brockmeyer
Edmund Dundreary .... Bill Vehr
Elfie Fey .... Black-Eyed Susan
Gilbert Fey .... Jack Mallory
Ghost .... ???

A Comedy in three acts. The action takes place in a theatre in
Mudville, U.S.A.

General Manager: Catherine Farinon Smith
Press: Alan Eichler, Marilyn Percy
Stage Manager: Richard Gibbs

* Closed Feb. 9, 1975 after limited run of 60 performances.

**Black-Eyed Susan, Charles Ludlam
in "Stage Blood"**

(John Stern Photo)

**Lola Pashalinski, Charles Ludlam
in "Bluebeard"**

144

(John Stern Photo)

EVERGREEN THEATRE
Opened Friday, April 18, 1975.*
The Ridiculous Theatrical Company presents:

BLUEBEARD

Written and Directed by Charles Ludlam; Set, Bobjack Callejo;
Lighting, Richard Currie; Costumes, Mary Brecht, Arthur Brady,
Bobjack Callejo, Mario Montez

CAST

Mrs. Maggot .... Jack Mallory
Sheemish .... John D. Brockmeyer
Lamia, the Leopard Woman .... Mario Montez
Baron Khanazar von Bluebeard .... Charles Ludlam
Sybil .... Black-Eyed Susan
Rodney Parker .... Bill Vehr
Miss Cubbidge .... Lola Pashalinski
Hecate .... Richard Currie
Her Train .... Arthur Brady, Richard Gibbs
The Serpent .... Larry

A Melodrama in three acts.

General Manager: Catherine Farinon Smith
Press: Alan Eichler, Marilyn Percy
Stage Manager: Richard Gibbs

* Closed June 22, 1975 after 48 performances.

ROUND HOUSE COMPANY

Robert Moss, Executive Director
Associate Producers, Joan Lowell, Ian Calderon; Production
Coordinator, Richard Novello; Technical Director, Peter
Matusewitch; General Manager, Alvin T. Kraizer

QUEENS THEATRE-IN-THE-PARK
March 29–30, 1975
(4 performances)
AN EVENING WITH MA BELL by Tony Giordano; Director,
Joseph R. Cali; Set, Sandi Marks; Lighting, David Kissel; Costumes,
Lorri Schneider; Stage Managers, Joseph Kavanagh, Jim Swaine.
CAST: Scotty Block, John Clarkson, Margaret Gwenver, Christine
Lavren, David McCarver, Donald Silva
April 10–13, 1975
(4 performances)
RHINEGOLD with book by Barry Keating, Jim Steinman; Music,
Jim Steinman; Lyrics, Direction and Choreography, Barry Keating;
Musical Director, Jez Davidson; Costumes, Bosha Johnson; Set,
Calvin Churchman; Lighting, Jim Chaleff; Stage Manager, Joel
Brehm. CAST: Johanna Albrecht, George Ayer, Alan Braunstein,
Sarah Harris, Mary Hendrickson, Pat Lavelle, Lester Malizia, How-
ard Meadow, Edwin Ownes, Ellen Parks, Chuck Richie, Tim Shea-
han, Frank Thompson, Ron Van Lieu

April 17–20, 1975
(4 performances)
IPHIGENIA IN AULIS by Euripides; Adapted and Directed by
Yannis Simonides; Original Music, George Prideaux; Choreogra-
pher, Nellie Karras; Designed by Philip Jung; Chorus Director, Kris
Leonakis; Stage Manager, Mary Charlotte Cummings. CAST: Len
Auclair, Aldo Bonura, Jane Burley, Allan Carlsen, Laurie Copland,
Anne DeSalvo, Spring Fairbank, Elene Kianos, Johanna Leister,
Neil Napolitan, Portia Patterson, William Preston, Ruth Wallman,
Ricky Walters
April 24–27, 1975
(4 performances)
THE CORONER'S PLOT by David Shumaker; Director, Alfred
Ringold; Set, Richard B. Williams; Costumes, David Murin; Light-
ing, Jeff Miller; Stage Manager, Judy Goldstein. CAST: Margaret
Ann Bauer, Kathleen Chalfant, Bruce Detrick, Carole Doscher,
Ronald Hale, Alice Elliott, Jen Jones, Keith McDermott, Alex
Reed, Patricia Richardson, H. Frederick Wessler, Ronald Wil-
loughby

May 8–11, 1975
(4 performances)
NEW YORK! NEW YORK! Producers, Dennis Andersen, Alice
Elliott; Material by Dennis Andersen, David Epstein, Allan Knee,
Philip Magdalany, Kenneth Pressman, Jeremiah Murray, Steven
Shea, Marsha Sheiness, Martin Sherman; Directors, Michael Pos-
nick, Russell Treyz, Robert Moss, Caymichael Patten, Joseph R.
Cali; Lighting, Jon Knudsen; Costumes, Jody Berke; Stage Manag-
ers, Georgia Fleenor, Joseph Kavanagh, Jim Swaine. CAST: Sudie
Bond, Maria Cellario, Dana Gladstone, Barbara Lee GoVan, Kristin
Jolliff, Jeffrey Kramer, Roy London, Mitchell McGuire, Linda Rob-
bins, Timothy Sheahan
May 29–June 1, 1975
(4 performances)
I REMEMBER THE HOUSE WHERE I WAS BORN by Dennis
Andersen; Director, Susan Einhorn; Set and Costume Coordinator,
Christina Weppner; Lighting, Jeremy Lewis; Stage Managers, Lillah
McCarthy, Bill Phillips. CAST: Margaret Gwenver, Peter Bartlett,
Rose Lischner, Mary Frances Walsh, Daniel Pollack, Richard Lieb-
man

Nathaniel Tileston Photos

Top Right: John Clarkson, Margaret Gwenver in
"An Evening with Ma Bell" Below: Sarah Harris,
Lynn Pitney, Mary Hendrickson, Lester Malizia,
Johanna Albrecht, Howard Meadow, Ron Van Lieu,
Frank Thompson, Edwin Owens, Ellen Parks, Pat
Lavelle, Timothy Sheahan, Chuck Richie, Alan
Braunstein, George Ayer in "Rhinegold" Right
Center: H. Frederick Wessler, Kathleen Chalfant,
Margaret Ann Bauer, Ronald Hale, Patricia
Richardson, upstairs: Bruce Detrick, Keith
McDermott, Jen Jones in "Coroner's Plot"

Mary Frances Walsh, Daniel Pollack, Margaret Gwenver,
Rose Lischner, Alan Jordan in "I Remember the House ..."

ROUNDABOUT THEATRE COMPANY

Gene Feist, Producing Director
Michael Fried, Executive Director
Ninth Season

ROUNDABOUT THEATRE/STAGE TWO
Opened Tuesday, July 2, 1974.*
The Roundabout Theatre Company presents the New York premiere of:

THE BURNT FLOWERBED

By Ugo Betti; Translated by Henry Reed; Director, Paul Aaron; Set, Holmes Easley; Costumes, Mimi Maxmen; Lighting, Timmy Harris; Musical Supervision, Philip Campanella; Sound, Gary Harris; Technician, Steve Wood; Assistant to the Director, Lucille King; Business Manager, Paul Gruber; Production Assistants, Rene Devlin, Karen Dyrland, Laura Mortenson, Jill Panfel, Joe Reddington, Marian Reddington, Amy Shecter; Assistant Production Manager, Robert DeMartino

CAST

Giovanni .... Paul Sparer
Tomaso .... Brian Davies
Luisa .... Jane White
Raniero .... David Byrd
Rosa .... Lauren Frost
Nicola .... Salem Ludwig

A Drama in three acts. The action takes place in the recent past in a country house near a European frontier.

Press: David Guc
Stage Manager: Ron Antone

* Closed Aug. 11, 1974 after 48 performances.

Paul Sparer, Jane White in "The Burnt Flower Bed"
(Martha Swope Photo)

ROUNDABOUT THEATRE/STAGE ONE
Opened September 27, 1974.*
Roundabout Theatre Company presents:

ALL MY SONS

By Arthur Miller; Director, Gene Feist; Set, Holmes Easley; Costumes, Mimi Maxmen; Lighting, Richard Winkler; Sound, Gary Harris; Original Score, Philip Campanella; Hairstylist, Paul Huxley; Assistant to the Director, Lucille King; Assistant Production Managers, James Grant, Lewis Mead; Assistants to the Producer, Fred Ayeroff, David Guc; Technical Associates, Tim Knipe, W. O'Brien, Joseph Reddington; Production Assistants, Steven Furman, Laura Mortensen, Andrea Graham, Diana Benites, Helen DeTore, Bob Giordano, Gayle Marriner

CAST

Joe Keller .... Hugh Marlowe
Dr. Jim Bayliss .... Kenneth Kimmins
Frank Lubey .... Rik Pierce
Sue Bayliss .... Janet Sarno
Lydia Lubey .... Jane Dentinger
Chris Keller .... Drew Snyder
Bert .... Matthew Byers
Kate Keller .... Beatrice Straight
Ann Deever .... Catherine Byers
George Deever .... Tom Keena

A Drama in three acts. The action takes place in the back of the Keller home in the outskirts of an American town in August of 1947.

General Manager: Paul Gruber
Press: George Siegal, Ronni Chasen
Stage Manager: Ron Antone

* Closed Nov. 17, 1974 after 60 performances.

Drew Snyder, Beatrice Straight, Catherine Byers, Hugh Marlowe, above: Janet Sarno, Kenneth Kimmins, Byers, Tom Keena, Marlowe, Straight

Martha Swope Photos

ROUNDABOUT THEATRE/STAGE TWO

Opened Tuesday, December 3, 1974.*
The Roundabout Theatre Company and Alfredo Viazzi present:

ROSMERSHOLM

By Henrik Ibsen; Director, Raphael Kelly; Set Design, Stuart Wurtzel; Costumes, Patrizia von Brandenstein; Lighting, Timmy Harris; Hairstylist, Paul Huntley; Assistant to the Director, Jacquie Berger; Technical Associates, Robert Hendricks, Tim Knipe, Lou Mead, Wick O'Brien, Joseph Reddington; Production Assistants, Andrea Christensen, Helena De Tore, Gayle Marriner

CAST

Rebekka West	Jane White
Miss Helseth	Virginia Payne
Professor Kroll	Stephen Scott
Johannes Rosmer	Bill Moor
Ulrik Brendel	Stefan Schnabel
Peter Mortensgaard	Steven Gilborn

A Drama in two acts. The action takes place at Rosmersholm, an old estate in Norway in the late 1800's.

General Manager: Paul Gruber
Press: Gerald Siegal
Stage Manager: J. R. Grant

Closed Dec. 29, 1974 after 32 performances.

Martha Swope Photos

Right: Jane White, Bill Moor

ROUNDABOUT THEATRE/STAGE ONE

Opened Tuesday, December 3, 1974.*
Roundabout Theatre Company presents the 200th anniversary production of:

THE RIVALS

By Richard Brinsley Sheridan; Director, Michael Bawtree; Set Design, Holmes Easley; Costumes, Susan Benson; Lighting, Clarke Dunham; Original Score, Philip Campanella; Sound, Gary Harris; Hairstylist, Paul Huntley; Assistant to the Director, Lucille King; Assistant Production Managers, James Grant, Lou Mead; Technical Associates, Robert Hendricks, Tim Knipe, Wick O'Brien, Joseph Reddington; Stage Attendants, Larry Leonti, Frank Luz, Gayle Marriner, Stephen Miller; Production Assistants, Gary Cavello, Andrea Christensen, Adriana de LaRosa, Helena DeTore, Candy Dunn, Trueman Kelly, Gayle Marriner, Laura Mortenson, Ivan Myier, Sharon Taylor, Jayne Wanger, Paul Zak; Costume Supervisor, Linda C. Schultz; Wardrobe, Carmen Hiser

CAST

Thomas	Arthur Anderson
Fag	Michael Tucker
Lucy	Elizabeth Owens
Lydia Languish	Kathleen O'Meara Noone
Julia	Susan Watson
Mrs. Malaprop	Jane Connell
Sir Anthony Absolute	Christopher Hewett
Captain Jack Absolute	Richard Monette
Faulkland	Dennis Lipscomb
Bob Acres	George Pentecost
Sir Lucius O'Trigger	John Newton
David	Arthur Anderson

A Comedy in two acts. The action takes place in Bath on an early summer's day in the late 18th Century.

General Manager: Paul Gruber
Press: Gerald Siegal, Ronni Chasen
Stage Manager: Ron Antone

* Closed Feb. 9, 1975 after 79 performances.

Christopher Hewett, Jane Connell, and above, entire cast of "The Rivals"

ROUNDABOUT THEATRE/STAGE ONE

Opened Tuesday, February 25, 1975.*
Roundabout Theatre Company presents the World Premiere of:

JAMES JOYCE'S DUBLINERS

By J. W. Riordan; Director, Gene Feist; Original Music and Lyrics, Philip Campanella; Based on "My Brothers Keeper" by Stanislaus Joyce; Set Design, Holmes Easley; Costumes, Christina Gianini; Lighting, Ian Calderon; Sound, Gary Harris; Hairstylist, Paul Huntley; Assistant to the Director, Katharine Stanton; Assistant Production Managers, James Grant, Lewis Mead; Costume Supervisor, Linda C. Schultz; Production Assistants, Jill Blair, Andrea Christensen, Cathy Doxy, Candy Dunn, Adriana de LaRosa, Adrea Graham, Laura Mortenson, Kathy Reid, Theresa Rivera, Valerie Roberts, Ron Sautter, Jayne Wenger, Leonard Williams, Paul Zak

CAST

John Joyce	Stan Watt
Mary Joyce	Ruby Holbrook
James Joyce	Martin Cassidy
Stanislaus Joyce	Ty McConnell
Young Jimmy Joyce/Butcher Boy/ Mike O'Brien	Michael Hagerty
William Murray	Walter Klavun
Josephine Murray	Justine Johnston
Kate Murray/Miss Parker/Young Woman	Erika Petersen
Holohan/Alleyne/Gallagher/Capuchine Priest/Dempsey/Henchy	Don Perkins
Fitzpatrick/Father Conmee/Sheehy/ Old Jack/Dowd	Frank Hamilton
D'Arcy/Bartender/Brother Kenny/ Matt Calahan/Dodd	Kent Rizley

A play in two acts. The action takes place in Dublin, Ireland, during a ten year period at the turn of the century.

General Manager: Paul Gruber
Press: George Siegal, Valerie Warner
Stage Manager: Ron Antone

* Closed May 4, 1975 after 80 performances.

Martha Swope Photos

Right: Martin Cassidy, Ruby Holbrook, Ty McConnell, also above with the cast of "James Joyce's Dubliners"

Grayson Hall, Fran Brill, Ronald Drake, Michael Goodwin in "What Every Woman Knows"

ROUNDABOUT THEATRE/STAGE ONE

Opened Wednesday, May 28, 1975.*
Roundabout Theatre Company presents:

WHAT EVERY WOMAN KNOWS

By James M. Barrie; Director, Gene Feist; Set Design, Holm Easley; Lighting, Ian Calderon; Costumes, Charles Gelatt; Orig Score, Philip Campanella; Sound, Gary Harris; Hairstylist, P Huntley; Production Manager, Ron Antone; Assistant Produc Managers, Lewis Mead, Joseph Reddington; Men's Hairstyles, G of Sadie Thompson; Dialect Coach, Gordon Jacoby; Assistants the Producers, Steven Evans, David Guc

CAST

James Wylie	Jeff Ru
Alick Wylie	Jack Bitt
David Wylie	Ron Fra
Maggie Wylie	Fran
John Shand	Michael Good
Comtesse de la Briere	Grayson
Lady Sybil Tenterden	Susan Ta
Mr. Venables	Ronald D

A play in four acts performed with one intermission. The ac takes place in the house of the Wylies who are the proprietors granite quarry in Northern Scotland, in a barber shop in Glas serving as Shand's committee rooms, in Mr. Shand's house in don, and at the country estate of the Comtesse de la Briere.

General Manager: Paul Gruber
Press: George Siegal, Valerie Warner
Stage Manager: Robert A. Lowe

* Closed July 27, 1975 after 71 performances.

Martha Swope Photo

THEATRE AT ST. CLEMENT'S

Kevin O'Connor, Artistic Director

ST. CLEMENT'S CHURCH
Opened Tuesday, June 4, 1974.*
Theatre at St. Clement's presents:

NUTS

By Tom Topor; Director, John Margulis; Designed by Norvid
Roos; Lighting, Margay Whitlock; Property Mistress, Amy Bergen-
feld

CAST

Walters	Alexander Courtney
Claudia	Lynn Oliver
Rose	Lee Sanders
Art	Henry Calvert
Peter	Michael Durrell

A Play in two acts.

Press: Alan Eichler, Marilyn Percy
Stage Managers: Mary Ellin Barrett, Margay Whitlock

Closed June 9, 1974 after 7 performances.

THEATRE AT ST. CLEMENT'S
Opened Thursday, October 9, 1974.*
St. Clement's presents:

FIGURES IN THE SAND

By Nathan Teitel; Director, Nick Havinga; Sets and Lighting, Ben
Edwards; Costumes, Jane Greenwood; Music, Teiji Ito; Sound,
Lewis Rosen; Lighting Coordinator, Gary Porto; Production Assis-
tants, Bernard Beauchamps, Davis C. Burroughs III, Rick Clafin,
Randall Dayton, Jan Eliasberg, Bob Griffin, Miklos Horvath, Bruce
Katzman, Paul Mowbray, Pat Stern, Amy Stoller

CAST

"Duet"

Man	Kevin O'Connor
Woman	Carol Teitel

The action takes place at the present time near the sea.

"Trio"

Man	Kevin O'Connor
Woman	Carol Teitel

The action takes place at the present time near the sea.

Press: Alan Eichler, Marilyn Percy
Stage Managers: Peter Carlson, Celia Lee

Closed Oct. 27, 1974 after limited engagement of 15 performances.

"The Fall and Redemption of Man"
(Gerard Barnier Photo)

ST. CLEMENT'S CHURCH
Opened Sunday, June 16, 1974.*
St. Clement's and Hamm and Clov Stage Company present:

THE FALL AND REDEMPTION OF MAN

By John Bowen; Director, Tom Tarpey; Music, Matthew Yasner;
Set, Guy Smith; Costumes, Richard Graziano; Lighting, Neil Maz-
zela

CAST

Satan/2nd Shepherd/Torturer's Assistant	Robert Blumenfeld
Cain/Herald/Caiphas	J. Kenneth Campbell
First Shepherd/First King/Peter/ Barabas	Maury Chaykin
Eve/Sheep/1st Mother/Woman of Jerusalem	Vivien Ferrara
Abel/Ass/Jesus/Porter	Michael Finn
Tree/Mary	Margot Hastings
Joseph/Judas/Herod Agrippa/Simon of Cyrene	Peter Kingsley
Gabriel/Woman of Jerusalem/Veronica/ Citizen	Diana Kirkwood
Angel/Citizen on urgent business/ Mak/Pilate	Bruce Kornbluth
Adam/Third Shepherd/Third King/ Annas	E. E. Norris
God/Herod/Man with pot/Knight-Torturer	Alvah Stanley
Green Horn/Gil/Mary Magdalene/ Second Mother/Angel	Holly Villaire

A Drama in two acts.

Press: Alan Eichler, Marilyn Percy
Stage Managers: Steve Nash, Dale Mosher

* Closed June 23, 1974 after limited engagement of 10 performances.

ST. CLEMENT'S CHURCH
Opened Monday, November 4, 1974.*
The Musical Theatre Lab at St. Clement's presents:

THE ROBBER BRIDEGROOM

Book and Lyrics, Alfred Uhry; Adapted from the story by Eudora
Welty; Music, Robert Waldman; Director, Gerald Freedman; Lighting, Gary Porto; Choreography, Don Redlich; Executive Producer,
Stephanie Copeland; Project Producer, Steven Woolf; a joint project
of The Stuart Ostrow Foundation and St. Clement's

CAST

Salome	Susan Berger
3rd Landlord/Indian	William Brenner
Rosamund	Rhonda Coullet
Mike Fink	John Getz
Airie/Raven	Cynthia Herman
Jaimie Lockhart	Raul Julia
Indian	Dana Kyle
2nd Landlord/Goat's Mother	Carolyn McCurry
1st Landlord/Big Harp	Bill Hunnery
Robber/Indian	Thomas Oglesby
Goat	Trip Plymale
Little Harp	Ernie Sabella
Robber/Indian	David Summers
Clement Musgrove	Steve Vinovich

Performed without intermission. The action takes place in Mississippi in legendary times.

Press: Alan Eichler
Stage Manager: Mary Burns

* Closed Nov. 9, 1975 after limited engagement of 6 performances.

ST. CLEMENT'S CHURCH

Opened Tuesday, November 19, 1974.*

St. Clement's (Lawrence Goossen, Administrative Director; Lewis Rosen, Production Director; Jean Halbert, Coordinator) presents The Proposition production of:

THE KING OF THE UNITED STATES

By Jean-Claude Van Itallie; Music, Richard Peaslee; Director, Allan Albert; Set, Scott Johnson; Lighting, Gary Porto; Musical Direction, Donald Sosin; Technical Director, Dale Mosher; Production Assistant, D. C. Burroughs

CAST

Politician	Raymond Baker
Policeman	Don Creech
Young Man	John Long
Etiquette Lady	Leila Martin
Mystery Writer	Marilyn Redfield
Call Girl	Michele Shay
Professor	Ronald Willoughby

Performed without intermission.

Press: Herb Striesfield
Stage Manager: Jay S. Hoffman

* Closed Dec. 1, 1974 after limited engagement of 12 performances.

Ronald Willoughby, Don Creech Top: Raymond Baker, Michele Shay in "King of the U.S."

ST. CLEMENT'S CHURCH

Opened Tuesday, December 17, 1974.*

Theatre at St. Clement's presents:

ENTER A FREE MAN

By Tom Stoppard; Director, Brian Murray; Sets, David Mitchell; Costumes, Lorye Watson; Lights, Pat Collins; Sound, Lewis Rosen; Assistant to the Director, Jeffrey Wachtel; Sound, Davis C. Burroughs III

CAST

Persephone	Alice Drummond
Linda	Swoosie Kurtz
George Riley	David Rounds
Harry	Scott Hylands
Able	J. T. Walsh
Brown	John Leighton
Carmen	James Hummert
Florence	Katherine McGrath

A play in two acts. The action takes place on July 5 and 6 at the present time.

Press: Alan Eichler, Marilyn Percy
Stage Managers: Suzanne Egan, Randall Dayton, Margay Whitlock

* Closed Jan. 19, 1975 after 25 performances.

ST. CLEMENT'S CHURCH

Monday, December 30, 1974.*

St. Clement's Career Orientation Program presents:

ICARUS'S MOTHER

By Sam Shepard; Director, Jeffrey Wachtel

CAST

Bill	Miklos Horvath
Jill	Celia Lee
Pat	Ellen Murray
Howard	Peter Carlson
Frank	Randy Dayton

* Presented for one performance only.

front: Swoosie Kurtz, Alice Drummond, back: J. T. David Rounds, Curt Dawson, Katherine McGrath, Hummert, John Leighton in "Enter a Free Man"

ST. CLEMENT'S CHURCH
Opened Thursday, February 20, 1975.*
The Vestry House at St. Clement's presents:

WAR BABIES

Alix Elias
Caren Kaye
Marsha Meyers
Jed Mills
Peter Riegert
Lenny Roberts
Renny Temple
John Welsh
Debbie White

An improvisational theatre company performing without inter-mission

Closed May 31, 1975 after 10 performances on weekends only.

ST. CLEMENT'S CHURCH
Opened Friday, February 28, 1975.*
Theatre at St. Clement's presents the Musical Theatre Lab production of:

JOE'S OPERA

By Tom Mande; Director, Robert Allan Ackerman; Musical Di-ction, Tom Mandel; Choreography, Edmond Kresley; Set Design, avid Sackeroff; Costumes, Kathi Horne; Lighting, David Sack-off, Michael Watson; Executive Producer, Stephanie Copeland; roject Producer, Richard Tauber; Sound, Tony Giovanetti; Pro-action Assistants, Peter Gelblum, Ilse Gordon

CAST

om/Convict/Marianne .... Zenobia Conkerite
e .... Richard Dunne
rk .... Victor Garber
d/Dancer/Convict .... Ronald Hall
d/State Trooper's Wife/
Convict/Judge .... Paul Kreppel
nabelle .... Armelia McQueen
gel/Convict/Judge .... Peter Norman
d/Waitress/Rosabelle .... Deborah Offner
alyst/Convict/Judge .... Tony Travis
d/Kid .... Gyl Waddy

A Work-in-progress in two acts.

Press: Alan Eichler, Marilyn Percy
Stage Managers: Marjorie Horne, Rita Calabro

Closed March 9, 1975 after limited engagement of 9 performances.

ST. CLEMENT'S CHURCH
Opened Sunday, April 6, 1975.*
Theatre at St. Clement's presents:

WORKERS

By Tom Griffin; Director, Bolen High; Setting, Leo Yoshimura; Lighting, Barley Harris; Costumes, Tina Watson; A project of Bolen High, Michael O'Rand, Steven Woolf; Technical Supervisor, Chip Burroughs; Assistant to the Director, Dennis Grimaldi; Technical Director, Doug Gray; Sound Design, Bob Bielecki; Production Assistant, Danny Mizell; Production Manager, Steven Woolf

CAST

Marvin	J. T. Walsh
Harry	Alan Mixon
Eddie	Steve Karp
Pete	Madison Arnold
Al	Ray Lynch
Timothy	Stephen Ivester
Nancy	Jane Anderson
Dawn	Ginger Flick
Carol	Linda Zernecke
Richard	Michael Sander
Bill	Donald Weed

A play in three acts. The action takes place at the present time during the summer in a warehouse.

General Manager: Michael O'Rand
Press: Alan Eichler, Marilyn Percy
Stage Managers: Lee Geisel, Barbara Rosenthal, Christopher Cara

* Closed Apr. 20, 1975 after a limited engagement of 12 perfor-mances.

ar Babies clockwise from left: **Peter Riegert, bbie White, Renny Temple, Marsha Meyers, Jed Mills, Caren Kaye, Alix Elias**

front: **J. T. Walsh, Ray Lynch, back: Steve Karp, Jane Anderson, Ginger Flick, Alan Mixon in "Workers"**

151

Opened Thursday, March 13, 1975.*
Theatre at St. Clement's presents the Medicine Show Theatre
Ensemble in:

FROGS

By Carl Morse, Richard Schotter; Directors, James Barbosa, Barbara Vann; Composers, Yenoin Guibbory, Robert Dennis, Jim Milton; Costumes, Patricia McGourty

CAST

James Barbosa	Davidson Lloyd
Ziska Baum	James Milton
John Bowers	Dan Morris
Chris Brandt	Alan Nebelthau
Kathleen Kelly	Barbara Vann
Derry Light	Elizabeth von Benken
	Ray Xifo

"An Irrational Comedy" performed without intermission.

Press: Alan Eichler, Marilyn Percy

* Closed March 23, 1975 after limited engagement of 12 performances.

Derry Light in "Frogs"

ST. CLEMENT'S CHURCH
Opened Wednesday, April 23, 1975.*
Theatre at St. Clement's presents:

WAKING UP TO BEAUTIFUL THINGS

Music and Lyrics, Jeffrey Roy; Director, Jeffrey Wachtel; Lighting, Gary Porto; Technical Supervisor, Chip Burroughs

CAST

Norman Begin
Richard Eber
Deborah Magid
Marcia Savella
Joanne Young

MUSICAL NUMBERS: "I Know a Song," "The Good Thing," "Beanstalk Song," "Awful Lot of Time," "Getting There," "Natural Kind of Love," "Never Did I Love You," "David's Song," "Let the Bad Times Stumble," "Time in the Snow," "Love Day," "Got to Try to Sing Our Song Again," "Couldn't Be Myself with You," "Open All Night," "Don't Play with Fire," "Circus," "We'll Build a Castle," "Morning Chases Dreams Away," "Parody Parade," "Waking Up to Beautiful Things."

Performed without intermission.

Press: Alan Eichler, Marilyn Percy
Stage Managers: Margay Whitlock, Walter Wood

* Closed Apr. 27, 1975 after limited engagement of 10 performances.

ST. CLEMENT'S CHURCH
Opened Friday, May 2, 1975.*
The Musical Theatre Lab of St. Clement's presents:

THE RED BLUE-GRASS WESTERN FLYER SHOW

Book and Lyrics, Conn Fleming; Music, Clint Ballard, Jr.; Director, Robert Brewer; Dances and Musical Staging, Dennis Grima[Set, John Falabella; Costumes, Bill Kellard, Michele Reisch; Lig[ing, Barley Harris; Sound, Tony Giovannetti; Executive Produc[Stephanie Copeland; Project Producer, Steven Woolf; Dance C[tain, Stephen deGhelder; Assistant to the Director, Joe Bricki[Assistant to the Choreographer, Baayork Lee

CAST

Big Emmit Childress	Maurice Copela[
Hattie Cox	Kate Wilkin[
Arlen	Conrad McLa[
Dolly	Barbara Cog[
Emma Lou	Kate Kell[
Scotty Young	Robert Pol[
George D. Hay	Larry Swan[
Swing Dancer	Forbsey Rus[

LOOKOUT MOUNTAIN DANCERS: Terry Brown, K[Crossley, Stephen deGhelder, Ellen Manning, John Scoullar, De[Woodhouse

SOUTHERN SUNSHINE SINGERS: Elinor Ellsworth, H[Hoffman, Michael David Laibson, Dan Kruger, Carmen Peter[Gerard Wagner

BROTHER BILL AND THE BLACK BOTTOM BOYS: [Falk, Dick Frank, Steve Mack, Jeff Waxman

"A Grand Ole Opry Musical Play" in two acts. The action [place in the Childress apartment in a Northern city, and on the s[of the Grand Ole Opry.

Press: Alan Eichler, Marilyn Percy
Stage Managers: Doug Gray, Lora Oxenreiter, Stephanie Re[

* Closed May 11, 1975 after limited engagement of 12 pe[mances.

THEATRE OF THE RIVERSIDE CHURCH

Arthur Bartow, Executive Producer

RIVERSIDE CHURCH
Opened Tuesday, November 12, 1974.*
Theatre of the Riverside Church presents the American Premiere of:

LEAVING HOME

By David French; Director, Arthur Bartow; Scenic Design, Alan M. Beck; Costumes, Pamela Dendy; Lighting, Lee A. Goldman; Movement Consultant, Nora Peterson; Managing Director, Eric M. Hamburger; Assistant Technical Director, Frank Herbert

CAST

Mary Mercer	Lenka Peterson
Ben Mercer	William Carden
Billy Mercer	Danny Corcoran
Jacob Mercer	Brendan Fay
Kathy Jackson	Maureen Silliman
Minnie Jackson	Marilyn Chris
Harold	John Leighton

A play in two acts. The action takes place on a November day in the late 1950's in Toronto, Canada.

Stage Manager: Thom Edlun

* Closed Dec. 1, 1974 after limited engagement of 16 performances.

Bert Andrews Photos

Right: Elliot Cukor, Harriet Hall, Michael Reynolds, Alice Rosengard, Kenneth Norris, William Newman in "Mister Runaway" Above: William Carden, Brendan Fay, Danny Corcoran, Lenka Peterson, Maureen Silliman, in "Leaving Home"

RIVERSIDE CHURCH
Opened Tuesday, January 21, 1975.*
Theatre of the Riverside Church (Arthur Bartow, Administrative Producer; Eric M. Hamburger, Managing Director) presents the American Premiere of:

MISTER RUNAWAY

By Liliane Atlan; English Version, Marc Prensky; Director, Arthur Bartow; Scenic Design, Alan M. Beck; Lighting, Lee A. Goldman; Costumes, Pamela Dendy; Properties, Suri Bieler; Assistant to the Director, Burton Crane; Wardrobe Master, John Ferdon

CAST

Grol (called Mr. Runaway)	William Newman
Christopher	Elliot Cuker
Frobbe	David Manson
Soldiers	Frank Herbert, Brian O'Connor
Captain	George Spelvin
Yossele	Kenneth Norris
Raissa	Alice Rosengard
Yona	Harriet Hall
Tamar's Doll	
Abracha	Michael Reynolds

The action takes place in Central Europe during the 1940's: in a totally destroyed Ghetto, in a truck in the fog, and in Rot-Bourg or the Valley of Bones.

Stage Managers: Thom Edlun, Brian O'Connor

Closed Feb. 9, 1975 after a limited engagement of 12 performances.

RIVERSIDE CHURCH
Opened Tuesday, March 4, 1975.*
Theatre of Riverside Church (Arthur Bartow, Executive Producer; Eric M. Hamburger, Managing Director) Discovery 74–75 presents the World Premiere of:

SHARK

By T. J. Camp III; Director, Dean Irby; Scenic Design, Alan M. Beck; Costumes, Pamela Dendy; Lighting, Frank Herbert; Technical Director, Lee A. Goldman; Properties, Suri Bieler; Sound, Thom Edlun; Wardrobe Master—Costume Coordinator, John Ferdon

CAST

Big Bill	F. William Parker
Elmore	Bruce Strickland
Carl	Raymond Serra
Junior	James Bond, Jr. III
Barry	Albert Grand Eggleston III
Drummond	Jay Hargrove
Lonnie	Robert Judd
May	Venida Evans
Sweetman	Carl Gordon
Hollobird	Arnold Johnson

Understudy: Nicolas Barnwell

A play in two acts. The action takes place at the present time on Labor Day in the caddy yard of an exclusive country club.

Stage Managers: Brian O'Connor, Tina Reddy

* Closed Mar. 16, 1975 after limited engagement of 12 performances. No photos available.

UNIVERSAL RELEVANCE GROUP ENTERPRISE IN A NATIONAL THEATER

Ronald Muchnick and Nathan George, Producers
Third Season

U.R.G.E.N.T. THEATER
Opened Thursday, July 11, 1974.*
Ronald Muchnick and Nathan George present the World Premiere of:

OVERNIGHT

By William Inge; Director, Nathan George; Setting, Michael Molly; Lighting, Cheryl Thacker; Production Assistant, Marge Eliot; Technical Coordinator, Lowell Copeland

CAST

Harry Broch .... Arthur Roberts
Muriel .... Carol Potter
Ray Hirsch .... William Mooney

A play in two acts. The action takes place in a modest apartment in an old, once grand building in downtown Los Angeles.

Press: Seymour Krawitz, Fred Hoot
Stage Manager: Gwen Anderson

* Closed July 24, 1974 after a limited engagement of 12 performances.

U.R.G.E.N.T. THEATER
Opened Wednesday, September 11, 1974.*
Ronald Muchnick and Nathan George present:

BIG FISH, LITTLE FISH

By Hugh Wheeler; Director, Richard Altman; Designed by Michael J. Hotopp and Paul dePass; Production Supervisor, Lowell Copeland

CAST

Edith Maitland .... Ruth Livingston
Jimmie Luton .... Richard Seff
William Baker .... Mark Fleischman
Basil Smythe .... Philip Lawrence
Hilda Rose .... Elaine Hyman
Ronnie Johnson .... Courtney Burr
Paul Stumpfig .... Bob Levine

A play in three acts and six scenes. The action takes place at the present time in William Baker's New York apartment during March.

Press: Seymour Krawitz, Fred Hoot
Stage Managers: Phillip Levien, Michele Korf

* Closed Sept. 29, 1974 after a limited engagement of 12 performances.

U.R.G.E.N.T. THEATER
Opened Tuesday, October 22, 1974.*
Ronald Muchnick and Nathan George present:

A SONG FOR NOW

Directed and Choreographed by Edward Roll; Musical Director, Patrick Holland; Designed by Calvin Churchman

CAST

Loni Zoe Ackerman   Jose Fernandez
Patrick Adiarte   Barbara Montgomery
Irene Cara   Rick Podell
Margery Cohen   Ron Recasner

A Musical Collage in progress.

Press: Seymour Krawitz, Fred Hoot
Stage Managers: Barry Steinman, Peter Trachtenberg

* Closed Nov. 9, 1974 after limited engagement of 12 performances.

U.R.G.E.N.T. THEATER
Opened Friday, November 29, 1974.*
Ronald Muchnick and Nathan George present:

IN HONORED MEMORY OF TED AND SPARKY

By Jay Broad; Directed by the author; Setting, David Chapman, Lighting, Jim Harrison

CAST

Ted Snyder .... Jack Ramage
Marty Washington .... William Jay
Charlie Revere .... Lou Bedford
Sparky Snyder .... Elaine Kerr
Georgia Washington .... Joan Lowell
Otto Beethoven .... Frank Hamilton
Huck Snyder .... Tim Wilson
Spike Snyder .... Clyde Burton
Tony Kraber .... Bert Hunter
Policeman .... Philip Levien

Press: Howard Atlee, Clarence Allsopp, Meg Gordean, Owen Levy
Stage Manager: Christopher Clark Dunlop

* Closed Dec. 14, 1974 after limited engagement of 12 performances. (A revised version of "The Killdeer" presented at the Public Theater last season. See THEATRE WORLD, Vol. 30.)

U.R.G.E.N.T. THEATER
Opened Wednesday, February 12, 1975.*
Under the aegis of Ronald Muchnick and Nathan George, U.R.G.E.N.T. presents:

EDGAR ALLAN POE: A CONDITION OF SHADOW
with
JERRY ROCKWOOD

A Characterization from the writings of Poe, selected by Jerry Rockwood; Music composed and performed by Thomas Wilt; Setting, Michael Molly; Lighting, Christopher Dunlop; Tour Management, Arthur Shafman; Voice of John Allan by Don Sobolik; Newspaper Voice, Barnard Hughes.

* Closed March 1, 1975 after limited engagement of 12 performances. Repeated May 30 and 31, 1975 at Hunter College Playhouse.

U.R.G.E.N.T. THEATER
Opened Thursday, March 6, 1975.*
Ronald Muchnick and Nathan George present the World Premiere of:

e. e. AS IS
or
"Damn Everything but the Circus"

An evening's entertainment by e. e. cummings. Selected and performed by William Mooney; Director, Henry Kaplan; Setting, Michael Molly; Lighting, Lee Mayman

Press: Howard Atlee, Clarence Allsopp, Meg Gordean, Owen Levy
Stage Manager: Barry Steinman

* Closed Mar. 22, 1975 after limited engagement of 12 performances.

Opened Wednesday, April 30, 1975.*
Under the aegis of Ronald Muchnick and Nathan George, U.R.G.E.N.T. presents the World Premiere of:

MIDNIGHT SPECIAL

By Clifford Mason; Director, Clifford Goodwin; Setting, David Chapman; Lighting, Priscilla Cooper; Technical Director, Christopher Clark Dunlop; Sound Consultant, Jeff Peters; Production Assistant, Maureen Bryan

CAST

Bull Dog	Norman Matlock
Andrew	Joseph Attles
White Lightnin'	Fred Morsell
Grease	Frank Adu
Slick	Taurean Blacque
Johnny Midnight	Vernon Washington
Eddy	Ken Foree
First Cop	Stephen Liska
Second Cop	Tom Kubiak
First Customer	Doug Jones
Second Customer	Hank Frazier
Third Customer	Maureen Bryan
Fourth Customer	Everrette Johns
Francine	Marlene Warfield
Miriam	Bette Howard
Young Blood	Obaka Adedunyo

A play in three acts. The action takes place in a neighborhood bar in Harlem.

Press: Howard Atlee, Clarence Allsopp, Meg Gordean, Owen Levy
Stage Managers: Vere Everrette Johns, Jr., Hope McKenzie

Closed May 15, 1975 after limited engagement of 10 performances.

Right: William Mooney in "e. e. As Is"
Top: Jerry Rockwood as Edgar Allan Poe

OFF BROADWAY PRODUCTIONS FROM OTHER SEASONS
THAT CLOSED THIS SEASON

Title	Opened	Closed	Performances
El Grande de Coca-Cola	2/13/73	4/13/75	1114
Don't Bother Me, I Can't Cope	4/19/72	10/26/74	1065
Moonchildren	11/4/73	10/20/74	394
When You Comin' Back, Red Ryder?	11/5/73	8/25/74	328
The Sea Horse	4/15/74	8/4/74	136
My Sister, My Sister	4/30/74	8/11/74	128
Camille	5/13/74	10/27/74	113
Short Eyes	3/13/74	8/4/74	102
In the Deepest Part of Sleep	5/28/74	6/30/74	32

SULLIVAN STREET PLAYHOUSE
Opened Tuesday, May 3, 1960.*
Lore Noto presents:

THE FANTASTICKS

Book and Lyrics, Tom Jones; Suggested by Edmond Rostand's play "Les Romanesques"; Music, Harvey Schmidt; Director, Word Baker; Original Musical Director and Arrangements, Julian Stein: Designed by Ed Wittstein; Associate Producers, Sheldon Baron, Dorothy Olim, Robert Alan Gold; Assistant to the Producer, Thad Noto; Production Assistant, John Krug; Original Cast Album, MGM Records.

CAST

The Narrator	Hal Robinson†1
The Girl	Virginia Gregory†2
The Boy	Michael-Glenn Smith†3
The Boy's Father	Lore Noto
The Girl's Father	Robert Tennenhouse†4
The Actor	Jay Hampton†5
The Man Who Dies	James Cook†6
The Mute	Robert Brigham†7
At the Piano	William F. McDaniel
At the Harp	Pattee Cohen

MUSICAL NUMBERS: Overture, "Try to Remember," "Much More," "Metaphor," "Never Say No," "It Depends on What You Pay," "Soon It's Gonna Rain," "Rape Ballet," "Happy Ending," "This Plum Is Too Ripe," "I Can See It," "Plant a Radish," "Round and Round," "They Were You," Finale.

A musical in two acts.

Press: David Powers
Stage Managers: Geoffrey Brown, Linda Harris, Kent McKeever

* Still playing May 31, 1975. For original production See THE-ATRE WORLD, Vol. 16.

† Succeeded by: 1. David Brummel, 2. Sarah Rice, Cheryl Horne, 3. Paul Killian, Ralph Bruneau, 4. Sy Travers, 5. Seamus O'Brien, Evan Thompson, 6. Jack Fogarty, 7. Paul W. Francis

Martha Swope Photos

James Cook, Seamus O'Brien

Lore Noto Above: David Brummel (top),
Sarah Rice, Ralph Bruneau

CHERRY LANE THEATRE
Opened Monday, May 17, 1971.*
(Moved August 10, 1971 to Promenade Theatre)
Edgar Lansbury, Stuart Duncan, Joseph Beruh present:

GODSPELL

Music and Lyrics, Stephen Schwartz; Conceived and Directed by John-Michael Tebelak; Based on "The Gospel According to St. Matthew;" Lighting, Barry Arnold; Costumes, Susan Tsu; Production Supervision, Nina Faso; Musical Director, Sheldon Markham; Associate Producer, Charles Haid; Musical Arrangement and Direction, Stephen Schwartz; Production Assistant, Mark Jacobson; Sound and Props, Ellen Katz; Assistant to Producers, Darrell Jonas; Original Cast Album by Bell Records.

CAST

Valda Aviks†	Jeremy Sage
Debbie Weems	Scotch Byerley
Marley Sims	Gary Imhoff
Leslie Ann Ray	Laurie Faso
Lloyd Bremseth	Don Scardino

MUSICAL NUMBERS: "Tower of Babble," "Prepare Ye the Way of the Lord," "Save the People," "Day by Day," "Learn Your Lessons Well," "Bless the Lord," "All for the Best," "All Good Gifts," "Light of the World," "Turn Back, O Man," "Alas for you," "By My Side," "We Beseech Thee," "On the Willows," Finale

A Musical in two acts and sixteen scenes.

General Manager: Al J. Isaac
Company Manager: Gail Bell
Press: Gifford/Wallace, Merle Frimark
Stage Manager: Jan Allred

* Still playing May 31, 1975. For original production see THE-ATRE WORLD, Vol. 28
† Others who appeared in the cast during the season were Damon Evans, Michael Hoit, Peter Jurasik, Danny Lipman, Patti Mariano, Gilmer McCormick, Tom Rolfing, Naomi Wexler, William Thomas, Jr.

Ellen M. Katz, William L. Smith Photos

Opened Thursday, March 22, 1973.*
Kermit Bloomgarden and Roger Ailes present the Circle Theatre Company production of:

THE HOT L BALTIMORE

By Lanford Wilson; Director, Marshall W. Mason; Setting, Ronald Radice; Costume Coordinator, Dina Costa; Assistant to Director, Rob Wolfson; Production Assistant, Noel Gilmore; Lighting, Marshall W. Mason; Assistant to the Producers, John Bloomgarden

CAST

Bill	William Wise
Girl	Faith Catlin[1]
Millie	Eunice Anderson
Mrs. Billotti	Lorraine Spritzer[2]
April	Jane Cronin
Mr. Morse	Peter Bosche[3]
Jackie	Lisa Jacobson
Jamie	Chip Zien[4]
Mr. Katz	Antony Tenuta[5]
Suzy	Jane Lowry[6]
Suzy's John	Burke Pearson
Paul Granger III	Ted LePlat[7]
Mrs. Oxenham	Louise Clay[8]
Cab Man	Richard A. Steel
Delivery Boy	Alan Wolfzahn[9]

UNDERSTUDIES: Girl, Jackie, Sandra Teller; Millie, Mrs. Oxenham, Mrs. Billotti, Suzy, Maryellen Flynn; Bill, Katz, Morse, Burke Pearson; Paul, Jamie, Roy Wolfson; Suzy's John, Richard A. Steel

A Comedy in three acts. The action takes place at the present time on Memorial Day in the lobby of the Hotel Baltimore in Baltimore, Md.

Press: Merlin Group, Betty Lee Hunt, Maria C. Pucci, Stanley F. Kaminsky
Stage Managers: William Bramlette, Burke Pearson

* Still playing May 31, 1975. Winner of 1973 Drama Critics Circle Award for Best American Play, Outer Critics Circle Award, and "Obie" Award as Best New Play. Opened Feb. 4, 1973 at the Circle Repertory Theatre and played 17 performances and 7 previews before moving to Circle in the Square.
† Succeeded by: 1. Heather MacRae, Trish Hawkins, Penny Peyser, 2. Alexandra Smith, 3. Sherman Lloyd, 4. Ron Paul Little, John Shuman, 5. Larry Spinelli, 6. Stephanie Gordon, Corie Sims, 7. Jonathan Hogan, Ted LePlat, 8. Maryellen Flynn, Molly Adams, 9. Rob Wolfson

Zane Lasky, Conchata Ferrell
Top: Stephanie Gordon

Mari Gorman, Antony Tenuta

VILLAGE GATE
Opened Tuesday, January 8, 1974.*
Phil Oesterman presents:

LET MY PEOPLE COME

Music and Lyrics, Earl Wilson, Jr.; Music Arranged and Conducted by Billy Cunningham; Choreography, Ian Naylor; Lighting, Centaur Productions; Produced and Directed by Phil Oesterman; Production Assistant, Michael Murphy; Wardrobe Coordinator, Dianemarie Lemon; Associate Music Director, Norman Bergen.

CAST

Christine Anderson†	Larry Paulette
Joe Jones	Marty Duffy
Tobie Columbus	Peachena
James Moore	Alan Evans
Daina Darzin	Jim Rise
Ian Naylor	Lola Howse
Lorraine Davidson	Denise Connolley

UNDERSTUDIES: Susan Solomon, David Patrick Kelly, Barry Pearl

ACT I: "Opening Number," "Mirror," "Whatever Turns You On," "Give It To Me," "Giving Life," "The Ad," "Fellatio 101," "I'm Gay," "Linda Georgina Marilyn and Me," "Dirty Words," "I Believe My Body," "The Show Business Nobody Knows," "Take Me Home with You," "Choir Practice," "And She Loved Me"

ACT II: "Poontang," "Come In My Mouth," "The Cunnilingus Champion of Company C," "Doesn't Anybody Love Anymore," "Let My People Come"

General Manager: Jay Kingwill
Company Manager: Robert H. Wallner
Press: Saul Richman, Fred Nathan
Stage Managers: Andie Wilson Kingwill, Ray Colbert

Still playing May 31, 1975. The following succeeded various members of the original cast during the season: Ray Colbert, James Morgan, Shezwae Powell, Christine Rubens, Dean Tait, Robin Charin, Stephan Burns, Steven Alex-Cole, Carl Deese, Judy Gibson, Jo Ann Lehmann, Edwina Lewis, Jim Rich, Tuesday Summers, Michael Poulos, Joanne Baron.

**Top: Tuesday Summers, Robin Charin
(R) Steven Alex-Cole, Marty Duffy**

**Ray Colbert, Tuesday Summers
Above: Christine Rubens, Steven Alex-Cole, Jim Rich**

MISS MOFFAT

Book, Emlyn Williams, Joshua Logan; Based on play "The Corn Is Green" by Emlyn Williams; Music, Albert Hague; Lyrics, Emlyn Williams; Director, Joshua Logan; Scenery and Lighting, Jo Mielziner; Costumes, Robert Mackintosh; Musical Direction, Jay Blackton; Orchestrations, Robert M. Freedman; Musical Numbers Staged by Donald Saddler; Associate Producer, Jim Milford; Production Associate, David Crain; Production Assistant, John Hillner; Hairstylist, Norman Allison; Incidental Music, Vocal and Dance Arrangements, Albert Hague; Additional Dance Music, Robert Rogers; Presented by Eugene V. Wolsk, Joshua Logan, Slade Brown; Opened at the Shubert Theatre in Philadelphia, Pa., Monday, Oct. 7, 1974 and closed there Thursday, Oct. 17, 1974 because of Miss Davis' illness.

CAST

Champ	Rudolf Lowe
Ty	Jaison Walker
Absie	Nat Jones
Zeke	Gian Carlo Esposito
Morgan Evans	Dorian Harewood
Jim	Kevin Dearinger
Jerry	Randy Martin
Larry	Michael Calkins
Mr. Jones	Lee Goodman
Mrs. Sprode	Anne Francine
Miss Ronberry	Dody Goodman
The Senator	David Sabin
Bessie Watty	Marion Ramsey
Miss Moffat	Bette Davis
Ole Mr. Pete	Avon Long
Marse Jeff	Gil Robbins

SCHOOLCHILDREN, PARENTS, ETC: Wendell Brown, Vicky Geyer, Yolande Graves, Helen Jennings, Betty Lynd, Pamela Palluzzi, Lacy Darryll Phillips, Sandra Philips, Janet Powell, Christine Tordenti

MUSICAL NUMBERS: "A Wonderful Game," "Pray for the Snow," "Here in the South," "Tomorrow," "There's More to a Man Than His Head," "Time's A-Flyin'," "You Don't Need a Nailfile in a Cornfield," "The Words Unspoken," "Peekaboo, Jehovah," "Go, Go, Morgan," "I Can Talk Now," "If I Weren't Me," "What Could Be Fairer Than That?," "The Debut I Owe," "I Shall Experience It Again."

A Musical in two acts and twelve scenes. The action takes place on and around a small plantation in a remote Southern part of the United States, and covers nearly three years early in this century.

General Managers: Wolsk & Azenberg
Company Manager: Martin Cohen
Press: Merle Debuskey, John L. Toohey
Stage Managers: Martin Herzer, David Taylor, Betty Lynd

Friedman-Abeles Photos

Dody Goodman, David Sabin, Bette Davis
Top Right: Bette Davis, Dody Goodman

Bette Davis, Marian Ramsey
Above: Bette Davis, Dorian Harewood

ATIONAL TOURING
COMPANIES

Failure to submit material unfortunately necessitated several omissions)

GOOD EVENING

y Peter Cook and Dudley Moore; Director, Jerry Adler; De-
ed by Robert Randolph; Production Assistant, Meg Simon;
rdrobe Supervisor, Ruth Tishman; Presented by Alexander H.
en and Bernard Delfont; Produced in association with Donald
gdon for Hemdale, Ltd.; An All-Star Forum Presentation.
ened Tuesday, February 4, 1975 at the National Theatre, Wash-
on, D.C. and still touring May 31, 1975.

CAST

PETER COOK
DUDLEY MOORE

RT I: "Hello," "On Location," "Madrigal," "Six of the Best,"
erman Lied," "Down the Mine," "One Leg Too Few," "Chan-
," "Soap Opera"

RT II: "Gospel Truth," "The Kwai Sonata," "The Frog and
ch," "An Appeal," "Tea for Two"

Comedy with music presented in two parts.
General Manager: Roy A. Somlyo
Company Manager: Charles Willard
Press: David Powers, Harry Davies
Stage Managers: Tom Urban, Phil DiMaggio

r original New York production, see THEATRE WORLD, Vol.

Peter Cook, Dudley Moore, also above

**Peter Cook, Dudley Moore,
also above**

IRENE

Book, Hugh Wheeler, Joseph Stein; From an adaptation by Harry Rigby; Based on original play by James Montgomery; Music, Harry Tierney; Lyrics, Joseph McCarthy; Additional Lyrics and Music, Charles Gaynor, Otis Clements; Musical Numbers Staged by Peter Gennaro; Original Production Supervised by Gower Champion; Production and Costumes Designed by Raoul Pene duBois; Lighting, David F. Segal; Music Direction, Robert Brandzel; Orchestrations, Ralph Burns; Dance Arrangements and Incidental Music, Wally Harper; Sound, Tony Alloy; Music Consultant and Coordinator, Joseph A. McCarthy; Associate Producer, Steven Beckler; Production Associate, Constance Montgomery; Tour Direction, Theatre NOW Inc.; Technical Director, Mitch Miller; Wardrobe Supervisor, Lucy Trama; Assistants to Peter Gennaro, Mary Ann Niles, Tony Stevens, David Evans; Hairstylist, John Mincieli; Production Assistant, Jeffrey Mont; Presented by Harry Rigby, Albert W. Selden and Jerome Minskoff. Opened Thursday, Sept. 13, 1974 at the Aerie Crown Theatre, Chicago, Ill. and closed May 3, 1974 at the Shubert in Boston, Mass.

CAST

Mrs. O'Dare	Patsy Kelly
Jane Burke	Penny Worth†1
Helen McFudd	Karen Weeden†2
Jimmy O'Flaherty	J.J. Epson
Irene O'Dare	Debbie Reynolds†3
Emmeline Marshall	Ruth Warrick
Clarkson	Albert Stephenson
Donald Marshall	Ron Husmann
Ozzie Babson	Ted Pugh†4
Madame Lucy	Hans Conried

DEBUTANTES: Christi Curtis, Mary Flowers, Silvia Hahn, Stephenie James, Jeanne Lehman, Merilee Magnuson, Jacqueline Payne, Kathryn Sandy

NINTH AVENUE FELLAS: Paul Charles, Dennis Edenfield, David Evans, J. J. Jepson, Stan Picus, Robert Rayow, Dennis Roth, Steve Short, Albert Stephenson

UNDERSTUDIES AND STANDBYS: Mrs. O'Dare, Thelma Lee; Mme. Lucy, Ozzie, Thomas Boyd; Irene, Jeanne Lehman; Carole Bishop, Kathryn Sandy; Swing Dancers, Judy Endacott, Steve Short

MUSICAL NUMBERS: "The World Must Be Bigger Than an Avenue," "The Family Tree," "Alice Blue Gown," "They Go Wild, Simply Wild," "An Irish Girl," "Stepping on Butterflies," "Mother Angel Darling," "The Riviera Rage," "The Last Part of Every Party," "We're Getting Away with It," "I'm Always Chasing Rainbows," "Irene," "The Great Lover Tango," "You Made Me Love You," Finale.

A Musical in two acts and eleven scenes.

General Managers: Theatre NOW, William Court Cohen, Edward H. Davis
Company Manager: G. Warren McClane
Stage Managers: Richard Hughes, Joe Lorden, Robert Corpora, Thomas Boyd

For original NY revival, see THEATRE WORLD, Vol. 29.
† Succeeded by: 1. Bette Glenn, 2. Carole Bishop, 3. Jane Powell, 4. Jess Richards

Top: Debbie Reynolds, Patsy Kelly
Right: Debbie Reynolds, Hans Conried

Ron Husmann, Debbie Reynolds, also above with Ruth Warrick

162

A LITTLE NIGHT MUSIC

Book, Hugh Wheeler; Suggested by Ingmar Bergman's film "Smiles of a Summer Night;" Music and Lyrics, Stephen Sondheim; Director, Harold Prince; Choreography, Patricia Birch; Scenic Production, Boris Aronson; Costumes, Florence Klotz; Lighting, Tharon Musser; Musical Direction, Richard Parrinello; Orchestration, Jonathan Tunick; Original Cast Album, Columbia Records; Wardrobe Supervisor, Colin Ferguson; Hairstylist, Richard Allen, David Carey; Assistant Conductor, Danny Troob; Production Supervisor, Ruth Mitchell; Presented by Harold Prince in association with Ruth Mitchell; Opened Tuesday, February 26, 1974 at the Forrest Theatre, Philadelphia, Pa., and closed Feb. 15, 1975 at the Shubert in Boston, Mass.

CAST

Mr. Lindquist	Elliott Savage
Mrs. Nordstrom	Kris Karlowski
Mrs. Anderssen	Marina MacNeal
Mr. Erlanson	Joe McGrath
Mrs. Segstrom	Karen Zenker
Fredrika Armfeldt	Marti Morris
Madame Armfeldt	Margaret Hamilton
Frid, her butler	Jonathan Banks
Henrik Egerman	Stephen Lehew
Anne Egerman	Virginia Pulos
Fredrik Egerman	George Lee Andrews
Petra	Mary Ann Chinn
Desiree Armfeldt	Jean Simmons
Bertrand, a page	James Ferrier
Count Carl-Magnus Malcolm	Ed Evanko
Countess Charlotte Malcolm	Andra Akers
Osa	Verna Pierce

UNDERSTUDIES: Desiree, Mary Ann Chinn; Mme. Armfeldt, Marina MacNeal; Fredrik, Count, Lindquist, Marshall Borden; Couness, Karen Zenker; Fredrika, Petra, Mrs. Segstrom, Mrs. Nordstrom, Mrs. Anderssen, Verna Pierce; Henrik, Frid, Erlanson, James Ferrier

MUSICAL NUMBERS: Overture, "Night Waltz," "Now," "Later," "Soon," "The Glamorous Life," "Remember?," "You Must Meet My Wife," "Liaisons," "In Praise of Women," "Every Day a Little Death," "A Weekend in the Country," "The Sun Won't Set," "It Would Have Been Wonderful," "Perpetual Anticipation," "Send in the Clowns," "The Miller's Son," Finale

A Musical in two acts. The action takes place at the turn of the century in Sweden.

General Manager: Howard Haines
Company Manager: John Caruso
Press: Mary Bryant, Gertrude Bromberg
Stage Managers: Ben Strobach, Patricia Drylie, Arlene Caruso

For original NY production, see THEATRE WORLD, Vol. 29.

Martha Swope Photos

Top Right: Margaret Hamilton, Jean Simmons
Below: Jean Simmons, Marti Morris

Jean Simmons (C)

George Lee Andrews, Ed Evanko

THE MAGIC SHOW

Book, Bob Randall; Songs, Stephen Schwartz; Magic, Doug Henning; Directed and Staged by Grover Dale; Setting, David Chapman; Costumes, Randy Barcelo; Lighting, Richard Nelson; Musical Director, Stephen Reinhardt; Dance Arrangements, David Spangler; Production Supervisor, Herb Vogler; Musical Conductor, Robert Billig; Associate Producer, Anan Pearlman; Audio, Robert Minor; Production Coordinator, Gary Gunas; Production Associate, Al Isaac; Presented by Edgar Lansbury, Joseph Beruh, Ivan Reitman; Opened Saturday, Dec. 21, 1974 at the Wilbur Theatre in Boston, Mass., and still touring May 31, 1975.

CAST

Magician	Peter DePaula
Cal	Pippa Pearthree
Feldman	Paul Keith
Charmin	Hester Lewellen
Donna	Susan Edwards
Dina	Signa Joy
Manny	Daniel Cass
Goldfarb	W. P. Dremak
Steve	Robert Brubach
Mike	Richard Balestrino
Goons	Joseph Abaldo, Bill Beyers, Betsy Lapka, Dara Norman
Off-Stage Voices	Hester Lewellen, W. P. Dremak

UNDERSTUDIES: Magician, Joseph Abaldo; Feldman, W. P. Dremak; Cal, Donna, Dara Norman; Charmin, Dina, Betsy Lapka; Manny, Richard Balestrino; Goldfarb, Brennan Roberts

A Magic Show with music performed without intermission.

General Management: Marvin A. Krauss Associates
Company Manager: Harold O. Kusell
Press: Gifford/Wallace, William Wilson, Merle Frimark
Stage Managers: William Falkner, Haig Shepherd, Joel Tropper

For original Broadway production, see THEATRE WORLD, Vol. 30.

Kenn Duncan Photos

Left: Peter DePaula, Pippa Pearthree, Paul Keith

Peter DePaula (chained)

Susan Edwards, Richard Balestrino, Robert Bruba Daniel Cass, Signa Joy, Paul Keith (C)

MY FAT FRIEND

By Charles Laurence; Director, Robert Moore; Scenery, William Ritman; Lighting, Martin Aronstein; Costumes, Sara Brook; Wardrobe Mistress, Penny Davis; Presented by James M. Nederlander by arrangement with Michael Godron; Opened Tuesday, Dec. 10, 1974 at the Fisher Theatre in Detroit, Mich., and closed Jan. 25, 1975 at the O'Keefe in Toronto, Can.

CAST

James .... John Lithgow
Henry .... George Rose
Vicky .... Lynn Redgrave
Tom .... Stephen C. Bradbury

UNDERSTUDIES: Vicky, Karen Shallo; Henry, John Clarkson; Tom, James, George Gitto

A Comedy in two acts and six scenes. The action takes place at the present time in Vicky's house and bookshop in a North Section of London.

Stage Managers: T. L. Boston, George Gitto

For original New York production, see THEATRE WORLD, Vol. 30.

Martha Swope Photos

Top: George Rose, Lynn Redgrave, John Lithgow

George Rose, Lynn Redgrave

NATIONAL SHAKESPEARE COMPANY

Artistic Director, Philip Meister; General Manager, Albert Schoemann; Managing Director, Elaine Sulka; Directors, Philip Meister (Merchant of Venice), Mario Siletti (Two Gentlemen of Verona), Neil Flanagan (The Miser); Scenery, Steven Rubin; Costumes, Cheryl Lovett; Tour Director, Mary Trone; Business Manager, Lloyd Kay; Company Manager, Richard Boddy; Press, Bill Errigo; Stage Managers, Murphy Guyer, Mark Blum, Thomas Bahring; Opened Sept. 23, 1974 Ulster County Community College, Stone Ridge, NY, and closed Apr. 25, 1975 at Rutgers University, Camden, N.J.

CAST

TWO GENTLEMEN OF VERONA by William Shakespeare

Duke of Milan	Larry Fishman
Valentine	Mark Blum
Proteus	S. Lockhart Fryer
Antonio/Second Outlaw	Warren Hansen Hansen
Thurio	Ronald Klein
Eglamour/Host/First Outlaw/ Panthino/William Shakespeare	Richard Boddy
Speed	Jack Powell
Launce	Thomas Bahring
Julia	Marilyn Hickey
Silvia	Kaaren Ragland
Lucetta/Dog	Michele Frankenberb

NATIONAL SHAKESPEARE COMPANY
THE MERCHANT OF VENICE by William Shakespeare

Antonio	Richard Boddy
Lorenzo	Thomas Bahring
Gratiano	Larry Fishman
Salario/Aragon	S. Lockhart Fryer
Bassanio	Murphy Guyer
Salanio/Morocco	Warren Hansen
Shylock	Ronald Klein
Launcelot Gobbo/Tubal/Duke/Punch and Judy Man	Jack Powell
Portia	Michele Frankenberg
Nerissa	Marilyn Hickey
Jessica	Kaaren Ragland

NATIONAL SHAKESPEARE COMPANY
THE MISER by Moliere

Harpagon	Jack Powell
Cleante	Mark Blum
Elise	Marilyn Hickey
Valere	S. Lockhart Fryer
Mariane	Kaaren Ragland
Anselm/Brindavoine	Warren Hansen
Frosine	Michele Frankenberg
Simon/Officer	Richard Boddy
Jacques	Larry Fishman
La Fleche	Murphy Guyer
Dame Claude	Ronald Klein
La Merluche	Thomas Bahring

Alan Carey Photos

Top Right: Ronald Klein in "Two Gentlemen of Verona" Below: Michele Frankenberg, Warren Hansen, Marilyn Hickey in "The Merchant of Venice"

S. Lockhart Fryer, Larry Fishman, Jack Powell in "The Miser"

THE NEW YORK THEATRE COMPANY

Artistic Director, Philip Meister; Managing Director, Elaine Sulka; General Manager, Albert Schoemann; Direction and Choreography, Richard Ronald Beebe; Sets, John Fallabella; Costumes, Kevin Woodworth; Tour Director, Mary Trone; Business Manager, Lloyd Kay; Company Manager, Dennis Sook, Rob Grandfors. Opened Tuesday, October 22, 1974 at Wofford College, Spartanburg, S.C., and closed March 25, 1975 at Ohio Northern University, Ada, Ohio.

PRODUCTIONS AND CASTS

THE FANTASTICKS by Tom Jones (Book and Lyrics) and Harvey Schmidt (Music)

Mute	Jim Hay
Hucklebee	Dennis Warning
Amy Bellamy	Lydia Roberts
Luisa	Joan W. Gardner†1
Matt	Martin Bestimt
El Gallo	Jeffrey Rockwell
Henry	Dennis Sook†2
Pianist	James Ferrario
Stage Manager	Dennis Sook

† Succeeded by: 1. Valerie Joy Miller, 2. Rob Granfors

THE APPLE TREE with Book, Music and Lyrics by Sheldon Harnick and Jerry Bock

"Adam and Eve"

Adam	Dennis Warning
Eve	Joan W. Gardner†1
Snake	Jeffrey Rockwell
Stage Manager: Jim Hay	

"The Lady or the Tiger"

Balladeer	Martin Bestimt
Soldiers	Jim Hay, Jeffrey Rockwell
Courtesan	Joan W. Gardner†1
Princess Barbara	Lydia Roberts
King Arik	Dennis Sook†3
Captain Sanjar	Jeffrey Rockwell
Nadjira	Joan W. Gardner†1
Tiger	Dennis Warning†2
Stage Manager: Dennis Warning†2	

"Passionella"

Narrator	Jim Hay
Ella/Passionella	Lydia Roberts
Reporter	Joan W. Gardner†1
Mr. Fallible	Dennis Sook†2
Director	Martin Bestimt
Starlet	Joan W. Gardner†1
Producer	Dennis Sook†2
Flip	Dennis Warning
Piano	James Ferrario
Stage Manager	Jeffrey Rockwell

BERLIN TO BROADWAY WITH KURT WEILL with text and format by Gene Lerner; Music, Kurt Weill

COMPANY

Martin Bestimt
Joan W. Gardner†1
Jim Hay
Lydia Roberts
Jeffrey Rockwell
Dennis Warning

Piano	James Ferrario
Stage Manager	Dennis Sook†2

* Succeeded by: 1. Valerie Joy Miller, 2. Rob Granfors, 3. Dennis Warning

Conrad Ward Photos

p Right: Lydia Roberts, Dennis Warning in "The Fantasticks" Below: Joan W. Gardner, Dennis Warning in "The Apple Tree" Bottom: James errario, Lydia Roberts, Dennis Warning, Joan W. dner, Martin Bestimp, Jeffrey Rockwell, Jim Hay in "Berlin to Broadway"

NOEL COWARD IN TWO KEYS

Two Plays by Noel Coward; Director, Vivian Matalon; Setting and Lighting, William Ritman; Costumes, Ray Diffen; Assistant to the Producers, Jerry Sirchia; Wardrobe Supervisor, Clarence Sims; Hairstylist, Michael Wasula; Associate Producers, Michael Kasdan, Michael Frazier; Presented by Richard Barr and Charles Woodward; Opened Monday, Feb. 17, 1975 at the Playhouse in Wilmington, Del., and still touring May 31, 1975.

CAST

"Come into the Garden, Maud"

Anna-Mary Conklin	Jessica Tandy
Felix, a waiter	Joel Parks
Verner Conklin	Hume Cronyn
Maud Caragnani	Anne Baxter

The action of both plays takes place at the present time in a private suite in a luxurious hotel in Switzerland.

"A Song at Twilight"

Hilde Latymer	Jessica Tandy
Felix, a waiter	Joel Parks
Hugo Latymer	Hume Cronyn
Carlotta Gray	Anne Baxter

STANDBYS: For Misses Tandy and Baxter, Ludi Claire; for Mr. Cronyn, Laurence Hugo; for Mr. Parks, Robert Rigamonti

General Manager: Michael Kasdan
Company Manager: Oscar Abraham
Press: Betty Lee Hunt Associates, Maurice Turet
Stage Managers: Paul Foley, Robert Rigamonti

For original New York production, see THEATRE WORLD, Vol. 30.

Friedman-Abeles Photos

Hume Cronyn, Joel Parks, Anne Baxter
Top: Hume Cronyn, Anne Baxter

Top: Jessica Tandy, Hume Cronyn

ODYSSEY

By Erick Segal; Music, Mitch Leigh; Director, Albert Marre; Choreography, Billy Wilson; Scenery and Lighting, Howard Bay; Costumes, Howard Bay, Ray Diffen; Musical Direction, Ross Reimueller; Orchestrations, Buryl Red; Dance Arrangements, Danny Holgate; Assistant to Choreographer, Jeff Phillips; Production Manager, Franco Gratale; Associate Conductor, Bruce Steeg; Production Assistants, Kay Vance, John Hillner; Wardrobe Supervisor, Byron Brice; Hairstylist, Gloria Rivera; Produced by Kennedy Center Productions; Opened Thursday, Dec. 19, 1974 at the John F. Kennedy Center for Performing Arts, Washington, D.C., and still touring May 31, 1975.

CAST

Odysseus	Yul Brynner
Penelope, his wife	Joan Diener
Telamachus, his son	Russ Thacker
Penelope's Suitors:	
Antinous	Martin Vidnovic
Agelaos	Greg Bell
Ktesippos	Bill Mackey
Eurymachus	Michael Mann
Leokritos	Brian Destazio
Pimteus	John Gorrin
Mulios	Jeff Phillips
Polybos	Derrick Bell
King Alkinoos	Shev Rodgers
Nausikaa, his daughter	Diana Davila
Nausikaa's Handmaidens:	
Therapina	Christine Uchida
Melantho	Cecile Santos
Hippodameia	P. J. Mann
Kerux, the herald	Garon Douglass
Kalypso, a nymph	Catherine Lee Smith
Polyphemus	Ian Sullivan

STANDBYS AND UNDERSTUDIES: Odysseus, Shev Rodgers; Penelope, Karen Shepard; Telamachus, Garon Douglass; Antinous, Agelaos, Alkinoos, Ian Sullivan; Nausikaa, Suzanne Sponsler; Swing Dancers, A. William Perkins, Suzanne Sponsler.

A Musical Play. The action takes place in and around Odysseus' palace on the island of Ithaka, and on various islands in Odysseus' travels—nine years after the Trojan War.

General Managers: Wolsk & Azenberg
Company Manager: Fred J. Cuneo
Press: John L. Toohey
Stage Managers: Patrick Horrigan, Gregory Allen Hirsch

**Right: Joan Diener, Yul Brynner
Top: Shev Rodgers, Diana Davila, Yul Brynner, Russ Thacker**

Yul Brynner, Catherine Lee Smith

Joan Diener

169

PIPPIN

Book, Roger O, Hirson; Music and Lyrics, Stephen Schwartz; Direction and Choreography, Bob Fosse; Scenery, Tony Walton; Costumes, Patricia Zipprodt; Lighting, Jules Fisher; Musical Direction, Milton Setzer; Orchestrations, Ralph Burns; Dance Arrangements, John Berkman; Dances and Musical Staging Reproduced by Kathryn Doby; Original Cast Album, Motown Records; Assistant to the Director, Lola Shumlin; Production Assistant, Camille Ranson; Hairstylist, Werner Sherer; Wardrobe Supervisor, Edward Myers; Presented by Stuart Ostrow in association with Theatre NOW, Inc; Tour Direction, American Theatre Productions, Inc.; Opened Friday, Sept. 20, 1974 at the Masonic Temple Theatre, Scranton, Pa., and closed Apr. 5, 1975 in Wilmington, Del.

CAST

Leading Player	Irving Lee
Pippin	Barry Williams
Charles	I. M. Hobson
Lewis	Adam Grammis
Fastrada	Louisa Flaningam
Sword Bearer	Danny Ruvolo
The Head	Guy Allen
Berthe	Dortha Duckworth
Beggar	Guy Allen
Peasant	Danny Ruvolo
Noble	Gary Flannery
Field Marshall	Loyd Sannes
Catherine	Carol Fox Prescott
Theo	Eric Brown

STANDBYS AND UNDERSTUDIES: Leading Player, Pippin, P. J. Benjamin; Charles, Guy Allen; Catherine, Laurie Skinner; Fastrada, Beverly Hartz; Lewis, Chuck Beard; Theo, Danny Ruvolo

General Managers: Joseph Harris, Ira Bernstein
Company Manager: Peter Russell
Press: Fred Weterick, Solters/Roskin
Stage Managers: John H. Lowe III, Kenneth Porter, Laurie Skinner

For original New York production, see THEATRE WORLD, Vol. 29.

Friedman-Abeles Photos

**Left: I. M. Hobson and cast
Top: Barry Williams, I. M. Hobson, Louisa
Flannigam, Adam Grammis**

Irving Lee and dancers

Dortha Duckworth

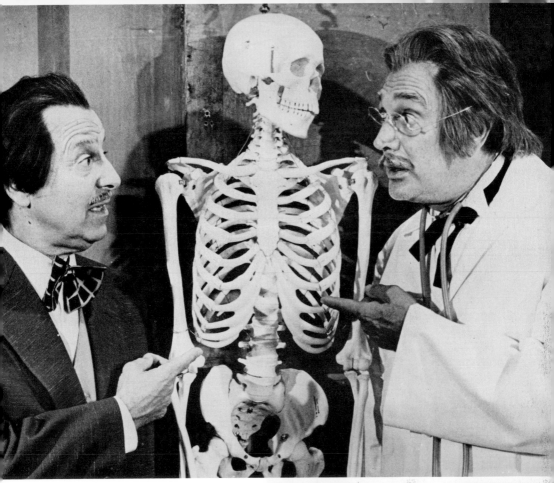

THE SUNSHINE BOYS

By Neil Simon; Director, Tom Porter; Scenery, Kert Lundell;
stumes, Albert Wolsky; Lighting, Tharon Musser; Wardrobe Su-
visor, Donald Grubler; Tour Direction, Columbia Artists Theat-
als Corp.; Presented by Emanuel Azenberg and Eugene V. Wolsk;
ened Friday, Oct. 11, 1974 in the Masonic Auditorium of Scran-
, Pa., and closed Apr. 17, 1975 in the Jesse Auditorium, Colum-
, Mo.

CAST

llie Clark	Robert Alda†
n Silverman	Harvey Siegel
Lewis	Arny Freeman
tient	Dennis Piatak
die	Joe Calvan
etch Nurse	Michele Dubou
rse O'Neill	Urylee Leonardos

A Comedy in two acts. The action takes place at the present time.

General Manager: Jose Vega
Company Manager: L. Liberatore
Press: David Lipsky
Stage Managers: Hal Halvorsen, Joe Calvan

r original New York production, see THEATRE WORLD, Vol.

Succeeded by Eddie Bracken

Top: Arny Freeman, Robert Alda

Eddie Bracken, Arny Freeman

NASH AT NINE

Verses and Lyrics, Ogden Nash; Music, Milton Rosenstock; Conceived and Directed by Martin Charnin; Sets, David Chapman; Costumes, Theoni V. Aldredge; Lighting, Martin Aronstein; At the pianos, Rod Derefinko, Brooks Morton; Associate Producer, Buddy Noro; Presented by Les Schecter and Barbara Schwei; Opened Tuesday, January 28, 1975 at Ford's Theatre, Washington, D. C., and closed March 16, 1975 at the Mechanic Theatre in Baltimore, Md.

CAST

Craig Stevens
Harvey Evans
Jane Summerhays
John Stratton

UNDERSTUDIES: Mr. Stevens, John Stratton; Mr. Evans-Mr. Stratton, Richard Crystal; Ms. Summerhays, Bonnie Hinson.

Performed without an intermission.

General Manager: Sherman Gross
Press: Les Schecter, Barbara Schwei
Stage Managers: F. R. McCall, Rich Rosdale

Right: Craig Stevens, Jane Summerhays

TREASURE ISLAND

Book, Tom Tippett; Adapted from the novel by Robert L Stevenson; Music and Lyrics, John Clifton; Director, Evan Tho son; lighting, Barry Arnold; Costumes, Jennie Cleaver; Setti John Nelson; Musical Direction and Arrangements, John Cli Executive Producer, Adelaide Sutherland; Assistant to the ducers, Ann Juliet Scott; Presented by A. Sutherland, Shepard, ton & Thompson in association with Theatre NOW, Inc.; Ope Monday, Jan. 20, 1975 at the DuPont Playhouse, Wilmington, I and closed Mar. 8, 1975 at the Shubert in New Haven, Conn.

CAST

Jim Hawkins	Joan Shep
Billy Bones/Dr. Livesey/Israel Hands	Evan Thom
Black Dog/Dick Johnson/Ben Gunn	Jerry Je
Blind Pew/Capt. Smollett/Tom Morgan	Bill S
Dirk/Job Anderson	Michael Bur
Squire Trelawny/George Merry	Alan Abr
Long John Silver	Christopher C

UNDERSTUDIES: Jim, Jerry Jerger; Long John Silver, E Thompson; General Understudy: Michael Burke†
MUSICAL NUMBERS: "Treasure Island," "I'll Buy Me a Sh "Gold," "That's What I Would Do," "Honest Sailors," "Yo-F "Let's Be Friends."

General Managers: Theatre NOW, Inc.
Company Managers: Donald Tirabassi, Marin Tirabassi
Press: Bill Steele
Stage Managers: Michael Sinclair, Michael Burke†
† Succeeded by Keith Perry

**Evan Thompson, Christopher Cable,
Joan Shepard in "Treasure Island"**

172

WHAT'S A NICE COUNTRY LIKE YOU DOING IN A STATE LIKE THIS?

Based on an original concept by Ira Gasman, Cary Hoffman and Bernie Travis; Directed and Choreographed by Miriam Fond; Lighting, Michael Langford; Costumes, Mary McReady; Producers, Susan Douglas Rubes, Marlene Smith, W. J. DeLaurentis; Presented by Young Peoples Theatre, Marlene Smith, W. J. DeLaurentis: Opened Monday, June 10, 1974 at Theatre in the Dell, Toronto, Canada, moved Mar. 17, 1975 to Firehall Restaurant, and still playing May 31, 1975.

CAST

Trudy Desmond†

Martin Short

Claude Tessier†

Andrea Martin†

Richard Whelan†

ACT I; "It's a Typically, Topical Revue," 'Massage a Trois," "Changing Partners," "I'm in Love with . . .," "I Believe in," "Haldeman und Ehrlichman and Klein," "Oi!," "Male Chauvinist Pig," "Street Suite: Street People, It's Getting Better, I Like Me," "Love Story," "The Cover-up," "Hallelujah," "Daniel Boone," "New York Suite: But I Love New York, Why Do I keep Going to the Theatre?," "I Found the Girl of My Dreams on Broadway," "A Mugger's Work Is Never Done"
ACT II: "1984," "Farewell First Amendment," "Watergate Waltz," "I'm in Love with . . .," "Johannesburg," "Fill'er Up," "Liberation Tango," "I'm Not Myself," "Porcupine Suite: People Are Like Porcupines, Bar Scene, Threesome, Bedroom Scene, A Scale of One to Ten," "Come on, Daisy," "Whatever Happened to the Communist Menace?," Finale.

A Satirical Musical of the '70's presented in two acts.

General Manager: W. J. DeLaurentis
Stage Manager: Don Thomas
Press: Marlene Smith

† Succeeded by Nancy Dolman, Mary Ann McDonald, Derk McGrath, Gerry Salsberg

Musical Director, Irwin Webb; Scenery and Lighting, Elizabeth Karsner; Costumes, Elinor Shalman; Press, Bill Watters Associates; Production Assistant, Charles H. Eglee; Presented by Executive Media; Opened Wednesday, Oct. 30, 1974 at the Meeting House Cabaret, Los Angeles, Cal., and still playing May 31, 1975.

CAST

Suzanne Astor

Lorry Goldman

Bill LaVallee

Trudy Desmond

Michael Scott

Musical Director, Robert Goldstone; Stage Design, Paul Fitzmaurice; Set and Lighting, Mark Rubinsky; Costumes, Thomas Neil Crater; Technical Director, Alfred Borden IV; Press, James McCormick; Stage Manager, Jerry Campbell; Presented by Michael Frazier, FLF Productions; Opened Thursday, Feb. 6, 1975 at the Cabaret—Just Jazz, in Philadelphia, Pa., and closed there Apr. 12, 1975.

CAST

Dan Levoff

Tom Offt

Mary Ann Robbins

Tina Marsh

Michael Tucci

Musical Director, Bruce Kellet; Set, Glenn Macdonald, Bert Woldring; Lighting, John Beatty; Stage Manager, Sid Kozak; Producer, Marlene Smith; Opened Wednesday, Apr. 16, 1975 at Stage West, Vancouver, Can., and still play May 31, 1975.

CAST

Joanie Bye

Marek Norman

Ruth Nicol

Jeff Hyslop

Edd Wright

Top Right: Claude Tessier, Andrea Martin, Richard Whelan, Trudy Desmond, Martin Short
(Robert C. Ragsdale Photo)

Below: Mary Ann McDonald, Gerry Salsberg, Nancy Dolman, Derek McGrath, Martin Short
(Paul Appleby Photo)

Bottom: Edd Wright, Joanie Bye, Marek Norman, Jeff Hyslop, Ruth Nichol
(Glen E. Erikson Photo)

AMERICAN SHAKESPEARE THEATRE

Stratford, Connecticut
June 11 through September 1, 1974
Twentieth Season
Artistic Director, Michael Kahn; Managing Director, William Stewart; Director of Educational Projects, Mary Hunter Wolf; Staff Repertory Director, Philip Taylor; Production Manager, Lo Hardin; Stage Managers, Walter W. Meyer, Stephen Nasuta; Wardrobe Mistress, Helen McMahon; Production Assistants, Steve Butler, Hayward Grainger, Roseann Isgro, Lowell Detweiler, Lawrence Casey, Larry Carpenter; Musical Director-Conductor, Judith Somogi; Business Manager, Donald Bundock; Press, Anne Marie Borger, Arts Counterparts, Bruce Wiener; Scenic Designer, John Conklin; Costume Designer, Jane Greenwood; Lighting Designer, Marc B. Weiss; Choreographer, Elizabeth Keen.

COMPANY

Elizabeth Ashley, Jeanne Bartlett, David Birney, Philip Carling, Larry Carpenter, Keir Dullea, Jack Gwillim, Fred Gwynne, Philip Kerr, William Larsen, Michael Levin, Roberta Maxwell, Tom McLaughlin, Caroline McWilliams, Joan Pape, Wyman Pendleton, Sarah Peterson, Kate Reid, David Rounds, John Seidman, Carole Shelley, Theodore Sorel, Donald Warfield, Gregg Almquist, Christine Baranski, Robert Beseda, Michael Houlihan, Joe Muzikar, Franklyn Seales.

REPERTOIRE

"Twelfth Night" directed by David William, "Romeo and Juliet" directed by Michael Kahn, "Cat on a Hot Tin Roof" directed by Michael Kahn

Martha Swope Photos

Right: Roberta Maxwell, Kate Reid in "Romeo and Juliet" Above: David Rounds, Fred Gwynne, John Seidman, Carole Shelley in "Twelfth Night"

**Keir Dullea, Elizabeth Ashley
in "Cat on a Hot Tin Roof"**

**Roberta Maxwell, David Birney
in "Romeo and Juliet"**

GLOBE OF THE GREAT SOUTHWEST

Odessa, Texas
June 21 through August 25, 1974
Sixth Season
Producing Director, Charles David McCally; Press, Wanda Snodgrass, John Bagwell, Pat Bodenhorn; Technical Director, Roger Titus; Stage Managers, Bob Gibson, Mark Wagner, Haskell Hestand, Charles Pogue; Guest Director, Claire Luce

COMPANY

Mary Jane Atkinson, Ev Lunning, Patricia McColm, Wayne Narey, Brenda Nickerson, Mark Wagner, Deanna Dunagan, Ad Cover, Charles Pogue, Barry S. Eisenberg, Roger Titus, James Daniels, Gregory Edwin Wurz, Timothy Jenkins, Ritch Brinkley

Doug Kremer, David Roberts, Haskell Hestand, Mike D. Morris, Joe Durham, Mary Jo Goss, Craig Cooper, Norman Nelson, Brett Elise McCally, Bob Gibson, Sabrina Green, Steve McGuire

REPERTOIRE

"Macbeth," "Twelfth Night," "The Imaginary Invalid"

John Bagwell Photos

Right: Wayne Narey, Patricia McColm in "Twelfth Night"

Ritch Brinkley, Brett Elise McCally in "The Imaginary Invalid"

James Daniels, Deanna Dunagan in "Macbeth"

GREAT LAKES SHAKESPEARE FESTIVAL

Lakewood, Ohio
July 6–September 28, 1974
Producer-Director, Lawrence Carra; Production Coordinator, Frederic Youens; Sets, Mark Pirolo, Michael Olich, Frederic Youens; Costumes, William French; Lighting, Frederic Youens; Stage Manager, Robert W. Pitman; Guest Director, Henry Hewes; Press, Ron Henry, William N. Rudman

COMPANY

Wesley Addy, Robert Allman, Carol Emshoff, Nathaniel Fuller, Tom Fuccello, Janet Hayes, Gregory Lehane, Kendall March, Keith Mackey, John Newton, Edith Owen, Robert W. Pitman, M. Jonathan Steele, Richard Yarnell

REPERTOIRE

"King Lear," "The Playboy of the Western World," "Measure for Measure," "Under the Gaslight," "Comedy of Errors"

James Fry Photos

Left: Kendall March, Gregory Lehane, Robert Allman in "Playboy of the Western World" Below: Wesley Addy, Tom Fuccello, Keith Mackey, Gregory Lehane in "King Lear"

Carol Emshoff, Edith Owen, Kendall March, Wesley Addy in "Under the Gaslight"

Keith Mackey, Kendall March, Gregory Lehane, Jonathan Steele in "Playboy of the Western World"

Victor Buono, Penelope Fuller
in "Henry IV, Part II"

Tim Matheson, Penelope Fuller
in "Romeo and Juliet"

NATIONAL SHAKESPEARE FESTIVAL

San Diego, California
June 4 through September 15, 1974
Twenty-fifth Season

Producing Director, Craig Noel; Art Director, Peggy Kellner; Coordinator, Tom Corcoran; Stage Managers, Ken Brocious, Carl Reggiardo, Stephen Storer; Assistant Designers, Scott Busath, Brigitte Sitte; Props, Steve Carmack, Roger Mask; Production Assistants, James Gill, Bennett E. McClellan; Sound, Nathan Haas; Dance Consultant, Vivan Woll; Press, William B. Eaton; Resident Composer, Conrad Susa; Fencing Master, Anthony DeLongis

COMPANY

Penelope Fuller, Wiley Harker, Carl Weintraub, Barry Kraft, Paul Baccus, Ralph Meyering, Jr., James Ryan, Anthony DeLongis, Tom Searle, Benjamin Stewart, Lois Foraker, John Glover, Sandy McCallum, Mary Layne, Karen Hensel Bailey, Holly Schoonover, Katherine Brecka, Eric Christmas, Michael Horton, Tom Ramirez, Marc Weishaus, Lanny Broyles, David Hewson, Margaret Fitzgerald, Benjamin Stewart, Jenifer Henn, Harry Frazier, Jacqueline De Haviland, Wiley Harker, Charles Goldman, Weldon Garrett, Tim Matheson, Leila Sardagna, Robert Cornthwaite, Derek Murcott, G. W. Bailey, Victor Buono, Chuck Halpern, Parlan McGaw, Michael Nowicki, Wilson Ochoa, David Meyers, Christopher Desmond, Rhys Stewart, Michael Byers, Nada Rowand, Robin Taylor, David Cahalan, Charles W. Mark

REPERTOIRE

"Twelfth Night" directed by Eric Christmas and Craig Noel, "Romeo and Juliet" directed by Diana Maddox, "King Henry IV, Part II" directed by Edward Payson Call, "Your Own Thing" directed and choreographed by Walter Willison

**Center: (L) Victor Buono, John Glover
in "Henry IV, Part II" (R) John Glover,
Lois Foraker, Eric Christmas, Benjamin
Stewart in "Twelfth Night"**

Robin Taylor, Michael Byers
in "Your Own Thing"

NEW JERSEY SHAKESPEARE FESTIVAL

Madison, N.J.
June 25–September 15, 1974
Tenth Season

Artistic Director, Paul Barry; Press, Ellen Barry; Stage Managers, Richard Gibson, Gary Porto; Scenic Designer-Technical Director, David M. Glenn; Costume Designer, Gay Beale Smith; Lighting Designer, Gary Porto; Treasurer, Philip Bennis; Directors of Educational Programs, Sylvia Felder, James R. Lee

COMPANY

Paul Barry, Ellen Barry, Greg Bell, Tom Brennan, Catherine Byers, John Capodice, Philip Hanson, J. C. Hoyt, Robert Machray, Timothy Meyers, Bill E. Noone, Martha Sherrill, Ronald Steelman, William Preston, Margery Shaw, and 72 interns

REPERTOIRE

"Measure for Measure," "Under Milk Wood," "J. B.," "Richard II," "Steambath"

Right: Ramon Ramos, Timothy Meyers, Greg Bell, John Greenleaf, Brian Lynner (kneeling) in "Richard II" Top: "Measure for Measure"

Bill Noone, Robert Machray, Philip Hanson in "J. B." Above: J. C. Hoyt, Greg Bell, John Capodice in "Richard II"

"Under Milk Wood" Above: Robert Machray, Timothy Meyers in "Steambath"

178

NEW YORK SHAKESPEARE FESTIVAL

Delacorte Theater-Central Park
New York, N.Y.
June 20–August 24, 1974
Eighteenth Season

Producer, Joseph Papp; Associate Producer, Bernard Gersten; Production Supervisor, David Eidenberg; Technical Coordinator, Rob Ingenthron; Stage Managers, D. W. Koehler, Jason Steven Cohen; Production Manager, Andrew Mihok; Assistant to the Producer, Gail Merrifield; Technical Director, Mervyn Haines, Jr.; Music Coordinator, Herbert Harris; Press, Merle Debuskey, Norman L. Berman; Production Associate, Meir Zvi Ribalow; Props, Deborah Pope; Wardrobe, James McGaha; Production Assistant, Richard Hirsch; Hairstylist, Dorman Alison; General Manager, David Black

June 20–July 20, 1974

PERICLES

By William Shakespeare; Director, Edward Berkeley; Assistant to the Director, Alexandra Elson; Settings, Santo Loquasto; Costumes, John Conklin; Lighting, Martin Aronstein; Music, William Penn; Dance and Mime, Dennis Nahat

CAST

Barnard Hughes (Gower/Chorus), Lex Monson (Antiochus/Fisherman), Carol Cole (Daughter of Antiochus/Diana), Lenny Baker (Thaliard/Boult), Steven Burleigh (Messenger/Knight), Randall Duk Kim (Pericles), Graham Brown (Helicanus/A Pander), Ted Swetz (Escanes/Fisherman), Richard Ramos (Cleon), Dimitra Arliss (Dionyza), Armand Assante (Leonine/Knight), Roland Sanchez (Pirate), Kenneth Marshall (Pirate), Bob Harders (Pirate), Tom Toner (Simonides/Cerimon), Charlotte Moore (Thaisa), Helen Stenborg (Lychorida), Marybeth Hurt (Marina), Gastone Rossilli (Knight/Lysimachus), Juan Palma (Knight), Michael Hammond (Philemon), Sasha von Scherler (A Bawd), Rise Collins (Companion to Marina)

July 25–August 24, 1974

THE MERRY WIVES OF WINDSOR

By William Shakespeare; Director, David Margulies; Settings, Santo Loquasto; Costumes, Carrie Robbins; Lighting, Martin Aronstein; Music, Robert Dennis; Dances, Donald Saddler

CAST

Tom Toner (Shallow), Lenny Baker (Slender), George Pentecost (Sir Hugh Evans), George Hearn (George Page), Barnard Hughes (Falstaff), Ernest Austin (Bardolph), Jaime Sanchez (Pistol), Dennis Tate (Nym), Michael Tucker (Simple), Deborah Offner (Ann Page), Kenneth McMillan (Host), Marilyn Sokol (Mistress Quickly), Danny DeVito (Rugby), David Hurst (Dr. Caius), Frederick Coffin (Fenton), Marcia Rodd (Mistress Page), Cynthia Harris (Mistress Ford), Joseph Bova (Ford), Matthew Douglas Anton (Robin), Richard Hamburger (John), Michael Hammond (Robert), Stephen Austin (William Page), Villagers: Michael Austin, Linda Howes, Reginald Vel Johnson, Sam McMurray, Davie Wier, Alan Woolf, Wendie Marks

July 24–August 18, 1974
Mobile Theater

WHAT THE WINE-SELLERS BUY

By Ron Milner; Director, Woodie King, Jr.; Setting, Leo Yoshimura; Costumes, Judy Dearing; Lighting, Lawrence Metzler

CAST

Herbert Rice (Steve), David Harris (Joe), Dick A. Williams (Rico), Juanita Clark (Mrs. Carlton) Loretta Greene (Mae), Gylan Kain (Hustler/George), Joan Pryor (Voice/Mrs. Harris), Sonny Jim Gaines (Jim), Yusef Iman (Old Bob), Ron Trice (Melvin), Starletta DePaur (Frances), Dianne Kirksey (Helen), Ramona King (Marilyn), Kyle Duncan (Red), Todd Davis (Hunt), Leon Pinkney (Pete/Cabdriver)
STANDBYS AND UNDERSTUDIES: Rico, Jim, Aaron, George, Roscoe Orman; Steve, Lawrence Hilton Jacobs; Old Bob, Harrison Avery; Cab Driver, David Harris; Rico, Gylan Kain

Friedman-Abeles Photos

Top Right: Barnard Hughes, Marybeth Hurt, Charlotte Moore, Randall Duk Kim in "Pericles" Below: Barnard Hughes in "Merry Wives of Windsor"

Juanita Clark, Herbert Rice in "What the Wine-Sellers Buy"

179

OREGON SHAKESPEARE FESTIVAL

Ashland, Oregon
June 15–September 15, 1974
Thirty-fourth Season

Founder-Development Consultant, Angus L. Bowmer; Production Director, Jerry Turner; General Manager, William Patton; Scenic Designer, Richard L. Hay; Lighting Designer, Steven A. Maze; Resident Directors, Laird Williamson, Jim Edmondson; Production Coordinator, Pat Patton; Technical Director, Andrew J. Traister; Director of Music, Todd Barton; Choreographer, Judith Kennedy; Vocal Coach, Cornelia Clemens; Costume Director, Richard Hieronymus; Stage Managers, Mark Harrison, Lyle Raper, James Verdery; Press, Janis Nelson, Ruth Brookman

COMPANY

Neville L. Archambault, Denis Arndt, Raye Birk, Jeff Brooks, Franklin Brown, David Q. Combs, Joseph V. DeSalvio, James A. Donadio, le Clanche du Rand, Jim Edmondson, Mona Lee Fultz, Kirk Gibson, Douglas Hadley, Michael Hall, Mark Harrison, Christine Healy, Will Huddleston, A. Bryan Humphrey, Jay Longan, John Mansfield, Judith Metskas, Eric Booth Miller, Margit Moe, Michael Kevin Moore, Mark D. Murphey, Todd Oleson, Victor Pappas, Shirley Patton, John Renforth, Richard Riehle, James Ringer, Diane Salinger, Warner Shook, Peter Silbert, Lee Stetson, Ernie Stewart, Mary Turner, Laird Williamson, Cal Winn
DANCERS: Barbara Barton, Odysseus Llowell, Sandy Lynch, Mary Molodovsky, JoAnn Johnson Patton, Marcia Pedrick, Richard Reynolds, T. J. Rizzo, Rebecca Robbins

REPERTOIRE

"Twelfth Night" directed by Jim Edmondson, "The Tragedy of Titus Andronicus" directed by Laird Williamson, "Hamlet" directed by Jerry Turner, "Two Gentlemen of Verona" directed by Laird Williamson, "Waiting for Godot" directed by Andrew J. Traister, "The Time of Your Life" directed by Pat Patton

Hank Kranzler Photos

Left: Ernie Stewart, Jeff Brooks, Cal Winn, Richard Riehle in "A Funny Thing Happened on the Way to the Forum" Top: Michael Kevin Moore, Jeff Brooks, Christine Healy in "Twelfth Night"

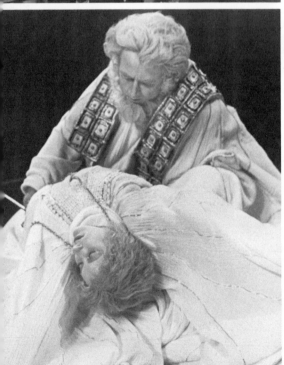

Denis Arndt, Christine Healy in "Titus Andronicus"   Raye Birk, Mary Turner in "Hamlet"

180

STRATFORD FESTIVAL OF CANADA

Stratford, Ontario
June 3–October 26, 1974
Twenty-second Season

General Manager, Bruce Swerdfager; Artistic Director, Jean Gascon; Associate Directors, William Hutt, Michael Bawtree; Executive Producer, John Hayes; Business Manager, Gerald J. Corner; Production Manager, Jack Hutt; Technical Directors, Robert Scales, Misha N. Tarasoff; Music Director, Raffi Armenian; Music Administrator, Stuart Knussen; Press, Mary Webb, Anne Selby, Barbara Van Luven; Company Manager, Max Helpman; Stage Managers, Vincent Berns, Paddy McEntee, Nora Polley, Elspeth Gaylor, Brian Longstaff, Catherine McKeehan; Directors, Jean Gascon, Michael Bawtree, Peter Dews, John Wood, Arif Hasnain; Designers, Leslie Hurry, Tanya Moiseiwitsch, Sam Kirkpatrick, Brian Jackson, Robert Prevost, Francois Barbeau, Grant Guy, Susan Benson, John Ferguson; Lighting, Gil Wechsler, Michael J. Whitfield.

COMPANY

Don Allison, Edward Atienza, Ken Atkinson, Michael Ball, Diana Barrington, Keith Batten, John Bayliss, Rod Beattie, Pat Bentley-Fisher, Jean Bergmann, Darryl Beschell, Mervyn Blake, Sara Botsford, Jean Francois Boucher, Bonnie Britton, Pamela Brook, Garnet Brooks, Daniel Jean Buccos, Michael Burgess, Eleanor Calbes, Douglas Campbell, Graeme Campbell, J. Kenneth Campbell, Barbara Carter, Patricia Collins, Jack Creley, Richard Curnock, Diana D'Aquila, John J. Dee, Diane Dewey, Sebastien Dhavernas, Martin Donley, Rosemary Dunsmore, Mary Lou Fallis, Donna Farron, Denise Fergusson, Edwina Follows, Maureen Forrester, Neil Freeman, Nancy Belle Fuller, Pat Galloway, Marilyn Gardner, Gabriel Gascon, Robert Godin, John Goodlin, Lewis Gordon, Luba Goy, Wanda Graham, Dawn Greenhalgh, Amelia Hall, David Hemblen, Edward Henry, Martha Henry, Jose Hernandez, Susan Hogan, Howard Hughes, Donald Hunkin, William Hutt, Sister Barbara Ianni, Tim Jones, Terry Judd, Joan Keane, Joel Kenyon, Sheena Larkin, Lise LaSalle, Jack Lemon, Dan Lichti, Anne Linden, Hardee T. Lineham, Michael Liscinsky, Ian Macdonald, Barry MacGregor, Phyllis Mailing, Marti Maraden, Serge Marquis, Robert Martin, Brian McKone, Susan Mitchell, Tony Moffat-Lynch, Sam Moses, Jan Muszynski, William Needles, Sean Neely, Rick Neilson, Lynda Neufeld, Wolfgang Oeste, Janis Orenstein, Nicholas Pennell, Brian Petchey, Kenneth Pogue, Douglas Rain, Derek Ralston, Duncan Regehr, Alvin Reimer, George Reinke, Jack Roberts, Paul Robertson, Pam Rogers, Stephen Russell, Jeffrey Skubowius, Penny Speedie, Phil Stark, John Stewart, Powys Thomas, Gordon Thomson, Robert Thomson, Sven van de Ven, Robert Vigod, Mel Weitzel, Johnathan Welsh, Jack Wetherall, Christina Williams, Larry Zacharko, Elias Zarou, Gene Zerna.

REPERTOIRE

"The Imaginary Invalid," "Pericles," "Love's Labour's Lost," "King John," "La Vie Parisienne," "The Summoning of Everyman," "The Medium," "Walsh Ready Steady Go"

Robert C. Ragsdale Photos

Top: "Love's Labour's Lost" (R) "King John"
Right Center: William Hutt in "The
Imaginary Invalid"

Nicholas Pennell, Mervyn Blake
in "Pericles"

THEATRE VENTURE '75

Beverly, Massachusetts
May 5–June 7, 1975

Managing Director, Stephan Slane; Assistant Manager, John B. Welch; Production Supervisor, Theda Taylor; Press, Peter Downs; Business Manager, Robert Dustman; Scenic Designer, Eve Lyon; Costumes, Steven B. Feldman; Lighting, Theda Taylor; Movement, Gui Andrisano; Production Staff: Ginger Andrews, Nancy Bogardus, Beth Newbold, Dan Richard Preston, Steven D. White

PRODUCTIONS AND CASTS

HAMLET by William Shakespeare; Director, Ada Brown Mather. CAST: David Kieran (Bernardo), David McKenny (Francisco), Ken Kliban (Horatio), John Tallman (Marcellus), Kristoffer Tabori (Hamlet), Lou Bedford (Claudius), Caroline McWilliams (Gertrude), Edward Stevlingson (Polonius), James Richards (Laertes), Laurie Heineman (Ophelia), Larry Dyekman (Rosencrantz), Bruce Kendall (Guildenstern), Jane Brenny (Gentlewoman), Robert Baines (Player King/Gravedigger), Players: Bruce Ackland, Caesar Del Trecco, Debbie Kidder, Aimee Oliver, Guards: Tony Anastasopoulos, John Eadie, Tom Hall, Paul Hunkins

THE AMERICAN DREAM by Edward Albee; Director, Jack Eddleman. CAST: Esther Benson (Mommy), Robert Baines (Daddy), Lois Holmes (Grandma), June Squibb (Mrs. Barker), Keith Baker (Young Man)

A MARRIAGE PROPOSAL by Anton Chekhov; Director, Jack Eddleman. CAST: Robert Baines (Chubukov) June Squibb (Natalia), Keith Baker (Ivan)

Peter Downs Photos

Lois Holmes, Keith Baker in "The American Dream"
Above: Keith Baker, June Squibb, Robert Baines in "The Marriage Proposal"

Top: Robert Baines, Kristoffer Tabori in "Hamlet"
Left: Laurie Heineman, Lou Bedford, Caroline McWilliams in "Hamlet"

PROFESSIONAL RESIDENT COMPANIES

(Failure to meet deadline unfortunately necessitated several omissions)

ACT: A CONTEMPORARY THEATRE

Seattle, Washington
June 1, 1974–May 31, 1975
Tenth Season

Artistic Director, Gregory A. Falls; General Manager, Andrew M. Witt; Press, Edna K. Hanna; Assistant General Manager, Warren Sklar; Audience Development, Robin Atkins; Administrative Assistant, Cindy Mueller; Directors, Gregory A. Falls, Robert Loper, Pirie MacDonald, M. Burke Walker, William F. West; Musical Director, Stan Keen; Set Designers, S. Todd Muffatti, Jerry Williams; Costumes, Lynn Lewis, Sally Richardson; Lighting, Phil Schermer; Technical Director, Dick Montgomery; Props, Shelley Henze Schermer, Patsy Parrish; Stage Manager, Eileen MacRae Murphy

COMPANY

Jack Axelrod, Patricia Estrin, Adrienne Marden, Sally Kniest, Janice Fuller, Lucian Scott, Joyce Reehling, Robert McCormack, John Gilbert, Hersha Parady, Robert E. Taeschner, Jonathan Estrin, Zouanne Henriot, Jerry M. Brinkman, David B. Williams, Patricia Barry, James Higgins, John Brandon, Ed Bordo, Julian Schembri, Robert Donley, Regina Bell, Earl Hindman, Barbara Caruso, Dean Gardner, Sue Patella, Gardner Hayes, Medora Moburg, Margaret Hilton, Bill Mullikin, Wayne Hudgins, Patricia Hodges, Ted D'Arms, Donald Ewer, Maureen Quinn, Marjorie Nelson, Steven Gilborn, Clayton Corzatte, Michael Byron, Steven J. Goddard, Gail Hebert, Noel Koran, Kathryn Luster, Ruth Kidder Roats, Marie Truty, William C. Witter

PRODUCTIONS

"The Hot l Baltimore, "Twigs," "A Streetcar Named Desire," "Count Dracula," "In Celebration," "The Chairs," "The Bald Soprano," "Godspell," "The Hollow Crown," "The Absurd Musical Revue for Children"

Greg Gilbert Photos

Right: Margaret Hilton, Clayton Corzatte, Julian Schembri in "The Chairs" Top: Robert Donley, Patricia Barry, Jonathan Estrin in "Twigs"

Barbara Caruso, Hersha Parady
in "A Streetcar Named Desire"

Ruth Kidder Roats, Noel Koran,
Wayne Hudgins in "Godspell"

183

ACTORS THEATRE OF LOUISVILLE

Louisville, Kentucky
October 10, 1974–June 1, 1975

Producing-Director, Jon Jory; Administrative Director, Alexander Speer; Associate Director, Trish Pugh; Press, Norma Eckroate; Assistant Administrative Director, Stewart Slater; Director of Apprentices, Marilee Hebert-Slater; Directors, Jon Jory, Charles Kerr, Christopher Murney, Elizabeth Ives, Adale O'Brien, Israel Hicks, Teri Ralston; Designers, Paul Owen, Kurt Wilhelm, Geoffrey T. Cunningham, Stephen McDowell, Richard Gould, Raymond C. Recht, James Stephens, Anne A. Gibson, Linus M. Carleton; Technical Directors, Joe Ragey, James Stephens; Costumiere, Mary Lou Owen; Stage Managers, Charles Kerr, Don Johnson, Elizabeth Ives, Tom Todd

COMPANY

G. W. Bailey, Jim Baker, Jadeen Barbor, Wanda Bimson, Bob Burrus, William Cain, David Canary, Susan Cardwell-Kingsley, Gary L. Carlson, Jeffrey Duncan Jones, Ray Fry, Margaret Gathright, Haskell Gordon, Michael Gross, Alfred Hinckley, Vinnie Holman, Jean Inness, Stephen James, Don Johnson, Victor Jory, Gail Kellstrom, Andrea Levine, Ric Mancini, Beverly May, Vaughn McBride, Adale O'Brien, Stephen Pearlman, Patricia Pearcy, John Pielmeier, Mary Ed Porter, Scott Porter, Teri Ralston, Kay Erin Thompson, Barrie Youngfellow

PRODUCTIONS

"That Championship Season," "The Real Inspector Hound/Red Peppers/Swan Song," "Luv," "The Threepenny Opera," "A Flea in Her Ear," "Jacques Brel Is Alive and Well and Living in Paris," "The Ballad of the Sad Cafe," "Noon/Welcome to Andromeda," "Relatively Speaking," "Sleuth"
AMERICAN PREMIERES: "Female Transport," "Count Dracula," "Frankenstein"

David S. Talbott, Richard Nugent Photos

Left: Victor Jory in "Swan Song"
Top: William Cain, Michael Robertson, Michael Gro͟
(on floor), Adale O'Brien, John Pielmeier, Jim Bake͟
in "Ballad of the Sad Cafe"

William Cain, Adale O'Brien
in "Relatively Speaking"

David Canary, Teri Ralston, Steve James, Andr͟
Levine (front) in "Jacques Brel Is Alive. . . ."

Tony Russel, Bettye Fitzpatrick, Lillian Evans
in "A Streetcar Named Desire"

Jo Alessandro Marks, Cristine Rose
in "The Contest"

ALLEY THEATRE

Houston, Texas
October 17, 1954–May 11, 1975

Producing Director, Nina Vance; Managing Director, Iris Siff; Press, Bob Feingold, George Jonte; Administrative Assistant, Toni Simon; Administrative Director, Bettye Gardner; Producing Associate, H. Wilkenfeld; Directors, Robert E. Leonard, Beth Sanford, William Trotman; Company Manager, Robert E. Leonard; Stage Managers, Bettye Fitzpatrick, George Anderson, Trent Jenkins; Production Assistants, Chris Fisher, Rozanne Gates, Malcolm McGee, David Schuster; Head of Design, William Trotman; Costumes, Barbara C. Cox; Sets, John Kenny; Lighting, Jonathan Duff, Paul Gregory; Music Director, Paul Dupree, Technical Director, William C. Lindstrom

COMPANY

dney Armus, Roger Baron, Ronald Bishop, Darlene Conley, Joph Costa, Philip Davidson, Christopher Fazel, Mark Keeler, Mike ibler, Simon L. Levy, David Okarski, Tony Russel, E. A. Sirianni, hepperd Strudwick, William Trotman, Edward Wittner, Cal Bedrd, Mimi Carr, Dan Carter, A. D. Cover, Caroline Crystal, Zan ailey, Barbara Daytree, Lillian Evans, Haskell Fitz-Simons, Barra Dennison Grant, Rosamond Hooper, Mary S. Irey, Trent Jenns, Tony Keyes, Kathryn Mosbacher, Amelia Parker, Bruce rter, Jean Proctor, Sharon Swink, David Wurst

PRODUCTIONS

Wilson," "The Man Who Came to Dinner," "Twelfth Night," "A eetcar Named Desire," "Tobacco Road," and *World Premiere* of e Contest" by Shirley Mezvinsky Lauro

Dome City Photos

p: Ronald Bishop, Lillian Evans, Philip Davidson,
. D. Cover in "The Man Who Came to Dinner"
) Shepperd Strudwick, Joseph Costa in "Wilson"

Sharon Swink, Cal Bedford
in "Twelfth Night"

185

AMERICAN CONSERVATORY
THEATRE

San Francisco, California
October 12, 1974–June 1, 1975

General Director, William Ball; Executive Producer, James B. McKenzie; Executive Director, Edward Hastings; Development Director, Edith Markson; Conservatory Director, Allen Fletcher; Stage Directors, William Ball, Allen Fletcher, Edward Hastings, James Dunn, Andrei Serban; Artists and Repertory Director, Robert Bonaventura; Directors in Residence, Eugene Barcone, Paul Blake; Production Director, Benjamin Moore; General Manager, Charles Dillingham; Dramaturge, Dennis Powers; Designers, Robert Blackman, Gregory Bolton, F. Mitchell Dana, Dirk Epperson, Robert Fletcher, Ralph Funicello, J. Allen Highfill, John Jensen, Robert Morgan, Bartholomeo Rago, Walter Watson; Press, Cheryle Elliott, Jim Kerber; Production Manager, Stan Grindstaff; Stage Managers, James Haire, James L. Burke, Diana Clarke, Raymond S. Gin

COMPANY

Hope Alexander-Willis, Rene Auberjonois, Andy Backer, Candace Barrett, Joseph Bird, Raye Birk, Earl Boen, Ronald Boussom, Bonita Bradley, Joy Carlin, Robert Chapline, Megan Cole, Daniel Davis, Barbara Dirickson, Peter Donat, Bobby F. Ellerbee, Sabin Epstein, Lou Ann Graham, Ross Graham, Charles Hallahan, Rick Hamilton, Lawrence Hecht, Elizabeth Huddle, Michael Hume, Charles H. Hyman, Daniel Kern, Randall Duk Kim, Ruth Kobart, Charles Lanyer, Anne Lawder, Deborah May, Robert Mooney, Fredi Olster, Frank Ottiwell, William Paterson, E. Kerrigan Prescott, Ray Reinhardt, Juanita Rice, Eve Roberts, Stephen Schnetzer, Sandra Shotwell, Anna Deavere Smith, Randall Smith, Anthony S. Teague, Sydney Walker, Marrian Walters, Al White, J. Steven White, Laird Williamson, James R. Winker, Rick Winter

PRODUCTIONS

"The Threepenny Opera," "Jumpers," "The Ruling Class," "King Richard III," "Horatio," "The Taming of the Shrew," "Pillars of the Community," "Street Scene," "Cyrano de Bergerac"

William Ganslen Photos

Rene Auberjonois, Fredi Olster in "The Ruling C
Above: Megan Cole, Daniel Davis in "Horati
Top: Fredi Olster, Anthony S. Teague in "Tamin
the Shrew"

186 Top: Marrian Walters, Randall Duk Kim in
"Richard III" Below: Hope Alexander-Willis,
Earl Boen, Ray Reinhardt in "Jumpers"

ARENA STAGE

Washington, D.C.
October 18, 1974–July 27, 1975

Producing Director, Zelda Fichandler; Executive Director, Thomas C. Fichandler; Associate Producer, George Touliatos; Directing Associate, Alan Schneider; Producing Associate, Hugh Lester; Assistant Executive Director, Alton Miller; Directors, Edward Payson Call, John Dillon, Zelda Fichandler, Gene Lesser, Alan Schneider, Carl Weber; Scenery, Karl Eigsti, David Jenkins, Ming Cho Lee; Costumes, Gwynne Clark, Linda Fisher, Marjorie Slaiman; Lighting, Hugh Lester, William Mintzer; Music Composers, Robert Dennis, Alan Laing, Richard Peaslee; Musical Director, Steven Ross; Stage Managers, Joseph A. Glosson, Terrence Kester, Roger Richardson, Gully Stanford, Douglas Wager; Technical Director, Henry R. Gorfein; Press, Alton Miller.

COMPANY

Stanley Anderson, Susan Stone Appleton, Peggy Atkinson, Richard Bauer, Gary Bayer, James Blendick, Roberts Blossom, Michael Burg, Ralph Byers, Thomas Carson, Leslie Cass, Jill Choder, Sarah Chodoff, Leonardo Cimino, Bryan Clark, Al Corbin, Terrence Currier, Carl G. Darchuk, Edna Dix, Carl Don, David Eric, Walter Flanagan, Henderson Forsythe, David Garrison, Mike Genovese, Valorie Grear, Ralph Glickman, Dexter Hamlett, Mark Hammer, Dorothea Hammond, Bob Harper, Patrick Hines, Zviah Igdalsky, Max Jacobs, Michael Jonnes, Caroline Kava, Terrence Kester, Gabriela Koczak, Mordecai Lawner, Lynn Ann Leveridge, Robert LuPone, Macon McCalman, Philip Mandelkorn, John Marriott, Wayne Maxwell, Michael Mertz, Gene S. Minkow, Moon, Peg Murray, Vivian Nathan, W. Thomas Newman, Don Plumley, Daniel Pollack, Robert Prosky, Eddy Ormond, Theresa O'Rourke, Elena Rimson, Paul Rudd, Ruth Sadler, Scott Schofield, Robert Shilton, David Silber, Anne Swift, Glenn Taylor, Douglas Wager, Lloyd Weber, Bruce Weitz, Eric Weitz, Dianne Wiest, Halo Wines, Howard Witt, Richard Wright, Max Wright, Wendell W. Wright, Jr., J. Zakkai, Ken Zimmerman, Robert Zukerman.
GUEST ARTISTS: Duro Ladipo and his Yoruba Folk Festival "Oba Koso," John Kani and Winston Ntshona in "Sizwe Banzi Is Dead" and "The Island"

PRODUCTIONS

"Death of a Salesman," "Who's Afraid of Virginia Woolf?," "The Front Page," "Julius Caesar," "The Last Meeting of the Knights of the White Magnolia," "The Dybbuk,"
PREMIERES: "The Ascent of Mount Fuji" (American Premiere), "Boccaccio" (World Premiere)

George De Vincent, Alton Miller Photos

Right: Lynn Ann Leveridge, Peggy Atkinson, Robert LuPone, Jill Choder in "Boccaccio" Top: Ken Zimmerman, Paul Rudd, Henderson Forsythe, Patrick Hines in "Last Meeting of the Knights ..."

Premiere of "The Ascent of Mt. Fuji"

Richard Bauer, Gary Bayer, Peg Murray in "Who's Afraid of Virginia Woolf?"

THE ASOLO STATE THEATER

Sarasota, Florida
June 1, 1974–May 31, 1975

Executive Director, Richard G. Fallon; Artistic Director, Robert Strane; Managing Director, Howard J. Millman; Director of Acting, Bernerd Engel; Director of Voice, Mary Corrigan; Guest Directors, Amnon Kabatchnik, Jim Hoskins, Steve Rothman, S. C. Hastie, Paxton Whitehead, John Dillon; Scenic Designer, Rick Pike; Costumes, Catherine King, Flozanne John, Paige Southard; Sound, Martin Petlock; Technical Director, Victor Meyrich; Press, Edith N. Anson; Stage Managers, Marian Wallace, Stephanie Moss; Guest Musical Director, Salli Parker

COMPANY

Burton Clarke, Bernerd Engel, Stephen Johnson, Henson Keys, William Leach, Philip LeStrange, Jillian Lindig, Barbara Reid McIntyre, Robert Murch, Ellen Novack, Nona Pipes, Walter Rhodes, Robert Strane, Isa Thomas, Bradford Wallace, Martha J. Brown, Max Gulack, Bette Oliver, Joan Rue, Denny Albee, Donna Aronson, John Behan, Joan Inwood, Ellen Olian-Bate, Valerie Ososky, Burmah Smith, Cristine Smith, William Turner, Vikkian, Lewis Agrell, Dottie Dee, James Donadio, Pat Hurley, Barry Klassel, Thomas Quimby, Anne Sandoe, Alan Smith, Cathy S. Chappell, Nora Chester, Janice Clark, Jim Crisp, Jr., John Gray, Stephen Joseph, David Kwiat, Clark Niederjohn, Patricia Oetken, Frederic-Winslow Oram, Donna Pelc, Bob Stallworth, Deborah Stewart, Steve Weaver, Romulus E. Zamora
GUEST ARTISTS: Patrick Crean, Terri Mastobueno, Carol Lee, Nancy Hanks, Martin Esslin, Maria Niles, Jim Hoskins, Salli Parker

PRODUCTIONS

"Inherit the Wind," "A Delicate Balance," "Arsenic and Old Lace," "Broadway," "Ring Round the Moon," "Macbeth," "Don Quixote of La Mancha," "Story Theatre," "There's One in Every Marriage," "Mistress of the Inn," "The Plough and the Stars," "Tobacco Road," "Heartbreak House," "The Sea," "Guys and Dolls"

Gary Sweetman Photos

Left: "Heartbreak House"
Top: Robert Murch, Jillian Lindig in "Ring Round the Moon"

"The Plough and the Stars"

"Arsenic and Old Lace"

188

Michael Tolaydo, Barbara Tarbuck, George Hosmer,
Nancy Snyder, David Darlow in "Straitjacket"

James Noble, Ann Buckles
in "Private Lives"

BARTER THEATRE

State Theatre of Virginia
Abingdon, Virginia
May 3, 1974–October 26, 1974

STAFF: Susan Strandberg, Ann Sehrt, Gayle Ruhlen, Marvin
oark, Bryan Rice, Raymond C. Recht, Eleanor Pickrell, H. Owen
hillips, Tony Partington, Rex Partington, Ellen Painter, Michael
antel, David Lohoeter, Sigrid Insull, Elizabeth Howe, Pearl
ayter, Kathryn Harris, Philip Giller, Clayton Austin, Bennet Ave-
t, Gregory Buch, Ruth Carr, Jo Leslie Collier, Kenneth Swiger,
san Tucker, Myron White

COMPANY

rney Connell Sutton, Nancy Elizabeth Snyder, Donna Gail
arcy, William E. Schleuter, Robert E. Rutland, Dorothy Marie
binson, Margaret Price, John W. Morrow, Jr., Paul A. Milikin,
tharine Manning, Randall Meade, John Medici, Raymond
nch, Margaret Lunsford, George Hosmer, Max Gulack, Sarah
xton, Mary Carney, Walter J. Carroll, Eric D. Conger, Joseph
sta, David Darlow, Joseph P. Edens III, Glynis Eileen Ellis,
chael Ellis, Shannon Eubanks, Gwyllum Evans, Barbara Tar-
ck, Nancy Tribush, Marsha Wischhusen

PRODUCTIONS

he Torch Bearers," "Candida," "Scapin," "The Odd Couple,"
rivate Lives," "Beyond the Fringe," "Ten Nights in a Barroom,"
hampagne Complex," "Silent Night, Lonely Night" and *PRE-
ERE* of "The Straitjacket"

Top: "Ten Nights in a Barroom"
(R) George Hosmer, John Medici,
Gwyllum Evans in "Scapin"

Michael Tolaydo, Cleo Holladay
in "Candida"

189

CENTER THEATRE GROUP
AHMANSON THEATRE

Los Angeles, California
October 8, 1974–May 10, 1975
Eighth Season

Managing Director, Robert Fryer; Manager, Charles Mooney; Assistant Manager, Barbara Stocks; Production Associate, Robert Linden; Production Coordinator, Michael Grossman; Production Administrator, Ralph Beaumont; Press, Allan, Ingersoll, Sega & Henry-Rupert Allan, Farrar Cobb; Technical Supervisor, H. R. Poindexter; Administrative Coordinator, Joyce Zaccaro; Stage Managers, Don Winton, Milt Commons

PRODUCTIONS AND CASTS

PRIVATE LIVES by Noel Coward; Director, John Gielgud; Sets, Anthony Powell; Costumes, Germinal Rangel; Lighting, H. R. Poindexter; Production Manager, Mitchell Erickson; Producer, Arthur Cantor. CAST: Maggie Smith, John Standing, Remak Ramsay, Niki Flacks, Marie Tommon (See Broadway Calendar)
A MOON FOR THE MISBEGOTTEN by Eugene O'Neill; Director, Jose Quntero; Scenery and Lighting, Ben Edwards; Costumes, Jane Greenwood; Producers, Elliot Martin, Lester Osterman Productions. CAST: Jason Robards, Colleen Dewhurst, Tom Clancy, John O'Leary, Edwin J. McDonough
MACBETH by William Shakespeare; Director, Peter Wood; Sets and Lighting, H. R. Poindexter; Costumes, Sam Kirkpatrick; Music, Robert Prince; A CTG-Ahmanson Production. CAST: Charlton Heston, Venessa Redgrave, John Ireland, Richard Jordan, John Devlin, William Ian Gamble, Gary Krawford, Patricia Wynand, George McDaniel, Harold Oblong, Benjamin Stewart, William Rhys, John Ventantonio, Susan French, Billy Simpson, Larkin Ford, Anthony DeLongis, Charles Gregory, Tom Henschel, Rory Kelly, Daniel Zippi
RING ROUND THE MOON by Jean Anouilh; Adapted by Christopher Fry; Director, Joseph Hardy; Production Designed by Anthony Powell; Lighting, H. R. Poindexter; Incidental Music Composed by Maurice Jarre; A CTG-Ahmanson Production. CAST: Michael York, Glynis Johns, Kitty Winn, Joan Van Ark, Rosemary Murphy, Kurt Kasznar, Keene Curtis, Penny Fuller, Paul Shenar, Anne Seymour, William Schallert, Darlene Conley, Antonia Ellis, Curt Gareth, Erik Howell, Kat Quillen, Lucian Scott, Woody Skaggs, Lesley Woods

CENTER THEATRE GROUP
MARK TAPER FORUM

Los Angeles, California
June 1, 1974–June 30, 1975

Artistic Director, Gordon Davidson; General Manager, Frank von Zerneck; Director New Theatre for Now, Edward Parone; Manager New Theatre for Now, William P. Wingate; Director Forum/-Laboratory, Robert Greenwald; Press, Richard Kitzrow, Thomas Brocato, Anthony Sherwood, Dennis Hammer; Design Consultant, Peter Wexler; Staff Lighting Designer, Tharon Musser; Technical Supervisor, H. R. Poindexter; Production Manager, John DeSantis; Technical Director, Robert Calhoun; Production Stage Managers, David Barber, Don Winton, Madeline Puzo, Milt Commons; Staff Directors, Robert Greenwald, John Dennis

PRODUCTIONS AND CASTS

SAVAGES by Christopher Hampton; Director, Gordon Davidson; Designers, Sally Jacobs, John Gleason. CAST: Erik Arbiso, Susan Brown, Art Burns, Michael Ivan Cristofer, Soledad de Oram, Ted Flores, Ken R. Ganado, Martyn Green, Robert Huerta, Frank Michael Liu, Joseph Maher, Fredd Morgan, Nilak, Cliff Osmond, Mauricio Palma, Ben Piazza, Ruth Pinedo, Henry Santillan, Fred Sannoya, Milcha C. Scott, Vito Scotti, Daniel Sullivan, David Villa, Ronald Yates Warden, David White, Muni Zano
JUNO AND THE PAYCOCK by Sean O'Casey; Director, George Seaton; Designers, John Conklin, Dorothy Jeakins, Donald Harris. CAST: Anthony Auer, Art Burns, Duchess Dale, Gilbert Girion, John Glover, William Glover, Nicholas Hammond, Mary Jackson, Jack Lemmon, Walter Matthau, Sandy McCallum, Sean McClory, Charles Thomas Murphy, Laurie Prange, Peggy Rea, Dennis Robertson, William Schallert, Martin Speer, Maureen Stapleton, Mary Wickes, Victor Vitartas

Maureen Stapleton, Laurie Prange, John Glover, Walter Matthau, Jack Lemmon, Nicholas Hammond in "Juno and the Paycock"

Upper Center: Michael York, William Schallert, Anne Seymour, Glynis Johns, Kurt Kasznar in "Ring Round the Moon" Below: Vanessa Redgrave, Charlton Heston in "Macbeth"

Tom Clancy, Jason Robards, Colleen Dewhurst in "Moon for the Misbegotten"

THE DYBBUK by S. Ansky; Newly Adapted by John Hirsch; Director, John Hirsch; Designers Maxine Graham, Mark Negin, Pat Collins; Music Composer, Alan Laing; Musical Supervisor, John Berkman. CAST: Alan Bergmann, Charles Briscoe, Gene Castle, Robert Corff, Jo Davidson, Alfred Dennis, Lisa Donaldson, Stefan Fischer, Herb Foster, Bert Freed, Harvey Gold, Cindi Haynie, John Hesley, Marvin Kaplan, John LaMotta, Marilyn Lightstone, Stephanie Liss, Adrienne Marden, Melora Marshall, Jean-Paul Mustone, Nehemiah Persoff, V. Phipps-Wilson, Steven Rotblatt, Joseph Ruskin, Don Samuels, Constance Sawyer, Joseph R. Sicari, George Sperdakos, Michael Strong, Anne Turner, Lou Wagner, Helene Winston

ME AND BESSIE conceived by Will Holt and Linda Hopkins; Director, Robert Greenwald; Designers, Donald Harris, Pete Menefee; Musical Director, Tony Berg; Special Dance Sequences, Lester Wilson. CAST: Gerri Dean, Linda Hopkins, Lester Wilson

SIZWE BANZI IS DEAD and THE ISLAND both devised by Athol Fugard, John Kani, Winston Ntshona; Director, Athol Fugard; Designers, Stuart Wurtzel, Bill Walker, John DeSantis. CAST: John Kani, Winston Ntshona

Steven Keull Photos

NEW THEATRE FOR NOW
"IN THE WORKS: II" FESTIVAL

Edward Parone, Director
Stage Managers: Nancy Norris, Madeline Puzo

THE DEATH AND LIFE OF JESSE JAMES by Len Jenkin; Director, Jeff Bleckner; Designers, Robert Clair La Vigne, Marilyn Rennagel; Musical Director, Richie Jenkin. CAST: Edith Diaz, David Dukes, Gerrit Graham, James Greene, Scott Hylands, Michael McNeilly, Arthur Metrano, Karmin Murcelo, Frederick Neumann, Claudette Nevins, Lupe Ontiveros, Andy Robinson, Herman Poppe, Paul Rubenfeld, Robert Symonds, Susan Tyrrell, James Victor

ME AND BESSIE—Director, Robert Greenwald; Designers, Donald Harris, Terence Tam Soon; Musical Coordinator, Tony Berg. CAST: Gerri Dean, Linda Hopkins, Lester Wilson

LA GRANDE CARPA DE LOS RASQUACHIS by El Teatro Campesino; Directed by the company; Designer, Donald Harris. CAST: Feliz Alvarez, Lily Alvarez, Sal Bravo, Allen David Cruz, Socorro Cruz, Jose Delgado, Julio Gonzalez, Andres Valenzuela Gutierrez, Ernesto Hernandez, Carlos Martinez, Jr., Diana Rodriguez, Daniel Valdez, Daniel Villalva

INPROVISATIONAL THEATRE PROJECT

Stage Manager: Ron Rudolph

WINTER COMPANY: Director, John Dennis; Writer, Doris Baizley; Designers, Ron Rudolph, Donald Harris, Marianna Elliott. CAST: Janet Johnson, Kenneth Manney, Michael McNeilly, Tony Papenfuss, Loren Pickford, Thomas M. Pollard, Sharon Ullrick, Rick Vartorella

SPRING COMPANY: Director, John Dennis; Writer, Doris Baizley; Designers, Ron Rudolph, Joe Tompkins. CAST: Nathan Cook, Stefan Fischer, Aileen Fitzpatrick, Ron Grant, Michael McNeilly, Thomas M. Pollard, Rick Vartorella, Alfred Woodard

FORUM/LABORATORY

Director, Robert Greenwald; Production Manager, Ron Rudolph; Stage Managers, Miranda Barry, Leonard Ellis, Ellyn Gersh, Richard Johnson, John Megna, Pat Ryker, Bethe Ward, Becky Weimer

PIN 411: Conceived and Directed by Ron Rudolph; Video Tapes, Nina Sobel, John Sturgeon; Photographs, John Gulager; Poetry, David James

LADY LAZARUS: Director, Vickie Rue; Designers, Ron Rudolph, Barbara Ling, Jim Reva; Musical Director, Lori Alexander. CAST: Tyne Daly, Barra Grant, Madge Sinclair

THE IMPROVISATIONAL WORKSHOP: Director, John Dennis. CAST: Laura Campbell, John Koch, Hal Landon, Jr., Michael McNeilly, Thomas M. Pollard, Sharon Ullrick, Rick Vartorella

KILLER IN PIECES by Susan Miller; Director, Jeremy Blahnik; Designer, Becky Weimer. CAST: Indus Arthur, Barbara Boles, Nea Deen, Herb Foster, Bill Gerber

PRESIDENT WILSON IN PARIS by Ron Blair; Director, Gordon Hunt; Designer, Ron Rudolph. CAST: Marjorie Battles, Keene Curtis, Cliff DeYoung

WITNESS TO THE CONFESSION as conceived by Jack Voorhies and Robert Ravan; Music Composed by Laura Nyro; Director, Robert Ravan; Choreography, Jack Voorhies; Designers, Doug Oliver, Charles E. Hurley II, Margaretrose; Music arranged by Miles Goodman, Tony Berg. CAST: George Ball, Tim Bowman, Danny Vitus, Judy Kaye, Amanda McBroom, Mark Montgomery, Trina Parks

CROSS COUNTRY by Susan Miller; Director, Vickie Rue. CAST: Henry Hoffman, Lee McCain, Robin Strasser, Sharon Ullrick

SIGNALS by John O'Brien; Conceived and Directed by Michael Griggs; Designers, Ron Rudolph, Leonard Ellis; Music, Ron Grant. CAST: Jakob Been, Burke Byrnes, Marcus Cato, Peter Frankland, Gilbert Girion, Andrew Griggs, Peter Kastner, John O'Brien

THE AMAZING FLIGHT OF THE GOONEY BIRD by Dory Previn; Music and Lyrics, Dory Previn; Director, Robert Greenwald; Designers, Robert Zentis, Patricia Ryker; Musical Direction, Tony Berg. CAST: Susan French, Joan Hackett, Thelma Houston, Judy Kaye, Ben Piazza

THE MOTHER JONES AND MOLLIE BAILEY FAMILY CIRCUS by Megan Terry; Directors, Jeremy Blahnik, Vickie Rue; Designers, Ron Rudolph, Barbara Ling, Louise Hayter. CAST: Seth Allen, Jane Connell, Liebe Gray, J. J. Lewis, Richard Marion, John Megne, Julie Payne, V. Phipps-Wilson, William Shepard, Susan Tyrrell, Sharon Ullrick, Virginia Wing

UPON A DYING LADY by William Butler Yeats; Director, Susan Burkhalter; Designer, Barbara Ling. CAST: Susan Burkhalter, Max Roberts, Winston Tong

THE KILLING OF YABLONSKI by Richard Nelson; Director, John Dennis; Designers, Richard Johnson, Ron Rudolph, Julie Weiss. CAST: Frank Christi, Johana de Winter, Cliff DeYoung, John D. Gowans, Donald Hotton, Janet Johnston, Tony Papenfuss, Vic Tayback

op: Frederick Neumann, Gerrit Graham, Herman **ppe,** James Greene, Scott Hylands in "Death and **ife of Jesse James" Below:** Bert Freed, Marilyn **ightstone,** Nehemiah Persoff in "The Dybbuk"

Gerri Dean, Linda Hopkins, Lester Wilson
in "Me and Bessie"

191

CALIFORNIA ACTORS THEATRE

Los Gatos, California
January 3–July 12, 1975

Artistic Director, Peter Nyberg; Producing Director, Sheldon Kleinman; Directors, Peter Nyberg, James Dunn, John Reich, Michael Posnick, Milton Lyon; Set and Lighting, Steve T. Howell, Peter Nyberg, Ronald E. Krempetz, Donald Cate; Costumes Marcia Frederick; Stage Managers, Frank Silvey, Ron Schultz; Press, Barbara Carpenter, Technical Director, Terry Cermak

COMPANY

Phoebe Alexander, Frank Boyd, Georg Stanford Brown, Tyne Daly, Lola Fisher, Michael Keenan, Sandy McCallum, Tom McCorry, Brian Moore, Peter Nyberg, Anne Occhiogrosso, Michael Prichard, Roxann Pyle, Carolyn Reed, Carl Reggiardo, Kurtwood Smith, Sheila Stephenson, David Steirs, Martin Ferrero, Karen Hensel, Amy Johnston, Victor Pappas, Mary Simonton, Paul Ventura

PRODUCTIONS

"Happy End," "The Happy Hunter," "Detective Story," "Old Times," "The Servant of Two Masters," "Lady Audley's Secret," and *WORLD PREMIERE* of "Roses Don't Grow Here No More/-Darlin' Boy" by Tom McCorry

Peter Nyberg Photos

Left: Tom McCorry, Sandy McCallum, Amy Johnston, Michael Keenan, Carl Reggiardo in "Darlin' Boy" Top: Michael Prichard, Michael Keenan, Tom McCorry, Sandy McCallum in "Roses Don't Grow Here Anymore"

Peter Nyberg, Brian Moore, Carolyn Reed
in "Happy End"

Michael Prichard, Carolyn Reed, Victor Papp
in "The Servant of Two Masters" Above: Geo
Stanford Brown, Frank Thompson, Michael
Prichard in "Detective Story"

CINCINNATI PLAYHOUSE IN THE PARK

Cincinnati, Ohio
October 17, 1974–June 29, 1975

Producing Director, Thomas Kelly; Associate Director, Lani [Ba]ll; General Manager, Patt Dale; Business Manager, Audry Tel[le]r; Press, Jerri Roberts, Lanni Johnston Brengel; Sets, Eric Head; [Li]ghting, John Gleason; Costumes, Susan Tsu; Stage Managers, [Ke]nneth Leavee, Vicky West; Technical Director, Nick Davis

PRODUCTIONS AND CASTS

[T]ARTUFFE by moliere; English verse translation by Richard Wil[be]r; Director, Daniel Sullivan; Music, Worth Gardner. CAST: [Ge]orge Brengel, J. Kenneth Campbell, Peter Covette, Neil Flana[ga]n, Richard Greene, Lynn Milgram, Austin Pendleton, Teri Ral[sto]n, Carl Reggiardo, Jayne Rizzo, Dee Victor, Eda Zahl

[W]HO'S AFRAID OF VIRGINIA WOOLF? by Edward Albee; [Di]rector, Garland Wright; Set, John Scheffler; Lighting, Marc B. [W]eiss. CAST: J. Kenneth Campbell, Bette Ford, James Ray, Eda [Za]hl

[A]RSENIC AND OLD LACE by Joseph Kesselring; Director, An[tho]ny Stimac; Set, John Scheffler. CAST: Sydney Blake, Gibby [Br]and, James Cook, Nancy Cushman, Eddie Jones, William Metzo, [Da]vid Ringer, Reid Shelton, Bob Stocker, Raymond Thorne, Dee [Vic]tor, Gene Wolters

[TH]AT CHAMPIONSHIP SEASON by Jason Miller; Director, [Ala]n Dillson; Set, John Scheffler. CAST: James Cook, Eddie Jones, [Wi]lliam Metzo, Reid Shelton, Raymond Thorne

[TH]E HOT L BALTIMORE by Lanford Wilson; Director, Daniel [Su]llivan. CAST: Lani Ball, Gibby Brand, Michael Buzek, Ray Fry, [Fra]nk Geraci, David Lyman, Charlene Mathies, Ruth Maynard, [Jo]an O'Connor, Jill O'Hara, Joan Pape, James Roman, Tracy Brooks [Sw]ope, Dee Victor

[OH]! COWARD! with Words and Music by Noel Coward; Devised [by] Roderick Cook; Director, Garland Wright; Music, Worth Gard[ner]; Choreography, Gary Menteer. CAST: Alan Brasington, Bonnie [Fr]anklin, Leonard Frey

Sandy Underwood Photos

Top: James Ray, Bette Ford in "Who's Afraid of Virginia Woolf?" (R) Teri Ralston, Austin Pendleton in "Tartuffe"

Alan Brasington, Bonnie Franklin, Leonard Frey in "Oh! Coward!"

193

CLARENCE BROWN THEATRE COMPANY

Knoxville, Tennessee
October 18, 1974–February 14, 1975

Directors, Anthony Quayle, Ralph G. Allen, N. Wandalie Henshaw; Scenic Designer, Robert M. Cothran; Costumes, Marianne Custer; Lighting/Technical Director, Robert C. Field; Sceneshop Director, Michael Garl; Costumiere/Technical Director, Judi Rice; Stage Managers, Paul A. Foley, Walter B. Smith

COMPANY

Ken Costigan, Jay Doyle, Gwyllum Evans, Richard Galuppi, Albert Harris, Earle Hyman, Harriet Nichols, Anthony Quayle, Susan Ringwood, Eric Schneider, Walter B. Smith, Cynthia Woll, Maria Alexandra Wozniak, and *GUEST ARTIST* Eva LeGallienne

PRODUCTIONS

"Everyman," "The Second Shepherd's Play," "An Elizabethian Miscellany," "Shakespeare and His Contemporaries," "Scenes from Shakespeare," "An Afternoon with Eva LeGallienne," "Playboy of the Western World," "Aristotle's Bellows"

Photos by Gordon Studio

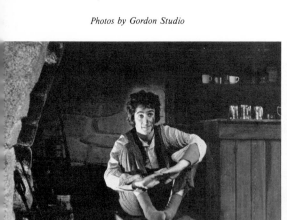 

Gwyllum Evans, Anthony Quayle, Wandalie Hens in "Everyman" (also below)

Harriet Nichols, Eric Schneider (also above) in "Playboy of the Western World"

Jay Doyle, Gwyllum Evans, Richard Galuppi in "The Second Shepherd's Play"

194

CLEVELAND PLAY HOUSE

Cleveland, Ohio
October 18, 1974–May 11, 1975
Fifty-ninth Season

Director, Richard Oberlin; Business Manager, James Sweeney; Associate Director, Larry Tarrant; Press, Ric Wanetik, William Lempke; Scenic Director, Richard Gould; Administrative Coordinator, Nelson Isekeit; Assistant Director, Robert Snook; Directors, Jonathan Farwell, Richard Halverson, Paul Lee, Evie McElroy, Richard Oberlin, Robert Snook, Larry Tarrant; Designers, Richard Gould, Eugene Hare, Barbara Leatherman, Joe Dale Lunday, Tim Zupancic; Costumes, Joe Dale Lunday, Harriet Cone, Bernadette O'Brien, Estelle Painter; Technical Director, David Fletcher; Props, David Smith; Stage Managers, Eugene Hare, Ben Letter, Daniel Morris, Stanley Suchecki, Larry Tarrant

COMPANY

Robert Allman, John Bergstrom, Norm Berman, John Buck, Jr., Brenda Curtis, Daniel Desmond, Jo Farwell, Jonathan Farwell, June Gibbons, Richard Halverson, Eugene Hare, Douglas Jones, Allen Leatherman, Gregory Lehane, Ben Letter, Evie McElroy, Daniel Mooney, Daniel Morris, Ralph Neeley, Richard Oberlin, Dale Place, Marilyn Schreffler, Robert Snook, Larry Tarrant, Haskell V. Anderson III, Tony Campisi, Dana Hart, Dee Hoty, Elizabeth McMahon, Leslie Rapp, Frederic Serino, Pamela Sprosty, Lora Beth Staley, William Turner, John Volpe, Nancy Ellen Weiss, Russell Wulff

GUEST ARTISTS: Ken Albers, Lief, Ancker, Jon Peter Benson, Jonathan Bolt, Tom Carson, C. C. Carter, Audrey Cobb, Marjorie Dawe, Marji Dodrill, Bill Francisco, Ibby Hardies, Charlotte Hare, Myrna Kaye, Theresa Kirby, Stanja Lowe, Edmund Lyndeck, Barbara Meek, Edith Owen, Dennis M. Romer, Dennis Rosa, William Rhys, Kerry Slattery, Fran Soeder, Vivienne Stotter, Paula Wagner, Bud Wendell, David Williams

PRODUCTIONS

"Happy End," "The Sea Horse," "Cat on a Hot Tin Roof," "The Freedom of the City," "Colette," "Hay Fever," "The Hot l Baltimore," "Richard III," "The Rivals," "The Prisoner of Second Avenue," *U.S. PREMIERE* of "Confession at Night," and *WORLD PREMIERE* of "The Count of Monte Cristo"

J. R. Burroughs, Barney Taxel Photos

Right: "Confession at Night"
Top: Brenda Curtis, Daniel Desmond, Jonathan Farwell in "The Count of Monte Cristo"

June Gibbons, Paula Wagner, Douglas Jones in "Cat on a Hot Tin Roof"

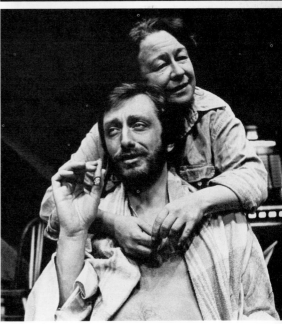

John Bergstrom, Evie McElroy in "The Sea Horse"

195

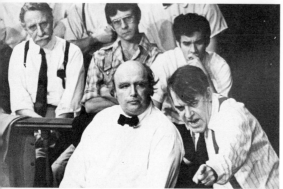

DALLAS THEATER CENTER

Dallas, Texas
October 8, 1974–August 16, 1975

Managing Director, Paul Baker; Assistant Director, Mary Sue Jones; Business Manager, Glenn Allen Smith; Press, Lynn Trammell; Stage Directors, Paul Baker, Randolph Tallman, Ken Latimer, Linda Daugherty; Sets, Mary Sue Jones, John Henson, George T. Green, Peter Wolf, Nancy Levinson, Virgin Beavers; Costumes, Celia Karston, Daryl Conner, Irene Corey, Kathleen Latimer, John Henson; Lighting, Sam Nance, Randy Moore, Robyn Flatt, Linda Blase, Sally Netzel

COMPANY

Yoichi Aoki, Linda Blase, Judith Davis, John Figlmiller, Robyn Flatt, John Henson, Allen Hibbard, Mary Sue Jones, Preston Jones, Kathleen Latimer, Ken Latimer, John Logan, Rebecca Logan, Steven Mackenroth, Joan Meister, Gary Moore, Norma Moore, Randy Moore, Louise Mosley, Sally Netzel, Mona Pursley, Bryant J. Reynolds, Synthia Rogers, Chelcie Ross, Margaret Tallman, Randolph Tallman, Jacque Thomas, Lynn Trammell

PRODUCTIONS

"Arsenic and Old Lace," "Tobacco Road," "Chemin de Fer," "Inherit the Wind," "Misalliance," "Journey to Jefferson," and *WORLD PREMIERE* of "The Bradleyville Trilogy (The Oldest Living Graduate, The Last Meeting of the Knights of the White Magnolia, Lu Ann Hampton Laverty Oberlander) by Preston Jones

Andy Hanson, Linda Blase Photos

Left: Barry Hope, Preston Jones in "Inherit the Wind" Top: Ken Latimer, John Logan, Robyn Flatt, Tommy Kendrick, Randy Moore, Drexel Riley in "Journey to Jefferson"

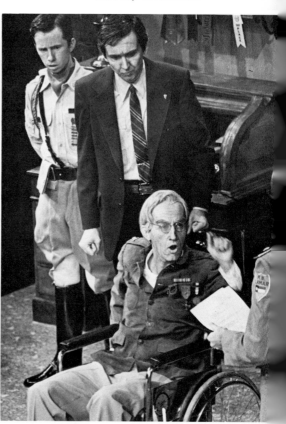

James Crump, Mary Sue Jones in "Tobacco Road"
196 **Above: Ella Mae Brainard, Jacque Thomas in "Arsenic and Old Lace"**

Tommy Kendrick, John Henson, Randy Moore, Allen Hibbard in "The Oldest Living Graduate"

DETROIT REPERTORY THEATRE

Detroit, Michigan
November 7, 1974–June 29, 1975

Artistic Director, Bruce E. Millan; Sets, Robert Katkowsky, Bruce E. Millan, Marianna Hoad; Lighting, Dick Smith; Costumes, Marianna Hoad; Sound, William Jennings; Stage Managers, Robert Williams, William Boswell

COMPANY

Del Bondie, Denise Sakunah DeLaney, Willie J. Jones, John Hardy, James Sephers, III, William Boswell, Thruman L. Briggs, Brenda Allen, Dee Andrus, Becky Cherveny, Frances A. Hansberry, Melissa Moran, Rosemary Berkley, Mark Murri, Marvin Jones, Ray Adams, Barbara Busby, Jesse Newton, Phyllis Grant, Scott Dennis, Charles Roseborough, Priscilla Kimbrough, Bill Banks, Edward Morin, Ruth Palmer

PRODUCTIONS

"Medea," "Dutchman," "Rocket to the Moon," "Tobacco Road," "Old Times"

Above: Robert Williams, Dee Andrus, Ruth Palmer "Old Times" Top: Barbara Busby, Jesse Newton "Tobacco Road" Below: Denise Sakunah Delaney in "Medea"

Dee Andrus, Willie J. Jones in "Dutchman"
Above: William Roswell, Melissa Moran, John Hardy in "Rocket to the Moon"

FOLGER THEATRE GROUP

Washington, D.C.
October 8, 1974–May 25, 1975

Producer, Louis W. Scheeder; Associate Producer, Ray Hanley; Press, Nan Randall; Assistant to the Producer, Cynthia Ferrell; Company Manager, Mary Ann deBarbieri; Technical Director, Thom Shovestull; Stage Managers, David M. Levine, Dorothy Maffei; Costumiere, Deborah Walthers

PRODUCTIONS AND CASTS

THE FARM *(American Premiere)* by David Story; Director, Louis W. Scheeder; Setting, David Chapman; Costumes, Bob Wojewodski; Lighting, Hugh Lester. CAST: Elizabeth Perry (Wendy), Lauri Peters (Jennifer), Anne Stone (Brenda), Roy Cooper (Slattery), Kate Wilkinson (Mrs. Slattery), John Calkins (Albert), Allan Carlsen (Arthur)

HENRY IV, PART ONE by William Shakespeare; Director, Paul Schneider; Music, Robert Dennis; Setting, William Mickley; Costumes, Joan Thiel; Lighting, Arden Fingerhut; Stage Fights, Ron Mangravite. CAST: James Cahill (Henry IV), Dan Szelag, John Christopher Jones, John Calkins, Paul Edwards, Robert Zukerman, Richard Sterne, Clement Fowler, Earl Hindman, Gerald Graham Brown, Miguel Alves, Clement Fowler, Stephen Lang, Donald C. Moore, Mark Robinson, Shepard Sobel, Richard Wright, Anne Stone, Elise Caitlin, Ruth Sadler, W. Ross McIntire, Kurt Feuer, Ted C. Sod, Gregory Mosel, Gilbert Oakley III, Kurt Feuer

THE TEMPEST by William Shakespeare; Director, Paul Schneider; Setting, Paul Zalon; Costumes, Bob Wojewodski; Choreography, Virginia Freeman; Music, William Penn; Lighting, Arden Fingerhut. CAST: M. Jan Dabrowski, Richard Vernon, Steven Gilborn, Peter Vogt, Ron Siebert, Paul C. Edwards, Larry McKisson, John Hertzler, Terry Hinz, Mark Robinson, Charles Morey, Elise Caitlin, Seret Scott, Mauree Barnes, Tom Carlson, Cole Eckhardt, Gregory Ford

HE'S GOT A JONES *(World Premiere)* By G. Tito Shaw; Director, Harold Shaw; Setting, Stuart Wurtzel; Costumes, Joan E. Thiel; Lighting, Betsy Toth; Music, E. L. James, Hilston Felton. CAST: Terry Alexander (Joe), Cecelia Norfleet (Gladys), Count Stovall (Joffrey), Cara Duff-MacCormick (Margaret)

Nan Randall, Robin Moyer Photos

Top Right: Lauri Peters, Anne Stone, Elizabeth Perry in "The Farm" Below: John Christopher Jones, James Cahill, John Calkins in "Henry IV, Part I"

Cecelia Norfleet, Terry Alexander in "He's Got a Jones"

Steven Gilborn in "The Tempest"

FORD'S THEATRE SOCIETY

Washington, D.C.
September 15, 1974–August 31, 1975

Executive Producer, Frankie Hewitt; Assistant, Maury Sutter; Administrative Director, Robert G. Buchanan; Press, Alma Viator, Wayne Knickel; Technical Director, Tom Berra; Wardrobe, Hillary Gibbs Paul

PRODUCTIONS AND CASTS

ME AND BESSIE by Will Holt and Linda Hopkins; Director, Robert Greenwald; Setting and Lighting, Donald Harris; Costumes, Terence Tam Soon; Musical Coordinator, Tony Berg. CAST: Linda Hopkins, Gerri Dean, Lester Wilson

LOVE'S LABOUR'S LOST and THE TAMING OF THE SHREW by William Shakespeare; Performed by the City Center Acting Company; Producing Director, Margot Harley; Executive Director, Porter Van Zandt. COMPANY: Nita Angeletti, Robert Bacigalupi, Brooks Baldwin, Gisela Caldwell, Peter Dvorsky, Gerald Gutierrez, Sandra Halperin, J. W. Harper, Elaine Hausman, Benjamin Hendrickson, Patti LuPone, Mary-Joan Negro, Richard Ooms, Mary Lou Rosato, Jared Sakren, David Schramm, Norman Snow, Roy K. Stevens, Nicolas Surovy, Sam Tsoutsouvas, William Wright

A TRIBUTE TO ROSALIND RUSSELL as produced by John Springer; Guest Narrator, John Charles Daly.

GABRIELLE with Book and Direction by Jose Quintero; Music, Gibert Becaud; Original Lyrics and Adaptations, Jason Darrow; From an Original Idea by Neal Du Brock; Set, Eugene Lee; Costumes, Franne Lee; Lighting, Jules Fisher; Musical Concepts and Orchestrations, Garry Sherman; Choreography, Dan Siretta; Musical Direction, William Cox; Stage Manager, Donald Walters. CAST: Tammy Grimes, Marilyn Cooper, Laurence Guittard, Robin Hoff, Danny Meehan, David Sabin

NASH AT NINE with Music by Milton Rosenstock; Conceived and Directed by Martin Charnin; Sets, David Chapman; Costumes, Theoni V. Aldredge; Lighting, Martin Aronstein; Produced in association with Les Schechter and Barbara Schwei; At the pianos, Rod Derefinko, Brooks Morton; General Manager, Sherman Gross; Stage Manager, F. R. McCall. CAST: Craig Stevens, John Stratton, Jane Summerhays, Harvey Evans

THE PORTABLE PIONEER AND PRAIRIE SHOW with Book and Lyrics by David Chambers; Music and Lyrics, Mel Marvin; Musical Director, Mel Marvin; Director, David Chambers; Set, James Bakkom; Lighting, Spencer Mosse; Costumes, William Henry; Production Manager, Frank Marino; Choreographer, Dennis Nahat. CAST: Terry Hinz, Prudence Wright Holmes, John Long, Ingrid Helga Sonnichsen, Lyle Swedeen, Donovan Sylvest, Mary Wright

LIGHT UP THE SKY by Moss Hart; Director, Harold J. Kennedy. CAST: Vivian Blaine, Celeste Holm, Sam Levene, Kay Medford, Skipp Lynch, Jack Collard, Donald Barton, Peggy Winslow, Harold J. Kennedy

GIVE 'EM HELL HARRY! By Samuel Gallu; Based on life and times of President Harry S. Truman; Director, Peter H. Hunt; Set, James Hamilton; Presented in association with Samuel Gallu and Thomas J. McErlane. CAST: James Whitmore

DIAMOND STUDS with Book by Jim Wann; Music and Lyrics, Bland Simpson, Jim Wann; Director, John L. Haber; Musical Staging, Patricia Birch; Costumes, Carol Spieer; Stage Managers, Ginny Freedman, William Yaggy. CAST: Dan Denerstein, Carolyn Dutton, Goud Edminds, Jimmy English, Gregory Fleeman, Homer Foil, Madison Mason, Cassandra Morgan, Connie O'Connell, Ron Osborne, Nick Plakias, Jeffryn Stephens, Ty Stephens, D. L. Taylor

Top Right: Lyle Swedeen, Terry Hinz, John Long, Prudence Wright Holmes, Ingrid Helga Sonnichsen, Donovan Sylvest in "The Portable Pioneer and Prairie Show"

(Steven Karafyllakis Photo)

Below: Cassandra Morgan, Gregory Fleeman, Dan Denerstein, Ron Osborne, Ty Stephens, Madison Mason in "Diamond Studs"

(Earl Robbin Photo)

James Whitmore in "Give 'Em Hell Harry!"

(Ken Howard Photo) **199**

GOODMAN THEATRE CENTER

Chicago, Illinois
October 9, 1973–June 16, 1974
(not included in THEATRE WORLD, Vol. 30)

Artistic Director, William Woodman; Managing Director, John Economos; Press, Rhona Schultz, Joanne Unkovskoy; Production Supervisor, Joseph DePauw; Stage Managers, James Greek, Peter DeNicola, James McDermott, Patrick Skelton, Joseph Drummond

PRODUCTIONS AND CASTS

THE FREEDOM OF THE CITY (*American Premiere*) by Brian Friel; Director, William Woodman; Sets, David Jenkins; Costumes, Alicia Finkel; Lighting, F. Mitchell Dana. CAST: Frances Hyland, Lenny Baker, Allan Carlsen, Maurice D. Copeland, Charles W. Noel, Edward Meekin, James Miller, Fred Michaels, Tony Mockus, Timothy W. Oman, Stephen Parr, Timothy Himes, Ian Williams, Frank Miller, Bob Swan, David Whitaker

A DOLL'S HOUSE by Henrik Ibsen; Translation, Christopher Hampton; Director, Tormod Skagestad; Set, John Scheffler; Costumes, Alicia Finkel; Lighting, G. E. Naselius. CAST: Carole Shelley, Philip Kerr, Anthony Mocus, Jeremiah Sullivan, Maureen Anderman, Viola Berwick, Cynthia Baker Johnson, Laurie Oleff, Mark Dold, Ross Porges, Staci Munic, Michael Kay, Thomas Krug

THE TOOTH OF CRIME by Sam Shepard; Director, Michael Kahn; Music, Tony Zito; Scenery, John Kasarda; Costumes, John David Ridge; Lighting, Gilbert Hemsley. CAST: Charles Siebert, Cynthia Dalbey, Jack Wallace, Michael Houlihan, Danny Goldring, Joe Bell, Bob Swan, Robert LuPone

TO BE YOUNG, GIFTED AND BLACK by Lorraine Hansberry; Adapted by Robert Nemiroff; Director, Patrick Henry; Costumes, Andrea Kalish; Scenery, Joseph Nieminski; Lighting, Daniel Adams. CAST: Reuben G. Greene, Colostine Boatwright, Myron Natwick, Kristine Cameron, Connie Mango, Amanda Ambrose, Noreen Walker, Larry D. Riley, Jackie Taylor

HENRY IV by William Shakespeare; A 3 act adaptation of Parts I and II by Richard Matthews; Director, Peter Wexler; Costumes, Virgil Johnson; Associate Director, Joseph Leon; Fights, Michael Tezla. CAST: Tom Atkins, George C. Hearn, Joseph Leon, Tony Mockus, Jack Roberts, David Selby, Delia Hattendorf, Edward Holmes, Louise Jenkins, Raleigh Miller, Karen Shallo, Ron Siebert, Roy K. Stevens, Michael Tezla, Eugene J. Anthony, Barry Cullison, Allison Giglio, Dean Hill, Michael Houlihan, Glenn Kovacevich, James Miller, Lu Ann Post, Randall Smith, Robert Swan, Ian Williams

GUYS AND DOLLS with Music and Lyrics by Frank Loesser; Book, Jo Swerling, Abe Burrows; Director, Gene Lesser; Choreography, Elizabeth Keen; Musical Direction, David Richards; Sets, James E. Maronek; Costumes, Nancy Potts; Lighting, William Mintzer. CAST: Viola Verwick, Terry Deck, Michael J. Fisher, Edward Holmes, Joseph Leon, Mary Louise, Don Perkins, Sheilah Rae, Paul Zegler, Eugene J. Anthony, John Bazzell, Suzi Bolen, Jim Carey, Vivian Facusse, Judy Fields, Nancy Grahn, Robert Hartigan, Bernardo Hiller, Patty Kozono, Jimmy Spinks, David Reed Staller, Wendy Stuart, Jerry Tullos, Laureen Valuch

David H. Fishman Photos

Left: Paul Zegler in "Guys and Dolls" Top: Allan Carlsen, Frances Hyland, Lenny Baker in "Freedom of the City" Below: Tom Atkins, Ron Siebert, Robert Swan, James Miller, Ian Williams, David Selby in "Henry IV"

Carole Shelley, Philip Kerr in "A Doll's House"

Amanda Ambrose, Jackie Taylor, Noreen Walker, Larry B. Filey, Colostine Boatwright, Reuben Greene in "To Be Young, Gifted and Black"

rian Murray, Swoosie Kurtz in "The Philanthropist"
Right: Maurice Copeland, William Roerick, Nancy
Marchand, Roger Omar Serbagi in "The Cherry
Orchard" Below: Martyn Green, Bruce Kornbluth,
Maurice Copeland, Brenda Forbes in "The Sea"

October 4, 1974–June 15, 1975

THE CHERRY ORCHARD by Anton Chekhov; Translation, Tyrone Guthrie, Leonid Kipnis; Director, Brian Murray; Scenery, David Mitchell; Costumes, Virgil Johnson; Lighting, Patricia Collins. CAST: Scott Brown, Maurice D. Copeland, Julie Garfield, Allison Giglio, Cecilia Hart, Edward Herrmann, Bruce Kornbluth, Ronald Koules, Leonard J. Kraft, Sonja Lanzener, Nancy Marchand, Fred Michaels, Jay E. Raphael, William Roerick, Louis Edmonds, Otto L. Schlesinger, Roger Omar Serbagi, Donovan Sylvest, Michael Tezla, Nancy Zala

THE SEA (American Premiere) by Edward Bond; Director, William Woodman; Scenery, David Jenkins; Costumes, James Edmund Brady, Lighting, F. Mitchell Dana. CAST: Eugene J. Anthony, Lenny Baker, Rebecca Balding, Joe Bell, Maurice Copeland, Helen Cutting, Brigid Duffy, Brenda Forbes, Allison Giglio, Martyn Green, Judith Ivey, Dennis Kennedy, Bruce Kornbluth

'TIS PITY SHE'S A WHORE by John Ford; Director, Michael Kahn; Sets, Robert U. Taylor; Costumes, Lawrence Casey; Lighting, John McLain; Choreographer, Beulah Abrahams; Fencing, Larry Carpenter. CAST: Christine Baranski, Robert Beseda, Frank Borgman, Valerie Charron, Louis Edmonds, Harry Epstein, Ellen Holly, Allison Giglio, Michael Houlihan, Charlotte Jones, Michael Levin, Seymour Penzner, Sarah Peterson, J. A. Preston, Hugh Reilly, Ralph Robbins, Franklyn Seales, Theodore Sorel, John Tillinger, Michael Tezla, Enka Vagenius, Annebelle Winston

THE PHILANTHROPIST by Christopher Hampton; Director, Michael Montel; Setting, Peter Wexler; Costumes, John David Ridge; Lighting, Ken Billington. CAST: Veronica Castang, Richard Clarke, Jarlath Conroy, Judith Ivey, Swoosie Kurtz, David H. Leary, Brian Murray

THE RESISTIBLE RISE OF ARTURO UI by Bertolt Brecht; adapted by George Tabori; Director, William Woodman; Settings, Joseph Nieminski; Costumes, John David Ridge; Lighting, Gilbert V. Hemsley, Jr. CAST: Eugene J. Anthony, Joe Bell, George Brengel, Robert Davis, Roger De Koven, Tony Flacco, Allison Giglio, Donna Haley, Louise Jenkins, Art Kassul, Dennis Kennedy, Gary Roppel, Ron Koules, Glenn Kovacevich, Paul Larson, Don Marson, Fred Michaels, Anthony M. Mockus, Neil Patrick, Charles Randall, Joe Rodgers, Joe Shea, Michael Tezla, Greg Von Dare, Kenneth Welsh, Paul Zegler

CHEMIN DE FER by Georges Feydeau; Translation, Suzanne Grossman, Paxton Whitehead; Director, Stuart Gordon; Sets, James Maronek; Costumes, James Edmund Brady; Lighting, F. Mitchell Dana. CAST: Keith Bjes, Warren Casey, Margaret Christopher, Arnold Coty, Arlene DeCoveny, Kathleen Doyle, Richard Fire, Dennis Franz, Richard Kline, Ron Koules, Raymond Nelson, Eugenie Ross-Leming, Michael Saad, Robert Swan, Ian Williams

David H. Fishman Photos

**Richard Kline, Richard Fire, Eugenie Ross-Lenning
in "Chemin de Fer" Above: Ken Welsh in "Arturo Ui"**

THE GUTHRIE THEATER COMPANY

Minneapolis/St. Paul, Minnesota
July 1, 1974–January 18, 1975

Artistic Director, Michael Langham; Associate Directors, Len Cariou, David Feldshuh, Gene Lion; Managing Director, Donald Schoenbaum; Production Manager, Jon Cranney; Directors, Michael Langham, Len Cariou, Michael Bawtree, Robert Benedetti; Designers, Desmond Heeley, John Jensen, Sam Kirkpatrick, Jack Barkla, Jack Edwards, Lowell Detweiler, Bruce Cana Fox; Composers, Dick Whitbeck, Stanley Silverman, John Cook, Henry Mollicone; Lighting, Duane Schuler, Richard William Tidwell, Richard Borgen, Gilbert V. Hemsley, Jr.; Stage Managers, Charlotte Green, Ron Bruncati, John Soliday; Voice and Movement, Fran Bennett; Fight Direction, Erik Fredricksen; Press, Charlotte Solomon Guindon

COMPANY

Maureen Anderman, Paul Ballantyne, Bernard Behrens, Fran Bennett, Drew Birns, James Blendick, Ivar Brogger, Blair Brown, Barbara Bryne, Len Cariou, Jeff Chandler, Patricia Conolly, Valery Daemke, Lance Davis, Robert Engels, Katherine Ferrand, Larry Gates, Peter Michael Goetz, James Harris, Henry J. Jordan, Nicholas Kepros, Mark Lamos, Gary Martinez, Macon McCalman, Eda Reiss Merin, Ken Ruta, August Schellenberg, William Schoppert, Frank Scott, Sheriden Thomas, Kenneth Welsh

PRODUCTIONS

"King Lear," "Love's Labour's Lost," "The Crucible," "Tartuffe," "The School for Scandal," "Everyman"

Right: "Love's Labour's Lost" Below: Katherine Ferrand, Ken Ruta in "Tartuffe" Top: "The Crucible"

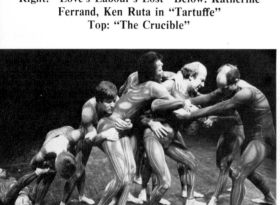

**Len Cariou, Blair Brown in "King Lear"
Above: "Everyman"**

202

Bernard Behrens, Blair Brown, Nicholas Kepros in "School for Scandal"

HARTFORD STAGE COMPANY

Hartford, Connecticut
September 20, 1974–June 15, 1975

Producing Director, Paul Weidner; Managing Director, Jessica L. Andrews; Press, Dave Skal; Business Manager, Alan Toman; Educational Programs, Ellen Jones; Technical Director, Paul Daniels; Directors, Marvin Feliz Camillo, Irene Lewis, Paul Weidner; Sets, John Conklin, Marjorie Kellogg, Hugh Landwehr, Santo Loquasto; Costumes, Sara Covalt, Linda Fisher, Paul Martino, Caley Summers; Lighting, Larry Crimmins, Peter Hunt; Stage Managers, Fred Hoskins, Gary Lamagna, Craig Watson

COMPANY

Ray Aranha, Evalyn Baron, Hollis Barnes, Louis Beachner, George Bowe, Jani Brenn, Larry Bryggman, Carlos Carrasco, Barbara Caruso, Jordan Charney, Joan Coe, Brenda Currin, David Downing, Eduardo Figueroa, Bernard Frawley, John Frey, Deloris Gaskins, Billy Gilmore, Tito Goya, Jerald Goralnick, Ted Graeber, Tana Hicken, Sharita Hunt, Anne Jackson, William Jay, Ben Jefferson, J. J. Johnson, Kurt Karibalis, Gary Lamagna, John Leighton, Leroy Lessane, Vera Lockwood, Richard Loder, Gale McNeeley, Claudia McNeil, Chu Chu Malave, Robert Maroff, Anderson Matthews, Ruth Maynard, Robert Moberly, Jack Murdock, Hannibal Penney, Jr., David O. Peterson, Jerry Reid, Rick Reid, Bill Reilly, Christopher S. Riley, Marilynn Scott, Seret Scott, Michael Shaffer, Geddeth Smith, Kenny Steward, Jack Swanson, Paul C. Thomas, Felipe Torres, Edgar Wilcock, Bari Willerford, Victoria Wood, Paul Woodard, Mary Wright, H. Richard Young, Victoria Zussin

PRODUCTIONS

"The Hot l Baltimore," "Short Eyes," "The Cherry Orchard," "A Raisin in the Sun," "Room Service," "Annelies Marie Frank: Witness," "A Clown's Corner Concert," "Spoon River," and *WORLD PREMIERE* of "Afternoon Tea" by Harvey Perr.

David Robbins Photos

Right: Anne Jackson, Bernard Frawley in "The Cherry Orchard" Above: Richard Loder, Bill Reilly in "Short Eyes" Top: David O. Petersen, Richard Loder, John Frey, Jack Swanson, Seret Scott, Tana Hicken in "The Hot l Baltimore"

Claudia McNeil, Deloris Gaskins, William Jay in "A Raisin in the Sun"

Jordan Charney, Barbara Caruso in "Afternoon Tea"

203

THE INNER CITY REPERTORY THEATRE COMPANY

Los Angeles, California
October 18, 1974–June 29, 1975

Executive Director, C. Bernard Jackson; Assistant, Elaine Kashiki; Press/Stage Manager, John C. Thorpe; Set and Lighting Designer, William Grant III: Costumes, Clarissa Morse; Lighting Designer/Stage Manager, Robert Jones

COMPANY

Chris Calloway, Gloria Calomee, Mel Carter, Terry Carter, Tony DeCosta, Jesse Dizon, Talya Ferro, Robert Garner, William Grant III, Xenia Gratsos, Olga James, Jeanne Joe, Charlene Jones, Abbey Lincoln, Kenneth Martinez, Ruby Millsap, Reginald Montgomery, Thomas Mosley, Nina Nicholas, Thalmus Rasulala, Beah Richards, Rosie Rodriguez, Mike Salcido, Marvin Samuels, Candi Sosa, Sonia Tavares, Wally Taylor, John C. Thorpe, Regina Werneck, Virginia Wing, Thomas Young

PRODUCTIONS

"The Second Earthquake" by C. B. Jackson, "Sweet Nutcracker" by C. B. Jackson, "Sortilegio" by Abdias do Nascimento, "Langston Hughes Said" adapted by C. B. Jackson, "Departure" by C. B. Jackson, "A Black Woman Speaks" by Beah Richards

Bruce Toliman. Michael Nelson Photos

Left: Tony DeCosta, Thomas Young, Mel Carter, Virginia Wing, Candi Sosa, Olga James in "Departure" Top: Mel Carter, Olga James, Reginald Montgomery, Virginia Wing, Marvin Samuels, Candi Sosa, Mike Salcido, Gloria Calomee in "The Second Earthquake"

**Gloria Calomee, Terry Carter in "Sortilegio"
Above: Jeanne Joe, John C. Thorpe
in "Sweete Nutcracker"**

**Beah Richards
in "A Black Woman Speaks"**

IOWA THEATER LAB

Iowa City, Iowa
June 1, 1974–May 31, 1975

Director, Ric Zank; Associate Director, George Kon; Administrative Director/Press, Gillian Richards

COMPANY

Christopher Amato
Ryan Cutrona
Scott Duncan
Rocky Greenberg
George Kon
Jamie Leo
Barry Meiners
Susan Rich
Helen Szablya

PRODUCTIONS: "The Naming," "Dancer without Arms," "Moby Dick"

Walt Dulaney Photos

**Right: Susan Rich, George Kon
in "Dancer without Arms"**

**George Kon, Kim Allen Bent
in "Dancer without Arms"**

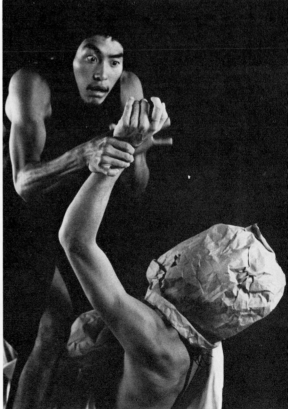

**George Kon, Barry Meiners
in "Dancer without Arms"**

JOHN F. KENNEDY CENTER FOR THE PERFORMING ARTS

Washington, D.C.
June 10, 1974–June 28, 1975

Chairman, Roger L. Stevens; Executive Director, Martin Feinstein; Music Director, Julius Rudel

PRODUCTIONS AND CASTS

PERFECT PITCH by Samuel Taylor; Director, Davey Marlin-Jones. CAST: Tammy Grimes, Jean-Pierre Aumont, Carole Cook, Cecilia Hart, Kate Harrington, Robert Anthony, Harold Gary
I DO! I DO! with Music by Harvey Schmidt; Book and Lyrics, Tom Jones; Staged by Lowell Purvis. CAST: Carol Burnett, Rock Hudson
LLOYD GEORGE KNEW MY FATHER by William Douglas-Hume; Director, Robin Midgley. CAST: Ralph Richardson, Meriel Forbes, Simon Merrick, Carolyn Lagerfelt, David Stoll, Daphne Anderson, Christopher Bernau, Norman Barrs.
SEESAW with Music by Cy Coleman; Lyrics, Dorothy Fields; Written, Directed, and Choreographed by Michael Bennett. CAST: John Gavin, Lucie Arnaz, Tommy Tune, Loida Iglesias, Ken Carr, Frolic Taylor, Chris Wilzak, Steve Anthony, Christine Barker, Robyn Blair, Naomi Boyd, Richard Christopher, Brandt Edwards, Jon Engstrom, Trudie Green, Nancy Lane, Frank Newell, Jeff Phillips, Linda Poser, Denise Richard, Brennan Roberts, Sachi Shimizu, William Swiggard, Sammy Williams, Jerry Yoder.
SUMMER by Hugh Leonard; Director, James D. Waring. CAST: Stephen Joyce, Lois Smith, Sydney Walker, Lois Markle, John Wylie, Pauline Flanagan, Davis Hall, Harriet Hall
DESIRE UNDER THE ELMS by Eugene O'Neill; Director, Jeffrey Hayden. CAST: Eva Marie Saint, James Broderick, James Broderick, Jerry Hardin, John D. McKinney, George Wilson, Terry Kingsley-Smith, Joe Hill, Laurette Hayden, Ben Jones, Diane Hill, Marianna Peterson, Mike Genovese
ODYSSEY (see National Touring Companies)
OWEN'S SONG based on works of Owen Dodson; Conceived, Directed and Choreographed by Glenda Dickerson, Mike Malone; Music, Clyde-Jacques Barrett, Dennis Wiley; Set, Ron Anderson; Lighting, Ron Truitt; Costumes, Quay Barnes Truitt. CAST: David Cameron, Amii, Lynda Gravatt, Lisa Sneed, Carol Maillard, Robert MacFadden, Carlton Poles, Skipper Driscoll, Loretta Rucker, Janifer Baker, Kiki, Alva Petway, Lynn Whitfield, Bernie Gibson, Ed DeShane, Charles Augins, Moon, Deborah Bridges, Lewis Cason, Ralph Glenmore, E. L. James, Zachery Minor, Robert Pittman
PRESENT LAUGHTER by Noel Coward; Director, Stephen Porter; Scenery, Oliver Smith; Costumes, Nancy Potts; Lighting, John Gleason. CAST: Douglas Fairbanks, Jr., Jane Alexander, Ilka Chase, Diana Van Der Vlis, Dorothy Blackburn, Roy Cooper, Paddy Croft, Lindsay Crouse, Bruce Heighley, Richard Neilson, George Pentecost

Richard Braaten Photos

**Top: Douglas Fairbanks, Jr., Jane Alexander
Below: Douglas Fairbanks, Jr., Ilka Chase
in "Present Laughter"**

**Yul Brynner, Joan Diener
in "Odyssey"**

**Douglas Fairbanks, Jr., Diana Van Der Vlis
in "Present Laughter"**

LONG WHARF THEATRE

New Haven, Connecticut
October 11, 1974–June 6, 1975

Artistic Director, Arvin Brown; Executive Director, M. Edgar Rosenblum; Dramaturge, John Tillinger; Administrative Associate, Alison Harris; Press, Rosalind Heinz, Dan Schay; Stage Directors, Arvin Brown, Ron Daniels, Barry Davis, Athol Fugard, Robin Gammell, Brooks Jones; Sets, John Conklin, Douglas Heap, David Jenkins, Marjory Kellogg, Steve Rubin, Virginia Dancy, Elmon Webb; Costumes, John Conklin, Jania Szatanski, Bill Walker; Lighting, Jamie Gallagher, Judy Rasmusson, Ronald Wallace; Stage Managers, Anne Keefe, Nina Seely, Jean Wiegel

PRODUCTIONS AND CASTS

SIZWE BANZI IS DEAD and THE ISLAND *(American premiere)* by Athol Fugard, John Kani, Winston Ntshona. CAST: John Kani, Winston Ntshona

THE SOLDIER'S TALE and THE KNIGHT OF THE BURNING PESTLE *World Premiere* of new adaptation of latter play with Music by Peter Schickele. CAST: David Byrd, Frederick Coffin, Cathryn Damon, Robin Gammell, Victor Garber, Haskell Gordon, Linda Hunt, Doug Lee, Michael Mullins, Eric O'Hanian, Teresa Wright, Randolyn Zinn

AH, WILDERNESS! with Richard Backus, Emery Battis, John Braden, Kevin Ellicott, Geraldine Fitzgerald, Don Gantry, Sean G. Griffin, Suzanne Lederer, Stephen Mendillo, Paul Rudd, Susan Sharkey, William Swetland, Christina Whitmore, Teresa Wright

PYGMALION with Emery Battis, Shirley Bryan, Mary Fogarty, Don Gantry, Sean G. Griffin, Suzanne Lederer, Carmen Mathews, Rex Robbins, Susan Sharkey, William Swetland, Christina Whitmore

YOU'RE TOO TALL, BUT COME BACK IN TWO WEEKS by Richard Venture *(World Premiere)* CAST: Mary Alice, Joyce Ebert, Hannibal Penney, Jr., Richard Venture, Beatrice Winde

AFORE NIGHT COME *(American Premiere)* by David Rudkin. CAST: Emery Battis, Frank Converse, Mary Fogarty, Sean G. Griffin, David Huffman, Joseph Maher, Stephen McHattie, Stephen Mendillo, Rex Robbins, William Swetland, George Taylor, John Tillinger, Christina Whitmore

RICHARD III with Emery Battis, Carolyn Coates, Paul Collins, David DeRosa, Nancy Donohue, Mary Fogarty, Robin Gammell, Don Gantry, Sean G. Griffin, James Hummert, Nancy Kelly, Joseph Maher, Stephen Mendillo, Lynn Milgrim, Hannibal Penney, Jr., John Roddick, Terrence Sherman, Josef Sommer, William Swetland, John Tillinger, Richard Venture, Rudolph Willrich

YOUNG PEOPLE'S THEATRE PRODUCTIONS: "Troubadour's Carnival," "Frolicks," "Creation of Myths," "Ticket to Tomorrow," "The Hour of Need," with January Eckert, Jack Hoffmann, Barbara MacKenzie, Barbara Nadel, Antonio Pandolfo, Terrence Sherman, Michaelan Sisti

William L. Smith Photos

Top Right: William Swetland, Geraldine Fitzgerald in "Ah, Wilderness" Below: Mary Alice, Richard Venture in premiere of "You're Too Tall, But Come Back in Two Weeks"

Robin Gammell as Richard III

Joseph Maher, Frank Converse in premiere of "Afore Night Come"

LORETTO-HILTON REPERTORY THEATRE

St. Louis, Missouri
October 1, 1974–April 30, 1975

Managing Director, David Frank; Consulting Director, Davey Marlin-Jones; General Manager, George Spalding; Stage Directors, John Dillon, Gene Lesser, Davey Marlin-Jones, Bert Houle, Sophie Wibaux, Bob DeFrank, David Frank, Dwight Schultz; Music Director, Tony Zito; Sets, Grady Larkins, John Kavelin; Costumes, Sigrid Insull, John David Ridge, Mary Strieff; Lighting, Peter E. Sargent, Vance Sorrells; Movement, Bob DeFrank; Choreographic Consultant, Darwin Knight; Music Arrangements, Nelson Sheeley; Stage Managers, Don Lamb, Glenn Dunn; Press, Sara Cramer; Company Manager, Nelson Sheeley; Technical Director, Jack Conant

COMPANY

Lewis Arlt, Brendan Burke, Robert Darnell, Bob DeFrank, Joneal Joplin, Wil Love, Jessica Richman, Arthur A. Rosenberg, Nelson Sheeley, Vance Sorrells, Henry Strozier, Margaret Winn, Bert Houle, Sophie Wibaux, James Anthony, Gregg Berger, Richard McGougan, Jessica Richman, Stephen Walker.
GUEST ARTISTS: Edmund Day, Patrick Desmond, Georgia Engel, Asa Harris, Francesca James, Louise Jenkins, Barbara Lester, Don Plumley, Robert Spencer, Renee Tadlock, Trinity Thompson

PRODUCTIONS

"Indians," "Caesar and Cleopatra," "The Crucible," "Trevor," "The Real Inspector Hound," "An Evening of Mime," "Oklahoma Heritage" and *World Premiere* of "Have I Stayed Too Long at the Fair?" (an original musical play based on the St. Louis World's Fair of 1904, by the Loretto-Hilton Theatre Company and staff under the direction of Davey Marlin-Jones)

Michael Eastman Photos

Top: Barbara Lester, Joneal Joplin, Katie Spillars, Lewis Arlt, Wil Love, Renee Tadlock in "The Crucible" Below: Lewis Arlt, Vance Sorrells, Arthur Rosenberg, Henry Strozier in "Have I Stayed Too Long at the Fair?" Below: Henry Strozier, Arthur A. Rosenberg, Wil Love in "Trevor"

**Renee Tadlock, Lewis Arlt
In "The Real Inspector Hound"**

**Joneal Joplin
in "Indians"**

Tom Pedi, Milton Selzer in "Sunshine Boys"
Right: Zoe Alexander, Tobi Brydon, W. B. Brydon
in "Old Times" Below: Carole Zorro, Francine
Baughman, Dixie Seatle in "Red Emma . . ."

MANITOBA THEATRE CENTRE

Winnipeg, Canada
October 18, 1974–May 24, 1975

Artistic Director, Edward Gilbert; General Manager, Gregory
Poggi; Press, Max Tapper, Cheryl Karpyshin; Production Manager,
Christopher Lester; Technical Director, Ken McKay; Directors,
John Going, Frances Hyland, Powys Thomas, George Luscombe,
Edward Gilbert, Hutchison Shandro, Alan Lund, Arif Hasnain,
Michael Mawson, Leon Major, Jeremy Gibson; Designers, Peter
Wingate, C. Zak, Christopher Lester, Alistair MacRae, Mark Negin,
Doug McLean, Murray Laufer, Hilary Corbett; Lighting, Bill Wil-
liams, Donald Acaster, Kent McKay, Christopher Lester, Gil
Wechsler, Eric Scott, Peter Van Johnson; Stage Managers, Dwight
Griffin, Eric Scott

PRODUCTIONS AND CASTS

THE SUNSHINE BOYS with Milton Selzer, Richard Kline, Tom
Pedi, Eddie Sprung, Brian Smegal, Wanda Wilkinson, Max Tapper,
Juanita Bethea
OLD TIMES with Zoe Alexander, W. B. Brydon, Tobi Brydon
ANDROCLES AND THE LION with Powys Thomas, Sam Moses,
Lewis Gordon, Pam Rogers, Jack Roberts, Don Allison
THE CHERRY ORCHARD with Pat Galloway, William Needles,
Diane D'Aquila, Mia Anderson, George Morfogen, James Hurdle,
Mervyn Blake, Christine Bennett, Hardee T. Lineham, Fiona Reid,
Edward Atienza, Jan Muszynski, Frank Adamson, Joseph Bahr,
Christopher Benson, Tania Dolovich, Fred Jansen, Joan Lawrence
THE BRAVE LITTLE TAILOR with Francine Baughman, Brenda
Devine, Raymond O'Neill, Duncan Regehr, Pam Rogers, James
Timmins
THE BOY FRIEND with Janis Dunning, Edda Gburek, Fiona
Reid, Bonnie Monaghan, Amanda Hancox, Pamela MacDonald,
Robert E. Landar, Jacques Lemay, Bill Orlowski, Evelyne Ander-
son, Barrie Wood, Jack Northmore, Claude Tessier, Edward Green-
halgh, Marilyn Boyle, Neil Guerin, Alan Blanchette, Claudette
Emond
FORGET-ME-NOT LANE with Derek Godfrey, Budd Knapp,
Brian Tree, Mary Savidge, R. H. Thomson, Charles Hudson, Vinetta
Strombergs, Irena Mayeska, Susan Hogan
HOSANNA with David Calderisi, Michael Hogan
RED EMMA, QUEEN OF THE ANARCHISTS with Carole
Zorro, Francine Baughman, R. H. Thomson, Leon Fermanian,
Dixie Seatle, Tom Celli, Dean Hawes, Charles Hudson, David Bolt,
Phillip Schreibman
THE KNACK with Clive Endersby, Robert Thomson, Jan Muszyn-
ski, Rosemary Dunsmore, Diane Laczko
TRELAWNY OF THE "WELLS" with Betty Leighton, James B.
Douglas, Allan Royal, Maja Ardal, Gerard Parkes, Ron Hastings,
Kenneth Wickes, Jennifer Phipps, Patricia Gage, Domini Blythe,
Neil Munro, Carole Galloway, Christine Foster, John Cutts, Claude
Bede, Joyce Campion, Jeff Braunstein, Martin Doyle, Blair Mascall
CRABDANCE with Helene Winston, Jim Mezon, Dennis
Thatcher, Roland Hewgill, Brian Richardson, John Gauthier, Rory
Runnells, Doug Millar

Gerry Kopelow Photos

George Morfogen, Pat Galloway in "The Cherry
Orchard" Above: "The Boy Friend" 209

Charles Sweigart, Richard Backus, David Stein, Jack Ryland in "Romeo and Juliet" (R) Lee Richardson, Eileen Heckart, Tom Poston in "Mother Courage" Below: Sharon Chazin, Richard Backus, Maria Tucci in "Beyond the Horizon"

McCARTER THEATRE COMPANY

Princeton, N.J.
October 10, 1974–April 6, 1975

President, Daniel Seltzeer; Producing Director, Michael Kahn; General Manager Edward A. Martenson; Press, Norman Lombino, Barbara Steele; Business Manager, Louise M. Bayer; Technical Director, Robert H. Rickner, Jr.; Production Manager, Charles Roden; Stage Managers, Stephen Nasuta, Peter James, Lee Schlosberg, Michael Novak; Production Assistant, Poco Smith; Scenic Designers, Robert U. Taylor, David Jenkins, Paul Zalon, John Conklin; Costumes, Jane Greenwood, Lawrence Casey, David James; Lighting, John McLain, Marc B. Weiss, David F. Segal

PRODUCTIONS AND CASTS

BEYOND THE HORIZON by Eugene O'Neill; Director, Michael Kahn. CAST: Richard Backus, Edward J. Moore, Hugh Reilly, Maria Tucci, Laurinda Barrett, Paul Larson, Camila Ashland, Sharon Chazin, Michael Houlihan, Daniel Seltzer

'TIS PITY SHE'S A WHORE by John Ford; Director, Michael Kahn. CAST: Hugh Reilly, Franklyn Seales, Christine Baranski, Charlotte Jones, Michael Levin, Al Freeman, Jr., Frank Borgman, John Tillinger, Michael Houlihan, Theodore Sorel, Ellen Holly, Sarah Peterson, Jack Gwillim, Seymour Penzner, Robert Beseda, David Farfinkel, Charles Owen, Roger Wellington, Lynne Dennis, Judith Shapiro, Leith Symington

MOTHER COURAGE AND HER CHILDREN by Bertolt Brecht; Director, Michael Kahn. CAST: Eileen Heckart, Maria Tucci, Charles Swigart, Philip Yankee, Rod Loomis, Ronald C. Frazier, Lee Richardson, Patrick Hines, Tom Poston, Ron Siebert, Michele Shay, John Seidman, C. W. Owen, Rod Loomis, Paul Larson, Roger Wellington, Jeff Ferguson, Ronald C. Frazier, Grayce Grant

KINGDOM OF EARTH by Tennessee Williams; Director, Garland Wright. CAST: David Pendleton, Marilyn Chris, Courtney Burr

ROMEO AND JULIET by William Shakespeare; Director, Michael Kahn. CAST: Daniel Seltzer, Charles Sweigart, E. E. Norris, Powers Boothe, Tom Everett, Larry Carpenter, Jack Ryland, William Larsen, Laurinda Barrett, Wyman Pendleton, Grayce Grant, Theodore Sorel, Richard Backus, Robert Beseda, Michael Houlihan, Charlotte Jones, Maria Tucci, Brian Petchey, Sarah Peterson, Julia MacKenzie, Sally Backus, Richard Dix, Tom Poston, Gregg Almquist, David Stein, Frank Esposito, Francesca Poston, Marshall Shnider, David Suehsdorf

Cliff Moore, John Stern Photos

Right Center: Courtney Burr, Marilyn Chris, David Pendleton in "Kingdom of Earth"

Ellen Holly, Al Freeman, Jr. in "Tis Pity She's a Whore"

MEADOW BROOK THEATRE

Rochester, Minnesota
October 10, 1974–May 18, 1975

Artistic Director, Terence Kilburn; Managing Director, David Robert Kanter; Stage Directors, Terence Kilburn, Donald Ewer, Charles Nolte, John Ulmer; Set Designers, Peter Hicks, David Weber, Susan Zsidisin, Lee Adey, Nancy Thompson, Thomas A. Aston; Costume Coordinator, Mary Lynn Bonnell; Lighting Designers, Jeffrey Schissler, Dan File, Lawrence Reed, Jean Montgomery, Robert Neu; Stage Managers, R. Joseph Mooney, Robert Neu, Douglas F. Goodman; Press, Rose Marie McClain, Linda D. Watson; Business Manager, Vincent L. Amman; Technical Director, Peter Hicks; Sound, Thomas D. Spence; Wardrobe, Linda J. Watson, Janice Scott

COMPANY

Jonathan Alper, John Bayliss, Patricia Collins, Donald Ewer, Jane Houdyshell, Marianne Muellerleile, Elisabeth Orion, Dennis Romer, Fred Thompson, Richard Riehle, Robert Grossman, David Combs, David Himes, Stephanie Lewis, Jack Mather, J. L. Dahlmann, Joyce Feurring, Cheryl Giannini, William Halliday, James Corrigan, Judith Cooper, Raye Bush, Richard Baird, Michael Pullin, Douglas Gens, Art Barsamian, Judson Barteaux, James Sims
GUEST ARTISTS: Diana Barrington, John Crawford, Harry Ellerbe, Edgar Meyer, Dorothy Blackburn, Booth Colman, Josephine Nichols, Douglas Travis, Susanne Peters, Joseph Shaw, Guy Stockwell, Brian Petchey, Steven Sutherland, Barbara Tarbuck, Geoff Garland, Priscilla Merrill, Evelyn Baron, Kate Billings, Sam Greenbaum, Terri McRay, Michele Mullen, Curt Williams, Eric Tavaris

PRODUCTIONS

"Tonight at 8:30," "Twelfth Night," "Harvey," "Death of a Salesman," "The Misanthrope," "See How They Run," "Come Back, Little Sheba," "The Drunkard"

Brendan Ross, Walt Bromley Photos

Right: Robert Grossman, Fred Thompson, Cheryl Giannini, Guy Stockwell, David Combs, Susanne Peters, William Halliday in "The Misanthrope" Above: J. L. Dahlmann, Booth Colman, Josephine Nichols, Douglas Travis, Jack Mather, David Himes, Robert Grossman in "Death of a Salesman" Top: Edgar Meyer, Dennis Romer, Harry Ellerbe, Dorothy Blackburn, Jack Mather, Jane Houdyshell in "Harvey"

David Combs, Guy Stockwell, Stephanie Lewis
in "Come Back, Little Sheba"

Diana Barrington, Dennis Romer
in "Twelfth Night"

MILWAUKEE REPERTORY THEATER COMPANY

Milwaukee, Wisconsin
September 13, 1974–June 28, 1975

Artistic Director, Nagle Jackson; Managing Director, Sara O'-Connor; Press, Michael Krawczyk; Directors, Nagle Jackson, Robert Lanchester, William McKereghan, Fredric H. Orner, Penelope Reed, Jeffrey Tambor; Sets, Christopher M. Idoine, Richard H. Graham; Costumes, Ellen M. Kozak, Elizabeth Covey; Lighting, Christopher M. Idoine, Duane Schuler; Stage Managers, Fredric H. Orner, Lyle Raper, Walter Schoen; Tour Manager, Jan Miner

COMPANY

Cheryl Anderson, Robert Dawson, Michael Duncan, Leslie Geraci, John Hancock, Rose Herron, Robert Lanchester, John Mansfield, Durward McDonald, William McKereghan, Andrew Miner, James Pickering, Penelope Reed, Joel Stedman, Stephen Stout, Jeffrey Tambor

GUEST ARTISTS: William Cain, Peggy Cowles, Janice Davies, Woody Eney, Tracy Friedman, Margaret Hilton, Michael Pierce, Susan Schoenfeld, Ruth Schudson, Owen Sullivan

PRODUCTIONS

"The Rehearsal," "Androcles and the Lion," "Richard II," "Big Fish, Little Fish," "Joe Egg," "The English Mystery Plays," "The Great Nebula in Orion," "The Dumb Waiter," the *American Premiere* of "Commitments and Other Alternatives" by Norman Kline, and the *World Premieres* of "Down by the Gravois (under the Anheuser-Busch)" by James Nicholson, "Clocks" by Carl Larsen, and "Chamber Piece" by Nagle Jackson.

Ric Sorgel Photos

Left: Joel Stedman, Rose Herron in "Down by the Gravois" Below: Robert Lanchester in "Richard II" Top: Leslie Geraci, Robert Lanchester, William Cain, Margaret Hilton in "The Rehearsal"

Woody Eney, Peggy Cowles
in "Joe Egg"

Michael Pierce, Stephen Stout
in "Androcles and the Lion"

Jack Bittner, John Broome in "Endgame"
Top: David Berman, Jeanne Ruskin in "Fog
and Mismanagement" Top Right: Joel Brooks,
Mary Testa in "Scrambled Eggs"

THE NEW REPERTORY PROJECT

Kingston, R.I.

Director, J. Ranelli; General Manager, Barry Grove; Designers,
Robert Steinberg, John Gleason, Fred Voelpel, Joy Spanabel; Musi-
al Director, Charles Cofone; Administrative Associate, Bonnie
Bosworth; Technical Director, Robert Steinberg; Costumes, Joy G.
panabel; Stage Managers, Arlene Elboim, David N. Feight, Mi-
hael Holland, Norman Johnson, Judith Swift

COMPANY

David Berman, Jack Bittner, Joel Brooks, John Broome, Victor
aroli, Michael Dantuono, John Gallogly, Robert Gutchen, Mau-
ce Klein, Jane Macdonald, Bruce Pomahac, A. William Perkins,
eanne Ruskin, Mary Testa, Nick Verrecchia

PRODUCTIONS

Antigone," "Endgame," "The Prague Spring," "Fog and Misman-
ement," "Scrambled Eggs," "Congo Square"

Robert Steinberg Photos

Mike Dantuono, David Berman, Joel Brooks
in "The Prague Spring"

213

OKLAHOMA THEATER CENTER

Oklahoma City, Oklahoma
October 2, 1974–April 20, 1975

Managing Director, Lyle Dye, Jr.; Business Manager, Russ Walton; Assistant, Pat Cacy; Technical Director, Robert Souders; Special Projects Coordinators, Judi McElroy, David McElroy; Designer, Costumer, Vicki Holden; Sets, Jerry Davis, Dale Hall, Steve Estes, Ray Larson, Van Alan Grubbs, William Sherry, Del Unruh; Lighting, Del Unruh, David Pape, Steve Estes, Craig Van-Winkle, Steve Bernstein, Jerry Davis

PRODUCTIONS AND CASTS

BAREFOOT IN THE PARK with Dana Nutt, David McElroy, Sandy Sanbar, Scotty Dallas, Sue Long, Clyde Martin

THE CRUCIBLE with Susan Ice, Tom Sheehan, Jennie Pollard, Robbie Holderman, Sara VanHorn, Diane Perkins, Janie Fried, Janice Coffman, Rick Rhodes, Flo Garner, Arlan Gill, Lance Reese, Joan Pickard, Gene Reeves, Curtis Michener, Nick Backes, Charles Unger, Mark Twomey, Joan McDonnald, Liza Burgess, Cynthia Henderson

JOE EGG with Rodger Smith, Mary Gordon Taft, Beck Burgess, Karen Massey, T. A. Minton, Jasmine Moran

STOP THE WORLD, I WANT TO GET OFF with John Swick, Malita Barron, S. S. Vaughn, Miriam McConnell, Scott Mills, Jeanie Cochran, Chris Guinn, Liessa Hinkle, Janet Loafman, Jane Norman, Teresa Thom, Helen Von Feldt

AN EVENING OF ONE ACTS with Vickie Watson, Johnathan Fain, Teri Quick, Dru Richman, John Webb, Robert Woods, David Earl Hodges, Michael Kelley, Vicki Ollie

THE TORCH-BEARERS with Katherine Frame, Charlie Dickerson, Barbara Wade Cox, Suzanne Charney, Mary Gordon Taft, Nick Backes, Clyde Martin, Floyd Nash, Catherine Wright, Steve Schmidt, Ken Hamilton, Kay Lehman

THAT CHAMPIONSHIP SEASON with Tom Schreier, David Earl Hodges, Todd VanEvery, Keith Burkart, Mark Kaplan

A THOUSAND CLOWNS with Rodger Smith, Alan Amick, Wes Collier, Emma Williams, Ken Hamilton, Charles Unger

THE MIRACLE WORKER with Thomas Sheehan, Joyce Bishop, Vernon Wall, Lisa McEwen, Jacqueline Wiley, Victor Wilson, Laurel VanHorn, David M. Scott, Sandy Sanbar, Jeanie Miller, Jennie Pollard, Derek Wilson, Kathy Bellamy, April Courtney, Denham Cramer, Jeffery Kizer, Todd McCoy, Melissa Norris, Lisa Voegeli

Pat Cacy Photos

Top Right: Rodger Smith, Alan Amick in "A Thousand Clowns" Below: Jeannie Miller, Lisa McEwen in "The Miracle Worker"

Miriam McConnell, John Swick in "Stop the World, I Want to Get Off"

Floyd Nash, Kathy Wright, Barbara Wade Cox, Suzanne Charney in "The Torchbearers"

PHILADELPHIA DRAMA GUILD

Philadelphia, Pennsylvania
November 19, 1974–April 20, 1975

Artistic Director, Douglas Seale; Assistant, Lillian Steinberg; Chairman of the Board of Directors, Elkins Wetherill; President, Sidney S. Bloom; Treasurer, Managing Director, James B. Freydberg; Stage Directors, Douglas Seale, Paxton Whitehead, Richard Maltby, Jr.; Sets, David Ballou; Costumes, Jane Greenwood, David Charles; Lighting, Lee Watson, Press, James E. McCormick; Properties, Blair Kersten, Allan Trumpler; Stage Managers, Jerry Nobles, Rusty Swope, Gerald Nobles

PRODUCTIONS AND CASTS

MISALLIANCE with Philip Kerr, Albert Sanders, Leah Chandler, Betty Leighton, Dillon Evans, Robert Pastene, James Valentine, Louise Troy, Heath Lamberts

ARDELE with Douglas Seale, Claudia Peluso, Leah Chandler, James Hurwitz, Angela Wood, Paxton Whitehead, James Valentine, Philip Kerr, Merry Ross, Jerri Iaia

THE IMPORTANCE OF BEING EARNEST with James Parsons, Philip Kerr, James Valentine, Patricia Falkenhain, Louise Troy, Myra Carter, Lu Ann Post, John Braden, William Preston, Jerri Iaia

LONG DAY'S JOURNEY INTO NIGHT with Robert Pastene, Geraldine Fitzgerald, Philip Kerr, John Glover, Regan O'Connell

James E. McCormick Photos

Right: Robert Pastene, Leah Chandler, James Valentine, Heath Lamberts in "Misalliance"
Top: Philip Kerr, Lu Ann Post in "The Importance of Being Earnest"

Geraldine Fitzgerald, Robert Pastene in "Long Day's Journey into Night"

Douglas Seale, James Valentine in "Ardele"

PAF: PERFORMING ARTS FOUNDATION

Huntington Station, N.Y.
October 4, 1974–May 17, 1975

General Manager, Peter Bellermann; Artistic Director, Joseph Brockett; Education Director, Kas Bendiner; Press, Gordon Forbes; Company Coordinator, Eleanor Lindsay; Production Supervisor, William Gensel; Designer, John Shane, Technical Director, Lee De-Weerdt; Costumes, Betsy Wood; Stage Manager, Paulette Licitra

PRODUCTIONS AND CASTS

BORN YESTERDAY with Ginger Drake, Raymond Singer, Richmond Hoxie, J. D. Ferrara, Donald Gantry, Vinnie Holman, Nick Savian, William Pardue, Judith Tillman

THE CARETAKER with Richard Council, Robert Whiting, Bill Pardue

ARSENIC AND OLD LACE with Kay Strozzi, Daniel Keyes, Robert Whiting, Philip Reeves, William Pisarra, Mary Hara, Virginia Drake, Jeffrey Haddow, Tom Sly, Ralph Roberts, William Pardue, Brian Driscoll

THE EFFECT OF GAMMA RAYS ON MAN-IN-THE-MOON MARIGOLDS with Eleanor Lindsay, Georgia Hester, Deborah Mayo, Elizabeth Donnelly, Kathy Goodwin

THE IMPORTANCE OF BEING EARNEST with Ronn Kistler, Richard Morris, Jason McAuliffe, Ann Mitchell, Deborah Mayo, Peggy Cosgrave, Doreen Dunn, Robert Whiting

STRAIGHT UP with Peggy Cosgrave, William Pardue, Brian Brownlee, Alexandra Stoddart, Ronn Kistler, Robert Whiting

**Alexandra Stoddart, Brian Brownlee
in "Straight Up"**
(Joan James Photo)

THE PROFESSIONAL PERFORMING COMPANY

Chicago, Illinois
January 2, 1975–May 3, 1975

Producer, H. Adrian Rehner; Co-Artistic Supervisors/Stage Directors, Lenard Norris, Jack Montgomery; Production Manager, Mary Cobb; Stage Manager, Joseph DePauw; Designer, Jack Montgomery; Costumes, David Bess; Technical Director, Gregory Von Dare; Properties/Scenic Artist, Beverly Sobieski; Sound, Robert James; Lighting Director/Designer, Jeffrey Shender; Production Assistant, Marcia Belton

COMPANY

Frank Barrett, Tom Gora, Kip Gillespie, Larry Hughes, Wafer Lewis, Leon Natker, Richard Pittman, Bernadine Rideau, Peggy Roeder, James Spinks, William Vines, Peter Zopp, Toimiken Three, Mary Rucker, Frankie Hill, Cheryl Stennis, Ralph Flannigan, Booker O'Quinn, Sandra Wallace, Marva Gilliams, Randy Lindsay, Louis Raymond, Sandra Marshall, Nancy Russ, Constance Weakley, Matina Hernandez, Willie Thomas, Audrey Ellis, Katherine Butler, Ricardo Young, Gloria Willis, Mary An Johnson, Ann Grose, Gayle Talbot, Jo Ann Jones

PRODUCTIONS

"Norman, Is That You?'" "Ceremonies in Dark Old Men," "Hamlet," "The Death and Times of Sneaky Fitch"

Raymond Hasch Photos

216 **Wafer Lewis, Bill Vines, Leon Natker
in "Norman, Is That You?" Above: "Hamlet"**

SEATTLE REPERTORY THEATRE

Seattle, Washington
October 16, 1974–June 15, 1975

Artistic Director, Duncan Ross; Producing Director, Peter Donnelly; Assistant Artistic Director, Arne Zaslove; Designers, Robert Dahlstrom, Eldon Elder, John Naccarato, John Wright Stevens; Costumes, Lewis D. Rampino; Lighting, Steven A. Maze, Richard Nelson; Technical Director, Floyd Hart; Production Manager, Marc Rush; Press, Shirley Dennis, Marnie Andrews; For Second Stage: Designers, W. Scott Robinson, Phil Schermer; Costumes, Ethel Anderson, Lewis D. Rampino; Lighting, Cynthia J. Hawkins, Phil Schermer, D. Edmund Thomas; Technical Director, Floyd Hart; Stage Managers, Jay Moran, Edwin C. Stone; Administrative Assistant, Charles Younger; Production Assistants, Michael Mayer, George Wakefield, Toby Corbett

COMPANY

Adrian Sparks, Robin Reeds, Loren Foss, Gastone Rossilli, Robert Loper, Ted D'Arms, William Preston, D. H. Panchot, Mark Metcalf, Marsha Wischhusen, Clayton Corzatte, Gerald Burgess, John Renforth, Erik Fredricksen, William Rongstad, Kimberly Ross, Jim Baker, Mark Buchan, Peter Hodges, Jerry Brinkman, Daryl Anderson, Eric Helland, Pamela Reed, Dan Mahar, Gregg Henry, David Boushey, C. W. Armstrong, Steve Elliott, Jeff Beatty, John Clark, Douglas Shofstall, John Smily, Stan Yale, Ted Hinkey, Tom Humphrey, David Clark, Dennis Ryan, Bill Hartmann, Bryce Butler, Steve Moe, Laurie Pilloud, Tamara Brown, Frances Haertel, Zoaunne, Deborah Offner, Gardner Hayes, Jo Leffingwell, Jim Etue, Deke Lundquist, Brady Smith, Judith Drake, Jan Devereaux, Leah Sluis, Marie Truty, Maureen Hawkins

PRODUCTIONS

MAINSTAGE: "Hamlet," "Life with Father," "Waltz of the Toreadors," "A Doll's House," "The Matchmaker," and *World Premiere* of "A Grave Understanding" by Lloyd Gold

SECOND STAGE: "Biography," "After Magritte" and "The Real Inspector Hound," "Lunchtime" and "Halloween," "The Architect and the Emperor of Assyria," "A Look at the Fifties"

GUEST ARTISTS: Christopher Walken as Hamlet; Biff McGuire and Jeannie Carson in "Life with Father" and director George Abbott; Marian Mercer, David Hurst, and Shirl Conway in "Waltz of the Toreadors" with director Harold Scott; Jeannie Carson, Hurd Hatfield, Curt Dawson in "A Doll's House" with director Eva LeGallienne; Shirl Conway and Donald Woods in "The Matchmaker" with director Word Baker; Valerie Harper and Anthony Zerbe in "Lunchtime" and "Halloween" with director Asaad Kelada

Right: Amelia Loren, Marjorie Nelson, Edwin Bordo, Pamela Burrell, John Gilbert in "The Real Inspector Hound" Above: Jay Garner, Deborah Offner, John Harkins in "A Grave Undertaking" Top: Curt Dawson, Jeannie Carson in "A Doll's House"

Loren Foss, Christopher Walken, Gastone Rossilli in "Hamlet"

Shirl Conway, Rod Pilloud, Donald Woods in "The Matchmaker"

217

STUDIO ARENA THEATRE

Buffalo, N.Y.
September 26, 1974–June 8, 1975
Tenth Season

Executive Producer, Neal Du Brock; Associate Producer, Paul Repetowski; Production Director, Gintare Sileika; Press, Blossom Cohan, Thomas M. Fontana; Business Manager, William E. Lurie; Assistant to Production Director, Jane Abbott; Stage Managers, Donald Walters, J. P. Valente; Technical Directors, Jim Crossley, David Hurlbert; Wardrobe, Diane R. Schaller; Props, Jean E. Russ; Sound, Michael Lamar.

PRODUCTIONS AND CASTS

I GOT A SONG (*World Premiere*) a view of life and times through the lyrics of E. Y. Harburg; Music, Harold Arlen, Vernon Duke, Sammy Fain, Burton Lane, Jay Gorney, Earl Robinson; Director, Harold Stone; Choreography, Geoffrey Holder; Set, R. J. Graziano; Costumes, Theoni V. Aldredge; Lighting, Tom Skelton. CAST D'Jamin Bartlett, Alan Brasington, Norma Donaldson, Bonnie Franklin, Miguel Godreau, Gilbert Price

COME BACK, LITTLE SHEBA by William Inge; Director, Warren Enters; Scenery, Bennet Averyt; Lighting, Peter Gill; Costumes, Lorena McDonald. CAST: Jan Sterling, James DeMunn, Bruce Detrick, Donald Keyes, Steve Martin, Todd Oppenheimer, Nancy Snyder, George Strath, Susan Willis, Mark Multerer

GABRIELLE (*World Premiere*) with the Music of Gilbert Becaud; Book and Direction, Jose Quintero; Original Lyrics, Jason Darrow; Set, Eugene Lee; Costumes, Franne Lee; Lighting, Jules Fisher; Choreography, Dania Krupska; Musical Direction, William Cox. CAST: Tammy Grimes, Marilyn Cooper, Laurence Guittard, Robin Hoff, Danny Meehan, David Sabin

DESIRE UNDER THE ELMS by Eugene O'Neill; Director, Warren Enters; Set, Stephen Hendrickson; Lighting, Peter Gill; Costumes, Linda Letta. CAST: Roy Cooper, Lawrie Driscoll, Carol Mayo Jenkins, Dermot McNamara, Alvah Stanley, Sean Patric Brennan, James DeMunn, Janis Goldman, Len Kadlubowski, Betty Lutes, Tom Mardirosian

13 RUE DE L'AMOUR by Georges Feydeau; Director Donald Moffat; Set, Michael Sharp; Costumes, Clifford Capone; Lighting, Robert Monk. CAST: Donald Moffat, Gwen Arner, Jessica James, David Laundra, Tom Mardirosian, Philip Minor, Alvah Stanley, Thomas M. Fontana, Len Kadlubowski, Patricia Weber

P.S. YOUR CAT IS DEAD! (*World Premiere*) by James Kirkwood; Set, William Ritman; Lighting, David Zierk; Costumes, Frank J. Boros. CAST: Keir Dullea, Tony Musante, Mary Hamill, Bill Moor, Antony Ponzini, Jennifer Warren, Peter White

GODSPELL with Music and Lyrics by Stephen Schwartz; Director, William R. Cox; Set, Jim Crossley; Costumes, Reet Pell; Lighting, David Zierk. CAST: Sue Benkin, Ann Marie Breen, Sean Patric Brennan, Scotch Byerley, Bruce D'Auria, George-Paul Fortuna, Helen Gelzer, Glynis Marie Grafton, Tony Hoty, Lynn Humphrey, Maggie Hyatt, Matt Landers, Margot Rose

THE LEGEND OF WU CHANG as Conceived and Directed by Tisa Chang; Set, Stephen Hendrickson; Lighting, Rober Monk; Costumes, Fredda Slavin. CAST: Ernest Abuba, Lori Tan Chinn, Lynette Chun, Alvin Lum, Tom Mardirosian, Tom Matsusaka, Dennis Sakamoto, Atsumi Sakato, Pamela Tokunaga, Peter Yoshida, Gregory Houston, Len Kadlubowski

Greenberg May Productions Photos

Top Right: Henderson Forsythe, Jan Sterling in "Come Back, Little Sheba" Below: Marilyn Cooper, David Sabin, Robin Hoff, Tammy Grimes, Danny Meehan, Laurence Guittard in "Gabrielle"

Gregory Houston, Ernest Abuba, Lynette Chu
Len Kadlubowski in "The Legend of Wu Chan

SYRACUSE STAGE

Syracuse, N. Y.
October 25, 1974 - April 5, 1975

Artistic Director, Arthur Storch; General Manager, Karl Ge-
vecker; Administrative Assistant, Anne Jennings; Press, Baird
Thompson; Technical Director, Mark Luking; Stage Managers,
Robert Colson, Denise Kasell; Stage Directors, Arthur Storch, John
Dillon, Pirie MacDonald, Thomas Gruenewald, John Going; Sets,
Stuart Wurtzel, David Chapman, Philip Gilliam, John Doepp; Cos-
tumes, James Berton Harris, Randy Barcelo, Lowell Detweiler,
Jerry Pannozzo, Whitney Blausen, Nanzi Adzima; Lighting, Wil-
liam Lyons, Jeff Davis, Arden Fingerhut, Judy Rasmuson; Choreog-
raphy, Frances Barbour.

PRODUCTIONS AND CASTS

LA RONDE with Kelly Wood, David Kagen, Faith Catlin, Jeffrey
DeMunn, Kathy Bruce, Merwin Goldsmith, Sandy Faison, Mitchell
McGuire, Jacqueline Bertrand, Earl Sydnor

HEDDA GABLER with Sheila Coonan, Anne Ives, James Secrest,
Sara Croft, Virginia Kiser, Merwin Goldsmith, Paul Collins

THE BUTTERFINGERS ANGEL (*World Premiere*) by William
Gibson; Director, Arthur Storch. CAST: Steve Vinovich, John Car-
penter, Kelly Wood, Faith Catlin, Mary Carter, Sally Sockwell, J.
Thomas Wierney, Rachael Potash, Haley Alpiar, Walter White,
Thomas MacGreevy, Merwin Goldsmith, Fred Stuthman, Mitchell
McGuire, Barbara Kudan, Ben Kapen, Sharon Ganjoian, Brad
Videki, Kevin Meikleham, Nancy Hahn, Barbara White, Robert
Stabile

THE IMPORTANCE OF BEING EARNEST with Thomas Mac-
Greevy, Ben Kapen, Robert Moberly, Anne Francine, Virginia
Kiser, Lois Holmes, Eren Ozker, Peter Bosche, Sally Sockwell

ARMS AND THE MAN with Eren Ozker, Patricia O'Connell,
Kelly Wood, Robert Moberly, David Kagen, Merwin Goldsmith,
Ben Kapen, Richard Yarnell

THE LITTLE FOXES with Leila Danette, Earl Sydnor, Margaret
Phillips, Robert Nichols, David Kagen, Virginia Kiser, Earl Rowe,
John Carpenter, Maia Danziger, Robert Blackburn

Rita Hammond Photos

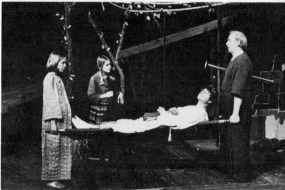

Right: Lois Holmes, Robert Moberly, Peter Bosche
in "The Importance of Being Earnest" Above: Faith
Catlin, John Carpenter, Steve Vinovich, Sharon
Ganjoian in "The Butterfingers Angel" Top: Robert
Nichols, Virginia Kiser, Earl Rowe, Margaret Phillips,
David Kagen, John Carpenter, Maia Danziger in
"The Little Foxes"

Jacqueline Bertrand, Earl Sydnor
in "La Ronde"

Sara Croft, James Secrest, Paul Collins
in "Hedda Gabler"

TRINITY SQUARE REPERTORY COMPANY

Providence, R. I.
October 31, 1974 - May 31, 1975

Director, Adrian Hall; Assistant, Marion Simon; Press, Dave Wynne, Patricia Schwadron; Musical Direction, Richard Cumming; Sets, Eugene Lee, Robert D. Soule; Lights, Eugene Lee, John McLain; Costumes, James Berton Harris, Betsey Potter; Technical Director, Shaun Curran; Properties, Sandra Nathanson; Stage Managers, William Radka, Beverly Andreozzi; Stage Directors, Adrian Hall, Brooks Jones, Word Baker, Larry Arrick

COMPANY

Robert Black, Robert J. Colonna, William Damkoehler, Lila Daniels, Lane Davies, Timothy John Donahue, John D. Garrick, Peter Gerety, Tom Griffin, Ed Hall, Richard Kavanaugh, Richard Kneeland, Marguerite Lenert, Howard London, Mina Manente, George Martin, Bruce McGill, Derek Meader, Barbara Meek, Julie Miterko, Nancy Nichols, Barbara Orson, Ben Powers, Margo Skinner, Daniel Von Bargen, Ricardo Wiley

GUEST ARTISTS: Barbara Damashek, Jan Farrand

PRODUCTIONS

"Jumpers," "The Emperor," "Seven Keys to Baldpate," and *PREMIERES* of "Well Hung" by Robert Lord, "Peer Gynt" by Adrian Hall and Richard Cumming, "Tom Jones" by Larry Arrick and Barbara Damashek

William L. Smith Photos

Right: George Martin, Mina Manente, Marguerite Lenert, William Damkoehler, Robert Black, Tom Griffin, Richard Jenkins in "Well Hung"
Top: "Tom Jones"

George Martin, Mina Manente,
Richard Kneeland in "Jumpers"

"Peer Gynt"

THEATRE FOR THE NEW CITY

New York, N. Y.
July 1, 1974 - June 30, 1975

Artistic Directors, George Bartenieff, Crystal Field; General Manager, Susan Gregg; Business Manager, Mary Thompson; Press, Jerry Jaffe, Howard Atlee; Stage Manager, Janet Paist; Stage Directors, Seth Allen, Mary Thompson, Emilio Cubeiro, Bill Hunt, Crystal Field, Ted Mornell, Susan George, Norman Marshall, Sande Shurin

COMPANY

Alvin Alexis, George Bartenieff, Sarah Brecht, D. J. Brien, Victor Eschbach, Paula Faber, John Farrell, Heven Felder, Ellen Foley, Victory Gatling, Diane George, Jerry Jaffe, Nina Karp, Mike Kushner, Jennifer Lee, Ilan Mamber, Margaret Miller, John Marino, Ken Phelps, Hank Sanders, Claudia Tedesco, Carla Torgrimson, Letitia York, Jeff Zinn

GUEST ARTISTS: Eric Bentley, Geraldine Fitzgerald

PRODUCTIONS

"Bond Roots," "Hoosick Falls," "La Bellilote," "High Time," "RA-D-IO Wisdom," "Ladies Night," "Charley Chestnut F.ides the I.R.T.," "Fat Fell Down." "Feast for Flies," "Sweet Suite"

George Bartenieff, Kristen Steen in "RA-D-IO Wisdom"
(David Street Photo)

THE THIRD EYE THEATRE

Denver, Colorado
November 27, 1974 - June 28, 1975

Producer-Director, Jean Favre; General Manager, June Favre; Associate Directors, Rick Schmidt, Eric Baldwin; Set Designs, Judy Graese, John Meredith; Lighting, Jean Favre; Costumes, Judy Graese, Janetta Turner, Tamara Arendt; Musical Direction, Judy Hangen, Beverly Mango; Choreographer, Ara Marx; Playwright in residence/Technical Director, Eric Baldwin; Press, Margaret Steckler-Prouse; Stage Managers, Brad Currier, David Lewis

COMPANY

Jean Favre, June Favre, Eric Baldwin, Jeannie Marlin, Danny Woods, Darcy Johnson, Paula Boltz, Eric Israelson, Harry Woods, Earline Israelson, Carolyn Harrison, Stephen Smith, Judy Graese, Mike Kimmerl, Todd Pietrafeso, Jennifer Wollerman, Helen Singer, Madeline Kimmel, T. Joe Chamberlin, Pandora Pipiringos, Brian Trampler, Ruie Allyn Halpin, Ken Pietrafeso, Brian Pietrafeso, Vesta Garcia, Tony McVicker, Sheila Johnson, Monica deFranco, J. Kevin Monahan, Barbara Ulrich, Willa Hatcher, Bruce Kerwood, Pat Mahoney, Paul Mast, Harold Aarons, John Meredith, Mike Franco, Bethany Haye, Jerry Reitmeyer, Gregory Boyle, Virginia Baldwin, Janice Matisse, Robert Turner, Al McKittrick, Terry McDonald, Arne Merchant, Kristin McNeil, Pamela Dunne, Jean-Claude Bleuze, Carol Meredith

PRODUCTIONS

"A Christmas Carol," "The Innocents," "Scenes from American Life," "Flamenco Fantasy," "Mary Stuart," "The Stoned Guest," "Ba-Ta-Clan," "Voices," and *World Premiere* of "The Moon" by Eric Baldwin

"Mary Stuart"
(Third Eye Theatre)

VIRGINIA MUSEUM THEATRE REPERTORY COMPANY

Richmond, Virginia
November 8, 1974 - April 13, 1975

Producing Director, Keith Fowler; General Manager, Loraine alde; Stage Directors, Rogert S. Cohen, Keith Fowler, James Kirkand, Ken Letner, Albert B. Reyes, Gene Snow; Music Director, illiam Marion Smith; Choreographer, Nat Horne; Scenic Design-s, deTeel Patterson Tiller, Richard Norgard; Costumes, Frederick . Brown; Lighting, Michael Watson, Cameron Grainger; Company anager, Rachael Lindhart; Press, Fred Haseltine, Michael P. ickey

COMPANY

Irwin Atkins, Janet Bell, Leigh Burch, Mel Cobb, Pamela Cos-llo, Monty Cones, Jim Cyrus, Maury Erickson, Keith Fowler, ank Geraci, Birdie M. Hale, Mark Hattan, Marie Goodman unter, James Kirkland, Ken Letner, Rachael Lindhart, Milledge osley, Carolyn Munson, Lynda Myles, Kathy O'Callaghan, K. pe O'Dell, Nona Pipes, William Pitts, Walter Rhodes, William ancil, Gene Snow, Margaret Thomson, Laurie Thorp

PRODUCTIONS

"Purlie," "Our Town," "Kaspar," "The Miser," "Much Ado ut Nothing," "Tobacco Road," and English language *PRE-IERE* of Maxim Gorki's "Our Father," translated and adapted by lliam Marion Smith, directed by Keith Fowler.

Leigh Burch, Mark Hattan in "Tobacco Road"
(Ron Jennings Photo)

YALE REPERTORY THEATRE

New Haven, Connecticut
October 4, 1974 - May 31, 1975

Artistic Director, Robert Brustein; Associate Director, Alvin Epstein; Managing Director, Robert J. Orchard; Business Manager, Abigail P. Fearon; Press, Jan Geidt; Designers, Michael H. Yeargan, Tony Straiges; Lighting Director, William B. Warfel; Production Supervisor, John Robert Hood; Technical Directors, Bronislaw Sammler, George Lindsay; Stage Managers, Frank S. Toro, Carol M. Waaser; Costumer, Gerda Proctor; Props, Hunter Nesbitt Spence; Assistant Managing Directors, Laurie Edelman, Marion Godfrey; Stage Directors, Andrzej Wajda, William Peters, Alvin Epstein, Michael Posnick, Jeff Bleckner, David Schweizer; Musical Directors/Conductors, Otto-Werner Mueller, Gary Fagin, Paul Schierhorn, Carol Lees, Walt Jones; Original Music, Zygmunt Konieczny, Jack Feldman; Directors, Andrzej Wajda, Atkin Pace; Costumes, Krystyna Zachwatowicz, William Ivey Long, Vittorio Capecce, Michael H. Yeargan, Jeanne Button, Atkin Pace, Zack Brown; Lighting, Krystyna Zachwatowicz, Lloyd S. Riford III, Stephe R. Woody, James F. Ingalls; Choreographer, Carmen de Lavallade

COMPANY

Linda Leigh Atkinson, Norma Brustein, Robert Brustein, Joseph Capone, Stephanie Cotsirilos, Elzbieta Czyzewska, Carmen de Lavallade, Jerome Dempsey, Francelle Stewart Dorn, Ralph Drischell, Christopher Durang, Alvin Epstein, Wesley Fata, Jeremy Geidt, Joe Grifasi, Hurd Hatfield, Walt Jones, Michael Lassell, Charles Levin, Christopher Lloyd, Lizbeth Mackay, Barry Marshall, John McAndrew, Kate McGregor-Stewart, R. Nersesian, Elizabeth Parrish, Ralph Redpath, John Rothman, Stephen Rowe, Paul Scheirhorn, Peter Mark Schifter, Meryl Streep, Rip Torn, Kay Tornburg, Mary Van Dyke, Frederic Warriner

PRODUCTIONS

"Happy End," "The Father," "A Midsummer Night's Dream," *American Premiere* of "The Possessed" adapted by Andrzej Wajda from the stage version by Albert Camus of the novel by Fyodor Dostoyevsky, *WORLD PREMIERES* of "The Idiots Karamazov" by Christopher Durang and Albert Innaurato, "Victory" a story theatre version by Alvin Epstein and Walt Jones based on the novel by Joseph Conrad, "The Shaft of Love" by Charles Dizenzo

Eugene Cook, William Baker Photos

Left: Carmen de Lavallade, Christopher Lloyd in "A Midsummer Night's Dream" Top: Jeremy Geidt, Alvin Epstein, Paul Schierhorn, Charles Levin, Ralph Drischell, Jerome Dempsey in "Happy End"

Norma Brustein, Jerome Dempsey in "The Possessed"

Elzbieta Czyzewska, Rip Torn in "The Father"

222

1975 THEATRE WORLD AWARD WINNERS

PETER BURNELL
of "In Praise of Love"

ZAN CHARISSE
of "Gypsy"

LOLA FALANA
of "Dr. Jazz"

PETER FIRTH
of "Equus"

223

DORIAN HAREWOOD
of "Don't Call Back"

MARCIA McCLAIN
of "Where's Charley?"

LINDA MILLER
of "Black Picture Show"

JOEL HIGGINS
of "Shenandoah"

JOHN SHERIDAN
of "Gypsy"

MARTI ROLPH
of "Good News"

DONNA THEODORE
of "Shenandoah"

SCOTT STEVENSEN
of "Good News"

1975 THEATRE WORLD AWARD PARTY
Awards Presented by COLLEEN DEWHURST and JULIE HARRIS

Peter Firth, Colleen Dewhurst
Below: Bette Davis

George Wojtasik, Julie Harris

Marcia McClain, Colleen Dewhu
Below: Julie Harris

Zan Charisse, John Sheridan, Bette
Davis, Donna Theodore

Peter Burnell, Joel Higgins, Scott Stevensen,
Linda Miller, Peter Firth

Thursday, May 29, 1975

Mark Daniels and wife, Tony Musante, Anita
Gillette, Kay Medford, John Springer
below: John Cullum

Bette Davis, Charles Bowden, Paul Giovanni, Peter
Shaffer, Kermit Bloomgarden, Colleen Dewhurst
Below: Peter Firth, Alec McCowen

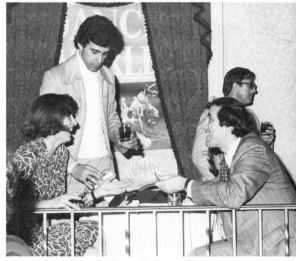

Scott Stevensen, Barbara Cook, Don Nute

Pamela Burrell, Peter Gatto,
Miles Kreuger, Jacques Crampon

ted, Evan Romero, Van Williams Photos

Maureen Anderman

Ralph Carter

Carol Channing

Clifton Davis

Tammy Grimes

PREVIOUS THEATRE WORLD AWARD WINNERS

1944–45: Betty Comden, Richard Davis, Richard Hart, Judy Holliday, Charles Lang, Bambi Linn, John Lund, Donald Murphy, Nancy Noland, Margaret Phillips, John Raitt

1945–46: Barbara Bel Geddes, Marlon Brando, Bill Callahan, Wendell Corey, Paul Douglas, Mary James, Burt Lancaster, Patricia Marshall, Beatrice Pearson

1946–47: Keith Andes, Marion Bell, Peter Cookson, Ann Crowley, Ellen Hanley, John Jordan, George Keane, Dorothea MacFarland, James Mitchell, Patricia Neal, David Wayne

1947–48: Valerie Bettis, Edward Bryce, Whitfield Connor, Mark Dawson, June Lockhart, Estelle Loring, Peggy Maley, Ralph Meeker, Meg Mundy, Douglass Watson, James Whitmore, Patrice Wymore

1948–49: Tod Andrews, Doe Avedon, Jean Carson, Carol Channing, Richard Derr, Julie Harris, Mary McCarty, Allyn Ann McLerie, Cameron Mitchell, Gene Nelson, Byron Palmer, Bob Scheerer

1949–50: Nancy Andrews, Phil Arthur, Barbara Brady, Lydia Clarke, Priscilla Gillette, Don Hanmer, Marcia Henderson, Charlton Heston, Rick Jason, Grace Kelly, Charles Nolte, Roger Price

1950–51: Barbara Ashley, Isabel Bigley, Martin Brooks, Richard Burton, James Daly, Cloris Leachman, Russell Nype, Jack Palance, William Smothers, Maureen Stapleton, Marcia Van Dyke, Eli Wallach

1951–52: Tony Bavaar, Patricia Benoit, Peter Conlow, Virginia de Luce, Ronny Graham, Audrey Hepburn, Diana Herbert, Conrad Janis, Dick Kallman, Charles Proctor, Eric Sinclair, Kim Stanley, Marian Winters, Helen Wood

1952–53: Edie Adams, Rosemary Harris, Eileen Heckart, Peter Kelley, John Kerr, Richard Kiley, Gloria Marlowe, Penelope Munday, Paul Newman, Sheree North, Geraldine Page, John Stewart, Ray Stricklyn, Gwen Verdon

1953–54: Orson Bean, Harry Belafonte, James Dean, Joan Diener, Ben Gazzara, Carol Haney, Jonathan Lucas, Kay Medford, Scott Merrill, Elizabeth Montgomery, Leo Penn, Eva Marie Saint

1954–55: Julie Andrews, Jacqueline Brookes, Shirl Conway, Barbara Cook, David Daniels, Mary Fickett, Page Johnson, Loretta Leversee, Jack Lord, Dennis Patrick, Anthony Perkins, Christopher Plummer

1955–56: Diane Cilento, Dick Davalos, Anthony Franciosa, Andy Griffith, Laurence Harvey, David Hedison, Earle Hyman, Susan Johnson, John Michael King, Jayne Mansfield, Sarah Marshall, Gaby Rodgers, Susan Strasberg, Fritz Weaver

1956–57: Peggy Cass, Sydney Chaplin, Sylvia Daneel, Bradford Dillman, Peter Donat, George Grizzard, Carol Lynley, Peter Palmer, Cliff Robertson, Pippa Scott, Inga Swenson

1957–58: Anne Bancroft, Warren Berlinger, Colleen Dewhurst, Richard Easton, Tim Everett, Eddie Hodges, Joan Hovis, Carol Lawrence, Jacqueline McKeever, Wynne Miller, Robert Morse, George C. Scott

1958–59: Lou Antonio, Ina Balin, Richard Cross, Tammy Grimes, Larry Hagman, Dolores Hart, Roger Mollien, France Nuyen, Susan Oliver, Ben Piazza, Paul Roebling, William Shatner, Pat Suzuki, Rip Torn

1959–60: Warren Beatty, Eileen Brennan, Carol Burnett, Patty Duke, Jane Fonda, Anita Gillette, Elisa Loti, Donald Madden, George Maharis, John McMartin, Lauri Peters, Dick Van Dyke

1960–61: Joyce Bulifant, Dennis Cooney, Nancy Dussault, Robert Goulet, Joan Hackett, June Harding, Ron Husmann, James MacArthur, Bruce Yarnell

1961–62: Elizabeth Ashley, Keith Baxter, Peter Fonda, Don Galloway, Sean Garrison, Barbara Harris, James Earl Jones, Janet Margolin, Karen Morrow, Robert Redford, John Stride, Brenda Vaccaro

1962–63: Alan Arkin, Stuart Damon, Melinda Dillon, Robert Drivas, Bob Gentry, Dorothy Loudon, Brandon Maggart, Julienne Marie, Liza Minnelli, Estelle Parsons, Diana Sands, Swen Swenson

1963–64: Alan Alda, Gloria Bleezarde, Imelda De Martin, Claude Giraud, Ketty Lester, Barbara Loden, Lawrence Pressman, Gilbert Price, Philip Proctor, John Tracy, Jennifer West

1964–65: Carolyn Coates, Joyce Jillson, Linda Lavin, Luba Lisa, Michael O'Sullivan, Joanna Pettet, Beah Richards, Jaime Sanchez, Victor Spinetti, Nicolas Surovy, Robert Walker, Clarence Williams III

1965–66: Zoe Caldwell, David Carradine, John Cullum, John Davidson, Faye Dunaway, Gloria Foster, Robert Hooks, Jerry Lanning, Richard Mulligan, April Shawhan, Sandra Smith, Lesley Ann Warren

1966–67: Bonnie Bedelia, Richard Benjamin, Dustin Hoffman, Terry Kiser, Reva Rose, Robert Salvio, Sheila Smith, Connie Stevens, Pamela Tiffin, Leslie Uggams, Jon Voight, Christopher Walken

1967–68: Pamela Burrell, Sandy Duncan, Julie Gregg, Bernadette Peters, Alice Playten, Brenda Smiley, David Birney, Jordan Christopher, Jack Crowder, Stephen Joyce, Michael Rupert, Russ Thacker

1968–69: Jane Alexander, David Cryer, Ed Evanko, Blythe Danner, Ken Howard, Lauren Jones, Ron Leibman, Marian Mercer, Jill O'Hara, Ron O'Neal, Al Pacino, Marlene Warfield

1969–70: Susan Browning, Donny Burks, Catherine Burns, Len Cariou, Bonnie Franklin, David Holliday, Katharine Houghton, Melba Moore, David Rounds, Lewis J. Stadlen, Kristoffer Tabori, Fredricka Weber

1970–71: Clifton Davis, Michael Douglas, Julie Garfield, Martha Henry, James Naughton, Tricia O'Neil, Kipp Osborne, Roger Rathburn, Ayn Ruymen, Jennifer Salt, Joan Van Ark, Walter Willison

1971–72: Jonelle Allen, Maureen Anderman, William Atherton, Richard Backus, Adrienne Barbeau, Cara Duff-MacCormick, Robert Foxworth, Elaine Joyce, Jess Richards, Ben Vereen, Beatrice Winde, James Woods

1972–73: D'Jamin Bartlett, Patricia Elliott, James Farentino, Brian Farrell, Victor Garber, Kelly Garrett, Mari Gorman, Laurence Guittard, Trish Hawkins, Monte Markham, John Rubinstein, Jennifer Warren, Alexander H. Cohen (Special Award)

1973-74: Mark Baker, Maureen Brennan, Ralph Carter, Thom Christopher, John Driver, Conchata Ferrell, Ernestine Jackson, Michael Moriarty, Joe Morton, Ann Reinking, Janie Sell, Mary Woronov, Sammy Cahn (Special Award)

Robert Drivas   **Cloris Leachman**   **Ron O'Neal**   **Liza Minnelli**   **Jason Robards**   **Gwen Verdon**

PULITZER PRIZE PRODUCTIONS

1918– Why Marry?, **1919–** No award, **1920–**Beyond the Horizon, **1921–**Miss Lulu Bett, **1922–**Anna Christie, **1923–**Icebound, **1924–**Hell-Bent fer Heaven, **1925–**They Knew What They Wanted, **1926–**Craig's Wife, **1927–**In Abraham's Bosom, **1928–**Strange Interlude, **1929–**Street Scene, **1930–**The Green Pastures, **1931–**Alison's House, **1932–**Of Thee I Sing, **1933–**Both Your Houses, **1934–**Men in White, **1935–**The Old Maid, **1936–**Idiot's Delight, **1937–**You Can't Take It with You, **1938–**Our Town, **1939–**Abe Lincoln in Illinois, **1940–**The Time of Your Life, **1941–**There Shall Be No Night, **1942–**No award, **1943–**The Skin of Our Teeth, **1944–**No award, **1945–**Harvey, **1946–**State of the Union, **1947–**No award, **1948–**A Streetcar Named Desire, **1949–**Death of a Salesman, **1950–**South Pacific, **1951–**No award, **1952–**The Shrike, **1953–**Picnic, **1954–**The Teahouse of the August Moon, **1955–**Cat on a Hot Tin Roof, **1956–**The Diary of Anne Frank, **1957–**Long Day's Journey into Night, **1958–**Look Homeward, Angel, **1959–**J. B., **1960–**Fiorello!, **1961–**All the Way Home, **1962–**How to Succeed in Business without Really Trying, **1963–**No award, **1964–**No award, **1965–**The Subject Was Roses, **1966–**No award, **1967–**A Delicate Balance, **1968–**No award, **1969–**The Great White Hope, **1970–**No Place to Be Somebody, **1971–**The Effect of Gamma Rays on Man-in-the-Moon Marigolds, **1972–**No award, **1973–**That Championship Season, **1974–**No award, **1975–**Seascape

NEW YORK DRAMA CRITICS CIRCLE AWARDS

1936–Winterset, **1937–**High Tor, **1938–**Of Mice and Men, Shadow and Substance, **1939–**The White Steed, **1940–**The Time of Your Life, **1941–**Watch on the Rhine, The Corn is Green, **1942–**Blithe Spirit, **1943–**The Patriots, **1944–**Jacobowsky and the Colonel, **1945–**The Glass Menagerie, **1946–**Carousel, **1947–**All My Sons, No Exit, Brigadoon, **1948–**A Streetcar Named Desire, The Winslow Boy, **1949–**Death of a Salesman, The Madwoman of Chaillot, South Pacific, **1950–**The Member of the Wedding, The Cocktail Party, The Consul, **1951–**Darkness at Noon, The Lady's Not for Burning, Guys and Dolls, **1952–**I Am a Camera, Venus Observed, Pal Joey, **1953–**Picnic, The Love of Four Colonels, Wonderful Town, **1954–**Teahouse of the August Moon, Ondine, The Golden Apple, **1955–**Cat on a Hot Tin Roof, Witness for the Prosecution, The Saint of Bleecker Street, **1956–**The Diary of Anne Frank, Tiger at the Gates, My Fair Lady, **1957–**Long Day's Journey into Night, The Waltz of the Toreadors, The Most Happy Fella, **1958–**Look Homeward Angel, Look Back in Anger, The Music Man, **1959–**A Raisin in the Sun, The Visit, La Plume de Ma Tante, **1960–**Toys in the Attic, Five Finger Exercise, Fiorello!, **1961–**All the Way Home, A Taste of Honey, Carnival, **1962–**Night of the Iguana, A Man for All Seasons, How to Succeed in Business without Really Trying, **1963–**Who's Afraid of Virginia Woolf?, **1964–**Luther, Hello, Dolly!, **1965–**The Subject Was Roses, Fiddler on the Roof, **1966–**The Persecution and Assassination of Marat as Performed by the Inmates of the Asylum of Charenton under the Direction of the Marquis de Sade, Man of La Mancha, **1967–**The Homecoming, Cabaret, **1968–**Rosencrantz and Guildenstern Are Dead, Your Own Thing, **1969–**The Great White Hope, 1776, **1970–**The Effect of Gamma Rays on Man-in-the-Moon Marigolds, Borstal Boy, Company, **1971–**Home, Follies, The House of Blue Leaves, **1972–**That Championship Season, Two Gentlemen of Verona, **1973–**The Hot l Baltimore, The Changing Room, A Little Night Music, **1974–**The Contractor, Short Eyes, Candide, **1975–**Equus, The Taking of Miss Janie, A Chorus Line

AMERICAN THEATRE WING
ANTOINETTE PERRY (TONY) AWARD PRODUCTIONS

1948–Mister Roberts, **1949–**Death of a Salesman, Kiss Me, Kate, **1950–**The Cocktail Party, South Pacific, **1951–**The Rose Tattoo, Guys and Dolls, **1952–**The Fourposter, The King and I, **1953–**The Crucible, Wonderful Town, **1954–**The Teahouse of the August Moon, Kismet, **1955–**The Desperate Hours, The Pajama Game, **1956–**The Diary of Anne Frank, Damn Yankees, **1957–**Long Day's Journey into Night, My Fair Lady, **1958–**Sunrise at Campobello, The Music Man, **1959–**J. B., Redhead, **1960–**The Miracle Worker, Fiorello! tied with Sound of Music, **1961–**Becket, Bye Bye Birdie, **1962–**A Man for All Seasons, How to Succeed in Business without Really Trying, **1963–**Who's Afraid of Virginia Woolf?, A Funny Thing Happened on the Way to the Forum, **1964–**Luther, Hello, Dolly!, **1965–**The Subject Was Roses, Fiddler on the Roof, **1966–** The Persecution and Assassination of Marat as Performed by the Inmates of the Asylum of Charenton under the Direction of the Marquis de Sade, Man of La Mancha, **1967–**The Homecoming, Cabaret, **1968–**Rosencrantz and Guildenstern Are Dead, Hallelujah, Baby!, **1969–**The Great White Hope, 1776, **1970–**Borstal Boy, Applause, **1971–**Sleuth, Company, **1972–**Sticks and Bones, Two Gentlemen of Verona, **1973–**That Championship Season, A Little Night Music, **1974–**The River Niger, Raisin, **1975–**Equus, The Wiz

| Molly Adams | Wil Albert | Johanna Albrecht | Gregg Almquist | Mary Ellen Ashley |

BIOGRAPHIES OF THIS SEASON'S CAST

AARON, DAVID. Born Sept. 19, 1947 in Denver, Colo. Attended U Denver. Made NY debut 1969 OB in "You're a Good Man, Charlie Brown," followed by NYSF's "Wars of Roses," "Richard III" and "Macbeth," "Accounting for Murder," "Bubbles," "Veil of Infamy."

AARON, JACK. Born May 1, 1933 in NYC. Attended Hunter Col., Actors Workshop. OB in "Swim Low Little Goldfish," "Journey of the Fifth Horse," "The Nest," "One Flew Over the Cuckoo's Nest," "The Birds," "The Pornographer's Daughter."

ABEL, WALTER. Born June 6, 1898 in St. Paul, Minn. Attended AADA. Made Bdwy debut in 1918 in "A Woman's Way," subsequently appearing in, among others, "Forbidden," "Back to Methuselah," "Square Peg," "As You Like It," "The Enemy," "Taming of the Shrew," "Hangman's House," "Beyond the Horizon," "Skidding," "The Seagull," "Mourning Becomes Electra," "When Ladies Meet," "Invitation to a Murder," "Merrily We Roll Along," "Wingless Victory," "Mermaids Singing," "Parlor Story," "Biggest Thief in Town," "Wisteria Trees," "The Long Watch," "Pleasure of His Company," "Night Life," "90 Day Mistress," "Saturday Sunday Monday."

ABRAHAM, F. MURRAY. Born Oct. 24, 1939 in Pittsburgh, Pa. Attended UTex. OB in 1967 in "The Fantasticks," followed by "An Opening in the Trees," "Fourteenth Dictator," "Young Abe Lincoln," "Tonight in Living Color," "Adaptation," "Survival of St. Joan," "The Dog Ran Away," "Fables," "Richard III," "Little Murders," "Scuba Duba," "Where Has Tommy Flowers Gone?," "Miracle Play," "Blessing," Bdwy debut "The Man In The Glass Booth" (1968), followed by "6 Rms Riv Vu.," "Bad Habits," "The Ritz."

ABRAMS, AMOS. Born Aug. 25, in Boone, N.C. Graduate of St. Andrews, and Yale. Made debut in 1969 OB in "Of Thee I Sing," Bdwy 1974 in "Saturday Sunday Monday."

ADAMS, MOLLY. Born in Portchester, NY. Graduate Smith College. Debut 1973 OB in "Older People," followed by "Hot 1 Baltimore."

AGRESS, TED. Born Apr. 20, 1945 in Brooklyn, NY. Attended Adelphi U. Bdwy debut 1965 in "Hello, Dolly!" followed by "Dear World," "Look Me Up" (OB), "Shenandoah."

ALBERT, WIL. Born Aug. 22, 1930 in NYC. Attended AmThWing. Debut 1959 OB in "Dinny and the Witches" followed by "Medea," "Spitting Image," "Water Hen," "Moonchildren," Bdwy 1965 in "Fade Out, Fade In."

ALBRECHT, JOHANNA. Born July 30, 1940 in Mass. Smith Col. graduate. Debut 1971 OB in "Six," followed by "Rhinegold," "Bloodshot Wine."

ALDREDGE, TOM. Born Feb. 28, 1928 in Dayton, O. Attended Dayton U., Goodman Theatre. Bdwy bow 1959 in "The Nervous Set," followed by "UTBU," "Slapstick Tragedy," "Everything in the Garden," "Indians," "Engagement Baby," "How the Other Half Loves," "Sticks and Bones," "Where's Charley?," OB in "The Tempest," "Between Two Thieves," "Henry V," "The Premise," "Love's Labour's Lost," "Troilus and Cressida," "Butter and Egg Man," "Ergo," "Boys In the Band," "Twelfth Night," "Colette," "Hamlet," "The Orphan," "King Lear," "Iceman Cometh."

ALEXANDER, JAMES. Born June 15, 1941 in Albany, Ore. Mich. State graduate. Bdwy debut 1968 in "House of Atreus," followed by "Arturo Ui," OB in "Marouf," "Falling Apart."

ALEXANDER, JANE. Born Oct. 28, 1939 in Boston, Mass. Attended Sarah Lawrence, UEdinburgh. Bdwy debut 1968 in "The Great White Hope" for which she received a Theatre World Award, followed by "6 Rms Riv Vu," "Find Your Way Home."

ALEXANDER, TERRY. Born Mar. 23, 1947 in Detroit, Mich. Wayne State U. graduate. Bdwy debut 1971 in "No Place to Be Somebody" OB in "Rashomon," "Glass Menagerie," "Breakout," "Naomi Court."

ALICE, MARY. Born Dec. 3, 1941 in Indianola, Miss. Studied with NEC, and appeared in its "Trials of Brother Jero" and "The Strong Breed" (1967); Bdwy debut 1971 in "No Place to Be Somebody," followed by "Duplex," "Thoughts," "Miss Julie," "House Party," "Terraces," "Heaven and Hell's Agreement," "In the Deepest Part of Sleep."

ALLEN, DEBORAH. Born Jan. 16, 1950 in Houston, Tex. Graduate Howard U. Debut OB 1972 in "Ti-Jean and His Brothers," Bdwy 1973 in "Raisin."

ALLINSON, MICHAEL. Born in London; attended Lausanne U., RADA. Bdwy bow 1960 in "My Fair Lady," followed by "Hostile Witness," "Come Live with Me," "Coco," OB in "Importance of Being Earnest," "Staircase."

ALLMON, CLINTON. Born June 13, 1941 in Monahans, Tex. Graduate Okla. State U. Bdwy debut 1969 in "Indians," OB in "The Bluebird," "Khaki Blue," "One Sunday Afternoon."

ALMQUIST, GREGG. Born Dec. 1, 1948 in Minneapolis Minn. Graduate U.Minn. Debut Off Broadway 1974 in "Richard III."

ALTMAN, JANE. Born Sept. 7 in Philadelphia, Pa. Temple U. graduate. Debut OB in "Importance of Being Earnest," followed by "Taming of the Shrew," "Candida," "A Doll's House," "Magda," "The Three Musketeers."

AMES, CINDY. Born in Brooklyn; Attended Actors Lab. Debut 1970 OB in "Hedda Gabler," followed by "Death of J.F.K.," "Dark Lady of the Sonnets," "Against the Sun."

ANDERMAN, MAUREEN. Born Oct. 26, 1946 in Detroit, Mich. Graduate U.Mich. Bdwy debut 1970 in ASF's "Othello," followed by "Moonchildren" for which she received a Theatre World Award, "An Evening with Richard Nixon and. . . .," "The Last of Mrs. Lincoln," "Seascape."

ANDERSON, ARTHUR. Born Aug. 29, 1922 in Staten Island, NY. Attended AmThWing. Made Bdwy debut 1937 in "Julius Caesar," followed by "Shoemakers' Holiday," "1776," OB in "Winkelberg," "The Doctor's Dilemma," "Zoo Story," "American Dream," "Gallows Humor," "The Rivals."

ANDERSON, DOUGLAS. Born June 26, 1948 in NYC. Graduate Carnegie-Mellon U. Bdwy debut 1969 in "Malcolm," followed by "Ulysses in Nighttown," OB in "Pinter Review," "Under Milk Wood," "Noye's Fludde," "Moonchildren."

ANDRE, JILL. Born Feb. 16, 1935 in NYC. Attended CCNY, Columbia. Debut OB 1952 in "Madwoman of Chaillot," followed by "Dark of the Moon," "Last Analysis," "Horsemen Pass By," "From Here inside My Head," "Kennedy's Children," "Stop the Parade," "Monkey, Monkey," "Battle of Angels," "Four Friends," "Augusta." On Bdwy in "Sunrise at Campobello," "Great White Hope," "An Evening with Richard Nixon and. . . ."

ANDRES, BARBARA. Born Feb. 11, 1939 in NYC. Graduate of Catholic U. Bdwy debut 1969 in "Jimmy," followed by "The Boy Friend," "Rodgers and Hart."

ANTHONY, ROBERT. Born May 10, 1941 in Newark, NJ. Attended Boston U., AADA. Off Bdwy in "Jerico-Jim Crow," "Bugs and Veronica," "Dirty Old Man," "Hamlet," "Othello," "Scuba Duba," "Salome," on Bdwy in "Man in the Glass Booth," "Butterflies Are Free."

ARBEIT, HERMAN. Born Apr. 19, 1925 in Brooklyn, NY. Attended CCNY, HB Studio, Neighborhood Playhouse. Debut 1959 OB in "The Golem," followed by "Awake and Sing," "A Delicate Balance," "Yentl the Yeshiva Boy."

ARBUS, ALLAN. Born Feb. 15 in NYC. Attended CCNY. Debut OB 1965 in "Cocktail Party," followed by "Uncle Vanya," "Julius Caesar," "The Tramp," "Golden Door," Bdwy bow 1974 in "Dreyfus in Rehearsal."

ARLEN, BILL. (formerly Christopher Coles) Born Nov. 4, 1952 in East Meadow, NY. Attended HB Studio, AADA. Made debut OB 1973 in "Call Me Madam," followed by "The Boy Friend."

ARLISS, DIMITRA. Born in Lorain, O. Attended Goodman Theatre. NY debut OB 1964 in "Trojan Women," followed by "Antigone," "Pericles," Bdwy in "Indians" (1969).

ARMSTRONG, CHERYL. Born Apr. 12, 1950 in Cleveland, Oh. Graduate Baldwin-Wallace Col. Bdwy debut 1974 in "Mack and Mabel."

ARNOLD, JEANNE. Born July 30 in Berkeley, Cal. UCal graduate. Debut OB 1955 in "Threepenny Opera," followed by "Take 5," "Demi-Dozen," "Medium Rare," "Put It in Writing," "Beggar's Opera," "Marry Me! Marry Me!," "Valentine's Day," Bdwy in "Happy Time," "Coco."

ARNOLD, MADISON. Born Feb. 7, 1935 in Allentown, Pa. Attended Columbia, UVienna, UBerlin. OB in "Lower Depths," "Much Ado about Nothing," "The Gamblers," "The Marriage," "Macbeth" (CP), "Basic Training of Pavlo Hummel," "Jungle of Cities," "Ride a Black Horse," "In the Boom Boom Room," Bdwy 1968 in "Man in the Glass Booth."

ASHLEY, ELIZABETH. Born Aug. 30, 1939 in Ocala, Fla. Attended Neighborhood Playhouse. Bdwy debut 1959 in "The Highest Tree," followed by "Take Her, She's Mine" for which she received a Theatre World Award, "Barefoot in the Park," "Ring Round the Bathtub," "Cat on a Hot Tin Roof."

ASHLEY, MARY ELLEN. Born June 11, 1938 in Long Island City, N Queens College graduate. Bdwy debut 1943 in "The Innocent Voyage," followed by "Bobino," "By Appointment Only," "Annie Get Your Gun," OB "Carousel," "Yentl the Yeshiva Boy," "Polly."

230

Luis Avalos

Verona Barnes

Peter Bartlett

Betsy Beard

Willard Beckham

ASTREDO, HUMBERT ALLEN. Born in San Francisco, CA. Attended SFU. NY debut 1967 OB in "Arms and the Man," followed by "Fragments," "Murderous Angels," "Beach Children," "End of Summer," "Knuckle," on Bdwy in "Les Blancs," "An Evening with Richard Nixon and. . . ."

ATKINS, TOM. Born in Pittsburgh. Graduate Duquesne U., AADA. With LCRep in "Unknown Soldier and His Wife," and "Cyrano," Bdwy 1967 in "Keep It in the Family," "Front Page," "The Changing Room," OB in "Whistle in the Dark," "Nobody Hears a Broken Drum," "Long Day's Journey into Night," "The Tempest."

ATKINSON, PEGGY. (formerly Peggy Longo) Born Oct. 1, 1943 in Bklyn. Attended Ithaca Col. Bdwy debut 1967 in "Fiddler on the Roof," followed by "Two Gentlemen of Verona," OB in "Boccaccio," "The Faggot," "One Free Smile," "One Cent Plain."

ATTLES, JOSEPH. Born Apr. 7, 1903 in Charleston, SC. Attended Harlem Musical Conservatory. Bdwy bow in "Blackbirds of 1928," followed by "John Henry," "Porgy and Bess," "Kwamina," "Tambourines to Glory," "The Last of Mrs. Lincoln," OB in "Jerico-Jim Crow," "Cabin in the Sky," "Prodigal Son," "Day of Absence," "Cry of Players," "King Lear," "Duplex," "Bubbling Brown Sugar."

AUSTIN, STEPHEN. Born Dec. 28, 1964 in NYC. Debut 1972 OB in "All the Way Home," followed by "Merry Wives of Windsor," "Richard III," "Midsummer Night's Dream."

AVALOS, LUIS. Born Sept. 2, 1946 in Havana, Cuba. Graduate NYU. Debut OB in "Never Jam Today," followed by "Rules for the Running of Trains," LC's "Camino Real," "Beggar on Horseback," "Good Woman of Setzuan," and "Kool Aid," "The Architect and the Emperor." "As You Like it," "El Grande de Coca Cola," "Zoo Story," "Payment as Pledged," "Armenians."

BACKUS, RICHARD. Born Mar. 28, 1945 in Goffstown, NH. Harvard graduate. Bdwy debut 1971 in "Butterflies Are Free," followed by "Promenade, All!" for which he received a Theatre Award, "Studs Edsel" (OB).

BAKER, LENNY. Born Jan. 17, 1945 in Boston, Mass. Graduate Boston U. Debut OB 1969 in "Frank Gagliano's City Scene," followed by "The Year Boston Won the Pennant," "The Time of Your Life," "Summertree," "Early Morning," "Survival of Joan," "Gallery," "Barbary Shore," "Merry Wives of Windsor," "Pericles." Bdwy 1974 in "Freedom of the City."

BAKER, MARK. Born Oct. 2, 1946 in Cumberland, Md. Attended Wittenberg U., Carnegie-Mellon U., Neighborhood Playhouse, AADA. Debut 1971 OB in "Love Me, Love My Children," Bdwy bow 1972 in "Via Galactica," followed by "Candide" for which he received a Theatre World Award.

BAL, HENRY KAIMU. Born Dec. 14, 1940 in Hawaii. Graduate of UHawaii, UCLA. Debut 1974 OB in "The Miser," followed by "Danton's Death," "Last Days of British Honduras," "Santa Anita '42."

BARBOUR, THOMAS. Born July 25, 1921 in NYC. Princeton, Harvard Graduate. Bdwy in "Portrait of a Queen," "Great White Hope," "Scratch," "The Lincoln Mask," OB in "Twelfth Night," "Merchant of Venice," "Admirable Bashville," "River Line," "The Lady's Not for Burning," "The Enchanted," "Antony and Cleopatra," "The Saintliness of Margery Kemp," "Dr. Willy Nilly," "Under the Sycamore Tree," "Epitaph for George Dillon," "Thracian Horse," "Old Glory," "Sjt. Musgrave's Dance," "Veil of Infamy," "Nestless Bird," "The Seagull."

BARGE, GILLIAN. Born May 27, 1940 in Sussex, Eng. Attended Birmingham Theatre School. Bdwy debut 1975 in "The Misanthrope."

BARNES, VERONA. Born June 2, 1940 in Wilson, NC. Graduate Winston-Salem State Col. Bdwy debut 1968 in "Great White Hope," OB in "Sleep," "Cherry Orchard," "House Party," "All God's Chillun."

BARRETT, LAURINDA. Born in 1931 in NYC. Attended Wellesley Col., AADA. On Bdwy in "Too Late the Phalarope," "The Girls in 509," "The Milk Train Doesn't Stop Here Anymore," "UTBU," "I Never Sang for My Father," in "The Misanthrope," "Palm Tree in a Rose Garden," "All is Bright."

BARRY, MATTHEW. Born Sept. 5, 1962 in NYC. Debut 1972 OB in "A Piece Fog," followed by "American Gothics," "All My Sons."

BARTENIEFF, GEORGE. Born Jan. 24, 1933 in Berlin, Ger. Bdwy bow 1947 "The Whole World Over," followed by "Venus Is," "All's Well That Ends Well," "Quotations from Chairman Mao Tse-Tung," "Death of Bessie Smith," "Cop-Out," "Room Service," "Unlikely Heroes," OB in "Walking to Waldheim," "Memorandum," "The Increased Difficulty of Concentration," "Tremony of the Wells," "Charley Chestnut Rides the IRT," "Radio (Wisdom) Sophia Part I."

BARTLETT, CHARLES. Born Aug. 18, 1941 in San Antonio, Tex. Graduate UNY. Bdwy debut 1970 in "Story Theatre," followed by "Metamorphosis," "Much Ado about Nothing," OB in "The Screens," "Marouf," "Blessing."

BARTLETT, D'JAMIN. Born May 21 in NYC. Attended AADA. Bdwy debut 1973 in "A Little Night Music" for which she received a Theatre World Award, OB in "The Glorious Age."

BARTLETT, PETER. Born Aug. 28, 1942 in Chicago. Attended Loyola U., LAMDA. Bdwy debut 1969 in "A Patriot for Me," followed by "Gloria and Esperanza," OB in "Boom Boom Room," "I Remember the House Where I Was Born."

BASS, EMORY. Born in Ga.; Bdwy bow 1952 in "Kiss Me, Kate," followed by "Teahouse of the August Moon," CC's "Pal Joey" and "Where's Charley!," "1776," "Lysistrata," "Bad Habits." OB in "Chic," "Bartleby," "Gay Divorce," "Boys from Syracuse," "By Jupiter."

BATTEN, TOM. Born in Oklahoma City, Okla. Graduate USC. Bdwy debut 1961 in "How to Succeed in Business . . . ," followed by "Mame," "Gantry," "Mack and Mabel."

BATTIS, EMERY. Born May 30, 1915 in Arlington, Mass. Harvard and Columbia graduate. Bdwy debut 1946 with American Repertory Theatre, followed by "House of Atreus," "Arturo Ui," "The National Health," OB in "Misalliance."

BAUER, BRUCE. Born July 5, 1944 in Santa Monica, CA. Attended Santa Monica Col. Bdwy bow 1975 in "The Ritz."

BAXTER, ANNE. Born May 7, 1923 in Michigan City, Ind. Attended Irvine Sch. Bdwy debut 1936 in "Seen but Not Heard," followed by "There's Always a Breeze," "Mme. Capet," "Square Root of Wonderful," "Applause," "Noel Coward in Two Keys."

BAYNE, RICHARD COOPER. Born Feb. 25, 1949 in Brooklyn, NY. Graduate NYU. Bdwy debut 1971 in "Hair," followed by "Seesaw," "Rachael Lily Rosenbloom," OB in "The Boy Friend."

BEACHNER, LOUIS. Born June 9, 1923 in Jersey City, NJ. Bdwy bow 1942 in "Junior Miss," followed by "No Time for Sergeants," "Georgy," "The Changing Room," "The National Health," "Where's Charley?," OB in "Time to Burn," "The Hostage."

BEAN, REATHEL. Born Aug. 24, 1942 in Mo. Graduate Drake U. OB in "America Hurrah," "San Francisco's Burning," "The Love Cure," "Henry IV," "In Circles," "Peace," "Journey of Snow White," "Wanted," "The Faggot," "Lovers."

BEARD, BETSY. Born Nov. 9, 1949 in Tulsa, Okla. Graduate UTulsa. Bdwy debut 1975 in "Shenandoah," followed by "Polly" OB.

BEARDSLEY, ALICE. Born Mar. 28, 1927 in Richmond, Va. UIowa graduate. Bdwy debut 1960 in "The Wall," OB in "Eastward in Eden," "In Good King Charles' Golden Days," "Leave It to Jane," "Camino Real," "A Man's a Man," "Cindy," "Boy on a Straight-back Chair," "Things," "The Kid," "Rag Doll."

BECHER, JOHN C. Born Jan. 13, 1915 in Milwaukee, Wisc. Graduate UWisc. Bdwy bow 1946 with Am. Rep. Theatre, followed by "Skipper Next to God," "Idiot's Delight," "Picnic," "Brigadoon" (CC), "No Time for Sergeants," "Ballad of the Sad Cafe," "Mame," "Harvey," "Gypsy," OB in "American Dream," "Death of Bessie Smith," "Happy Days," "Dumbwaiter," "Child Buyer," "That Thing at the Cherry Lane."

BECKER, EDWARD. Born in Astoria, NY. Attended AmThWing. Bdwy debut 1951 in "Paint Your Wagon," followed by "Silk Stockings," "Happy Hunting," "Body Beautiful," "Whoop-Up," "Bye Bye Birdie," "Family Affair," "Camelot," "Here's Love," "Illya Darling," "Brigadoon" (CC), "Mame," "Jimmy," "Ari," "Goodtime Charley."

BECKHAM, WILLARD. Born Nov. 6, 1948 in Hominy, Okla. Graduate Cleveland Inst. of Music. Debut OB 1972 in "Crazy Now," Bdwy 1974 in "Lorelei."

BEDFORD, BRIAN. Born Feb. 16, 1935 in Morley, Eng. Attended RADA. Bdwy bow 1960 in "Five Finger Exercise," followed by "Lord Pengo," "The Private Ear," "The Knack" (OB). "The Astrakhan Coat," "The Unknown Soldier and His Wife," "Seven Descents of Myrtle," "Jumpers," with APA in "Misanthrope," "Cocktail Party," and "Hamlet," "Private Lives," "School for Wives."

BEERS, FRANCINE. Born Nov. 26 in NYC. Attended Hunter Col., CCNY, HB Studio. Debut 1962 OB in "King of the Whole Damned World," followed by "Kiss Mama," "Monoply," "Cakes with Wine," Bdwy in "Cafe Crown," "6 Rms Riv Vu."

BELANGER, JOANNE. Born Feb. 26, 1945 in Chicago. Graduate Wayne State U., UIowa. Debut OB 1971 in "Dowager's Hump," followed by "The Red Hat," "Crystal and Fox," "Night Must Fall," "Falling Apart."

231

Harry Bellaver　　**Meg Bennett**　　**Jack Bittner**　　**Mary Boylan**　　**Robie Braun**

BELLAVER, HARRY. Born Feb. 12, 1905 in Hillsboro, Ill. Attended Brookwood Col. Bdwy bow 1931 in "House of Connelly," followed by "Night over Taos," "Carry Nation," "We, the People," "Threepenny Opera," "The Sellout," "Page Miss Glory," "Noah," "Black Pit," "How Beautiful with Shoes," "Russet Mantle," "St. Helena," "To Quito and Back," "Tortilla Flat," "Johnny 2 X 4," "Mr. Sycamore," "The World's Full of Girls," "Annie Get Your Gun," "That Championship Season."

BELLOMO, JOE. Born Apr. 12, 1938 in NYC. Attended Manhattan Sch. of Music. Bdwy bow 1960 in "New Girl in Town," followed by CC's "South Pacific" and "Guys and Dolls," OB in "Cindy," "Fantasticks."

BENNETT, MEG. Born Oct. 4, 1948 in Los Angeles. Graduate Northwestern U. Debut OB 1971 in "Godspell," on Bdwy 1972 in "Grease."

BENNETT, TONY. Born Aug. 3, 1926 in Long Island City, NY. Attended AmThWing. Bdwy debut 1974 in "Tony Bennett & Lena Horne."

BERDESHEVSKY, MARGO ANN. Born May 29, 1945 in NYC. Attended Northwestern U. OB in "Mary of Nijmeghen," "Objective Case," "Necessity of Being Polygamous," "Yerma," "The Basement," "Middle of the Night," "A Difficult Borning," "The Catch."

BEREZIN, TANYA. Born Mar. 25, 1941 in Philadelphia, Pa. Attended Boston U. Debut OB 1967 in "The Sandcastle." Member of Circle Rep. Theatre Co. from 1969, and has appeared in "Three Sisters," "Great Nubula in Orion," "him," "Amazing Activity of Charlie Contrare," "Battle of Angels," "Mound Builders."

BERGAN, JUDITH-MARIE. Born Nov. 25, 1951 in Indianapolis, Ind. Attended Goodman Theatre School. Debut 1974 OB in "Overruled."

BERGMAN, INGRID. Born Aug. 29, 1915 in Stockholm, Swed. Attended Royal Dramatic Theatre. Bdwy debut 1940 in "Liliom," followed by "Joan of Lorraine," "More Stately Mansions," "Capt. Brassbound's Conversion," "The Constant Wife."

BERNHEIM, SHIRL. Born Sept. 21, 1921 in NYC. Studied with Ouspenskaya. Debut 1967 OB in "A Different World," followed by "Stag Movie," "Middle of the Night," "Come Back, Little Sheba."

BERRY, ERIC. Born Jan. 9, 1913 in London. Graduate RADA. NY debut 1954 in "The Boy Friend," followed by "Family Reunion," "The Power and the Glory," "Beaux Stratagem," "Broken Jug," "Pictures in the Hallway," "Peer Gynt," "Great God Brown," "Henry IV," "The White House," "White Devil," "Charley's Aunt," "The Homecoming" (OB), "Capt. Brassbound's Conversion." "Pippin."

BILLINGTON, LEE. Born July 15, 1932 in Madison, Wisc. Attended UWisc. Bdwy debut 1969 in "But Seriously," OB in "Dance of Death," "3 by O'Neill," "Our Town," "Capt. Brassbound's Conversion," "Henry VIII," "Boy with a Cart," "Epicoene."

BISHOP, CAROLE. Born Feb. 28, 1944 in Colorado Springs, Colo. Bdwy debut 1967 in "Golden Rainbow," followed by "Promises, Promises," "On the Town," "Rachael Lily Rosenbloom," "A Chorus Line."

BITTNER, JACK. Born in Omaha, Neb. Graduate UNeb. NY debut OB in "Nathan the Wise," "Land of Fame," "Beggar's Holiday," "Rip Van Winkle," "Dear Oscar," "What Every Woman Knows."

BLAIR, PAMELA. Born Dec. 5, 1949 in Arlington, Vt. Attended Ntl. Acad. of Ballet. Made Bdwy debut in 1972 in "Promises, Promises," followed by "Sugar," "Seesaw," "Of Mice and Men," "Wild and Wonderful," OB in "Ballad of Boris K."

BLUE, ARLANA. Born Nov. 15, 1948 in Passaic, NJ. Attended NYSchool of Ballet. Debut 1971 OB in "Fear of Love," followed by "Paranoia Pretty," "Sgt. Pepper's Lonely Hearts Club Band."

BLUMENFELD, ROBERT. Born Feb. 26, 1943 in NYC. Rutgers and Columbia graduate. Bdwy debut 1970 in "Othello," OB in American Savoyards productions, "The Fall and Redemption of Man."

BOBBIE, WALTER. Born Nov. 18, 1945 in Scranton, Pa. Graduate UScranton, Catholic U. Bdwy debut 1971 in "Frank Merriwell," followed by "Grass Harp," "Grease," "Drat!" (OB), "Tricks."

BOGERT, WILLIAM. Born Jan. 25, 1936 in NYC. Yale graduate. Bdwy in "Man for All Seasons," "Hamlet," "Star Spangled Girl," "Cactus Flower," "Sudden and Accidental Re-education of Horse Johnson," OB in "Country Wife," "Taming of the Shrew," "Henry V," "Love's Labour's Lost," "A Gun Play," "The Real Inspector Hound," "Conflict of Interest," "Killdeer," "Rubbers," "Yankees 3 . . ."

BOHDAN, SERHIJ. Born Oct. 18, 1947 in Munich, Ger. Graduate Syracuse U. Bdwy debut 1974 in "Gypsy."

BOND, RUDY. Born Oct. 1, 1915 in Philadelphia. Attended UPa. Bdwy in "Streetcar Named Desire," "Bird Cage," "Two Blind Mice," "Romeo and Juliet," "Glad Tidings," "Golden Boy," "Fiorello," "Illya Darling," "Night Watch," OB in "O'Daniel," LCR's "After the Fall" and "Incident at Vichy," "Big Man," "Match-Play," "Papp," "Twelve Angry Men," "The Birds," "Joan of Lorraine," "Bread," "Armenians," "Dream of a Blacklisted Actor."

BOND, SUDIE. Born July 13, 1928 in Louisville, Ky. Attended Rollins Col. OB in "Summer and Smoke," "Tovarich," "American Dream," "Sandbox," "Endgame," "Theatre of the Absurd," "Home Movies," "Softly and Consider the Nearness," "Memorandum," "Local Stigmatic," "Billy," "New York! New York!," Bdwy in "Waltz of the Toreadors," "Auntie Mame," "The Egg," "Harold," "My Mother, My Father and Me," "The Impossible Years," "Keep It in the Family," "Quotations from Chrmn. Mao Tse-Tung," "American Dream," "Forty Carats," "Hay Fever," "Grease."

BONELLE, DICK. Born Apr. 11, 1936 in Houston, Tex. Graduate UHouston. Debut OB 1970 in "Lyle," followed by "Sugar" (Bdwy), "Carousel," "Call Me Madam," "Bus Stop."

BONGIOVANNI, GAETANO. Born Oct. 18, 1944 in Columbus, Ga. Bdwy debut 1967 in "Rosencrantz and Guildenstern Are Dead," followed by "Vivat! Vivat Regina!," OB in "Sjt. Musgrave's Dance," "The Zykovs."

BOOCKVOR, STEVE. Born Nov. 18, 1942 in NYC. Attended Queens Col., Juilliard. Bdwy debut 1966 in "Anya," followed by "A Time for Singing," "Cabaret," "Mardis Gras," "Jimmy," "Billy," "The Rothschilds," "Follies," "Over Here," "The Lieutenant."

BORDEN, MARSHALL. Born Aug. 10, 1935 in Howell, Mich. Graduate Wayne State, UDetroit. Bdwy debut 1970 in "The Cherry Orchard," followed by "We Interrupt This Program."

BORRELLI, JIM. Born Apr. 10, 1948 in Lawrence, Mass. Graduate Boston Col. NY Debut OB 1971 in "Subject to Fits," followed by "Grease."

BOVA, JOSEPH. Born May 25 in Cleveland, O. Graduate Northwestern U. Debut OB 1959 in "On the Town," followed by "Once upon a Mattress," "House of Blue Leaves," "Comedy," "The Beauty Part," NYSF's "Taming of the Shrew," "Richard III," "Comedy of Errors," "Invitation to a Beheading," "Merry Wives of Windsor," on Bdwy in "Rape of the Belt," "Irma La Douce," "Hot Spot," "The Chinese," "American Millionaire."

BOYLAN, MARY. Born in Plattsburg, NY. Attended Mt. Holyoke Col. Bdwy debut 1938 in "Dance Night," followed by "Susannah and the Elders," "The Walrus and the Carpenter," "Our Town," "Live Life Again," OB in "To Bury a Cousin," "Curley McDimple," "Blood," "Middle of the Night"(ELT), "Girls Most Likely to Succeed," "Biography for a Woman," "Women behind Bars."

BRAHA, HERB. (formerly Herb Simon) Born Sept. 18, 1946 in Hyannis, Mass. Attended Carnegie Tech. Debut 1971 OB in "Godspell."

BRANDEIS, RUTH. Born May 31, 1942 in NYC. Attended San Francisco State Col. OB in "Theatre of the Absurd," "Leave from Quintessence," "The Killers," "Nighthawks," "Against the Sun."

BRANNUM, TOM. Born June 17, 1941 in Shawnee, Pa. Bdwy debut 1961 in "Once There Was a Russian," followed by "Take Her, She's Mine," "We Bombed in New Haven," "Room Service," OB in "Mystery Play," "Shaft of Love."

BRANON, JOHN. Born Oct. 7, 1939 in Chicago, Ill. Attended Chicago City Col. Bdwy Debut 1968 in "The Guide," OB in "Scuba Duba," "Glorious Ruler," "42 Seconds from Broadway," "Against the Sun."

BRAUN, ROBIE. Born May 2, 1950 in Ponchatoula, La. Attended SE La. U. Debut 1975 OB in "Do I Hear a Waltz?"

BRAUNSTEIN, ALAN. Born Apr. 30, 1947 in Brooklyn. Debut OB 1962 in "Daddy Come Home," followed by "Rhinegold," on Bdwy in "Hair," "Jesus Christ Superstar," "Dude."

BREMSETH, LLOYD. Born July 27, 1948 in Minneapolis, Minn. Attended UMinn. Debut OB 1968 in "Kiss Rock," followed by "Klara," "Sweet Shopp Myriam," "Kiss Now," "Godspell."

BRENNAN, MAUREEN. Born Oct. 11, 1952 in Washington, DC. Attended UCincinnati. Bdwy debut 1974 in "Candide" for which she received a Theatr World Award.

BRESLIN, TOMMY. Born Mar. 24, 1946 in Norwich, Conn. Attended Ior Col. OB in "For Love or Money," "Freedom Is a Two-Edged Sword," "Who Who, Baby?," "Beggar on Horseback"(LC), "Moon Walk," "Dear Oscar Bdwy bow 1971 in "70 girls 70," followed by "Good News."

BRIDGES, BEAU. Born Dec. 9, 1941 in Los Angeles, CA. Attended UCL UHawaii. Bdwy debut 1966 in "Where's Daddy?," followed by "Who's W in Hell."

| Fran Brill | Stanley Brock | Gwendolyn Brown | Joseph Burke | Catherine Byers |

BRILL, FRAN. Born Sept. 30, 1946 in Pa. Attended Boston U. Bdwy debut 1969 in "Red, White and Maddox," followed by "What Every Woman Knows" (OB).

BROCK, STANLEY. Born July 7, 1931 in Brooklyn, NY. Attended AmTh-Wing. Debut 1972 OB in "Scuba Duba," followed by "20th Century Tar," Bdwy 1975 in "We Interrupt This Program."

BROCKSMITH, ROY. Born Sept. 15, 1945 in Quincy, Ill. Debut OB 1971 in "Whip Lady," followed by "The Workout," "Beggar's Opera," "Polly."

BROOKE, PAUL. Born Nov. 24, 1944 in London. Graduate King's Col. Debut OB 1974 in "Taming of the Shrew," and Bdwy 1974 in "Scapino."

BROOKES, JACQUELINE. Born July 24, 1930 in Montclair, NJ. Graduate UIowa, RADA. Bdwy debut 1955 in "Tiger at the Gates," followed by "Watercolor," "Abelard and Heloise," OB in "The Cretan Woman" for which she received a Theatre World Award, "The Clandestine Marriage," "Measure for Measure," "Duchess of Malfi," "Ivanov," "Six Characters in Search of an Author," "An Evening's Frost," "Come Slowly, Eden," "The Increased Difficulty of Concentration"(LC), "The Persians," "Sunday Dinner," "House of Blue Leaves," "A Meeting by the River," "Owners," "Hallelujah," "Dream of a Blacklisted Actor," "Knuckle."

BROOKS, GERALDINE. Born Oct. 29, 1925 in NYC. Attended Neighborhood Playhouse, AADA, Actors Studio. Bdwy debut 1944 in "Follow the Girls," followed by "Winter's Tale," "Time of the Cuckoo," "Brighttower," "Fiddler on the Roof"(JB).

BROWN, CHRISTOPHER J. Born in Port Chester, NY. Emerson Col. and Yale graduate. Bdwy debut 1975 in "The Ritz."

BROWN, DANIEL. Born June 9, 1947 in Little Rock, Ark. Graduate LSU. Debut 1972 OB in "Absolutely Time!," followed by "Secret Life of Walter Mitty," "Be Kind to People Week."

BROWN, GRAHAM. Born Oct. 24, 1924 in NYC. Graduate Howard U. OB in "Widower's Houses," "The Emperor's Clothes," "Time of Storm," "Major Barbara," "Land Beyond the River," "The Blacks," "Firebugs," "God Is a (Guess What?)," "An Evening of One Acts," "Man Better Man," "Behold! Cometh the Vanderkellans," "Ride a Black Horse," "Great MacDaddy," on Bdwy in "Weekend," "Man in the Glass Booth," "The River Niger," "Pericles," "Black Picture Show" (LC)

BROWN, GWENDOLYN. (formerly Gwen Saska) Born Sept. 9, 1939 in Mishawaka, Ind. Northwestern and Columbia graduate. Debut 1969 OB in "Geese," followed by "Macbeth," "In the Boom Boom Room."

BROWN, WALTER P. Born Apr. 18, 1926 in Newark, NJ. Attended Bklyn Cons. of Music. Bdwy bow in "Porgy and Bess," followed by "Fiorello!," "The Advocate," CC's "Guys and Dolls" and "South Pacific," "Kelly," "Hello, Dolly," "Raisin."

BROWNE, HARRY. Born Aug. 21, 1952 in Flemington, NJ. Graduate BostonU. Debut 1975 OB in "Down by the River Where the Waterlilies Are Disfigured."

BROWNING, ROD. Born Nov. 25, 1942 in Manhasset, NY. Attended Lon Morris Col. Debut 1966 OB in "All's Well That Ends Well," followed by Richard III," "Measure for Measure," "Mystery Play," "Breadwinner," Some People, Some Other People . . ."

BROWNING, SUSAN. Born Feb. 25, 1941 in Baldwin, NY. Graduate Penn. State. Bdwy bow 1963 in "Love and Kisses," followed by "Company" for which she received a Theatre World Award, "Shelter," "Goodtime Charley," OB in "Jo," "Dime A Dozen," "Seventeen," "Boys from Syracuse," "Collision Course," "Whiskey," "As You Like It," "Removalists."

BROWNLEE, BRIAN. Born July 6 in Virginia. Attended UNC, AADA. Debut 1972 OB in "We Bombed in New Haven," followed by "A Streetcar Named Desire"(LCR)., "The Rapists," "Give My Regards to Broadway."

BRUMMEL, DAVID. Born Nov. 1, 1942 in Brooklyn. Bdwy debut 1973 in "The Pajama Game," followed OB by "Cole Porter," "Fantasticks."

BRUNEAU, RALPH. Born Sept. 22, 1952 in Phoenix, Ariz. Graduate UNotre Dame. Debut 1974 OB in "The Fantasticks."

BRUNO, JEAN. Born Dec. 7, 1926 in Bklyn. Attended Hofstra Col., Feagin School. Bdwy debut 1960 in "Beg, Borrow or Steal," followed by "Midgie Purvis," "Music Man," "Family Affair," "Minnie's Boys," "The Lincoln Mask," "Lorelei," OB in "All That Fall," "Hector," "Hotel Paradiso," "Pigeons in the Park," "Ergo," "Trelawny of the Wells," "Song for the First of May."

BRYAN, SHIRLEY. Born Oct. 12, 1917 in Cleveland, O. Western Reserve and NYU graduate. Bdwy debut 1974 in "The National Health."

BRYAN, WAYNE. Born Aug. 13, 1947 in Compton, CA. Graduate UCal. Santa Barbara. Bdwy debut 1974 in "Good News," followed by "Rodgers and Hart."

BRYNNER, YUL. Born June 15, 1915 in Sakhalin Island, Japan. Bdwy debut 1946 in "Lute Song," followed by "The King and I," "Odyssey."

BUCHTRUP, BJARNE. Born Aug. 11, 1942 in Copenhagen, Den. Appeared in ballet, on Bdwy in "Finian's Rainbow," "Annie Get Your Gun," "Oklahoma!," "Come Summer," "Minnie's Boys," "Ari," "No, No, Nanette," "Gigi," OB in "Fiddler on The Roof" (JB).

BUCKLEY, BETTY. Born July 3, 1947 in Big Spring, Tex. Graduate TCU. Bdwy debut 1969 in "1776," followed by "Pippin," OB in "Ballad of Johnny Pot," "What's a Nice Country like You Doing in a State Like This?," "Circle of Sound."

BURKE, JOSEPH. Born Apr. 16, 1945 in Philadelphia, Pa. Graduate UMd. Bdwy debut 1974 in "Good News."

BURNELL, PETER. Born Apr. 29, 1950 in Johnstown, NY. OB in "Henry IV," "Antony and Cleopatra," "The Tempest," "Macbeth," "Olathe Response," "Ubu Roi/Ubu Bound," Bdwy debut 1974 in "In Praise of Love" for which he received a Theatre World Award.

BURR, COURTNEY. Born May 22, 1948 in NYC. Attended UConn. Debut OB 1973 in "The Children's Mass," followed by "Big Fish, Little Fish."

BURR, LONNIE. Born May 31, 1943 in Dayton, Ky. Graduate UCal., UCLA. Debut OB 1971 in "Look Where I'm At," followed by "Broadway," Bdwy bow 1974 in "Mack and Mabel."

BURRELL, PAMELA. Born Aug. 4, 1945 in Tacoma, Wash. Bdwy debut 1966 in "Funny Girl," followed by "Arms and the Man" (OB) for which she received a Theatre World Award, "Where's Charley?"

BURSTEIN, MIKE. Born July 1, 1945 in The Bronx, NY. Bdwy debut 1968 in "The Megilla of Itzik Manger," followed by "Inquest," "Wedding in Shtetl" (OB).

BURSTYN, ELLEN. Born Dec. 7, 1932 in Detroit, Mich. Attended Actors Studio. Bdwy debut 1957 (then known as Ellen McRae) in "Fair Game," followed by "Same Time, Next Year."

BUTLER, RHODA. Born July 25, 1949 in Sanford, Me. Attended Centenary Col. Debut OB 1974 in "Fashion," Bdwy 1974 in "Candide," followed by "Goodtime Charley."

BYERS, CATHERINE. Born Oct. 7 in Sioux City, I. Graduate UIowa, LAMDA. Bdwy debut 1971 in "The Philanthropist," followed by "Don't Call Back," OB in "Petrified Forest," "All My Sons."

CABLE, CHRISTOPHER. Born Mar. 18, 1930 in Alameda, Ca. Graduate UCal. Debut 1965 OB in "Garden of Heavenly Faucets," followed by "The Drunkard," "Treasure Island."

CAHILL, JAMES. Born May 31, 1940 in Brooklyn. Bdwy debut 1967 in "Marat/deSade," OB in "The Hostage," "The Alchemist," "Johnny Johnson," "Peer Gynt," "Timon of Athens," "An Evening for Merlin Finch," "The Disintegration of James Cherry," "Crimes of Passion," "Rain," "Screens," "Total Eclipse," "Entertaining Mr. Sloane."

CALLOWAY, BRIAN. Born July 17, 1934 in London, Eng. Attended HB Studio. Debut 1970 OB in "War of the Roses," followed by "Down by the River Where Waterlilies Are Disfigured Every Day."

CALVERT, HENRY. Born Jan. 8, 1920 in Chicago, Ill. Attended AmThWing. OB credits: "The Prodigal," "Hamlet," "Miss Julie," "Country Girl," "There Is No End," "America Hurrah," "Spiro Who?," "And Whose Little Boy Are You?," "Nuts."

CANNING, JAMES J. Born July 2, 1946 in Chicago, Graduate DePaul U. Debut 1972 in "Grease."

CAPERS, VIRGINIA. Born Sept. 22, 1925 in Sumter, SC. Attended Juilliard. Bdwy debut 1973 in "Raisin."

CARBERRY, JOSEPH. Born May 5, 1948 in NYC. Debut OB 1974 in "Short Eyes."

CARDEN, WILLIAM. Born Feb. 2, 1947 in NYC. Attended Lawrence U., Brandeis U. Debut OB 1974 in "Short Eyes," followed by "Leaving Home."

Frank Carey   **Rosanna Carter**   **Walter Charles**   **Louise Clay**   **David Clarke**

CAREY, DAVID. Born Nov. 16, 1945 in Brookline, Mass. Graduate Boston U., Ohio U. Debut 1969 OB in "Oh, What a Wedding," followed by "Let's Sing Yiddish," "Dad, Get Married," "Light, Lively and Yiddish," "Wedding in Shtetl," "Big Winna."

CAREY, FRANK. Born Oct. 12, 1934 in Tarrytown, NY. Attended AADA. Debut OB 1960 in "Nat Turner," followed by "The Brick and the Rose," "Black Quartet," "Little Bit," Bdwy bow 1972 in "Don't Play Us Cheap."

CARLIN, CHET. Born Feb. 23, 1940 in Malverne, NY. Graduate Ithaca Col., Catholic U. Bdwy bow 1972 in "An Evening with Richard Nixon and . . . ," OB in "Under Gaslight," "Lou Gehrig Did not Die of Cancer," "Graffiti!," "Crystal and Fox," "Golden Honeymoon," "Arms and the Man."

CARLSEN, ALLAN. Born Feb. 7 in Chicago. Attended UPa. Bdwy debut 1974 in "The Freedom of the City.", followed by OB "The Morning after Optimism," "Iphigenia in Aulis."

CARRUTHERS, JAMES. Born May 26, 1931 in Morristown, NJ. Attended Lafayette Col. Debut 1959 OB in "Our Town," followed by "Under the Sycamore Tree," "Misalliance," "The Hostage," "Telemachus Clay," "Shadow of a Gunman," "Masks."

CARTER, MARY. Born Oct. 3, 1938 in Washington, DC. Attended Peabody Cons. Debut 1969 OB in "The Glorious Ruler," followed by "Why Hanna's Skirt Won't Stay Down."

CARTER, ROSANNA. Born Sept. 20 in Rolle Town, Exuma, Bahamas. Trained at Negro Ensemble Workshop. OB in "Lament of Rasta Fari," "Burghers of Callais," "Scottsboro Boys," "Les Femmes Noires."

CARTER, THELMA LOUISE. Born July 16 in Gary, Ind. Studied with Stella Adler. Debut 1975 OB in "Liberty Call."

CASSIDY, TIM. Born Mar. 22, 1952 in Alliance, O. Attended UCinncinnati. Bdwy debut 1974 in "Good News."

CASTANG, VERONICA. Born Apr. 22, 1938 in London. Attended Sorbonne. Bdwy debut 1966 in "How's the World Treating You?," followed by "The National Health," OB in "The Trigon," "Sjt. Musgrave's Dance," "Saved," "Water Hens," "Self-Accusation," "Kaspar," "Ionescapade."

CATER, JOHN. Born Jan. 17, 1932 in London, Eng. Attended RADA. Bdwy debut 1974 in "London Assurance."

CATLIN, FAITH. Born Sept. 19, 1949 in Troy, NY. Graduate Boston U. Debut OB 1969 in "Pequod," followed by "Approaching Simone," "Summer Brave," "Hot l Baltimore," "American Glands," "The Catch," "Augusta."

CHACE, DOROTHY. Born in North Bergen, NJ. Attended SF State Col., Stanford, Yale. Bdwy debut 1969 in "3 Men on a Horse," followed by LCRep's "Caucasian Chalk Circle," and "Cyrano," OB in "Screens," "Total Eclipse," "Babylon," "Hothouse."

CHANNING, CAROL. Born Jan. 31, 1921 in Seattle, Wash. Attended Bennington Col. Bdwy debut 1941 in "No for an Answer," followed by "Let's Face It," "Proof through the Night," "Lend an Ear" for which she received a Theatre World Award, "Gentlemen Prefer Blondes," "Wonderful Town," "The Vamp," "Show Girl," "Hello, Dolly!," "Four on a Garden," "Lorelei."

CHAPIN, HARRY. Born Dec. 7, 1941 in NYC. Attended Cornell. Bdwy debut 1975 in "The Night That Made America Famous" for which he wrote the music and lyrics.

CHARISSE, ZAN. Born Nov. 14, 1951 in NYC. Debut 1971 OB in "Look Me Up," Bdwy bow 1974 in "Gypsy" for which she received a Theatre World Award.

CHARLES, WALTER. Born Apr. 4, 1945 in East Stroudsburg, Pa. Graduate Boston U. Bdwy debut 1973 in "Grease."

CHARNEY, JORDAN. Born in NYC. Graduate Bklyn Col. OB in "Harry, Noon and Night," "A Place for Chance," "Hang Down Your Head and Die," "The Pinter Plays," "Telemachus Clay," "Zoo Story," "Viet Rock," "MacBird," "Red Cross," "The Glorious Ruler," "Waiting for Godot," "Slow Memories," "One Flew over the Cuckoo's Nest," "The Boy Who Came to Leave," "The Cretan Bull," "Naomi Court," Bdwy in "Slapstick Tragedy," "The Birthday Party."

CHARTOFF, MELANIE. Born Dec. 15, 1948 in New Haven, Conn. Graduate Adelphi U. Debut 1971 OB in "The Proposition," followed by "Do I Hear a Waltz?," Bdwy bow 1972 in "Via Galactica."

CHINN, LORI. Born in Seattle, Wash. Bdwy debut 1970 in "Lovely Ladies, Kind Gentlemen," OB in "Coffins for Butterflies," "Hough in Blazes," "Peer Gynt," "King and I," "Children," "Secret Life of Walter Mitty," "Bayou Legend."

CHRIS, MARILYN. Born May 19, in NYC, Attended CCNY. Appeared in "The Office," "Birthday Party," "7 Descents of Myrtle," "Lenny," OB in "Nobody Hears a Broken Drum," "Fame," "Judas Applause," "Junebug Graduates Tonight," "Man Is Man," "In the Jungle of Cities," "Good Soldier Schweik," "The Tempest," "Ride a Black Horse," "Screens," "Kaddish," "Lady from the Sea," "Bread," "Leaving Home."

CHRISMAN, CAROLYN. Born in NYC. Off Bdwy in "Games," "Fantastic Gardens," "Home Again," "Something for Kitty Genovese," "Greenwillow," "Dinner at the Ambassador's," "The Boy Friend," "Man's Estate."

CHRISTIAN, ROBERT. Born Dec. 27, 1939 in Los Angeles. Attended UCLA. OB in "The Happening," "Hornblend," "Fortune and Men's Eyes," "Boys in the Band," "Behold! Cometh the Vanderkellans," "Mary Stuart," "Narrow Road to the Deep North," "Twelfth Night," "The Past Is the Past," "Going through Changes," "Black Sunlight," "Terraces," Bdwy in "We Bombed in New Haven," "Does a Tiger Wear a Necktie?," "An Evening with Richard Nixon," "All God's Chillun."

CHRISTMAS, DAVID. Born May 2, 1942 in Pasadena, Ca. Attended Pasadena City Col., HB Studio. Bdwy debut 1970 in "Grin and Bare It," OB in "Butter and Egg Man," "Dames at Sea," "Give My Regards to Broadway."

CHRISTOPHER, RICHARD. Born Nov. 1, 1948 in Ft. Knox, Ky. Graduate SW. La. U. Bdwy debut 1973 in "Seesaw," followed by "Three Musketeers" (OB).

CINKO, PAULA. Born Dec. 14, 1950. Debut 1972 OB in "A Quarter for the Ladies Room." Bdwy debut 1974 in "Good News."

CISSEL, CHUCK. Born Oct. 3, 1948 in Tulsa, Okla. Graduate UOkla. Bdwy debut 1971 in "Purlie," followed by "Lost in the Stars," "Via Galactica," "Don't Bother Me, I Can't Cope," "A Chorus Line."

CLARK, JACQUELINE. Born June 21, 1949 in Portland, Ore. Attended UPortland, HB Studio. Bdwy debut 1973 in "Desert Song," followed by "Where's Charley?"

CLARKE, DAVID. Born Aug. 30, 1908, in Chicago, Ill. Attended Butler U. Bdwy bow 1934 in "Roadside," followed by "Let Freedom Ring," "Bury the Dead," "Washington Jitters," "200 Were Chosen," "Journey Man," "Abe Lincoln in Illinois," "See the Jaguar," "The Emperor's Clothes," "A View from the Bridge," "Ballad of the Sad Cafe," "Inquest," "Of Mice and Men," OB in "Madam, Will You Walk," "Rose."

CLARKE, RICHARD. Born Jan. 31, 1933 in Eng. Graduate UReading. With LCRep in "St. Joan," "Tiger at the Gates," "Cyrano de Bergerac," Bdwy debut 1970 in "Conduct Unbecoming."

CLARKSON, JOHN. Born Jan. 19, 1932 in London. Graduate Oxford U. NY debut OB 1971 in "Murderous Angels," followed by "An Evening with Ma Bell," "Staircase," Bdwy bow 1973 in "No Sex Please, We're British."

CLAY, LOUISE. Born Mar. 3, 1938 in Lafayette, La. LSU graduate. Bdwy debut 1966 in "Marat/deSade," followed by "Mike Downstairs," OB in "Rondelay," "The Hot l Baltimore."

CLAY, NICHOLAS. Born Sept. 18, 1946 in London, Eng. Attended RADA. Bdwy debut 1975 in "The Misanthrope."

CLOSE, GLENN. Born Mar. 19, 1947 in Greenwich, Conn. Graduate William & Mary Col. Bdwy debut 1974 with Phoenix Co. in "Love for Love," "Member of the Wedding," and "Rules of the Game."

COATES, CAROLYN. Born Apr. 29, 1930 in Oklahoma City, Okla. Attended UCLA. OB in "The Innocents," "The Balcony," "Electra," "The Trojan Women" for which she received a Theatre World Award, "A Whitman Portrait," "Party on Greenwich Avenue," "Club Bedroom," "A Scent of Flowers," "Effect of Gamma Rays on Man-in-the-Moon Marigolds," LCRep's "Country Wife," "Condemned of Altona," "Caucasian Chalk Circle," and "Disintegration of James Cherry," Bdwy in "Death of Bessie Smith," "American Dream," "Fire!," "All Over."

CODY, PAT. Born Dec. 30, 1950 in Hoboken, NJ. Graduate Hollins Col. NYU. Bdwy debut 1974 in "Gypsy."

COFFIN, FREDERICK. Born Jan. 16, 1943 in Detroit. Graduate UMich. Debut 1971 OB in "Basic Training of Pavlo Hummel," followed by "Much Ado about Nothing," "King Lear," "As You Like It," "Boom Boom Room," "Merry Wives of Windsor," Bdwy bow 1975 in "We Interrupt This Program."

COGGIN, BARBARA. Born Feb. 27 in Chattanooga, Tenn. Attended Peabody Col. Bdwy debut 1970 in "Lovely Ladies, Kind Gentlemen," OB in "The Drunkard," "One for the Money, etc.," "Judy: A Garland of Songs," "Rag Doll."

| Barbara Colby | Dennis Cooney | Patricia Conwell | Barry Corbin | Joan Copeland |

COLBY, BARBARA. Born July 2, 1940 in NYC. Attended Carnegie Tech, Sarbonne. Bdwy debut 1965 in "The Devils," OB in "Under Milkwood," "6 Characters in Search of an Author," "Murderous Angels," "Richard III," "A Doll's House."

COLE, KAY. Born Jan. 13, 1948 in Miami, Fla. Bdwy debut 1961 in "Bye Bye Birdie," followed by "Stop the World I Want to Get Off," "Roar of the Greasepaint . . . ," "Hair," "Jesus Christ Superstar," "Words and Music," "Chorus Line," OB in "The Cradle Will Rock," "Two if by Sea," "Rainbow," "White Nights," "Sgt. Pepper's Lonely Hearts Club Band."

COLES, ZAIDA. Born Sept. 10, 1933 in Lynchburg, Va. OB credits: "The Father," "Pins and Needles," "Life and Times of J. Walter Smintheus," "Cherry Orchard," "Bayou Legend," Bdwy in "Weekend," "Zelda."

COLLIER, ANN. Born Aug. 15, 1946 in Fitzgerald, Ga. Attended Players Workshop. Debut 1975 OB in "Women behind Bars."

COLLINS, PAUL. Born July 25, 1937 in London, Eng. Attended Los Angeles City and State Col., Actors Studio. OB credits: "Say Nothing," "Cambridge Circus," "The Sea," on Bdwy in "Royal Hunt of the Sun," "A Minor Adjustment."

COLLINS, STEPHEN. Born Oct. 1, 1947 in Des Moines, I. Graduate Amherst Col. Bdwy debut 1972 in "Moonchildren," followed by "No Sex Please, We're British," "The Ritz," OB in "Twelfth Night," "More Than You Deserve," "Macbeth" (LC), "Last Days of British Honduras."

COLTON, CHEVI. Born In NYC. Attended Hunter Col. OB in "Time of Storm," "Insect Comedy" (CC). "The Adding Machine," "O Marry Me," "Penny Change," "The Mad Show," "Jacques Brel Is Alive. . . . ," "Bits and Pieces," Bdwy in "Cabaret."

COLUMBUS, TOBIE. Born May 14, 1951 in Detroit, Mich. Graduate Wayne State U. Debut OB 1974 in "Let My People Come."

COMBS, DEBORAH. Born July 2, 1951 in Tucson, Ariz. Attended UOkla., AMDA. Debut 1974 OB in "The Boy Friend."

CONAWAY, JEFF. Born Oct. 5, 1950 in NYC. Attended NYU. Bdwy debut 1960 in "All the Way Home," followed by "Grease."

CONNELL, JANE. Born Oct. 27, 1925 in Berkeley, Ca. Attended UCal. OB credits: "Shoestring Revue," "Three-penny Opera," "Pieces of Eight," "Demi-Dozen," "She Stoops to Conquer," "Drat!," "The Real Inspector Hound," "The Rivals," Bdwy in "New Faces of 1956," "Drat! The Cat!," "Mame," "Dear World," "Lysistrata."

CONNELL, KATHY. Born Sept. 16, in NYC. Attended Finch Col. Debut 1974 OB in "The Desperate Hours."

CONNOLLEY, DENISE. Born Nov. 19, 1951 in Brooklyn, NY. Attended HB Studio. Debut 1974 OB in "Let My People Come."

CONWAY, KEVIN. Born May 29, 1942 in NYC. Debut 1968 OB in "Muzeeka," followed by "Saved," "Plough and the Stars," "One Flew over the Cuckoo's Nest," "When You Comin' Back, Red Ryder?," on Bdwy in "Indians," "Moonchildren," "Of Mice and Men."

CONWELL, PATRICIA. Born Aug. 17, 1951 in Mexico City, Mex. Graduate Incarnate Word Col. Debut 1974 OB in "Pericles" (NYSF), followed by Bdwy bow in "Love for Love" (1974).

COOK, PETER. Born in England in 1937. Attended Cambridge. Bdwy debut 1962 in "Beyond the Fringe," followed by "Good Evening."

COOLEY, DENNIS. Born May 11, 1948 in Huntington Park, Ca. Attended Northwestern U. Bdwy debut 1970 in "Hair," followed by "Jesus Christ Superstar," "Creation of the World and Other Business," "Where's Charley?"

COONEY, DENNIS. Born Sept. 19, 1938 in NYC. Attended Fordham U. OB in "Whisper to Me," "Every Other Girl" for which he received a Theatre World Award, "In a Summer House," LCR's "Tiger at the Gates," and "Cyrano de Bergerac," on Bdwy in "Ross," "Love and Kisses," "Lion in Winter," "The Last of Mrs. Lincoln," "Sherlock Holmes."

COOPER, PEGGY. Born Mar. 31, 1931 in Huntington, WVa. Graduate Baldwin-Wallace Conserv. Bdwy debut 1968 in "Zorba," followed by "La Strada," "The Rothschilds," "Goodtime Charley."

COPELAND, JOAN. Born June 1, 1922 in NYC. Attended Bklyn Col., AADA. Debut 1945. OB in "Romeo and Juliet," followed by "Othello," "Conversation Piece," "Delightful Season," "End of Summer," Bdwy in "Sundown Beach," "Detective Story," "Not for Children," "Handful of Fire," "Something More," "The Price," "Two by Two."

COPELAND, MAURICE D. Born June 13, 1911 in Rector, Ark. Graduate Pasadena Playhouse. Bdwy debut 1974 in "The Freedom of the City."

CORBIN, BARRY. Born Oct. 16, 1940 in LaMesa, Tex. Attended Texas Tech. Bdwy debut 1969 in ASF's "Othello," followed OB with "Masquerade," "Crystal and Fox," "Holy Ghosts."

CORRAL, JOSEPH. Born Mar. 6, 1945 in New Orleans, La. Graduate UFla., HB Studio. Debut 1973 OB in "Medea," followed by "Richard III."

CORY, KENNETH. Born July 21, 1941 in Hanover, Pa. Studied with Stella Adler. Bdwy debut 1971 in "Company," followed OB "Out of This World," "Be Kind to People Week."

COSTER, NICOLAS. Born Dec. 3, 1934 in London. Attended Neighborhood Playhouse. Bdwy bow 1960 in "Becket," followed by "90 Day Mistress," "But Seriously," "Twigs," OB in "Epitaph for George Dillon," "Shadow and Substance," "Thracian Horses," "O, Say Can You See," "Happy Birthday, Wanda June," "Naomi Court."

COUNCIL, RICHARD. Born Oct. 1, 1947 in Tampa, Fla. Graduate UFla. Debut OB 1973 in "Merchant of Venice," followed by "Ghost Dance," "Look We've Come Through," "Arms and the Man."

COURTNEY, ALEXANDER. Born Mar. 21, 1940 in NYC. Appeared OB in "Hamlet," "Othello," "The Wild Duck," "War and Peace," "Nuts," Bdwy in "Rosencrantz and Guildenstern Are Dead."

COWLES, MATTHEW. Born Sept. 28, 1944 in NYC. Attended Neighborhood Playhouse. Bdwy bow 1966 in "Malcolm," "The Indian Wants the Bronx," "Triple Play," "Stop, You're Killing Me!," "The Time of Your Life," "Foursome," "Kid Champion."

CRAIG, DONALD. Born Aug. 14, 1941 in Abilene, Tex. Graduate Hardin-Simmons Col., UTex. Debut 1975 OB in "Do I Hear a Waltz?"

CRESWELL, SAYLOR. Born Nov. 18, 1939 in Pottstown, Pa. Graduate Brown U. Debut OB 1968 in "Carving a Statute," "Room Service."

CRISCUOLO, LOUIS. Born Jan. 23, 1934 in NYC. Attended Actors Studio. Debut OB 1964 in "Matty, the Moron, and the Madonna," followed by "Hooray! It's a Glorious Day," "Smith," "Rubbers," "Yanks 3, Detroit 0," Bdwy in "Man of La Mancha," "Hurry Harry."

CRITTENDEN, JORDAN. Born Sept. 22, 1937 in Wichita, Kan. Graduate Kansas U. Debut 1974 OB in "Some People, Some Other People, and What They Finally Do"

CROMWELL, DAVID. Born Feb. 16, 1946 in Cornwall, NY. Graduate Ithaca Col. Debut OB 1968 in "Up Eden," followed by "In the Boom Boom Room."

CRONIN, JANE. Born Apr. 4, 1936 in Boston, Mass. Attended Boston U. Bdwy debut 1965 in "Postmark Zero," OB in "Bald Soprano," "One Flew over the Cuckoo's Nest," "Hot l Baltimore."

CRONYN, HUME. Born July 18, 1911 in London, Ont., Can. Attended McGill U., AADA. Bdwy debut 1934 in "Hipper's Holiday," followed by "Boy Meets Girl," "High Tor," "Room Service," "There's Always a Breeze," "Escape This Night," "Off to Buffalo," "Three Sisters," "Weak Link," "Retreat to Pleasure," "Mr. Big," "Survivors," "Four-poster," "Madam, Will You Walk" (OB), "The Honeys," "A Day by the Sea," "Man in the Dog Suit," "Triple Play," "Big Fish, Little Fish," "Hamlet," "Physicists," "Delicate Balance," "Hadrian VII," "Promenade, All," "Noel Coward in Two Keys," LC's "Krapp's Last Tape," "Happy Days," and "Act without Words."

CROWLEY, EDWARD. Born Sept. 5, 1926 in Lewiston, Me. Attended AADA. Bdwy debut 1958 in "Make a Million," followed by "Family Way," OB in "Admirable Bashville," "Evening with GBS," "Once around the Block," "I Want You," "Lion in Love," "Telemachus Clay," "Hair," "How to Steal an Election," "In the Matter of J. Robert Oppenheimer," "Evening for Merlin Finch," "Dylan," "Val, Christie and Others," "Danton's Death."

CROXTON, DARRYL. Born Apr. 5, 1946 in Baltimore, Md. Attended AADA. Appeared OB in "Volpone," "Murder in the Cathedral," "The Taking of Miss Jane," Bdwy debut 1969 in "Indians."

CRYER, DAVID. Born Mar. 8, 1936 in Evanston, Ill. Attended DePauw U. OB in "The Fantasticks," "Streets of New York," "Now Is the Time for All Good Men," "Whispers on the Wind," "The Making of Americans," "Portfolio Revue," on Bdwy in "110 in the Shade," "Come Summer," for which he received a Theatre World Award, "1776," "Ari," "Leonard Bernstein's Mass.," "Desert Song."

CULLUM, JOHN. Born Mar. 2, 1930 in Knoxville, Tenn. Graduate U. Tenn. Bdwy bow 1960 in "Camelot," followed by "Infidel Caesar," "The Rehearsal," "Hamlet," "On A Clear Day You Can See Forever" for which he received a Theatre World Award, "Man of LaMancha," "1776," "Vivat! Vivat Regina!," "Shenandoah," OB in "Three Hand Reel," "The Elizabethans," "Carousel," "In the Voodoo Parlor of Marie Leveau," "The King and I" (JB).

Bill Cwikowski **Norma Darden** **Brian Davies** **Carole Demas** **Jeffrey DeMunn**

CUNNINGHAM, JOHN. Born June 22, 1932 in Auburn, NY. Darmouth and Yale graduate. OB in "Love Me Little," "Pimpernel," "The Fantasticks," "Love and Let Love," "The Bone Room," Bdwy in "Hot Spot," "Zorba," "Company," "1776."

CURRY, CHRISTOPHER. Born Oct. 22, 1948, in Grand Rapids, Mich. Graduate UMich. Debut 1974 OB in "When You Comin' Back, Red Ryder?"

CURTIS, KEENE. Born Feb. 15, 1925 in Salt Lake City, U. Graduate UUtah. Bdwy bow 1949 in "Shop at Sly Corner," with APA in "School for Scandal," "The Tavern," "Anatole," "Scapin," "Right You Are," "Importance of Being Earnest," "Twelfth Night," "King Lear," "The Seagull," "Lower Depths," "Man and Superman," "Judith," "War and Peace," "You Can't Take it with You," "Pantagleize," "Cherry Orchard," "Misanthrope," "Cocktail Party," "Cock-a-Doodle Dandy" and "Hamlet," "A Patriot for Me," "The Rothschilds," "Night Watch," "Via Galactica," OB in "Colette," "Ride across Lake Constance."

CWIKOWSKI, BILL. Born Aug. 5, 1945 in Newark, NJ. Graduate Monmouth and Smith Cols. Debut 1972 OB in "Charlie the Chicken," followed by "Summer Brave," "Desperate Hours," "Mandragola."

CYPKIN, DIANE. Born Sept. 10, 1948 in Munich, Ger. Attended Bklyn Col. Bdwy debut 1966 in "Let's Sing Yiddish," followed by "Papa Get Married," "Light, Lively and Yiddish," OB in "Yoshke Musikant," "Stempenyu," "Big Winner."

DALBY, CYNTHIA. Born Nov. 1, 1944 in Spencer, Iowa. Graduate Northwestern U. Bdwy debut 1969 in "Play It Again, Sam."

DALE, JIM. Born 1936 in Rothwell, Eng. Made NY debut 1974 OB with Young Vic Co. in "Taming of the Shrew," followed by "Scapino" that moved to Bdwy.

DAMON, CATHRYN. Born Sept. 11 in Seattle, Wash. Bdwy debut 1954 in "By the Beautiful Sea," followed by "The Vamp," "Shinbone Alley," "A Family Affair," "Foxy," "Flora, The Red Menace," "UTBU," "Come Summer," "Criss-Crossing," "A Place for Polly," "Last of the Red Hot Lovers," OB in "Boys from Syracuse," "Secret Life of Walter Mitty," "Show Me Where The Good Times Are," "Effect of Gamma Rays on Man-in-the-Moon Marigolds," "Siamese Connections," "Prodigal," "Down by the River . . ."

DANA, LEORA. Born Apr. 1, 1923 in NYC. Attended Barnard Col., RADA. Bdwy debut 1947 in "Madwoman of Chaillot," followed by "Happy Time," "Point of No Return," "Sabrina Fair," "Best Man," "Beekman Place," "The Last of Mrs. Lincoln," "The Women," "Mourning Pictures," OB in "In the Summer House," "Wilder's Triple Bill," "Collision Course," "Bird of Dawning Singeth All Night Long," "Increased Difficulty of Concentration," "Place without Mornings."

DANIELE, GRACIELA. Born Dec. 8, 1939 in Buenos Aires. Bdwy debut 1964 in "What Makes Sammy Run?," followed by "Here's Where I Belong," "Promises, Promises," "Follies," "Chicago."

DARDEN, NORMA JEAN. Born Nov. 4 in Newark, NJ. Graduate Sarah Lawrence Col. Bdwy debut 1968 in "Weekend," OB in "Underground," "Les Femmes Noires," "Uncle Tom's Cabin."

DARZIN, DAINA. Born Jan. 10, 1953 in Spokane, Wash. Attended Carnegie-Mellon U. Debut OB 1974 in "Let My People Come."

DAVIDSON, JACK. Born July 17, 1936 in Worcester, Mass. Graduate Boston U. Debut 1968 OB in "Moon for the Misbegotten," followed by "Battle of Angels," "Midsummer Night's Dream," Bdwy 1972 in "Capt. Brassbound's Conversion."

DAVIDSON, LORRAINE. Born Oct. 11, 1945 in Boston, Mass. Attended HB Studio. Debut OB 1974 in "Let My People Come."

DAVIES, BRIAN. Born Nov. 15, 1939 in South Wales. Attended Indiana U. Bdwy bow 1959 in "Sound of Music," followed by "A Funny Thing Happened on the Way to the Forum," OB in "The Circle," "The Burnt Flower Bed."

DAVILA, DIANA. Born Nov. 5, 1947 in NYC. Bdwy debut 1967 in "Song of the Grasshopper," followed by "The Prime of Miss Jean Brodie," "Two Gentlemen of Verona," OB in "What the Butler Saw," "The Refrigerators," "People Are Living There," "Last Analysis," "The Seducers."

DAVIS, BETTE. Born Apr. 5, 1908 in Lowell, Mass. Attended John Murray Anderson School of Theatre. NY debut 1929 in "The Earth Between," followed by "Broken Dishes," "Solid South," "Two's Company," "World of Carl Sandburg," "Night of the Iguana."

DAVIS, STEVEN. Born Feb. 26, 1947 in Lafayette, Ind. Attended Southern Ill. U. Debut 1971 OB in "The Dirtiest Show in Town," followed by "Why Hanna's Skirt Won't Stay Down."

DAWSON, CURT. Born Dec. 5, 1941 in Kansas. RADA graduate. Debut OB 1968 in "Futz," followed by "Boys in the Band," "Not Now, Darling," "White Nights," "Enter a Free Man," Bdwy 1975 in "Absurd Person Singular."

DEAVEN, JOHN BRUCE. Born Nov. 6, 1947 in Harrisburg, Pa. Graduate Ohio U. Debut 1973 OB in "Tubstrip."

DE BEER, GERRIT. Born June 17, 1935 in Amsterdam. Bdwy debut 1965 in "Pickwick," followed by "Illya Darling," "Zorba," "Pajama Game," "All Over Town."

DEE, BLANCHE. Born Jan. 18, 1936 in Wheeling, WVa. Graduate Bklyn. Col. Debut 1967 OB in "Rimers of Eldritch," followed by "Tom Paine," "Sunset," "Yentl the Yeshiva Boy," Bdwy in "Grin and Bare It."

DEERING, OLIVE. Bdwy debut 1932 in "Girls in Uniform," followed by "Growing Pains," "Picnic," "Daughters of Atreus," "Eternal Road," "Winged Victory," "Skydrift," "Front Page," "Marathon '33," OB in "Ceremony of Innocence," "Two by Tennessee."

DeKOVEN, ROGER. Born Oct. 22, 1907 in Chicago, Ill. Attended UChicago, Northwestern, Columbia. Bdwy bow 1926 in "Juarez and Maximilian," followed by "Mystery Man," "Once in a Lifetime," "Counsellor-at-Law," "Murder in the Cathedral," "Eternal Road," "Brooklyn U.S.A.," "The Assassin," "Joan of Lorraine," "Abie's Irish Rose," "The Lark," "Hidden River," "Compulsion," "Miracle Worker," "Fighting Cock," OB in "Deadly Game," "Steal the Old Man's Bundle," "St. Joan," "Tiger at the Gates," "Walking to Waldheim," "Cyrano de Bergerac," "An Enemy of the People."

DEITCH, DAN. Born Oct. 26, 1945 in San Francisco, Cal. Graduate Princeton, Harvard, LAMDA. Bdwy debut 1972 in "Grease," OB in "Troilus and Cressida."

D'ELIA, CHET. Born Nov. 19, 1944 in Bridgeport, Conn. Attended Boston Conserv. Bdwy debut 1974 in "Mack and Mabel," followed by "The Lieutenant."

DELL, GABRIEL. Born Oct. 7, 1930 in Barbadoes, BWI. On Bdwy in "Dead End," "Tickets, Please," "Ankles Aweigh," "Prisoner of Second Avenue," CC's "Can-Can," "Wonderful Town," and "Oklahoma!," "Marathon '33," "Anyone Can Whistle," "Sign in Sidney Brustein's Window," "Luv," "Something Different," "Fun City," OB in "Chocolates," "Adaptation," "Where Do We Go from Here?"

DeMAIO, PETER. Born in Hartford, Conn. Attended New School, Juilliard. Debut OB 1961 in "Threepenny Opera," followed by "Secret Life of Walter Mitty," "Dark of the Moon," "Welcome to Black River," "Last Breeze of Summer." Bdwy in "Billy," "Indians," "The Changing Room."

DEMAS, CAROLE. Born May 26, 1940 in Bklyn. Graduate UVt., NYU. OB in "Morning Sun," "The Fantasticks," "How to Steal an Election," "Rondelay," Bdwy debut 1965 in "Race of Hairy Men," followed by "Grease."

DeMUNN, JEFFREY P. Born Apr. 25, 1947 in Buffalo, NY. Graduate Union Col. Debut 1975 OB in "Augusta."

DENGEL, JAKE. Born June 19, 1933 in Oshkosh, Wis. Graduate Northwestern U. Debut OB in "The Fantasticks," followed by "Red Eye of Love," "Fortuna," "Abe Lincoln in Illinois," "Dr. Faustus," "An Evening with Garcia Lorca," "Shrinking Bride," APA's "Cock-a-Doodle Dandy" and "Hamlet," "Where Do We Go from Here?," Bdwy in "Royal Hunt of the Sun," "The Changing Room."

DENNIS, RONALD. Born Oct. 2, 1944 in Dayton, O. Debut OB 1966 in "Show Boat," followed by "Of Thee I Sing," "Moon Walk," "Please Don't Cry," Bdwy 1975 in "A Chorus Line."

DENNIS, SANDY. Born Apr. 27, 1937 in Hastings, Neb. Bdwy debut 1957 in "The Dark at the Top of the Stairs," followed by "Burning Bright" (OB), "Face of a Hero," "Complaisant Lover," "A Thousand Clowns" for which she received a Theatre World Award, "Any Wednesday," "Daphne in Cottage D," "How the Other Half Loves," "Let Me Hear You Smile," "Absurd Person Singular."

DeSHIELDS, ANDRE. Born Jan. 12, 1946 in Baltimore, Md. Graduate UWisc. Bdwy debut 1973 in "Warp," followed by "Rachel Lily Rosenbloom," "The Wiz," OB in "2008½."

DEVLIN, JOHN. Born Jan. 26, 1937 in Cleveland, O. Graduate Carnegie Tech. Bdwy debut 1964 in "Poor Bitos," followed by "Billy," "Vivat! Vivat Regina!," OB in "Richard III," "King Lear."

| ianne Oyama Dixon | Richard Donat | Alice Drummond | Pi Douglass | Doreen Dunn |

DEWHURST, COLLEEN. Born in Montreal, Can. Attended Downer Col., AADA. Bdwy debut 1952 in "Desire under the Elms," followed by "Tamburlaine the Great," "Country Wife," "Caligula," "All the Way Home," "Great Day in the Morning," "Ballad of the Sad Cafe," "More Stately Mansions," "All Over," "Mourning Becomes Electra," "Moon for the Misbegotten." OB in "Taming of the Shrew," "The Eagle Has Two Heads," "Camille," "Macbeth," "Children of Darkness" for which she received a Theatre World Award, "Antony and Cleopatra" (CP), "Hello and Goodbye," "Good Woman of Setzuan" (LC), "Hamlet" (NYSF).

DIENER, JOAN. Born Feb. 24, 1934 in Cleveland, O. Attended Sarah Lawrence Col. Bdwy debut 1948 in "Small Wonder," followed by "Season in the Sun," "Kismet" for which she received a Theatre World Award, "Cry for Us All," "Man of La Mancha."

DILLON, DENNY. Born May 18, 1951 in Cleveland, O. Graduate Syracuse U. Bdwy debut 1974 in "Gypsy."

DIXON, DIANNE OYAMA. Born Mar. 24, 1954 in Nashville, Tenn. Stephens Col. graduate. Debut 1975 OB in "The Taking of Miss Janie."

DIXON, MacINTYRE. Born Dec. 22, 1931 in Everett, Mass. Graduate Emerson Col. OB in "Quare Fellow," "Plays for Bleecker St.," "Stewed Prunes," "Cat's Pajamas," "Three Sisters," "3 X 3," "Second City," "Mad Show," "Meeow!" "Lotta," "Rubbers," Bdwy in "Xmas in Las Vegas," "Cop-Out," "Story Theatre," "Metamorphoses," "Twigs," "Over Here."

DONAT, RICHARD. Born June 1, 1941 in Kentville, NS, Can. Attended UBritish Col., Ntl. Theatre School. Bdwy debut 1974 in "Hosanna."

DONNELLY, JAMIE. Bdwy debut 1965 in "Flora the Red Menace," followed by "You're a Good Man, Charlie Brown," (OB), "George M!," "Rodgers and Hart," "Rocky Horror Show."

DORRIN, JOHN. Born July 17, 1920 in Omaha, Neb. Attended LACC. Bdwy bow 1944 in "Song of Norway," followed by "Kismet," "Silk Stockings," "Most Happy Fella," "Best Man," "My Fair Lady," "What Makes Sammy Run?," "Fade Out—Fade In," "Annie Get Your Gun," "Finian's Rainbow," "St. Joan," "I'm Solomon," "New Girl in Town" (OB).

DOTRICE, ROY. Born May 26, 1925 in Guernsey, Channel Islands. Bdwy debut 1967 in "Brief Lives" in which he returned in 1974.

DOUGLASS, PI. Born in Sharon, Conn. Attended Boston Conserv. Bdwy debut 1969 in "Fig Leaves Are Falling," followed by "Hello, Dolly!," "Georgy," "Purlie," "Ari," "Jesus Christ Superstar," "Selling of the President," "The Wiz," OB in "Of Thee I Sing."

DOVA, NINA. Born Jan. 15, 1926 in London, Eng. Attended Neighborhood Playhouse. Debut OB 1954 in "I Feel Wonderful," followed by "A Delicate Balance," Bdwy in "Zorba," "The Rothschilds," "Saturday Sunday Monday."

DOW, R. A. Born Aug. 30, 1941 in Cambridge, Mass. Graduate UPa. Debut OB 1970 in "The Dirtiest Show in Town," followed by "Baba Goya," "Nourish the Beast," "Hothouse," "Action."

DOWNING, DAVID. Born July 21, 1943 in NYC. OB in "Day of Absence," "Happy Ending," "Song of the Lusitanian Bogey," "Ceremonies in Dark Old Men," "Man Better Man," "The Harangues," "Brotherhood," "Perry's Mission," "Rosalee Pritchett," "Dream on Monkey Mt.," "Ride a Black Horse," "Ballet behind the Bridge," "Please Don't Cry and Say No," "Richard III," Bdwy in "Raisin."

DOWNING, VIRGINIA. born Mar. 7, in Washington, DC. Attended Bryn Mawr. OB in "Juno and the Paycock," "Man with the Golden Arm," "Palm Tree in a Rose Garden," "Play with a Tiger," "The Wives," "The Idiot," "Medea," "Mrs. Warren's Profession," "Mercy Street," "Thunder Rock," "Pygmalion," "The First Week in Bogota," Bdwy in "Father Malachy's Miracle," "Forward the Heart," "The Cradle Will Rock," "A Gift of Time," "We Have Always Lived in the Castle."

DOYLE, KATHLEEN. Born Nov. 7, 1947 in Hyattsville, Md. Graduate Goodman School. NY debut 1971 with LCRep in "Ride across Lake Constance," "Mary Stuart," "Twelfth Night," and "The Crucible."

DRIVAS, ROBERT. Born Nov. 20, in Chicago. Bdwy debut 1958 in "The Firstborn," followed by "One More River," "The Wall," "Lorenzo," "Irregular Verb to Love," "And Things That Go Bump in the Night," "The Ritz," OB in "Mrs. Dally Has a Lover" for which he received a Theatre World Award, "Sweet Eros," "Where Has Tommy Flowers Gone," "Breeze from the Gulf."

DRUMMOND, ALICE. Born May 21, 1929 in Pawtucket, RI. Attended Pembroke Col. OB in "Royal Gambit," "Go Show Me a Dragon," "Sweet of You to Say So," "Gallows Humor," "American Dream," "Giants' Dance," "Carpenters," "Charles Abbott & Son," "God Says There Is No Peter Ott," "Enter a Free Man," Bdwy debut 1963 in "Ballad of the Sad Cafe," followed by Malcolm," "The Chinese," "Thieves."

DUFF-MacCORMICK, CARA. Born Dec. 12 in Woodstock, Can. Attended AADA. Debut 1969 OB in "Love Your Crooked Neighbor," followed by "The Wager," "Macbeth" (LC), "A Musical Merchant of Venice," Bdwy 1972 in "Moonchildren" for which she received a Theatre World Award, followed by "Out Cry."

DUKES, DAVID. Born June 6, 1945 in San Francisco, Ca. Attended Mann College. Bdwy debut 1971 in "School for Wives," followed by "Don Juan," "The Play's the Thing," "The Visit," "Chemin de Fer," "Holiday," "Rules of the Game," "Love for Love."

DULLEA, KEIR. Born May 30, 1936 in Cleveland, NJ. Attended Neighborhood Playhouse. Debut OB 1959 in "Season of Choice," Bdwy in "Dr. Cook's Garden," "Butterflies Are Free," "P.S. Your Cat Is Dead."

DUNMORE, BEATRICE. Born Feb. 10, 1963 in NYC. Bdwy debut 1975 in "All God's Chillun Got Wings."

DUNN, DOREEN. Born Oct. 2, 1946 in Bath, Maine. Graduate Northwestern U. Debut 1975 OB in "Celebration," followed by "The Three Musketeers."

DURRELL, MICHAEL. OB 1961 in "Worm in the Horseradish," "Butterfly Dream," "Phedre," "MacBird," "A Maid's Tragedy," APA's "Cherry Orchard," "Pantagleize," "Misanthrope," "Cock-a-Doodle Dandy," and "Hamlet," "Nuts," Bdwy 1973 in "Emperor Henry IV."

EARLEY, CANDICE. Born Aug. 18, 1950 in Ft. Hood, Tex. Attended Trinity U. Bdwy debut 1971 in "Hair," followed by "Jesus Christ Superstar," "Grease."

EBER, RICHARD. Born Nov. 5, 1946 in Boston, Mass. Graduate UMass. Debut 1970 OB in "A Christmas Carol," followed by "Apartment to Let," "Circus," "Waking Up to Beautiful Things," "The Three Musketeers."

EBERT, JOYCE. Born June 26, 1933 in Homestead, Pa. Graduate Carnegie Tech. Debut 1956 OB in "Liliom," followed by "Sign of Winter," "Asmodee," "King Lear," "Hamlet," "Under Milkwood," "Trojan Women," "White Devil," "Tartuffe," Bdwy 1971 in "Solitaire/Double Solitaire."

EDE, GEORGE. Born Dec. 22, 1931 in San Francisco, Cal. Bdwy debut 1969 in "A Flea in Her Ear," followed by "Three Sisters," "The Changing Room," "The Visit," "Chermin de Fer," "Holiday," "Love for Love," "Rules of the Game," "Member of the Wedding."

EDMONDS, LOUIS. Born Sept. 24, 1923 in Baton Rouge, La. Attended Carnegie Tech. OB in "Life in Louisiana," "Way of the World," "The Cherry Orchard," "Uncle Vanya," "Duchess of Malfi," "Ernest in Love," "The Rapists," "Amoureuse," Bdwy in "Candide," "Maybe Tuesday," "The Killer," "Passage to India," "Fire!"

EDWARDS, ANNIE JOE. Born Sept. 15, 1949 in Birmingham, Ala. Graduate Dillard U. Bdwy debut 1975 in "Dr. Jazz," followed by "Be Kind to People Week" (OB).

EDWARDS, BRANDT. Born Mar. 22, 1947 in Holly Springs, Miss. Graduate UMiss. NY debut 1975 off and on Bdwy in "A Chorus Line."

EDWARDS, DENNIS. Born Dec. 28, 1916 in London, Eng. Attended King's Col., Fay Compton Studio. Bdwy debut 1974 in "As You Like It."

ELIC, JOSIP. Born Mar. 10, 1921 in Butte, Mont. Attended Wisc. U. Debut OB in "Threepenny Opera," followed by "Don Juan in Hell," "Leave It to Jane," "Comic Strip," "Coriolanus," "Too Much Johnson," "Stag Movie," "Rise and Fall of Burlesque Humor," Bdwy in "Hamlet," "Baptiste," "West Side Story," "Sign in Sidney Brustein's Window," "Kelly."

ELIO, DONNA. Born Oct. 30, 1962 in Paterson, NJ. Bdwy debut 1974 in "Gypsy."

ELKINS, FLORA. Born July 28 in NYC. Attended Neighborhood Playhouse. Bdwy debut 1961 in "Rhinoceros," OB in "Ardele," "Geranium Hat," "Othello," "Troilus and Cressida," "Baal," "Stephen D," "Candle in the Wind," "A Touch of the Poet."

ELLIN, DAVID. Born Jan. 10, 1925 in Montreal, Can. Attended AADA. Bdwy in "Swan Song," "West Side Story," "Education of Hyman Kaplan," "Light, Lively and Yiddish," OB in "Trees Die Standing," "Mirele Efros," "End of All Things Natural," "Yoshe Kalb," "Fiddler on the Roof" (JB).

ELLIOTT, ALICE. Born Aug. 22, 1950 in Durham, NC. Graduate Carnegie-Mellon U., Goodman Theatre. Debut 1972 OB in "In the Time of Harry Harass," followed by "American Gothics," "Bus Stop."

ELLIOTT, PATRICIA. Born July 21, 1942 in Gunnison, Colo. Graduate U. Colo., London Academy. Debut with LCRep 1968 in "King Lear," and "A Cry of Players," followed OB in "Henry V," "The Persians," "A Doll's House," "Hedda Gabler," "In Case of Accident," "Water Hen," "Polly," Bdwy bow 1973 in "A Little Night Music" for which she received a Theatre World Award.

| Tricia Ellis | Woody Eney | Boni Enten | Damon Evans | Mary Fogarty |

ELLIS, TRICIA. Born Nov. 29, 1949 in Beverly Hills, Ca. Attended UCLA. Debut OB 1975 in "The Three Musketeers."

ENEY, WOODY. Born June 8, 1937 in Canberra, Aust. Attended RADA. Debut OB 1974 in "The Desperate Hours."

ENNIS, FLLOYD. Born June 29, 1926 in Philadelphia Pa. Studied with Stella Adler. Debut 1961 OB in "The Octoroon," followed by "Kid Champion."

ENO, TERRY R. Born June 5, 1946 in Miami, Fla. Attended Miami U., HB Studio. Bdwy debut in "Irene" followed by "Good News," OB in "Buy Bonds Buster."

ENSERRO, MICHAEL. Born Oct. 5, 1918 in Soldier, Pa. Attended Allegheny Col., Pasadena Playhouse. Bdwy in "Me and Molly," "Passion of Josef D," "Song of the Grasshopper," "Mike Downstairs," "Camino Real," "Saturday Sunday Monday," OB in "Penny Change," "Fantasticks," "The Miracle," "The Kitchen," "Rome, Rome," "The Jar."

ENTEN, BONI. Born Feb. 20, 1947 in Baltimore, Md. Attended TCU. Bdwy debut 1965 in "Roar of the Greasepaint," followed by "Rocky Horror Show," OB in "You're a Good Man, Charlie Brown," "Oh! Calcutta!," "Salvation," "The Real Inspector Hound."

EPSTEIN, PIERRE. Born July 27, 1930 in Toulouse, France. Graduate UParis, Columbia. Bdwy bow 1962 in "A Shot in the Dark," followed by "Enter Laughing," "Bajour," "Black Comedy," "Thieves," "Fun City," OB in "Incident at Vichy," "Threepenny Opera," "Too Much Johnson," "Second City," "People vs. Ranchman," "Promenade," "Cakes with Wine," "Little Black Sheep."

ESTERMAN, LAURA. Born Apr. 12, in NYC. Attended Radcliffe, London's AMDA. Debut 1969 OB in "The Time of Your Life" (LCR), followed by "Pig Pen," "The Carpenters," "Ghosts," "Waltz of the Toreadors," "MacBeth" (LC), "The Seagull," "Rubbers," "Yanks 3, Detroit 0," Bdwy 1974 "God's Favorite."

EVANKO, ED. Born in Winnipeg, Can. Studied at Bristol Old Vic. Bdwy debut 1969 in "Canterbury Tales" for which he received a Theatre World Award, OB in "Love Me, Love My Children," "Leaves of Grass."

EVANS, DAMON. Born Nov. 24, 1950 in Baltimore, Md. Studied at Boston Cons. Debut 1971 OB in "A Day in the Life of Just about Everyone," followed by "Love Me, Love My Children," "Don't Bother Me, I Can't Cope," "Godspell," Bdwy bow 1971 in "The Me Nobody Knows," followed by "Lost in the Stars," "Via Galactica."

EVERETT, JAKE. Born Oct. 1, 1946 in Eugene, Ore. Graduate UOre., Wayne State U. Debut OB 1973 in "Tubstrip" followed by "Roomers."

EVERSON, JOHN. Born May 21, 1947 in Dawson, Minn. Graduate UWisc. Bdwy debut 1974 in "Grease," followed by "The Ritz."

FANCY, RICHARD. Born Aug. 2, 1943 in Evanston, Ill. Attended LAMDA Debut OB 1973 in "The Creeps," followed by "Love One Another."

FANN, ALBERT. Born Feb. 21, 1933 in Cleveland, O. Attended Cleveland Inst of Music. Debut 1970 OB in "King Heroin," Bdwy 1975 in "The Wiz."

FARENTINO, JAMES. Born Feb. 24, 1938 in Brooklyn. Attended AADA. Bdwy debut 1961 in "Night of the Iguana," followed by "Death of a Salesman," OB in "Days and Nights of Beebee Fenstermaker," "In the Summer House," LC's "Streetcar Named Desire" for which he received a Theatre World Award.

FARR, KIMBERLY. Born Oct. 16, 1948 in Chicago. UCLA graduate. Bdwy debut 1972 in "Mother Earth," OB in "More than You Deserve," "The S.S. Benchley," "At Sea with Benchley."

FAWCETT, ROGER. Born Apr. 28, 1943 in Brooklyn, NY. Attended AmTh-Wing. Debut OB 1962 in "Murder in the Cathedral," followed by "Infernal Machine," "Oldest Trick in the World," "Hollow Crown," "The Skin of Our Teeth," "I Can't Go on without You, Minna Mandelbaum," "The Three Musketeers."

FAYE, ALICE. Born May 5, 1915 in NYC. Bdwy debut 1931 in "George White's Scandals," followed by "Good News" (1974).

FELDER, CLARENCE. Born Sept. 2, 1938 in St. Matthews, SC. Debut OB 1964 in "The Room," followed by "Are You Now or Have You Ever Been," Bdwy 1969 in "Red, White and Maddox," "Love for Love," "Rules of the Game."

FELDSHUH, TOVAH. Born Dec. 27 in NYC. Graduate Sarah Lawrence Col. Bdwy debut 1973 in "Cyrano," followed by "Dreyfus in Rehearsal," "Rodgers and Hart," OB in "Yentl the Yeshiva Boy," "Straws in the Wind."

FERNANDES, YUYE. Born Nov. 9, 1948 in Wareham, Mass. Graduate Smith Col. Debut OB 1970 in "Pig," followed by "Silver Queen," "La Gente," "Inner City," "Three Musketeers," Bdwy 1974 in "Scapino."

FERRELL, CONCHATA. Born Mar. 28, 1943 in Charleston, WVa. Graduate Marshall U. Debut 1973 OB in "The Hot 1 Baltimore," "The Sea Horse" for which she received a Threatre World Award, "Battle of Angels."

FIRE, RICHARD. Born Nov. 12, 1945 in Paterson, NJ. Graduate Rutgers, UWisc. Bdwy debut 1973 in "Warp!"

FIRTH, PETER. Born Oct. 27, 1953 in Bradford, Eng. Bdwy debut 1974 in "Equus" for which he received a Theatre World Award.

FISKE, ELLEN. Born May 1, in Paterson, NJ. Graduate Wilmington Col., Ohio U. Debut OB 1974 in "Arms and the Man."

FITCH, ROBERT. Born Apr. 29, 1934 in Santa Cruz, Cal. Attended U Santa Clara. Bdwy debut 1961 in "Tenderloin," followed by "Do Re Mi," "My Fair Lady" (CC), "Girl Who Came to Supper," "Flora the Red Menace," "Baker Street," "Sherry," "Mack and Mabel," "Henry, Sweet Henry," "Mame," "Promises, Promises," "Coco," "Lorelei," OB in "Lend an Ear," "Half-Past Wednesday," "Anything Goes," "Crystal Heart," "Broadway Dandies," "One Cent Plain."

FITZGERALD, GERALDINE. Born Nov. 24, 1914 in Dublin, Ire. Bdwy debut 1938 in "Heartbreak House," followed by "Sons and Soldiers," "Doctor's Dilemma," "King Lear," "Hide and Seek," OB in "Cave Dwellers," "Pigeons," "Long Day's Journey into Night," "Everyman and Roach."

FITZPATRICK, KELLY. Born Dec. 31, 1937 in Mt. Kisco, NY. Graduate Hobart Col. Bdwy debut 1971 in "Abelard and Heloise," followed by OB in "The Trial of Denmark Vesey," "Oakville," "Mississippi Moonshine," "Trees in the Wind," "Hothouse," "The True History of Squire Jonathan . . ."

FLACKS, NIKI. Born Apr. 7, 1943 in Daytona Beach, Fla. Attended Northwestern, UMinn. Bdwy debut 1966 in "Dinner at 8," followed by "Private Lives," "Candide."

FLANAGAN, NEIL. Born May 3, 1934 in Springfield, Ill. Debut 1966 OB in "Fortune and Men's Eyes," followed by "Haunted Host," "Madness of Lady Bright," "Dirtiest Show in Town," "The Play's the Thing," "As You Like It," "Hedda Gabler," "Design for Living," "him," "Partnership," "Down by the River . . . ," "Lisping Judas," Bdwy in "Sheep on the Runway," "Secret Affairs of Mildred Wild."

FLANDERS, ED. Born in 1934 in Minnesota. Bdwy debut 1967 in "The Birthday Party," followed by "A Man for all Seasons," "The Crucible," "Trial of the Catonsville 9," "Moon for the Misbegotten."

FLEISCHMAN, MARK. Born Nov. 25, 1935 in Detroit, Mich. Attended UMich. Bdwy debut 1955 in "Tonight in Samarkand," followed by "A Distant Bell," OB in "What Every Woman Knows," "Lute Song," "The Beautiful People," "Big Fish, Little Fish."

FLETCHER, JACK. Born Apr. 21, 1921 in Forest Hills, NY. Attended Yale. On Bdwy in "Trial Honeymoon," "She Stoops to Conquer," "Romeo and Juliet," "Ben Franklin in Paris," "Drat! The Cat!," "Lysistrata," "Lorelei," OB in "Comic Strip," "Way of the World," "Thieves' Carnival," "Amorous Flea," "American Hamburger League," "The Time of Your Life," CC's "Can-Can," "Cyrano," and "Wonderful Town."

FLINT, JOHN. Born Aug. 1, 1929 in London, Eng. Bdwy debut 1956 in "Troilus and Cressida," followed by "As You Like It."

FLIPPIN, LUCY LEE. Born July 23, 1943 in Philadelphia, Pa. Graduate Northwestern U. Debut OB 1970 in "The Playground," followed by "Shoestring Revue," "Rip Van Winkle," "Midsummer Night's Dream."

FLYNN, MARYELLEN. Born Aug. 22, 1940 in Boston, Mass. Attended Fordham U., AADA. Debut 1963 OB in "Pullman Car Hiawatha," followed by "Babes Don't Cry Anymore," "Guimpes and Saddles," "Hot 1 Baltimore," "Battle of Angels."

FOGARTY, JACK. Born Oct. 23, 1923 in Liverpool, Eng. Attended Fordham and Columbia U. Debut 1952 OB in "No Exit," followed by "Hogan's Goat," "Sweeney Todd," "The Fantasticks."

FOGARTY, MARY. Born in Manchester, NH. Debut 1959 OB in "The Well of the Saints," followed by "Shadow and Substance," "Nathan, the Wise," Bdwy 1974 in "The National Health."

FONDA, HENRY. Born May 16, 1905 in Grand Island, Neb. Attended UMinn. Bdwy debut 1929 in "Game of Love and Death," followed by "I Love You Wednesday," "Forsaking All Others," "New Faces of 1934," "The Farmer Takes a Wife," "Mr. Roberts," "Point of No Return," "Caine Mutiny Court Martial," "Two for the Seesaw," "Silent Night, Lonely Night," "Critic's Choice," "A Gift of Time," "Generation," "Our Town," "Clarence Darrow."

Frances Foster   Arthur French   Lauren Frost   Peter Friedman   Patricia Gaul

FOOTE, GENE. Born Oct. 30, 1936 in Johnson City, Tenn. Attended ETSU. Bdwy debut 1961 in "Unsinkable Molly Brown," followed by "Bajour," "Sweet Charity," "Golden Rainbow," "Applause," "Pippin," "Chicago," "Celebration" (OB).

FORBES, BRENDA. Born Jan. 14, 1909 in London. Bdwy debut 1931 in "Barretts of Wimpole Street," followed by "Candida," "Lucrece," "Flowers of the Forest," "Pride and Prejudice," "Storm over Patsy," "Heartbreak House," "One for the Money," "Two for the Show," "Three to Make Ready," "Yesterday's Magic," "Morning Star," "Suds in Your Eyes," "Quadrille," "The Reluctant Debutante," "Loves of Cass McGuire," "Darling of the Day," "The Constant Wife."

FORSLUND, CONNIE. Born June 19, 1950 in San Diego, Cal. Graduate NYU. Debut OB 1972 in "The Divorce of Judy and Jane," followed by "The Cretan Bull," "The Kiss-Off," Bdwy 1973 in "The Women."

FORSTER, JOHN. Born Apr. 1, 1948 in Philadelphia, Pa. Harvard U. graduate. Debut Ob 1974 in "Pretzels."

FOSTER, FRANCES. Born June 11 in Yonkers, NY. Bdwy debut 1955 in "The Wisteria Trees," followed by "Nobody Loves an Albatross," "Raisin in the Sun," "The River Niger," "First Breeze of Summer," OB in "Take a Giant Step," "Edge of the City," "Tammy and the Doctor," "The Crucible," "Happy Ending," "Day of Absence," "An Evening of One Acts," "Man Better Man," "Brotherhood," "Akokawe," "Rosalee Pritchett," "Sty of the Blind Pig," "Ballet behind the Bridge," "Good Woman of Setzuan" (LC) "Behold! Cometh the Vanderkellans," "Orrin."

FRANCIS, ARLENE. Born Oct. 20, 1908 in Boston, Mass. Attended Finch Col. Bdwy debut 1936 in "Horse Eats Hat," followed by "The Women," "All That Glitters," "Michael Drops In," "Journey to Jerusalem," "Doughgirls," "Overtons," "French Touch," "Cup of Trembling," "My Name is Aquilon," "Metropole," "Little Blue Light," "Late Love," "Once More with Feeling," "Beekman Place," "Mrs. Dally," "Dinner at 8," "Gigi," "Don't Call Back."

FRANKLIN, BONNIE. Born Jan. 6, 1944 in Santa Monica, Cal. Attended Smith Col. UCLA. Debut OB 1968 in "Your Own Thing," followed by "Dames at Sea," "Drat!," "Carousel" (JB), Bdwy bow 1970 in "Applause" for which she received a Theatre World Award.

FRANKLIN, NANCY. Born in NYC. On Bdwy in "Happily Never After," "The White House," "Never Live over a Pretzel Factory," OB in "Buffalo Skinner," "Power of Darkness," "Oh, Dad, Poor Dad . . . ," "Theatre of Peretz," "Seven Days of Mourning," "Here Be Dragons," "Beach Children," "Safe Place."

FRAZIER, RONALD C. Born Feb. 18, 1942. Graduate Carnegie Tech. Bdwy debut 1970 in "Wilson in the Promise Land," followed by "Enemy of the People," "What Every Woman Knows," "Death Story."

FREED, SAM. Born Aug. 29, 1948 in York, Pa. Graduate Pa. State U. Debut OB 1972 in "The Proposition," followed by "What's a Nice Country Like You . . . ," Bdwy 1974 in "Candide."

FREEMAN, AL, JR. Born in 1934 in San Antonio, Tex. Attended CCLA. On Bdwy in "The Long Dream," "Tiger, Tiger, Burning Bright," "Living Premise," "Blues for Mr. Charlie," "Dozens," "Look to the Lilies," OB in "Slave," "Dutchman," "Trumpets of the Lord," "Medea," "The Great Mac-Daddy."

FRENCH, ARTHUR. Born in NYC. Attended Bklyn Col. OB 1962 in "Raisin' Hell in the Sun," "Ballad of Bimshire," "Day of Absence," "Happy Ending," "Jonah," "Black Girl," "Ceremonies in Dark Old Men," "An Evening of One Acts," "Man Better Man," "Brotherhood," "Perry's Mission," "Rosalee Pritchett," "Moonlight Arms," "Dark Tower," Bdwy 1971 in "Ain't Supposed to Die a Natural Death," followed by "The Iceman Cometh," "All God's Chillun Got Wings."

FRENCH, BRUCE. Born July 4, 1945 in Reinbeck, Ia. Graduate UIowa. Debut 1972 OB in "Shadow of a Gunman," followed by "End of Summer," "Heathen Piper."

FREY, LEONARD. Born Sept. 4, 1938 in Brooklyn. Attended Cooper Union, Neighborhood Playhouse. OB in "Little Mary Sunshine," "Funny House of a Negro," "Coach with Six Insides," "Boys in the Band," "Time of Your Life," "Beggar on Horseback," "People Are Living There," "Twelfth Night," "Troilus and Cressida," on Bdwy in "Fiddler on the Roof," "The National Health."

FRIEDMAN, PETER. Born Apr. 24, 1949 in NYC. Graduate Hofstra U. Debut OB 1971 in "James Joyce Memorial Liquid Theatre," Bdwy 1973 in "The Visit," "Chemin de Fer," followed by "Love for Love," "Rules of the Game."

FROST, LAUREN. Born Feb. 7, 1945 in Fairfield, Conn. Graduate Carnegie-Mellon U. Debut 1974 OB in "A Sneaky Bit to Raise the Blind," followed by "Pick Pack Pock Puck," "The Burnt Flower Bed."

FULLER, PENNY. Born in 1940 in Durham, NC. Attended Northwestern U. Credits include "Barefoot in the Park," "Cabaret," "Richard III," "As You Like It," "Henry IV," "Applause."

GABEL, MARTIN. Born June 19, 1912 in Philadelphia, Pa. Attended Lehigh U., AADA. Bdwy debut 1935 in "Dead End," followed by "Julius Caesar," "Danton's Death," "King Lear," "Reclining Figure," "Will Success Spoil Rock Hunter?," "The Rivalry," "Big Fish, Little Fish," "Children from Their Games," "Sheep on the Runway," "In Praise of Love."

GABLE, JUNE. Born June 5, 1945 in NY. Graduate Carnegie Tech. OB in "MacBird," "Jacques Brel Is Alive and Well and Living In Paris," "A Day in the Life of Just about Everyone," "Mod Donna," "Wanted," "Lady Audley's Secret," "Candide."

GALE, DAVID. Born Oct. 2, 1936 in England. Debut 1958 OB in "Elizabeth the Queen," followed by "Othello," "White Devil," "Baal," "What Do They Know about Love Uptown," "Joe Egg," "The Trial," "Dumbwaiter," Bdwy 1974 in "Of Mice and Men."

GALLAGHER, HELEN. Born in 1926 in Brooklyn, NY. Bdwy debut 1947 in "Seven Lively Arts," followed by "Mr. Strauss Goes to Boston," "Billion Dollar Baby," "Brigadoon," "High Button Shoes," "Touch and Go," "Make a Wish," "Pal Joey," "Guys and Dolls," "Finian's Rainbow," "Oklahoma!," "Pajama Game," "Bus Stop," "Portofino," "Sweet Charity," "Mame," "Cry for Us All," "No, No, Nanette," "Hothouse" (OB).

GANTRY, DONALD. Born June 11, 1936 in Philadelphia, Pa. Attended Temple U. Bdwy debut 1961 in "One More River," OB in "The Iceman Cometh," "Children of Darkness," "Here Come the Clowns," "Seven at Dawn," "Long Day's Journey into Night," "Enclave."

GARBER, VICTOR. Born Mar. 16, 1949 in London, Can. Debut 1973 OB in "Ghosts" for which he received a Theatre World Award, followed by "Joe's Opera."

GARDENIA, VINCENT. Born Jan. 7 in Italy. Debut OB 1956 in "Man with the Golden Arm," followed by "Brothers Karamazov," "Power of Darkness," "Machinal," "Gallows Humor," "Endgame," "Little Murders," "Passing through from Exotic Places," "Carpenters," Bdwy in "The Visit," "The Cold Wind and the Warm," "Rashomon," "Only in America," "The Wall," "Daughters of Silence," "Seidman and Son," "Dr. Fish," "Prisoner of Second Avenue," "God's Favorite."

GARDNER, RICK. Born Feb. 27, 1945 in Detroit, Mich. Graduate Wayne State U. Bdwy debut 1968 in "Golden Rainbow," OB in "Two if by Sea," "Gay Company."

GARFIELD, DAVID. Born Feb. 6, 1941 in Brooklyn, NY. Columbia, Cornell graduate. OB in "Hang Down Your Head and Die," "Government Inspector," "Old Ones," Bdwy in "Fiddler on the Roof," "The Rothschilds."

GARFIELD, JULIE. Born Jan. 10, 1946 in Los Angeles. Attended UWisc., Neighborhood Playhouse. Debut OB 1969 in "Honest-to-God Schnozzola," "East Lynne," "The Sea," followed by "Uncle Vanya" for which she received a Theatre World Award, Bdwy in "The Good Doctor," "Death of a Salesman."

GARFIELD, KURT. Born Jan. 10, 1931 in The Bronx, NY. Attended Goodman Theatre. Bdwy debut 1970 in "Sheep on the Runway," OB in "Dylan," "The Screens," "Payment as Pledged," "Richard III."

GARRETT, BOB. Born Mar. 2, 1947 in NYC. Graduate Adelphi U. Debut OB 1971 in "Godspell," Bdwy in "Grease."

GARRETT, KELLY. Born Mar. 25, 1948 in Chester, Pa. Attended Cincinnati Cons. Bdwy debut 1972 in "Mother Earth" for which she received a Theatre World Award, followed by "Words and Music," "The Night That Made America Famous."

GASSELL, SYLVIA. Born July 1, 1923 in NYC. Attended Hunter Col. Bdwy debut 1952 in "The Time of the Cuckoo," followed by "Sunday Breakfast," "Fair Game for Lovers," "Inquest," OB in "U.S.A.," "Romeo and Juliet," "Electra," "A Darker Flower," "Fragments," "Goa," "God Bless You, Harold Fineberg," "Philosophy in the Boudoir," "Stag Movie," "The Old Ones."

GAUL, PATRICIA. Born Oct. 31 in Philadelphia, Pa. Debut 1972 OB in "And They Put Handcuffs on Flowers," followed by "Rainbow," "In the Boom Boom Room," "Dance with Me."

GAVALA, YULA. Born in 1948 in Komotini, Greece. Debut 1974 OB in "Medea," followed by "Electra."

GAVON, IGORS. Born Nov. 14, 1937 in Latvia. Bdwy bow 1961 in "Carnival," followed by "Hello, Dolly," "Marat/deSade," "Billy," "Sugar," "Mack and Mabel," OB in "Your Own Thing," "Promenade," "Exchange," "Nevertheless They Laugh," "Polly."

| **Steven Gelfer** | **Kathy K. Gerber** | **Kenneth Gilman** | **Mary-Pat Green** | **Sean G. Grif** |

GAZZARA, BEN. Born Aug. 28, 1930 in NYC. Attended CCNY. Bdwy debut 1953 in "End as a Man" for which he received a Theatre World Award, followed by "Cat on a Hot Tin Roof," "Hatful of Rain," "Night Circus," "Strange Interlude," "Traveller without Luggage," "Hughie," "Duet."

GELFER, STEVEN. Born Feb. 21, 1949 in Brooklyn, NY. Graduate NYU, Ind. U. Debut 1968 OB in "West Side Story," followed by "Beggar's Opera," "Do I Hear a Waltz?," Bdwy 1974 in "Gypsy."

GEMIGNANI, RHODA. Born Oct. 21, 1940 in San Francisco, Cal. Graduate SF State Col. Bdwy debut 1968 in "Cabaret," OB in "In the Voodoo Parlour of Marie Leveau," "Mert and Phil."

GENISE, LIVIA. Born Oct. 15, 1949 in Brooklyn. Attended UIll. Bdwy debut 1972 in "Via Galactica," OB in "White Nights," "New Girl in Town."

GENNARO, MICHAEL. Born Sept. 20, 1950 in NYC. Graduate UNotre Dame, Neighborhood Playhouse. Debut 1975 OB in "The Three Musketeers," followed by "Godspell."

GERARD, LINDA. Born Dec. 24, 1938 in Trenton, NJ. Attended Finch Col., AmThWing. Bdwy debut 1965 in "Funny Girl," OB in "Look Me Up," "The Magic of Jolson."

GERBER, KATHY K. Born July 18, 1946 in Baltimore, Md. Attended UMd., AADA. Debut 1975 OB in "The Zykovs."

GIBBS, SHEILA. Born Feb. 16, 1947 in NYC. Graduate NYU. Bdwy debut 1971 in "Two Gentlemen of Verona," OB in "Last Days of British Honduras."

GIBSON, JUDY. Born Sept. 11, 1947 in Trenton, NJ. Graduate Rider Col. Bdwy debut 1970 in "Purlie," followed by "Seesaw," "Rachel Lily Rosenbloom," OB in "Sensations," "Manhattan Arrangement," "Two if by Sea," "Let My People Come."

GIERASCH, STEFAN. Born Feb. 5, 1926 in NYC. On Bdwy in "Kiss and Tell," "Snafu," "Billion Dollar Baby," "Montserrat," "Night Music," "Hatful of Rain," "Compulsion," "Shadow of a Gunman," "War and Peace" (APA). "Of Mice and Men," OB in "7 Days of Mourning," "AC/DC," "Owners," "Nellie Toole & Co.," "The Iceman Cometh."

GILBERT, LOU. Born Aug. 1, 1909 in Sycamore, Ill. Bdwy debut 1945 in "Common Ground," followed by "Beggars Are Coming to Town," "Truckline Cafe," "Dream Girl," "The Whole World Over," "Volpone," "Hope Is a Thing with Feathers," "Sundown Beach," "Detective Story," "Enemy of the People," "Anna Christie," "The Victim," "Whistler's Grandmother," "His and Hers," "Abie's Irish Rose," "Highway Robbery," "Streetcar Named Desire," "Good as Gold," "Diary of Anne Frank," "The Egg," "In the Counting House," "Great White Hope," "Creation of the World and Other Business," "Much Ado about Nothing," OB in "A Month in the Country," "Big Man," "Dynamite Tonight," "Good Woman of Setzuan," "The Three Sisters," "The Tempest," "King Lear," "Baba Goya," "As You Like It," "Nourish the Beast," "The Old Ones."

GILCHRIST, REBECCA. Born June 10, 1948 in Parkersburg, WVa. Graduate WVa. U. Debut OB 1972 in "The Proposition," Bdwy debut 1974 in "Grease."

GILMAN, KENNETH. Born Nov. 18, 1946 in Revere, Mass. Graduate Bowling Green State U. Debut 1974 OB in "The Wager," followed by "Lotta," "Weigh In—Weigh Out."

GILMAN, LARRY. Born Apr. 3, 1950 in NYC. Graduate Franklin & Marshall Col. Debut OB 1973 in "Tubstrip," Bdwy bow 1975 in "The Ritz."

GLENN-SMITH, MICHAEL. Born July 2, 1945 in Abilene, Tex. Attended NTex. State U. Bdwy debut 1969 in "Celebration," followed OB by "The Fantasticks," "Once I Saw a Boy Laughing," "Celebration," "Philemon."

GOLDSTEIN, ALLAN. Born Mar. 19, 1949 in Brooklyn, NY. Graduate UDenver, UCopenhagen; Debut 1973 OB in "Moon," followed by "Trial by Jury," "Offending the Audience," "Battle of Angels."

GOLONKA, ARLENE. Born Jan. 23, 1938 in Chicago, Ill. Attended Goodman Theatre, Actors Studio. Bdwy debut 1958 in "Night Circus," followed by "Take Me Along," "Come Blow Your Horn," "Ready When You Are, C. B.," "One Flew over the Cuckoo's Nest," OB in "Ladies of the Alamo."

GOODFRIEND, LYNDA. Born Oct. 31, 1950 in Miami, Fla. Graduate Southern Methodist U. OBdwy debut 1973 in "No Strings," followed by "Dancing Picture Show," Bdwy 1974 in "Good News."

GOODMAN, ROBYN. Born Aug. 24, 1947 in NYC. Graduate Brandeis U. Debut OB 1973 in "When You Comin' Back, Red Ryder?", followed by "Richard III."

GOODWIN, MICHAEL. Born in Virginia, Minn. Bdwy debut 1969 in "A Patriot for Me," followed by "Charley's Aunt," "The Ambassador," "Cyrano," OB in "Colette," "Hamlet," "What Every Woman Knows."

GORBEA, CARLOS. Born July 3, 1938 in Santurce, PR. Graduate Fordham U. Bdwy debut 1964 in "West Side Story," followed by "Fiddler on the Roof, "Cabaret," "Candide," OB in "Time of Storm," "Theatre in the Street."

GORDON, CARL. Born Jan. 20, 1932 in Richmond, Va. Bdwy bow 1966 i "Great White Hope," followed by "Ain't Supposed to Die a Natural Death," OB in "Day of Absence," "Happy Ending," "Strong Breed," "Trials of Brothe Jero," "Kongi's Harvest," "Welcome to Black River," "Shark," "Orrin an Sugar Mouth."

GORDON, MARK. Born in NYC; Attended AmThWing. OB in "Desire unde the Elms," "Man Who Never Died," "The Iceman Cometh," "Deep Are th Roots," "Caretaker," "Third Ear," "Conerico Was Here to Stay," Bdwy i "Moon Beseiged," "Compulsion," "The Devils," "Of Mice and Men."

GORDON, PEGGY. Born Dec. 26, 1949 in NYC. Attended Carnegie Tech Debut OB 1971 in "Godspell."

GORDON, RUTH. Born Oct. 30, 1896 in Wollaston, Mass. Attended AADA Bdwy debut 1915 in "Peter Pan," followed by "Seventeen," "Clarence," "Satu day's Children," "Serena Blandish," "Hotel Universe," "Church Mouse, "Three Cornered Moon," "Ethan Frome," "Country Wife," "Doll's House, "Three Sisters," "Over 21," "Leading Lady," "Smile of the World," "Match maker," "Good Soup," "My Mother, My Father and Me," "A Very Ric Woman," "Loves of Cass McGuire," "Dreyfus in Rehearsal."

GRACIE, SALLY. Born in Little Rock, Ark. Attended Neighborhood Play house. Bdwy debut 1942 in "Vickie," followed by "At War with the Army, "Dinosaur Wharf," "Goodbye Again," "Major Barbara," "Fair Game," "Bu Seriously," OB in "Naomi Court."

GRAINGER, GAWN. Born Oct. 12, 1940 in Holywood, Ire. Bdwy debut 196 with Bristol Old Vic in "Romeo and Juliet," "Measure for Measure," an "Hamlet," followed by "There's a Girl in My Soup," "The Misanthrope."

GRANDY, FRED. Born June 29, 1948 in Sioux City, Io. Harvard graduate Debut OB 1971 in "The Proposition," followed by "Green Julia," "The Bo Who Came to Leave," "Pretzels," "Boom Boom Room."

GRANGER, MICHAEL. Born May 14, 1923 in Kansas City, Mo. Debut 196 OB in "A Man's a Man," followed by "Joan of Lorraine," "Danton's Death, "The Alchemist," "Eastwind," "Caucasian Chalk Circle," "Country Wife," "A Doll's House."

GREEN, MARY-PAT. Born Sept. 24, 1951 in Kansas City, Mo. Attende UKan. Bdwy debut 1974 in "Candide."

GREENE, ELLEN. Born Feb. 22 in NYC. Attended Ryder Col. Debut 197 in "Rachel Lily Rosenbloom," followed by "In the Boom Boom Room."

GREENE, REUBEN. Born Nov. 24, 1938 in Philadelphia, Pa. With APA i "War and Peace," "You Can't Take It with You," and "Pantagleize," OB i "Jerico-Jim Crow," "Happy Ending," "Boys in the Band."

GREENE, RICHARD. Born Jan. 8, 1946 in Miami, Fla. Graduate Fla. Atlan tic U. Debut 1971 with LCRep in "Macbeth," followed by "Play Strindberg, "Mary Stuart," "Narrow Road to the Deep North," "Twelfth Night," "Th Crucible," "The Zykovs."

GREGORY, WILL. Born Nov. 18, 1928 in Glasgow, Scot. Attended Wester Reserve U., Cleveland Play House. OB in "Orpheus Descending," "Summe and Smoke," "Streetcar Named Desire," "Eclipse Day," "Psalm for Fat Tues days," "Give My Regards to Broadway," Bdwy in "Cactus Flower," "A Warn Body," "Front Page."

GREY, JOEL. Born Apr. 11, 1932 in Cleveland, O. Attended Cleveland Neighborhood Playhouses. OB 1956 in "The Littlest Revue," followed b "Harry, Noon and Night," Bdwy debut 1951 in "Borscht Capades," subse quently in "Come Blow Your Horn," "Stop the World—I Want to Get Off, "Half a Sixpence," "Cabaret," "George M!," "Goodtime Charley."

GRIFFIN, SEAN G. Born Oct. 14, 1942 in Limerick, Ire. Graduate Notr Dame, UKan. Bdwy debut 1974 in "The National Health."

GRIFFITH, DONALD M. Born Feb. 2, 1947 in Chicago, Ill. Graduate Loyo U. Debut OB 1971 in "Contributions," followed by "The Me Nobody Knows, "Clara's Ol' Man," LCR's "Merchant of Venice," and "A Streetcar Name Desire," "A Matter of Time."

GRODIN, CHARLES. Born Apr. 21, 1935 in Pittsburgh, Pa. Attende UMiami, Pittsburgh Playhouse. Bdwy debut 1962 in "Tchin-Tchin," followe by "Absence of a Cello," "Same Time, Next Year," OB in "Hooray! It' Glorious Day," "Steambath."

GROH, DAVID. Born May 21, 1939 in NYC. Graduate Brown U., LAMD. Debut OB 1963 in "The Importance of Being Earnest," followed by "Elizabe the Queen" (CC), "The Hot l Baltimore."

Joan Hackett   **Stanley Grover**   **Mary Hamill**   **Gary Harger**   **Delphi Harrington**

GROVER, EDWARD. Born Oct. 23, 1932 in Los Angeles, Ca. Graduate UToledo, UTex. Bdwy bow 1965 in "Postmark Zero," OB in "Ivanov," "Trip to Bountiful," "Six Characters in Search of an Author," "Misalliance," "The Alchemist," "Little Black Sheep."

GROVER, STANLEY. Born Mar. 28, 1926 in Woodstock, Ill. Attended UMo. Appeared in "Seventeen," "Wish You Were Here," "Time Remember'd," "Candide," "13 Daughters," "Mr. President," CC's "South Pacific," "Finian's Rainbow," and "King and I," "Lyle" (OB), "Company," "Desert Song," "Don't Call Back."

GUEST, CHRISTOPHER. Born Feb. 5, 1948 in NYC. Attended Bard Col., NYU. Bdwy bow 1970 in "Room Service," followed by "Moonchildren," OB in "Little Murders," "National Lampoon's Lemmings," "East, Lynne."

GUITTARD, LAURENCE. Born July 16, 1939 in San Francisco, Cal. Graduate Stanford U. Bdwy debut 1965 in "Baker Street," followed by "Anya," "Man of La Mancha," "A Little Night Music" for which he received a Theatre World Award, "Rodgers and Hart."

GUNN, MOSES. Born Oct. 2, 1929 in St. Louis, Mo. Graduate Tenn. AIU, UKan. OB in "Measure for Measure," "Bohikee Creek," "Day of Absence," "Happy Ending," "Baal," "Hard Travelin'," "Lonesome Train," "In White America," "The Blacks," "Titus Andronicus," "Song of the Lusitanian Bogey," "Summer of the 17th Doll," "Kongi's Harvest," "Daddy Goodness," "Cities in Bezique," "Perfect Party," "To Be Young, Gifted and Black," "Sty of the Blind Pig," "Twelfth Night," Bdwy in "A Hand Is on the Gate," "Othello," "First Breeze of Summer."

GUNTON, BOB. Born Nov. 15, 1945 in Santa Monica, Ca. Attended UCal. Debut 1971 OB in "Who Am I?," followed by "The Kid," "Desperate Hours."

GWILLIM, JACK. Born Dec. 15, 1915 in Canterbury, Eng. Attended Central Sch. of Speech. Bdwy debut 1956 with Old Vic in "Macbeth," "Romeo and Juliet," "Richard II," "Troilus and Cressida," followed by "Laurette," "Ari," "Lost in the Stars," "The Iceman Cometh," "The Constant Wife."

GWYNNE, FRED. Born July 10, 1926 in NYC. Harvard graduate. Bdwy debut 1952 in "Mrs. McThing," followed by "Love's Labour's Lost," "Frogs of Spring," "Irma La Douce," "Here's Love," "The Lincoln Mask," "More Than You Deserve" (OB), "Cat on a Hot Tin Roof."

HACKETT, JOAN. Born Mar. 1 in NYC. Attended Actors Studio. OB debut 1959 in "A Clearing in the Woods," followed by "Call Me by My Rightful Name" for which she received a Theatre World Award, Bdwy bow 1959 in "Much Ado about Nothing," subsequently "Peterpat," "Park," "Night Watch."

HAGERTY, MICHAEL. Born Sept. 2, 1951 in Cincinnati, O. Graduate Carnegie-Mellon U. Debut 1975 OB in "Dubliners."

HALL, ALBERT. Born Nov. 10, 1937 in Boothton, Ala. Columbia graduate. Debut 1971 OB in "Basic Training of Pavlo Hummel," followed by "Duplex" (LC), "Wedding Band," "Are You Now or Have You Ever Been," "As You Like It," "Miss Julie," "Black Picture Show," "Yankees 3, Detroit 0," Bdwy in "Ain't Supposed to Die a Natural Death," "We Interrupt This Program."

HALL, GEORGE. Born Nov. 19, 1916 in Toronto, Can. Attended Neighborhood Playhouse. Bdwy bow 1946 in "Call Me Mister," followed by "Lend an Ear," "Touch and Go," "Live Wire," "Boy Friend," "There's a Girl in My Soup," "An Evening with Richard Nixon . . .," "We Interrupt This Program," OB in "The Balcony," "Ernest in Love," "A Round with Ring," "Family Pieces," "Carousel," "Case against Roberta Guardino," "Marry Me! Marry Me!," "Arms and the Man."

HALLIDAY, GORDON. Born Apr. 2, 1952 in Providence, RI. Attended RI Col., AADA. Bdwy Debut 1975 in "Shenandoah."

HALLOW, JOHN. Born Nov. 28, 1942 in NYC. Attended Neighborhood Playhouse. Bdwy bow 1954 in "Anastasia," followed by "Ross," "Visit to a Small Planet," "Foxy," "Oh, Dad, Poor Dad . . .," "Ben Franklin in Paris," "3 Bags Full," "Don't Drink the Water," "Hadrian VII," "Tough to Get Help," "Do I hear a Waltz?" (OB).

HAMILL, MARY. Born Dec. 29, 1943 in Flushing, NY. Graduate UDallas. Debut OB 1969 in "Spiro Who?," followed by "What the Butler Saw," "Siamese Connections," "The Boy Who Came To Leave," "A Difficult Borning," Bdwy in "4 on a Garden," "P.S. Your Cat Is Dead."

HAMILTON, MARGARET. Born Dec. 9, 1902 in Cleveland, O. Attended Cleveland Playhouse. Bdwy debut 1932 in "Another Language," followed by "Dark Tower," "Farmer Takes a Wife," "Outrageous Fortune," "The Men We Marry," "Fancy Meeting You Again," CC's "Annie Get Your Gun," "Goldilocks," "UTBU," LC's "Show Boat" and "Oklahoma," "Come Summer," "Our Town."

HAMILTON, ROGER. Born in San Diego, Cal., May 2, 1928. Attended San Diego Col., RADA. OB in "Merchant of Venice," "Hamlet," "Live Like Pigs," "Hotel Passionato," "Sjt. Musgrave's Dance," Bdwy in "Someone Waiting," "Separate Tables," "Little Moon of Alban," "Luther," "The Deputy," "Rosencrantz and Guildenstern Are Dead," "The Rothschilds," "Pippin."

HANLEY, KATIE. Born Jan. 17, 1949 in Evanston, Ill. Attended Carnegie-Mellon U. Debut 1971 OB in "Godspell," followed by "Grease."

HANSON, IAN. Born June 15, 1947 in Manchester, Eng. Attended Guildhall School of Music and Drama. Bdwy debut 1974 in "As You Like It."

HARE, WILL. Born Mar. 30, 1919 in Elkins, WVa. Attended Am. Actors Theatre. Credits: "The Eternal Road," "The Moon Is Down," "Suds in Your Eye," "Only the Heart," "The Visitor," "Trip to Bountiful," "Witness for the Prosecution," "Marathon '33," OB in "The Viewing," "Winter Journey," "Dylan," "Older People," "Crystal and Fox," "Long Day's Journey into Night," "Boom Boom Room," "Old Times," "Dream of a Blacklisted Actor."

HAREWOOD, DORIAN. Born Aug. 6, in Dayton, O. Attended UCincinnati Conservatory. Bdwy debut 1972 in "Two Gentlemen of Verona," followed by "Over Here," "Don't Call Back" for which he received a Theatre World Award.

HARGER, GARY. Born Aug. 19, 1951 in New Haven, Conn. Ithaca Col. graduate. Bdwy debut 1975 in "Shenandoah."

HARPER, CHARLES THOMAS. Born Mar. 29, 1949 in Carthage, NY. Graduate Webster Col. Debut 1975 OB in "Down by the River Where Waterlilies Are Disfigured Every Day."

HARRINGTON, DELPHI. Born Aug. 26 in Chicago, Ill. Graduate Northwestern U. Debut 1960 OB in "Country Scandal," followed by "Moon for the Misbegotten," "Baker's Dozen," "The Zykovs," Bdwy in "Thieves," "Everything in the Garden."

HARRIS, BAXTER. Born Nov. 18, 1940 in Columbus, Kan. Attended UKan. Debut 1967 OB in "America Hurrah!," followed by "The Reckoning," "Wicked Women Revue," "More Than You Deserve," "Pericles," "him," "Battle of Angels," "Down by the River. . . ."

HARRIS, CYNTHIA. Born in NYC. Graduate Smith Col. Bdwy debut 1963 in "Natural Affection," followed by "Any Wednesday," "Best Laid Plans," "Company," OB in "The Premise," "Three by Wilder," "America Hurrah," "White House Murder Case," "Mystery Play," "Bad Habits," "Merry Wives of Windsor," "Beauty Part."

HARRIS, JULIE. Born Dec. 2, 1925 in Grosse Point, Mich. Attended Yale. Bdwy debut 1945 in "It's a Gift," followed by "Henry V," "Oedipus," "The Playboy of the Western World," "Alice in Wonderland," "Macbeth," "Sundown Beach" for which she received a Theatre World Award, "The Young and The Fair," "Magnolia Alley," "Montserrat," "The Member of the Wedding," "I Am a Camera," "Mlle. Colombe," "The Lark," "Country Wife," "Warm Peninsula," "Little Moon of Alban," "A Shot in the Dark," "Marathon '33," "Ready When You Are, C. B.," "Hamlet" (CP), "Skyscraper," "40 Carats," "And Miss Reardon Drinks A Little," "Voices," "The Last of Mrs. Lincoln," "The Au Pair Man" (LC), "In Praise of Love."

HARRISON, REX. Born Mar. 5, 1908 in Huyten, Eng. Attended Liverpool Col. Bdwy debut 1936 in "Sweet Aloes," followed by "Anne of a Thousand Days," "Bell, Book and Candle," "Venus Observed," "The Love of Four Colonels," "My Fair Lady," "Fighting Cock," "Emperor Henry IV," "In Praise of Love."

HARVEY, KENNETH. Born Dec. 25, 1918 in Montreal, Can. Bdwy debut 1951 in "Top Banana," followed by "John Murray Anderson's Almanac," "Grand Prize," "Pipe Dream," OB in "Phoenix '55," "Augusta."

HASTON, GERALD. Born May 30, 1947 in Bryn Mawr, Pa. Attended UCLA. Bdwy debut 1972 in "Ambassador," followed by "New Girl in Town" (OB).

HAWKINS, TRISH. Born Oct. 30, 1945 in Hartford, Conn. Attended Radcliffe, Neighborhood Playhouse. Debut OB 1970 in "Oh! Calcutta!" followed by "Iphigenia," "The Hot l Baltimore" for which she received a Theatre World Award, "him," "Come Back, Little Sheba," "Battle of Angels," "Mound Builders."

HAWTHORNE, NIGEL. Born Apr. 5, 1929 in Coventry, Eng. Bdwy debut 1974 in "As You Like It."

HAYES, EVERY. Born Sept. 1, 1949 in Montclair, NJ. OB in "Step Lively, Boys," "Croecus and the Witch," "The Flies," "Ups and Downs of Theophilus Maitland," Bdwy in "Purlie," "Don't Bother Me, I Can't Cope," "All Over Town."

Tiger Haynes

Brenda Holmes

Dan Held

Cheryl Horne

Nicholas Hormann

HAYLE, DOUGLAS. Born Jan. 11, 1942 in Trenton, NJ. Graduate AADA. OB in "Henry IV," "Romeo and Juliet," "King Lear," "A Cry of Players," "In the Matter of J. Robert Oppenheimer," "The Miser," "Trelawny of the Wells," "Oh, Lady! Lady!," "Desperate Hours."

HAYNES, TIGER. Born Dec. 13, 1907 in St. Croix, VI. Bdwy bow 1956 in "New Faces," followed by "Finian's Rainbow," "Fade Out—Fade In," "The Pajama Game," "The Wiz."

HEARN, GEORGE. Born June 18, 1934 in St. Louis, Mo. Southwestern Col. graduate. In NYSF's "Macbeth," "Antony and Cleopatra," "As You Like It," "Richard III," "Merry Wives of Windsor," "Midsummer Night's Dream," OB in "Horseman, Pass By," Bdwy in "A Time for Singing," "Changing Room."

HECKART, EILEEN. Born Mar. 29, 1919 in Columbus, O. Graduate Ohio State U. Debut OB in "Tinker's Dam," followed by Bdwy in "Our Town," "They knew What They Wanted," "The Traitor," "Hilda Crane," "In Any Language," "Picnic" for which she received a Theatre World Award, "Bad Seed," "View from the Bridge," "Dark at the Top of the Stairs," "Invitation to a March," "Pal Joey," "Everybody Loves Opal," "And Things That Go Bump in the Night," "Barefoot in the Park," "You Know I Can't Hear You When the Water's Running," "Mother Lover," "Butterflies Are Free," "Veronica's Room."

HEFFERNAN, JOHN. Born May 30, 1934 in NYC. Attended CCNY, Columbia, Boston U. OB in "The Judge," "Julius Caesar," "Great God Brown," "Lysistrata," "Peer Gynt," "Henry IV," "Taming of the Shrew," "She Stoops to Conquer," "The Plough and the Stars," "Octoroon," "Hamlet," "Androcles and the Lion," "A Man's a Man," "Winter's Tale," "Arms and the Man," "St. Joan" (LCR), "Peer Gynt"(CP), "Memorandum," "Invitation to a Beheading," "Shadow of a Gunman," "The Sea," Bdwy in "Luther," "Tiny Alice," "Postmark Zero," "Woman Is My Idea," "Morning, Noon and Night," "Purlie," "Bad Habits."

HELD, DAN. Born May 20, 1948 in NYC. Graduate Hofstra U. Debut 1973 OB in "You Never Know," followed by "El Grande de Coca Cola," "Wings."

HELFEND, DENNIS. Born Mar. 15, 1939 in Los Angeles. Attended UCLA. Debut 1968 OB in "The Mad Show," followed by "American Gothics," "The Inn at Lydda," Bdwy in "Man in the Glass Booth."

HENNING, DOUG. Born May 3, 1947 in Winnipeg, Can. Graduate McMaster U. Bdwy debut 1974 in "The Magic Show."

HENRITZE, BETTE. Born May 3 in Betsy Layne, Ky. Graduate U. Tenn. OB in "Lion in Love," "Abe Lincoln in Illinois," "Othello," "Baal," "Long Christmas Dinner," "Queens of France," "Rimers of Eldritch," "Displaced Person," "Acquisition," "Crime of Passion," "Happiness Cage," NYSF's "Henry VI," "Richard III," "Older People," "Lotta," Bdwy debut 1948 in "Jenny Kissed Me," followed by "Pictures in the Hallway," "Giants, Sons of Giants," "Ballad of the Sad Cafe," "The White House," "Dr. Cook's Garden," "Here's Where I Belong," "Much Ado about Nothing," "Over Here."

HERMAN, CYNTHIA. Born July 23, 1947 in Peoria, Ill. Graduate Juilliard. Bdwy debut 1974 in "Three Sisters," followed by "Beggar's Opera," "Measure for Measure," "Scapin."

HERRMANN, EDWARD. Born July 21, 1943 in Washington, DC. Graduate Bucknell U., LAMDA. Debut 1970 OB in "Basic Training of Pavlo Hummel," followed by NYSF's "Midsummer Night's Dream," Bdwy 1972 in "Moonchildren."

HESTON, CHARLTON. Born Oct. 4, 1922 in Evanston, Ill. Graduate Northwestern U. Bdwy bow 1947 in "Antony and Cleopatra," followed by "Leaf and Bough," "Design for a Stained Glass Window" for which he received a Theatre World Award, "Mister Roberts" (CC), "The Tumbler."

HIGGINS, JOEL. Born Sept. 28, 1943 in Bloomington, Ill. Graduate Mich. State U. Bdwy debut 1975 in "Shenandoah" for which he received a Theatre World Award.

HIGGINS, MICHAEL. Born Jan. 20, in Bklyn. Attended Theatre Wing. Bdwy bow 1946 in "Antigone," followed by "Our Lan'," "Romeo and Juliet," "The Crucible," "The Lark," "Equus," OB in "White Devil," "Carefree Tree," "Easter," "The Queen and the Rebels," "Sally, George and Martha," "L'Ete," "Uncle Vanya," "The Iceman Cometh."

HINCKLEY, ALFRED. Born Sept. 22, 1920 in Kalamazoo, Mich. Graduate NYU. Bdwy bow 1959 in "Legend of Lizzie," followed by "Subways Are for Sleeping," "Man for All Seasons," "Impossible Years," "More Stately Mansions," "That Championship Season," OB in "A Clearing in the Woods," "Long Voyage Home," "Diff'rent," "Rimers of Eldritch," "People vs Ranchman," "Steambath," "Harry Outside."

HINES, PATRICK. Born Mar. 17, 1930 in Burkesville, Tex. Graduate Tex. U. Debut OB in "Duchess of Malfi," followed by "Lysistrata," "Peer Gynt," "Henry IV," "Richard III," Bdwy bow 1959 in "Great God Brown," subsequently "Passage to India," "The Devils," "Cyrano," "The Iceman Cometh."

HIRSON, ALICE. Born Mar. 10, 1929 in NYC. Attended AADA. Bdwy debut 1964 in "Traveller without Luggage," followed by "The Investigation," OB in "All Is Bright," "Breadwinner."

HITT, ROBERT. Born Sept. 11, 1942 in Washington, DC. Graduate ULouisville, Yale. Debut 1975 OB in "The Zykovs."

HOFF, ROBIN. Born Jan. 4, 1952 in Washington, DC. Studied at Harkness House. Debut OB 1974 in "Carousel," followed by "Fiddler on the Roof" (JB).

HOFFMAN, JANE. Born July 24 in Seattle, Wash. Attended UCal. Bdwy debut 1940 in " 'Tis of Thee," followed by "Crazy with the Heat," "Something for the Boys," "One Touch of Venus," "Calico Wedding," "Mermaids Singing," "Temporary Island," "Story for Strangers," "Two Blind Mice," "The Rose Tattoo," "The Crucible," "Witness for the Prosecution," "Third Best Sport," "Rhinoceros," "Mother Courage and Her Children," "Fair Game for Lovers," "A Murderer among Us," OB in "American Dream," "Sandbox," "Picnic on the Battlefield," "Theatre of the Absurd," "Child Buyer," "A Corner of the Bed," "Someone's Comin' Hungry," "Increased Difficulty of Concentration," "American Hamburger League," "Slow Memories," "Last Analysis," "Dear Oscar," "Hocus-Pocus."

HOGAN, JONATHAN. Born June 13, 1951 in Chicago, Ill. Graduate Goodman Theatre. Debut OB 1972 in "The Hot l Baltimore," followed by "Mound Builders," "Harry Outside."

HOLDEN, HAL. Born Aug. 25, 1938 in Brookhaven, Miss. Graduate Northwestern U. Debut OB 1969 in "Of Thee I Sing," followed by "Masks."

HOLGATE, RONALD. Born May 26, 1937 in Aberdeen, SD. Attended Northwestern U., New Eng. Cons. Debut 1961 OB in "Hobo," followed by "Hooray, It's a Glorious Day," Bdwy in "A Funny Thing Happened on the Way to the Forum," "Milk and Honey," "1776," "Saturday Sunday Monday."

HOLLAND, ANTHONY. Born Oct. 17, 1933 in Brooklyn, NY. Graduate UChicago. OB in "Venice Preserved," "Second City," "Victim of Duty," "New Tenant," "Dynamite Tonight," "Quare Fellow," "White House Murder Case," "Waiting for Godot," on Bdwy in "My Mother, My Father and Me," "We Bombed in New Haven," "Dreyfus in Rehearsal."

HOLLIDAY, POLLY. Born in Jasper, Ala. Attended Ala. Col., Fla. State U. Debut 1964 OB in "Orphee," followed by "Dinner on the Ground," "Wedding Band," "Girls Most Likely to Succeed," "Carnival Dreams," Bdwy bow 1974 in "All over Town."

HOLLY, ELLEN. Born Jan. 17, 1931 in NYC. Graduate Hunter Col. Debut OB 1955 in "2 for Fun," followed by "Salome," "A Florentine Tragedy," "Tevya and His Daughters," "Othello," "Moon on a Rainbow Shawl," "Antony and Cleopatra," "Funny House of a Negro," "Midsummer Night's Dream," "Cherry Orchard," Bdwy in "Too Late the Phalarope," "Face of a Hero," "Tiger, Tiger Burning Bright," NYSF's "Henry V," and "Taming of the Shrew," "A Hand Is on the Gate," "King Lear."

HOLLY, JOHN. Born May 6, 1944 in St. Louis, Mo. Graduate Ariz. State U. Bdwy debut 1973 in "Grease," OB in "Call Me Madam."

HOLMES, BRENDA. Born Mar. 19, 1954 in Jamestown, NY. With Harkness Ballet before Bdwy debut 1974 in "Lorelei."

HOLMES, PRUDENCE WRIGHT. Born in Boston, Mass. Attended Carnegie Tech. Debut 1971 OB in "Godspell," followed by "Polly."

HOPKINS, ANTHONY. Born Dec. 31, 1937 in Port Talbot, South Wales. Attended Cardiff Col. of Music and Drama, RADA. Bdwy debut 1974 in "Equus."

HORNE, CHERYL. Born Nov. 15 in Stamford, Conn. Graduate SMU. Debut 1975 OB in "The Fantasticks."

HORMANN, NICHOLAS. Born Dec. 22, 1944 in Honolulu, Ha. Graduate Oberlin, Yale. Bdwy debut 1973 in "The Visit," followed by "Chemin de Fer," "Holiday," "Love for Love," "Rules of the Game," "Member of the Wedding."

HORNE, LENA. Born June 30, 1917 in Brooklyn, NY. Bdwy debut 1934 in "Dance with Your Gods," followed by "Jamaica," "Tony Bennett and Lena Horne Sing."

HOUSE, RON. Born in Chicago. Attended Wilson Col., Roosevelt U. Debut OB 1973 in "El Grande de Coca Cola," followed by "Bullshot Crummond."

HOWARD, KEN. Born Mar. 28, 1944 in El Centro, Cal. Yale graduate. Bdwy debut 1968 in "Promises, Promises," followed by "1776" for which he received a Theatre World Award, "Child's Play," "Seesaw," "Little Black Sheep" (LC).

Linda Hunt   **James Hummert**   **Lisa Jacobson**   **Page Johnson**   **Ruth Jaroslow**

HOWELL, ERIK. Born in Dothan, Ala. Attended William & Mary Col. Debut 1966 OB in "The Fantasticks," followed by "Who's Who, Baby?"

HUFFMAN, DAVID. Born May 10, 1945 in Berwin, Ill. Bdwy debut 1971 in "Butterflies Are Free," followed by OB's "Small Craft Warnings," "Entertaining Mr. Sloane."

HUGHES, BARNARD. Born July 16, 1915 in Bedford Hills, N.Y. Attended Manhattan Col. OB in "Rosmersholm," "A Doll's House," "Hogan's Goat," "Line," "Older People," "Hamlet" "Merry Wives of Windsor," "Pericles," Bdwy in "The Ivy Green," "Dinosaur Wharf," "Teahouse of the August Moon" (CC), "A Majority of One," "Advise and Consent," "The Advocate," "Hamlet," "I Was Dancing," "Generation," "How Now, Dow Jones?," "Wrong Way Light Bulb," "Sheep On The Runway," "Abelard and Heloise," "Much Ado about Nothing," "Uncle Vanya," "The Good Doctor," "All Over Town."

HUGHES, TRESA. Born Sept. 17, 1929 in Washington, DC. Attended Wayne U. OB in "Electra," "The Crucible," "Hogan's Goat," "Party on Greenwich Avenue," "Fragments," "Passing Through from Exotic Places," "Beggar On Horseback" (LC), "Early Morning," "The Old Ones," Bdwy in "Miracle Worker," "Devil's Advocate," "Dear Me, The Sky Is Falling," "Last Analysis," "Spofford," "Man in the Glass Booth," "Prisoner of Second Avenue."

HULCE, THOMAS. Born Dec. 6, 1953 in Plymouth, Mich. Graduate N.C. School of Arts. Bdwy debut 1975 in "Equus."

HUMMERT, JAMES. Born June 30, 1944 in USA. Graduate UConn. Debut OB 1969 in "Three Cuckolds," followed by "Murder in the Cathedral," "Restoration of Arnold Middleton," "Enter a Free Man," Bdwy in "The Changing Room."

HUNT, LINDA. Born Apr. 2, 1945 in NYC. Attended Goodman Theatre School. Debut OB 1972 in NYSF's "Hamlet," followed by "Down by the River Where the Waterlilies are Disfigured Every Day."

HUNT, W. M. Born Oct. 9 in St. Petersburg, Fla. Graduate UMich. Debut OB 1973 in "The Proposition," followed by "The Glorious Age."

HYMAN, EARLE. Born Oct. 11, 1926 in Rocky Mount, NC. Attended New School, Theatre Wing. Bdwy debut 1943 in "Run, Little Chillun," followed by "Anna Lucasta," "Climate of Eden," "Merchant of Venice," "Othello," "Julius Caesar," "The Tempest," "No Time for Sergeants," "Mr. Johnson" for which he received a Theatre World Award, "St. Joan," "Hamlet," "Waiting for Godot," "Duchess of Malfi," "Les Blancs," OB in "The White Rose and the Red," "Worlds of Shakespeare," "Jonah," "Life and Times of J. Walter Smintheus," "Orrin," "Cherry Orchard," "House Party," "Carnival Dreams."

HYMAN, ELAINE. Born in Detroit, Mich. Graduate Columbia U. Bdwy debut 1962 in "General Seeger," followed by "Say Darling," OB in "Javelin," "Night of the Dunce," "What the Butler Saw," "Children, Children," "Big Fish, Little Fish."

IACANGELO, PETER. Born Aug. 13, 1948 in Brooklyn, NY. Attended Hofstra U. Bdwy debut 1968 in "Jimmy Shine," OB in "One Flew over the Cuckoo's Nest," "Moonchildren."

IMPERT, MARGARET. Born June 4, 1946 in Elmira, NY. Graduate Rollins Col. Debut OB 1973 in "Girls Most Likely to Succeed," followed by "The Cretan Bull," "Look, We've Come Through," "Rag Doll."

IRVING, GEORGE S. Born Nov. 1, 1922 in Springfield, Mass. Attended Leland Powers Sch. Bdwy bow 1943 in "Oklahoma!," followed by "Call Me Mister," "Along Fifth Avenue," "Two's Company," "Me and Juliet," "Can-Can," "Shinbone Alley," "Bells are Ringing," "The Good Soup," "Tovarich," "A Murderer among Us," "Alfie," "Anya," "Galileo" (LC), "The Happy Time," "Up Eden" (OB), "4 on a Garden," "An Evening with Richard Nixon and . . ." "Irene," "Who's Who in Hell," "All over Town."

JACKSON, ERNESTINE. Born Sept. 18 in Corpus Christi, Tex. Graduate Del Mar Col., Juilliard. Debut 1966 in LC's "Show Boat," followed by "Finian's Rainbow" (CC), "Hello, Dolly!," "Applause," "Jesus Christ Superstar," "Tricks," "Raisin" for which she received a Theatre World Award.

JACKSON, LEONARD. Born Feb. 7, 1928 in Jacksonville, Fla. Graduate Fiske U. Debut 1965 OB in "Troilus and Cressida," followed by "Henry V," "Happy Ending," "Day of Absence," "Who's Got His Own?," "Electronic Nigger and Others," "Black Quartet," "Five on the Blackhand Side," "Boesman and Lena," "Murderous Angels," "Chickencoop Chinaman," "Karl Marx Play," "Prodigal Sister," Bdwy in "Great White Hope," "Lost in the Stars."

JACOBSON, LISA. Born Oct. 16 in Yokahama, Japan. Graduate Peabody, Ohio U. Debut OB 1973 in "The Hot l Baltimore."

JAMESON, MICHAEL. Born Nov. 7, 1945 in Wilmington, Del. Graduate UDel., Ind. U. Debut 1975 in "Liberty Call."

JAMROG, JOE. Born Dec. 21, 1932 in Flushing, NY. Graduate CCNY. Debut OB 1970 in "Nobody Hears a Broken Drum," followed by "Tango," "And Whose Little Boy Are You?," "When You Comin' Back, Red Ryder?," "Drums at Yale," "The Boy Friend."

JANSEN, JIM. Born July 27, 1945 in Salt Lake City, U. Graduate UUtah. NYU. Debut OB 1973 in "Moonchildren," Bdwy 1974 in "All over Town."

JARKOWSKY, ANDREW. Born in NYC. Graduate CCNY. Debut OB 1974 in "Festival of Short Plays," followed by "Cakes with Wine."

JAROSLOW, RUTH. Born May 22 in Brooklyn, NY. Attended HB Studio. Debut 1964 OB in "That 5 A.M. Jazz," Followed by "Jonah," Bdwy in "Mame," "Fiddler on the Roof," "The Ritz."

JARRETT, JERRY. Born Sept. 9, 1918 in Brooklyn, NY. Attended New Theatre School. Bdwy debut 1948 in "At War with the Army," followed by "Gentlemen Prefer Blondes," "Stalag 17," "Fiorello," "Fiddler on the Roof," OB in "Waiting for Lefty," "Nat Turner," "Me Candido," "That 5 A.M. Jazz," "Valentine's Day."

JARVIS, GRAHAM. Born Aug. 25, 1930 in Toronto, Can. Attended Williams Col. Bdwy bow 1957 in "Orpheus Descending," followed by "Egghead," "Man in the Dog Suit," "Much Ado about Nothing," "Best Man," "Romulus," "The Investigation," "Halfway Up the Tree," "Rocky Horror Show," OB in "Adaptation," "More Than You Deserve."

JAY, DAVID. Born June 4, 1961 in Worcester, Mass. Debut 1971 OB in "Waiting for Godot," followed by "Macbeth" "Richard III," Bdwy 1972 in "Lost in the Stars."

JAY, DON. Born in Calif. Bdwy debut 1965 in "The Zulu and the Zayda," followed by "Hello, Dolly!," "Two Gentlemen from Verona," "Raisin."

JENNINGS, HELEN. Born Oct. 28, 1964 in NYC. Bdwy debut 1972 in "Dude," followed by "All God's Chillun Got Wings."

JEROME, TIMOTHY. Born Dec. 29, 1943 in Los Angeles, Ca. Graduate Ithaca Col., Manhattan School of Music. Bdwy debut 1969 in "Man of La Mancha," followed by "The Rothschilds," "Creation of the World and Other Business," OB in "Beggars Opera," "Pretzels."

JOHNS, ANDREW. Born June 10, 1949 in London, Eng. Attended RADA. Bdwy debut 1974 in "As You Like It."

JOHNS, GLYNIS. Born Oct. 5, 1923 in Pretoria, S.Af. Bdwy debut 1952 in "Gertie," followed by "Major Barbara," "Too True to Be Good," "A Little Night Music."

JOHNSON, PAGE. Born Aug. 25, 1930 in Welch, W. Va. Graduate Ithaca Col. Bdwy bow 1951 in "Romeo and Juliet," followed by "Electra," "Oedipus," "Camino Real," "In April Once" for which he received a Theatre World Award, "Red Roses for Me," "The Lovers," "Equus," OB in "The Enchanted," "Guitar," "4 in 1," "Journey of the Fifth Horse," APA's "School for Scandal," "The Tavern" and "The Seagull," "Odd Couple," "Boys In The Band," "Medea."

JOHNSTON, GAIL. Born Aug. 8, 1943 in Far Rockaway, NY. Attended Hofstra Col., Hunter Col. Bdwy Debut 1959 in "Juno," followed by "Tenderloin," "Do Re Mi," OB in "Streets of NY," "Shoemaker's Holiday," "Out of This World" "Things Are Getting Better."

JOHNSTON, JUSTINE. Born June 13 in Evanston, Ill. OB debut 1959 in "Little Mary Sunshine," followed by "The Time of Your Life" (CC), "The Dubliners," Bdwy in "Pajama Game," "Milk and Honey," "Follies," "Irene," "Molly."

JONES, CHARLOTTE. Born Jan. 1, in Chicago. Attended Loyola, DePaul U. OB in "False Confessions," "Sign of Jonah," "Girl on the Via Flaminia," "Red Roses for Me," "Night is Black Bottles," "Camino Real," "Plays for Bleecker St.," "Pigeons," "Great Scot!" "Sjt. Musgrave's Dance," "Papers," "Johnny Johnson," "Beggar's Opera," "200 Years of American Furniture," Bdwy in "Camino Real," "Buttrio Square," "Mame," "How Now Dow Jones."

JONES, JAMES EARL. Born Jan. 17, 1931 in Arkabutla, Miss. Graduate Mich U. OB in "The Pretender," "The Blacks," "Clandestine on the Morning Line," "The Apple," "A Midsummer Night's Dream," "Moon on a Rainbow Shawl" for which he received a Theatre World Award. "PS 193," "Last Minstrel," "Love Nest," "Bloodknot," "Othello," "Baal," "Danton's Death" (LC), "Boesman and Lena," "Hamlet" (NYSF) "Cherry Orchard," Bdwy in "The Egghead," "Sunrise at Campobello," "The Cool World," "A Hand is on the Gate," "Great White Hope," "Les Blancs," "King Lear," "The Iceman Cometh," "Of Mice and Men."

JORDAN, ALAN. Born Mar. 21, 1943 in Toronto, Can. Graduate Neighborhood Playhouse. Debut 1974 OB in "The Proposition," followed by "Battle of Angels."

Dick Joslyn

Dolores Kenan

Alan Kass

Nancy Killmer

Ken Kliban

JORDAN, RICHARD. Born July 19, 1938 in NYC. Attended Harvard U. Bdwy bow 1961 in "Take Her, She's Mine," followed by "Bicycle Ride to Nevada," APA's "War and Peace," and "Judith," "Generation," "A Patriot for Me," OB in "All's Well That Ends Well," "Trial of the Catonsville 9."

JOSLYN, DICK. Born Dec. 24, 1948 in Davenport, Ia. Graduate UMd., LACC. Debut 1974 OB in "Tubstrip."

JULIA, RAUL. Born Mar. 9, 1940 in San Juan, PR. Graduate UPR. OB in "Macbeth" "Titus Andronicus" (CP), "Theatre in the Streets," "Life Is a Dream," "Blood Wedding," "Ox Cart," "No Exit," "Memorandum," "Frank Gagliano's City Scene," "Your Own Thing," "Persians," "Castro Complex," "Pinkville," "Hamlet," "King Lear," "As You Like it," "Emperor of Late Night Radio," Bdwy bow 1968 in "The Cuban Thing," followed by "Indians," "Two Gentlemen of Verona," "Via Galactica," "Where's Charley?"

KAGAN, DIANE. Born in Maplewood, NJ. Graduate Fla. State U. Debut OB 1963 in "Asylum," followed by "Days and Nights of Beebee Fenstermaker," "Death of the Well-Loved Boy," "Madam de Sade," "Blue Boys," "Alive and Well in Argentina," "Little Black Sheep," Bdwy in "Chinese Prime Minister," "Never Too Late," "Any Wednesday," "Venus Is," "Tiger at the Gates" (LC).

KAHAN, JUDY. Born May 24, 1948 in NYC. Graduate Boston U. Debut OB 1971 in "The Proposition," followed by "Godspell," "Pretzels," Bdwy in "A Little Night Music."

KAPRAL, JANET. Born in Brno, Czech. Graduate Marquette U. Debut OB 1970 in "Trelawny of the Wells," followed by "I Love Thee Freely," "Amoureuse."

KARIN, RITA. Born Oct. 24, 1919 in Warsaw, Poland. Bdwy debut 1960 in "The Wall," followed by "A Call on Kuprin," "Penny Wars," OB in "Pocket Watch," "Scuba Duba," "House of Blue Leaves," "Yentl the Yeshiva Boy."

KARNILOVA, MARIA. Born Aug, 3, 1920 in Hartford, Conn. Bdwy debut 1938 in "Stars in Your Eyes," followed by "Call Me Mister," "High Button Shoes," "Two's Company," "Hollywood Pinafore," "Beggar's Opera" (CC), "Kaleidoscope" (OB), "Gypsy," "Miss Liberty," "Out of This World," "Bravo Giovanni," "Fiddler on the Roof," "Zorba," "Gigi," "God's Favorite."

KARP, STEVE. Born Apr. 5, 1943 in Mt. Vernon, NY. Graduate Tufts U., AADA. Debut 1969 OB in Light Opera of Manhattan productions, followed by "The Changing Room" (Bdwy), "Richard III" (OB).

KARR, DENNIS. Born Dec. 12, 1952 in Hartford, Conn. Bdwy debut 1974 in "Gypsy."

KARR, PATTI. Born July 10 in St. Paul, Minn. Attended TCU. Bdwy debut 1953 in "Maggie," followed by "Carnival in Flanders," "Pipe Dream," "Bells Are Ringing," "New Girl in Town," "Body Beautiful," "Bye Bye Birdie," "New Faces of 1962," "Come on Strong," "Look to the Lilies," "Different Times," "Lysistrata," "Seesaw," "Irene," "Pippin," OB in "A Month of Sundays," "Up Eden."

KASS, ALAN. Born Apr. 23, 1928 in Chicago, Ill. Graduate CCNY. Bdwy bow 1968 in "Golden Rainbow," followed by "Sugar," OB in "Guitar," "Be Kind to People Week."

KASZNAR, KURT. Born Aug. 12, 1913 in Vienna, Aus. Studied with Max Reinhardt. Bdwy debut 1936 in "Eternal Road," followed by "The Army Play by Play," "Joy to the World," "Make Way for Lucia," "Montserrat," "Happy Time," "Waiting for Godot," "Seventh Heaven," "Six Characters in Search of an Author" (OB), "Look after Lulu," "Sound of Music," "Barefoot in the Park."

KATZMAN, DREW. Born Apr. 24, 1947 in NYC. Attended Syracuse U., HB Studio. Debut OB 1975 in "Philemon."

KAYE, ANNE. Born Sept. 6, 1942 in New Haven, Conn. Attended Emerson Col., AMDA. Debut OB 1967 in "Now Is the Time for All Good Men," followed by "Have I Got One for You," "Fantasticks," "Mahagonny," "Val, Christie and the Others," Bdwy 1974 in "Good News."

KAYE, STUBBY. Born Nov. 11, 1918 in NYC. Bdwy debut 1950 in "Guys and Dolls," followed by "Li'l Abner," "Everybody Loves Opal," "Good News."

KEAGY, GRACE. Born Dec. 16 in Youngstown, O. Attended New Eng. Cons. Debut 1974 OB in "Call Me Madam," followed by Bdwy bow 1975 in "Goodtime Charley."

KEARNS, MICHAEL. Born Jan. 8 in St. Louis, Mo. Attended AADA, Goodman Theatre. Debut 1974 OB in "Tubstrip."

KEEFE, ADAM. Born Jan. 8, 1931 in the Bronx, NY. Debut 1970 OB in "Nature of the Crime," followed by "Dream of a Blacklisted Actor," "Against the Sun."

KELLER, JEFF. Born Sept. 8, 1947 in Brooklyn. Graduate Monmouth Col. Bdwy debut 1974 in "Candide."

KELLY, NANCY. Born Mar. 25, 1921 in Lowell, Mass. Attended Bentley School. Bdwy debut 1931 in "Give Me Yesterday," followed by "One Good Year," "Susan and God," "Flare Path," "Big Knife," "Season in the Sun," "Twilight Walk," "Bad Seed," "The Genius and the Goddess," "The Rivalry," "A Mighty Man Is He," "Giants, Sons of Giants," "Who's Afraid of Virginia Woolf?," "Quotations from Chairman Mao Tse-Tung."

KENAN, DOLORES. Born June 7 in Bellevue, Ky. Graduate Xavier U., Goodman Theatre. Debut 1974 OB in "The Killdeer," followed by "Wedding Band," "Summer Brave," "Bus Stop."

KERR, DEBORAH. Born Sept. 30, 1921 in Helensburgh, Scot. Attended Phyllis Smale School of Drama. Bdwy debut 1953 in "Tea and Sympathy," followed by "Seascape."

KERR, PHILIP. Born Apr. 9, 1940 in NYC. Attended Harvard U., LAMDA. Bdwy debut 1969 in "Tiny Alice," followed by "A Flea in Her Ear," "Three Sisters," "Hamlet" (OB), "Jockey Club Stakes."

KEYES, DANIEL. Born Mar. 6, 1914 in Concord, Mass. Attended Harvard. Bdwy debut 1954 in "The Remarkable Mr. Pennypacker," followed by "Bus Stop," "Only in America," "Christine," "First Love," "Take Her, She's Mine," "Baker Street," "Dinner at 8," "I Never Sang for My Father," "Wrong Way Light Bulb," "A Place for Polly," "Scratch," "Rainbow Jones," OB in "Our Town," "Epitaph for George Dillon," "Plays for Bleecker Street," "Hooray! It's A Glorious Day!," "Six Characters in Search of an Author," "Sjt. Musgrave's Dance," "Arms and the Man," "Mourning Becomes Electra," "Salty Dog Saga."

KILEY, RICHARD. Born Mar. 31, 1922 in Chicago. Attended Loyola U. Bdwy debut 1953 in "Misalliance" for which he received a Theatre World Award, followed by "Kismet," "Sing Me No Lullaby," "Time Limit!" "Redhead," "Advise and Consent," "No Strings," "Here's Love," "I Had a Ball," "Man of La Mancha" (also LC), "Her First Roman," "The Incomparable Max," "Voices," "Absurd Person Singular."

KILLIAN, PHIL. Born July 30 in Charlotte, NC. Graduate Northwestern U. Debut OB 1972 in "The Fantasticks."

KILLMER, NANCY. Born Dec. 16, 1936 in Homewood, Ill. Graduate Northwestern U. Bdwy debut 1969 in "Coco," followed by "Goodtime Charley."

KIMBROUGH, CHARLES. Born May 23, 1936 in St. Paul, Minn. Graduate Ind. U., Yale, Bdwy bow 1969 in "Cop-Out," followed by "Company," "Love for Love," "Rules of the Game," "Candide," OB in "All in Love," "Struts and Frets," "Troilus and Cressida."

KIMMINS, KENNETH. Born Sept. 4, 1941 in Brooklyn, NY. Graduate Catholic U. Debut 1966 OB in "The Fantasticks," followed by "Adaptation," "All My Sons," Bdwy in "Fig Leaves are Falling," "Gingerbread Lady," "Company," "Status Quo Vadis," "Magic Show."

KINGSLEY, PETER. Born Aug. 14, 1945 in Mexico City, Mex. Graduate Hamilton Col., LAMDA. Debut 1974 OB in "Coco."

KIRK, LISA. Born Sept. 18, 1925 in Brownsville, Pa. Bdwy debut 1945 in "Goodnight, Ladies," followed by "Allegro," "Kiss Me, Kate," "Here's Love," "Mack and Mabel."

KIRSCH, CAROLYN. Born May 24, 1942 in Shreveport, La. Bdwy debut 1963 in "How to Succeed . . .," followed by "Folies Bergere," "La Grosse Valise," "Skyscraper," "Breakfast at Tiffany's," "Sweet Charity," "Hallelujah, Baby!," "Dear World," "Promises, Promises," "Coco," "Ulysses in Nighttown.," "A Chorus Line."

KISER, TERRY. Born Aug. 1, 1939 in Omaha, Neb. Graduate U. Kan. Debut OB 1966 in "Night of the Dunce," followed by "Fortune and Men's Eyes" for which he received a Theatre World Award, "Horseman, Pass By," "Frank Gagliano's City Scene," "The Ofay Watcher," "Castro Complex," "In Case of Accident," "The Children," "More Than You Deserve," Bdwy in "Paris Is Out," "Shelter.," "God's Favorite."

KLAVUN, WALTER' Born May 8, 1906 in NYC. Graduate Yale U. Bdwy debut 1928 in "Say When," followed by "No More Ladies," "Arms for Venus," "Annie Get Your Gun," "Twelfth Night," "Dream Girl," "Auntie Mame," "Say, Darling," "Desert Incident," "How to Succeed in Business . . .," "What Makes Sammy Run," "Twigs," OB in "Mornings at 7," "Dandy Dick," "The Dubliners."

KLIBAN, KEN. Born July 26, 1943 in Norwalk, Conn. Graduate UMiami, NYU. Bdwy debut 1967 in "War and Peace," OB in "Puppy Dog Tails," "Istanbul," "Persians," "him," "Elizabeth the Queen," "Boom Boom Room."

Eleanore Knapp   **Roger Kozol**   **Carolyn Lagerfelt**   **Frank Langella**   **Christine Lavren**

KLINE, RICHARD. Born Apr. 29, 1944 in NYC. Graduate Queen's Col., Northwestern U. Debut 1971 OB in LCRep's "Mary Stuart," followed by "Narrow Road to the Deep North," "Twelfth Night," "The Crucible," "We Bombed in New Haven."

KNAPP, ELEANORE. Born in Passaic, NY. Graduate Western Reserve U. Career in opera before Bdwy debut 1965 in "Man of La Mancha," OB in "The Prime of Miss Jean Brodie."

KNIGHT, WILLIAM. Born Dec. 6, 1934 in Los Angeles. Graduate CCLA. Bdwy debut 1970 in "Oh! Calcutta!," followed by "An Evening with Richard Nixon . . .," OB in "The Minister's Black Veil.," "Santa Anita '42."

KNOWLES, CHRISTOPHER. Born May 4, 1959 in Brooklyn, NY. Debut OB 1973 in "The Life and Times of Joseph Stalin," followed by "A Mad Man, A Mad Giant, A Mad Dog. . . .," Bdwy 1975 in "A Letter for Queen Victoria."

KOLOGI, MARK. Born Mar. 23, 1954 in Jersey City, NJ. AADA graduate. Bdwy debut 1975 in "Don't Call Back."

KOZOL, ROGER. Born June 5, 1947 in Boston, Mass. Graduate Harvard, U., Stanford U. Debut 1974 OB in "Godspell," followed by "New Girl in Town."

KRAUS, PHILIP. Born May 10, 1949 in Springville, NY. Carnegie Tech graduate. Bdwy debut 1973 in "Shelter," followed by "Equus."

KUHLMAN, RON. Born Mar. 6, 1948 in Cleveland, O. Graduate Ohio U. Debut 1972 OB in "A Maid's Tragedy," followed by "A Chorus Line" (Bdwy 1975).

KURTZ, MARCIA JEAN. Born in the Bronx. Juilliard Graduate, Debut 1966 OB in "Jonah," followed by "America Hurrah," "Red Cross," "Muzeeka," "Effects of Gamma Rays. . . .," "Year Boston Won the Pennant," "The Mirror," "The Orphan," "Action," Bdwy in "The Chinese and Dr. Fish."

KURTZ, SWOOSIE. Born Sept. 6, 1944 in Omaha, Neb. Attended USCal., LAMDA. Debut 1968 OB in "The Firebugs," followed by "The Effect of Gamma Rays. . . .," "Enter a Free Man."

LAGERFELT, CAROLYN. Born Sept. 23 in Paris, France. AADA graduate. Bdwy debut 1971 in "The Philanthropist," followed by "Four on a Garden," "Jockey Club Stakes," "The Constant Wife," OB in "Look Back in Anger."

LAIL, BARBARA. Born Apr. 6, 1950 in New Orleans, La. Debut 1970 OB in "You're a Good Man, Charlie Brown," followed by "Godspell," Bdwy 1974 in "Good News."

LANCASTER, LUCIE. Born Oct. 15, 1907 in Chicago. Bdwy debut 1947 in "Heads or Tails," followed by "Mr. Pickwick," "The Girl Who Came to Supper," "Bajour," "How Now, Dow Jones," "Little Boxes" (OB), "70 girls 70," "Pippin."

LANDERS, MATT. Born Oct. 21, 1952 in Mohawk Valley, NY. Attended Boston Cons. Debut OB 1974 in "Godspell," followed by Bdwy 1975 in "Grease."

LANDIS, JEANETTE. Born Apr. 4 in England. Attended National Theatre School. Bdwy debut 1966 in "Marat/deSade," followed by "There's One in Every Marriage," "Elizabeth I," "Love for Love," "Rules of the Game," "Member of the Wedding."

LANE, NANCY. Born June 16, 1951 in Passaic, NJ. Attended Va. Commonwealth U., AADA. Debut 1975 OB and Bdwy in "A Chorus Line."

LANGELLA, FRANK. Born in 1940; graduate Syracuse U. OB in "The Immoralist," "Good Day," "Old Glory," "White Devil," "A Cry of Players," Bdwy bow 1975 in "Seascape."

LANGFORD, BONNIE. Born July 22, 1964 in Hampton Court, Middlesex, Eng. Bdwy debut 1974 in "Gypsy."

LANNING, JERRY. Born May 17, 1943 in Miami, Fla. Graduate USCal. Bdwy debut 1966 in "Mame" for which he received a Theatre World Award, followed by "1776," "Where's Charley?," OB in "Memphis Store Bought Teeth," "Berlin to Broadway," "Sextet."

LANSBURY, ANGELA. Born Oct. 16, 1925 in London, Eng. Bdwy debut 1957 in "Hotel Paradiso," followed by "A Taste of Honey," "Anyone Can Whistle," "Mame," "Dear World," "Gypsy."

LANSING, JOHN. Born Oct. 16, 1949 in Baldwin, NY. Attended Hofstra Col. Bdwy debut 1972 in "The Sign in Sidney Brustein's Window," followed by "Grease."

LARSEN, WILLIAM. Born Nov. 20, 1927 in Lake Charles, La. Attended UTex. On Bdwy in "Ballad of the Sad Cafe," "Half a Sixpence," "Funny Girl," "Halfway up a Tree," "There's a Girl in My Soup," "Dear World," "Cat on a Hot Tin Roof," OB in "The Crucible," "Fantasticks," "Legend of Lovers," "Twelfth Night," "The Tavern," "Lower Depths," "School for Scandal," "Troilus and Cressida," "Murderous Angels."

LARSON, PAUL. Born Dec. 22, 1918 in Detroit, Mich. Attended St. Francis Col. Bdwy debut 1949 in "The Father," followed by "Dylan," "The Investigation," OB in "Spoon River Anthology," "The Subject Was Roses."

LASKY, ZANE. Born Apr. 23, 1953 in NYC. Attended Manhattan Com. Col., HB Studio. Debut OB 1973 in "The Hot l Baltimore," followed by "Prodigal.", Bdwy 1974 in "All over Town."

LASSER, LOUISE. Born in NYC. Attended Brandeis U. Bdwy debut 1962 in "I Can Get It for You Wholesale," followed by "Henry, Sweet Henry," "The Chinese and Dr. Fish," "The Third Ear" (OB), "Thieves."

LAUGHLIN, SHARON. Graduate UWash. Bdwy debut 1964 in "One by One," OB in "Henry IV, "Huui, Huui," "Mod Donna," "Subject to Fits," "The Minister's Black Veil," "Esther," "Rag Doll," "Four Friends."

LAURENCE, JAMES HOWARD. Born Sept. 23, 1945 in Chicago, Ill. Attended Ind.U., HB Studio. Bdwy debut 1969 in "Henry V," followed OB in "The Moths," "El Grande de Coca Cola."

LAVIN, LINDA. Born Oct. 15, 1939 in Portland, Me. Graduate William & Mary Col. Bdwy bow 1962 in "A Family Affair," followed by "Riot Act," "The Game Is Up," "Hotel Passionato," "It's a Bird . . . It's Superman!," "On a Clear Day You Can See Forever," "Something Different," "Cop-Out," "Last of the Red Hot Lovers," "Story Theatre," "The Enemy Is Dead," OB in "Wet Paint" for which she received a Theatre World Award.

LAVREN, CHRISTINE. Born Sept. 7, 1944 in Victoria, Tex. Bdwy debut 1971 in "Four on a Garden," followed OB by "An Evening with Ma Bell," "Fame."

LAWRENCE, DELPHI. Born Mar. 23, 1932 in London, Eng. Attended RADA. Debut 1972 OB in "The Divorce of Judy and Jane," followed by "Dylan," "The Elizabethans," Bdwy 1975 in "The Constant Wife."

LAWS, STEVE. Born Oct. 15, 1937 in NYC. Debut OB 1974 in "What the Wineseller Buys."

LAWSON, DAVID. Born Feb. 13, 1955 in NYC. Attended Antioch Col., NYU. Bdwy debut 1974 in "Gypsy."

LEA, BARBARA. Born Apr. 10, 1929 in Detroit, Mich. Graduate Wellesley, San Fernando State Col. Debut 1961 OB in "The Painted Days," followed by "Do I Hear a Waltz?"

LEARY, DAVID. Born Aug. 8, 1939 in Brooklyn, NY. Attended CCNY. Debut 1969 OB in "Shoot Anything That Moves," followed by "Macbeth," "The Plough and the Stars," Bdwy 1974 in "The National Health."

LEDERER, SUZANNE. Born Sept. 29, 1948 in Great Neck, NY. Graduate Hofstra U. Bdwy debut 1974 in "The National Health."

LEET, WILLIAM. Born Mar. 27, 1945 in Baton Rouge, La. Attended Southeastern La. Col. Debut OB 1968 in "Boys in the Band," followed by "All the King's Men," "Black Picture Show," Bdwy 1969 in "The American Dream."

LEGRAND, MICHEL. Born Feb. 24, 1932 in Paris, France. Attended National Conservatory. Bdwy debut 1974 in "Andy Williams with Michel Legrand."

LEIBMAN, RON. Born Oct. 11, 1937 in NYC. Attended Ohio Wesleyan, Actors Studio. Bdwy debut 1963 in "Dear Me, the Sky Is Falling," followed by "Bicycle Ride to Nevada," "The Deputy," "We Bombed in New Haven" for which he received a Theatre World Award, "Cop-Out," OB in "The Academy," "John Brown's Body," "Scapin," "Legend of Lovers," "Dead End," "Poker Session," "The Premise," "Transfers," "Room Service," "Love Two."

LEIGH-HUNT, BARBARA. Born Dec. 14, 1935 in Bath, Eng. Appeared in NY with Old Vic in 1959, with Bristol Old Vic in 1967, "Sherlock Holmes."

LeMASSENA, WILLIAM. Born May 23, 1916 in Glen Ridge, NJ. Attended NYU. Bdwy bow 1940 in "Taming of the Shrew," followed by "There Shall Be No Night," "The Pirate," "Hamlet," "Call Me Mister," Inside U.S.A.," "I Know, My Love," "Dream Girl," "Nina," "Ondine," "Fallen Angels," "Redhead," "Conquering Hero," "Beauty Part," "Come Summer," "Grin and Bare It," "All over Town," OB in "The Coop," "Brigadoon," "Life with Father," "F. Jasmine Addams."

LeNOIRE, ROSETTA. Born Aug. 8, 1911 in NYC. Attended Theatre Wing. Bdwy debut 1936 in "Macbeth," followed by "Bassa Moona," "Hot Mikado," "Marching with Johnny," "Janie," "Decision," "Three's a Family," "Destry Rides Again," "Finian's Rainbow," "South Pacific," "Sophie," "Tambourines to Glory," "Blues for Mr. Charlie," "Great Indoors," "Lost in the Stars," OB in "Bible Salesman," "Double Entry," "Clandestine on the Morning Line," "Cabin in the Sky," "Lady Day," LC in "Show Boat,""A Cry of Players," and "Streetcar Named Desire."

| Tom Leo | Anna Levine | Miller Lide | Carol Jo Lugenbeal | J. Frank Lucas |

LEO, TOM. Born Nov. 28, 1936 in Teaneck, NJ. Graduate UToronto. Debut OB 1974 in "More Than You Deserve.", followed by "Beethoven/Karl."

LEON, JOSEPH. Born June 8, 1923 in NYC. Attended NYU, UCLA. Bdwy debut 1950 in "Bell, Book and Candle," followed by "Seven Year Itch," "Pipe Dream," "Fair Game," "Gazebo," "Julia, Jake and Uncle Joe," "Beauty Part," "Merry Widow," "Henry, Sweet Henry," "Jimmy Shine," "All over Town," OB in "Come Share My House," "Dark Corners," "Interrogation of Havana," "Are You Now or Have You Ever Been."

LeROUX, MADELEINE. Born May 28, 1946 in Laramie, Wyo. Graduate U Cape Town. Debut OB 1969 in "The Moondreamers," followed by "Dirtiest Show in Town," "Rain," "Troilus and Cressida," "2008½," "Glamour, Glory, Gold," "Lisping Judas," "Why Hanna's Skirt Won't Stay Down," "Women behind Bars." Bdwy 1972 in "Lysistrata."

LESSANE, LEROY. Born Aug. 5, 1942 in NYC. Debut 1970 OB in "Gandhi," followed by "Snowbound King," "Ballad of Johnny Pot," "A Man Is a Man," "Last Days of British Honduras," Bdwy 1972 in "Capt. Brassbound's Conversion."

LEVENE, SAM. Born Aug. 28, 1905 in NYC. Graduate AADA. Bdwy debut 1927 in "Wall Street," followed by "3 Men on a Horse," "Dinner at 8," "Room Service," "Margin for Error," "Sound of Hunting," "Light up the Sky," "Guys and Dolls," "Hot Corner," "Fair Game," "Make a Million," "Heartbreak House," "Good Soup," "Devil's Advocate," "Let It Ride" "Seidman & Son," "Cafe Crown," "Last Analysis," "Nathan Weinstein, Mystic, Conn.," "The Impossible Years," "Paris Is Out," "A Dream out of Time" (OB), "The Sunshine Boys,," "Dreyfus in Rehearsal."

LEVIN, MICHAEL. Born Dec. 8, 1932 in Minneapolis, Minn. Graduate UMinn. Bdwy debut 1965 in "Royal Hunt of the Sun," followed by "End of All Things Natural" (OB), LCRep's "Camino Real," "Operation Sidewinder" and "Good Woman of Setzuan."

LEVINE, ANNA. Born Sept. 18, 1955 in NYC. Attended Actors Studio. Debut 1975 OB in "Kid Champion."

LEWIS, ABBY. Born Jan. 14, 1910 in Mesilla Park, NMex. Graduate NMex. U. Bdwy debut 1934 in "Richard III," followed by "You Can't Take It with You," "Macbeth," "The Willow and I" "The Chase," "Four Winds," "Howie," "Riot Act," "Life with Father," "70 Girls 70," "We Interrupt This Program."

LIDE, MILLER. Born Aug. 10, 1935 in Columbia, SC. Graduate USC, AmTh-Wing. Debut 1961 OB in "Three Modern Japanese Plays," followed by "Trial at Rouen," "Street Scene," "Joan of Arc at the Stake," Bdwy in "Ivanov" (1966), "Halfway up the Tree," "Who's Who in Hell," "We Interrupt This Program."

LINDSEY, GENE. Born Oct. 26, 1936 in Beaumont, Tex. Graduate Baylor, Southwestern U. OB in "Gogo Loves You," "By Jupiter," "Bernstein's Theatre Songs," "Deer Park," "Brainchild," "Rag Doll," Bdwy bow 1969 in "My Daughter, Your Son,"

LINTNER, ROBERT. Born Oct. 21, 1950 in Madison, Neb. Graduate Midland Col. Debut 1975 OB in "The Three Musketeers."

LIPSCOMB, DENNIS. Born Mar. 1, 1942 in Brooklyn, NY. Graduate Clarkson Col.,UIowa, LAMDA. Debut 1975 OB in "The Rivals."

LIPSON, CLIFFORD. Born Feb. 10, 1947 in Providence, RI. Attended Neighborhood Playhouse, AMDA. Bdwy bow 1970 in "Hair," OB in "Great Scot!," "Hooray, It's a Glorious Day," "The Indian Wants the Bronx," "Salvation," "Shaft of Love."

LIPSON, PAUL. Born Dec. 23, 1913 in Brooklyn. Attended Ohio State, Theatre Wing. Bdwy bow 1942 in "Lily of the Valley," followed by "Heads or Tails," "Detective Story," "Remains to Be Seen," "Carnival in Flanders," "I've Got Sixpence," "The Vamp," "Bells Are Ringing," "Fiorello" (CC), "Sound of Music," "Fiddler on the Roof," OB in "Deep Six the Briefcase," "The Inn at Lydda."

LISTMAN, RYAN. Born Dec. 30, 1939 in Newark, NJ. With LCRep in "St. Joan," "Tiger at the Gates," and "Cyrano de Bergerac," OB in "Utopia," "Until the Monkey Comes," "Fortune and Men's Eyes," "Spiro Who?," "Blueberry Mountain."

LITTLE, CLEAVON. Born June 1, 1939 in Chickasha, Okla. Attended San Diego State U., AADA. Debut OB 1967 in "MacBird," followed by "Hamlet," "Someone's Coming Hungry," "Ofay Watcher," "Scuba Duba," "Narrow Road to the Deep North," "Great MacDaddy," Bdwy "Jimmy Shine," "Purlie," "All over Town."

LITTLE, DAVID. Born Mar. 21, 1937 in Wadesboro, NC. Graduate William & Mary Col., Catholic U. Debut OB 1967 in "MacBird," followed by "Iphigenia in Aulis," "Antony and Cleopatra," "Antigone," "Enemy of the People," Bdwy bow 1974 in "Thieves."

LITTLE, RON PAUL. Born Apr. 2, 1949 in New Haven, Conn. UConn. graduate. Debut OB 1973 in "Thunder Rock," followed by "Summer Brave," "The Hot l Baltimore."

LLOYD, BERNARD. Born Jan. 30, 1934 in Newport, S. Wales. Graduate Keele U., RADA. Bdwy debut 1974 in "London Assurance."

LoBIANCO, TONY. Born Oct. 19, 1936 in NYC. Bdwy debut 1966 in "The Office," followed by "Royal Hunt of the Sun," "Rose Tattoo," "90 Day Mistress," "The Goodbye People," OB in "Three-penny Opera," "Answered the Flute," "Camino Real," "Oh, Dad, Poor Dad. . .," "Journey to the Day," "Zoo Story," "Nature of the Crime," "Incident at Vichy," "Tartuffe," "Yankees 3, Detroit O."

LoGRIPPO, JOE. Born Apr. 3, 1939 in Yonkers, NY. Graduate Bucknell U. Debut OB 1968 in "Day the Lid Blew Off," followed by "Futz," "Hallelujah," "Petrified Forest," "Breakout," "Desperate Hours."

LOMBARD, MICHAEL. Born Aug. 8, 1934 in Brooklyn. Graduate Bklyn Col., Boston U. OB in "King Lear," "Merchant of Venice," "Cages," "Pinter Plays," "LaTurista," "Elizabeth the Queen" (CC), "Room Service," "Mert and Phil," Bdwy in "Poor Bitos," "The Devils," "Gingerbread Lady," "Bad Habits."

LONDON, ROY. Born May 3, 1943 in NYC. Antioch Col. graduate. Bdwy debut 1967 in "Little Murders," followed by "The Birthday Party," "Gingham Dog," OB in "Three by de Ghelderode," "Once in a Lifetime," "Viet Rock," "America Hurrah," "Monopoly," "New York! New York!," "End of Summer."

LONG, AVON. Born June 18, 1910 in Baltimore, Md. Attended New Eng. Cons. Bdwy debut 1942 in "Porgy and Bess," followed by "Memphis Bound," "Carib Song," "Beggar's Holiday," "Don't Play Us Cheap," OB in "Ballad of Jazz Street," "Bubbling Brown Sugar."

LONG, TAMARA. Born Nov. 7, 1941 in Oklahoma City. Graduate Okla. U. Debut OB 1968 in "Dames At Sea," Bdwy 1974 in "Lorelei."

LOOMIS, ROD. Born Apr. 21, 1942 in St. Albans, Vt. Graduate Boston U, Brandeis U. Debut 1972 OB in "Two if by Sea," followed by "You Never Know," "Uncle Vanya."

LOWE, LARRY. Born Feb. 10, 1946 in Cleveland, O. Attended Philander Smith Col., AADA. Debut 1973 OB in "Holy Moses," followed by "Pop," "The Prodigal Sister."

LOWERY, MARCELLA. Born Apr. 27, 1946 in Jamaica, NY. Graduate Hunter Col. Debut 1967 OB in "Day of Absence," followed by "American Pastoral," "Ballet behind the Bridge," "Jamimma," "A Recent Killing," "Miracle Play.", "Welcome to Black River," "A Member of the Wedding" (Bdwy 1975).

LUBAR, CYNTHIA. Born Apr. 16, 1954 in White Plains, NY. OB in "Life and Times of Sigmund Freud," "Deafman Glance," "Overture to Ka Mountain . . ." "Ka Mountain and Guardenia Terrace," "Cyndi," "Life and Times of Joseph Stalin," Bdwy debut 1975 in "A Letter for Queen Victoria."

LUCAS, JEANNE. Born July 15 in Detroit, Mich., Graduate UMich. HB Studio. Debut 1974 OB in "Portfolio Revue." ·

LUCAS, J. FRANK. Born in Houston, Tex. Graduate Tex. Christian U. Debut OB 1943 in "A Man's House," followed by "Coriolanus," "Edward II," "Long Gallery," "Trip to Bountiful," "Orpheus Descending," "Guitar," "Marcus in the High Grass," "Chocolates," "To Bury a Cousin," "One World at a Time," Bdwy 1974 in "Bad Habits."

LUDWIG, KAREN. Born Oct. 9, 1942 in San Francisco, Ca. Bdwy credits: "The Deputy," "The Devils," OB in "Trojan Women," "Red Cross," "Muzeeka," "Huui, Huui," "Our Late Night," "The Seagull."

LUDWIG, SALEM. Born July 31, 1915 in Brooklyn. Attended Bklyn Col. Bdwy bow 1946 in "Miracle in the Mountains," followed by "Camino Real," "Enemy of the People," "All You Need Is One Good Break," "Inherit the Wind," "Disenchanted," "Rhinoceros," "Three Sisters," "Zulu and the Zayda," "Moonchildren," OB in "Brothers Karamazov," "Victim," "Troublemaker," "Man of Destiny," "Night of the Dunce," "Corner of the Bed," "Awake and Sing," "Prodigal," "Babylon," "The Burnt Flowerbed,."

LUGENBEAL, CAROL JO. Born July 14, 1952 in Detroit, Mich. Graduate U.S. International U. Bdwy debut 1974 in "Where's Charley?"

| Denise Lute | Richard Lupino | Heather MacRae | Anthony Mannino | Liz Marks |

LUPINO, RICHARD. Born Oct. 29, 1929 in Hollywood, Ca. Attended LACC, RADA. Bdwy debut 1956 in "Major Barbara," followed by "Conduct Unbecoming," "Sherlock Holmes."

LuPONE, PATTI. Born Apr. 21, 1949 in Northport, NY. Juilliard graduate. Debut 1972 OB in "School for Scandal," followed by "Women Beware Women," "Next Time I'll Sing to You," "Lower Depths," Bdwy in "Three Sisters," "Measure for Measure," "Next Time I'll Sing to You," "Beggar's Opera," "Scapin."

LUTE, DENISE. Born Aug. 2, 1954 in NYC. Attended HB Studio. Debut 1975 OB in "Harry Outside."

LYMAN, DOROTHY. Born Apr. 18, 1947 in Minneapolis, Minn. Attended Sarah Lawrence Col. Debut OB in "America Hurrah," followed by "Pequod," "American Hamburger League," "Action."

LYNCH, RICHARD. Born Feb. 12, 1940 in Brooklyn, NY. Attended Actors Studio. Bdwy debut 1965 in "The Devils," followed OB by "Live Like Pigs," "One Night Stands of a Noisy Passenger," "Things That Almost Happen," "12 Angry Men," "The Orphan," "Action."

LYNDECK, EDMUND. Born Oct. 4, 1925 in Baton Rouge, La. Graduate Montclair State Col., Fordham U. Bdwy debut 1969 in "1776," followed by "The King and I" (JB), OB in "Mandragola," "A Safe Place," "Amoureuse."

MacCAULEY, MARK. Born Dec. 11, 1948 in NYC. Attended UInd. Debut 1969 OB in "Crimes of Passion," followed by "Anna K.," "Godspell."

MacDONALD, PIRIE. Born Mar. 24, 1932 in NYC. Graduate Harvard U. Debut OB 1957 in "Under Milk Wood," followed by "Zoo Story," Bdwy in "Shadow and Substance," "Golden Fleecing," "Big Fish, Little Fish," "Death of a Salesman."

MACE, DAVID. Born Nov. 7, 1945 in London, Eng. Attended Guildhall Sch. Bdwy debut 1974 in "As You Like It."

MacGRATH, LEUEEN. Born July 3, 1914 in London, Eng. Attended RADA. Bdwy debut 1948 in "Edward, My Son," followed by "The Enchanted," "High Ground," "Fancy Meeting You Again," "Love of Four Colonels," "Tiger at the Gates," "Potting Shed," "The Seagull" (OB).

MACKENZIE, WILL. Born July 24, 1938 in Providence, RI. Graduate Brown U. Bdwy debut 1965 in "Half a Sixpence," followed by "Hello, Dolly!," "Sheep on the Runway," "Scratch," "Much Ado about Nothing," OB in "Wonderful Town," "Put It in Writing," "Morning Sun," "Brigadoon" (CC), "As You Like It," "Music! Music!" (CC), "Look Back in Anger."

MacRAE, HEATHER. Born in NYC. Attended Colo. Woman's Col. Bdwy debut 1968 in "Here's Where I Belong," followed by "Hair," OB in "Hot 1 Baltimore."

MAGGART, BRANDON. Born Dec. 12, 1933 in Carthage, Tenn. Graduate U. Tenn. OB in "Sing Muse!," "Like Other People," "Put It In Writing" for which he received a Theatre World Award, "Wedding Band," Bdwy in "Kelly," "New Faces of 1968," "Applause," "Lorelei," "We Interrupt This Program."

MAGGIORE, CHARLES. Born Mar. 19, 1936 in Valley Stream, NY. Attended Bates, Col., Adelphi U., Neighborhood Playhouse. Bdwy debut 1967 in "Spofford," OB in "Six Characters in Search of an Author," "Rivals," "The Iceman Cometh," "Othello," "The Elizabethans," "Three Musketeers."

MAGID, KAREN. Born June 2, 1949 in Cleveland, O. Graduate Ohio U. Debut OB 1974 in "Pop," followed by "A Funny Thing Happened on the Way to the Forum," "Anyone Can Whistle."

MAGUIRE, GEORGE. Born Dec. 4, 1946 in Wilmington, Del. Graduate UPa. Debut 1975 OB in "Polly."

MAHER, JOSEPH. Born Dec. 29, 1933 in Westport, Ire. Bdwy bow 1964 in "Chinese Prime Minister," followed by "Prime of Miss Jean Brodie," "Henry V," "There's One in Every Marriage," "Who's Who in Hell," OB in "The Hostage," "Live Like Pigs," "Importance of Being Earnest," "Eh?" "Local Stigmatic," "Mary Stuart," "The Contractor."

MALLORY, VICTORIA. Born Sept. 20, 1948 in Virginia. Graduate AMDA. Debut 1968 in "West Side Story" (LC), followed by "Carnival" (CC'68), "Follies," "A Little Night Music."

MANCINI, RIC. Born Apr. 16, 1933 in Brooklyn, NY. Attended Bklyn Col. Debut OB 1966 in "A View from the Bridge," followed by "All My Sons," "Night of the Iguana," "5 Finger Exercise," "Heloise," "Soon Jack November," "Beach Children."

MANNINO, ANTHONY. Born June 16, 1944 in Altoona, Pa. Graduate Cal. State, UCLA. Debut 1975 OB in "Kid Champion."

MARCH, ELLEN. Born Aug. 18, 1948 in Brooklyn. Graduate AMDA. Debut OB 1967 in "Pins and Needles," Bdwy 1973 in "Grease."

MARCHAND, NANCY. Born June 19, 1928 in Buffalo, NY. Carnegie Tech graduate. Debut 1951 in CC "Taming of the Shrew," followed by "Merchant of Venice," "Much Ado About Nothing," "The Balcony" (OB), "Three Bags Full," "After the Rain," "The Alchemist," "Yerma," "Cyrano de Bergerac," "Mary Stuart," "Enemies," "The Plough and the Stars," "Forty Carats," "And Miss Reardon Drinks a Little," "Veronica's Room."

MARGULIES, DAVID. Born Feb. 19, 1937 in NYC. Graduate CCNY. Debut 1958 OB in "Golden Six," followed by "Six Charactors in Search of an Author," "Tragical Historie of Dr. Faustus," "Tango," "Little Murders," "Seven Days of Mourning," "Last Analysis," "An Evening with the Poet Senator," "Kid Champion," Bdwy 1973 in "The Iceman Cometh."

MARIANO, PATTI. Born June 12, 1945 in Philadelphia, Pa. Bdwy debut 1957 in "Music Man," followed by "Bye Bye Birdie," "Sail Away," "I Had a Ball," "George M!," OB in "Country Girl," "Me and Juliet," "Godspell."

MARKS, LIZ. (formerly Linda Helen Marks) Born June 18, 1952 in Richmond, Va. Graduate UCincinnati. Debut 1974 OB in "The Boy Friend."

MARLOWE, HUGH. Born Jan. 30, 1911 in Philadelphia, Pa. Attended Pasadena Playhouse. Bdwy bow 1936 in "Arrest That Woman," followed by "Kiss the Boys Goodbye," "Young Couple Wanted," "The Land Is Bright," "Lady in the Dark," "It Takes Two," "Laura," "Duet for Two Hands," "Rabbit Habit," "Woman Is My Idea," OB in "Deer Park," "Postcards," "All My Sons."

MARLOWE, LYNN. Born Oct. 13, 1952 in Springfield, Ill. Graduate UIll. Debut OB 1975 in "Do I Hear a Waltz?"

MAROFF, ROBERT. Born Jan. 22, 1934 in Brooklyn. Debut OB 1974 in "Short Eyes."

MARR, RICHARD. Born May 12, 1928 in Baltimore, Md. Graduate UPa. Bdwy in "Baker Street," "How to Succeed . . .," "Here's Where I Belong," "Coco," "The Constant Wife," OB in "Sappho," "Pilgrim's Progress," "Pimpernel," "Witness," "Antiques," "Two by Tennessee."

MARSEN, PAMELA WILD. Born Aug. 18, 1946 in New Orleans, La. Graduate Sophie Newcomb Col., Columbia U. Debut OB 1974 in "The Desperate Hours."

MARSHALL, SID. Born July 15, 1941 in Mt. Pleasant, NY. Attended Dramatic Workshop. Bdwy debut 1972 in "Lost in the Stars," followed by "The Night That Made America Famous," OB in "Bachelor Toys," "Sambo," "Armored Dove," "Your Own Thing."

MARSHALL, WILL SHARPE. Born Jan. 12, 1947 in East Chicago, Ind. Graduate Brown U. Debut OB 1969 in "The Drunkard," Bdwy in "Butterflies Are Free," "A Little Night Music."

MARTIN, LEILA. Born Aug. 22, 1932 in NYC. Bdwy debut 1944 in "Peepshow," followed by "Two on the Aisle," "Wish You Were Here," "Guys and Dolls" (CC), "Best House in Naples," "Henry, Sweet Henry," "The Wall," "Visit to a Small Planet," "The Rothschilds," OB in "Ernest in Love," "Beggar's Opera," "King of the U.S.," "Philemon."

MASIELL, JOE. Born Oct. 27, 1939 in Bklyn. Studied at HB Studio. Debut 1964 OB in "Cindy," followed by "Jacques Brel Is Alive. . . .," "Sensations," "Leaves of Grass," "How to Get Rid of It," "A Matter of Time," Bdwy in "Dear World," "Different Times," "Jacques Brel is Alive . . ."

MASON, MARSHA. Born Apr. 3, 1942 in St. Louis, Mo. Attended Webster Col. Debut OB 1967 in "Deer Park," followed by "It's Called the Sugar Plum," "Happy Birthday, Wanda June," "Richard III," Bdwy bow 1973 in "The Good Doctor."

MASONER, GENE. Born Jan. 22, in Kansas City, Kan. Attended UKan., HB Studio. Debut OB 1969 in "Your Own Thing," followed by "White Devil," "Cherry," "3 Drag Queens from Daytona," Bdwy 1975 in "Shenandoah."

MATHEWS, CARMEN. Born May 8, 1918 in Philadelphia, Pa. RADA graduate. Bdwy debut 1938 in "Henry IV," followed by "Hamlet," "Richard II," "Harriet," "Cherry Orchard," "The Assassin," "Man and Superman," "Ivy Green," "Courtin' Time," "My Three Angels," "Holiday for Lovers," "Night Life," "Lorenzo," "The Yearling," "Delicate Balance," "I'm Solomon," "Dear World," "Ring Round the Bathtub," "Ambassador."

MATHEWS, WALTER. Born Oct. 10, 1926 in NYC. Graduate NYU, Ohio U. Bdwy debut 1951 in "St. Joan," followed by "The Long Dream," "King Lear," "Mr. Roberts," "Equus."

MATHIS, SHERRY. Born Feb. 2, 1949 in Memphis, Tenn. Attended Memphis State U. Bdwy debut 1973 in "A Little Night Music."

MATSUSAKA, TOM. Born Aug. 8, in Wahiawa, Ha. Graduate Mich. State U. Bdwy bow 1968 in "Mame," followed (OB) by "Jungle of Cities," "Ride the Winds," "Santa Anita '42."

| Jade McCall | Linda McClure | Everett McGill | Beverlee McKinsey | Michael Melling |

MAURICE, MICHAEL A. Born Feb. 17, 1952 in Detroit, Mich. Attended Mich. State U., Actors Studio. Debut 1975 OB in "The Three Musketeers."

MAY, WINSTON. Born Feb. 3, 1937 in Mammoth Spring, Ark. Graduate Ark. State U., AmThWing. Debut OB 1967 in "The Man Who Washed His Hands," followed by "King Lear," "Candida," "Trumpets and Drums," "Otho the Great," "Uncle Vanya," "Servant of Two Masters," "The Play's the Thing," "Autumn Garden."

McCALL, JADE. Born Sept. 13, 1941 in Richland Center, Wisc. Attended Ariz. State U. Debut 1974 OB in "Tubstrip."

McCALL, JANET. Born June 26, 1935 in Washington, DC. Graduate Penn. State. Debut 1960 OB in "Golden Apple," followed by "Life Is a Dream," "Tatooed Countess," "The Bacchantes," "Jacques Brel is Alive. . . .," "How to Get Rid of It," Bdwy in "Camelot," "1776," "Two by Two," "Jacques Brel Is Alive . . ."

McCARTHY, KEVIN. Born Feb. 15, 1914 in Seattle, Wash. Attended UMinn. Bdwy debut 1938 in "Abe Lincoln in Illinois," followed by "Flight to the West," "Winged Victory," "Truckline Cafe," "Joan of Lorraine," "Death of a Salesman," "Anna Christie," "Deep Blue Sea," "Red Roses for Me," "Day the Money Stopped," "Two for the Seasaw," "Advise and Consent," "Something about a Soldier," "Three Sisters," "A Warm Body," "Cactus Flower," "Happy Birthday, Wanda June," OB in "The Children," "The Rapists," "Harry Outside."

McCARTY, MARY. Born in 1923 in Kansas. Bdwy debut 1948 in "Sleepy Hollow" for which she received a Theatre World Award, followed by "Small Wonder," "Miss Liberty," "Bless You All," "A Rainy Day in Newark," "Follies," "Chicago."

McCAULEY, WILLIAM. Born Nov. 20, 1947 in Philadelphia, Pa. Graduate Northwestern U., Goodman Theatre. Bdwy debut 1974 in "Saturday Sunday Monday."

McCLAIN, MARCIA. Born Sept. 30, 1949 in San Antonio, Tex. Graduate Trinity U. Debut 1972 OB in "Rainbow," followed by Bdwy bow 1974 in "Where's Charley?" for which she received a Theatre World Award.

McCLURE, LINDA. Born Sept. 6, 1947 in Santa Monica, Cal. Graduate UCLA. Bdwy debut 1974 in "Lorelei."

McCONNELL, TY. Born Jan. 13, 1940 in Coldwater, Mich. Graduate UMich. Debut OB 1962 in "The Fantasticks," followed by "Promenade," "Contrast," "Fashion," "The Dubliners," Bdwy in "Lion in Winter," "Dear World."

McCOWEN, ALEC. Born May 26, 1925 in Tunbridge Wells, Eng. Attended RADA. Bdwy debut 1951 in "Antony and Cleopatra," followed by "Caesar and Cleopatra," "King Lear," "Comedy of Errors," "After the Rain," "Hadrian VII," "The Philanthropist," "The Misanthrope."

McGANN, MICHAELJOHN. Born Feb. 2, 1952 in Cleveland, O. Graduate Ohio U. Debut 1975 OB in "The Three Musketeers."

McGILL, EVERETT. Born Oct. 21, 1945 in Miami Beach, Fla. Graduate UMo., RADA. Debut OB 1971 in "Brothers," followed by "The Father," "Enemies," Bdwy 1974 in "Equus."

McGRATH, DON. Born Mar. 3, 1940 in Pittsburgh, Pa. Graduate Duquesne U., NYU, AMDA. Debut 1970 OB in "Madwoman of Chaillot," followed by "Oedipus at Colonnus," "Sigfried in Stalingrad," "Mother & Son & Co.," "Miracle of St. Anthony," "Miss Collins, the English Chairman," "St. Joan," "Myth Oedipus," Bdwy 1975 in "The Lieutenant."

McGRATH, KATHERINE. Born Dec. 11, 1944 in Winchester, Mass. Attended Boston Cons., RADA. Debut OB in "The Bacchants," followed by "Perry's Mission," "The Real Inspector Hound," "Enter a Free Man."

McGREEVEY, ANNIE. Born in Brooklyn, NY. Graduate AADA. Bdwy debut 1971 in "Company," followed by "The Magic Show," OB in "Booth Is Back in Town."

McGUIRE, BIFF. Born Oct. 25, 1926 in New Haven, Conn. Attended Mass. State Col. Bdwy in "Make Mine Manhattan," "South Pacific," "Dance Me a Song," "The Time of Your LIfe," (CC&LC), "A View from the Bridge," "Greatest Man Alive," "The Egghead," "Triple Play," "Happy Town," "Beg, Borrow or Steal," "Finian's Rainbow" (CC) "Beggar on Horseback" (LC), "Father's Day," "Trial of the Catonsville 9," "Present Tense" (OB), "Streetcar Named Desire."

McGUIRE, MITCHELL. Born Dec. 26, 1936 in Chicago, Ill. Attended Goodman Theatre, Santa Monica City Col. OB in "The Rapists," "Go, Go, Go, God Is Dead," "Waiting for Lefty," "The Bond," "Guns of Carrar," "Oh, Calcutta!," "New York! New York!"

McHATTIE, STEPHEN. Born Feb. 3 in Antigonish, N.S. Graduate Acadia U, AADA. With NYSF in "Henry IV," on Bdwy in "The American Dream" ('68), OB in "Richard III," "The Persians," "Pictures in the Hallway" (LC), "Now There's Just the Three of Us," "Anna K.," "Twelfth Night" (LC), "Mourning Becomes Electra," "Alive and Well in Argentina," "The Iceman Cometh."

McKAY, ANTHONY. Born Sept. 25, 1946 in Paterson, NJ. Graduate Carnegie-Mellon U. Debut 1974 OB in "Moonchildren," followed by "The First Breeze of Summer" (also Bdwy 1975)

McKAY, TONY. Born on Cat Island, Bahamas. NY debut 1962 OB in "Moon on a Rainbow Shawl," followed by "The Brighter Shading," "Man Better Man," "Danton's Death."

McKECHNIE, DONNA. Born in Nov. 1944 in Detroit. Bdwy debut 1961 in "How to Succeed. . . ." followed by "Promises, Promises," "Company," "On the Town," "Music! Music!" (CC), "A Chorus Line."

McKENZIE, RICHARD. Born June 2, 1930 in Chattanooga, Tn. Attended UMo., UTenn., RADA. Bdwy debut 1969 in "Indians," followed by "The National Health," OB in "Whistle in the Dark," "Nobody Hears a Broken Drum," "Uncle Vanya."

McKINSEY, BEVERLEE. Born Aug. 9 in Oklahoma. Graduate UOkla. Debut OB 1962 in "P.S. 193," followed by "Love Nest," "Dutchman," "Mert and Phil," Bdwy in "Who's Afraid of Virginia Woolf?," "Barefoot in the Park."

McMARTIN, JOHN. Born in Warsaw, Ind. Attended Columbia. Debut OB 1959 in "Little Mary Sunshine" for which he received a Theatre World Award, foloowed by Bdwy in "The Conquering Hero," (1968) "Blood, Sweat and Stanley Poole," "Children from Their Games," "Rainy Day in Newark," "Too Much Johnson" (OB), "Sweet Charity," "Follies," "Great God Brown," "Don Juan," "The Visit," "Chemin de Fer," "Love for Love," "Rules of the Game."

McMILLAN, KENNETH. Born July 2, 1934 in Brooklyn. Bdwy debut 1970 in "Borstal Boy," OB in "Red Eye of Love," "King of the Whole Damn World," "Little Mary Sunshine," "Babes in the Wood," "Moonchildren," "Merry Wives of Windsor," "Where Do We Go from Here?", "Kid Champion."

McNAMARA, DERMOT. Born Aug. 24, 1925 in Dublin, Ire. Bdwy bow 1959 in "A Touch of the Poet," followed by "Philadelphia, Here I Come," "Donnybrook," "Taming of the Shrew," OB in "The Wise Have Not Spoken," "3 by Synge," "Playboy of the Western World," "Shadow and Substance," "Happy as Larry," "Sharon's Grave," "A Whistle in the Dark," "Red Roses for Me," "The Plough and the Stars," "Shadow of a Gunman," "No Exit," "Stephen D," "Hothouse," "Home Is the Hero," "Sunday Morning Bright and Early."

McWILLIAMS, CAROLINE. Born Apr. 4, in Seattle, Wash. Attended Carnegie Tech, Pasadena Playhouse. Bdwy debut 1971 in "The Rothschilds," followed by "Cat on a Hot Tin Roof," OB in "An Ordinary Man."

MEARS, DeANN. Born in Ft. Fairfield, Me. Attended Westbrook Col. Debut 1961 OB in "Decameron," followed by "Ernest in Love," "Sound of Silence," "House of Blue Leaves," "Desire under the Elms," "Arthur," Bdwy in "Too True to Be Good," "Tiny Alice," "Abelard and Heloise."

MEDOFF, MARK. Born Mar. 19, 1940 in Mt. Carmel, Ill. Graduate UMiami, Stanford U. Debut 1974 OB in "When You Comin' Back, Red Ryder?" which he wrote.

MELLINGER, MICHAEL. Born May 30, 1929 in Kochel, Ger. Attended Central Sch. of Speech and Drama, London. Bdwy debut 1974 in "Sherlock Holmes."

MERIN, EDA REISS. Born July 31 in NYC. Attended Hunter Col. Bdwy debut 1939 in "My Heart's in the Highlands," followed by "Trio," "Lovers," "Sophie," "A Flag Is Born," "A Far Country," OB in "Private Life of the Master Race," "Tower beyong Tragedy," "Square in the Eye," "Huui, Huui," "Inner Journey," "Good Woman of Setzuan," "A Doll's House," "Hedda Gabler."

MERSON, SUSAN. Born Apr. 25, 1950 in Detroit, Mich. Graduate Boston U. Bdwy debut 1974 in "Saturday Sunday Monday."

METCALF, MARK. Born Mar. 11 in Findlay, O. Attended UMich. Debut OB 1973 in "Creeps," followed by "The Tempest" (LC), "Beach Children."

MICHAELS, BERT. Born Dec. 22, 1943 in NYC. Attended UMiami. Bdwy debut 1965 in "Baker Street," followed by "La Grosse Valise," "Half a Sixpence," "Man of La Mancha," "Cabaret," "Canterbury Tales," "Ulysses in Nighttown," "Mack and Mabel."

MICHAELS, PATRICIA. Born in Riverside, Cal. Bdwy debut 1965 in "Baker Street," followed by "La Grosse Valise," "It's a Bird . . . It's Superman!," "Cabaret," "Canterbury Tales," "Mack and Mabel."

Lynn Milgrim   **Ross Miles**   **Jan Miner**   **Fred Morsell**   **Maureen Moore**

MICHAELS, STUART. Born Oct. 31, 1940 in Manchester, Conn. Attended Emerson Col., HB Studio. Debut 1971 OB in "June Moon," followed by "Against the Sun," "The Seasons."

MICHAELS, TIMMY. Born Mar. 6, 1963 in NYC. Debut 1969 OB in "Seven Days of Mourning," followed by "A Midsummer Night's Dream."

MILES, ROSS. Born in Poughkeepsie, NY. Bdwy debut 1962 in "Little Me," followed by "Baker Street," "Pickwick," "Darling of the Day," "Mame," "Jumpers," "Goodtime Charley."

MILGRIM, LYNN. Born Mar. 17, 1944 in Philadelphia, Pa. Graduate Swarthmore, Harvard U. Debut OB 1969 in "Frank Gagliano's City Scene," followed by "Crimes of Passion," "Macbeth," "Charley's Aunt," "The Real Inspector Hound."

MILLER, LINDA. Born Sept. 16, 1942 in NYC. Graduate Catholic U. Debut 1975 OB in "Black Picture Show" for which she received a Theatre World Award.

MILLER, MICHAEL. Born Sept. 1, 1931 in Los Angeles. Attended Bard Col. OB debut 1961 in "Under Milk Wood," followed by "The Lesson," "A Memory of 2 Mondays," "Little Murders," "Tom Paine," "Morning, Noon and Night," "Enemy of the People" (LC). "Whitsuntide," "Say When," "Case Against Roberta Guardino," "Dandelion Wine," Bdwy in "Ivanov," "Black Comedy," "Trial of Lee Harvey Oswald."

MILLS, STEPHANIE. Born in 1959 in Brooklyn, NY. Bdwy debut 1975 in "The Wiz."

MINER, JAN. Born Oct. 15, 1917 in Boston. Debut 1958 OB in "Obligato," followed by "Decameron," "Dumbbell People," "Autograph Hound," Bdwy in "Viva Madison Avenue," "Lady of the Camelias," "Freaking out of Stephanie Blake," "Othello," "Milk Train Doesn't Stop Here Anymore," "Butterflies Are Free," "The Women," "Pajama Game," "Saturday Sunday Monday."

MINTUN, JOHN. Born Jan. 16, 1941 in Decatur, Ill. Princeton graduate. Debut OB 1969 in "Get Thee to Canterbury," followed by "Boys in the Band," "The Rabinowitz Gambit," "Happy Halloween," "Esther," "The Inn at Lydda," "Carnival Dreams," Bdwy 1975 in "The Ritz."

MITCHELL, JAMES. Born Feb. 29, 1920 in Sacramento, Cal. Attended LACC. Bdwy bow 1944 in "Bloomer Girl," followed by "Billion Dollar Baby," "Brigadoon" for which he received a Theatre World Award, "Paint Your Wagon," "Carousel" (CC), "First Impressions," "Carnival," "Deputy," "Mack and Mabel," OB in "Threepenny Opera," "Livin' the Life," "Winkelberg," "The Father."

MIXON, ALAN. Born Mar. 15, 1933 in Miami, Fla. Attended UMiami. Bdwy bow 1962 in "Something about a Soldier," followed by "Sign in Sidney Brustein's Window," "The Devils," "The Unknown Soldier and His Wife," "Love Suicide at Schofield Barracks," "Equus," OB in "Suddenly Last Summer," "Desire under the Elms," "Trojan Women," "Alchemist," "Child Buyer," "Mr. and Mrs. Lyman," "A Whitman Portrait," "Iphigenia in Aulis," "Small Craft Warnings," "Mourning Becomes Electra," "The Runner Stumbles."

MOONEY, WILLIAM. Born in Bernie, Mo. Attended UColo. Bdwy debut 1961 in "A Man for All Seasons," followed by "A Place for Polly," OB in "Half Horse, Half Alligator," "Strike Heaven on the Face," "Conflict of Interest," "Overnight."

MOOR, BILL. Born July 13, 1931 in Toledo, O. Attended Northwestern, Denison U. Bdwy debut 1964 in "Blues for Mr. Charlie," followed by "Great God Brown," "Don Juan," "The Visit," "Chemin de Fer," "Holiday," "P.S. Your Cat Is Dead," OB in "Dandy Dick," "Love Nest," "Days and Nights of Beebee Fenstermaker," "The Collection," "The Owl Answers," "Long Christmas Dinner," "Fortune and Men's Eyes," LC's "King Lear" and "Cry of Players," "Boys in the Band," "Alive and Well in Argentina," "Rosmersholm."

MOORE, CHARLOTTE J. Born July 7, 1939 in Herrin, Ill. Attended Smith Col., Washington U. Bdwy debut 1972 in "The Great God Brown," followed by "Don Juan," "The Visit," "Chemin de Fer," "Holiday," "Love for Love," "Member of the Wedding."

MOORE, EDWARD J. Born June 2, 1935 in Chicago, Ill. Graduate Goodman Theatre. Bdwy debut 1967 in "After the Rain," followed OB by "White House Murder Case," "The Sea Horse" which he wrote.

MOORE, MAUREEN. Born Aug. 12, 1951 in Wallingford, Conn. Attended Carnegie-Mellon U. Bdwy debut 1974 in "Gypsy."

MOOSE, G. EUGENE. Born July 23, 1951 in Kilgore, Tex. Attended Tex. Wesleyan Col. Bdwy debut 1975 in "The Lieutenant."

MORENO, RITA. Born Dec. 11, 1931 in Humacao, PR. Bdwy debut 1945 in "Skydrift," followed by "West Side Story," "Sign in Sidney Brustein's Window," "Last of the Red Hot Lovers," "The National Health," "The Ritz."

MORIARTY, MICHAEL. Born Apr. 5, 1941 in Detroit, Mich. Graduate Dartmouth, LAMDA. Debut OB 1963 in "Antony and Cleopatra," followed by "Peanut Butter and Jelly," Bdwy in "Trial of the Catonsville 9," "Find Your Way Home" for which he received a Theater World Award, "Richard III" (LC).

MORRIS, MARTI. Born June 8, 1949 in Clarksburg, WVa. Graduate UWVa. Debut in 1972 OB in "The Fantasticks," followed by "Riverwind" (ELT), Bdwy 1974 in "Candide."

MORSELL, FRED. Born Aug. 3, 1940 in NYC. Graduate Dickinson Col. Debut OB 1971 in "Any Resemblance to Persons Living or Dead," followed by LC's "Enemies," and "Merchant of Venice," "Enclave," "Esther," "Nightlight," Bdwy in "Love for Love," "Rules of the Game," "Member of the Wedding."

MORTON, JOE. Born Oct. 18, 1947 in NYC. Attended Hofstra U. Debut OB 1968 in "Month of Sundays," followed by "Salvation," "Charlie Was Here and Now He's Gone," Bdwy in "Hair," "Two Gentlemen of Verona," "Tricks," "Raisin" for which he received a Theatre World Award.

MOSKIN, DAVID. Born Apr. 29, 1961 in Teaneck, NJ. Bdwy debut 1971 in "The Grass Harp," followed by "The Rothschilds," "Seesaw," OB in "Do I Hear a Waltz?"

MULLINS, MICHAEL. Born Aug. 23, 1951 in Salem, Va. Attended NC Sch. of Arts. Debut OB 1973 in "L'Ete."

MURNEY, CHRISTOPHER. Born July 20, 1943 in Narragansett, RI. Graduate URI, UNH, Penn State U. Bdwy debut 1973 in "Tricks," followed by "Mack and Mabel."

MURPHY, ROSEMARY. Born Jan. 13, 1927 in Munich, Ger. Attended Neighborhood Playhouse, Actors Studio. Bdwy debut 1950 in "Tower Beyond Tragedy," followed by "Look Homeward, Angel," "Period of Adjustment," "Any Wednesday," "Delicate Balance," "Weekend," "Death of Bessie Smith," "Butterflies Are Free."

MURRAY, BRIAN. Born Oct. 9, 1939 in Johannesburg, SA. Debut 1964 OB in "The Knack," followed by "King Lear" (LC), Bdwy in "All in Good Time," "Rosencrantz and Guildenstern Are Dead," "Sleuth."

MUSANTE, TONY. Born June 30, 1936 in Bridgeport, Conn. Oberlin Col. graduate. Debut OB 1960 in "Borak," followed by "The Balcony," "Theatre of the Absurd," "Half-Past Wednesday," "The Collection," "Tender Heel," "Kiss Mama," "Mme. Mousse," "Zoo Story," "Match-Play," "Night of the Dunce," "A Gun Play," Bdwy bow 1975 in "P.S. Your Cat Is Dead."

NAGEL, ALICE. Born in Brooklyn, NY. Graduate Boston U., Adelphi U., HB Studio. Bdwy debut 1974 in "The National Health," "All God's Chillun Got Wings," OB in "You're a Good Man, Charlie Brown," "House of Blue Leaves," "Night Must Fall," "Caucasian Chalk Circle."

NASTASI, FRANK. Born Jan. 7, 1923 in Detroit, Mich. Graduate Wayne U., NYU. OB in "Bonds of Interest," "One Day More," "Nathan the Wise," "The Chief Things," "Cindy," "Escurial," "Shrinking Bride," "Macbird," "Cakes with the Wine," Bdwy in "Lorenzo," "Avanti."

NEBIOL, GARY. Born Aug. 27, 1943 in NYC. Debut 1972 OB in "Present Tense," followed by "Parades Shall Follow."

NEEDHAM, PETER. Born Aug. 20, 1932 in Nottingham, Eng. Graduate RADA. Bdwy debut 1956 in "Macbeth," followed by "Romeo and Juliet," "Richard II," "Troilus and Cressida," "The Misanthrope."

NELSON, BARRY. Born in 1925 in Oakland, Ca. Bdwy debut 1943 in "Winged Victory," followed by "Light Up the Sky," "The Moon Is Blue," "Wake Up, Darling," "Rat Race," "Mary, Mary," "Nobody Loves an Albatross," "Cactus Flower," "Everything in the Garden," "Only Game in Town," "Fig Leaves Are Falling," "Engagement Baby," "Seascape."

NELSON, GENE. Born Mar. 24, 1920 in Seattle, Wash. Bdwy debut 1942 in "This is the Army," followed by "Lend an Ear," for which he won a Theatre World Award, "Follies," "Music! Music!" (CC), "Good News."

NETTLETON, DENISE. Born June 9, 1948 in Branford, Can. Bdwy debut 1974 in "Grease."

NEUBERGER, JAN. Born Jan. 21, 1953 in Amityville, NY. Attended NYU. Bdwy debut 1974 in "Gypsy."

NEVILLE, JOHN. Born May 2, 1925, in London, Eng. Attended RADA. Bdwy debut 1956 in "Romeo and Juliet," followed by "Richard II," "Hamlet," "Twelfth Night," "Sherlock Holmes."

NEVILLE-ANDREWS, JOHN. Born Aug. 23, 1948 in Woking Surrey, Eng. Attended Westminster Tech. Col. Debut OB 1973 in "El Grande de Coca-Cola," followed by "Bullshot Crummond."

NEWLEY, ANTHONY. Born Sept. 21, 1931 in London, Eng. Bdwy debut 1956 in "Cranks," followed by "Stop the World—I Want to Get Off," "The Roar of the Greasepaint, The Smell of the Crowd," "Anthony Newley and Henry Mancini."

NEWMAN, STEPHEN D. Born Jan. 20, 1943 in Seattle, Wash. Stanford graduate. Debut 1971 OB in Judith Anderson's "Hamlet," followed by "School for Wives," "Beggar's Opera," "Pygmalion," "In the Voodoo Parlour of Marie Leveau," "Richard III," "Santa Anita '42," "Polly," Bdwy in "An Evening with Richard Nixon and . . . ," "Emperor Henry IV."

NEWMAN, WILLIAM. Born June 15, 1934 in Chicago, Ill. Graduate UWash., Columbia U. Debut 1972 OB in "The Beggar's Opera," followed by "Are You Now or Have You Ever Been . . . ?," "Conflict of Interest," "Mr. Runaway," Bdwy in "Over Here," "Rocky Horror Show."

NEWTON, JOHN. Born Nov. 2, 1925 in Grand Junction, Colo. Graduate UWash. Debut 1951 OB in "Othello," followed by "As You Like It," "Candida," "Candaules Commissioner," "Sextet," LCR's "The Crucible" and "Streetcar Named Desire," "The Rivals," Bdwy in "Weekend" (1968).

NICHOLLS, ALLAN. Born Apr. 8, 1945 in Montreal, Can. Bdwy debut 1969 in "Hair," followed by OB in "Inner City," "Dude," OB in "Sgt. Pepper's Lonely Hearts Band . . ."

NICKERSON, E. LYNN. Born Mar. 12, 1948 in Akron, O. Graduate St. Olaf Col. Debut 1975 OB in "Medea and Jason," followed by "Man on the Moon."

NICKERSON, SHANE. Born Jan. 29, 1964 in Miami, Fla. Bdwy debut 1972 in "Pippin."

NICOL, LESSLIE. Born May 27 in Dundee, Scot. NY debut OB in "Man with a Load of Mischief," Bdwy 1973 in "Grease."

NILES, MARY ANN. Born May 2, 1933 in NYC. Attended Miss Finchley's Ballet Acad. Bdwy debut in "Girl from Nantucket," followed by "Dance Me a Song," "Call Me Mister," "Make Mine Manhattan," "La Plume de Ma Tante," "Carnival," "Flora the Red Menace," "Sweet Charity," "George M!," "No, No, Nanette," "Irene," OB in "The Boys from Syracuse," CC's "Wonderful Town" and "Carnival."

NILES, RICHARD. Born May 19, 1946 in NYC. Graduate NYU. Debut 1969 OB in "Sourball," followed by "Innocent Thoughts and Harmless Intentions," Bdwy in "And Miss Reardon Drinks a Little," "Don't Call Back."

NOBLE, JAMES. Born Mar. 5, 1922 in Dallas, Tex. Attended SMU. Bdwy bow 1949 in "The Velvet Glove," followed by "Come of Age," "A Far Country," "Strange Interlude," "1776," OB in "Wilder's Triple Bill," "Night of the Dunce," "Rimers of Eldritch," "The Acquisition," "A Scent of Flowers," "A Touch of the Poet."

NOLEN, JOYCE. Born Oct. 5, 1949 in Philadelphia, Pa. Debut 1967 OB in "Curley McDimple," followed by Bdwy in "Different Times," "A Matter of Time."

NUTE, DON. Born Mar. 13, in Connellsville, Pa. Attended DenverU. Debut OB 1965 in "The Trojan Women," followed by "Boys in the Band," "Mad Theatre for Madmen," "The Eleventh Dynasty," "About Time," "The Urban Crisis," "Christmas Rappings," "The Life of Man," "A Look at the Fifties."

NYE, GENE. Born Feb. 23, 1939 in Brooklyn, NY. Graduate Hofstra U. OB in "Too Much Johnson," "Elizabeth the Queen," "Trelawny of the Wells," Lion Co. productions.

O'CONNOR, KEVIN. Born May 7, in Honolulu. Attended UHawaii, Neighborhood Playhouse. Debut 1964 OB in "Up to Thursday," followed by "Six from LaMama," "Rimers of Eldritch," "Tom Paine," "Boy on the Straightback Chair," "Dear Janet Rosenberg," "Eyes of Chalk," "Alive and Well in Argentina," "Duet," "Trio," "The Contractor," Bdwy (1970) "Gloria and Esperanza," "Kool Aid" (LC), "The Morning after Optimism," "Figures in the Sand."

O'LEARY, JOHN. Born May 5, 1926 in Newton, Mass. Graduate Northwestern U. Bdwy debut 1962 in "General Seeger," OB in "Picture of Dorian Gray," "Rimers of Eldritch," "Big Broadcast," "Car."

OLIVER, LYNN. Born Sept. 18 in San Antonio, Tex. Graduate UTex., UHouston. Debut OB 1970 in "Oh! Calcutta!," followed by "In the Boom Boom Room," "Redhead," "Blood," "Two Noble Kinsmen."

OLIVER, ROCHELLE. Born Apr. 15, 1937 in NYC. Attended Bklyn Col. Bdwy debut 1960 in "Toys in the Attic," followed by "Harold," "Who's Afraid of Virginia Woolf?," "Happily Never After," OB in "Brothers Karamazov," "Jack Knife," "Vincent," "Stop, You're Killing Me," "Enclave," "Bits and Pieces."

OLSON, MARILYN. Born Feb. 2, 1948 in Chicago, Ill. Graduate Western Ill. U. Bdwy debut 1974 in "Gypsy."

O'NEAL, RON. Born Sept. 1, 1937 in Utica, NY. Attended Ohio State U. Debut 1968 OB in "American Pastoral," followed by "No Place to Be Somebody" for which he received a Theatre World Award, "Dream on Monkey Mountain," Bdwy in "All over Town."

OPATOSHU, DAVID. Born Jan. 30, 1918 in The Bronx, NY. Attended CCNY. Bdwy debut 1940 in "Night Music," followed by "Clinton Street," "Man of Tomorrow," "Me and Molly," "Flight into Egypt," "Reclining Figure," "Silk Stockings," "Once More with Feeling," "The Wall," "Bravo Giovanni," "Lorenzo," "Does a Tiger Wear a Necktie?," OB in "Yoshe Kalb," "Big Winner."

ORBACH, JERRY. Born Oct. 20, 1935 in NYC. Attended Northwestern U. Bdwy debut 1961 in "Carnival," followed by "Guys and Dolls," "Carousel," "Annie Get Your Gun," "The Natural Look," "Promises, Promises," "6 Rms Riv Vu," "Chicago," OB in "Threepenny Opera," "The Fantasticks," "The Cradle Will Rock," "Scuba Duba."

ORFALY, ALEXANDER. Born Oct. 10, 1935 in Brooklyn. Appeared in "South Pacific" (LC), "How Now, Dow Jones," "Ari," "Sugar," "Cyrano," OB in "The End of All Things Natural," "Mahogonny," "Johnny Johnson," "Ride the Winds," "Polly."

ORIN, RENEE. Born Oct. 25 in Slatington, Pa. Attended Carnegie Tech. Debut 1951 OB in "Good News," followed by "The Great Magician," "Riverwind," "Augusta," Bdwy in "Plain and Fancy," "Cafe Crown," "Slapstick Tragedy," "Show Me Where the Good Times Are," "Plaza Suite."

OSHEN, GABRIEL. Born Oct. 8, 1950 in NYC. Bdwy debut 1974 in "Equus."

OTTENHEIMER, ALBERT M. Born Sept. 6, 1904 in Tacoma, Wash. Graduate UWash. Bdwy debut 1946 in "Affair of Honor," followed by "West Side Story," "Deputy," OB in "Monday's Heroes," "Tiger," "Mother Riba," "A Christmas Carol," "Juno and the Paycock," "Italian Straw Hat," "The Iceman Cometh," "Call It Virtue," "The Immoralist," "The Cat and the Canary," "Exhaustion of Our Son's Love," "Deadly Game," "Brother Gorski," "The Kid," "Holy Ghosts," "Yentl the Yeshiva Boy."

OWENS, ELIZABETH. Born Feb. 26, 1938 in NYC. Attended New School, Neighborhood Playhouse. Debut 1955 OB in "Dr. Faustus Lights the Lights," followed by "The Lovers" (Bdwy), "Chit Chat on a Rat," "The Miser," "The Father," "The Importance of Being Earnest," "Candida," "Trumpets and Drums," "Oedipus," "Macbeth," "Not Now Darling" (Bdwy), "Uncle Vanya," "Misalliance," "Master Builder," "American Gothics," "The Play's the Thing," "The Father," "Death Story," "The Rivals."

OYSTER, JIM. Born May 3, 1930 in Washington, DC. OB in "Coriolanus," "The Cretan Woman," "Man and Superman," Bdwy in "Cool World," "Hostile Winners," "The Sound of Music," "The Prime of Miss Jean Brodie," "Who's Who in Hell."

PAGE, GERALDINE. Born Nov. 22, 1924 in Kirksville, Mo. Attended Goodman Theatre. OB in "7 Mirrors," "Summer and Smoke" for which she received a Theatre World Award, "Macbeth," "Look Away," Bdwy debut 1953 in "Midsummer," followed by "The Immoralist," "The Rainmaker," "The Innkeepers," "Separate Tables," "Sweet Bird of Youth," "Strange Interlude," "Three Sisters," "P.S. I Love You," "The Great Indoors," "White Lies," "Black Comedy," "The Little Foxes," "Angela," "Absurd Person Singular."

PALMER, LELAND. Born June 16, 1945 in Port Washington, NY. Bdwy debut 1966 in "Joyful Noise," followed by "Applause," "Pippin," OB in "Your Own Thing."

PALMER, PETER. Born Sept. 20, 1931 in Milwaukee, Wis. Attended UIll. Bdwy debut 1956 in "Li'l Abner" for which he received a Theatre World Award, followed by "Brigadoon" (CC), "Lorelei."

PALMER, STACY. Born in 1930 in Little Valley, NY. Attended UBuffalo, AADA. Debut OB 1971 in "Middle of the Night," followed by "Ah! Wine!" "Sweet Suite."

PALMIERI, JOSEPH. Born Aug. 1, 1939 in Bklyn. Attended Catholic U. With NYSF 1965-6, "Cyrano de Bergerac" (LCR), OB in "Butter and Egg Man," "Boys in the Band," "Beggar's Opera," Bdwy in "Lysistrata," "Candide."

PANKIN, STUART. Born Apr. 8, 1946 in Philadelphia, Pa. Graduate Dickinson Col., Columbia U. Debut OB 1968 with NYSF in "Wars of the Roses," followed by "Richard III," "Timon of Athens," "Cymbeline," "Mary Stuart," "Narrow Road to the Deep North," "Twelfth Night," "The Crucible," "Wings," "A Glorious Age."

PAPE, JOAN. Born Jan. 23, 1944 in Detroit, Mich. Graduate Purdue U., Yale. Debut 1972 in "Suggs" (LC), Bdwy in "The Secret Affairs of Mildred Wild," "Cat on a Hot Tin Roof," OB in "Bloomers."

PARKS, CHARLES. Born Feb. 27, 1940 in Santiago, Chile. Attended Boston U. Debut 1966 OB in "Automobile Graveyard," followed by "Where Do We Go From Here?"

PARSONS, ESTELLE. Born Nov. 20, 1927 in Lynn, Mass. Attended Boston U., Actors Studio. OB in "Threepenny Opera," "Automobile Graveyard," "Mrs. Dally Has a Lover" for which she received a Theatre World Award, "In the Summer House," "Monopoly," "Peer Gynt," "Mahagonny," "Silent Partner," "Barbary Shore," "Oh Glorious Tintinnabulation," with LCR in "East Wind," "Galileo," "People Are Living There," and "Mert and Phil," Bdwy in "Happy Hunting," "Whoop-Up!," "Beg, Borrow or Steal," "Ready When You Are, C. B.," "Malcolm," "Seven Descents of Myrtle," "A Way of Life," "And Miss Reardon Drinks a Little."

PASSELTINER, BERNIE. Born Nov. 21, 1931 in NYC. Graduate Catholic U. OB in "Square in the Eye," "Sourball," "As Virtuously Given," "Now Is the Time for All Good Men," "Rain," "Kaddish," "Against the Sun," "End of Summer," "Yentl, the Yeshiva Boy," Bdwy in "The Office," "The Jar."

PATTON, LUCILLE. Born in NYC; attended Neighborhood Playhouse. Bdwy debut 1946 in "A Winter's Tale," followed by "Topaze," "Arms and the Man," "Joy to the World," "All You Need Is One Good Break," "Fifth Season," "Heavenly Twins," "Rhinoceros," "Marathon '33," "The Last Analysis," "Dinner at 8," "La Strada," "Unlikely Heroes," "Love Suicide at Schofield Barracks," OB in "Ulysses in Nighttown," "Failures," "Three Sisters," "Yes, Yes, No, No," "Tango," "Mme. de Sade."

PAULETTE, LARRY. Born Apr. 10, 1949 in Steubenville, O. Attended UCinn. Debut OB 1974 in "Let My People Come."

PELUSO, LISA. Born July 29, 1964 in Philadelphia, Pa. Bdwy debut 1974 in "Gypsy."

PENDLETON, DAVID. Born Nov. 5, 1937 in Pittsburgh, Pa. Graduate Lincoln U., CCNY. Bdwy debut 1971 in "No Place to Be Somebody," OB in "Screens," "Don't Bother Me, I Can't Cope," "Blueberry Mountain."

Mary Ann Niles

Don Nute

Lynn Oliver

Peggy Pope

Gilbert Price

PENDLETON, WYMAN. Born Apr. 18, 1916 in Providence, RI. Graduate Brown U. Bdwy in "Tiny Alice," "Malcolm," "Quotations from Chairman Mao Tse-Tung," "Happy Days," "Henry V," "Othello," "There's One in Every Marriage," "Cat on a Hot Tin Roof," OB in "Gallows Humor," "American Dream," "Zoo Story," "Corruption in the Palace of Justice," "Giant's Dance," "Child Buyer," "Happy Days," "Butter and Egg Man."

PENDREY, MICHAEL. Born Apr. 13, 1941 in Taft, Ca. Graduate UCBerkeley, Neighborhood Playhouse. Bdwy debut 1969 in "The Great White Hope," followed by "Dreyfus in Rehearsal."

PENN, EDWARD. Born in Washington, DC. Studied at HB Studio. Debut 1965 OB in "The Queen and the Rebels," followed by "My Wife and I," "Invitation to a March," "Of Thee I Sing," "Fantasticks," "Greenwillow," "One for the Money," "Dear Oscar," "Speed Gets the Poppys," "Man with a Load of Mischief." Bdwy bow 1975 in "Shenandoah."

PENTECOST, GEORGE. Born July 15, 1939 in Detroit, Mich. Graduate Wayne State, UMich. With APA in "Scapin," "Lower Depths," "The Tavern," "School for Scandal," "Right You Are," "War and Peace," "The Wild Duck," "The Show-Off," "Pantagleize," and "The Cherry Orchard," OB in "The Boys in the Band," "School for Wives," "Twelfth Night," "Enemies," Bdwy in "The Merry Wives of Windsor," "The Rivals," "The Visit," "Chemin de Fer," "Holiday."

PENZNER, SEYMOUR. Born July 29, 1915 in Yonkers, NY. Attended CCNY. OB in "Crystal Heart," "Guitar," Bdwy in "Oklahoma!," "Finian's Rainbow," "Call Me Madam," "Paint Your Wagon," "Can-Can," "Kean," "Baker Street," "Man of La Mancha."

PERCASSI, DON. Born Jan. 11 in Amsterdam, NY. Bdwy debut 1964 in "High Spirits," followed by "Walking Happy," "Coco," "Sugar," "Molly," "Mack and Mabel," "A Chorus Line."

PERKINS, ANTHONY. Born Apr. 4, 1932 in NYC. Attended Rollins Col., Columbia U. Bdwy debut 1954 in "Tea and Sympathy" for which he received a Theatre World Award, followed by "Look Homeward, Angel," "Greenwillow," "Harold," "Star Spangled Girl," "Steambath" (OB), "Equus."

PERKINS, DON. Born Oct. 23, 1928 in Boston, Mass. Emerson Col. graduate. OB in "Drums under the Window," "Henry VI," "Richard III," "The Dubliners," Bdwy 1970 in "Borstal Boy."

PETERS, BERNADETTE. Born Feb. 28, 1948 in Jamaica, NY. Bdwy debut 1967 in "Girl in the Freudian Slip," followed by "Johnny No-Trump," "George M!" for which she received a Theatre World Award, "La Strada," "On the Town," "Mack and Mabel," OB in "Curley McDimple," "Penny Friend," "Most Happy Fella," "Dames at Sea," "Nevertheless They Laugh."

PETERSEN, ERIKA. Born Mar. 24, 1949 in NYC. Attended NYU. Debut 1963 OB in "One Is a Lonely Number," followed by "I Dreamt I Dwelt in Bloomingdale's," "F. Jasmine Addams," "The Dubliners."

PETERSON, LENKA. Born Oct. 16, 1925 in Omaha, Neb. Attended UIowa. Bdwy debut 1946 in "Bathsheba," followed by "Harvest of Years," "Sundown Beach," "Young and Fair," "Grass Harp," OB in "Mrs. Minter," "American Night Cry," "Leaving Home."

PETRICOFF, ELAINE. Born in Cincinnati, O. Graduate Syracuse U. Bdwy debut 1971 in "The Me Nobody Knows," OB in "Hark!," "Ride the Winds," "Cole Porter," Bdwy debut 1973 in "Grease."

PEYSER, PENNY. Born Feb. 9, 1951 in NYC. Emerson Col. graduate. Debut 1975 OB in "Diamond Studs," followed by "Hot l Baltimore."

PIAZZA, BEN. Born July 30, 1934 in Little Rock, Ark. Attended Princeton U., Actors Studio. Bdwy bow 1958 in "Winesburg, Ohio," followed by "Kataki" for which he received a Theatre World Award, "A Second String," "Fun Couple," "Who's Afraid of Virginia Woolf?," "Song of the Grasshopper," "Death of Bessie Smith," OB in "American Dream," "Deathwatch," "Zoo Story," "Endgame."

PICKLES, CHRISTINA. Born Feb. 17, 1938 in England. Attended RADA. With APA in "School for Scandal," "War and Peace," "The Wild Duck," "Pantagleize," "You Can't Take It with You," "The Seagull," "The Misanthrope," Bdwy in "Inadmissible Evidence," "Who's Who in Hell," "Sherlock Holmes."

PIERCE, RIK. Born Jan. 21, 1939 in NYC. Attended UPittsburgh. OB in "Call It Virtue," "The Experiment," "All My Sons," Bdwy bow 1968 in "Avanti!"

PIGOTT-SMITH, TIMOTHY. Born May 13, 1946 in Rugby, Eng. Graduate Bristol U., Bristol Old Vic Theatre School. Bdwy debut 1974 in "Sherlock Holmes."

PITCHFORD, DEAN. Born July 29, 1951 in Honolulu, Hawaii. Graduate Yale U. Debut 1971 OB in "Godspell," Bdwy 1973 in "Pippin."

PLAYTEN, ALICE. Born Aug. 28, 1947 in NYC. Attended NYU. Bdwy debut 1960 in "Gypsy," followed by "Oliver," "Hello, Dolly!," "Henry, Sweet Henry" for which she received a Theatre World Award, "George M!," OB in "Promenade," "Last Sweet Days of Isaac," "National Lampoon's Lemmings," "Valentine's Day."

PLUMLEY, DON. Born Feb. 11, 1934 in Los Angeles, Ca. Pepperdine Col. graduate. Debut 1961 OB in "The Cage," followed by "A Midsummer Night's Dream," "Richard II," "Cymbeline," "Much Ado about Nothing," "Saving Grace," "A Whistle in the Dark," "Operation Sidewinder," "Enemy of the People," "Back Bog Beast Bait," "The Kid," Bdwy 1974 in "Equus."

POLITO, PHILIP. Born Feb. 17, 1944 in Hackensack, NJ. Graduate Ill. Wesleyan U., Yale. Bdwy debut 1969 in "1776," OB in "As You Like It," "Boom Boom Room."

PONAZECKI, JOE. Born Jan. 7, 1934 in Rochester, NY. Attended Rochester U., Columbia. Bdwy bow 1959 in "Much Ado About Nothing," followed by "Send Me No Flowers," "Call on Kuprin," "Take Her, She's Mine," "Fiddler on the Roof," "Xmas in Las Vegas," "3 Bags Full," "Love in E-Flat," "90 Day Mistress," "Harvey," "Trial of the Catonsville 9," "Country Girl," "Freedom of the City," OB in "The Dragon," "Muzeeka," "Witness," "All Is Bright," "The Dog Ran Away," "Dream of a Blacklisted Actor."

PONZINI, ANTONY. Born June 1. Attended Neighborhood Playhouse, Actors Studio. Debut 1959 OB in "The Breaking Wall," followed by "Oh, Dad, Poor Dad . . . ," "Glory in the Flower," "Purification," Bdwy in "Arturo Ui," "P.S. Your Cat Is Dead."

POPE, PEGGY. Born May 15, 1929 in Montclair, NJ. Attended Smith Col. On Bdwy in "Doctor's Dilemma," "Volpone," "Rose Tattoo," "Harvey," "School for Wives," "Dr. Jazz," OB in "Muzeeka," "House of Blue Leaves," "New Girl in Town."

PORTER, STAN. Born July 1, 1928 in Brooklyn, NY. Bdwy debut 1967 in "Hello, Solly!," OB in "Jacques Brel Is Alive and Well and Living in Paris," followed by "Big Winner."

POSER, LINDA. Born in Los Angeles, Cal. Graduate San Francisco State U. Debut 1973 OB in "Call Me Madam," followed by "The Boy Friend."

POSTON, RICHARD. Born Apr. 7, 1922 in Columbus, O. Attended Northeastern U., New Eng. Cons. Bdwy debut 1948 in "The Insect Comedy," followed by "The Mikado," "Stalag 17," "The Chase," OB in "The Rise and Fall of Burlesque Humor."

POSTON, TOM. Born Oct. 17, 1921 in Columbus, O. Attended Bethany Col., AADA. Bdwy debut 1947 in "Cyrano de Bergerac," followed by "Insect Comedy," "King Lear," "Stockade," "Grand Prize," "Will Success Spoil Rock Hunter?," "Goodbye Again," "Romanoff and Juliet," "Drink to Me Only," "Golden Fleecing," "Come Play with Me" (OB), "Conquering Hero," "Come Blow Your Horn," "Mary, Mary," "But Seriously," "40 Carats," "A Funny Thing Happened on the Way to the Forum."

POTTER, DON. Born Aug. 15, 1932 in Philadelphia, Pa. Debut 1961 OB in "What a Killing," followed by "Sunset," "You're a Good Man, Charlie Brown," "One Cent Plain," Bdwy 1974 in "Gypsy."

POWERS, JOEL. Born May 27, 1947 in Wallkill, NY. Graduate Boston U. OB in "Like It Is," "The Visit," Bdwy bow 1975 in "The Lieutenant."

POWERS, NEVA RAE. Born in Oakland City, Ind. Graduate Cincinnati Cons. Debut 1974 OB in "The Boy Friend."

PRESTON, ROBERT. Born June 8, 1918 in Newton Highlands, Mass. Attended Pasadena Playhouse. Bdwy debut 1951 in "20th Century," followed by "The Male Animal," "Men of Distinction," "His and Hers," "The Magic and the Loss," "Tender Trap," "Janus," "Hidden River," "Music Man," "Too True to Be Good," "Nobody Loves an Albatross," "Ben Franklin in Paris," "The Lion in Winter," "I Do! I Do!," "Mack and Mabel."

PRESTON, WILLIAM. Born Aug. 26, 1921 in Columbia, Pa. Graduate Pa. State U. Debut OB 1972 in "We Bombed in New Haven," followed by "Hedda Gabler," "Whisper into My Good Ear," "A Nestless Bird," "Friends of Mine," "Iphigenia in Aulis."

PRICE, GILBERT. Born Sept. 10, 1942 in NYC. Attended AmThWing. Bdwy bow 1965 in "Roar of the Greasepaint . . . ," followed by "Lost in the Stars," "The Night That Made America Famous," OB in "Kicks & Co.," "Fly Blackbird," "Jerico-Jim Crow" for which he received a Theatre World Award, "Promenade," "Slow Dance on the Killing Ground," "Six," "Melodrama Play."

PRICE, PAUL B. Born Oct. 7, 1933 in Carteret, NJ. Attended Pasadena Playhouse. Debut 1960 OB in "Dead End," followed by "Banquet for the Moon," "O Say Can You See," "Dumbwaiter," "Live Like Pigs," "Medea," "4H Club," "Waiting for Godot," Bdwy in "A Cook for Mr. General," "Let Me Hear You Smile," "The Ritz."

Tom Quinn

Gina Ramsel

Lee Roy Reams

Joy Rinaldi

Jess Richards

PRYOR, NICHOLAS. Born Jan. 28, 1935 in Baltimore, Md. Attended Yale. Bdwy in "Small War on Murray Hill," "Egghead," "Love Me Little," "Who's Afraid of Virginia Woolf?," OB in "Borak," "Party for Divorce," "Boys in the Band," "Scott and Zelda," "Thieves."

PYSHER, ERNIE. Born in Youngstown, O. Graduate Youngstown State U. Bdwy debut 1974 in "Good News," followed by "The Night That Made America Famous," OB in "Carousel."

QUARRY, RICHARD. Born Aug. 9, 1944 in Akron, O. Graduate UAkron, NYU. Bdwy bow 1970 in "Georgy," followed by "Oh! Calcutta!," "Grease."

QUINN, TOM. Born Oct. 6, 1934 in NYC. Attended Indiana U., CCNY. Debut 1974 OB in "Moonchildren," followed by "Boom Boom Room."

RADIGAN, MICHAEL. Born May 2, 1949 in Springfield, Ill. Graduate Springfield Col., Goodman Theatre. Debut 1974 in "Music! Music!" (CC), followed by "Broadway Dandies," (OB).

RAE, CHARLOTTE. Born Apr. 22, 1926 in Milwaukee, Wis. Northwestern graduate. Bdwy debut 1952 in "3 Wishes for Jamie," followed by "Li'l Abner," "The Beauty Part," "Pickwick," "Morning, Noon and Night," "The Chinese," OB in "Threepenny Opera," "Littlest Revue," "Beggar's Opera," "New Tenant," "Victims of Duty," "Henry IV," "Whiskey," "Boom Boom Room."

RAE, SHEILAH. Born Apr. 27, 1946 in Chicago, Ill. Graduate UMich. Bdwy debut 1967 in "Fiddler on the Roof," followed by "Applause," "Selling of the President," OB in "Horror Show," "Iphigenia."

RAGNO, JOSEPH. Born Mar. 11, 1936 in Bklyn. Attended Allegheny Col. Debut 1960 OB in "Worm in the Horseradish," followed by "Elizabeth the Queen," "A Country Scandal," "The Shrike," "Cymbeline," "Love Me, Love My Children," "Interrogation of Havana," "The Birds," "Armenians," Bdwy in "Indians," "The Iceman Cometh."

RALSTON, TERI. Born Feb. 16, 1943 in Holyoke, Colo. Graduate SF State Col. Debut 1969 OB in "Jacques Brel Is Alive . . . ," Bdwy 1970 in "Company," followed by "A Little Night Music."

RAMOS, RICHARD. Born Aug. 23, 1941 in Seattle, Wash. Graduate UMinn. Bdwy debut 1968 in "House of Atreus," followed by "Arturo Ui," OB in "Adaptation," "Screens," "Lotta," "The Tempest," "A Midsummer Night's Dream."

RAMSAY, LOUIE. Born Nov. 25, in South Africa. Attended RADA. Bdwy debut 1975 in "The Misanthrope."

RAMSAY, REMAK. Born Feb. 2, 1937 in Baltimore, Md. Princeton Graduate. OB in "Hang Down Your Head and Die," "The Real Inspector Hound," Bdwy in "Half a Sixpence," "Sheep on the Runway," "Lovely Ladies, Kind Gentlemen," "On the Town," "Jumpers," "Private Lives."

RAMSEL, GINA. Born Feb. 10, 1950 in El Reno, Okla. Graduate SMU. Bdwy debut 1974 in "Lorelei."

RAMSEY, DAVID. Born Nov. 15, in Shawnee, Okla. Attended UIowa. OB in "Holy Moses," "Jesse James," "The Kid," Bdwy debut 1974 in "Equus."

RANDALL, CHARLES. Born Mar. 15, 1923 in Chicago, Ill. Attended Columbia U. Bdwy bow 1953 in "Anastasia," followed by "Enter Laughing," "Trial of Lee Harvey Oswald," OB in "The Adding Machine," "Cherry Orchard," "Brothers Karamazov," "Susan Slept Here," "Two for Fun," "Timon of Athens."

RANDELL, RON. Born Oct. 8, 1920 in Sydney, Aust. Attended St. Mary's Col. Bdwy debut 1949 in "The Browning Version," followed by "A Harlequinade," "Candida," "World of Suzie Wong," "Sherlock Holmes."

RAPHAEL, GERRIANNE. Born Feb. 23, 1935 in NYC. Attended New School, Columbia U. Bdwy in "Solitaire," "Guest in the House," "Violet," "Goodbye, My Fancy," "Seventh Heaven," "Li'l Abner," "Saratoga," "Man of La Mancha," OB in "Threepenny Opera," "The Boy Friend," "Ernest in Love," "Say When," "The Prime of Miss Jean Brodie."

RAVEN, ELSA. Born Sept 21, 1929 in Charleston, SC. Attended Charleston Col. Bdwy debut 1959 in "Legend of Lizzie," OB in "Taming of the Shrew," "In a Bar in a Tokyo Hotel," "The Web and the Rock," "Safe Place."

RAYE, ROBERT. Born Sept. 2, 1954 in Phoenix, Ariz. Debut OB 1974 in "The Boy Friend."

RAYSON, BENJAMIN. Born in NYC. Bdwy debut 1953 in "Can-Can," followed by "Silk Stockings," "Bells Are Ringing," "A Little Night Music."

REAMS, LEE ROY. Born Aug. 23, 1942 in Covington, Ky. Graduate U. Cinn. Cons. Bdwy debut 1966 in "Sweet Charity," followed by "Oklahoma!" (LC), "Applause," "Lorelei."

REARDON, NANCY. Born June 28, 1942 in NYC. Bdwy debut 1964 in "Poor Bitos," followed by "The Right Honourable Gentleman," "Odd Couple," "Black Comedy," "The Unknown Soldier and His Wife," "Arturo Ui," "Fame," OB in "Charles Abbott & Son," "She Stoops to Conquer."

REDFIELD, DENNIS. Born Feb. 23, 1943 in Orange, Ca. Graduate ENMex. U., Cal. State U. Debut 1971 OB in "James Joyce Memorial Liquid Theatre," Bdwy 1974 in "The Hashish Club."

REDFIELD, MARILYN. Born May 2, 1940 in Chicago, Ill. Graduate Vassar, Harvard U., HB Studio. Debut 1973 OB in "The Rainmaker," followed by "Monologia," "Mod Madonna," "King of the U.S."

REDGRAVE, LYNN. Born in London Mar. 8, 1943. Attended Central Sch. of Speech. Bdwy debut 1967 in "Black Comedy," followed by "My Fat Friend."

REED, ALAINA. Born Nov. 10, 1946 in Springfield, O. Attended Kent State U. Bdwy debut in "Hair," followed by "Sgt. Pepper's Lonely Heart's Club Band" (OB).

REED, ALEXANDER. Born June 9, 1916 in Clearfield, Pa. Graduate Columbia U. Debut OB 1956 in "Lady from the Sea," followed by "All the King's Men," "Death of Satan," "The Balcony," "Call Me by My Rightful Name," "Studs Edsel," "The Coroner's Plot," on Bdwy in "Witness," "Lost in the Stars."

REED, GAVIN. Born June 3, 1935 in Liverpool, Eng. Attended RADA. Debut OB 1974 in "Taming of the Shrew," followed by "French without Tears," Bdwy 1974 in "Scapino."

REES, ROGER. Born May 5, 1946 in Abersystwyth, Wales. Bdwy debut 1974 in "London Assurance."

REID, KATE. Born Nov. 4, 1930 in London. Attended Toronto U. Bdwy debut 1962 in "Who's Afraid of Virginia Woolf?," followed by "Dylan," "Slapstick Tragedy," "The Price," "Freedom of the City," "Cat on a Hot Tin Roof."

REILLY, CHARLES NELSON. Born Jan. 13, 1931 in NYC. Attended Conn.U. OB in "Nightcar," "Fallout," "Lend an Ear," "Parade," "Inspector General," "3 Times 3," "Apollo of Bellac," Bdwy bow 1960 in "Bye Bye Birdie," followed by "How to Succeed in Business . . . ," "Hello, Dolly!," "Skyscraper," "God's Favorite."

REMME, JOHN. Born Nov. 21, 1935 in Fargo, NDak. Debut 1972 OB in "One for the Money," Bdwy 1975 in "The Ritz."

REINKING, ANN. Born Nov. 10, 1949 in Seattle, Wash. Attended Joffrey Sch., HB Studio. Bdwy debut 1969 in "Cabaret," followed by "Coco," "Pippin," "Over Here" for which she received a Theatre World Award, "Goodtime Charley."

REVILL, CLIVE. Born Apr. 18, 1930 in Wellington, NZ. Attended Rongotai Col. Bdwy debut 1952 in "Mr. Pickwick," followed by "Irma La Douce," "Oliver!," "Sherry!," "The Incomparable Max," "Sherlock Holmes."

REXROAD, DAVID. Born Jan. 11, 1950 in Parkersburg, WVa. Graduate WVa. U. Debut OB 1973 in "The Fantasticks."

RHYS, WILLIAM. Born Jan. 2, 1945 in NYC. Graduate Wesleyan U. Bdwy debut 1969 with National Theatre of the Deaf, followed by "The Changing Room," "Birth" (OB).

RICE, SARAH. Born Mar. 5, 1955 in Okinawa. Attended Ariz. State U. Debut 1974 OB in "The Fantasticks."

RICHARDS, JESS. Born Jan. 23, 1943 in Seattle, Wash. Attended UWash. Bdwy debut 1966 in "Walking Happy," followed by "South Pacific" (LC), "Blood Red Roses," "Two by Two," "On the Town" for which he received a Theatre World Award, "Mack and Mabel," OB in "One for the Money."

RICHARDS, JON. Born in Wilkes Barre, Pa. Bdwy in "Tobacco Road," "Arsenic and Old Lace," "Love or Money," "Gramercy Ghost," "Bad Seed," "Sunrise at Campobello," "Sail Away," "A Murderer among Us," "A Very Rich Woman," "Roar like a Dove," "Elizabeth the Queen," "3 Bags Full," "Woman Is My Idea," "Does a Tiger Wear a Necktie?," OB in "Leave It to Jane," "One Flew over the Cuckoo's Nest," "Come Back, Little Sheba," "Room Service."

RICHARDS, PAUL-DAVID. Born Aug. 31, 1935 in Bedford, Ind. Graduate Indiana U. Bdwy debut 1959 in "Once upon a Mattress," followed by "Camelot," "It's Superman!," "A Joyful Noise," "1776," OB in "Black Picture Show."

RIDDLE, GEORGE. Born May 21, 1937 in Auburn, Ind. OB in "Eddie Fey," "The Prodigal," "The Fantasticks," "Huui, Huui," "The Glorious Age."

RIGG, DIANA. Born July 20, 1938 in Doncaster, Eng. Attended RADA. Bdwy debut 1964 in "Comedy of Errors," followed by "King Lear," "Abelard and Heloise," "The Misanthrope."

RILEY, ED. Born Apr. 1, 1933 in Kulpmont, Pa. Attended Georgetown U. OB in "Little Mary Sunshine," Bdwy 1969 in "The Front Page," followed by "Gypsy."

RINALDI, JOY. Born in Yonkers, NY. Graduate Stephens Col., AADA. Debut OB 1969 in "Satisfaction Guaranteed," Bdwy 1973 in "Grease."

RITTER, KATHRYN. Born Aug. 1, 1948 in NYC. Attended NYU. Bdwy debut 1974 in "Candide."

Chita Rivera   **William Robertson**   **Marcia Rodd**   **Chris Romilly**   **Gloria Rossi**

RIVERA, CHITA. Born Jan. 23, 1933 in Washington, DC. Attended AmSch. of Ballet. Bdwy debut 1950 in "Guys and Dolls," followed by "Call Me Madam," "Can-Can," "Shoestring Revue" (OB), "Seventh Heaven," "Mr. Wonderful," "West Side Story," "Bye Bye Birdie," "Bajour," "Chicago."

RIVERA, MARTIN. Born July 1, 1952 in NYC. Attended NYU. OB in "Madness of Lady Bright," "The Pledge," "Belches and Well Fair," "Everybody Knows My Business," "Lovers."

ROBARDS, JASON. Born July 26, 1922 in Chicago, Ill. Attended AADA. Bdwy debut 1947 with D'Oyly Carte, followed by "Stalag 17," "The Chase," "Long Day's Journey into Night" for which he received a Theatre World Award, "The Disenchanted," "Toys in the Attic," "Big Fish, Little Fish," "A Thousand Clowns," "Hughie," "The Devils," "We Bombed in New Haven," "The Country Girl," "Moon for the Misbegotten," OB in "American Gothic," "The Iceman Cometh," "After the Fall," "But for Whom Charlie."

ROBBINS, JANA. Born Apr. 18, 1947 in Johnstown, Pa. Stephens Col. graduate. Bdwy debut 1974 in "Good News."

ROBBINS, MARLA JANE. Born Nov. 2, 1944 in NYC. Bryn Mawr graduate. Bdwy debut 1969 in "Morning, Noon and Night," OB in "The Bear," "Beyond Desire," "Deep Six the Briefcase," "Dear Nobody," "Richard III."

ROBBINS, REX. Born in Pierre, SDak. Bdwy debut 1964 in "One Flew over the Cuckoo's Nest," followed by "Scratch," "The Changing Room," "Gypsy," OB in "Servant of Two Masters," "The Alchemist," "Arms and the Man," "Boys in the Band."

ROBERTS, ARTHUR. Born Aug. 10, 1938 in NYC. Graduate Harvard U. Debut 1964 OB in "Hamlet," followed by "Galileo," "Boys in the Band," "Anna K.," "Overnight," Bdwy 1970 in "Borstal Boy."

ROBERTS, DORIS. Born in St. Louis, Mo. Attended Actors Studio, Neighborhood Playhouse. Bdwy debut 1956 in "The Desk Set," followed by "Have I Got a Girl for You," "Malcolm," "Marathon '33," "Under the Weather," "The Office," "The Natural Look," "Last of the Red Hot Lovers," "Secret Affairs of Mildred Wild," OB in "Death of Bessie Smith," "American Dream," "Color of Darkness," "Don't Call Me By My Rightful Name," "Christy," "Boy in the Straight-back Chair," "A Matter of Position," "Natural Affection," "Time of Your Life" (CC), "Bad Habits," "Ladies at the Alamo."

ROBERTS, MARILYN. Born Oct. 30, 1939 in San Francisco, Ca. Graduate SF State Col. Debut 1963 OB in "Telemachus Clay," followed by "The Maids," "The Class," "Gabriella," "Tom Paine," "Futz," "Candaules Commissioner," "Persia," "Masque of St. George and The Dragon," "Split Lip," "Mert and Phil."

ROBERTS, TONY. Born Oct. 22, 1939 in NYC. Graduate Northwestern U. Bdwy bow 1962 in "Something about a Soldier," followed by "Take Her, She's Mine," "Last Analysis," "The Cradle Will Rock" (OB), "Never Too Late," "Barefoot in the Park," "Don't Drink the Water," "How Now, Dow Jones," "Play It Again, Sam," "Promises, Promises," "Sugar," "Absurd Person Singular."

ROBERTSON, JANE. Born May 17, 1948 in Bartlesville, Okla. Attended UOkla. Debut 1970 OB in "Shoestring Revues," followed by "DuBarry Was a Lady," "Buy Bonds Buster," Bdwy 1975 in "A Matter of Time."

ROBERTSON, WILLIAM. Born Oct. 9, 1908 in Portsmouth, Va. Graduate Pomona Col. Bdwy debut 1936 in "Tapestry in Grey," followed by "Cup of Trembling," "Liliom," "Our Town," OB in "Uncle Harry," "Shining Hour," "Aspern Papers," "Madame Is Served," "Tragedian in spite of Himself," "Kibosh," "Sun-Up," "The Last Pad," "Hamlet," "Girls Most Likely to Succeed," "The Petrified Forest," "The Minister's Black Veil," "Santa Anita," "Babylon," "Midsummer Night's Dream," "A Touch of the Poet," "The Zykovs."

ROBIN, NAOMI. Born Mar. 18, 1948 in Brooklyn, NY. Graduate Brooklyn Col. Debut 1963 OB with American Savoyards, followed by "The Awakening of Spring," "House of Blue Leaves," "Booth Is Back in Town," "Arms and the Man."

ROBINSON, HAL. Born in Bedford, Ind. Graduate Ind. U. Debut 1971 OB in "Memphis Store-Bought Teeth," followed by "From Berlin to Broadway," "The Fantasticks."

RODD, MARCIA. Born July 8 in Lyons, Kan. Attended Northwestern U., Yale Col. Debut OB in "O Say Can You See L.A.," "Cambridge Circus," "Mad Show," "Madame Mousse," "Love and Let Love," "Your Own Thing," "Merry Wives of Windsor," Bdwy debut 1964 in "Love in E-Flat," followed by "Last of the Red Hot Lovers," "Shelter."

RODDICK, JOHN. Born Oct. 5, 1944 in Melbourne, Aust. Graduate Melbourne U. Debut OB 1971 in "James Joyce Memorial Liquid Theatre," followed by "The Contractor," "Macbeth" (LC).

RODGERS, JERRY. Born Aug. 20, 1941 in Stockton, Ca. Graduate UPortland. Debut 1971 OB in "Miss Lizzie," followed by "Shakuntala," "Life in Bed," "Rainbow Rape Trick."

RODGERS, SHEV. Born Apr. 9, 1928 in Holister, Cal. Attended SF State Col. Bdwy bow 1959 in "Redhead," followed by "Music Man," "Man of La Mancha" (also LC), OB in "Get Thee to Canterbury," "War Games," "Moonchildren."

RODRIGUEZ, EDWARD. Born Mar. 11, 1946 in Bayamon, PR. Graduate AMDA. Debut 1974 OB in "How to Get Rid of It."

ROERICK, WILLIAM. Born Dec. 17, 1912 in NYC. Bdwy bow 1935 in "Romeo and Juliet," followed by "St. Joan," "Hamlet," "Our Town," "Importance of Being Earnest," "The Land is Bright," "Autumn Hill," "This Is the Army," "Magnificent Yankee," "Tonight at 8:30," "The Heiress," "Medea," "Macbeth," "Burning Glass," "Right Honourable Gentleman," "Marat/deSade," "Homecoming," "We Bombed in New Haven," "Elizabeth the Queen" (CC), "Waltz of the Toreadors," OB in "Madam, Will You Walk," "Come Slowly, Eden," "A Passage to E. M. Forster," "Trials of Oz."

ROFFMAN, ROSE. Has appeared OB in "La Madre," "Harold Pinter Plays," "Arthur Miller Double Bill," "Happy Hypocrite," "Under Gaslight," "Beaux Stratagem," "Tea Party," "The Boy Friend."

ROFFRANO, ALBERT. Born May 16, 1947 in Brooklyn, NY. Bdwy debut 1968 in "Henry V," followed by "The Misanthrope."

ROGAN, PETER. Born May 11, 1939 in County Leitrim, Ire. Bdwy debut 1966 in "Philadelphia, Here I Come!," OB in "The Kitchen," "Nobody Hears a Broken Drum," "Picture of Dorian Gray," "Macbeth," "Sjt. Musgrave's Dance," "Stephen D.," "People Are Living There," "The Plough and the Stars," "Look Back in Anger."

ROGERS, GIL. Born Feb. 4, 1934 in Lexington, Ky. Attended Harvard. OB in "The Ivory Branch," "Vanity of Nothing," "Warrior's Husband," "Hell Bent fer Heaven," "Gods of Lightning," "Pictures in the Hallway," "Rose," "Memory Bank," "A Recent Killing," "Birth" "Come Back, Little Sheba," Bdwy debut 1968 in "The Great White Hope."

ROLPH, MARTI. Born March 8 in Los Angeles, Ca. Occidental Col. graduate. Bdwy debut 1971 in "Follies," followed by "Good News" for which she received a Theatre World Award.

ROMILLY, CHRIS. Born Oct. 19, 1950 in NYC. Graduate Cornell U. Debut 1974 OB in "The Desperate Hours."

ROSE, GEORGE. Born Feb. 19, 1920 in Bicester, Eng. Bdwy debut with Old Vic 1946 in "Henry IV," followed by "Much Ado about Nothing," "A Man for All Seasons," "Hamlet," "Royal Hunt of the Sun," "Walking Happy," "Loot," "My Fair Lady" (CC '68), "Canterbury Tales," "Coco," "Wise Child," "Sleuth." "My Fat Friend."

ROSE, NORMAN. Born June 23, 1917 in Philadelphia, Pa. Graduate George Washington U. Bdwy in "Cafe Crown," "St. Joan," "Land of Fame," "Richard III," "Fifth Season," OB in "Career," "Hemingway Hero," "Wicked Cooks," "Empire Builders," "The Old Ones."

ROSEN, ROBERT. Born Apr. 24, 1954 in NYC. Attended Indiana U., HB Studio. Bdwy debut 1975 in "Shenandoah."

ROSKAM, CATHRYN. Born May 30, 1943 in Hempstead, NY. Middlebury Col. graduate. Debut 1970 OB in "Gandhi," followed by "Autumn Garden."

ROSSI, GLORIA. Born Nov. 16, 1946 in San Francisco, Cal. Attended SF State, Syracuse U. Bdwy debut 1973 in "The Desert Song," followed by "Gypsy."

ROUNDS, DAVID. Born Oct. 9, 1938 in Bronxville, NY. Attended Denison U. Bdwy debut 1965 in "Foxy" followed by "Child's Play" for which he received a Theatre World Award, "The Rothschilds," "The Last of Mrs. Lincoln," "Chicago," OB in "You Never Can Tell," "Money," "The Real Inspector Hound," "Epic of Buster Friend," "Enter a Free Man."

ROWE, HANSFORD. Born May 12, 1924 in Richmond , Va. Graduate URichmond. Bdwy debut 1968 in "We Bombed in New Haven," OB in "Curley McDimple," "The Fantasticks," "Last Analysis," "God Says There Is No Peter Ott," "Mourning Becomes Electra," "Bus Stop."

RUBINSTEIN, JOHN. Born Dec. 8, 1946 in Los Angeles. Attended UCLA. Bdwy debut 1972 in "Pippin" for which he received a Theatre World Award.

RUDD, PAUL. Born May 15, 1940 in Boston, Mass. OB in "Henry IV," followed by "King Lear," "A Cry of Players," "Midsummer Night's Dream," "An Evening with Merlin Finch," "In the Matter of J. Robert Oppenheimer," "Elagabalus," Bdwy in "The Changing Room," "The National Health."

Richard Sabellico   **Marcia Savella**   **Richard Sanders**   **Isabel Segovia**   **Robert Schlee**

RULE, CHARLES. Born Aug. 4, 1928 in Springfield, Mo. Bdwy bow 1951 in "Courtin' Time," followed by "Happy Hunting," "Oh, Captain!," "Conquering Hero," "Donnybrook," "Bye, Bye Birdie," "Fiddler on the Roof," "Henry, Sweet Henry," "Maggie Flynn," "1776," "Cry for All of Us," "Gypsy," "Goodtime Charley."

RULE, SEAN. Born Apr. 6, 1961 in NYC. Bdwy debut 1974 in "Gypsy."

RUPERT, MICHAEL. Born Oct. 23, 1951 in Denver, Colo. Attended Pasadena Playhouse. Bdwy debut 1968 in "The Happy Time" for which he received a Theatre World Award, followed by "Pippin."

RUSSAK, GERARD. Born Sept. 11, 1927 in Paterson, NJ. Attended NY Col. of Music. Bdwy bow 1967 in "Marat/deSade," followed by "Zorba," OB in "The Fantasticks."

RUSSELL, DAVID. Born Aug. 9, 1949 in Allenwood, Pa. Ithaca Col. graduate. Bdwy debut 1975 in "Shenandoah."

RUST, ALAN. Born June 27 in Mansfield, O. Graduate Adrian Col., Ohio U. Debut OB 1973 in "Broadway," followed by "The Three Musketeers."

RYAN, CHARLENE. Born in NYC. Bdwy debut 1964 in "Never Live over a Pretzel Factory," followed by "Sweet Charity," "Fig Leaves Are Falling," "Coco," "A Funny Thing Happened on the Way to the Forum," "Chicago."

RYAN, MICHAEL. Born Mar. 19, 1929 in Wichita, Kan. Attended St. Benedict's Col., Georgetown U., Stella Adler Studio. Bdwy in "Advise and Consent," "Complaisant Lover," OB in "Richard III," "King Lear," "Hedda Gabler," "The Barroom Monks," "Portrait of the Artist as a Young Man," "Autumn Garden," "Naomi Court."

RYDER, RICHARD. Born Aug. 20, 1942 in Rochester, NY. Attended Colgate U., Pratt Inst. Bdwy debut 1972 in "Oh, Calcutta!," followed by "Via Galactica," OB in "Rain," "Oh, Pshaw!," "The Dog beneath the Skin," "Polly," "Lovers."

RYLAND, JACK. Born July 2, 1935 in Lancaster, Pa. Attended AFDA. Bdwy debut 1958 in "The World of Suzie Wong," followed by "A Very Rich Woman," "Henry V," OB in "A Palm Tree in a Rose Garden," "Lysistrata," "The White Rose and the Red," "Old Glory," "Cyrano de Bergerac," "Mourning Becomes Electra."

SABELLICO, RICHARD. Born June 29, 1951 in NYC. Attended C. W. Post Col. Bdwy debut 1974 in "Gypsy."

SADUSK, MAUREEN. Born Sept. 8, 1948 in Brooklyn, NY. Attended AADA. Debut 1969 OB in "We'd Rather Switch," followed by "O Glorious Tintinnabulation," "New Girl in Town."

ST. JOHN, MARCO. Born May 7, 1939 in New Orleans, La. Graduate Fordham U. Bdwy bow 1964 in "Poor Bitos," followed by "And Things That Go Bump in the Night," "The Unknown Soldier and His Wife," "Weekend," "40 Carats," APA's "We Comrades Three" and "War and Peace," OB in "Angels of Anadarko," "Man of Destiny," "Timon of Athens," "Richard III."

SANCHEZ, JAIME. Born Dec. 19, 1938 in Rincon, PR. Attended Actors Studio. Bdwy bow 1957 in "West Side Story," followed by "Oh, Dad, Poor Dad, . . .," "Midsummer Night's Dream," OB in "The Toilet," "Conerico Was Here to Stay" for which he received a Theatre World Award, "Ox Cart," "The Tempest," "Merry Wives of Windsor."

SANDERS, HONEY. Born Dec. 24, 1928 in Brooklyn, NY. Attended Hofstra U. Bdwy debut 1961 in "13 Daughters," followed by "Mame," "Education of Hyman Kaplan," "Heathen," CC's "South Pacific," and "Rose Tattoo," OB in "She Shall Have Music," "Tobacco Road," "Fiddler on the Roof" (JB).

SANDERS, RICHARD. Born Aug. 23, 1940 in Harrisburg. Pa. Graduate Carnegie Tech., LAMDA. Bdwy debut 1973 in "Raisin."

SANDY, GARY. Born Dec. 25, 1945 in Dayton, O. Attended Wilmington Col., AADA. Bdwy debut 1974 in "Saturday Sunday Monday," OB in "Pequod," "Children's Mass."

SANFORD, JANE. Born March. 15, 1943 in NYC. Graduate Carnegie Tech. Bdwy debut 1970 in "Gloria and Esperanza," OB in "Moondreamers," "Lost Jazz," "Where Do We Go from Here?"

SANTELL, MARIE. Born July 8 in Brooklyn, NY. Bdwy debut 1957 in "Music Man," followed by "A Funny Thing Happened on the Way . . .," "Flora the Red Menace," "Pajama Game," "Mack and Mabel," OB in "Hi, Paisano," "Boys from Syracuse," "Peace," "Promenade," "The Drunkard," "Sensations."

SARNO, JANET. Born Nov. 18, 1933 in Bridgeport, Conn. Graduate S. Conn. Teachers Col., Yale U. Bdwy debut 1963 in "Dylan," OB in "Six Characters in Search of an Author," "Who's Happy Now," "Closing Green," "Fisher," "Survival of St. Joan," "The Orphan," "All My Sons."

SAUNDERS, JANET. Born March 26 in NYC. Debut 1974 OB in "Broadway Dandies."

SAVELLA, MARCIA. Born Nov. 6, 1947 in Cranston, RI. Graduate UConn. Bdwy debut 1973 in "The Iceman Cometh," OB in "Circus."

SCARDINO, DON. Born in Feb. 1949 in NYC. Attended CCNY. On Bdwy in "Loves of Cass McGuire," "Johnny No-Trump," "My Daughter, Your Son," OB in "Shout from the Rooftops," "Rimers of Eldritch," "The Unknown Soldier and His Wife," "Godspell," "Moonchildren," "Kid Champion."

SCHACT, SAM. Born Apr. 19, 1936 in The Bronx. Graduate CCNY. OB in "Fortune and Men's Eyes," "Cannibals," "I Met a Man," "The Increased Difficulty of Concentration" (LCR), "One Night Stands of a Noisy Passenger," "Owners," Bdwy in "The Magic Show."

SCHLEE, ROBERT. Born June 13, 1938 in Williamsport, Pa. Lycoming Col. graduate. Debut 1972 OB in "Dr. Selavy's Magic Theatre," followed by "Hotel for Criminals."

SCHMIDT, HARVEY. Born Sept. 12, 1929 in Dallas Tex. Graduate UTex. Debut 1974 OB in "Portfolio Revue." Composer of "The Fantasticks," "110 in the Shade," "I Do! I Do!," "Celebration," "Colette."

SCHNABEL, STEFAN. Born Feb. 2, 1912 in Berlin, Ger. Attended UBonn, Old Vic. Bdwy bow 1937 in "Julius Caesar," followed by "Shoemaker's Holiday," "Glamour Preferred," "Land of Fame," "Cherry Orchard," "Around the World in 80 Days," "Now I Lay Me Down to Sleep," "Idiot's Delight" (CC), "Love of Four Colonels," "Plain and Fancy," "Small War on Murray Hill," "A Very Rich Woman," "A Patriot for Me," OB in "Tango," "In the Matter of J. Robert Oppenheimer," "Older People," "Enemies," "Little Black Sheep," "Rosmersholm."

SCHREIBER, AVERY. Born Apr. 9, 1935 in Chicago, Ill. Goodman Theatre graduate. Debut 1965 OB in "Second City at Square East," followed by "Conerico Was Here to Stay," Bdwy in "Metamorphoses," "Dreyfus in Rehearsal."

SCOTT, GEORGE C. Born Oct. 18, 1927 in Wise, Va. OB in "Richard II" for which he received a Theatre World Award, followed by "As You Like It," "Children of Darkness," "Desire under the elms," Bdwy in "Comes a Day," "Andersonville Trial," "The Wall," "General Seeger," "Little Foxes," "Plaza Suite," "Uncle Vanya."

SCOTT, LEA. Born Oct. 5 in NYC. Debut 1962 OB in "The Blacks," followed by "No Place to Be Somebody," "Black Electra," "Soon Jack November," "Arrin and Sugar-Mouth."

SCOTT, SERET. Born Sept. 1, 1949 in Washington, DC. Attended NYU Debut OB 1969 in "Slave Ship," followed by "Ceremonies in Dark Old Men," "Black Terror," "Dream," "One Last Look," "My Sister, My Sister."

SCOTT, STEPHEN. Born Feb. 8, 1928 in London, Eng. Attended Central Speech School. Bdwy debut 1967 in "There's a Girl in My Soup," followed by "Borstal Boy," "Vivat! Vivat Regina!," OB in "Rosmersholm."

SCOTT, STEVE. Born Oct. 11, 1949 in Denver, Colo. Graduate UDenver Debut 1971 OB in "The Drunkard," followed by "Summer Brave," Bdwy 1975 in "The Ritz."

SEFF, RICHARD. Born Sept. 23, 1927 in NYC. Attended NYU. Bdwy debut 1951 in "Darkness at Noon," OB in "Big Fish, Little Fish."

SEGAL, KATHRIN KING. Born Dec. 8, 1947 in Washington, DC. Attended HB studio. Debut 1969 OB in "Oh! Calcutta!," followed by "The Drunkard," "Alice in Wonderland," "Pirates of Penzance," "Portfolio Revue," "Phi lemon."

SEGOVIA, ISABEL. Born June 17, 1943 in Peru. Attended UCuzco. Debu 1971 OB in "Yerma," followed by "Life Is a Dream," "House of Fools," "Don Juan Tenorio," "Electra Garrigo," "Uncle Vanya," "Miracle for Maggie."

SELBERT, MARIANNE. Born June 26, 1946 in NYC. Bdwy debut 1966 in "Cabaret," followed by "Canterbury Tales," "Mack and Mabel."

SELDES, MARIAN. Born Aug. 23, 1928 in NYC. Attended Neighborhood Playhouse. Bdwy debut 1947 in "Medea," followed by "Crime and Punishment," "That Lady," "Tower Beyond Tragedy," "Ondine," "On High Ground," "Come of Age," "Chalk Garden," "The Milk Train Doesn't Stop Here Anymore," "The Wall," "A Gift of Time," "A Delicate Balance," "Before You Go," "Father's Day," "Equus," in "Diff'rent," "Ginger Man," "Mercy Street," "Candle in the Wind."

SELL, JANIE. Born Oct. 1, 1941 in Detroit, Mich. Attended UDetroit. Debut OB 1966 in "Mixed Doubles," followed by "Dark Horses," "Dames at Sea," Bdwy in "George M!," "Irene," "Over Here" for which she received a Theatre World Award.

SEMES, RENEE. Born Feb. 27, 1947 in NYC. Attended NYU. Bdwy debut 1974 in "Candide."

Marilyn Seven **Keenan Shimizu** **Anna Shaler** **Dino Shorte** **Alexandra Smith**

SENTER, JERRY. Born Aug. 24, 1948 in Tulsa, Okla. Graduate Baylor U., AADA. Debut 1974 OB in "The Boy Friend."

SERABIAN, LORRAINE. Born June 12, 1945 in NYC. Graduate Hofstra U. OB in "Sign of Jonah," "Electra," "Othello," "Secret Life of Walter Mitty," "Bugs and Veronica," "Trojan Women," "American Gothics," "Gallows Humor," Bdwy in "Cabaret," "Zorba."

SERBAGI, ROGER. Born July 26, 1937 in Waltham, Mass. Attended AmTh-Wing. Bdwy debut 1969 in "Henry V," OB in "A Certain Young Man," "Awake and Sing," "The Partnership."

SEVEN, MARILYN. Born March 22 in Boston, Mass. Graduate Vassar Col. Debut 1974 OB in "The Boy Friend."

SEVRA, ROBERT. Born Apr. 15, 1945 in Kansas City, Mo. Graduate Stanford U., UMich. Debut 1972 OB in "Servant of Two Masters," followed by "Lovers."

SEYMOUR, JAMES. Born Dec. 5, 1948 in Short Hills, NJ. Graduate Boston U. Debut 1969 in "Next Voyage of the Pequod," followed by "Approaching Simone," "Small Craft Warnings," "Moonchildren," "The Zykovs."

SEYMOUR, JOHN D. Born Oct. 24, 1897 in Boston, Mass. Attended Colgate U. Bdwy debut 1918 in "Out There," followed by "Richard III," "Dearest Enemy," "Blood Money," "Barretts of Wimpole Street," "Sweet Adeline," "Cyrano de Bergerac," "Pride and Prejudice," "Susan and God," "The Moon Is Down," "Eastward in Eden," "The Vigil," "Light up the Sky," "Sacred Flame," CC's "Pal Joey," "The King and I," and "Life with Father," "We Interrupt This Program," OB in "12 Angry Men."

SHAKAR, MARTIN. Born Jan. 1, 1940, in Detroit, Mich. Attended Wayne State U. OB in "Lorenzaccio," "Macbeth," "The Infantry," "Americana Pastoral," "No Place To Be Somebody," "The World of Mrs. Solomon," "And Whose Little Boy Are You?," "Investigation of Havana," "Night Watch," "Owners," "Actors," "Richard III," "Transfiguration of Benno Blimpie," Bdwy bow 1969 in "Our Town."

SHALER, ANNA. Born Apr. 8, 1940 in NYC. Bennington Col. graduate. Bdwy debut 1965 in "The Devils," followed by "Nathan Weinstein, Mystic, Conn.," "6 Rms Riv Vu," OB in "Trojan Women," "White Devil," "Philosophy in the Boudoir," "Where Do We Go from Here?"

SHARKEY, SUSAN. Born Dec. 12, 1948 in NYC. Graduate UAriz. Debut 1968 OB in "Guns of Carrar," "Cuba Si," "Playboy of the Western World," "Good Woman of Setzuan," "Enemy of the People," "People Are Living There," "Narrow Road to the Deep North," "Enemies," "The Plough and the Stars," "The Sea," "The Zykovs."

SHELLEY, CAROLE. Born Aug. 16, 1939 in London, Eng. Bdwy debut 1965 in "The Odd Couple," followed by "The Astrakhan Coat," "Loot," "Noel Coward's Sweet Potato," "Little Murders" (OB), "Hay Fever," "Absurd Person Singular."

SHAWHAN, APRIL. Born Apr. 10, 1940 in Chicago. Debut OB 1964 in "Jo," followed by "Hamlet," "Oklahoma!" (LC), "Mod Donna," Bdwy in "Race of Hairy Men," "3 Bags Full" for which she received a Theatre World Award, "Dinner at 8," "Cop-Out," "Much Ado about Nothing," "Over Here."

SHELTON, SLOANE. Born Mar. 17, 1934 in Asheville, NC. Attended Berea Col., RADA. Bdwy debut 1967 in "Imaginary Invalid," followed by "Touch of the Poet," "Tonight at 8:30," "I Never Sang for My Father," OB in "Androcles and the Lion," "The Maids," "Way of the World," "Dark of the Moon," "Basic Training of Pavlo Hummel," "Felix," "Bits and Pieces," "The Runner Stumbles."

SHENAR, PAUL. Born Feb. 12, 1936 in Milwaukee, Wis. Graduate UWisc. Bdwy debut 1969 in "Tiny Alice," followed by "Three Sisters," OB in "Six Characters in Search of an Author."

SHERIDAN, JOHN. Born May 9, 1947 in Newton, Mass. OB in "Your Own Thing," "Best Foot Forward," "Beggar on Horseback," Bdwy in "No, No, Nanette," "Gypsy" for which he received a Theatre World Award.

SHIMIZU, KEENAN. Born Oct. 22, 1956 in NYC. Graduate HS Performing Arts. Bdwy 1965 in CC's "South Pacific" and "The King and I," OB in "Rashomon," "The Year of the Dragon," "The Catch."

SHIMONO, SAB. Born in Sacramento, Cal. Graduate UCal. Bdwy bow 1965 in "South Pacific" (CC), followed by "Mame," "Lovely Ladies, Kind Gentlemen," OB in "Santa Anita," "Ride the Winds."

SHORTE, DINO. Born in Tifton, Ga. Neighborhood Playhouse graduate. Debut OB 1973 in "The Cream of the Crop," followed by "The Mummer's Play," "In White America," "Shoes," "Antigone," "As You Like It," Bdwy bow 1974 in "Who's Who in Hell," followed by "We Interrupt This Program."

SHULL, RICHARD B. Born Feb. 24, 1929 in Elmhurst, NY. Graduate Iowa State U. Bdwy debut 1954 in "Black-Eyed Susan," followed by "Wake Up, Darling," "Red Roses for Me," "I Knock at the Door," "Pictures in the Hallway," "Have I Got a Girl for You," "Minnie's Boys," "Goodtime Charley," OB in "Purple Dust," "Journey to the Day," "American Hamburger League."

SIEBERT, CHARLES. Born Mar. 9, 1938 in Kenosha, Wisc. Graduate Marquette U., LAMDA. Appeared in "Richard III" (CP), "Galileo" (LC), on Bdwy in "Jimmy Shine," "Gingerbread Lady," "Sticks and Bones," "Lysistrata," "The Changing Room," "Cat on a Hot Tin Roof," OB in "Wilde," "Rubbers."

SIEBERT, RONALD H. Born in Kenosha, Wis. Graduate UWis., Brandeis U. Bdwy debut 1973 in "The Changing Room," followed by "The Iceman Cometh."

SILBER, DONALD. Born Dec. 11, 1936 in Utica, NY. Attended Colgate, Syracuse U. Bdwy debut 1965 in "Royal Hunt of the Sun," followed by "The Constant Wife," OB in "Hamp," "The Glorious Ruler."

SILLS, PAWNEE. Born in Castalia, NC. Attended Bklyn Col. Debut OB 1962 in "Raisin Hell in the Sun," followed by "Mr. Johnson," "Black Happening," "One Last Look," "NY and Who to Blame It On," "Cities in Bezique," "I'd Go to Heaven if I was Good," "Oakville, U.S.A.," "Hocus-Pocus."

SILVER, JOE. Born Sept. 28, 1922 in Chicago, Ill. Attended UIll., AmTh-Wing. Bdwy bow 1942 in "Tobacco Road," followed by "Doughgirls," "Heads or Tails," "Nature's Way," "Gypsy," "Heroine," "Zulu and the Zayda," "You Know I Can't Hear You When the Water's Running," "Lenny," OB in "Blood Wedding," "Lamp at Midnight," "Joseph and His Brethern," "Victors," "Shrinking Bride," "Family Pieces," "Cakes with the Wine."

SILVER, STUART. Born June 29, 1947 in Hollywood, Ca. Attended URochester, AADA. Debut 1969 OB in "Little Murders," followed by "Seven Days of Mourning," "Dance Wi' Me," "Wanted," "The Making of Americans," "Dance with Me."

SIMMONDS, STANLEY. Born July 13 in Brooklyn, NY. Attended Roosevelt Col. Bdwy debut 1927 in "My Maryland," followed by "castles in the Air," "Simple Simon," "If the Shoe Fits," "Brigadoon"(CC), "Call Me Madam," "Silk Stockings," "Li'l Abner," "Fiorello," "Let It Ride," "I Can Get It for You Wholesale," "How to Succeed in Business . . . ," "Pickwick," "Kelly," "Half a Sixpence," "How Now, Dow Jones," "Maggie Flynn," "Jimmy," "Mack and Mabel."

SIMMONS, KEITH. Born June 2, 1955 in Jamaica, NY. Bdwy debut 1973 in "Seesaw," followed by "Raisin."

SIMPSON, STEVE. Born Sept. 3, 1947 in Perryton, Tex. Graduate UOkla. Wake Forest U. Debut OB 1973 in "The Soldier," followed by "Thieves Carnival," "The Desperate Hours."

SIMS, CORIE. Born Apr. 13, 1948 in NYC. Graduate Hofstra U. Debut OB 1970 in "You're a Good Man, Charlie Brown," followed by "The Hot l Baltimore."

SIMS, MARLEY. Born Feb. 23, 1948 in NYC. Attended NYU. Bdwy debut 1971 in "The Me Nobody Knows," followed by "Godspell" (OB).

SINDEN, DONALD. Born Oct. 9, 1923 in Plymouth, Eng. Attended Webber-Douglas School. After 33 years in the London theatre, made his Bdwy debut 1974 in "London Assurance."

SINDEN, LEON. Born July 20, 1927 in Sussex, Eng. Bdwy debut 1963 in "Semi-Detached," followed by "London Assurance" 1974.

SKALA, LILIA. Born in Vienna; graduate UDresden. Bdwy debut 1941 in "Letters to Lucerne," followed by "With a Silk Thread," "Call Me Madam," "Diary of Anne Frank," "Threepenny Opera" (CC), "Zelda," "40 Carats," "Medea and Jason" (OB).

SLAVIN, SUSAN. Born Nov. 21 in Chicago, Ill. Attended HB Studio. Debut 1968 OB in "The Mad Show," followed by "Dark of the Moon," "Sidnee Poet Heroical."

SMALL, NEVA. Born Nov. 17, 1952 in NYC. Bdwy debut 1964 in "Something More," followed by "Impossible Years," "Henry, Sweet Henry," "Frank Merriwell," OB in "Ballad for a Firing Squad," "Tell Me Where the Good Times Are," "How Much, How Much?," "F. Jasmine Addams," "Macbeth" (LC), "Yentl, the Yeshiva Boy."

SMITH, ALEXANDRA. Born Apr. 25, 1944 in Sydney, Aust. Graduate Poston U. Debut 1974 OB in "The Hot l Baltimore."

Barrey Smith **Hope Stansbury** **Jeff Spielman** **Patricia Stewart** **Jean-Pierre Stewart**

SMITH, BARREY. Born in Presque Isle, Me. Graduate Wheaton Col., Princeton. Bdwy debut 1973 in "Grease."

SMITH, CAMERON. Born Aug. 13 in Dayton, O. Graduate Ohio U. Debut 1975 OB in "The Three Musketeers."

SMITH, GWENDOLYN. Born Mar. 17, 1966 in NYC. Attended American Ballet Theatre School. Debut 1975 OB in "A Midsummer Night's Dream."

SMITH, LOIS. Born Nov. 3, 1930 in Topeka, Kan. Attended UWash. Bdwy debut 1952 in "Time Out for Ginger," followed by "The Young and Beautiful," "Wisteria Trees," "Glass Menagerie," "Orpheus Descending," OB in "Sunday Dinner," "Present Tense," "The Iceman Cometh," "Harry Outside."

SMITH, MAGGIE. Born Dec. 28, 1934 in Ilford, Eng. Attended Oxford Playhouse School. Bdwy debut in "New Faces of 1956," followed by "Private Lives" (1975).

SNELL, DAVID. Born Oct. 4, 1942 in Baltimore, Md. Graduate Hamilton Col., Catholic U. Debut OB 1970 in "Wars of Roses," followed by "Macbeth," "Beggar's Opera," "The Fantasticks," "Bits and Pieces," Bdwy 1973 in "Shelter."

SNYDER, DREW. Born Sept. 25, 1946 in Buffalo, NY. Graduate Carnegie Tech. Bdwy debut 1968 with APA in "Pantagleize," followed by "Cocktail Party," "Cock-a-doodle Dandy," and "Hamlet," NYSF's "Henry VI," "Richard III," and "Sticks and Bones," "The Cretan Bull," "All My Sons."

SOBOLOFF, ARNOLD. Born Nov. 11, 1930 in NYC. Attended Cooper Union. OB in "Threepenny Opera," "Career," "Brothers Karamazov," "Vincent," "Bananas," "Papp," "Camino Real" (LCR) "Are You Now or Have You Ever Been," "Music! Music!" "The Sea," Bdwy in "Mandingo," "The Egg," "Beauty Part," "One Flew over the Cuckoo's Nest," "Anyone Can Whistle," "Bravo Giovanni," "Sweet Charity," "Mike Downstairs," "Cyrano."

SOLEN, PAUL. Born Mar. 27, 1941 in Cincinnati, O. Bdwy debut 1964 in "Hello, Dolly!," followed by "Breakfast at Tiffany's," "Dear World," "Pippin," "Chicago."

SOLIN, HARVEY. Born Oct. 17 in NYC. Attended CCNY, Actors Studio. Debut 1960 OB in "Ring Round the Moon," followed by "Sign of Jonah," "Worm in the Horseradish," "A Man's a Man," "Next Time I'll Sing to You," "Louis and the Elephant," "Penthouse Legend," "The Advertisement."

SOMMER, JOSEF. Born June 26, 1934 in Greifswald, Ger. Graduate Carnegie Tech. Bdwy bow 1970 with ASF's "Othello," followed by "Children, Children," "Trial of the Catonsville 9," LCR's "Enemies," and "Merchant of Venice," "Full Circle," "Who's Who in Hell," OB in "The Dog Ran Away."

SPAISMAN, ZIPORA. Born Jan. 2, 1920 in Lublin, Poland. Debut OB 1955 in "Lonesome Ship," followed by "In My Father's Court," "Thousand and One Nights," "Eleventh Inheritor," "Enchanting Melody," "Fifth Commandment," "Bronx Express," "Melody Lingers On," "Yoshke Muzikant," "Stempenyu," "Generations of Green Fields."

SPEISER, FRANK. Born in Cuba in 1944. Graduate UBridgeport, Yale. Bdwy debut 1971 in "Lenny," followed by OB "The World of Lenny Bruce."

SPIELMAN, JEFF. Born Nov. 9, 1951 in Shakopee, Minn. Graduate Macalester Col. Bdwy debut 1974 in "Good News."

SPINELLI, LARRY. Born July 20, 1931 in NYC. Debut 1971 OB in "One Flew over the Cuckoo's Nest," followed by "Soon," "The Hot l Baltimore."

STADLEN, LEWIS J. Born Mar. 7, 1947 in Brooklyn. Attended Neighborhood Playhouse. Bdwy debut 1970 in "Minnie's Boys" for which he received a Theatre World Award, followed by "Happiness Cage" (OB), "The Sunshine Boys," "Candide."

STALEY, JAMES. Born May 20, 1948 in Oklahoma City. Graduate Okla. U. Bdwy debut 1972 in "Promenade, All!," followed by "Of Mice and Men," OB in "Siamese Connections" and "Felix."

STANSBURY, HOPE. Born Nov. 23, 1945 in NYC. OB in "Henry and Henrietta," "Just before the War with the Eskimos," "Run to the Sea," "Chocolates," "Couchmates," "Paderefski," "Howies," "Women behind Bars."

STAPLETON, MAUREEN. Born June 21, 1925 in Troy, NY. Attended HB Studio. Bdwy debut 1946 in "Playboy of the Western World," followed by "Antony and Cleopatra," "Detective Story," "Bird Cage," "Rose Tattoo" for which she received a Theatre World Award, "The Emperor's Clothes," "The Crucible," "Richard III," "The Seagull," "27 Wagons Full of Cotton," "Orpheus Descending," "The Cold Wind and the Warm," "Toys in the Attic," "Glass Menagerie," "Plaza Suite," "Norman, Is That You?," "Gingerbread Lady," "Country Girl," "Secret Affairs of Mildred Wild."

STARK, DOUGLAS. Born Aug. 4, 1916. Attended UVa. Bdwy bow 1938 in "Everywhere I Roam," followed by "Three Sisters," "The Man Who Killed Lincoln," "The Trial of Lee Harvey Oswald," "Holy Ghosts"(OB).

STARK, MOLLY. Born in NYC. Graduate Hunter Col. Debut OB 1969 in "Sacco-Vanzetti," followed by "Riders to the Sea," "Medea," "One Cent Plain," Bdwy 1973 in "Molly."

STARR, BILL. Born July 6 in San Francisco. Attended HB Studio. Bdwy debut 1959 in "Take Me Along," followed by "Molly Brown," "All American," "Nowhere to Go But Up," "Something More," "Fade Out—Fade In," "High Spirits," "It's Superman," "Illya, Darling," "Drat! The Cat," "A Funny Thing Happened on the Way to the Forum," "Via Galactica," "The Night That Made America Famous."

STATTEL, ROBERT. Born Nov. 20, 1937 in Floral Park, NY. Graduate Manhattan Col. Debut OB 1958 in "Heloise," followed by "When I Was a Child," "Man and Superman," "The Storm," "Don Carlos," "Taming of the Shrew," NYSF's "Titus Andronicus," "Henry IV," "Peer Gynt," and "Hamlet," LCR's "Danton's Death," "Country Wife," "Caucasian Chalk Circle," and "King Lear," "Iphigenia in Aulis," "Ergo," "The Persians," "Blue Boys," "The Minister's Black Veil," "Four Friends," Bdwy in "A Patriot for Me."

STEELE, BILL. Born Nov. 25 in Springfield, Mass. Graduate Yale U. Bdwy debut 1955 in "Tonight in Samarkand," OB in "Noah," "What Every Woman Knows," "Proposals and Propositions," "The Crucible," "Open 24 Hours," "Satisfaction Guaranteed," "Treasure Island."

STENBORG, HELEN. Born Jan. 24, 1925 in Minneapolis, Minn. Attended Hunter Col. OB in "A Doll's House," "A Month in the Country," "Say Nothing," "Rosmersholm," "Rimers of Eldrich," "Trial of the Catonsville 9," "Hot l Baltimore," "Pericles," "A Doll's House," Bdwy in "Sheep on the Runway."

STEPHENS, GARN. Born in Tulsa, Okla. Graduate Calif. Western U. Pasadena Playhouse. Debute 1972 OB and Bdwy in "Grease."

STERLING, JAN. Born Apr. 3, 1923 in NYC. Attended Fay Compton's School. Bdwy debut 1938 in "Bachelor Born," followed by "When We Are Married," "Grey Farm," "This Rock," "Rugged Path," "Dunnigan's Daughter," "This Too Shall Pass," "Present Laughter," "Two Blind Mice," "Small War on Murray Hill," "Perfect Setup," "Front Page," OB in "Friday Night," "Come Back, Little Sheba."

STERN, JOSEPH. Born Sept. 3, 1940 in Los Angeles, Cal. Graduate UCLA. Debut 1967 OB in "MacBird," followed by "The Homecoming," "Henry IV," "Last Analysis," "Cymbeline," "The Hot l Baltimore."

STERNHAGEN, FRANCES. Born Jan. 13, 1932 in Washington, DC. Vassar Graduate. OB in "Admirable Bashful," "Thieves' Carnival," "Country Wife," "Ulysses in Nighttown," "Saintliness of Margery Kemp," "The Room," "A Slight Ache," "Displaced Person," "Playboy of the Western World" (LC), Bdwy in "Great Day In the Morning," "Right Honourable Gentleman," with APA in "Cocktail Party" and "Cock-a-doodle Dandy," "The Sign in Sidney Brustein's Window," "Enemies" (LC), "The Good Doctor," "Equus."

STEVENS, FRAN. Born Mar. 8 in Washington, D.C. Attended Notre Dame, Cleveland Playhouse. Has appeared in "Pousse Cafe," "Most Happy Fella," "A Funny Thing Happened on the Way to the Forum," "How Now Dow Jones," "Her First Roman," "Cry for Us All," "On the Town," OB in "Frank Gagliano's City Scene," "Debris," "Polly."

STEVENS, JEREMY. Born Mar. 16, 1938 in Brooklyn, NY. Brooklyn Col. graduate. OB in "This Side of Paradise," "The Fourth Wall," "Saturday Night," Bdwy 1974 in "Fame."

STEVENS, JON. Born June 21, 1946 in Midland, Tex. Attended Tex. Tech. U. Debut 1968 OB in "Your Own Thing," followed by "Inn at Lydda."

STEVENSEN, SCOTT. Born May 4, 1951 in Salt Lake City, U. Attended USCal. Bdwy debut 1974 in "Good News" for which he received a Theatre World Award.

STEVENSON, MARGOT. Born Feb. 8, 1918 in NYC. Brearley School graduate. Bdwy debut 1932 in "Firebird," followed by "Evensong," "A Party," "Barretts of Wimpole Street," "Symphony," "Truly Valiant," "Call It a Day," "Stage Door," "You Can't Take It with You," "Golden Wings," "Little Women"(CC), "Rugged Path," "Leading Lady," "The Young and Beautiful," "The Apple Cart," "Triple Play," "Lord Pengo," "Hostile Witness," OB in "Autumn Ladies and Their Lovers Lovers."

STEWART, JEAN-PIERRE. Born May 4, 1946 in NYC. Graduate CCNY. Appeared OB in "Henry IV," "King Lear," "Cry of Players," "In the Matter of J. Robert Oppenheimer," "The Miser," "Long Day's Journey into Night," "American Night Cry," "King Lear," "The Old Ones."

STEWART, PATRICIA. Born Aug. 29, 1939 in Bronxville, NY. Graduate St. Lawrence U. Debut OB 1963 in "Best Foot Forward," followed by "The Ginger Man," "Dr. Faustus," "Kid Champion," "Wood Painting," "The Artists," "Elagabalus."

| Susan Sullivan | Scot Stewart | Carol Swarbrick | Tony Tanner | Carol Teitel |

STEWART, RAY. Born Apr. 21, 1932 in San Benito, Tex. Graduate UTex. OB in "Black Monday," "Conerico Was Here to Stay," "Second City," "Play," "Experiment," "Fantasticks," "King Lear," "Cry of Players," "Inner Journey," "Mary Stuart," "Narrow Road to the Deep North," "Bone Room," Bdwy 1970 in "Postcards."

STEWART, SCOT. Born June 3, 1941 in Tylertown, Miss. Graduate USMiss. Debut 1975 OB in "New Girl in Town."

STIERS, DAVID OGDEN. Born Oct. 31, 1942 in Peoria, Ill. Attended UOre., Juilliard. Debut OB 1972 in "School for Scandal," followed by "Lower Depths," "The Hostage," "Women Beware Women," Bdwy in "Three Sisters," "Measure for Measure," "Beggar's Opera," "Scapin," "Ulysses in Nighttown," "The Magic Show."

STILLER, JERRY. Born June 8, 1931 in NYC. Graduate Syracuse U., HB Studio. Debut 1953 OB in "Coriolanus," followed by "The Power and the Glory," "Golden Apple," "Measure for Measure," "Taming of the Shrew," "Carefree Tree," "Diary of a Scoundrel," "Romeo and Juliet," "As You Like It," "Two Gentlemen of Verona," Bdwy 1975 in "The Ritz."

STOCKING, ROBERT. Born Sept. 3, 1941 in Vicksburg, Miss. Attended Chicago City Col. Debut 1967 OB in "Trials of Brother Jero," followed by "Candaules Commissioner," "The Strong Breed," "No Place to Be Somebody," "Ballet behind the Bridge," "Uncle Tom's Cabin."

STOCKWELL, JEREMY. Born in Houston, Tex. Graduate UTex. Debut 1969 OB in "Fortune and Men's Eyes," followed by "Nightride," "Rainbow Rape Trick."

STOVALL, COUNT. Born Jan. 15, 1946 in Los Angeles, Cal. Graduate UCal. Debut OB 1973 in "He's Got a Jones," followed by "In White America," "Rashomon," "Sidnee Poet Heroical."

STRAIGHT, BEATRICE. Born Aug. 2, 1916 in Old Westbury, NY. Attended Dartington Hall. Bdwy debut 1934 in "Bitter Oleander," followed by "Twelfth Night," "Land of Fame," "Wanhope Building," "Eastward in Eden," "Macbeth," "The Heiress," "The Innocents," "Grand Tour," "The Crucible," "Everything in the Garden," OB in "Sing Me No Lullaby," "River Line," "Ghosts," "All My Sons."

STUTHMAN, FRED. Born June 27, 1919 in Long Beach, Cal. Attended UCal. Debut 1970 OB in "Hamlet," followed by "Uncle Vanya," "Charles Abbot & Son," "She Stoops to Conquer," "Master Builder," "Taming of the Shrew," "Misalliance," "Merchant of Venice," "Conditions of Agreement," "The Play's the Thing," "Ghosts," "The Father," "The Hot l Baltimore," Bdwy 1975 in "Sherlock Holmes."

SULKA, ELAINE. Born in NYC. Graduate Queens Col., Brown U. Debut OB 1962 in "Hop, Signor!," followed by "Brotherhood," "Brothers," Bdwy in "Passion of Josef D," "Medea." Co-founder of Ntl. Shakespeare Co., and The Cubiculo where she has appeared in over 25 original productions and revivals.

SULLIVAN, BRAD. Born Nov. 18, 1931 in Chicago, Ill. Graduate UMaine, AmThWing. Debut 1961 OB in "Red Roses for Me," followed by "South Pacific" (LC), "Hothouse."

SULLIVAN, JEREMIAH. Born Sept. 22, 1937 in NYC. Graduate Harvard U. Bdwy debut 1957 in "Compulsion," followed by "The Astrakhan Coat," "Philadelphia, Here I Come!," "A Lion in Winter," "Hamlet," OB in "Ardele," "A Scent of Flowers," "House of Blue Leaves," "Four Friends."

SULLIVAN, SUSAN. Born Nov. 18, in NYC. Graduate Hofstra U. Bdwy debut 1968 in "Avanti!," followed by "Jimmy Shine," OB in "The Beauty Part."

SUNDINE, JOHN PATRICK. Born Oct. 1, 1952 in Davenport, Iowa. Attended UIll., Augustana Col., Juilliard. Bdwy debut 1975 in "Man on the Moon."

SWARBRICK, CAROL. Born Mar. 20, 1948 in Inglewood, Ca. Graduate UCLA, NYU. Debut 1971 OB in "Drat!," followed by "The Glorious Age."

SYMINGTON, DONALD. Born Aug. 30, 1925 in Baltimore, Md. Bdwy debut 1947 in "Galileo," followed by "Mourning Pictures," CC's "Caesar and Cleopatra," "Dream Girl," and "Lute Song," "A Girl Can Tell," OB in "Suddenly Last Summer," "Lady Windermere's Fan," "Rate of Exchange," "Shrinking Bride," "Murderous Angels," "An Evening with the Poet Senator."

SYLVESTRE, CLEO. Born Apr. 19 in Hitchin, Eng. Attended Kalia Conti Stage School. Bdwy debut 1974 with Young Vic in "Scapino."

TABORI, KRISTOFFER. Born Aug. 4, 1952 in Calif. Bdwy debut 1969 in "The Penny Wars," followed by "Henry V," OB in "Emile and the Detectives," "Guns of Carrar," "A Cry of Players," "Dream of a Blacklisted Actor," "How Much, How Much?" for which he received a Theatre World Award, "The Wager."

TANANIS, ROBERT. Born Mar. 22, 1939 in Pittsburgh, Pa. St. Vincent Col. graduate. Bdwy debut 1967 in "Spofford," OB in "Damn Yankees," "Gay Company."

TANDY, JESSICA. Born June 7, 1909 in London. Attended Greet Acad. Bdwy debut 1930 in "The Matriarch," followed by "Last Enemy," "Time and the Conways," "White Steed," "Geneva," "Jupiter Laughs," "Anne of England," "Yesterday's Magic," "Streetcar Named Desire," "Hilda Crane," "Four-poster," "Honeys," "Day by the Sea," "Man in the Dog Suit," "Triple Play," "Five Finger Exercise," "Physicists," "Delicate Balance," "Home," "All Over," LCR's "Camino Real," "Not I" and "Happy Days," "Noel Coward in Two Keys."

TANNER, TONY. Born July 27, 1932 in Hillingdon, Eng. Attended Webber-Douglas School. Bdwy debut 1966 in "Half a Sixpence," followed by "No Sex Please, We're British," "Sherlock Holmes," OB in "Little Boxes," "The Home-coming."

TARBUCK, BARBARA. Born Jan. 15, 1942 in Detroit, Mich. Graduate UMich., LAMDA. Debut OB 1970 in LC's "Landscape" and "Silence," followed by "Amphitryon," "Birthday Party," "The Crucible," "The Carpenters," "Great American Refrigerator," "Evening with Sylvia Plath," "Biography for a Woman," "Hothouse."

TARPEY, TOM. Born June 3, 1943 in NYC. Attended Carnegie-Mellon U., LAMDA. Debut OB 1969 in "The Glorious Ruler," followed by "Crimes of Passion," "A Meeting at the River," "Strindberg," Bdwy in "Othello," "Uncle Vanya."

TATE, DENNIS. Born Aug. 31, 1938 in Iowa City, Ia. Attended Iowa U. OB in "Black Monday," "The Blacks," "The Hostage," "Bohikee Creek," "Happy Bar," "Trials of Brother Jero," "Strong Breed," "Goa," "Electronic Nigger," "Black Quartet," "Life and Times of J. Walter Smintheus," "Jazznite," "Cherry Orchard," "Phantasmagoria Historia . . . ," "Merry Wives of Windsor," Bdwy 1970 in "Les Blancs."

TAYLOR, CLARICE. Born Sept. 20, in Buckingham County, Va. Attended New Theater School. Debut 1943 OB in "Striver's Row," followed by "Major Barbara," "Family Portrait," "Trouble in Mind," "The Egg and I," "A Medal for Willie," "Nat Turner," "Simple Speaks His Mind," "Gold Through the Trees," "The Owl Answers," "Song of the Lusitanian Bogey," "Summer of the 17th Doll," "Kongi's Harvest," "Daddy Goodness," "God Is a (Guess What?)," "An Evening of One Acts," "5 on the Black Hand Side," "Man Better Man," "Day of Absence," "Brotherhood," "Akokawe," "Rosalee Pritchett," "Sty of the Blind Pig," "Duplex" (LC), "Wedding Band," Bdwy 1975 in "The Wiz."

TAYLOR, GEORGE. Born Sept. 18, 1930 in London. Attended AADA. Debut 1972 in NYSF's "Hamlet," followed by "Enemies" (LC), Bdwy in "Emperor Henry IV," "The Contractor"(OB), "The National Health."

TAYLOR, HOLLAND. Born Jan. 14, 1943 in Philadelphia, Pa. Graduate Bennington, Col. Bdwy debut 1965 in "The Devils," followed by "Butley," "We Interrupt This Program," OB in "Poker Session," "The David Show," "Tonight in Living Color," "Colette," "Fashion," "Nightlight."

TAYLOR, IAN. Born Oct. 23, 1937 in Kingston, Eng. Attended Queen Mary Col., ULondon. Bdwy debut 1974 in "Scapino."

TEITEL, CAROL. Born Aug. 1, 1929 in NYC. Attended AmThWing. On Bdwy in "The Country Wife," "The Entertainer," "Hamlet," "Marat/deSade," "All over Town," OB in "Way of the World," "Plough and the Stars," "The Anatomist," "Country Scandal," "Under Milk Wood," "The Bench," "7 Days of Mourning," "Duet," "Trio," "Figures in the Sand," "The Old Ones."

THACKER, RUSS. Born June 23, 1946 in Washington, DC. Attended Montgomery Col. Debut 1967 in "Life with Father" (CC), followed OB by "Your Own Thing" for which he received a Theatre World Award, "Dear Oscar," "Once I saw A Boy Laughing," Bdwy in "Grass Harp," "Heathen," "Music! Music!" (CC).

THEODORE, DONNA. Born July 25, 1945 in Oakland, Ca. Debut 1974 OB in "Oh, Lady, Lady," Bdwy 1975 in "Shenandoah" for which she received a Theatre World Award.

THOMAS, ERNEST. Born Mar. 26, 1954 in Gary, Ind. Graduate Ind. State U., AADA. Debut OB 1973 in "Miracle Play," Bdwy 1974 in "Love for Love," followed by "A Member of the Wedding."

THOMAS, WILLIAM, JR. Born in Columbus, O. Graduate Ohio State U. Debut OB 1972 in "Touch," followed by "Natural," "Godspell."

257

Ken Tigar

Kathleen Tolan

Kenneth Urmston

Sasha von Scherler

William Van Hunte

THOMPSON, EVAN. Born Sept. 3, 1931 in NYC. Graduate UCal. Bdwy bow 1969 in 'Jimmy,' followed by OB "Mahagonny," "Treasure Island."

THOMPSON, SADA. Born Sept. 27, 1929 in Des Moines, Iowa. Graduate Carnegie Tech. Debut 1953 OB in "Under Milk Wood," followed by "A Clandestine Marriage," "Murder in the Cathedral," "White Devil," "Carefree Tree," "Misanthrope," "USA," "River Line," "Ivanov," "Last Minstrel," "An Evening for Merlin Finch," "The Effect of Gamma Rays on Man-in-the-Moon Marigolds," Bdwy in "Festival," "Juno," "Johnny No-Trump," "American Dream," "Happy Days," "Twigs," "Saturday Sunday Monday."

THOMPSON, TAZEWELL. Born May 27, 1948 in NYC. Attended Actors Co. School. Debut 1968 OB in "Goa," Bdwy 1974 in "The National Health."

THURSTON, TED. Born Jan. 9, 1920 in St. Paul, Minn. Attended Drake U., Wash. U. Bdwy debut 1951 in "Paint Your Wagon," followed by "Girl in Pink Tights," "Kismet," "Buttrio Square," "Seventh Heaven," "Most Happy Fella," "Li'l Abner," "13 Daughters," "Happiest Girl in Town," "Let It Ride," "Sophie," "Luther," "Cafe Crown," "I Had a Ball," "Wonderful Town" (CC), "Celebration," "Gantry," "Wild and Wonderful," OB in "Bible Salesman," "Smith," "Fiddler on the Roof" (JB), "Celebration."

TIGAR, KEN. Born Sept. 24, 1942 in Chelsea, Mass. Harvard graduate. Debut OB 1973 in "Thunder Rock," followed by "Baba Goya," "Nourish the Beast," "Festival of Short Plays," "Rashomon," "Mississippi Moonshine," "Gallows Humor."

TILLINGER, JOHN. Born June 28, 1938 in Tabriz, Iran. Attended URome. Bdwy debut 1966 in "How's the World Treating You?," followed by "Halfway up the Tree," "The Changing Room," OB in "Tea Party," "Pequod," "A Scent of Flowers," "Crimes of Passion."

TIRELLI, JAIME. Born Mar. 4, 1945 in NYC. Attended UMundial, AADA. Debut 1975 OB in "Rubbers," "Yanks 3, Detroit O."

TOBIN, MATHEW. Born Aug. 10, 1933 in Indianapolis, Ind. Graduate Carnegie Tech. Debut OB 1959 in "Hasty Heart," followed by "Boys from Syracuse," "Mad Show," "Boys in the Band," "Empire Builders," "Lyle," "Survival of St. Joan," "Any Resemblance to Persons Living or Dead," "Festival of Short Plays," "Kaboom," "Room Service," "Drums at Yale," Bdwy in "Redhead," "Love Suicide at Schofield Barracks."

TOLAN, KATHLEEN. Born Aug. 10, 1950 in Milwaukee, Wisc. Attended NYU, HB Studio. Debut 1974 OB in "Hothouse," followed by "More Than You Deserve," "Wicked Women Revue."

TOMMON, MARIE. Born Apr. 13, 1945 in Eng. Attended AADA. Bdwy debut 1975 in "Private Lives."

TONER, TOM. Born May 25, 1928 in Homestead, Pa. Graduate UCLA. Bdwy debut 1973 in "Tricks," followed OB in "Pericles," "Merry Wives of Windsor," "Midsummer Night's Dream," "Richard III."

TORRES, ANDY. Born Aug. 10, 1945 in Ponce, PR. Attended AMDA. Bdwy debut 1969 in "Indians," followed by "Purlie," "Don't Bother Me, I Can't Cope," "The Wiz," OB in "Billy Noname."

TOVATT, ELLEN. Born in NYC. Attended Antioch Col., LAMDA. Debut OB 1962 in "Taming of the Shrew," Bdwy in "The Great God Brown," "The Visit," "Chemin de Fer," "Holiday," "Love for Love," "Rules of the Game."

TOWB, HARRY. Born July 27, 1925 in Larne, Ire. Attended Belfast Tech. Col. Bdwy debut 1966 in "Under the Weather," followed by "Sherlock Holmes."

TRAVOLTA, JOHN. Born Feb. 18, 1954 in Englewood, NJ. Debut 1972 OB in "Rain," Bdwy in "Grease," "Over Here."

TRIGGER, IAN J. Born Sept. 30, 1942 in Eng. Graduate RADA. NY debut OB 1973 in "Taming of the Shrew" followed by "Scapino," "True History of Squire Jonathan . . .," Bdwy 1974 in "Scapino."

TUCCI, MARIA. Born June 19, 1941 in Florence, Italy. Attended Actors Studio. Bdwy debut 1963 in "The Milk Train Doesn't Stop Here Anymore," followed by "Rose Tattoo" (CC) "Little Foxes," "The Cuban Thing," "Great White Hope," "School for Wives," OB in "Corruption in the Palace of Justice," "Five Evenings," "Trojan Women," "White Devil," "Horseman, Pass By," "Yerma," "Shepherd of Avenue B."

TUCKER, DUANE. Born Feb. 17, 1948 in NYC. Graduate Columbia U. OB in "Captains Folly," "Henry IV," "Hinkemann," "Macbeth," "St. George and the Dragon," "Bus Stop."

TYRRELL, BRAD. Born May 30, 1943 in Miami, Fla. Attended UKan., HB Studio. Debut OB 1974 in "Man with a Load of Mischief," Bdwy 1975 in "Goodtime Charley."

TYRRELL, JOHN. Born Nov. 24, 1948 in Perth Amboy, NJ. Graduate Marquette U., Neighborhood Playhouse. Bdwy debut 1974 in "Equus."

TYRRELL, SUSAN. Born in San Francisco. Bdwy debut 1952 in "Time out for Ginger," OB in "The Knack," "Futz," "A Cry of Players," "The Time of Your Life," "Camino Real."

ULLMANN, LIV. Born Dec. 16, 1938 in Touro, Japan. Made NY debut 1975 at Lincoln Center in "A Doll's House."

URMSTON, KENNETH. Born Aug. 6, 1929 in Cincinnati, O. Attended Xavier U. Bdwy debut 1950 in "Make a Wish," followed by "Top Banana," "Guys and Dolls," "John Murray Anderson's Almanac," "Can-Can," "Silk Stockings," "Oh Captain!," "Bells Are Ringing," "Redhead," "Madison Avenue," "Tenderloin," "We Take the Town," "Lovely Ladies, Kind Gentlemen," "Follies," "Pippin."

USTINOV, PETER. Born Apr. 16, 1921 in London, Eng. Attended London Theatre School. Bdwy debut 1957 in "Romanoff and Juliet," followed by "Photo Finish," "Who's Who in Hell."

VAHANIAN, MARC. Born Apr. 17, 1956 in Detroit, Mich. Attended AADA. Debut 1969 in "The Time of Your Life" (LC), followed by OB "Last Days of British Honduras."

VALE, MICHAEL. Born June 28, 1922 in Brooklyn, NY. Attended New School. Bdwy debut 1961 in "The Egg," followed by "Cafe Crown," "Last Analysis," "Impossible Years," "Saturday Sunday Monday," OB in "Autograph Hound," "Moths," "Now There's the Three of Us," "Tall and Rex," "Kaddish," "42 Seconds from Broadway," "Sunset."

VAN, BOBBY. Born Dec. 6, 1930 in NYC. Bdwy debut 1950 in "Alive and Kicking," followed by "On Your Toes," "No, No, Nanette," "Dr. Jazz."

VAN ARK, JOAN. Born June 16, 1943 in NYC. Attended Yale U., Actors Studio. Bdwy debut 1965 in "Barefoot in the Park," followed by "School for Wives" for which she received a Theatre World Award, "Rules of the Game."

VAN BENSCHOTEN, STEPHEN. Born Aug. 27, 1943 in Washington, DC. Graduate LaSalle Col., Yale. Debut 1967 OB in "King John," Bdwy in "Unlikely Heroes," "Grease."

VAN DEVERE, TRISH. Born Mar. 9, 1947 in Englewood Cliffs, NJ. Graduate Ohio Wesleyan U. Debut 1967 OB in "Kicking Down the Castle," followed by Bdwy 1975 in "All God's Chillun Got Wings."

VAN HUNTER, WILLIAM. Born Feb. 1, 1947 in Worcester, Mass. Graduate Nassau Col., Syracuse U. Debut 1975 OB in "The Three Musketeers."

VAN SCOTT, GLORY. Attended Goddard Col. Bdwy debut 1954 in "House of Flowers," followed by "Kwamina," "Great White Hope," "A Matter of Time," OB in "Carmen Jones," "Porgy and Bess," "Show Boat," "Fly Blackbird," "Prodigal Son," "Who's Who, Baby?," "Billy No-Name," "Don't Bother Me, I Can't Cope."

VATSKE, ROBERTA. Born June 4, 1945 in New Haven, Conn. Conn. Col. graduate. Debut 1967 in "Brigadoon" (CC), followed by "Carnival," OB in "Marriage by Lanternlight."

VENTANTONIO, JOHN. Born Aug. 13, 1943 in Orange, NJ. Attended AADA. Bdwy debut 1969 in "Our Town," followed by "Othello."

VERDON, GWEN. Born Jan 13, 1926 in Culver City, Ca. Bdwy debut 1950 in "Alive and Kicking," followed by "Can-Can" for which she received a Theatre World Award, "Damn Yankees," "New Girl in Town," "Redhead," "Sweet Charity," "Children, Children," "Chicago."

VICTOR, PETER. Born Nov. 22, 1939 in NYC. Graduate RPI, NYU. Debut 1974 OB in "In the Boom Boom Room."

VITA, MICHAEL. Born in 1941 in NYC. Studied at HB Studio. Bdwy debut 1967 in "Sweet Charity," followed by "Golden Rainbow," "Promises, Promises," "Chicago," OB in "Sensations," "That's Entertainment."

VON SCHERLER, SASHA. Born Dec. 12 in NYC. Bdwy debut 1959 in "Look after Lulu," followed by "Rape of the Belt," "The Good Soup," "Great God Brown," "First Love," "Alfie," "Harold," "Bad Habits," OB in "Admirable Bashville," "The Comedian," "Conversation Piece," "Good King Charles' Golden Days," "Under Milk Wood," "Plays for Bleecker Street," "Ludlow Fair," "Twelfth Night," "Sondra," "Cyrano de Bergerac," "Crimes of Passion," "Henry VI," "Trelawny of the Wells," "Screens," "Soon Jack November," "Pericles," "Kid Champion."

WALKEN, CHRISTOPHER. Born Mar. 31, 1943 in Astoria, NY. Attended Hofstra U. Bdwy debut 1958 in "J. B.," followed by "High Spirits," "Baker Street," "The Lion in Winter," "Measure For Measure" (CP), "Rose Tattoo" (CC'66) for which he received a Theatre World Award, "Unknown Soldier and His Wife," "Rosencrantz and Guildenstern Are Dead," "Scenes from American Life," (LC), "Cymbeline" (NYSF), LC's "Enemies," "The Plough and the Stars," "Merchant of Venice," "The Tempest," "Troilus and Cressida," and "Macbeth," OB in "Best Foot Forward," "Iphigenia In Aulis," "Lemon Sky," "Kid Champion."

| Marie Wallace | Craig Wasson | Robin Wesley | Stan Watt | Christinea Whitmore |

WALKER, KATHRYN. Born in Jan. in Philadelphia, Pa. Graduate Wells Col., Harvard, LAMDA. Debut 1971 OB in "Slag," followed by "Alpha Beta," "Kid Champion," Bdwy 1973 in "The Good Doctor," "Mourning Pictures."

WALKER, MICHAEL. Born Mar. 11, 1950 in Kenya. Bdwy debut 1974 in "Sherlock Holmes."

WALKER, PETER. Born July 24, 1927 in Mineola, NY. Studied with Stella Adler. Bdwy debut 1955 in "Little Glass Clock," followed by "Dear World," "Follies," "Where's Charley?"

WALLACE, MARIE. Born May 19, 1939 in NYC. Attended NYU. OB in "Electra," "Harlequinade," "Bell, Book and Candle," "Mert and Phil," Bdwy in "Gypsy," "The Beauty Part," "Nobody Loves an Albatross," "Right Honourable Gentleman," "The Women."

WALLACH, ELI. Born Dec. 7, 1915 in Brooklyn, NY. Graduate UTex, CCNY. Bdwy bow 1945 in "Skydrift," followed by "Henry VIII," "Androcles and the Lion," "Alice in Wonderland," "Yellow Jack," "What Every Woman Knows," "Antony and Cleopatra," "Mr. Roberts," "Lady from the Sea," "Rose Tattoo" for which he received a Theatre World Award, "Mlle. Colombe," "Teahouse of the August Moon," "Major Barbara," "The Cold Wind and the Warm," "Rhinoceros," "Luv," "Staircase," "Promenade, All!," "Waltz of the Toreadors," "Saturday Sunday Monday," OB in "The Chairs," "The Tiger," "The Typists."

WALTERS, CASEY. Born June 25, 1916 in Boston, Mass. Attended Leland Powers School. Bdwy debut 1948 in "Mr. Roberts," OB in "The First Week in Bogota."

WARD, DOUGLAS TURNER. Born May 5, 1930 in Burnside, La. Attended UMich. Bdwy bow 1959 in "A Raisin in the Sun," followed by "One Flew over the Cuckoo's Nest," "Last Breeze of Summer," OB in "The Iceman Cometh," "The Blacks," "Pullman Car Hiawatha," "Bloodknot," "Happy Ending," "Day of Absence," "Kongi's Harvest," "Ceremonies in Dark Old Men," "The Harangues," "The Reckoning," "Frederick Douglass through His Own Words," "River Niger."

WARD, JANET. Born Feb. 19 in NYC. Attended Actors Studio. Bdwy debut 1945 in "Dream Girl," followed by "Anne of the Thousand Days," "Detective Story," "King of Friday's Men," "Middle of the Night," "Miss Lonelyhearts," "J.B.," "Cheri," "The Egg," "Impossible Years," "Of Love Remembered," OB in "Chapparal," "The Typists and The Tiger," "Summertree," "Dream of a Blacklisted Actor," "Cruising Speed 600MPH," "One Flew over the Cuckoo's Nest," "Love Gotta Come by Saturday Night," "Home Is the Hero."

WARDWELL, JOHN. Born in Rockland, Me. Graduate UMaine, Oxford. Bdwy debut 1967 in "90 Day Mistress," followed by "Nathan Weinstein, Mystic, Connecticut," "Fire!," OB in "Single Man at a Party," "In White America," "All the King's Men," "Fireworks," "We Bombed in New Haven," "The Contractor," "The Dog Ran Away," "Richard III."

WARFIELD, MARLENE. Born June 19, 1941 in Queens, NY. Attended Actors Studio. Bdwy debut 1968 in "The Great White Hope" for which she received a Theatre World Award, OB in "The Blacks," "All's Well That Ends Well," "Volpone," "Taming of the Shrew," "Who's Got His Own," "Elektra," "2 by Cromwell," "Midsummer Night's Dream."

WARREN, JENNIFER. Born Aug. 12, 1941 in NYC. Graduate UWisc. Debut 1967 OB in "Scuba Duba," followed by "Trees in the Wind," Bdwy 1972 in "6 Rms Riv Vu" for which she received a Theatre World Award, followed by "P.S. Your Cat Is Dead."

WARREN, JOSEPH. Born June 5, 1916 in Boston, Mass. Graduate Denver U. Bdwy debut 1951 in "Barefoot in Athens," followed by "One Bright Day," "Love of Four Colonels," "Hidden River," "The Advocate," "Philadelphia, Here I Come," "Borstal Boy," "Lincoln Mask," OB in "Brecht on Brecht," "Jonah," "Little Black Sheep."

WASHINGTON, VERNON. Born Aug. 10, 1927 in Hartford, Conn. Attended Wholter School of Drama. OB in "Cabin in the Sky," "The Strong Breed," "Trials of Brother Jero," "Scuba Duba," "Hocus-Pocus."

WASSON, CRAIG. Born Mar. 15, 1954 in Ontario, Ore. Attended Lane Community Col., UOre. Bdwy debut 1975 in "All God's Chillun Got Wings."

WATERSTON, SAM. Born Nov. 15, 1940 in Cambridge, Mass. Graduate Yale. Bdwy bow 1963 in "Oh, Dad, Poor Dad . . . ," followed by "First One Asleep Whistle," "Halfway up the Tree," "Indians," "Hay Fever," "Much Ado about Nothing," OB in "As You Like It," "Thistle in My Bed," "The Knack," "Fitz," "Biscuit," "La Turista," "Posterity For Sale," "Ergo," "Muzeeka," "Red Cross," "Henry IV," "Spitting Image," "I Met A Man," "Brass Butterfly," "Trial of the Catonsville 9," "Cymbeline," "Hamlet," "A Meeting by the River," "The Tempest," "A Doll's House."

WATSON, DOUGLASS. Born Feb. 24, 1921 in Jackson, Ga. Graduate UNC. Bdwy bow 1947 in "The Iceman Cometh," followed by "Antony and Cleopatra" for which he received a theatre World Award, "Leading Lady," "Richard III," "Happiest Years," "That Lady," "Wisteria Trees," "Romeo and Juliet," "Desire under the Elms," "Sunday Breakfast," "Cyrano de Bergerac," "Confidential Clerk," "Portrait of a Lady," "Miser," "Young and Beautiful," "Little Glass Clock," "Country Wife," "Man for All Seasons," "Chinese Prime Minister," "Marat/deSade," "Prime of Miss Jean Brodie," "Pirates of Penzance," "The Hunter" (OB), NYSF's "Much Ado about Nothing," "King Lear," and "As You Like It," "Over Here."

WATSON, SUSAN. Born Dec. 17, 1938 in Tulsa, Okla. Attended Juilliard. Bdwy debut 1960 in "Bye Bye Birdie," followed by "Carnival," "Ben Franklin in Paris," "A Joyful Noise," "Celebration," "Beggar on Horseback" (LC), "No, No, Nanette," OB in "The Fantasticks," "Lend an Ear," "Follies of 1910," "Carousel," "Oklahoma!," "Where's Charley?," "Rivals," "Bone Room."

WATT, BILLIE LOU. Born June 20, 1924 in St. Louis, Mo. Attended Northwestern U. Bdwy bow 1945 in "Little Women," followed by "Barefoot Boy with Cheek," "King of Hearts," "Tough to Get Help," OB in "Autumn Garden."

WATT, STAN. Born Jan. 23, 1930 in Quincy, Mass. Graduate Carnegie Inst. Bdwy debut 1958 in "The Next President," followed by "A Taste of Honey," "Roman Candle," "Playroom," "Jennie," OB in "A Clearing in the Woods," "Roots," "Borac," "All the King's Men," "Blue Boy in Black."

WEAVER, FRITZ. Born Jan. 19, 1926 in Pittsburgh, Pa. Graduate UChicago. Bdwy debut 1955 in "Chalk Garden" for which he received a Theatre World Award, followed by "Protective Custody," "Miss Lonelyhearts," "All American," "Lorenzo," "The White House," "Baker Street," "Child's Play," "Absurd Person Singular," OB in "The Way of the World," "White Devil," "Doctor's Dilemma," "Family Reunion," "The Power and the Glory," "Great God Brown," "Peer Gynt," "Henry IV," "My Fair Lady" (CC).

WEEKS, JAMES RAY. Born Mar. 21, 1942 in Seattle, Wash. Graduate UOre., AADA. Debut 1972 in LCR's "Enemies" "Merchant of Venice," and "Streetcar Named Desire," followed by "49 West 87th" (OB), Bdwy bow in "My Fat Friend," then "We Interrupt This program."

WELCH, CHARLES C. Born Feb. 2, 1921 in New Britain, Conn. Attended Randall Sch., AmThWing. Bdwy debut 1958 in "Cloud 7," followed by "Donny Brook," "Golden Boy," "Little Murders," "Holly Go Lightly," "Darling of the Day," "Dear World," "Follies," "Status Quo Vadis," "Shenandoah," OB in "Half-Past Wednesday," "Oh, Lady! Lady!"

WELDON, CHARLES. Born June 1, 1940 in Wetumka, Okla. Bdwy debut 1969 in "Big Time Buck White," followed OB by "Ride a Black Horse," "Long Time Coming and a Long Time Gone," "Jamimma," "River Niger," "In the Deepest Part of Sleep."

WESLEY, ROBIN. Born July 9, 1951 in NYC. Graduate Hofstra U. Debut 1975 OB in "Wings," followed by "The Glorious Age."

WESTON, JIM. Born Aug. 2, 1942 in Montclair, NJ. Attended Manchester Col., AADA. Bdwy bow 1969 in "Red, White and Maddox," followed by "Lovely Ladies, Kind Gentlemen," "Grease," "Over Here," OB in "She Loves Me," "Ballad of Johnny Pot," "A Gun Play."

WHITE, CHARLES. Born Aug. 29, 1920 in Perth Amboy, NJ. Graduate Rutgers U., Neighborhood Playhouse. Credits include "Career," "Cloud 7," "Gypsy," "Philadelphia, Here I Come!," "Inherit the Wind," "Comes a Day," "Front Page," "Dandelion Wine"(OB).

WHITE, JANE. Born Oct. 30, 1922 in NYC. Attended Smith Col. Bdwy debut 1942 in "Strange Fruit," followed by "Climate of Eden," "Take a Giant Step," "Jane Eyre," "Once upon a Mattress," "The Cuban Thing," OB in "Razzle Dazzle," "Insect Comedy," "The Power and the Glory," "Hop, Signor," "Trojan Women," "Iphigenia in Aulis," "Cymbeline," "Burnt Flowerbed," "Rosmersholm."

WHITESIDE, ANN. Born in Philadelphia, Pa. Attended Chestnut Hill Col. Bdwy debut 1955 in "A Roomful of Roses," followed by "Wake Up, Darling," OB in "Jumping Fool," "Olathe Response," "Picnic."

WHITMORE, CHRISTINEA. Born Dec. 24, 1952 in Derby, Conn. Attended Adelphi U., HB Studio. Bdwy debut 1974 in "The National Health."

WHITMORE, JAMES. Born Oct. 1, 1922 in White Plains, NY. Attended Yale. Bdwy debut 1947 in "Command Decision," followed by "A Case of Libel," "Inquest," "Will Rogers' U.S.A."

WHITTON, PEGGY. Born Nov. 30, 1950 in Pa. Debut 1973 OB in "Baba Goya," followed by "Arthur."

Horton Willis   **Lisa Wilkinson**   **Richard Woods**   **Jo Ann Yeoman**   **Jerry Zaks**

WIDDOES, KATHLEEN. Born Mar. 21, 1939 in Wilmington, Del. Attended Paris' Theatre des Nations. Bdwy debut 1958 in "The Firstborn," followed by "World of Suzie Wong," "Much Ado About Nothing," OB in "Three Sisters," "The Maids," "You Can't Take It with You," "To Clothe the Naked," "World War 2-1/2," "Beggar's Opera," "As You Like It," "Midsummer Night's Dream."

WILCOX, RALPH. Born Jan. 30, 1951 in Milwaukee, Wisc. Attended UWisc. Debut 1971 OB in "Dirtiest Show in Town," followed by "Broadway," "Miracle Play," Bdwy in "Ain't Supposed to Die a Natural Death," "The Wiz."

WILKINSON, KATE. Born Oct. 25 in San Francisco, Cal. Attended San Jose State Col. Bdwy debut 1967 in "Little Murders," followed by "Johnny No-Trump," "Watercolor," "Postcards," "Ring Round the Bathtub," "Last of Mrs. Lincoln," OB in "La Madre," "Earnest in Love," "Story of Mary Surratt," "Bring Me a Warm Body," "Child Buyer," "Rimers of Eldritch," "A Doll's House," "Hedda Gabler," "Real Inspector Hound," "The Contractor,."

WILKINSON, LISA. Born in NYC. Graduate NYU. Debut OB 1970 in "Slave Ship," followed by "Don't Fail Your Lovin' Daddy, Lily Plum," Bdwy 1974 in "Candide."

WILLIAMS, ANDY. Born Dec. 3, 1928 in Wall Lake, Iowa. Bdwy debut 1974 in "Andy Williams at the Uris."

WILLIAMS, BARBARA. Born May 24 in Milwaukee, Wisc. Attended Northwestern U. Bdwy in "Damn Yankees," "Music Man," "Different Times," OB in "Streets of NY," "Horse Opera."

WILLIAMS, DICK ANTHONY. Born Aug. 9, 1938 in Chicago. Debut 1968 OB in "Big Time Buck White," followed by "Jamimma," "What the Winesellers Buy," Bdwy in "Ain't Supposed to Die a Natural Death," "We Interrupt This Program."

WILLIAMS, REX. Born May 23, 1914 in NYC. Bdwy debut 1935 in "If This Be Treason," followed by "Hitch Your Wagon," "Too Many Heroes," "Knights of Song," "Man with the Blond Hair," "Rugged Path," "Portrait in Black," "Rat Race," "Dreyfus in Rehearsal."

WILLIAMS, SAMMY. Born Nov. 13, 1948 in Trenton, NJ. Bdwy debut 1969 in "The Happy Time," followed by "Applause," "Seesaw," "A Chorus Line."

WILLIAMS, STEPHEN. Born Jan. 30, 1948 in Nottingham, Eng. Attended Webber-Douglas Acad. Bdwy debut 1975 in "The Misanthrope."

WILLIS, HORTON. Born Apr. 13, 1946 in Magnolia, Ark. Graduate Baylor U., AMDA. Debut 1968 OB in "Your Own Thing," followed by "And Puppy Dog Tails," "Mississippi Moonshine."

WILLIS, SUSAN. Born in Tiffin, O. Attended Carnegie Tech., Cleveland Play House. Debut 1953 OB in "Little Clay Cart," followed by "Love and Let Love," "The Glorious Age," Bdwy in "Take Me Along," "Gypsy," "Dylan," "Come Live with Me," "Cabaret."

WILLISON, WALTER. Born June 24, 1947 in Monterey Park, Calif. Bdwy debut 1970 in "Norman, Is That You?," followed by "Two by Two" for which he received a Theatre World Award, "Wild and Wonderful," "Pippin."

WILLMOTT, ROD. Born Aug. 9, 1939 in Cambridge, Eng. Bdwy debut 1974 in "As You Like It."

WILLOUGHBY, RONALD. Born June 3, 1937 near Goss, Miss. Graduate Millsaps Col., Northwestern U. Debut 1963 OB in "Walk in Darkness," followed by "Little Eyolf," "Antony and Cleopatra," "Balm in Gilead," "Dracula: Sabbat," "The Faggot," "King of the U.S."

WILSON, ELEANOR. Born in Chester, Pa. Attended Hollins Col., Pasadena and Cleveland Playhouses. Bdwy debut 1956 in "The Eagle Has Two Heads," followed by "The Silver Whistle," "The Wayward Saint," "Weekend," OB in "Dandelion Wine."

WILSON, MARY LOUISE. Born Nov. 12, 1936 in New Haven, Conn. Graduate Northwestern. OB in "Our Town," "Upstairs at the Downstairs," "Three-penny Opera," "A Great Career," "Whispers on the Wind," "Beggar's Opera," Bdwy in "Hot Spot," "Flora, the Red Menace," "Criss-Crossing," "Promises, Promises," "The Women," "Gypsy."

WILSON, ROBERT M. Born Oct. 4, 1944 in Waco, Tex. Graduate UTex., Pratt Inst. Bdwy debut 1975 in "A Letter for Queen Victoria."

WINDE, BEATRICE. Born Jan. 5 in Chicago, Ill. Debut 1966 OB in "In White America," followed by "June Bug Graduates Tonight," "Strike Heaven on the Face." Bdwy 1971 in "Ain't Supposed to Die a Natural Death" for which she received a Theatre World Award.

WINN, KITTY. Born in 1944 in Washington, DC. Graduate Boston U. Bdwy debut 1969 in "Three Sisters," followed OB by "Hamlet," "Knuckle."

WINTERSOLE, BILL. Born July 30, 1931 in Portsmouth, O. Graduate UKy., UCLA, USC. Debut OB 1959 in "Victims of Duty," followed by "What the Winesellers Buy."

WISE, WILLIAM. Born May 11, 1940 in Chicago, Ill. Attended Bradley U., Northern Ill. U. Debut 1970 OB in "Adaptation/Next," followed by "Hot 1 Baltimore."

WOLFE, JOEL. Born Sept. 19, 1936 in NYC. Graduate CCNY. Debut 1968 OB in "Ergo," followed by "Room Service," "The Co-op," Bdwy 1975 in "All over Town."

WOLFSON, ROB. Born Dec. 3, 1953 in NYC. Debut 1974 OB in "The Hot l Baltimore."

WOOD, G. Born Dec. 31, 1919 in Forrest City, Ark. Graduate Carnegie Tech, NYU. Bdwy bow 1953 in "Cyrano de Bergerac," followed by "Richard III," "Shangri-La," "The Crucible," "Seagull," "Imaginary Invalid," "A Touch of the Poet," "Tonight at 8:30," "Henry V," "Who's Who in Hell," OB in "La Ronde," "Cradle Song," "The Lesson," "Thor with Angels," "A Box of Watercolors," "Tobias and the Angels," "Potting Shed."

WOODS, RICHARD. Born May 9, 1930 in Buffalo, NY. Graduate Ithaca Col. Bdwy in "Beg, Borrow or Steal," "Capt. Brassbound's Conversion," "Sail Away," "Coco," "Last of Mrs. Lincoln," "Gigi," "Sherlock Holmes," OB in "The Crucible," "Summer and Smoke," "American Gothic," "Four-In-One," "My Heart's in the Highlands," "Eastward in Eden," "The Long Gallery," "The Year Boston Won the Pennant" and "In the Matter of J. Robert Oppenheimer" (LC), with APA in "You Can't Take It with You," "War and Peace," "School for Scandal," "Right You Are," "The Wild Duck," "Pantagleize," "Exit the King," "The Cherry Orchard," "Cock-A-Doodle Dandy," and "Hamlet."

WORONOV, MARY. Born Dec. 8, 1946 in Brooklyn, NY. Graduate Cornell U. Debut OB 1968 in "Kitchenette," followed by "Clearing House," "Queen of Greece," "Two Noble Kinsmen," "Boom Boom Room" for which she received a Theatre World Award, "Women behind Bars."

WRIGHT, TERESA. Born Oct. 27, 1918 in NYC. Bdwy debut 1938 in "Our Town," followed by "Life with Father," "Dark at the Top of the Stairs," "Mary, Mary," "I Never Sang for My Father," "Death of a Salesman," OB in "Who's Happy Now," "A Passage to E. M. Forster."

XIFO, RAY. Born Sept. 3, 1942 in Newark, NJ. Graduate Don Bosco Col. Debut OB 1974 in "The Tempest," followed by "Frogs."

YEOMAN, JOANN. Born Mar. 19, 1948 in Phoenix, Ariz. Graduate Ariz. State U., Purdue U. Debut 1974 OB in "The Boy Friend."

YOSHIDA, PETER. Born Sept. 29, 1945 in Chicago, Ill. Graduate UIll., Princeton U., AADA, AmThWing. Debut 1965 OB in "Coriolanus," followed by "Troilus and Cressida," "Santa Anita '42."

YOUNG, H. RICHARD. Born Mar. 13, 1930 in Port Huron, Mich. Attended Mich. State U. Debut OB 1974 in "Short Eyes."

ZAHL, EDA. Born Nov. 27, 1948 in NYC. Bennington Col. graduate. Bdwy debut 1972 in "The Country Girl," OB in "The Battering Ram."

ZAKS, JERRY. Born Sept. 7, 1946 in Germany. Graduate Dartmouth, Smith Col. Bdwy debut 1973 in "Grease," OB in "Death Story," "Dream of a Black-listed Actor," "Kid Champion."

ZALA, NANCY. Born July 10, 1936 in NYC. Graduate St. Andrews U. Debut OB 1967 in "In Circles," followed by "I Am a Camera," "Woman at the Tomb," "O Marry Me," "Medea," "One Sunday Afternoon."

ZANG, EDWARD. Born Aug. 19, 1934 in NYC. Graduate Boston U. OB in "Good Soldier Schweik," "St. Joan," "Boys in the Band," "The Reliquary of Mr. and Mrs. Potterfield," "Last Analysis," "As You Like It," "More Than You Deserve," "Polly."

ZELLER, MARK. Born Apr. 20, 1932 in NYC. Attended NYU, Juilliard. Bdwy debut 1956 in "Shangri-La," followed by "Happy Hunting," "Wonderful Town" (CC), "Saratoga," "Ari," OB in "Candle in the Wind," "Margaret's Bed."

ZENKER, KAREN. Born Jan. 9, in Columbus, O. Attended Ohio State U. Debut OB 1974 in "Carousel" (JB), followed by "The Three Musketeers."

ZOLLO, MISSIE. Born May 26, 1949 in NYC. Graduate Emerson Col., Neighborhood Playhouse. Debut 1974 OB in "Boom Boom Room."

ZORICH, LOUIS. Born Feb. 12, 1924 in Chicago, Ill. Attended Roosevelt U. OB in "Six Characters in Search of an Author," "Crimes and Crimes," "Henry V," "Thracian Horses," "All Women Are One," "Good Soldier Schweik," "Shadow of Heroes," "To Clothe the Naked," "Sunset," Bdwy in "Becket," "Moby Dick," "The Odd Couple," "Hadrian VII," "Moonchildren," "Fun City," "Goodtime Charley."

ZWICK, JOEL. Born Jan. 11, 1942 in Brooklyn, NY. Graduate Bklyn Col. Debut 1967 OB in "Macbird!," followed by "Dance with Me."

OBITUARIES

LARRY ALPERT, 56, actor and comedian, died March 9, 1975 of a heart attack in Ellenville, N.Y. Among his Broadway appearances were "Bagels and Yox," "A Tree Grows in Brooklyn," and "Let It Ride." More recently he had been appearing in nightclubs. No reported survivors.

LILLIAN ARNOLD, 69, a talent representative, died June 2, 1974 in NYC. Surviving are a sister and a brother.

OLGA BACLANOVA, 74, Russian-born stage and film star, died Sept. 6, 1974 in Vevey, Switz. She came to the U.S. in 1926 with the Moscow Art Theatre. In addition to several films, she appeared on stage in "Lysistrata," "Carmencita and the Soldier," "Love and Death," "The Fountain," "The Miracle," "Grand Hotel," "Twentieth Century," "Idiot's Delight," "$25 an Hour," "Murder at the Vanities," "Mahogany Hall," and "Claudia." She leaves her husband, Richard Davis, and a son by a previous marriage, Nicholas Soussanin, Jr.

JOSEPHINE BAKER, 68, St. Louis-born singer-dancer, died Apr. 12, 1975 of a cerebral hemorrhage in her adopted Paris, where she had lived since 1925. She became a French citizen in 1937. She was one of France's greatest music hall stars, and was appearing in a revue celebrating her 50 years as an entertainer when she had a stroke. She had appeared on Broadway in "Shuffle Along," "Cotton Club Revues," "Ziegfeld Follies of 1936," and her own one-woman shows—the last was at the Palace Theatre in 1973. She was separated from her third husband, musician Jo Bouillon. Surviving are her 12 adopted orphans of various nationalities. She had been awarded the Croix de Guerre and the Legion of Honor for her work during WW2.

JACK BENNY, 80, stage, vaudeville, nightclub, radio, film, and tv comedian, died Dec. 26, 1974 of cancer of the pancreas in his Beverly Hills, Ca., home. Born Benjamin Kubelsky in Waukegan, Ill., he began his career as a violinist, but ultimately became one of the best loved masters of timing and comedy in the world. He portrayed himself as timid, stingy, vain, and never older than 39. In reality, he was modest, generous, and raised millions for charitable organizations. For 47 years he was married to Sadie Marks who appeared with him as Mary Livingstone. Beginning in 1931, and for the next 32 years without interruption, he had his own show on radio or tv. On Broadway he appeared in "The Great Temptations," as headliner at the Palace Theatre, and in his one-man shows, the last in 1963. Surviving are his widow, and an adopted daughter.

MICHAEL BENTHALL, 55, British director-producer, and former actor, died Sept. 6, 1974 in London. From 1953–1962 he was director of the Old Vic and brought it to NY in 1954, 1956, and 1958 with a variety of Shakespeare's plays. For Broadway he directed "The Millionairess," "As You Like It," "Antony and Cleopatra," "Caesar and Cleopatra," "Man and Boy," and "Coco." No reported survivors.

OUIDA BERGERE, 88, actress, writer for stage and screen, and former talent agent, died Nov. 29, 1974 in NYC. She made her Broadway debut in 1911 in "The Stranger," and subsequently wrote several plays, including "Suburbia Comes to Paradise," "The Vicious Circle," "That Woman," and "Sherlock Holmes." She was the widow of Basil Rathbone, and is survived by a brother.

EDNA BEST, 74, British stage and film actress, died Sept. 18, 1974 in Geneva, Switz. Her Broadway debut was in 1925 in "These Charming People," followed by "The Constant Nymph," "Come with Me," "The High Road," "There's Always Juliet," "Delicate Story," "Yankee Point," "The Browning Version," "Harlequinade," "Captain Brassbound's Conversion," "First Lady," "Jane," "Ladies of the Corridor," "Mlle. Colombe," and "Quadrille." Surviving are twin sons by her first husband, actor Seymour Beard, and a daughter, actress Sarah Marshall, by her second husband, actor Herbert Marshall. Her third husband, Nat Wolff, predeceased her.

PAMELA BRITTON, 51, stage, screen and tv actress, died of a brain tumor June 17, 1974 in Chicago. She was appearing at the Arlington Park Theatre. She had starred on Broadway in "Brigadoon," and toured in "Oklahoma!" and "Guys and Dolls." She appeared in several films, and was a regular on the tv series "My Favorite Martian" and "Blondie." She is survived by her husband, hotel executive Arthur Steel, and a daughter.

CLIVE BROOK, 87, English stage and film actor, died Nov. 17, 1974 in his London home. After success on the London stage, he moved to Hollywood. He had appeared in over 100 films, and on Broadway in "Second Threshold." Surviving are a daughter, actress Faith Brook, and a son, playwright Lyndon Brook.

BETTY BRUCE, 54, dancer and comedienne on stage, screen, and tv, died July 18, 1974 of cancer in NYC. From the ballet companies of Michael Fokine and George Balanchine, she graduated to Broadway, and appeared in such productions as "The Boys from Syracuse," "Keep off the Grass," "High Kickers," "Something for the Boys," "Up in Central Park," and "Gypsy." She is survived by a son, Louis Satenstein, and her mother.

GRANT CODE, 78, actor, dancer and teacher, died June 28, 1974 in his NYC apartment. His Broadway debut was with Jane Cowl in "Madame X," and subsequently he acted in "Too Late the Phalarope," "The Hostage," "Galileo," "Dylan," "Legend of Lizzie," "Lost in the Stars," "Summer and Smoke," "In the Jungle of Cities," "Trelawny of the Wells." He appeared in tv's "Sgt. Bilko," "Naked City," and "Serpico." He had been public relations director of the Brooklyn Museum. No reported survivors.

JULIA COHN, 73, lawyer and former actress, died of a heart attack on Apr. 10, 1975. Before devoting her full time to being a labor and theatrical lawyer, she appeared in "Subway Express," "Peace on Earth," "Theodora, the Queen," and "St. Helena." She represented Actors Equity in contract negotiations. Surviving are her husband, lawyer Benjamin Algase, and a daughter.

Olga Baclanova (1933)

Edna Best (1953)

Grant Code (1970)

Katharine Cornell (1960)

Lili Darvas (1970)

Jerry Dodge (1968)

ROBERT COLEMAN, JR., 74, drama critic for 40 years, died Nov. 27, 1974 in NYC. He began writing drama criticism in 1924, subsequently becoming drama editor of the Morning Telegram, then of the Daily Mirror until it ceased publication in 1963 when he retired. His widow survives.

RICHARD CONTE, 59, stage, screen and tv actor, died Apr. 15, 1975 after a heart attack and stroke in Los Angeles. Before going to Hollywood, he appeared in several Broadway plays, including "Jason" and "The Family." He was featured or starred in over 50 films. Surviving is his second wife, and an adopted son.

KATHARINE CORNELL, 81, one of the great actresses of the American theatre, died of pneumonia June 9, 1974 in her home in Vineyard Haven, Mass. She made her stage debut in 1915, and from 1925 until her retirement in 1961 she represented theatre of quality in such plays as "The Green Hat," "The Barretts of Wimpole Street," "Romeo and Juliet," "Candida," "The Letter," "Alien Corn," "St. Joan," "The Doctor's Dilemma," "Bill of Divorcement," "The Three Sisters," "No Time for Comedy," "Antigone," "Antony and Cleopatra," "That Lady," "The Constant Wife," "The Prescott Proposals," "Rose Burke," "The Dark Is Light Enough," "The Firstborn," and her last, "Dear Liar." For 40 years she was married to producer-director Guthrie McClintic who died in 1961. A cousin survives.

INEZ COURTNEY, 67, stage and film actress, died Apr. 5, 1975 in Neptune, N.J. Before going to Hollywood in the 1930's, she appeared in "The Wild Rose," "Good News," "Spring Is Here," and "America's Sweetheart." No reported survivors.

PERQUETA COURTNEY, 80, former musical comedy actress, died Nov. 26, 1974 in NYC. During the 1920's and 1930's she appeared in several musicals, including "Tumble Tumble" and "Merry Merry." She leaves two sons and a daughter. She was the widow of band leader Reggie Childs.

PATRICIA CUTTS, 43, British stage, screen and tv actress, committed suicide in her London apartment Sept. 11, 1974. She came to NY in 1955 to be a panelist on the quiz show "Down You Go." Subsequently she appeared on Broadway in "The Matchmaker," "Kean," and "Any Wednesday." No reported survivors.

LILI DARVAS, 72, Hungarian-born stage, film and tv actress, died July 22, 1974 in her NYC apartment. Before her Broadway debut in 1944 in "Soldier's Wife," she was a recognized actress in Budapest, and became a leading member of Max Reinhardt's company with which she first appeared in the U.S. in 1927. Other NY productions in which she performed were "Hamlet," "Bravo," "Cry of the Peacock," "Horses in Midstream," "Hidden River," "Waltz of the Toreadors," "Cheri," "Far Country," "First Love," "My Mother, My Father, and Me," "Happiness," "The Miser," and "Les Blancs." She was the widow of playwright Ferenc Molnar for whom he wrote several plays. There were no immediate survivors.

JERRY DODGE, 37, actor-singer-dancer, died in his NYC apartment Oct. 31, 1974 of chemical poisoning. He had been under medical treatment for a virus infection. He was currently in the musical "Mack and Mabel." His other credits include "Bye Bye Birdie," "110 in the Shade," "Hello Dolly!" "George M!," "Desert Song," Off Broadway in "Sap of Life," "One Flew over the Cuckoo's Nest," and "Blue Boys." He leaves his mother.

EDWARD EMERSON, 65, stage, screen and tv actor, and writer, died Apr. 11, 1975 in NYC. Among his Broadway credits are "Hilda Cassidy," "Heigh-Ho, Everybody," "Spring Fever," "The Milky Way," and "Crime Marches On." His widow survives.

BRENDAN FAY, 54, stage, film and tv actor, died of a heart attack on Feb. 7, 1975 while rehearsing an Off Broadway play. He made his Broadway debut in 1959 in "Legend of Lizzie," followed by "First Love," "Borstal Boy," and was Off Broadway in "Heloise," "Threepenny Opera," "Donogoo," "King of the Whole Damned World," "Wretched the Lion-Hearted," "Time of the Key," "Thistle in My Bed," "Posterity for Sale," "Stephen D," "King Lear," "Cry of Players," "Brothers," "Wrong Side of the Moon," "Atheist in a Foxhole," and "Thieves' Carnival." Surviving are his mother and two sisters.

CARL FISHER, 65, general manager of many Broadway productions, died Dec. 21, 1974 at his home in Redding, Conn. Among his many credits are "Lily Turner," "20th Century," "Three Men on a Horse," "Boy Meets Girl," "Room Service," "Brother Rat," "Pal Joey," "Arsenic and Old Lace," "This Is the Army," "Call Me Madam," "Pajama Game," "West Side Story, "Fiorello!," "A Funny Thing Happened on the Way . . . ," "Fiddler on the Roof," "Cabaret," and "Follies." Surviving are his third wife, a daughter by his first wife, and an adopted son.

MICHAEL FLANDERS, 53, British actor, lyricist, and humorist, died Apr. 14, 1975 while on vacation in Wales. Since 1943 he had performed from a wheel chair because of the effects of polio. He was best known for his long and productive association with composer-comedian, Donald Swann. They appeared together on Broadway and on tour in "At the Drop of a Hat" and "At the Drop of Another Hat." He is survived by his wife and two daughters.

WALTER FRIED, 69, producer-general manager of many Broadway successes, died of a heart ailment May 28, 1975 in NYC. Among the many productions with which he was associated are "Death of a Salesman," "All My Sons," "Middle of the Night," "Life with Father," "Raisin in the Sun," "Time of the Cuckoo," "Purlie Victorious," "The Owl and the Pussycat," "The Moon Is Down," "Hallelujah Baby!," "Come Blow Your Horn," and "Irene." He is survived by his widow, two daughters, and a son.

JACK GAVER, 68, drama critic and Broadway columnist for United Press International, died Dec. 16, 1974 in NYC. He came to NY in 1929; became a member of Drama Critics Circle in 1948, and edited its prize plays from 1935–55. His widow survives.

MARTYN GREEN, 75, London-born actor and singer, died Feb. 8, 1975 of a blood infection in Hollywood, CA. He was probably best known for his performances in Gilbert and Sullivan operettas with the D'Oyly Carte Co. that had NY seasons in 1934, 1939, and 1947. He moved to NY in 1953 and subsequently appeared in "Misalliance," Chartok's Gilbert and Sullivan Co., "Shangri-La," "Child of Fortune," "Visit to a Small Planet," "Black Comedy," "Canterbury Tales," "Charley's Aunt," "The Incomparable Max," and Off Bdwy in "Drums under the Windows," "Red Roses for Me," and "Carricknabauna." In 1959 he lost his left leg in an accident, but it did not interfere with the progress of his career. Surviving are his third wife, and a daughter.

JEANNE GREENE, 69, an actress in the 1920's and 1930's, died Apr. 14, 1975 of cancer in NYC. Among her credits are "Four Walls," "Kibitzer," "Oh Promise Me," "Wonder Boy," "Not So Fast," "The Whole Town's Talking," "The Buccaneer," "The Bunk of 1926," "Mozart," "Be So Kindly," "Mulatto," "Morning Star," "Veneer," and "The K Guy." She leaves a son, Joseph Hilton, and a daughter, Iris Haines.

JAMES HAYES, 60, tv director-producer, and former actor, died of cancer May 17, 1975 in Norwalk, Conn. He appeared in "Hamlet" with Leslie Howard, "The Fireman's Flame," "First Stop Heaven," and "Steps Leading Up." In the 1940's he joined NBC where he became a director and producer. He was later a vice president of Benton & Bowles, and president of P.D.I. Films. He is survived by his widow, and four sons by a previous marriage.

LAURENCE C. HAYES, 71, actor, died of heart complications Nov. 17, 1974 in NYC. A native of Maine, he has been in the theatre for over 50 years in such productions as "Arsenic and Old Lace," "New Moon," and for 12 years in "Harvey," originally and on tour. Surviving are his widow and a daughter.

GEORGE HIROSE, retired actor, died Aug. 9, 1974 in NYC. He appeared in "The Mikado," "If This Be Treason," "See My Lawyer," and "13 Daughters," generally as an oriental. He was also a singer, and more recently had been busy with tv commercials. No reported survivors.

C. MAURICE HOLLAND, age unreported, former actor, radio and tv producer-director, died Nov. 14, 1974 of a heart attack at his home in Greenwich, Conn. He began his career in vaudeville, appeared on Broadway in the 1920's, in silent films, and for more than 10 years was producer-director of the "Kraft Television Theatre." Surviving are his widow, a son, and three daughters.

GENEVIEVE HOUGHTON, 78, former musical comedy actress, singer, and vaudeville performer, died Nov. 14, 1974 in North Bergen, NJ., after a lengthy illness. She had appeared in "The Only Girl," "Katinka," and several Victor Herbert productions. She was the widow of William Sully with whom she played all the major vaudeville circuits. Surviving are two sons.

WARREN HULL, 71, radio and tv master of ceremonies, and former stage and film actor, died Sept. 14, 1974 in Waterbury, Conn. He began his career in Shubert operettas before getting leading roles in "The Student Prince," "My Maryland," "Rain or Shine," and "Follow Through." He was probably best known as the host of the radio and tv show "Strike It Rich." He is survived by his widow, three sons, a stepson, and two stepdaughters.

KATHERINE HUPALO, 85, actress, died Sept. 7, 1974 in Ridgewood, NJ. For more than forty years she was a leading dramatic actress in the Ukrainian Art Theatre in this country. No reported survivors.

MURIEL HUTCHISON, 60, stage and film actress, died Mar. 24, 1975 of cancer in NYC. Among her credits are "The Amazing Dr. Clitterhouse," "The Man Who Came to Dinner," and "The Vigil." She was the widow of art dealer John Nicholson. After her marriage in 1953 she retired from the stage to operate an art gallery with her husband. No immediate survivors.

ELAINE IVANS, 75, actress, died Apr. 5, 1975 in NYC. She had appeared in "Mrs. Partridge Presents," "The Love Habit," "Headquarters," "Just Life," "Crime Marches On," and "Life with Father." No reported survivors.

HELEN JACOBSON, 53, producer and author, died Nov. 17, 1974 after a lengthy illness in Los Angeles. Her credits include "See the Jaguar," "Abraham Cochrane," "After the Rain," and "Fly Blackbird." A son and daughter survive.

ETHEL JAFFEE, 61, stage and tv actress, died Sept. 27, 1974 in Norwalk, Conn., after injuries suffered in an automobile accident. She is survived by her husband, lawyer Sydney Kweskin, and two sons.

ALLEN JENKINS, 74, stage, screen and tv actor, died July 20, 1974 in Santa Monica, CA., of complications following lung surgery. On Broadway he had roles in "Checkers," "Pitter Patter," "Rain," "What Price Glory?," "The Last Mile," "Front Page," "Five Star Final," "Blessed Event," and "Something for the Boys." He appeared in over 175 films, and was the cab driver in the tv series "Hey Jeannie." Surviving are a son and two daughters.

GREER JOHNSON, 54, playwright and music and dance critic for Cue Magazine, was found dead in his apartment in NYC on Oct. 30, 1974. Among his credits are "Mrs. Patterson" produced in 1954 starring Eartha Kitt. He leaves his mother and a sister.

HAZEL JONES, 79, English-born actress, died Nov. 13, 1974 in NYC. After appearing in over 50 London productions, she made her Broadway debut in 1945 in "Pygmalion," followed by "The First Mrs. Frazer," "Gayden," "The Living Room," "The Entertainer," and "Tea Party." No reported survivors.

JACOB KALICH, 83, actor, playwright, director, and producer for the Yiddish theatre, died of cancer Mar. 16, 1975 in his Lake Mahopac, NY home. After appearing in Bucharest and London, he came to the U.S. in 1914. He produced, directed, and acted in "Yankele," "Tzipke," "Gypsy Girl," "Girl of Yesterday," "Oh, What a Life!." He was married to actress Molly Picon who survives.

Martyn Green (1953)

Warren Hull (1936)

Allen Jenkins (1937)

Otto Kruger (1960)

Francine Larrimore (1951)

Fredric March (1963)

GEORGE KELLY, 87, playwright, died June 18, 1974 in Bryn Mawr, Pa. He began his career in vaudeville and turned to writing. His plays include "The Torchbearers," "The Show-Off," "Reflected Glory," "The Deep Mrs. Sykes," "The Fatal Weakness," and "Craig's Wife" which won the Pulitzer Prize. A bachelor, he was the uncle of Princess Grace of Monaco.

MAURICE KELLY, 59, stage and film actor, and former dancer, died of a heart attack Aug. 28, 1974 in Hollywood. On Broadway he appeared in "Between the Devil," "Leave It to Me," "Oklahoma!," and "This Is the Army!." Seven children survive.

WALTER KINSELLA, 74, stage, radio and tv actor, died May 11, 1975 in Englewood, NJ. Among his many Broadway credits are "What Price Glory?," "The Road to Rome," and "Blessed Event." On radio he was a regular on "Dick Tracy," "Mr. and Mrs. North," and "Stella Dallas," on tv in "Martin Kane," and the "Jackie Gleason Show." Surviving are a daughter and a son.

LEE KINSOLVING, 36, stage, film and tv actor, died Dec. 4, 1974 in Palm Beach, Fla. where he was manager of an art gallery. He leaves his parents, a sister and two brothers.

OTTO KRUGER, 89, stage, film, radio, and tv actor, died of a stroke Sept. 6, 1974 in Los Angeles. For many years he was a leading matinee idol of the theatre, and his credits include "Natural Law," "Gypsy Trail," "Adam and Eva," "Straw," "Alias Jimmy Valentine," "The Royal Family," "Private Lives," "Counselor-at-Law," "The Meanest Man in the World," "To the Ladies," "Nervous Wreck," "Karl and Anna," "Game of Life and Death," "The Moon Is Down," "Little A," "Laura," "Time for Elizabeth," and "The Smile of the World." He appeared in over 100 films, and was host of Lux Radio Theatre, and Lux Video Theatre. He is survived by his widow, former actress Sue MacManamy, and a daughter.

ETHEL MAE LAKE, 73, former Ziegfeld girl, died of cancer March 7, 1975 in NYC. She had appeared in "Chu Chin Chow," "Sunny," "Aphrodite," "Listen, Lester," and "No, No, Nanette." A daughter survives.

ROSEMARY LANE, 61, one of the singing Lane Sisters, died in Hollywood Nov. 25, 1974 of complications caused by pulmonary obstruction and diabetes. After singing with Fred Waring's Pennsylvanians, she appeared in several films. She was the star of the Broadway success "Best Foot Forward." Surviving are two sisters, Lola and Priscilla, and a daughter.

FRANCINE LARRIMORE, 77, French-born stage and film actress, died of pneumonia Mar. 7, 1975 in her NYC home. She made her Broadway debut in 1910 as a child actress in "Where There's a Will," subsequently appearing in "A Fool There was," "Over Night," "Some Baby," "Fair and Warmer," "Here Comes the Bride," "Parlor, Bedroom and Bath," "Scandal," "Nice People," "Nobody's Business," "Chicago," "Let Us Be Gay," "Brief Moment," "Shooting Star," and "Spring Song." Her last role was in 1946 in "Temporarily Mrs. Smith." Surviving are two brothers, Louis and Paul Adler, and cousins Luther and Stella Adler.

BURTON LENIHAN, 86, retired operetta and recording star, died July 1, 1974 in Chagrin Falls, Ohio. His credits include "Alma," "The Firefly," "Somebody's Sweetheart," "The Student Prince," "The Crinoline Girl." Several nieces and nephews survive.

MICHAEL LEWIS, 44, actor, died Mar. 6, 1975 in Summit, NJ. Son of the late Dorothy Thompson and Sinclair Lewis, he appeared in "Quadrille," "Small War on Murrary Hill," "Once There Was a Russian," "The Visit," "Hidden Stranger," "Little Moon of Alban," "A Man for All Seasons," "On a Clear Day You Can See Forever," "Henry VIII," "Darling of the Day," and "Soldiers." Surviving are his widow, a daughter, and two sons.

JACKIE "MOMS" MABLEY, 78, nee Loretta Aikin, comedienne of vaudeville, films, stage, radio and tv, died May 23, 1975 in White Plains, NY. She appeared on Broadway in "Swinging the Dream," and "Blackbirds," among others. A daughter and son survive.

MARJORIE MAIN, 85, stage and film actress, died Apr. 10, 1975 in Los Angeles, CA. After appearing on stage in such plays as "Cheating Cheaters," "Yes or No," "The Wicked Age," "Salvation," "Burlesque," "Dead End," and "The Women." She went to Hollywood in 1936 and subsequently had roles in over 100 films. She was the widow of Dr. Stanley Krebs.

FREDRIC MARCH, 77, nee Frederick Bickel, stage and film actor, died of cancer Apr. 14, 1975 in Los Angeles. He made his stage debut in 1920 in "Deburau," followed by "Yr. Obedient Husband," "The American Way," "Hope for a Harvest," "The Skin of Our Teeth," "A Bell for Adano," "Years Ago," "Now I Lay Me Down to Sleep," "An Enemy of the People," "Autumn Garden," "Long Day's Journey into Night ," and "Gideon." He appeared in 69 films. Surviving are his widow, actress Florence Eldridge, and an adopted son and daughter.

ILONA MASSEY, 62, Hungarian-born stage, film, radio and tv actress-singer, died Aug. 20, 1974 in Bethesda, Md. She appeared on Broadway in the long-running "Ziegfeld Follies" of 1943, and in 11 films. She is survived by her fourth husband, retired Gen. Donald Dawson.

RUTH MATTESON, 65, stage and radio actress, died Feb. 5, 1975 in Westport, Conn. She had appeared in "Geraniums in My Window," "Wingless Victory," "Barchester Towers," "Parnell," "What a Life!," "Spring Dance," "One for the Money," "Male Animal," "Merry Widow," "Tomorrow the World," "In Bed We Cry," "Antigone," "Park Avenue," "Clutterbuck," "The Relapse," "The Happiest Millionaire," "There Was a Little Girl." She was a regular on "The Aldrich Family" radio series. Surviving is her husband, Curt Peterson, retired advertising executive.

ELOISE McELHONE, 53, tv panelist and radio actress, died of a heart attack July 1, 1974 in her NYC home. She is survived by two daughters.

NAN McFARLAND, 58, stage and tv actress, died of cancer Dec. 31, 1974 in Stamford, Conn. She had appeared in "Macbeth," "Arsenic and Old Lace," "Cyrano de Bergerac," "Othello," "Angel Street," "The Alchemist," "A Streetcar Named Desire," "Long Voyage Home," "The Wild Duck," "The Chase," "My Three Angels," "The Hot Corner," "Bus Stop," and "Auntie Mame." A brother survives.

CLAUDIA MORGAN, 62, stage, film and radio actress, died Sept. 17, 1974 in NYC. Made her debut at 16 in "Gypsy April," and subsequently appeared in "Top o' the Hill," "Dancing Partner," "A Modern Virgin," "People on the Hill," "Thoroughbred," "False Dreams, Farewell," "Gentlewoman," "Are You Decent?," "Bridal Quilt," "The Lord Blesses the Bishop," "A Lady Detained," "DeLuxe," "Accent on Youth," "On Stage," "Call It a Day," "Corespondent Unknown," "And Stars Remain," "Masque of Kings," "Storm over Patsy," "In Clover," "Merely Murder," "Wine of Choice," "The Man Who Came to Dinner," "The Sun Field," "Ten Little Indians," "Venus Observed," "The Apple Cart," "A Fig Leaf in her Bonnet." She was Nora Charles in the popular radio series "The Thin Man." Surviving is her fourth husband, W. Kenneth Leone.

RAY MORGAN, age not reported, tv and radio actor, announcer, and narrator, died of cancer Jan. 5, 1975 in Englewood, NJ. He was co-host or announcer for such shows as "We the People," "Gang Busters," "Counterspy," "Toast of the Town," "Studio One," "Kraft Music Hall," "Robert Montgomery Presents," and "The Ted Mack Amateur Hour." He is survived by his widow and a daughter.

KATHERINE MURRAY, 80, retired actress, singer, and Ziegfield Girl, died Aug. 12, 1974 in her Rye, N.Y. home. She had appeared in "The Quaker" and several "Ziegfield Follies." She was the widow of Frederick Shoninger. A stepdaughter, a brother and a sister survive.

GERTRUDE NIESEN, 62, singer, comedienne, and actress on stage, in tv, films, radio and nightclubs, died Mar. 27, 1975 in Glendale, Cal. She had appeared in "Calling All Stars," "Ziegfeld Follies of 1936," "Follow the Girls," and "Gentlemen Prefer Blondes" (on the West Coast). She leaves her husband, Albert Greenfield.

LARRY PARKS, 60, stage and film actor, died of a heart attack Apr. 13, 1975 in his home in Studio City, Cal. His Broadway credits include "Golden Boy," "Bells Are Ringing," "The Tunnel of Love," "Beg, Borrow or Steal," and "Love and Kisses." He had roles in over 30 films. Surviving are his widow, actress Betty Garrett, and two sons.

MARJORIE PETERSON, 68, actress, singer and dancer, died of a heart attack Aug. 19, 1974 in her NYC apartment. She had appeared in "Annie Dear," "Greenwich Village Follies," "Earl Carroll's Vanities," "Countess Maritza," "The Red Robe," "The Perfumed Lady," "Creeping Fire," "Pre-Honeymoon," "It's a Gift," "Great to Be Alive," and "A Date with April." Her mother survives.

MARY PHILIPS, 74, retired stage and film actress, died of cancer Apr. 22, 1975 in Santa Monica, Cal. She had appeared in "Apple Blossoms," "The Old Soak," "The Tavern," "The Song and Dance Man," "Both Your Houses'," "Merrily We Roll Along," "Spring Thaw," and "Chicken Every Sunday." She was divorced from actor Humphrey Bogart, and the widow of actor Kenneth MacKenna. Her brother-in-law, designer Jo Mielziner, survives.

ARTHUR PIERSON, 73, Norwegian-born actor-director-writer for stage, film, and tv, died Jan. 1, 1975 in Santa Monica, Cal. He had appeared on Broadway in such plays as "Lost Horizon," and "Night of January 16." Surviving are his widow and son.

EDWARD PLATT, 58, stage, radio, tv actor and singer, died of natural causes Mar. 19, 1974 in his home in Santa Monica, Cal. After singing with Paul Whiteman's band for two years, he appeared on Broadway in "All in Fun," "Allegro," "Silver Whistle," "Texas, Li'l Darlin'," "20th Century," "The Shrike," "Stalag 17," and "Oh, Captain." He was the Chief on the "Get Smart" tv series. He leaves his widow, a daughter, and two sons.

ROY ROBERTS, 69, stage, film, and tv actor, died May 28, 1975 in Los Angeles, Cal. After several seasons in touring companies, he appeared on Broadway in "Hooray for What," "Sailor Beware," "Boy Meets Girl," "Room Service," "Everybody's Welcome," "Inside Story," "Zero Hour," "Old Man Murphy," "Keeper of the Keys," "Carnival in Flanders," and "The Old Foolishness." He had roles in over 1000 films. Surviving is his widow.

ROBERT ROUNSEVILLE, 60, singer, actor, and teacher, died of a heart attack Aug. 6, 1974 in his NYC Carnegie Hall studio. Although best known as an operatic tenor, he appeared on Broadway in "Babes in Arms," "Two Bouquets," "Knickerbocker Holiday," "Higher and Higher," "Up in Central Park," "Show Boat," "Merry Widow," "Candide," "Brigadoon," and "Man of La Mancha." He is survived by his widow, a son and a daughter.

VELMA ROYTON, 81, London-born stage and tv actress, died July 25, 1974 in NYC. Among her Broadway credits are "Little Women," "I Know My Love," "The Heiress," "Pygmalion," and five years in "My Fair Lady." No reported survivors.

JULIA SANDERSON, 87, retired vaudeville, radio and musical comedy star, died Jan. 27, 1975 in her home in Springfield, Mass. Her career began at 13 and she retired in 1943 when her husband, actor Frank Crumit, died. She made her NY debut in "Winsome Winnie," and subsequently starred in "The Dairy Maid," "The Arcadians," "The Siren," "Fantana," "Sunshine Girl," "The Canary," "Rambler Rose," "Kitchy Koo," "Tangerine," "Moonlight," "No, No, Nanette," "Oh, Kay!," and "Queen High." With her third husband, Mr. Crumit, she became part of a popular singing duo on radio for many years. No reported survivors.

DOROTHY STONE, 69, musical comedy actress, died Sept. 24, 1974 in her home in Montecito, Cal. She made her debut with her father, actor Fred Stone, in 1923 in "Stepping Stones," followed by "Criss-Cross," "Three Cheers," "Show Girl," "Smiling Faces," "The Gay Divorcee," "As Thousands Cheer," "Hurrah for What," "You Can't Take It with You," and "The Red Mill." Surviving are her two sisters, former actresses Paula and Carol Stone.

ROBERT STRAUSS, 61, stage, tv and film character actor, died from a stroke Feb. 20, 1975 in NYC. He had appeared on Broadway in "Having Wonderful Time," "Catherine Was Great," "Nelly Bly," "Detective Story," "20th Century," "Stalag 17," and "Portofino." He is survived by his second wife, and three children by his former marriage.

ED SULLIVAN, 73, Broadway columnist and host of his long-running tv variety show, died of cancer Oct. 13, 1974 in NYC. On his tv show that lasted for 23 years, he presented a wide variety of entertainers, and introduced to tv audiences many stars and future stars. His survivors include a daughter and five grandchildren.

Claudia Morgan (1952)

Mary Philips (1947)

Edward Platt (1958)

265

William Tabbert (1949)

Nancy Wickwire (1957)

Blanche Yurka (1950)

ELLIOTT SULLIVAN, 66, stage, film and tv actor, died June 2, 1974 while on a visit to Los Angeles. His Broadway credits include "The Passion Play," "Winged Victory," "Lysistrata," "Brigadoon," "Skydrift," and "Compulsion." He had been living in London for 11 years. He leaves his widow, a son and a daughter.

JACQUELINE SUSANN, 53, popular novelist, and former actress, died of cancer Sept. 21, 1974 in NYC. She had appeared in 21 plays, including "A Lady Says Yes," "Between Covers," "The Madwoman of Chaillot," and co-authored "Lovely Me." Her "Valley of the Dolls" was the best-selling novel of all times. Surviving are her husband, producer Irving Mansfield, and a son.

WILLIAM TABBERT, 53, actor and lyric tenor, died of a heart attack Oct. 19, 1974 while rehearsing for a nightclub act in NYC. He made his Broadway debut in 1943 in "What's Up?," subsequently appearing in "Follow the Girls," "Seven Lively Arts," "Billion Dollar Baby," "Three to Make Ready," Lt. Cable in "South Pacific," and "Fanny." He leaves his widow, former dancer Evelyn Rainey, and three children.

EDNA THOMAS, 88, actress, died of a heart condition and respiratory complications July 22, 1974 in NYC. She appeared with the Lafayette Players in Harlem before making her Broadway debut in 1926 in "Lulu Belle." Among her credits are "Porgy," "Run, Little Chillun," "Macbeth," "Harriet," "Strange Fruit," "A Streetcar Named Desire," "The Enforcer," and "Take a Giant Step." She was the widow of Lloyd Thomas and left no survivors.

WILLIAM A. TIERNEY, age unreported, retired vaudevillian and actor, died Dec. 21, 1974 in Boca Raton, Fla. He had appeared in, among others, "Silver Whistle," "Front Page," "Teahouse of the August Moon," "Finian's Rainbow," "A Hole in the Head," "The Shrike," and an "Oklahoma!" revival. A sister survives.

JOHN L. TOOHEY, 58, theatrical press agent, and short story writer, died of cancer Feb. 9, 1975 in Brighton, Mass. He had represented such Broadway productions as "Life with Father," "Mr. Wonderful," "Will Success Spoil Rock Hunter?," and "Bells Are Ringing." He also wrote "A History of the Pulitzer Prize Plays," and "On Plays, Playwrights and Playgoers." Surviving are his widow, and three daughters.

MARY URE, 42, a leading British stage and screen actress, died accidentally Apr. 3, 1975 from a mixture of alcohol and barbiturates, within a few hours after a successful opening in a new play in London. Her first success was "Look Back in Anger" in both London and New York. Her other Broadway roles were in "Duel of Angels," and "Old Times." She is survived by her husband actor Robert Shaw, and four children.

HENRY WADSWORTH, 72, stage and film actor, died Dec. 5, 1974 in NYC. He made his Broadway debut in 1927 in the title role of "Tommy," and for many years was the perennial juvenile. His last role was in 1950 in "The Happy Time." He also played the juvenile in over 30 films, in addition to others. No reported survivors.

WALTER DARE WAHL, 78, nee Walter Kalwara, retired comedian on stage and in vaudeville, died June 23, 1974 in Metamoris, Pa. He was also world lightweight wrestling champion from 1911 to 1916. His Broadway credits include "Ziegfeld Follies," "Earl Carroll's Vanities," "Life Begins at 40," "Top Banana," and "Star-Spangled Rhythm," among others. Two sons survive.

GEORGE WELBES, 40, stage and tv actor, died of a cerebral hemorrhage Oct. 17, 1974 in NYC. He appeared in "Oh Say Can You See L. A.," "The Other Man," "Oh, Calcutta!," "One Flew over the Cuckoo's Nest." Surviving is his son and two sisters.

WILLIAM WHITMAN, 49, stage actor, died Sept. 4, 1974 in San Francisco, Cal., after surgery for a kidney ailment. He had appeared in "Jane," "The Way of the World," "Six Characters in Search of an Author," "I Am a Camera," "Getting Married" and "Buoyant Billions." In recent years he had been working with the San Francisco Poverty Theatre of which he was a co-founder. A sister survives.

NANCY WICKWIRE, 48, stage and tv actress, died of cancer July 10, 1974 in San Francisco, Cal., where she had been appearing with the American Conservatory Theatre. Her NY credits include "Jane," "Dial 'M' for Murder," "St. Joan," "The Grand Prize," "The Way of the World," "Cherry Orchard," "Measure for Measure," "Girl of the Golden West," "As You Like It," "A Clearing in the Woods," "Rosmersholm," "Seidman & Son," "The Golden Age," "Abraham Cochrane," "Traveller without Luggage," and "Here's Where I Belong." No reported survivors.

P. G. WODEHOUSE, 93, English-born lyricist, playwright, and one of this century's most prolific writers of light fiction, died of a heart attack Feb. 14, 1975 in Southampton, NY. He wrote 97 novels, 300 short stories, 33 musicals, and 18 plays including "A Gentleman of Leisure," "A Thief for a Night," "Miss Springtime," "Have a Heart," "Leave It to Jane," "Riviera Girl," "Oh, Lady, Lady," "Sitting Pretty," "Oh, Kay," "Anything Goes." Although he had become an American citizen, he was knighted by Queen Elizabeth on New Year's Day 1975. His widow survives.

STANLEY YOUNG, 69, playwright, poet, publisher and literary reviewer, died of cancer Mar. 22, 1975 in Huntington, NY. His plays were "Robin Landing," "Bright Rebel," "Ask My Friend Sandy," "Mr. Pickwick," and "Laurette," based on the life of Laurette Taylor. Surviving are his widow, and three children from a former marriage.

BLANCHE YURKA, 86, stage and film actress, died of arteriosclerosis June 6, 1974 in NYC. Her Broadway career began in 1907 in "The Warrens of Virginia," and her last performance was Off Broadway in 1970 in "The Madwoman of Chaillot." Her credits include "Hamlet," "The Wild Duck," "Goat Song," "Hedda Gabler," "Lady from the Sea," "Lysistrata," "Troilus and Cressida," "Carrie Nation," "Romeo and Juliet," "Gloriana," "The Wind Is Ninety," "Temper the Wind," "Jane Eyre," "Dinner at 8," "The Carefree Tree," "Diary of a Scoundrel." She was divorced from the late Ian Keith.

INDEX

269

271

272

273

278

279

283

284

288